See Criminal Law
Charleton Heston —
another movie

LAST RIGHTS?

Euthenasia - Francis Bacon coined
"Good Death"

- Catholic church says is obligation to use ordinary
means: therapuetic & aveilable, and not place
strain on society or family. Un-ordinary- one is
lacking.

EUTHEnasia - v. vague word

Direct & Voluntary - shoot self, jump off bridge, or - paralyzed, say
kill me

Indirect & voluntary - don't treat me anymore, so I die from
my condition

Direct & involuntary - I don't ask, you just do it - infant euthenasia

Indirect & involuntary - patient doesn't say don't treat, but we
don't anyway.

P.V.S. - persistant vegetative state

OK
principle of dual effect - will the good in spite of foreseeable evil
not apposite

MICHAEL M. UHLMANN is a senior fellow at the Ethics and Public Policy Center and a professor of government in the Washington program of Claremont McKenna College. A graduate of Yale University, he received a law degree from the University of Virginia Law School and a doctorate in political philosophy from the Claremont Graduate School.

LAST RIGHTS?

Assisted Suicide and Euthanasia Debated

Edited by
MICHAEL M. UHLMANN

ETHICS AND PUBLIC POLICY CENTER
WASHINGTON, D.C.

WILLIAM B. EERDMANS PUBLISHING COMPANY
GRAND RAPIDS, MICHIGAN

Published jointly 1998 by the Ethics and Public Policy Center and
Wm. B. Eerdmans Publishing Co.
255 Jefferson Ave. S.E., Grand Rapids, Mich. 49503

Printed in the United States of America

03 02 01 00 99 98   7 6 5 4 3 2

Library of Congress Cataloging-in-Publication Data

Last rights? : assisted suicide and euthanasia debated /
edited by Michael M. Uhlmann.
p.   cm.
Includes bibliographical references and index.
ISBN 0-8028-4199-6 (pbk. : alk. paper)
1. Assisted suicide. 2. Euthanasia. 3. Right to die.
I. Uhlmann, Michael M.
R726.L379 1998
179.7—dc21   97-41104
CIP

Contents

IV. LEGAL PERSPECTIVES

About This Book

My first debt of gratitude goes to my colleagues at the Ethics and Public Policy Center, that oasis of civil discourse where the first things are still gladly learned and gladly taught: to George Weigel, its former president, who proposed the project, and to Elliott Abrams, its current president, who oversaw its completion; to Robert Royal, whose criticisms were unfailingly wise and gently proffered; to William Brailsford, whose knowledge of publishing is exceeded only by his love of good books; to my research assistants, Scott Croft and Eric Gregory, whose hard work and enthusiasm extended even to nights and weekends, and to Marianne Geers, whose infectious cheerfulness lightened the burdens of production; and, above all, to Carol Griffith, my indefatigably patient editor, whose discriminating editorial judgment and uncompromising professionalism are *sans pareil*.

I am very grateful to the Lynde and Harry Bradley Foundation, whose interest and generosity made completion of the project possible. Finally, I thank the authors whose learning is displayed in these pages. I have benefited greatly from their instruction and am pleased to present it to a wider audience.

All the essays in this book were previously published elsewhere except the Part One essay and the introductions. I am grateful to the many publishers for permission to use their works in this way. Details of original publication are given in the paragraph identifying the author of each piece. The Ethics and Public Policy Center does not hold the copyright on any of these reprinted materials. A few editorial points:

Omissions are shown by ellipses and can range from a few words

ix

to several pages. Square brackets [like this] usually indicate additions by us for clarification. Most of the subheads were added for this volume.

As in any volume of reprinted material, some facts may now be obsolete. A reference such as "a few years ago" would refer to the time of the original publication.

The notes have been somewhat standardized, and some have been abridged or eliminated; note numbering may therefore differ from that of the original publication.

We have tried to be accurate about representing the works as they were previously published. However, the original publications should be used when complete accuracy is required.

Introduction

During the next decade, assisted suicide and euthanasia could well become the dominant social and moral issue in the United States. The subject has been brought into sharp political focus by the actions of Jack Kevorkian, the sometime Michigan pathologist who has "assisted" fifty or more persons to their deaths, and by efforts in numerous states to alter or abolish long-standing statutory or common-law prohibitions against assisted suicide. In a dramatic legal turn, two federal courts of appeal determined in 1996 that terminally ill persons and certain others have a constitutionally protected right to assistance in ending their lives. Although both rulings were overturned by the Supreme Court in June 1997, the opinions of the justices ensure that the subject will be in the forefront of legislative and public debate for many years to come.

If and when the debate is resolved, it is unlikely to be resolved through the invocation of handy catch-phrases. Those who begin by declaring their support for the "right to die" or the "duty to sustain life" may shrink from the full implications of such slogans once they are revealed. This should not be surprising, for the questions raised in this debate are of the utmost gravity: What is the value of a human life? When does life cease, and what are our obligations when it does? By what moral license may a human being claim the right to end his own life, and what moral duties fall upon doctors or others who are asked to assist him? What, indeed, is the purpose of medicine, and to what extent should the doctor-patient relationship be regulated? Should the law guide or follow behavior in this area, and who should decide, courts or legislatures? To raise these questions—and they only scratch the surface of the matter—is to realize at once that they cannot be answered in haste or by means of the formulaic responses that so often dominate political discussion.

The causes of the current agitation are numerous and complex, but a few general observations are in order.

First, generally improved living conditions, better health care, and dramatic developments in medical technology now make possible the continuance of life well beyond what was considered "natural" in the past. The result is that many people (and not only the elderly) who yesterday might have been left to die because nothing could be done to help them are today able to enjoy lives relatively free of debilitating pain or illness. But the same medical technology that effects these miraculous cures and gives hope to the afflicted can also sustain biological existence over many years for patients who are, or will soon be, clinically dead. When medical technology can, so to speak, cheat death, critical decisions must be made about the most appropriate course of treatment and the conditions under which it may or should be withdrawn.

Such decisions raise difficult issues for medical professionals. On the one hand, physicians are trained to fight disease aggressively and to prolong life; but sometimes a patient's life can be sustained only by making him totally dependent on feeding tubes, respirators, or other machinery, often with little or no prospect for improvement. On the other hand, neither doctors nor their patients are prepared to forgo technology that offers a chance of recovery. For every patient whose condition seems hopeless, there is another who has undergone a near-miraculous cure.

Contemporary medicine, in short, seems to be caught in a dilemma created by medical technology itself. Antibiotics, respirators, and diverse other means of repairing, replacing, or replicating the functions of defective bodily organs have brought untold benefits to many suffering patients, but they can also produce patients whose quality of life—to use a much abused phrase—is as bad as, and even worse than, their condition before treatment. For example, just how aggressively should a 75-year-old patient with heart or kidney failure be treated? Indeed, what is the proper protocol for distinguishing between *this* septuagenarian and *that* one?

Medical professionals can scarcely be faulted for failing to provide hard, consistent, or comfortable answers to such knotty questions. And their attempts to do so have been complicated by legal changes that were supposed to clarify or simplify critical medical decisions at the end of life. During the past two decades, for example, virtually all states have formally recognized the right of patients to forgo treatment, including artificial nutrition and hydration essential to life. And virtually all have given legal sanction to advanced directives such as "living wills" and durable powers of attorney that permit patients to designate a surrogate to decide whether life-sustaining treatment should continue. The legal basis for refusing treatment derives from a long recognized common-law right to be free from bodily interference without consent. Some argue that such a right necessarily implies a degree of sovereignty over personal existence broad enough to include the right to end one's life—if need be, with the assistance of others. In this view, if patients and doctors have the right to terminate treatment when the result will be death, they should also have the right to speed things along, especially when the alternative is a lingering or painful death.[1]

Those opposed to this view contend that the right to terminate treatment implies no such thing. Medicine and law have long recognized a relatively bright-line distinction between killing and letting die, they say, and once that line is erased, the legitimation of assisted suicide will by irresistible logic lead to the killing of patients without their knowledge or consent.[2]

Debate on this profoundly important issue occurs against the backdrop of increased concern about the cost of health care. In an age in which government, directly or indirectly, pays for a large proportion of medical care, and when most Americans receive their medical care through bureaucratized health-maintenance organizations, budgetary concerns necessarily assume great importance. Quite apart from everything else, one fact alone assures that fiscal questions will weigh heavily in the forthcoming debate: during the next fifty years, there will be a five-fold increase in the number of people over 85 living in the United States.[3] With fertility rates at an all-time low, and with health care consuming a large portion of national wealth, the tax base available to support an aging population will face unprecedented strain. No less than doctors, the American people will find themselves confronting grave questions not only about the moral value of maintaining life but about its economic value as well.

Recent events in Oregon may provide a window into the future for the nation as a whole. In 1994, the voters of that state enacted by plebiscite what is unquestionably the most permissive physician-assisted suicide law in the world. Shortly after the measure passed, it was announced that assisted suicide would be a covered procedure under the publicly funded state health plan. Sometime after that, it was announced that the Oregon health plan (like that of many other states) would not offer public funding for expensive medications, such as protease inhibitors, used in the treatment of AIDS.[4] Whatever one may think about the wisdom of these decisions, the larger point is that in a cost-conscious health-care system, providers of medical treatment are likely to face increasing pressure to justify their decisions in terms of social utility. If so, assisted suicide may acquire a new and potentially sinister aspect.[5] If the pattern in Oregon is replicated in other states, the very government that is by law bound to protect life may involve itself in tipping the scales against the maintenance of life.

Finally, the debate over assisted suicide and euthanasia occurs at a time when once-settled ethical opinions about life and death no longer claim the widespread allegiance they once had. The prohibition against actively taking human life, whether one's own or another's, lies at the very center of the moral tradition of Western civilization and still retains enormous power, even among those who do not consider themselves formally religious. But arrayed against this tradition are various moral theories holding that morality arises not from God or from the laws of nature but from individual choice. Man, it is said, is an autonomous being, and never more so than when the question of his own life is in the balance; he has a right to end his life, or, as the argument is sometimes stated, a right to determine the time and manner of his own death. The argument between these two camps, though dressed in contemporary philosophical vocabulary, in fact has an ancient lineage. Moral opposition to suicide extends back through the thought of Plato and Aristotle to the Book of Genesis. Indeed, in many respects, the argument at the close of the twentieth century is little more than a replay of the argument between Stoic and Epicurean philosophers and the Church Fathers during the early centuries of Christianity.

Inevitably, in a constitutional system dedicated to protecting the rights of the individual, moral claims quickly become legal claims. Philosophical teachings, which once worked their way slowly through the culture by means of the classroom and the book, can now be enacted into law relatively quickly, often through judicial rulings that can impose a new or controversial ethical norm more or less by fiat. Perhaps the most dramatic illustration of this phenomenon occurred in the 1973 *Roe v. Wade* decision, in which the Supreme Court in effect rewrote the abortion laws of the entire country despite widespread opposition. Since then, the abortion cases have been the principal means by which the philosophical claims for autonomous individualism have entered the American constitutional bloodstream.

One thing more: those cases appear to have introduced and constitutionally blessed the proposition that under certain circumstances Human Being A may end the life of Human Being B. Of course, the abortion cases rest on the assumption that the victim, an unborn child, is not a human being possessing rights that the law is bound to respect. Nevertheless, in the eyes of many, including federal judges sitting in assisted-suicide litigation, the abortion cases yield a constitutional doctrine carrying implications far beyond the question of abortion itself. The moral and legal argument necessary to justify the right to terminate the life of an unborn child is said to justify also the right to take one's own life—and, by extension, the right of others to assist one in doing so.[6]

In our time, restraints upon the exercise of individual autonomy at the end of life thus begin with a kind of presumption against them. According to the new view, arguments relying on centuries-old prohibitions are not enough; the law should now have to demonstrate affirmatively the grounds of its continued opposition to assisted suicide. If the liberty guaranteed by the Constitution includes the right to control one's own destiny, it would arguably include the right to determine the time and manner of one's death. Absent a reasonable or even compelling demonstration to the contrary, the law should not be allowed to interfere with such a right.

On the other side, it is argued that so broad an understanding of autonomy has never been and is not now the true philosophical understanding on which the American Constitution rests. To recognize a right to assisted suicide would put many lives at risk and threaten the very liberties that government was instituted to protect.[7]

The debate, then, is clearly joined—in medicine, in morals, and in law. Few issues in American policy are freighted with greater importance for individual citizens or the society of which they are a part.

The essays that follow will introduce the reader to some of the grand themes that have animated similar debates in the past and continue to inform the moral and legal framework of contemporary discussion. The essay that constitutes Part One, CLASSICAL, CHRISTIAN, AND EARLY MODERN THOUGHT, provides a historical overview of moral philosophy and theology from Plato to Kant. Part Two, CONTEMPORARY MORAL AND THEOLOGICAL PERSPECTIVES, carries the debate into our own era with ten essays by notable moral teachers and commentators. Here the reader will encounter arguments as diverse as those of Peter Singer, who radically repudiates much of the Western moral tradition, and those of Pope John Paul II, who argues that that tradition was never more relevant.

In Part Three, MEDICAL PERSPECTIVES, Edmund D. Pellegrino asks us to think—again—about the Hippocratic Oath, while Jack Kevorkian, Timothy E. Quill, and Derek Humphry argue that the right to suicide is both rational and compassionate. Leon R. Kass explains why doctors must not kill. D. Alan Shewmon argues that allowing doctors to kill will place them—and us—on a slippery slope. Herbert Hendin recounts the Dutch experience with assisted suicide. And H. Tristram Englehardt, Jr., examines the issue of assisting young children to die.

Part Four, LEGAL PERSPECTIVES, has as its centerpiece excerpts from the opinions in two landmark cases on assisted suicide, which are then critiqued by Victor G. Rosenblum. Alan Meisel surveys the legal consensus on forgoing life-sustaining treatment, while Robert A. Sedler and Yale Kamisar lock horns on whether the Constitution establishes a right to die. Next comes a "model state act" for regulating physician-assisted suicide, followed by a critique in which Daniel Callahan and Margot White argue that such acts contain more loopholes than protections. The section concludes with the June 1997 Supreme Court opinions in *Washington v. Glucksberg* and *Vacco v. Quill*.

A word on this anthology: the already vast literature on suicide, assisted suicide, and euthanasia continues to grow, and judgments will inevitably differ on what ought (or ought not) to be included in a collection of this sort. I enter the plea that though the introductions inevitably reflect my own opinions, the volume as a whole gives a fair representation to diverse points of view. Readers who venture no further will acquire a solid and sophisticated introduction to the subject. The issues raised here are not dry academic questions. If this book does nothing else, I hope it makes clear that, in debating the rules that will determine whether and how we may end our lives, no one can afford to be a bystander.

PART ONE

Classical, Christian, and Early Modern Thought

1

Western Thought on Suicide: From Plato to Kant

Michael M. Uhlmann

Western thought on suicide, assisted suicide, and euthanasia is a complex subject with a copious literature. To think about these matters is to confront some of the central questions of the human condition: belief in God and the immortality of the soul, the nature of moral and legal obligation, and the origin of one's duties to neighbor and self, to name only a few. The thinkers who are discussed in the following essay represent only some of the high points in a long religious and philosophical tradition whose richness and subtlety often elude summary or paraphrase.

Beyond the difficulty of selecting only a few figures from a rich tradition, and of separating out views on suicide and euthanasia from broader questions about the human condition, there is a further difficulty in any survey of this kind. To extract an argument from a few paragraphs or pages of longer works demands close attention to context. One can easily be misled. In the second book of Thomas More's *Utopia,* for example, the practice of suicide and assisted suicide by the citizens of a make-believe kingdom appears in a favorable light, and some have taken this as an indication that More endorsed these practices. But nothing else in the life of this devout Catholic provides the slightest evidence for such a conclusion. Moreover, the rhetorical structure of the work features a playful More "reporting" what an imaginary visitor claims to have observed in an equally imaginary land. *Utopia* is a highly ironic, satirical work. It seems an unlikely setting for More—who, after all, went to the block for his religious convictions—to reveal his apostasy from one of the oldest and most settled moral teachings of Christianity.

A somewhat different contextual problem is presented by the thought of Plato, which comes down to us in the form of dramatic dialogues in which the chief interlocutor is, with but few exceptions, Socrates. Yet there is no simple identity between Plato's thought and that of any of his characters, including Socrates. The late Allan Bloom put it well:

> There is a Platonic teaching, but it is no more to be found in any of the speeches than is the thought of Shakespeare to be found in the utterances of any particular character. That thought is in none of the parts but somehow in the whole, and the process of arriving at it is more subtle than that involved in reading a treatise.[1]

Plato's opinion of suicide, moreover, must be extrapolated from a few short exchanges in three dialogues whose themes range far beyond questions raised by suicide. To lift these exchanges out of their context risks a disservice both to the integrity of the dialogue and to the subtlety of Plato's argument about suicide.

Analogous difficulties occur with many of the other thinkers whose writings form the cornerstone of the Western tradition on the morality of taking one's own life. This essay will serve as a surrogate for the absent texts, which are too voluminous to include, on the understanding that it is but a crude roadmap to the territory. There is, in the end, no adequate substitute for consulting the original works of the great minds.

CLASSICAL AND CHRISTIAN VIEWS: PLATO, ARISTOTLE, AUGUSTINE, AQUINAS

Without question, the most powerful influence on Western thought about suicide is Christian theology, which originates in the Jewish Scriptures' account of the creation of man in God's image. By marking man's nature with a divine character, God intended not only to bestow upon human life a special dignity but to limit man's sovereignty over his own existence.[2] That limitation is expressed, among other places, in the commandment "Thou shalt not kill," which affirms the goodness of life as a divine gift and God's abhorrence at the shedding of human blood.[3]

Although this understanding first appeared in God's revelation to the Jews, and although Jewish law forbade suicide accordingly, the New Testament furnished the teaching with a new and universal dimension: belief in the mystery of the Incarnation—God become flesh through the union of divine and human nature in the person of Jesus Christ. With its affirmation of charity as man's highest duty and the promise of heavenly reward to those who die in God's grace, Christianity produced an optimism that was utterly alien to the prevailing ethos at the time of Christ's birth, indeed to any that had gone before. Here was a belief that, by giving an eternal dimension to suffering and death, also gave new meaning to life. God was no longer remote, impersonal, or indifferent: in taking human form, he showed his love for man through the redemptive act of Christ's death and resurrection, promising salvation to all who were faithful to his word. For the faithful Christian, death was no longer an end but the doorway to eternal life.[4]

W. H. Lecky, the historian of European morals, aptly captures the way in which Christian belief altered the meaning of life and death in the ancient world:

> Considered as immortal beings, destined for the extremes of happiness or of misery, and united to one another by a special community of redemption, the first and most manifest duty of the Christian man was to look upon his fellow men as sacred beings and from this notion grew up the eminently Christian idea of the sanctity of human life. . . . [I]t was one of the most important services of Christianity that besides quickening greatly our benevolent affections it definitely and dogmatically asserted the sinfulness of all destruction of human life as a matter of amusement or of simple convenience, and thereby formed a new standard higher than any which then existed in the world. . . . This minute and scrupulous care for human life and human virtue in the humblest form, in the slave, the gladiator, the savage, or the infant, was indeed wholly foreign to the genius of Paganism. It was produced

by the Christian doctrine of the inestimable value of each immortal soul.[5]

In the course of time, these teachings and the dispositions habituated by them altered pagan attitudes toward suicide. Even Auguste Comte, that rigorously atheistic father of modern positivism, recognized Christianity's prohibition of suicide as one of its singular contributions to civilization.[6]

Comte of course was aware, in ways that most people today are not, of the customs and opinions that preceded the arrival of Christianity. The history of the Jews, significantly, is notable for the rarity of suicide, but among other peoples the practice seems to have been fairly widespread. Among the Greeks, for example, it was tolerated if not always formally approved, especially as a response to untreatable, painful illness or fear of ignominy. Early Greek physicians apparently felt little compunction about providing poisons to those who wished to end their lives. In the fourth century B.C., however, a school associated with the name of Hippocrates challenged the reigning medical orthodoxy by forbidding its members to assist others in the act of suicide. Although a distinctly minority view at the outset, the Hippocratic disposition grew in influence even before the rise of Christianity. In time, it was adapted to Christian purposes by the early Church Fathers and ultimately became the dominant medical ethic of the Western world.[7] Hippocratic teaching on assisted suicide and euthanasia appears to have derived from the Pythagoreans, who held that human beings possessed immortal souls that were deemed to be pieces of fallen divinity. Although entombed in the body, the soul could be purified through the study of philosophy and mathematics and eventually liberated, thereafter migrating to its heavenly home.[8]

Plato (427-347 B.C.)

Athough Pythagorean doctrine comes down to us mainly in fragments or by hearsay, its influence can be traced in a number of Platonic dialogues. The most important of these for our purposes is the *Phaedo,* which recounts a conversation between Socrates and a few friends during his last hours as he awaits execution.[9] The *Phaedo* presents Plato's most elaborate discussion of the immortality of the soul and the implications of that belief for human behavior. In a brief exchange at the beginning of the dialogue, Socrates is asked to explain the absolute ban on suicide advocated by the Pythagoreans and other religious teachers, and to reconcile it with his own opinion that death may sometimes be preferable to life Socrates restates what he understands the religious teaching to be: life is not ours to do with as we will because we have been placed in a kind of "prison" or "guard post" by the gods and are therefore not free to run away. He says that while this doctrine is not easy to understand, it does seem correct to him that the gods are our guardians and that we are but their possessions.

This passage has been the subject of much discussion among commentators, especially as it turns upon the reference to life as a kind of prison.[10] Does it mean prison in the sense of jail, as if one were being punished for some pre-natal sin? If so, it would seem to follow that we are not free to escape until that offense is properly atoned for, that is, until the gods permit us to go. This interpretation would seem to imply a radical opposition between soul and body, such that the only true freedom lies in death. That view clashes, however, with the general teaching of the *Phaedo,* which is that one can, and should, seek freedom by mastering bodily needs and desires through philosophy. By alluding to life as a kind of prison, therefore, Socrates may have had another meaning in mind. One thoughtful commentator has suggested that "prison" here means something more akin to "protective custody," i.e., that we are held in life, so to speak, by the gods until such time as we can properly care for ourselves.[11]

That would explain why Socrates does not oppose the popular religious teaching that the gods are benevolent and know what is best for us. It would also explain why Socrates can simultaneously argue that our bodies are an impediment to the pursuit of wisdom *and* that we are not morally free to end our lives for the sake of what we imagine to be a less encumbered condition. Absent some divinely sanctioned necessity of the sort that has now come upon him, Socrates says, we are not permitted to take our own lives.[12] Physical existence is, one might say, an irreducibly paradoxical good: our bodies are constantly drawing us away from the contemplation of the highest things, yet they are the instrument through which we learn to overcome obstacles, and by learning to overcome them we prepare ourselves for life after death in the company of the gods.

The so-called suicide passage of the *Phaedo* is a brief introductory exchange in a longer work that argues for the philosophical life as the best way of life because it entails the perfection of a human being's highest part, his rational soul. Such a life necessarily requires a habituated detachment from bodily demands, so that the soul may partake more fully in the contemplation of that which is unchanging and eternal. Socrates contends that philosophy is in effect a lifelong practice in learning how to die; death is not be feared but is to be welcomed as a release from the encumbrances of the body.

But if death is the gateway to unencumbered contemplation of the highest things, should it not be more hurriedly sought? Socrates makes no such argument. It is one thing, apparently, to welcome death when it comes and quite another thing to seek it actively. While Socrates does not flatly condemn suicide as always and everywhere immoral, he comes very close to that view. He grants to the act no general license, and least of all does he suggest or imply that it should be a matter of individual preference. His teaching seems to be that taking one's life would be morally acceptable if and only if one could be objectively certain that one's *soul* would be improved by the act. The general argument of the *Phaedo* indicates that such certainty is almost always beyond our grasp. Accordingly, we must, he says, "keep ourselves pure until god himself sets us free."[13]

Some further light may be shed by a passage in the *Republic,* the dialogue in which Plato discusses the character of a political regime in accord with perfect justice.[14] In the course of prescribing the best form of medicine for such a community, Socrates criticizes medical practice that prolongs life only through detailed regimens that consume virtually all of a patient's activity. A life utterly given over to bodily demands, Socrates implies, lacks a necessary condition for the virtuous life; and in cases where there is no prospect for recovery, it is better to cease treatment. Some read this passage as indicating Plato's support for suicide, at least for the incurably ill. But there are at least three reasons why this seems unlikely. First, Plato would have chosen an exceedingly roundabout way of making an argument about which he expressed strong doubt in the *Phaedo.* Second, withdrawing treatment and suicide are not always morally equivalent (in the case of withdrawal, death is caused by the underlying disease, not by the intentional act of patient or physician). Third, it must be noted that

Socrates is here concerned not with suicide as such but with subjecting the medical art to the architectonic governance of philosophical wisdom. Taken in that context, the passing comment in the *Republic* appears to be little more than a confirmation of the general argument of the *Phaedo*—that undue preoccupation with the body can interfere with man's duty to perfect his soul.

A brief discussion of suicide also occurs in Plato's *Laws,* his effort to construct a regime that is informed by philosophical understanding while being only an imperfect rendition of the philosophically perfect political community sketched in the *Republic*.[15] The dialogue is one of only a few in which someone other than Socrates is the philosophical protagonist. His place is taken by a nameless elder, referred to as the "Athenian Stranger." The passage discussing suicide occurs in the prologue to a detailed elaboration of a legal code that seeks to orient its subjects toward a life of moral virtue. At the outset the Stranger regrets that such a code should be necessary: noble character rather than fear of punishment should be the chief security of good behavior. But, the Stranger says, as "we are not now legislating . . . for heroes or the children of gods." For lesser mortals, whose behavior is less reliable, the law must act as surrogate for insufficient virtue. Even so, the law may be limited in its capacity to prevent particularly heinous crimes, whose cause will be found in character of an unusually debased sort. In such cases, legal punishment may not suffice as a deterrent. Those disposed to commit heinous crimes should be encouraged to purify themselves, sacrifice to the gods, and seek the company of virtuous men. If such steps are unavailing, the Stranger says that it would be better if those of incorrigible character "[departed] from this life."[16]

This somewhat cryptic comment, which appears to be at odds with the teaching of the *Phaedo,* should be read in the light of a subsequent passage, where suicide is harshly condemned as a species of heinous crime in itself. There, one who commits suicide is to be accorded ignominious burial, on a par with those who murder members of their own family. In a word, the political community must be reminded that suicide is a grave offense against its good order and the wishes of the gods. Nevertheless, the Stranger adds that three classes of suicide should be spared such opprobrious treatment: (1) those who are forced to take their own lives subject to judicial decree (in the manner, for example, of Socrates); (2) those who are compelled by "some intolerable and inevitable misfortune"; and (3) those who find themselves in "some disgrace that is beyond remedy and endurance."[17] Some read this passage as a movement away from the near-absolute disapprobation of suicide contained in the *Phaedo*. The Stranger, however, is here concerned with the amelioration of punishment rather than with the moral justification of suicide *per se*. Moreover, the actor in all three examples must be understood to be acting under some kind of powerful duress, whether legal, physical, social, or emotional. He does not act entirely as a free agent who is capable of making a rational choice; he is, so to speak, not himself. In the absence of such duress, death by his own hand is, and must be understood by others as, a species of "sloth and unmanly cowardice."[18]

Aristotle (384-322 B.C.)

Plato's general condemnation of suicide is supported by his student Aristotle, who shares with his teacher the preeminent position at the head of the Western philosophical tradition. Together, their views constitute the foundation on which philosophers and theologians of the Christian era built their opposition to suicide, as modified by the light of biblical revelation. Whereas Plato's argument is subtle and at times paradoxical, Aristotle's is characteristically straightforward and more overtly didactic; and whereas Plato's is woven dialectically from discussions in three dialogues, Aristotle's must be gleaned from a few brief references in his *Nichomachean Ethics*.

In general, it may be said that Aristotle takes no exception to Plato's general condemnation of suicide. That may indeed explain why he is less interested in the question of suicide *per se* than in a generic question of which suicide is but an illustration: Is it possible to do oneself an injustice?[19] His answer is regrettably brief and not easy to tease out. A few pages prior to this discussion, Aristotle has concluded that "no one can suffer injustice voluntarily, because no one can wish to be harmed."[20] As a voluntary act, then, suicide cannot be unjust to the actor. The implication would seem to be that suicide is morally permissible.

Aristotle's argument, however, contains an additional element:

though suicide may not be an injustice against oneself in a strict sense, the law nevertheless forbids it, and a just man will not contravene the law. Such an argument may strike the modern reader as quaint at best, perhaps even wrong-headed. That is because we understand law quite differently than Aristotle did. Our conceptions of legal obligation derive from characteristically modern theories of the state, according to which government comes into being by means of a social contract, for the purpose of securing individual rights. Aristotle, by contrast, believed that political life was natural to man and essential to the perfection of moral virtue. For him, the law is not a collection of statutes designed to secure rights originating in some pre-political human condition, but an authoritative set of rules whose goal is to habituate citizens to a life of virtue.[21] Because man is by nature a political animal, obedience to legal commands is an essential part of political justice, i.e., the obligation he owes to the political community. Although suicide may not be an injustice against oneself in the strict sense, it is, Aristotle says, an injustice against the political community whose existence is essential to one's own well-being.

Are we to infer, therefore, that in the absence of legal prohibition, Aristotle would have no objection to suicide? Or may suicide be morally objectionable in some other way? The only illustration Aristotle offers is that of a suicidal act committed in "a fit of passion."[22] The implication is that suicide may be unjust not only because it contravenes the law, but also because it offends against the virtue of moderation. This reading is supported by a passage in Book III of the *Ethics,* during Aristotle's discussion of courage. Arguing that courage is the virtuous mean between cowardice and foolhardiness, he offers a number of examples, culminating in a description of the heroic soldier. Fearlessness in the face of death, particularly in combat, is the mark of a courageous man, but "to seek death in order to escape from poverty, or the pangs of love, or from pain and sorrow, is not the action of a courageous man, but rather of a coward; for it is weakness to fly from troubles, and the suicide does not endure death because it is noble to do so, but to escape from evil."[23] This passage would seem to preclude justification of suicide on account of economic hardship, severe emotional distress, or physical infirmity —three of the most common justifications for "rational" suicide throughout the ages.

The Stoics

Perhaps the principal *locus classicus* for these justifications will be found in the thought of that highly eclectic and adaptive school of ancient philosophy known as Stoicism, which flourished in variant forms among Greek and Roman gentlemen during the four centuries surrounding the birth of Christ. Although no single text can be called the authoritative statement of Stoicism (it underwent considerable change over time), its adherents tended to share certain core opinions.[24] Stoic ethical teaching mirrored Platonic beliefs in many respects—for example, that living well was in effect learning how to die, and that living well required the virtues of prudence, justice, courage, and moderation. But whereas for Plato the practice of virtue found its ultimate expression in the contemplative life, the Stoic wise man was honored less for his devotion to philosophy than for the calm resignation he brought to life's contingencies. This difference is no doubt rooted in Stoic cosmology, which understood the universe in terms of endlessly repeated cycles of birth and decay. An emphatically materialist doctrine, Stoicism acknowledged only corporeal substances as real. Even ostensibly immaterial substances such as "God" or reason are commonly explained in material terms by reference to air currents or creative fire. The universe is periodically destroyed by fire only to come into being again to repeat its prior existence, down to the smallest detail.

In a philosophy so profoundly materialistic and deterministic, there was no room for the concept of personal immortality. Death held no fear for Plato because, for the wise man at least, it freed him from bodily constraints and enabled his soul to partake of eternal being. The Stoics also preached courage in the face of death, but for quite different reasons. In the words of one commentator,

> In the main, they taught a version of *natural personal dissolution* according to which the tiny pneuma indwelling within each person dispersed at the moment of death to reunite with the world-soul Pneuma of God. . . . Individuality and personality effectively ceased with death. Death was viewed as natural and inevitable resolution of life itself. Hence only a fool would attempt to oppose death; the wise man would arrange to meet it head on if he could, timing his exit from this world with the aplomb of a thoughtful dinner guest who seeks to avoid boring or detaining his hosts. Hence the wise

man withdraws from life's banquet in just the right way, under just the right circumstances.[25]

As Professor John Finnis has pointed out, "the Stoic thesis . . . seems to be essentially an expression of piety directed toward a world-order whose order might well be regarded as not altogether admirable, and whose outcome might equally be regarded as a matter of indifference to us."[26] There is nobility, certainly, in the Stoic understanding of virtue, which owes much to the thought of Plato and Aristotle, but it seems to lack a compelling sense of purpose. To borrow from Professor Finnis once again: "Boldly [the Stoic] will declare that, if you wish to compare one's choice of aim in life with a man aiming a spear at a target, then you must admit that the ultimate good, end, or aim that such a man has in view is *not* the target, *nor* the hitting of it, but the aiming it straight!"[27]

This account goes a long way toward explaining the Stoics' opinion about suicide, which they appear to have embraced in a mood just short of enthusiasm. One ancient commentator articulated five separate grounds used by the Stoics to justify suicide.[28] A thoughtful modern student of the subject has expanded the list to eight, which he divides roughly into two categories, "heroic" and "non-heroic." The heroic group includes the desire to escape shame and dishonor, to demonstrate total devotion to one's country, to end unrelieved grief over the death of a loved one, and to atone for the death one has accidentally dealt to another. In the non-heroic category are the desire to escape persistent and degrading poverty, to be reunited in death with a deceased loved one, to escape the boredom and futility of life, and to escape a relentlessly painful illness or injury.[29] To consider this list is to realize at once how far we have come from the arguments of Plato and Aristotle—and how close we are to arguments commonly encountered in our own time. Indeed, it may be said that there is little in contemporary justifications for suicide that is not prefigured in some way in the various rationales furnished by the Stoics.

Augustine (354-420)

To turn from the writings of classical antiquity to those of Christianity is to experience a remarkable intellectual and psychological sea-change. Among the tasks facing early Christian thinkers was to explain their beliefs, insofar as possible, in terms that made sense among the then dominant philosophical schools. Few were more adept or forceful in this effort than St. Augustine of Hippo, the towering figure of the early Christian West, who remains a primary spiritual and intellectual inspiration for Christians in the twentieth century. Among his many writings are two that are on almost everyone's short list of Great Books: his spiritual autobiography, *The Confessions,* and his profound meditation on politics, philosophy, and history, *The City of God.* The latter, which was prompted by the barbarians'sack of Rome in 410, sought to accomplish three purposes at once: to defend against the charge that the spread of Christianity caused Rome's decline; to demonstrate the inadequacies of pagan religion and philosophy; and to articulate a comprehensive philosophy of history in the light of the Incarnation.[30]

Augustine argues that the central feature of history since the Fall is the struggle within the human soul, testing whether its love will be given to the City of God or to the City of Man. By the former he means the spiritual community of those who are prepared to follow the teaching and example of Jesus Christ, and who seek to be united with him in heaven. By the latter, he means those who devote themselves exclusively to the vainglorious pursuit of the world and the flesh. Membership in the City of God is the only true path to inner peace in this world and happiness in the next. The allure of the City of Man is rooted in self-love; despite its temporary charms and pleasures, it is bound to produce dissatisfaction, misery, turmoil, and endless war. Its pretensions cannot satisfy man's deepest yearning, the desire to know God. The human heart is restless, says Augustine, and will find no repose unless directed toward God as its final end.

In describing the two cities, Augustine is of course speaking only figuratively. Both cities exist, so to speak, in the heart of everyone, and within all political communities. Virtuous action, though necessary and desirable, does not in and of itself determine which of the two cities one belongs to. The only true determinant is the purity of the human heart, which can be known by God alone. This view of Augustine's, it will be noted, bears a certain resemblance to Plato's theory of the good life, although at Augustine's hands the theory has acquired a profoundly Christian eschatology. Augustine defines man at one point as "a rational soul using a mortal and earthly body,"[31] a doctrine again reminiscent of Plato's discussion in the *Phaedo,* where the body is likened to a kind of guard-house for the soul that one may not quit without divine permission. Augustine reinforces Plato's objection to suicide with a forceful reminder to Christians of their duty to obey the commands of the one true God and to endure suffering in imitation of Jesus Christ.

Augustine's most extensive discussion of suicide is found in the opening sections of Book I of *The City of God.* Much of the first five books is directed against the fashionable accusation that Rome's decline and fall were directly proportional to the rise of Christianity. By orienting people to the service of a heavenly kingdom, so the argument went, Christianity had undermined Roman virtue and patriotism, which were grounded in citizen loyalty to the gods of the city. The gods of Rome had justly taken offense and, in anger, levied their revenge upon the city. If the Christian God were the one true God, Rome would not have been abandoned to the assault of the barbarians.

Augustine responds that, far from corrupting Rome, Christian virtue had given new direction and vitality to a faltering and demonstrably debauched moral order. He argues that the moral standards of Rome were either hopelessly contradictory or, at best, inferior to those emanating from Christianity. At best, he says, Rome practiced a kind of mock virtue; its greatest citizens performed heroic deeds, but their efforts were guided less by love of virtue rightly understood than by the desire for glory. The much vaunted history of the city before the arrival of Christianity was in fact a history of incessant strife and bloodshed, spiraling ever downward until it reached a fatal crisis. As for the Roman deities, it was apparent that Romans themselves failed to take their gods seriously, and when they did, their seeming devotion was more an expression of their own vanity than an act of genuine religious piety.

Augustine on Suicide

It is in this context that Augustine first addresses the question of suicide. He notes the case of certain Christian virgins who had been raped by the barbarian invaders and who had not avenged their defilement. The only virtuous course of action in such cases, pagan critics said, would have been to imitate the famous Roman noble-woman Lucretia, who assuaged the dishonor of her rape through suicide. Augustine replies that no story better illustrates the deficiency of Roman ethics when compared to those of Christianity. Consider the irony, he says: Lucretia, though innocent of moral complicity in her own defilement, felt it necessary to kill herself in order to vindicate her virtue! What kind of virtue is that? Augustine asks. We are forbidden by God to take the life of an innocent victim, but how is killing oneself any less an act of homicide? And how is it virtuous to compound one immoral act with another? An innocent victim has no valid ground for punishing herself; it would be as if she took upon herself the guilt of the perpetrator. The Christian women, though defiled, sought neither to avenge the crime nor to compound it by killing themselves. Their refusal exhibited true virtue and heroism. Theirs was not the glory prized by the world, but the glory of God's praise for obedience to his law.

Having established by example a general proposition about the immorality of killing, whether it be of another or of oneself, Augustine turns to Scripture for support. The Bible, he says, rejects suicide, even for the sake of avoiding evil. The divine commandment against killing is general in nature and, he says, clearly includes suicide no less than homicide. True, he says, not all homicide is killing in the biblical sense; it is permissible, for example, to kill in obedience to a legitimate edict or in a just war—but suicide fits neither category. It is also true, Augustine concedes, that God appears to have given his specific approval to killing or suicide in certain rare instances recorded in the Bible: the command to Abraham, as a test of his faith, to slay Isaac, for example; and the command to Samson to pull down the temple, thereby killing himself as well as his captors. Such circumstances are exceptional, however, and the lesson to be drawn from them, Augustine argues, is not that Scripture is ambiguous in its teaching, but that homicide, whether of another or of oneself, is forbidden unless expressly sanctioned by divine command.

Augustine next addresses the Stoic argument that suicide under certain conditions reveals greatness of soul. More often than not, Augustine argues, it shows the very opposite—either cowardliness, vanity, or just plain foolishness, and he cites the case of one Theombratus, who exhibited all three weaknesses. Theombratus had little tolerance for pain and even less, apparently, for the low esteem in which he was held by others. Finally, he was so inspired by what he understood to be the teaching of the *Phaedo* that he killed himself—the faster, it was said, to acquire immortality of soul. But Theombratus misread Plato's intention, Augustine says: if the philosopher himself chose not to follow such a course, clearly he meant to discourage suicide even when motivated by a desire for immortality.

Augustine then discusses a second category of women who were widely celebrated within the Christian community as heroic martyrs for their faith—those who took their own lives rather than submit to the lust of their ravishers. He expresses compassion for their action but believes them mistaken in judgment. First, it is futile to seek refuge from the ills of this world at the risk of incurring those of the next. Second, another's sin can never pollute the soul of an innocent victim, but taking one's own life could. Third, no one should commit suicide on account of her own sins, for she has all the more need of repentance in this world. And finally, one who defies God's command against killing herself cannot hope for a better life after death.

Is it ever licit to take one's own life in order to avoid sin? Augustine replies that if the argument had any merit, the most sensible thing would be to commit suicide immediately after baptism in an effort to avoid any occasion of sin whatsoever. For the Christian, committing one evil to avoid another is never permitted. The way to combat sin, rather, is through repentance, purification of soul, and humble submission to the will of the loving God, who took human form in the person of Jesus Christ.

Taken whole, Augustine's argument attempts to address the most common justifications for suicide that were offered during the early Christian era: the desire to avoid sin, to escape worldly troubles, to expiate guilt, to seek a better life, or to escape another's aggression. None of these, according to Augustine, can be squared with Christian teaching rightly understood. In other writings, though not in *The City of God,* Augustine addresses suicide in the specific context of the Donatist heresy.[32] The Donatists, who had a substantial following in the early fourth century, believed many of their fellow Christians to be lax in religious belief and practice and cowardly in the face of persecution. Preaching a militantly aggressive Christianity, the more extreme Donatists engaged in defiant and violent acts against public authority in the hope of stirring a popular uprising. The most fanatical among them even endeavored to provoke their own death at the hands of others, believing they would thereby ensure their salvation through martyrdom. Augustine's condemnation of their behavior is severe and uncompromising.

Augustine was not the first Christian thinker to argue against suicide, nor did he construct a Christian position out of thin air. He was the first, however, to set the argument down more or less systematically in one place, weaving it from pagan and scriptural sources alike to form what might be called the base-line Christian case against suicide. For centuries after his death, his argument exerted strong influence over the development of Western thought, customs, and law.[33]

Thomas Aquinas (1225-1274)

From Augustine we move forward some 900 years, during which the Augustinian argument against suicide had become the reigning orthodoxy of Christendom. In the thirteenth century, the argument was refined and restated by Thomas Aquinas, who holds the premier position among Christian teachers of the Middle Ages. Like Augustine, he was at once a theologian, a philosopher, and a saint, who coursed masterfully over everything from cosmology and ontology to politics and ethics. And like Augustine, he drew upon both pagan and Christian sources, reconstituting them into a new synthesis that for many centuries after his death exerted an extraordinary influence. Whereas Augustine relied for the most part on neo-Platonic philosophical teaching, which he thought particularly congenial to Christian belief, Aquinas made abundant use of Aristotle, whose writings had only recently been rediscovered in the West.[34]

For Aquinas, as for Aristotle, all things possess a specific nature that determines the type of activity appropriate to that nature. The character of a thing's nature is determined, in turn, by its final cause or end. The final cause of an acorn, for example, is an oak tree, and the activity by which it becomes an oak exhibits the perfection of its nature — in Aristotelian terminology, the actualization of its potentiality. With respect to human activity, Aquinas follows Aristotle in arguing that man's nature directs him toward the end of achieving happiness. Unlike acorns, of course, human beings can choose among various goods and may err in selecting those that constitute true happiness. If men are true to their natures, however, they will seek to actualize those attributes that denote human excellence objectively considered. For Aristotle, whose metaphysics lacked any sense of eternity, happiness is a temporal good only; but for Aquinas, whose vision of the good was not limited to the temporal sphere, the ultimate good for man can be achieved only through the vision of God in heaven. Again, men are free to choose other goals, but Aquinas judges actions as good or bad depending on their compatibility with man's final end.[35]

Whereas Aristotle neither knew of nor claimed any authority beyond human reason, Aquinas, as a devout Christian, acknowledged the existence of a supernatural order. The whole of the universe, natural and supernatural, is governed by "Divine Reason's conception of things," which Aquinas calls "eternal law."[36] The eternal law is expressed both through explicit revelation (Scripture), which Aquinas calls "Divine law," and through natural law, which Aquinas defines as the participation of human reason in the eternal law. Explicit divine revelation, then, is not the only source of human wisdom. Moral truths can be established by means of reason alone. Of course, moral propositions are not always self-evident, but Aquinas would argue that with proper habituation and mature reflection, their truth can be established independently of any particular commandment of God. Taken together, these moral propositions constitute the natural law. In defining the natural law as the "rational creature's participation in the eternal law,"[37] Aquinas does not mean that its content is dictated by the specific divine instruction, but that, through reason, man can know and be bound by the moral order of the created universe.

With this by way of background, we are better able to appreciate Aquinas's treatment of suicide. In general, he concurs with Augustine on both theological and philosophical grounds and, indeed, begins his discussion by quoting from *The City of God*. Like Augustine, he specifically condemns suicide by virgins for the sake of protecting their chastity, and he agrees that the divine commandment against killing covers suicide no less than homicide. In short, suicide is always forbidden unless specifically commanded by God (as in the case of Samson). But while tracking the sense of Augustine's argument closely, Aquinas gives it a characteristically Thomistic twist by emphasizing certain features that were either understated or merely implicit in Augustine or not addressed at all by him.[38] First, Aquinas argues—drawing on Aristotle—that it is in the nature of every living being to wish to preserve itself. To take one's own life is therefore not only a violation of God's commandment, but an act contrary to the natural law. Second, Aquinas emphasizes that suicide is an act of injustice against the political community. Here again he draws upon Aristotle in understanding political life as natural to man and essential to his well-being. No one is entitled to makes rules for himself in disregard of the laws of the community, as if he were the solitary citizen and sole ruler of his own *polis*. Third, Aquinas condemns suicide as an arrogation of the power over life and death that rightly belongs to God alone. Man's sovereignty over himself, evidenced by his free will, does not extend to the manner of his passing from this world to the next.

EARLY MODERN VIEWS: DONNE, HUME, AND KANT

With Aquinas's refinements to Augustine's argument, the Christian case against suicide is essentially developed in full. Subsequent comments by others are largely glosses on Thomistic themes. For the next five centuries, religious doctrine, philosophical argument, and civil law remained steadfast, if not adamant, in their opposition to suicide. To be sure, orthodox Christian teaching on this point was not always uniformly applauded, at least in private, but dissent is hardly unique to its position on suicide. The strength of the Church's political status and the vigor with which it defended its doctrines relegated dissenting opinion to the social margins.[39]

Nevertheless, cracks began to appear in the finely wrought edifice. With the Renaissance came a more audacious kind of thinking that gloried in the rediscovery of the pagan world and challenged the intellectual symmetry of the Middle Ages. Hard upon it came the Protestant Reformation, and by the end of the seventeenth century the doctrinal unity of Christendom had been irreparably shattered. With its disintegration, religious dissent, once branded as heresy, became widespread. Not surprisingly, this same era raised new questions about what had long been understood as the settled issue of suicide.

Among the first of the post-Reformation figures to write favorably about suicide was the French humanist Michel de Montaigne (1533-1592), who sympathetically recounted pagan customs hospitable to suicide but refrained from a direct attack upon the traditional Christian position.[40] Notwithstanding the free thinking fashionable among intellectuals in this period, Montaigne and a few others stand virtually alone in their approval of suicide. The leading Protestant reformers, for example, did not depart from the orthodox case against suicide laid down by Augustine and Aquinas, and continued to condemn the practice as the vilest of sins. The subject is widely discussed in the seventeenth century among the English Puritans, whose members showed a propensity for suicide far greater than that of the population as a whole. An interesting correlation was identified by the nineteenth-century sociologist Emile Durkheim, who reported that Protestants took their own lives at significantly higher rates than did Catholics. His explanation was that by encouraging greater freedom of inquiry and individual expression of belief, Protestantism also encouraged, albeit unintentionally, a departure from traditional Catholic reasoning on suicide.[41]

John Donne (1572-1631)

Whatever the explanation for the rise in suicide, the doctrinal prohibition of the churches did not change. Indeed, perhaps the most interesting document on the subject in the seventeenth century is notable precisely for its departure from the uniform ethical teaching of both Protestantism and Catholicism. Its author was a man of considerable learning and, later in life, of considerable piety as well. John Donne is best known to the modern world as the author of some of the finest poetry in the English language. But literature was not his only claim to fame. Though raised in a devout Catholic household whose members suffered much for their faith, Donne eventually became an Anglican cleric and the dean of St. Paul's, the most important pulpit in England.[42]

Donne set down his reflections on suicide during a period of extreme economic and emotional hardship, when his worldly prospects seemed unusually dim and some years before he entered upon a priestly vocation. *Biathanatos* (a bastardization of a Greek word that had come to mean "violent death") is as somber and melancholic as the mood that inspired it. Indeed, Donne openly acknowledged that he frequently thought of suicide, and the work may be no less a therapeutic than an intellectual exercise. Although he never formally disavowed its arguments, he refused to authorize its publication during his lifetime. The work circulated privately among friends and acquaintances but reached a larger audience after Donne's son published it twenty years after his father's death and some forty years after its creation.[43]

Biathanatos is, as far as we know, the first work in English to break with the previously settled disposition on suicide established by Augustine and Aquinas. The form of Donne's argument roughly parallels that of the *Summa Theologiae:* the first part is entitled "Of Law and Nature," the second, "Of the Law of Reason," and the third, "Of the Law of God." The title page declares the general character of the argument that will follow:

> A Declaration of that Paradox or Thesis, that
> Self-homicide is not so naturally a Sin that
> it may never be otherwise;
>
> wherein the Nature and the Extent of
> all those Laws which seem to be violated
> by this Act are diligently surveyed.[44]

To the argument that all living things naturally incline to their own preservation, Donne replies that some men seem, equally naturally, to yearn for death. Pious Christians, he argues, may be particularly prone to see death as but the natural stepping-stone to man's proper supernatural end, a heavenly afterlife: "If that which I affect by death be a truly better good, wherein is the other, stricter law of nature, which is rectified reason, violated?"[45] Is the yearning for death that ennobled so many Christian martyrs to be condemned as *contra naturam?* Donne concedes that while the desire for death, like many other human desires, can be corrupted by selfish or base motives, it should not for that reason be condemned out of hand. Deciding whether suicide is properly natural to man, Donne says, requires us to understand the intentions that direct some to take their own lives.

In the second part of his argument, Donne critiques the notion that suicide is an offense against the political community. The prohibition of suicide by civil law, he argues, says little about its status as an immoral act. The law, after all, condemns many things that are not immoral. True, an epidemic of suicide would clearly injure the social order, but the universal prohibition favored by moralists ignores those exceptional cases where the chief effect of the law is to condemn some to extended suffering. Here, as in the first part of his argument, Donne insists that a proper assessment of suicide must include an analysis of the actor's intent; a hypothetical effect on society is insufficient reason to proscribe the act as always and everywhere immoral.

In its concluding section, *Biathanatos* takes issue with traditional scriptural exegesis holding that suicide contravenes the law of God. Donne acknowledges the weight of the doctrinal tradition but is struck by the fact that Scripture nowhere *explicitly* condemns suicide. Moreover, the suicides recounted in the Bible are too various to be explained by Augustine's effort to condemn as morally illicit all those not specifically authorized by God. Once again, he argues that the only way to determine the morality of suicide is to assess the actor's motive; and as Scripture is notably silent on this point, Donne concludes that we are at liberty to say that not all suicides are necessarily contrary to God's will. One must distinguish between suicide in general and suicide directed toward the glory of God (as with martyrdom, for example), or suicide that is motivated by the welfare of others in accordance with Christian charity. In the end, God is the only fitting judge of the morality of such behavior, because he and he alone can know the hearts of those who die by their own hand.

For all its apparent daring at the time, it is a curiously conservative case that Donne makes. He gives no general license to suicide. Far from it. In lawyer-like fashion (Donne was a barrister as well as a student of Christian doctrine), he picks away at what he considers to be the most vulnerable points in the traditional argument, parrying here, thrusting there, but driving always toward a narrowly circumscribed conclusion: suicide directed by self-interest cannot be morally justified; suicide directed by a proper Christian motivation can be. Indeed, the piety of Donne's argument may be its most striking element. Though heretical in his time, it seems tame by contemporary standards. Donne's devotion to Christian religious practice and most traditional doctrines is palpable. There is not the slightest bow in *Biathanatos* to philosophical skepticism, and only a hint of what we would today describe as an argument for individual autonomy. Nonetheless, Donne's break with the hitherto uniform Christian tradition gave a certain indirect support to the older, pagan views against which Augustine had warred.

Although *Biathanatos* was roundly condemned in the years immediately following its publication, Donne's idiosyncratic yet pious doubts must have seemed a mere diversion to those who later launched a full frontal assault upon the intellectual and political citadels of Christianity. For the apostles of the Enlightenment, Augustine, Aquinas, Luther, and Calvin (among others) were so many purveyors of religious superstition whose teachings legitimated despotism and imprisoned minds in ignorance. Man's reason, uncorrupted by the false idols of religious revelation, would henceforth become the instrument of his liberation from the intellectually sterile and morally corrupting myths of the past. Given the wholly secular premises and spirit of the Enlightenment project, it was inevitable that traditional theological and philosophical objections to suicide would also be subjected to critical scrutiny.

David Hume (1711-1776)

In this respect, perhaps no one embodied Enlightenment enthusiasms with greater rigor than David Hume, the father of modern skepticism. Hume turned the harsh glare of reason upon reason itself and concluded, among other things, that moral distinctions have no rational basis. Few thinkers rival Hume's influence in the modern world, especially in the English-speaking countries, and although he himself was not a relativist, it is to his thought that much of today's fashionable relativism is greatly indebted. His principal works include *A Treatise on Human Nature* (a revised version of which was entitled *An Enquiry Concerning Human Understanding*), a multi-volume history of England, and numerous essays on politics and philosophy.[46] Although Hume did not affirm an unqualified autonomy for the individual, the force of his general philosophy virtually ensured that such qualifications as he continued to hold would themselves erode under the acidic effects of his own skepticism. Two and a half centuries have passed since Hume presented his views on suicide to the world, but the qualitative distance between his philosophy and main currents of our age is much shorter. Hume was celebrated in his own day for his historical and political works; his more profound philosophical works were ignored or misread. In our own time, his philosophical suppositions are among the most powerful of the age, and his essay on suicide is the touchstone of modern sensibility on the subject.[47]

Hume stands in the tradition of English empiricism, whose founding father, John Locke, in the late seventeenth century launched a withering attack upon the then fashionable theory of innate ideas, insisting that all knowledge comes from experience. Hume, however, takes Locke a step further. He defines experience in terms of "perceptions," which he says are of two kinds: "impressions" and "ideas." Impressions are constituted by our sensations, physical and emotional; ideas are but copies or images of impressions. The difference between impressions and ideas is one of degree, not kind: impressions strike us forcefully (e.g., touch, smell, hatred), ideas less so.

But if all knowledge arises from sensory impressions, and if ideas are but copies or representations of those impressions, how is it possible to have true (as opposed to merely suppositional) knowledge of reality? Regarding reality as a whole, we would seem to be in a position similar to that of a deaf man, who would be unable to form the idea of musical sound. On this predicate, Hume was unable to establish a rational demonstration of existence of the self—there being no exact impressions corresponding to the entity described by the personal pronoun "I." In similar fashion, he denied the principle of causation. What we call causation, he argued, was simply a result of our observing sequential events and assuming that the first in time caused the second. The presumed causal relationship is not in the events we behold but in our own minds.[48]

Not surprisingly, Hume's general philosophical skepticism carried over into his ethical teaching, where he argued that opinions about morals cannot ultimately be proved true or false. As he put it in a famous passage:

In every system of morality, which I have hitherto met with, I have always remarked, that the author proceeds for some time in the ordinary way of reasoning, and establishes the being of God, or makes observations concerning human affairs; when of a sudden I am surprised to find, that instead of the usual copulations, *is,* and *is not,* I meet with no proposition that is not connected with an *ought* or an *ought not.* This change is imperceptible; but is, however, of the last consequence. For as this *ought,* or *ought not,* expresses some new relation or affirmation, it is necessary that it should be observed and explained; and at the same time that a reason should be given, for what seems altogether inconceivable, how this new relation can be a deduction from others, which are entirely different from it. . . . [T]his small attention would . . . let us see, that the distinction of vice and virtue is not founded merely on the relations of objects, nor is perceived by reason.[49]

Morality, in short, cannot be inferred from factual experience. What we call virtue and vice is really our ascription to events of our own feelings and sentiments, which, Hume says, are ultimately rooted in our sense of what is pleasant and unpleasant.

Hume is at some pains, however, to save this theory from the jaws of mere subjectivism. The path by which he undertakes to do so consistently with his theories of ideas and morality is complex and cannot detain us here. It is worth remarking, however, that this path leads to an essentially utilitarian concept of ethics. Although, on Hume's terms, an objective sense of right and wrong cannot be established satisfactorily by reason, human beings seem nevertheless to possess a certain moral sense associated with the mores of their society. We give moral approval not only to those things that are immediately agreeable or useful to ourselves, but also to those that are agreeable or useful to others. Self-interest is modulated by a certain natural sociability or sympathy with our fellow man that induces us to assent to what is useful to society at large. Our passions and feelings are aroused, pleasantly or unpleasantly, by things that affect the lives of others. Hume thus softens the subjectivism of his ethical theory by extending the range of objects or actions that please or displease us as individuals to include those that please or displease us as members of a social order whose proper functioning is important to each individual's existence. His thought thus paved the way for the utilitarian calculus that would later be developed by Jeremy Bentham and John Stuart Mill.

Hume's Answer to Religious Objections

Hume's philosophical skepticism and his defense of individual autonomy in moral decision-making create the crucible in which his essay on suicide is formed. In general, it may be said that he brings the argument back to a position first fully articulated by the Stoics: when persistent grave misfortune, particularly in matters of health, robs one of the enjoyment of life, death by one's own hand can be a reasonable and welcome alternative. Unlike the Stoics, of course, Hume had to contend with a widely venerated and, by his time, thoroughly institutionalized religious opposition to suicide. To be sure, Hume does not believe that religious arguments can make any valid claim upon the mind of man; but he thinks it necessary to address the effects of those arguments upon the minds of others. He does this in part by recasting the Thomistic arguments—though he does not to refer to Aquinas by name—in a fashion that makes them seem ridiculous.

The core argument Hume chooses to address is that suicide encroaches upon "the office of divine providence," thereby "disturbing the order of the universe."[50] He reduces this claim to the idea that all life belongs to God in the same manner that one may be said to own a piece of property. If so, Hume implies, God is a very careless protector of his possessions. Men die from all kinds of causes; floods, fire, and disease, for example, all carry men away. Are we then to assume that God causes these things to happen? If so, why do we suddenly assume that his intention does not run to our own life-taking? Clearly, God does not superintend the universe in its details, and because he does not, men are not bound to act as if he did. Besides, if we are morally bound by the Creator to save our lives, should we not also be equally bound to protect them against lesser risks? Yet men place themselves in danger all the time without a thought of incurring divine displeasure.

Carrying the argument one step further, Hume suggests that perhaps suicide offends not only against God's ownership of our lives but also against the natural order of the universe he created. But, he counters, men disturb the natural order all the time for the benefit of what they deem to be a larger good. If we may divert the Nile or dam the Danube, "where then is the crime of turning a few ounces of blood from their natural channel?"[51]

Finally, Hume argues that not all suicides arise from prideful rebellion against God. Many are the consequence of abject misery that can no longer be endured. Surely the desire to eliminate pain and suffering cannot be evil in and of itself, especially if the suicide acknowledges his gratitude to God for such good as befell him before his misfortune.

Hume's Case for Suicide

Having disposed of the religious objections, at least in a recast form, Hume then undertakes to make an affirmative case for suicide by arguing that, far from offending the good order of the political community, it may sometimes bring it benefit. He does this by means of particular hypothetical examples. What obligation does a retired person owe to his community? At best, his contribution is small, and if social obligations are reciprocal, so the community's duty to him ought to be comparably diminished. By the same token, there is clearly some limit on the nature of these obligations. "I am not obliged to do a small good to society at the expense of a great harm to myself: When then should I prolong a miserable existence, because of some frivolous advantage which the public may perhaps receive from me?"[52] Hume then extends this argument to the case of a sick person whose contribution to the body politic is at best marginal. His suicide, by removing a piddling social benefit, works no very great harm, whereas if his suffering is great, his suicide could effect a net social gain. The same is even truer for one who no longer takes pleasure in life but remans a burden to those around him. In such a case, Hume says, suicide would dispense both an individual and a social benefit, as it would in the case of a captured spy who fears that the enemy will torture him into revealing things injurious to his country.

Hume's carefully chosen examples are designed to build a case for his general thesis. As religion can offer no rationally binding scruples, one should be able to do with one's life as one wishes, subject to this utilitarian calculus: if the benefit to be gained by relieving oneself of unhappiness outweighs the social benefit of continued life, suicide is morally defensible.

With Donne and Hume, the most important elements are in place for what will become, in the twentieth century, the dominant argument for suicide: the questioning, and then the rejection, of religion as an authoritative source of opposition; the displacement of divine and natural law by individual autonomy as the ground of moral decision-making; and the acknowledgment that social utility may sometimes qualify the sovereignty of the individual will. To these might be added a fourth element, powerfully present in contemporary discussion but traceable to Donne and Hume and, from them, back to the Stoics: the argument from compassion, i.e., the proposition that some lives seem so miserable that continued existence is a cruel punishment rather than a blessing. The full elaboration of this position did not occur all at once, but over the past two hundred years, Hume's argument has gradually acquired the force of a dogmatic opinion every bit equal, in its possession of men's minds today, to the hold that religious claims had in the centuries preceding Hume's assault.

That outcome was not immediately apparent, however, in the late eighteenth century. Hume's critics, of whom there were many, were alarmed by the implications of his radical skepticism and sought to correct his errors. Clearly, no simple assertion of dogmatic authority would suffice; the mold of religious unity had been broken by the Reformation, and the ethical symmetry that had generally prevailed even after the Reformation no longer possessed the metaphysical certitude of the pre-Enlightenment era. Could reason reassert itself against the rationalist assaults of Hume and others like him, who could find no enduring philosophical ground for moral ideas? This, among other things, was the task set for himself by Immanuel Kant, the pre-eminent figure of the German Enlightenment, who said that Hume's attack on reason had wakened him from his "dogmatic slumbers."

Moral Philosophy and the Scientific Revolution

The condition of moral philosophy in the late eighteenth century may be described roughly as follows. The revolution in the natural sciences that had become manifest during the preceding two hundred years caused doubt about the metaphysical assumptions that had dominated Western thought for a millennium or more. Those assumptions, emanating from both biblical revelation and the philosophy of Plato and Aristotle, conceived of the universe as one of identifiable design and purpose. According to traditional Judeo-Christian belief,

God not only created the universe but superintended his handiwork. He gave man a special dignity by creating him in His own image and likeness, and he ordained rules for man's behavior toward his Creator, toward himself, and toward his neighbor. According to Plato and Aristotle, the right ordering of man's soul reflected and corresponded to a universe of ordered purposes. To live well meant to live in accordance with virtue, which was understood, in turn, not simply by reference to utilitarian calculation, but by reference to those goods and actions appropriate to the perfection of man's nature.

The new discoveries in astronomy, physics, chemistry, and biology, however, seemed to suggest an alternative basis for understanding the universe in general and human nature in particular. God may have created the universe, but there was little evidence—little, at least, that could be confirmed by science—that he cared for his creation or intervened in its subsequent history. Reason and faith, which in the Christian view were previously understood to share compatible metaphysical suppositions, now appeared to rest on wholly different grounds and to require altogether separate justifications. With the rise of modern science, God was sometimes likened to an intelligent if somewhat absent-minded watchmaker who set nature in motion and then promptly forgot about it. Rather than operating in accordance with providential rules of divine origin and purpose, nature was now said to behave according to demonstrable laws of mathematical physics that operated with apparent indifference to the fate of the human things. The universe, in short, appeared to be governed more by mechanical necessity than by discernible rational purpose, divine or otherwise—a conclusion that had enormous consequences for understanding human action no less than planetary motion.

The antinomy between the suppositions and discoveries of natural science, on the one hand, and the principles of traditional theology and philosophy, on the other, did not appear all at once. Indeed, most scientists and philosophers of the early modern period retained their religious conviction, believing that rigorous scientific method and logical deduction would eventually shed confirming light on the tenets of religious faith. Just as Newtonian physics had demonstrated the laws of motion, so it was at first believed that an analogous scientific reasoning would provide a defensible explanation for man's place in the universe and for the rules of human behavior.

But the high confidence of the first generations of modern thinkers that a scientific rationale for human action could be established eventually gave way. The efforts of those who, like Descartes, sought to comprehend the whole of reality by synthesizing the laws of natural science and the laws of human action within a single overarching metaphysical construct proved unavailing. In the end, these finely wrought systems based on mathematical deduction were unable to withstand the critique of the empiricists, who argued that mathematical propositions, while perfectly logical, could not convey information about reality as such. The only true form of knowledge, they insisted, was that which comes to us through sense-perception and experience. This critique reached its apogee in the philosophical skepticism of Hume, who concluded that it was impossible to demonstrate a rational ground for objective moral choice. What we call morality, he argued, was entirely a matter of individual preference. Reason, in his view, was merely a slave of our passions.

Immanuel Kant (1729-1804)

This was the intellectual atmosphere in which the moral philosophy of Immanuel Kant arose. It is impossible in a short space—or even, for that matter, in a longer one—to give a succinct distillation of Kantian thought. It is elegant, complex, prolix, and difficult to understand; yet there is no gainsaying its influence upon the modern world. More than any other philosopher, Kant captured the predicament of man in the wake of the modern scientific revolution. On the one hand, man is subject to the same deterministic laws that appear to govern the rest of the physical universe; on the other, he is the one creature that is capable of rational reflection and conscious of freedom and moral obligation. Whether these two views could be reconciled, and if so, how, are the central questions animating Kant's philosophical enterprise.[53]

While accepting the findings of natural science and their implicit refutation of traditional metaphysics, Kant nevertheless argued that the world of mechanical causality did not encompass the whole of reality. There appeared to him to be a domain of supersensible reality that was accessible to man, yet not fully accounted for either in the new physics or in the philosophical speculation built upon that foundation. How Kant reached this conclusion is beyond our purpose here. We must content ourselves with a few conclusionary statements that provide a necessary backdrop to his position on suicide.

In general, it may be said that Kant undertook to demonstrate that Hume's critique of metaphysics extended to the presumed certitudes of natural science itself. In Hume's account, the only sure basis for knowledge derived from our sense-experience; but that being the case, how could Hume be sure there was no other reality than that which presented itself to our senses? How could he be sure that (as presumed by science) nature was everywhere uniform in its operations? And how could one who was unable to find a rational basis for causation accept the truth of scientific findings that necessarily recognized, indeed rested upon, the validity of causal relationships? Again, if the only sure knowledge is that which arises from sense-perceptions, what prevents these impressions from being simply a jumbled mass of data? While Kant, like Hume, rejected the theory of innate ideas that had attracted many of his predecessors, he nevertheless argued that man possessed the capacity to order and synthesize sense-experience in ways that the empiricists could not account for.

On the question of morality, Kant generally accepted Hume's argument that one could not rationally deduce an "ought" from an "is," but he also believed that ostensibly empirical explanations of human nature failed to explain two features of human behavior that for Kant were palpably obvious and significant: men are conscious of their freedom, and their actions are informed by a sense of moral obligation. These observations suggested to Kant the possibility of understanding morality as something other than choices dictated by our passions. Man was for Kant a kind of hybrid creature, governed by mechanical causality like the rest of the physical universe, yet capable of acting as a morally free agent. Armed with that insight, Kant undertook to reestablish morality on an entirely new ground, one that rejected the discredited metaphysical assumptions of the past while at the same time purporting to save morality from the abyss of subjectivity created by Hume's theory of autonomous individualism.

For Hume and other philosophical skeptics, it will be recalled, moral imperatives were entirely conditional; there was no rational basis for confirming their truth other than by reference to the preferences or desires of the actor. Kant, by contrast, sought to demonstrate the rationality of a second type of imperative, one that bore no relation to the motives of, while imposing moral obligation upon, the actor. Kant's demonstration of this argument is notably difficult to understand and cannot be easily recapitulated without an elaborate discussion of his overall philosophical stance. Suffice it to say here that Kant concluded that although morality originates in the individual will, not everything willed by the individual will necessarily be moral. Morality, in short, is not something "out there" awaiting to be discovered in, or deduced from, the facts of nature. Nor is it, as Hume argued, a mere function of individual preference. The very nature of morality, Kant contended, is inextricably intertwined with the concept of duty, and duty, if it is to have meaning at all, must oblige all men everywhere. The idea of moral obligation loses all coherence if it means one thing for this person in this circumstance but another thing for that person in that circumstance. The proper goal of moral philosophy is to articulate a concept of duty that simultaneously recognizes the centrality of human will while avoiding the chaos of subjectivity prompted by Hume's and similar arguments.

Kant's solution to this problem was to argue that an action is moral only when the agent acts from a good will, and that a good will is one that arises exclusively from a sense of duty. The moral worth of an action, he claimed, is determined not by its practical results (e.g., self-interest or social utility) but by the maxim on which the agent acts. A good will, in short, is one that acts out of respect for the obligation of moral law itself. This raises the obvious question of how a good man can ascertain the rule that ought to define his duties. Kant's answer is framed as follows: "I am never to act otherwise than so I can also will that my maxim should become a universal law."[54] Kant referred to this formula as the "categorical imperative," meaning that it was always and everywhere binding. When the categorical imperative is properly understood and applied, Kant believed that it established the case for objective morality on an entirely new ground, one that could be defended against both the facts of natural science and the arguments of philosophical skeptics. Kant's claim, whether valid or not, has greatly influenced the course of subsequent moral speculation.

Kant's View of Suicide

Although Kant nowhere provides a systematic analysis of the problem of suicide, he does use suicide to illustrate broader philosophical arguments and the proper application of the categorical imperative.[55] In one such famous example, he hypothesizes a man whose various misfortunes bring him to the brink of despair. Despite his condition, the man remains able and willing to make rational moral decisions. May he take his own life if he concludes that continuing to live will cause him more pain than pleasure? Kant answers that the animating maxim for such an argument proceeds from self-love. But self-love, he argues, is unable to justify suicide, because self-love necessarily presupposes the actor's continued existence. By ending his existence, the actor would contradict the basis for the maxim on which he proposed to act. Self-love cannot justify eliminating the conditions without which self-love could not exist. The maxim on which the would-be suicide proposes to act could not be made universal without destroying the very ground on which the possibility of morality rests.[56]

This argument has been criticized for appearing to rely on an undemonstrated teleological assumption about self-love, i.e., that it is necessarily directed toward self-preservation. May not self-love cause one to prefer not to live if life brings more pain than pleasure? One response is that this criticism misses Kant's larger point, which is that moral action, rightly understood, cannot be determined by the self-interested circumstances of the actor. As Professor Tom Beauchamp points out, "The bottom line [for Kant] seems to be that suicide is immoral because it attacks the moral order itself: Suicide makes self-love the end of action, and the moral agent's life becomes a means to this end in abandonment of its proper ends."[57] In Kant's own words, "To destroy the subject of morality in one's own person is to root out the existence of morality itself from the world, so far as this is in one's power; and yet morality is an end in itself."[58]

May suicide grounded on one's duty to others, rather than on self-love, be justified? Here Kant is notoriously obscure. He gives the example of a person who contracts rabies from a dog-bite and kills himself so as not to infect others. In such cases, the actor's motives are clearly mixed—the desire to end his own pain, the desire not to inflict it on others—but it is not clear on Kantian premises where the correct moral judgment ought to lie. Although Kant makes it clear that self-interested motives alone cannot suffice for a genuinely moral act, he would presumably bless a selfless concern for others as the basis for a noble and universalizable maxim of action. Indeed, he defends the suicide of Cato precisely on the grounds of its selfless patriotism, adding, however, that it is "the only example which has given the world the opportunity of defending suicide."[59] This abrupt and sharply limiting qualification suggests a certain wariness on Kant's part about the permissibility of suicide even where the actor's intention is noble.

In another example, Kant argues (contrary to St. Augustine) that if "a woman cannot preserve her life . . . except by surrendering her person to the will of another, she is bound to give up her life rather than dishonor humanity in her own person, which is what she would be doing in giving herself up as a thing to the will of another. The preservation of one's life is, therefore, not the highest duty."[60] Why this should be so is not immediately apparent in the example given. If Kant's point is that death can sometimes be preferable to moral degradation, it is hard to see how the woman can be morally degraded by an act to which she does not consent (which was precisely Augustine's point in arguing against suicide with respect to the Christian rape victims in Rome). It may be that Kant was merely trying to distinguish between killing oneself and allowing oneself to be killed, and arguing that the latter may be defensible in certain circumstances whereas the former is not. He does not, unfortunately, enlighten us further.

For all the puzzlement created by Kant's failure to discuss such examples in detail, he otherwise makes plain (a) that only the most compelling *moral* reasons could ever justify the taking of one's own life and (b) that such reasons are virtually non-existent. The most common reasons adduced to justify suicide—despair, fear of bodily degradation, the avoidance of pain, indeed a self-regarding calculation of any sort— fall short of this criterion. So insistent is Kant on the purity of will as a necessary condition for a moral act that he seems loath to acknowledge even a slight qualification. While he found Cato's suicide morally defensible, he said it was "the only example of its kind."

Kant's opposition to suicide in a sense brings us full circle. In it we hear echoes of the Platonic and Judeo-Christian arguments that our lives are not ours to dispose of as we will, and that although man is free to choose how to lead his life, and although he is capable of ending it, he is nevertheless obliged to do his duty. The ground of Kant's argument is radically different from that of his ancient predecessors, but his conclusion is strikingly similar. Whether he succeeded in his goal of refuting moral skepticism and reestablishing a case for objective morality remains a matter of dispute.

Hume's argument defending subjective moral choice is powerfully appealing in our time because it contains, literally, something for everyone. In hands less civilized than his, it has been used to justify a kind of radical subjectivism that Hume himself would have deplored. But that it has not utterly swamped the modern conscience is due in part to the rigor of Kant's critique. For all the differences between Kant and his pre-Enlightenment predecessors, by revealing the unexamined assumptions and fragilities on which modern philosophy rests, he opened a door that makes it possible to entertain thoughts and converse with minds that the Enlightenment believed it had buried once and for all. And in that conversation, twentieth-century man may rediscover that some truths, though they lack a modern pedigree, are nevertheless essential to his survival.

PART TWO

Contemporary Moral and Theological Perspectives

Contemporary Moral and Theological Perspectives: An Introduction

In the long historical debate regarding suicide and euthanasia, the major fissure runs between those who assert, whether on religious or on philosophical grounds, that we may not end our lives when it pleases us to do so, and those who argue that human beings have a moral right to control their own destiny. The rationalists of the Enlightenment believed they had once and for all banished religion to the realm of superstition, and Hume believed he had sealed their case in regard to suicide. There is, he contended, no defensible argument to confirm the unique sacredness of human life; when the burdens of life outweigh its benefits, a rational case for suicide is established.

Kant undertook to refute the ground of Hume's skepticism, while conceding important features of Hume's argument against the power of reason to arrive at objective moral judgments. Kant thought that by reestablishing the ground for moral decision-making in human will, and by rooting that will in a rule of moral duty that was always and everywhere applicable, he could prevent its descent into mere subjectivity.

Whether Kant succeeded in refuting Hume is a question for another time and place, but one of the enduring legacies of the argument between these two sons of the Enlightenment was the emphasis placed by both on individual autonomy in moral questions. Indeed, it may be said that much of the modern world knows no other moral vocabulary. That much will become apparent in many of the essays that follow. The attentive reader will also note, however, the persistence of the old moral reasoning that both Hume and Kant, in quite different ways, thought it necessary to abandon.

In the first essay, **A. Alvarez** draws our attention to what might be called the dark side of the prohibition of suicide. In the past, the enforcement of laws against suicide could indeed be draconian, as he graphically illustrates. Prior to the modern era, however, penal codes were bloody and pitiless across a broad front, not just for suicide. Still, Alvarez provides a useful reminder of how good intentions can lead to beastly results. The harshness of pre-modern law regarding suicide may have been driven in part, as Alvarez suggests, by a primordial fear of death, but another motive may also have been at work—the belief that the despair from which suicide derives is a common human temptation, so strong that it has to be addressed with the utmost severity.

This temptation, Alvarez argues, was exacerbated by early Christian teaching: by extolling the example of Christ's death and the promise of heavenly reward to those who suffered in his name, Christianity created "a powerful incentive for suicide." Certainly, that appears to have been the case among heretical sects such as the Donatists, but few Christian martyrs believed as the Donatists did, and the Church Fathers were virtually unanimous in condemning their beliefs. Alvarez does not distinguish between those who intend to kill themselves, and do, and those who—like Socrates and Jesus—do not will their own death but are prepared to accept death meted out by others. St. Augustine's argument, by contrast, rests in large part on the distinction between what Alvarez would call death lust and a willingness to suffer martyrdom for the sake of Christ. For Alvarez, it is a distinction without a difference.

At the core of Alvarez's argument is a theological judgment: that whereas the consequences of polytheism are "tolerance, a respect for individual freedom, [and] a civilized breathing space," the consequences of monotheism are "dogmatism, fanaticism, and persecution." On Alvarez's own evidence, however, polytheistic Rome was notable for its barbarity, no less to its own citizens than to its enemies. And while it is true, as he points out, that many cruelties have been committed in the name of Christianity, toleration and individual freedom have also flourished under the aegis of Christian teaching. When

Christ said, "Render unto Caesar the things that are Caesar's, and unto God the things that are God's," he limited the power of the state as no religion had before. In so doing, Christians would argue, he created the very "civilized breathing space" Alvarez wishes to celebrate.

Brutality of the sort Alvarez describes disappeared from the law long ago. Suicide is now understood largely as a medical problem rather than as a crime deserving punishment. The decriminalization of suicide, however, was not based on any claim of personal autonomy or individual rights; it was grounded, rather, in compassion for the victim and his family. Although suicide is no longer a crime, assisting another to take his life is still forbidden by statute or common law in virtually all states. In recent years, however, the argument for autonomy has acquired new force both in morals and in law, most notably in matters of sexual behavior and abortion rights. It is now being extended to issues involving death and dying.

Ronald Dworkin, who generally supports that argument, undertakes to refute some of the commonly asserted rationales against limiting personal autonomy in the matter of one's death. In the 1990 Supreme Court decision *Cruzan v. Director, Missouri Department of Health,* the question was whether life-sustaining treatment could be terminated for a comatose patient who for some years had exhibited few signs of significant cognitive function. The parents and doctors of Nancy Cruzan had been denied permission to terminate treatment because there was no "clear and convincing" evidence, as required by Missouri law, that Nancy would have wished such a fate for herself. On appeal, a sharply divided Supreme Court upheld the Missouri rule.

In his analysis of the Supreme Court's ruling, Dworkin raises an important philosophical question: What, exactly, is the moral basis for the state's interest in preserving human life? The rationale provided by Chief Justice Rehnquist seemed to presume that all human life has an irreducible intrinsic value, but Dworkin questions whether that presumption can be justified on non-religious grounds. Not all human life is equally valuable, he argues, and seeking to maintain Cruzan's life robs it of the very dignity the defenders of the statute seek to preserve. Whose interests are served, Dworkin asks, by requiring the maintenance of life-support measures for persons in a persistent vegetative state?

In the narrow framing of the *Cruzan* facts, Dworkin's argument has great appeal, but can its application be limited to patients in a persistent vegetative state? Dworkin does not address that question directly in the main body of his essay, but in an addendum, he praises a more recent federal court decision declaring a broad constitutional right to assisted suicide. What ought to have been the central question in *Cruzan,* he suggests, was obscured by the relatively narrow factual situation in which the case arose. In Dworkin's view, the real issue was Nancy's right of personal autonomy. Since she could not exercise that right herself, her parents and doctors should have been able to exercise it for her. Dworkin seems to suggest that the Supreme Court focused on the wrong question: the issue was not whether the state has authority to protect life, but whether its authority could be used to keep people alive against their—in this case, their imputed—will.

Whereas Ronald Dworkin sees suicide and (by extension) assisted suicide as morally grounded in the right of individual autonomy, **Hadley V. Arkes** argues that autonomy of will is an insufficient moral justification, not only for suicide but for all human action. The tendency of the modern age, Arkes points out, is to justify behavior on grounds of personal preference or pleasure. But the inadequacy of that position becomes apparent, he says, the minute we encounter another who says that *his* preference or pleasure is to inflict harm on *us.* In that case, we would be quick to say that there is no right to do a wrong. But in saying that such behavior is wrong for others, we are necessarily obliged to give reasons that move from subjective to objective principles of judgment. "If the ground of the act is incoherent or indefensible," Arkes says, "the wrong of the act is utterly unaffected by the question of whether the act is performed on others or on ourselves."

Arkes applies this argument to suicide and assisted suicide. The claim of a right to die, he says, rests on the proposition "that the principles that restrain killing in relation to all other persons do not bind the individual when he is acting solely on himself." Arkes undertakes to demonstrate the logical incoherence of this proposition through a series of hypothetical examples, the burden of which is that the moral restraints limiting our actions toward others also limit our actions toward ourselves. If it is wrong for a racial bigot to kill another on account of race, it would be equally wrong for him to kill himself upon discovering that he had the same racial ancestry. Similarly, if it is morally unjustifiable for another to kill an AIDS patient because he is suffering, so it is unjustifiable for the patient to kill himself. The obverse is equally true: if it is right to kill oneself on the grounds of race or physical infirmity, it would follow that it is right to kill another on the same grounds.

By conceding the sovereignty of the individual will in suicide and assisted suicide, Arkes says, many judges and doctors embrace a kind of moral reasoning they would otherwise be reluctant to accept. But having embraced that reasoning in one situation, they may be unable to deny its application to situations where they are loath to affirm it. The rules of morality, Arkes concludes, possess an inner logic that cannot be altered at will.

In the next selection, **Margaret Pabst Battin** provides a historical overview of physician-assisted suicide—the economic, medical, and demographic conditions that have brought the issue to the fore, the major arguments for and against legalization, and the ethical dilemmas that would arise after legalization. Contemporary debate, in her view, reflects four trends: (1) the "new epidemiology," which has dramatically increased life expectancy and changed the causes of death; (2) increased "attention to patient autonomy"; (3) the decreasing role of traditional religious and moral assumptions regarding death and dying; and (4) the rising cost of medical care, especially among the old. The confluence of these trends, Battin argues, will continue to erode resistance to physician-assisted suicide.

Battin sees two major ethical arguments in favor of legalization: the argument from personal autonomy and the argument from mercy. The opposition counters that killing is intrinsically wrong, that other, morally indefensible forms of licensed killing will inevitably follow, and that physician-assisted suicide will radically alter the doctor-patient relationship. Battin finds this opposing argument to be unpersuasive. We would do well, she says, to prepare for the coming of physician-assisted suicide—by developing better counseling techniques for those who contemplate death, by establishing regulatory safeguards against manipulation and coercion by families and physicians, and by training medical personnel in state-of-the-art methods for inducing painless death.

The **Ramsey Colloquium**, named for the late Princeton ethicist

Paul Ramsey, is a group of Jewish and Christian scholars that convenes periodically to consider questions of ethics, religion, and public life. In November 1991 the group reaffirmed the moral necessity of distinguishing between killing and letting die, and warned that to abandon this principle would open the door to other forms of medicalized killing. Their statement argues that moral claims arising from autonomy and from mercy are difficult to limit. If assisted suicide or euthanasia is justified by self-determination, how, the Colloquium asks, can it be limited to the terminally ill? If it is justified by the desire to relieve suffering, why should that relief be limited to those who request it?

Merely to ask such questions is to answer them, the Ramsey group implies: once the boundary between killing and letting die is crossed, there will be no logical stopping point. Pressure will mount to apply the new principle to an expanding category of cases. The law will cease to be the protector of the vulnerable and become instead a license for their elimination. Medicine will be tragically transformed as health-care professionals become technicians of managed death. For society at large as well as for doctors, the Colloquium statement concludes, we ought to affirm the ancient moral principle, "Always to care, never to kill."

Rabbi **Byron L. Sherwin** summarizes Jewish thought on assisted suicide and euthanasia in the next essay. According to the classic Jewish tradition, an individual's life is not his own to dispose of as he will; he holds it, as it were, in trust for God. "Life being sacred," Sherwin points out, "every effort must be made to preserve each moment of life, even to the moment of death." It follows that a person is prohibited from inflicting self-injury, including suicide, and that another person may not help to bring about or accelerate his death. Withdrawal of treatment may be licit under narrowly defined circumstances. While active euthanasia is almost universally condemned by the classic and even contemporary rabbinical texts, Sherwin argues that it may be permissible where death is imminent and inevitable, and where the patient is suffering extreme anguish.

Those who worry about the new medical ethic described by Margaret Battin and the Ramsey Colloquium will be troubled more deeply by the views of **Peter Singer**, who argues that the "traditional doctrine of the sanctity of human life" is in "deep trouble." Its defenders are really doing little more than patching up a decaying edifice. Singer undertakes to show why the old doctrine deserves to die and what its replacement should look like. He calls for a new "Copernican revolution," not in physics and astronomy but in ethics. Its chief target: Judeo-Christian religious belief, and particularly the idea that human beings are at the center of the ethical universe.

The old sanctity-of-life ethic, Singer says, was defined by five now obsolete "commandments," such as, "Treat all human life as of equal worth." He proposes five new commandments, beginning with "Recognize that the worth of human life varies." Singer is nothing if not provocative. Among the more arresting features of his argument is his conclusion that the right to life is not limited to members of *homo sapiens*. Those who possess the right, whether human or non-human, he calls "persons." But Singer goes even further: not all human beings are persons. Not surprisingly, these beliefs give him a different perspective on ethical dilemmas such as the definition of brain death, the moral status of newborn infants, and the right to abortion and euthanasia.

Physician and philosopher **Leon R. Kass** might agree with Singer that the sanctity-of-life ethic needs attention. Rather than discarding it, however, Kass undertakes to clear away some of the confusion that often attends popular discussion. Phrases like "sanctity of life" and "death with dignity," he says, are at best shorthand slogans that can obscure as often as they instruct. By taking the argument beyond the slogans, we will discover that the sacredness of life and the dignity of death not only are not in opposition but are integral parts of a single understanding.

In an extended reflection on the biblical account of man's creation and the divine commandment not to kill, Kass concludes that the sacredness of human life is inextricably bound up with man's God-like dignity. Although this understanding is most tellingly revealed in the Bible, Kass believes that it also confirmed by man's consciousness of his own being. In the exercise of his freedom and in his ability to deliberate about what is right and wrong, man confirms his unique status in the created order. Kass acknowledges that the dignity of man can be debased by "the bizarre mechanical companions" that often attend medicated, institutionalized death in modern society. But true dignity is more than the absence of "external indignities" and cannot be affirmed merely by "pulling plugs and taking poison." The answer to the "medicalized bureaucratization" of death lies, rather, in affirming the moral quality of man's existence. Voluntary euthanasia does not make sense as a gesture of personal dignity, says Kass, and its legalization is far more likely to coerce the medically vulnerable than to increase their freedom. Nor is it consistent with man's dignity to treat him like a lesser animal. In the very act of asking for death, man demonstrates that he cannot be regarded as "a dumb animal." What desperately ill patients need is not death by deliverance but a "bolstering of the human, especially in its dying moments." As for involuntary euthanasia, Kass argues that we must never treat persons— even those in a persistent vegetative state—as if they were things. In the end, we must say no to killing, "for it is precisely the setting of fixed limits on violating human life that makes possible our efforts at dignified relations with our fellow man."

The pontificate of **John Paul II**, the spiritual leader of the world's Roman Catholics, has been notable for its efforts to revivify the foundations of religious faith and proper moral behavior. In a series of public letters, the Pope has undertaken to teach both Catholics and non-Catholics about their moral obligations to God, one another, and themselves. Perhaps the most emphatic of these letters was "The Gospel of Life," issued in March 1995, in which John Paul attacked a new intellectual climate that had, he said, created a "culture of death."

While "The Gospel of Life" ranges across many issues of contemporary relevance, it is particularly pointed in its discussion of "crimes against life" committed in the name of autonomous individualism— abortion, suicide, and euthanasia. John Paul notes that assisted suicide and euthanasia are often prompted by compassionate motives; nevertheless, intentionally causing another's death is "a grave violation" of both God's law and the law of nature. Drawing on a long Catholic tradition, the Pope distinguishes between assisted suicide and the termination of aggressive medical treatment and points out that heroic gestures on the part of patient or doctor are not morally required. Similarly, the use of palliatives that may incidentally hasten death is ethically acceptable. But involuntary euthanasia is, he says, indistinguishable from murder; it is the victimization of the weak at the hands of the strong and a breach of the mutual trust without which no society can survive.

The Lutheran ethicist **Gilbert Meilander** rounds out this section by differentiating the Christian perspective on euthanasia from that of a well-intended but non-believing humanitarian. He begins with what he calls "the paradigm case" for euthanasia, as formulated by James Rachels: "The person (1) is deliberately killed, (2) would have died soon anyway, (3) was suffering terrible pain, and (4) asked to be killed, and (5) the motive of killing was mercy—to provide the person with as good a death as possible under the circumstances." Although these criteria are appealing to the modern ear, Meilander argues that they cannot, in the end, command our loyalty.

If we agree that it is morally licit not to resuscitate a terminally ill patient who is suffering terribly, why should we hesitate to hasten his end by active means? Because, says Meilander, it is necessary to distinguish between aim and result. While the patient is dead in either case, in the latter instance we *intend* death, whereas in the former we do not. That distinction, Meilander says, is crucial. Some might concede the distinction but then argue that the relief of suffering makes killing morally permissible. This "consequentialist" argument is common these days, but in Meilander's view, there is no end to the mischief that can be done in the name of relieving another's suffering.

Meilander concludes by reflecting on the Christian understanding of death and dying, in which "the fundamental imperative is not 'minimize suffering' but 'maximize love and care.'" In the Christian vision, he says, "love can never include in its meaning hastening a fellow human toward the evil of death, nor can it mean a refusal to acknowledge death when it comes as an evil (but not the greatest evil)."

2

The History of Suicide

A. Alvarez

A man was hanged who had cut his throat, but who had been brought back to life. They hanged him for suicide. The doctor had warned them that it was impossible to hang him as the throat would burst open and he would breathe through the aperture. They did not listen to his advice and hanged their man. The wound in the neck immediately opened and the man came back to life again although he was hanged. It took time to convoke the aldermen to decide the question of what was to be done. At length the aldermen assembled and bound up the neck below the wound *until he died.* Oh my Mary, what a crazy society and what a stupid civilization.[1]

Thus Nicholas Ogarev writing to his mistress Mary Sutherland around 1860, with news from the London papers. Ogarev was an alcoholic Russian exile of mildly revolutionary politics, the son of a wealthy landowner and close friend of Alexander Herzen's; his mistress was a good-natured prostitute whom he had reformed and was slowly educating. I suspect that it took two complete outsiders, one of them an

---

A. Alvarez is a poet, novelist, and literary critic who lives in London. Among his non-fiction books are *Life After Marriage* and *Offshore*. This essay is reprinted and abridged by permission from his book *The Savage God* (London: Weidenfeld & Nicolson, 1973).

enlightened and political foreigner, to notice the barbarity of a situation that the newspaper had reported simply as an unexpected twist to a public execution, odd enough to be newsworthy but not otherwise sufficiently shocking or remarkable to require comment.

Yet by pursuing their poor suicide with such weird vindictiveness —condemning a man to death for the crime of having condemned himself to death—the London aldermen were acting according to a venerable tradition sanctified by both church and state. The history of suicide in Christian Europe is the history of official outrage and unofficial despair. Both can be measured by the dry, matter-of-fact tone in which the accepted enormities were described. Writing in 1601, the Elizabethan lawyer Fulbecke says that the suicide "is drawn by a horse to the place of punishment and shame, where he is hanged on a gibbet, and none may take the body down but by the authority of a magistrate." In other words, the suicide was as low as the lowest criminal. Later another great legal authority, Blackstone, wrote that the burial was "in the highway, with a stake driven through the body,"[2] as though there were no difference between a suicide and a vampire. The chosen site was usually a crossroads, which was also the place of public execution, and a stone was placed over the dead man's face; like the stake, it would prevent him from rising as a ghost to haunt the living.

Apparently the terror of suicides lasted longer than the fear of vampires and witches: the last recorded degradation of the corpse of a suicide in England took place in 1823, when a man called Griffiths was buried at the intersection of Grosvenor Place and King's Road, Chelsea. But even then self-murderers were not left in peace: for the next fifty years the bodies of unclaimed and destitute suicides went to the schools of anatomy for dissection.

With variations, similar degradations were used all through Europe. In France, varying with local ground rules, the corpse was hanged by the feet, dragged through the streets on a hurdle, burned, thrown on the public garbage heap. At Metz, each suicide was put in a barrel and floated down the Moselle, away from the places he might wish to haunt. In Danzig, the corpse was not allowed to leave by the door; instead it was lowered by pulleys from the window; the window frame was subsequently burned. Even in the civilized Athens of Plato, the suicide was buried outside the city and away from other graves; his self-murdering hand was cut off and buried apart. So, too, with minor variations in Thebes and Cyprus. Sparta, true to form, was so severe in its ruling that Aristodemus was punished posthumously for deliberately seeking death in the battle of Plataea.[3]

In Europe these primitive revenges were duly dignified and made economically profitable to the state by law. As late as 1670 Le Roi-Soleil himself incorporated into the official legal code all the most brutal practices concerning the degradation of the corpse of a suicide, adding that his name was to be defamed *ad perpetuam rei memoriam;* nobles lost their nobility and were declared commoners; their escutcheons were broken, their woods cut, their castles demolished. In England a suicide was declared a felon *(felo de se)*. In both countries his property reverted to the crown. . . .

In France, these laws lasted at least until 1770, and, indeed, were twice reinforced in the eighteenth century. The confiscation of the suicide's property and defamation of his memory finally disappeared with the Revolution; suicide is not mentioned in the new penal code of 1791.[4] Not so in England, where the laws concerning the confiscation of property were not changed until 1870, and an unsuccessful suicide could still be sent to prison as late as 1961. Thus the phrase "suicide while the balance of his mind was disturbed" was evolved by lawyers as a protection against the inanities of the law, since a verdict of *felo de se* would deprive the dead man of a religious burial and his inheritors of his estate. . . .

In primitive societies, the mechanics of revenge are simple: either the suicide's ghost will destroy his persecutor for him, or his act will force his relatives to carry out the task, or the iron laws of the tribe will compel the suicide's enemy to kill himself in the same manner. It depends on the customs of the country. In any case, suicide under these conditions is curiously unreal; it is as though it were committed in the certain belief that the suicide himself would not really die. Instead, he is performing a magical act that will initiate a complex but equally magic ritual ending in the death of his enemy.

So the primitive horror of suicide, which survived so long in Europe, was of blood evilly spilled and unappeased. In practice, this meant that suicide was equated with murder. Hence, presumably, the custom of punishing the body of a suicide as though he were guilty of a capital crime, by hanging it from a gibbet. Hence too the terminology of the act. "Suicide," which is a Latinate and relatively abstract word, appeared late. The *Oxford English Dictionary* dates the first use as 1651; I found the word a little earlier in Sir Thomas Browne's *Religio Medici,* written in 1635, published in 1642. But it was still sufficiently rare not to appear in the 1755 edition of Dr. Samuel Johnson's *Dictionary.* Instead, the phrases used were "self-murder," "self-destruction," "self-killer," "self-homicide," "self-slaughter"— all expressions reflecting the associations with murder.

The Church's Ban on Suicide

They also reflect the difficulty the Church had in rationalizing its ban on suicide, since neither the Old nor the New Testament directly prohibits it. There are four suicides recorded in the Old Testament —Samson, Saul, Abimelech, and Achitophel—and none of them earns adverse comment. In fact, they are scarcely commented on at all. In the New Testament, the suicide of even the greatest criminal, Judas Iscariot, is recorded as perfunctorily; instead of being added to his crimes, it seems a measure of his repentance. Only much later did the theologians reverse the implicit judgment of St. Matthew and suggest that Judas was more damned by his suicide than by his betrayal of Christ. In the first years of the Church, suicide was such a neutral subject that even the death of Jesus was regarded by Tertullian, one of the most fiery of the early Fathers, as a kind of suicide. He pointed out, and Origen agreed, that Jesus voluntarily gave up the ghost, since it was unthinkable that the Godhead should be at the mercy of the flesh. Whence John Donne's comment in *Biathanatos,* the first formal defense of suicide in English: "Our blessed Savior . . . chose that way for our Redemption to sacrifice his life, and profuse his blood."[5]

The idea of suicide as a crime comes late in Christian doctrine, and as an afterthought. It was not until the sixth century that the Church finally legislated against it, and then the only biblical authority was a special interpretation of the Sixth Commandment, "Thou shalt not kill." The bishops were urged into action by St. Augustine, but he, as Rousseau remarked, took his arguments from Plato's *Phaedo,* not from the Bible. Although Augustine's arguments were sharpened by the suicide mania that was, above all, the distinguishing mark of the early Christians, ultimately his reasons were impeccably moral. Christianity was founded on the belief that each human body is the vehicle of an immortal soul that will be judged not in this world but in the next. And because each soul is immortal, every life is equally valuable. Since life itself is the gift of God, to reject it is to reject him and to frustrate his will; to kill his image is to kill him—which means a one-way ticket to eternal damnation.

The Christian ban on suicide, like its ban on infanticide and abortion, was, then, founded on a respect for life utterly foreign to the indifference and casual murderousness of the Romans. But there is a paradox: as David Hume pointed out, monotheism is the only form of religion that can be taken seriously, because only monotheism treats the universe as a single, systematic, intelligible whole; yet dogmatism, fanaticism, and persecution are its consequences; whereas polytheism, which is intellectually absurd and a positive obstacle to scientific understanding, produces tolerance, a respect for individual freedom, a civilized breathing space. So with suicide: when the bishops decided it was a crime, they were in some way emphasizing the moral distance traveled from pagan Rome, where the act was habitual and even honored. Yet what began as moral tenderness and enlightenment finished as the legalized and sanctified atrocities by which the body of the suicide was degraded, his memory defamed, his family persecuted. So although the idea of suicide as a crime was a late, relatively sophisticated invention of Christianity, more or less foreign to the Judeo-Hellenic tradition, it spread like a fog across Europe because its strength came from primitive fears, prejudices, and superstitions that had survived despite Christianity, Judaism, and Hellenism.

The Savage Mind and Suicide

Given the barbarity of the Dark and early Middle Ages, it was no doubt inevitable that the savage mind should once again have its day. The process was much the same as that by which the Christian calendar took over the pagan festivals, and the first Spanish missionaries in Mexico invented saints to whom they could dedicate the churches they built on the altar of each Aztec and Mayan god. In the modern business world this process is called "buying the good will" of a defunct firm. As far as suicide is concerned, Christianity bought up the pagan bad will.

Yet there is evidence that even to the savage mind, the horror of suicide did not always come naturally. The primitive fear of the dead may have been overpowering, particularly the terror of the spirits of those who had died unnaturally and willfully, murdered or by their own hand. It was largely as a protection against these restless and unappeased ghosts that the whole ornate complex of taboos was elaborated.[6] But to be afraid of the vengeful dead is something rather different from being afraid of death itself. Thus in some warrior societies whose gods were those of violence and whose ideal was bravery, suicide was often looked on as a great good. . . .

To promote the idea of violent death as glorious was an efficient way of preserving a properly warlike spirit; the Pentagon might have been spared some of its . . . embarrassment in Vietnam had it been able to instill its conscripts with the same primitive virtues. Thus the ancient Scythians regarded it as the greatest honor to take their own lives when they became too old for their nomadic way of life, thereby saving the younger members of the tribe both the trouble and the guilt of killing them. Quintus Curtius described them graphically:

> Among them exists a sort of wild and bestial men to whom they give the name of sages. The anticipation of the time of death is a glory in their eyes, and they have themselves burned alive as soon as age or sickness begins to trouble them. According to them, death, passively awaited, is a dishonor to life; thus no honors are rendered those bodies which old age has destroyed. Fire would be contaminated if it did not receive the human sacrifice still breathing.[7]

Durkheim called this style of suicide "altruistic"; one of the supreme examples is Captain Oates, who walked out to his death in the Antarctic snow in order to help Scott and his other doomed companions. But where the whole of a tribe's morality and mythology made it seem that suicide was a way to a better life, the motives of those who took their own lives were evidently not altogether pure and self-sacrificing. They were, instead, intensely narcissistic. . . . Since death was both inevitable and relatively unimportant, suicide ultimately became more a matter of pleasure than of principle: one sacrificed a few days or years on this earth in order to feast with the gods eternally in the next. It was, essentially, a frivolous act.

In contrast, a serious suicide is an act of choice, the terms of which are entirely those of this world; a man dies by his own hand because he thinks the life he has not worth living. Suicides of this kind are usually thought to be an index of high civilization, for the simple reason that the act goes against the most basic of instincts, that of self-preservation. But it is not necessarily so. For example, the Tasmanian aborigines died out not just because they were hunted like kangaroos for an afternoon's sport, but also because a world in which this could happen was intolerable to them; so they committed suicide as a race by refusing to breed. Ironically, perhaps, and as though to confirm the aborigines' judgment, the mummified remains of the old lady who was the last to survive have been preserved by the Australian government as a museum curiosity. Similarly, hundreds of Jews put themselves to death at Masada rather than submit to the Roman legions. . . .

The despair that ends with racial suicide is a peculiarly pure phenomenon and proportionately rare. Only under the most extreme conditions does the psychic mechanism of self-preservation go into reverse for a whole nation, unsanctioned by morality or belief and unswayed by zealotry. In a less pure, more complex culture, where death is accepted casually but beliefs are no longer simple and morality fluctuates, within limits, according to the individual, the question of suicide becomes urgent in another way. The supreme example is that of the Romans, who turned the ancient world's toleration of suicide into a high fashion.

Suicide in Ancient Greece

The toleration began with the Greeks. The taboos against suicide which obtained even in Athens—where the corpse was buried outside the city, its hand cut off and buried separately—were linked with the more profound Greek horror of killing one's own kin. By inference, suicide was an extreme case of this, and the language barely distinguishes between self-murder and murder of kindred. Yet in literature and philosophy the act passes more or less without comment, certainly without blame. The first of all literary suicides, that of Oedipus' mother, Jocasta, is made to seem praiseworthy, an honorable way out of an insufferable situation. Homer records self-murder without comment, as something natural and usually heroic. . . . So far as the records go, the ancient Greeks took their lives only for the best possible reasons: grief, high patriotic principle, or to avoid dishonor.

Their philosophical discussion of the subject is proportionately detached and balanced. The keys were moderation and high principle. Suicide was not to be tolerated if it seemed like an act of wanton disrespect to the gods. The Pythagoreans rejected suicide out of hand since for them, as for the later Christians, life itself was the discipline of the gods. In the *Phaedo,* Plato made Socrates repeat this Orphic doctrine approvingly before he drank the hemlock. He used the simile —often to be repeated later—of the soldier on guard duty who must not desert his post, and also that of man as the property of the gods, who are as angry at our suicide as we would be if our chattels destroyed themselves.

Aristotle used much the same argument, though in a more austere way: suicide was "an offense against the state" because, as a religious offense, it polluted the city and, economically, weakened it by destroying a useful citizen. That is, it was an act of social irresponsibility. Logically, this is no doubt impeccable. But it also seems curiously irrelevant to the act of suicide. It is not, I mean, a style of argument likely to impinge on the state of mind of a man about to take his own life. The fact that it was considered to be so cogent—Aristotle's huge authority apart—implies a curiously cool and detached attitude to the problem of suicide.

In contrast, Plato's arguments are less simple, more subtle. Socrates' sweetly reasonable tone repudiates suicide, yet at the same time he makes death seem infinitely desirable; it is the entry to the world of ideal presences of which earthly reality is a mere shadow. In the end, Socrates drinks the hemlock so cheerfully and has argued so eloquently for the benefits of death that he has set an example for others. The Greek philosopher Cleombrotus is said to have been inspired by the *Phaedo* to drown himself, and Cato read the book through twice the night before he fell on his own sword.

Plato also allowed for moderation in the other sense. He suggested that if life itself became immoderate, then suicide became a rational, justifiable act. Painful disease or intolerable constraint were sufficient reasons to depart. And this, when the religious superstitions faded, was philosophical justification enough. Within a hundred years of Socrates' death, the Stoics had made suicide into the most reasonable and desirable of all ways out. Both they and the Epicureans claimed to be as indifferent to death as to life. For the Epicureans the principle was pleasure: whatever promoted that was good, whatever produced pain was evil. For the Stoics the ideal was vaguer, more dignified: that of life in accordance with nature. When it no longer seemed to be so, then death came as a rational choice befitting a rational nature. Thus Zeno, the founder of the school, is said to have hanged himself out of sheer irritation when he stumbled and wrenched his finger; he was ninety-eight at the time. His successor Cleanthes died with equally philosophical aplomb. As a cure for a gumboil he was ordered to starve himself. Within two days the gumboil was better and his doctor put him back on an ordinary diet. But Cleanthes refused. "As he had advanced so far on his journey towards death, he would not now retreat"; he duly starved himself to death.

Classical Greek suicide, then, was dictated by a calm, though slightly excessive, reasonableness. In Athens, as in the Greek colonies of Marseilles and Ceos, where hemlock was developed and whose customs inspired Montaigne to his eloquent defense of noble suicide, the magistrates kept a supply of poison for those who wished to die. All that was required was that they should first plead their cause before the Senate and obtain official permission. The precepts were clear:

> Whoever no longer wishes to live shall state his reasons to the Senate, and after having received permission shall abandon life. If your existence is hateful to you, die; if you are overwhelmed by fate, drink the hemlock. If you are bowed with grief, abandon life. Let the unhappy man recount his misfortune, let the magistrate supply him with the remedy, and his wretchedness will come to an end.[8]

These early Stoics brought to the subject of their own death the same degree of nicety that Henry James reserved for morals. And this was appropriate, since the question of how they died became for them the final measure of discrimination. Plato had justified suicide when external circumstances became intolerable. The Greek Stoics developed and rationalized this attitude according to their ideal of life in accordance with nature.

Suicide in Ancient Rome

The advanced Stoicism of the later Roman Empire was a further development of Plato; the argument was essentially the same, but now the circumstances were internalized. When the inner compulsion became intolerable, the question was no longer whether or not one should kill oneself but how to do so with the greatest dignity, bravery, and style. To put it another way, it was an achievement of the Greeks to empty suicide of all the primitive horrors and then gradually to discuss the subject more or less rationally, as though it were not invested with much feeling, one way or another. The Romans, on the other hand, reinvested it with emotion, but in doing so, turned the emotions upside down. In their eyes suicide was no longer morally evil; on the contrary, one's manner of going became a practical test of excellence and virtue. . . .

I mentioned the belief that the more sophisticated and rational a society becomes, the further it travels from superstitious fears and the more easily suicide is tolerated. Roman Stoicism would seem to be the ultimate example of this. Stoic writing is full of exhortations to suicide, the most famous of which is Seneca's:

> Foolish man, what do you bemoan, and what do you fear? Wherever you look there is an end of evils. You see that yawning precipice? It leads to liberty. You see that flood, that river, that well? Liberty houses within them. You see that stunted, parched, and sorry tree? From each branch liberty hangs. Your neck, your throat, your heart are all so many ways of escape from slavery. . . . Do you enquire the road to freedom? You shall find it in every vein in your body.[9]

It is a beautiful and cadenced piece of rhetoric. But where most rhetoric is a protection from reality—a verbal armor the writer puts between himself and the world—Seneca finally practiced his precepts: he stabbed himself to avoid the vengeance of Nero, who had once been his pupil. His wife, Paulina, refused to be left behind and died with him in the same way.

One other example is enough to set the tone of the times. It is the advice of Seneca's ascetic friend Attalus to one Marcellinus, who was suffering from an incurable disease and was contemplating suicide:

Be not tormented, my Marcellinus, as if you were deliberating any great matter. Life is a thing of no dignity or importance. Your very slaves, your animals, possess it in common with yourself: but it is a great thing to die honorably, prudently, bravely. Think how long you have been engaged in the same dull course: eating, sleeping, and indulging your appetites. This has been the circle. Not only a prudent, brave or a wretched man may wish to die, but even a fastidious one.[10]

Again, there was no gap between rhetoric and reality. Marcellinus took his friend's advice and starved himself to death, a "fastidious" answer to the wild indulgence of Tiberius's Rome. In doing so, he also joined the company of some of the most distinguished men of the ancient world. . . . John Donne's list of notable suicides of the classical world runs to three pages, including the witty comments; Montaigne produced a host of others. Both chose more or less at random from many hundreds of possibilities; and these, in turn, were only a fraction of those who died in the Roman fashion.

The evidence is, then, that the Romans looked on suicide with neither fear nor revulsion, but as a carefully considered and chosen validation of the way they had lived and the principles they had lived by. . . . To live nobly also meant to die nobly and at the right moment. Everything depended on the dominant will and a rational choice.

This attitude was reinforced by Roman law. There were no revenges, no degradation, no evidence of fear or horror. Instead the law was the law—practical. According to Justinian's *Digest,* suicide of a private citizen was not punishable if it was caused by "impatience of pain or sickness, or by another cause," or by "weariness of life . . . lunacy, or fear of dishonor." Since this covered every rational cause, all that was left was the utterly irrational suicide "without cause," and that was punishable on the grounds that "whoever does not spare himself would much less spare another."[11] In other words, it was punished because it was irrational, not because it was a crime. There were other exceptions, but they were even more strictly practical: it was a crime for a slave to kill himself for the simple reason that he represented to his master a certain capital investment. . . . In Roman law the crime of suicide was strictly economic. It was an offense against neither morality nor religion, only against the capital investments of the slave-owning class or the treasury of the state.

The icy heroism of all this is admirable, even enviable, but it also seems, at least from our perspective, curiously unreal. It seems impossible that life and behavior could ever be quite so rational, and the will, at the moment of crisis, quite so dependable. That the Romans were able to act as though this were so indicates an extraordinary inner discipline—a discipline of the soul they did not believe in. But it also says something about the monstrous civilization of which they were part.

I suggested earlier that only comparatively recently has death ceased to be casual and public. In imperial Rome this casualness reached that point of lunacy where the crowd, for its entertainment, would be satisfied with nothing less than death. Donne quotes a learned source who says that in one month thirty thousand men died in gladiatorial shows.[12] Frazer says that at one time people would offer themselves for execution to amuse the public for five *minae* (about £50), the money to be paid to their heirs; he adds that the market was so competitive that the candidates would offer to be beaten to death rather than beheaded, since that was slower, more painful, and so more spectacular.[13] Perhaps, then, Stoic dignity was a last defense against the murderous squalor of Rome itself. When those calm heroes looked around them they saw a life so unspeakable, cruel, wanton, corrupt, and apparently unvalued that they clung to their ideals of reason much as the Christian poor used to cling to their belief in paradise and the goodness of God despite, or because of, the misery of their lives on this earth. Stoicism, in short, was a philosophy of despair; it was not a coincidence that Seneca, who was its most powerful and influential spokesman, was also the teacher of the most vicious of all Roman emperors, Nero.

From Stoic Calm to Christian Hysteria

Perhaps this is why Stoic calm was so easily assimilated into the religious hysteria of the early Christians. Rational suicide was a kind of aristocratic corollary of vulgar blood lust. Christianity, which began as a religion for the poor and rejected, took that blood lust, combined it with the habit of suicide, and transfered both into a lust for martyrdom. The Romans may have fed Christians to the lions for sport, but they were not prepared for the fact that the Christians welcomed the animals as instruments of glory and salvation. "Let me enjoy those beasts," said Ignatius, "whom I wish more cruell than they are; for if they will not attempt me, I will provoke and draw them by force."[14] The persecution of the early Christians was less religious and political than a perversion of their own seeking.

For the sophisticated Roman magistrates, Christian obstinacy was mostly an embarrassment: as when the Christians refused to make the token gestures toward established religion that would save their lives or, failing that, refused to avail themselves of the convenient pause between judgment and execution in which to escape. Embarrassment moved into irritation when the would-be martyrs, student revolutionary tacticians before their day, responded to clemency with provocation. And it finished with boredom: an African proconsul, surrounded by a mob of Christians baying for martyrdom, shouted to them, "Go hang and drown your selves and ease the Magistrate."[15] Others, no less bored, were less forbearing. The glorious company of martyrs came to number thousands of men, women, and children who were beheaded, burned alive, flung from cliffs, roasted on gridirons, and hacked to pieces—all more or less gratuitously, of their own free will, as so many deliberate acts of provocation. Martyrdom was a Christian creation as much as a Roman persecution.

Just as the early Christians took over the Roman religious festivals, so they also took over the Roman attitudes toward death and suicide, and in doing so, magnified them theologically, distorted them, and finally turned them upside down. To the Romans of every class, death itself was unimportant. But the way of dying—decently, rationally, with dignity, and at the right time—mattered intensely. Their way of death, that is, was the measure of their final value of life.

The early Christians showed this same indifference to death but changed the perspective. Viewed from the Christian heaven, life itself was at best unimportant, at worst evil; the fuller the life, the greater the temptation to sin. Death, therefore, was a release awaited or sought out with impatience. In other words, the more powerfully the Church instilled in believers the idea that this world was a vale of tears and sin and temptation, where they waited uneasily until death released them into eternal glory, the more irresistible the temptation to suicide became. Even the most stoical Romans committed suicide only as a last resort; they at least waited until their lives had become intolerable. But for the primitive Church, life was intolerable whatever its conditions. Why, then, live unredeemed when heavenly bliss is only a knife stroke away? Christian teaching was at first a powerful incitement to suicide.

The Allure of Martyrdom

The early Fathers had another inducement, almost as powerful as heavenly bliss. They offered posthumous glory: the martyrs' names celebrated annually in the church calendar, their passing officially recorded, their relics worshiped. Tertullian, the most bloodthirsty of the Fathers, who explicitly forbade his flock even to attempt to escape persecution, also proffered them the sweetest of recompenses, revenge: "No City escaped punishment, which had shed Christian blood."[16] The martyrs would peer down from paradise and see their enemies tortured eternally in hell.

But above all, martyrdom afforded certain redemption. Just as baptism purged away original sin, so martyrdom wiped out all previous transgressions. It was as much a guarantee of paradise to the Christians as violent death was to the Vikings and the Iglulik Eskimos. The only difference was that the martyrs died not as warriors but as passive victims; the war they fought was not of this world, and all their victories were Pyrrhic. We are back, by another route, with frivolous suicide.

Theologically, the argument was irresistible, but to respond to it required a zealotry that touched on madness. Donne remarked, unwillingly and with some embarrassment, that "those times were affected with a disease of this natural desire of such a death. . . . For that age was growne so hungry and ravenous of it [martyrdom], that many were baptized only because they would be burnt, and children taught to vexe and provoke Executioners, that they might be thrown into the fire."[17] It culminated in the genuine lunacy of the Donatists, whose lust for martyrdom was so extreme that the Church eventually declared them heretics. Gibbon elegantly described their weird and ambiguous glory:

> . . . [The Donatists] sometimes forced their way into the courts of justice and compelled the affrighted judge to give orders for their execution. They frequently stopped travellers on the public highways and obliged them to inflict the stroke of martyrdom by promise of a reward, if they consented—and by the threat of instant death, if they refused to grant so very singular a favor. When they

were disappointed of every other resource, they announced the day
on which, in the presence of their friends and brethren, they should
cast themselves headlong from some lofty rock; and many preci-
pices were shown, which had acquired fame by the number of these
religious suicides.[18]

The Donatists flourished—if that is the word—in the fourth and fifth
centuries and inspired their contemporary St. Augustine to the comment: ". . . to kill themselves out of respect for martyrdom is their
daily sport."

But Augustine also recognized the local dilemma of Christian
teaching: if suicide was allowed in order to avoid sin, then it became
the logical course for all those fresh from baptism. That sophistry,
combined with the suicide mania of the martyrs, provoked him into
arguments to prove suicide to be "a detestable and damnable wicked-
ness," mortal sin greater than any that could be committed between
baptism and a divinely ordained death. I have already mentioned that
the first of the arguments Augustine used was derived from the Sixth
Commandment, "Thou shalt not kill." Thus the man who killed
himself broke this commandment and became a murderer. Moreover,
if a man killed himself to atone for his sins, he was usurping the
function of the state and the church; and if he died innocent in order
to avoid sin, then he had his own innocent blood on his hands—a
worse sin than any he might commit, since it is impossible for him
to repent. Finally, Augustine took over Plato's and the Pythagoreans'
argument that life is the gift of God, and our sufferings, being divinely
ordained, are not to be foreshortened by one's own actions; to bear
them patiently is a measure of one's greatness of soul. Thus, to take
one's own life proved only that one did not accept the divine will.

The Church Door Closes

Augustine's large authority and the excesses of the presumptive
martyrs finally swung opinion against suicide. In A.D. 533 the Council
of Orleans denied funeral rites to anyone who killed himself while
accused of a crime. And in doing so, they were not merely following
Roman law that had been formulated to safeguard the state's rights to
the suicide's inheritance. Instead, they were condemning suicide both

as a crime in itself and also as a crime more serious than others, since ordinary criminals were still allowed a properly Christian burial. Thirty years later this seriousness was recognized without qualification by canon law. In 562 at the Council of Braga, funeral rites were refused to all suicides regardless of social position, reason, or method. The final step was taken in 693 by the Council of Toledo, which ordained that even the *attempted* suicide should be excommunicated.

The door had slammed shut. The decent alternative of the Romans, the key to paradise of the early Christians, had become the most deadly of mortal sins. Where St. Matthew recorded the suicide of Judas Iscariot without comment—implying by his silence that it in some way atoned for his other crimes—later theologians asserted that he was more damned for killing himself than for betraying Christ. St. Bruno, in the eleventh century, called suicides "martyrs for Satan," and two centuries later St. Thomas Aquinas sealed up the whole question in the *Summa:* suicide, he said, is a mortal sin against God, who has given us life; it is also a sin against justice and against charity.

Yet even there, in what was to be the center of Christian doctrine, Aquinas takes his arguments from non-Christian sources. The sin against God derives ultimately, like Augustine's similar argument, from Plato. The sin against justice—by which he means the in-dividual's responsibilities to his community—harks back to Aristotle. As for the sin against charity, Aquinas means that instinctive charity which each man bears toward himself—that is, the instinct of self-preservation that man has in common with the lower animals; to go against that is a mortal sin, since it is to go against nature. That reason was first used by the Hebrew general Josephus to dissuade his soldiers from killing themselves after they had been defeated by the Romans. (He also used Plato's argument.)

But however un-Christian the sources of the arguments, suicide became, in the long, superstitious centuries between Augustine and Aquinas, the most mortal of Christian sins. Augustine had attacked suicide as a preventive measure: the cult of martyrdom had got out of hand and was, anyway, no longer relevant to the situation of the Church in the fourth century. Moreover, it was an offense against that respect for life as the vehicle of the soul that was the essence of Christ's teaching; to love one's neighbor as oneself makes no sense if to kill oneself is also permitted.

Yet the fact remained that suicide, thinly disguised as martyrdom, was one of the rocks on which the Church had first been founded. So perhaps the absoluteness with which the sin was condemned and the horrors of the vengeance visited on the dead bodies of the suicides were directly proportional to the power the act exerted on the Christian imagination, and to the lingering temptation to escape the snares of the flesh by the shortest, most certain way. Thus when the Albigensians, in the early thirteenth century, followed the example of the early saints and suicidally sought martyrdom, they were thought only to have compounded the damnation that their other heresies had already earned them. In doing so, they justified the terrible savagery with which they were butchered.

Fedden believes that Augustine's teaching and canon law acted together to release all those primitive terrors of suicide that are repressed in more rational periods. Perhaps. But what also occurred was somehow more profound: what began as a preventive measure finished as a kind of universal character change. An act that during the first flowering of Western civilization had been tolerated, later admired, and later still sought as the supreme mark of zealotry, became finally the object of intense moral revulsion. When, in the late Renaissance, the question of the individual's right to take his own life once more arose, it seemed to be challenging the whole structure of Christian belief and morals. Hence the deviousness with which men like John Donne began once again to argue the case for suicide after a gap of more than a thousand years. Hence, too, the note of hoarse moral rectitude of their detractors, that earnest certainty which could dispense with argument because it had behind it the whole massive weight of the Church's authority. The increasingly outspoken and rational arguments of the philosophers—Voltaire, Hume, Schopenhauer—did more or less nothing to shake this moral certainty, although as time went on the pious denunciations became shriller, less assured, more outraged.

From the Individual to Society

It took the counterrevolution of science to change all this. Henry Morselli, an Italian professor of psychological medicine and Durkheim's most distinguished predecessor in the use of statistics to analyze the problem of suicide, wrote in 1879: "The old philosophy of individualism had given to suicide the character of liberty and spontaneity, but now it became necessary to study it no longer as the expression of individual and independent faculties, but certainly as a social phenomenon allied with all the other racial forces."[19]

The shift is from the individual to society, from morals to problems. Socially, the gains were enormous: the legal penalties gradually dropped away; the families of successful suicides no longer found themselves disinherited and tainted with the suspicion of inherited insanity; they could bury their dead and grieve for them in much the same way as any other bereaved. As for the unsuccessful suicide, he faced neither the gallows nor prison but, at worst, a period of observation in a psychiatric ward; more often, he faced nothing more piercing than his own continuing depression.

Existentially, however, there were also losses. The Church's condemnation of self-murder, however brutal, was based at least on a concern for the suicide's soul. In contrast, a great deal of modern scientific tolerance appears to be founded on human indifference. The act is removed from the realm of damnation only at the price of being transformed into an interesting but purely intellectual problem, beyond obloquy but also beyond tragedy and morality. There seems to me remarkably little gap between the idea of death as a fascinating, slightly erotic happening on a television screen and that of suicide as an abstract sociological problem. Despite all the talk of prevention, it may be that the suicide is rejected by the social scientist as utterly as he was by the most dogmatic Christian theologians. Thus even the author of the entry on suicide in the *Encyclopedia of Religion and Ethics* writes, with unconcealed relief: "Perhaps the greatest contribution of modern times to the rational treatment of the matter is the consideration . . . that many suicides are non-moral and entirely the affair of the specialist in mental diseases."

The implication is clear: modern suicide has been removed from the vulnerable, volatile world of human beings and hidden safely away in the isolation wards of science. I doubt if Ogarev and his prostitute mistress would have found much in the change to be grateful for.

3

Do We Have a Right to Die?

Ronald Dworkin

The tragedy of Nancy Cruzan's life is now part of American constitutional law. Before her automobile accident in 1983, she was an energetic 24-year-old recently married woman. Her injuries deprived her brain of oxygen for fourteen minutes, and left her in what doctors describe as a permanent vegetative state. Only the lower part of her brain stem continued to function. She was unconscious and oblivious to the environment, though she had reflexive responses to sound and perhaps to painful stimuli. She was fed and hydrated through tubes implanted in her stomach, and other machines performed her other bodily functions. She was washed and turned regularly, but all of her limbs were contracted and her fingernails cut into her wrists.

For months after the accident her parents and her then husband pressed doctors to do everything possible to restore her to some kind of life. But when it became plain that she would remain in a vegetative

Ronald Dworkin is a professor of law at New York University and the University Professor of Jurisprudence at Oxford University. He is the author of *Life's Dominion: An Argument About Abortion, Euthanasia, and Individual Freedom* (1993). This essay is reprinted by permission from his most recent book, *Freedom's Law: The Moral Reading of the American Constitution* (Cambridge: Harvard University Press, 1996). The main part of the essay was written in January 1991 and the Addendum in May 1994.

state until she died, which might mean for thirty more years, her parents, who had become her legal guardians, asked the state hospital to remove the tubes and allow her to die at once. Since the hospital refused to do so without a court order, the parents petitioned a Missouri court, which appointed a guardian *ad litem* (a special guardian appointed to represent her in these proceedings) to offer arguments why it should not grant that order. After a hearing the court granted the order on the ground that it was in Cruzan's best interests to be permitted to die with some dignity now rather than to live on in an unconscious state.

The guardian *ad litem* felt it his duty to appeal the order to the Missouri supreme court, though he told that court that he did not disagree with the decision. But the supreme court reversed the lower court's decision: it held that Cruzan's legal guardians had no power to order feeding stopped without "clear and convincing" evidence that she herself had decided, when competent, not to be fed in her present circumstances. Though a friend had testified that Cruzan had said, in a conversation soon after the death of her grandmother, that she would not want to be kept alive if she could not really live, the supreme court held that this testimony was not adequate evidence of the necessary decision.

Cruzan's parents appealed to the United States Supreme Court: their lawyers argued that the Missouri decision violated her right not to be subjected to unwanted medical treatment. The Court had not previously ruled on the question how far states must respect that right. On June 25, 1990, by a five-to-four vote, the Court refused to reverse the Missouri decision: it denied that Cruzan had a constitutional right that could be exercised by her parents in these circumstances.

The Opinions

The main opinion was written by Chief Justice Rehnquist, and he was joined by Justices Kennedy and White. Many newspaper reports and comments on the case declared that, although the Court had refused the Cruzan family's request, it had nevertheless endorsed a general constitutional right of competent people to decide that they should not be kept alive through medical technology. The *New York Times,* for example, said that the Court had decided that "the Constitution protects a person's liberty to reject life-sustaining technology," and congratulated the Court for a "monumental example of law adjusting to life." The *Washington Post* headline read, "Court Rules Patient's Wishes Must Control 'Right to Die.'"

It is important to notice, however, that Rehnquist took care to say that he and the two justices who joined his opinion were not actually deciding that people have a right to die. He said they were assuming such a right only *hypothetically,* "for purposes of this case," and he emphasized that he thought it still an open question whether even a competent person's freedom to die with dignity could be overridden by a state's own constitutional right to keep people alive.[1] Although the logic of past cases would embrace a "liberty interest" of a competent person to refuse artificially delivered food and water, he said, "the dramatic consequences involved in refusal of such treatment would inform the inquiry as to whether the deprivation of that interest is constitutional."

Even if we do assume that people have a constitutional right to refuse to be kept alive if they become permanently vegetative, Rehnquist said, Missouri did not infringe that right. It only insisted that people must exercise that right for themselves, while still competent, and do so in a formal and unmistakable way, by executing a "living will," for example. The United States Constitution does not prohibit states from adopting strict evidentiary requirements of that sort, he said. The Constitution does not require Missouri to recognize what most people would think was very strong evidence of Cruzan's convictions, that is, her serious and apparently well-considered statements to a close friend soon after a relative's death.

Justices O'Connor and Scalia, though they agreed to uphold the Missouri supreme court's decision, filed separate concurring opinions. O'Connor made an important practical point: that instead of drafting a living will describing precisely what should not be done to keep them alive, many people would prefer to designate someone else—a relative or close friend—to make those decisions for them when the need arises.[2] She stated her own view that the Constitution gave people that right, and emphasized that the Court's decision against Cruzan's parents was not to the contrary, since Cruzan had made no formal designation.

Scalia's concurring opinion was of a very different character. He repeated his extraordinarily narrow view of constitutional rights: that the Constitution, properly interpreted, allows the states to do anything that it does not expressly forbid. Since, he said, the Constitution "says nothing" about people's rights to control their own deaths, there is no question of any constitutional right of that sort, and state legislatures are free to make any decision they wish about what can be done to people to keep them technically alive. Scalia left little doubt about his own views of what a sensible state legislature would decide; he said that no reasonable person would wish to inhabit a body that was only technically alive. But, he said, the Constitution does not require state legislatures to be either reasonable or humane.

Justice Brennan dissented in an opinion joined by Justices Marshall and Blackmun. Brennan's opinion, one of the last he delivered before his retirement, was a valedictory address that made even plainer how much his humanity and intelligence will be missed. He pointed out the main fallacy in Rehnquist's opinion: it is inconsistent to assume that people have a right not to be given medical care contrary to their wishes, and yet to allow the state to impose evidentiary rules that make it unlikely that an incompetent person's past wishes will actually be discovered. "Even someone with a resolute determination to avoid life-support under circumstances such as Nancy's," he said, "would still need to know that such things as living wills exist and how to execute one. . . . For many, the thought of an ignoble end, steeped in decay, is abhorrent. A quiet, proud death, bodily integrity intact, is a matter of extreme consequence."

Justice Stevens dissented separately. He criticized the majority for not having enough regard for Cruzan's best interests, and stressed the religious basis of Missouri's case. "Not much may be said with confidence about death," he wrote, "unless it is said from faith, and that alone is reason enough to protect the freedom to conform choices about death to individual conscience."

In August 1990 Cruzan's parents petitioned the lower court that had initially decided in their favor with what they called new evidence: three more friends had come forward prepared to testify that she had told them, too, that she would not want to live as a vegetable. Though this evidence was of the same character as that which the Missouri supreme court had earlier said was not sufficiently "clear and convincing," the state attorney general decided this time not to oppose the parents' petition. Within a few days feeding and hydration were stopped, and Cruzan was given medication to prevent pain. She died on December 26.

The State's Interest

When competent people refuse medical treatment that is necessary to save their lives, doctors and legal officials may face a dilemma. They have an ethical and legal obligation both to act in the patient's best interests and to respect his autonomy, his right to decide for himself what will be done with or to his body. These obligations may be in conflict, because a patient may refuse treatment the doctors think essential. Rehnquist introduced a third consideration into the constitutional issue. He contrasted the patient's autonomy not just with his or her own best interests but also with the *state's* interest in "protecting and preserving life." In most cases when a competent person refuses life-saving aid—for example, when he refuses an essential blood transfusion on religious grounds—there is no difference between what most people would regard as his best interests and the state's interest in keeping him alive, because it is assumed that it is in his best interests to live. But in some cases—when the patient is in great pain, for example, and cannot live very long even with treatment— the state's supposed interest in keeping him alive may conflict with his own best interests, not only as he but as most people would judge these.

If we accept that some state policy might be served by prolonging life even in such cases, then two constitutional issues are presented. Does a state have the constitutional power to impose life-saving medical treatment on a person against his will, that is, in defiance of his autonomy, when it believes that treatment is in his own best interests? Does it have the constitutional power to impose such treatment for its own purposes, even when it concedes that this is *against* his best interests, that is, in defiance of the normal rule that patients should not be given medical treatment that is bad for them?

The law of most American states seems settled that the autonomy of a competent patient will be decisive in all such cases, and that doctors may not treat him against his will either for his sake or for the sake of some social interest in keeping him alive. The Supreme

Court had never explicitly decided that the Constitution compels states to take that position, though in the present case, as I said, Rehnquist assumed hypothetically that it does.

In the case of people who are unconscious or otherwise incompetent, however, and who did not exercise their right of self-determination when they were able to do so, the distinction between their own best interest and the alleged interest of the state in keeping them alive is of great importance, as Rehnquist's opinion, carefully examined, makes clear. He offered two different, though not clearly distinct, arguments why Missouri has a right to tip the scales in favor of keeping comatose people alive by demanding "clear and convincing" evidence that they had decided they would rather die. His first argument appealed to the best interests of incompetent people. He said that a rule requiring evidence of a formal declaration of a past decision to die, before life support can be terminated, benefits people who have become comatose because it protects them against guardians who abuse their trust, and because a decision not to terminate is always reversible if documented evidence of a formal past decision emerges later. His second argument is very different: it appeals not to the interests of comatose patients but to Missouri's supposed independent interests in keeping such patients alive. He said that a state has its own legitimate reasons for protecting and preserving life, which "no one can gainsay," and that Missouri is therefore entitled for its own sake to tip the evidentiary scales against termination.

Rehnquist treats these as cumulative arguments: he thinks that taken together they justify Missouri's evidentiary rule. I shall consider them separately, however, because they raise very different issues, and because, though Rehnquist mentions the second only obliquely and in passing, it has important implications for other constitutional issues, including the abortion controversy, and so deserves separate study.

Argument 1: For the Incompetent

Rehnquist devotes most of his opinion to the first argument: that the Missouri rule is in the best interests of most of the thousands of people who live in a permanent vegetative state and did not sign living wills when they could. That seems implausible. Many people who are now in that position talked—as Nancy Cruzan did in conversations with her friends—and acted in ways that make it very likely that they would have signed a living will had they anticipated their own accidents. The Missouri rule flouts rather than honors their autonomy. Many others, at least in the opinions of their family and others who know them best, almost certainly would have decided that way if they had ever considered the matter. The Missouri rule denies them what they probably would have chosen. Why is so indiscriminate a rule necessary? Why would it not be better to allow lower courts to decide each case on the balance of probabilities, so that a court might decide that on the best evidence Nancy Cruzan would have chosen to die, as the initial Missouri court in fact did decide?

While Rehnquist concedes that Missouri's rigid rule may sometimes lead to a "mistake," he says that the Constitution does not require states to adopt procedures that work perfectly. But his arguments that the Missouri rule would even in general work to the benefit of incompetent people are question-begging: they reflect a presumption that it is normally in the best interests of permanently comatose people to live, so that they should be kept alive unless there is decisive evidence that they have actually decided to the contrary. It is true that in some situations a presumption of that kind is sensible. A state need not accept the judgment of devout Jehovah's Witnesses, for example, that it would be in the best interests of an unconscious relative not to have a blood transfusion that would bring him back to conscious life, even if the state would accept his own decision not to be treated were he conscious. But the reason why we think that is that we believe life and health are fundamentally so important that no one should be allowed to reject them on behalf of someone else.

No such assumption is plausible when the life in question is only the insensate life of the permanently vegetative. That kind of life is not valuable to anyone. Some people, no doubt, would want to be kept alive indefinitely in such a state out of religious convictions: they might think that failing to prolong life as long as possible is insulting to God, for example. But even *they* do not think that it is in *their* interests to live on; most such people would hope, I think, for an early death in that situation, though one in which everything had been done to prolong life. They would regard an early death as an instance of God's mercy.

But Rehnquist is so far in the grip of the presumption that life is of great importance even to people in a vegetative state that he argues, at times, as if the Cruzan family's petition were a proceeding *against* their daughter. He says that the state is entitled to act as a "shield" for the incompetent, and he cites cases in which the Supreme Court required that government have "clear and convincing" evidence of fault before deporting someone, or depriving him of citizenship, or terminating his parental rights. In such cases constitutional law properly tips the scales against punitive action, because, as in an ordinary criminal trial, a mistake on one side, against the defendant, is much more serious than a mistake on the other. Cruzan's case is not an adversary proceeding, however. Her own parents are seeking relief *on her behalf*, and fairness argues for only one thing: the most accurate possible identification of what Nancy Cruzan's wishes were and where her interests now lie.

Some of Rehnquist's arguments depend not on the assumption that it is normally in the interests of a permanently comatose person to continue living, but on the equally implausible assumption that continued life in those circumstances is never against such a person's interests. This is the premise of his argument, for example, that it is better to keep a comatose patient alive than to allow her to die, even if the chances of recovery are infinitesimal, because the latter decision is irreversible. He assumes that someone in Nancy Cruzan's position suffers no disadvantage in continuing to live, so that if there is only the barest conceivable possibility of some extraordinary medical discovery in the future, however remote that may seem now, it must be on balance in the patient's interests to continue living as long as possible.

If the only things people worried about, or wanted to avoid, were pain and other unpleasant physical experiences, then of course they would be indifferent about whether, if they became permanently comatose, their bodies continued to live or not. But people care about many other things as well. They worry about their dignity and integrity, and about the view other people have of them, how they are conceived and remembered. Many of them are anxious that their relatives and friends not have to bear the burdens, whether emotional or financial, of keeping them alive. Many are appalled by the thought of resources being wasted on them that might be used for the benefit of other people who have genuine, conscious lives to lead.

These various concerns explain the horror so many people feel at the idea of existing pointlessly for years as a vegetable. They think that a bare biological existence, with no intelligence or sensibility or sensation, is not a matter of indifference, but something bad for them, something that damages their lives considered as a whole. This was the view Nancy Cruzan expressed to her friend after her grandmother's death. Rehnquist seems depressingly insensitive to all these concerns. In any case, his assumption—that people lose nothing when permission to terminate their lives is refused—ignores them. A great many people, at least, believe the contrary: that a decision to keep them alive would cheat them forever of a chance to die with both dignity and consideration for others, and that to be deprived of that chance would be a great and irreversible loss.

Of course, given the devastating importance of the decision to terminate life support, a state may impose strenuous procedural constraints on any doctor's or guardian's decision to do so. The state may require guardians to show, for example, in an appropriate hearing before a judge or hospital committee or some other suitable body, and with appropriate medical support, that there is no genuine hope that the victim will ever become competent again. It may require guardians to show, moreover, that there is no persuasive reason to think the patient would have preferred to have life support continued. It may also adopt suitable precautions to ensure that the decision is made by people solely concerned with the patient's wishes and interests; it may specify, for example, that the decision not be made by guardians who would gain financially by the patient's early death. Though these and other procedural constraints may somewhat increase the chance that a patient who would have wished to die is kept alive, they can plausibly be described as in the best interests of patients overall, or in the interests of protecting their autonomy.

The Cruzan family satisfied all such requirements, however. There is no evidence that Nancy Cruzan had any religious beliefs that would have led her to prefer mere biological life to death. On the contrary, the evidence of her serious conversations strongly suggested—to put it at its weakest—that she would vigorously oppose being kept alive. Since Missouri itself paid the full cost of her treatment, the family had no financial incentive to allow her to die. So the state's evidentiary procedures cannot reasonably be said to have been in Cruzan's best interests, or in the best interests of vegetative patients generally. If Missouri's rule is constitutional, it must be for some other reason.

Argument 2: For the State

We must therefore turn to Rehnquist's second, much less developed argument: that Missouri can impose evidentiary requirements, even if that is against Cruzan's interests and those of other permanently incompetent people, in order to protect its own interests in preserving life. Rehnquist said that "societal" and "institutional" issues are at stake, as well as individual ones, that no one can "gainsay" Missouri's "interest in the protection and preservation of human life."

No doubt Missouri pressed this argument, and perhaps Rehnquist adopted it, with an eye to the abortion controversy. In 1989's abortion case, *Webster v. Missouri Reproductive Services,* Missouri cited its own sovereign interest in preserving all human life as justification for refusing to allow abortions to be performed in state-financed medical facilities. Even *Roe v. Wade,* the 1973 decision that established a woman's limited right to an abortion, acknowledged that a state has a legitimate concern with protecting the life of a fetus. Though Justice Blackmun said, in that case, that a state's right to protect a fetus is outweighed by a woman's right of privacy during the first two trimesters of pregnancy, he held that the state's right was sufficiently strong thereafter to allow a state to make most third-trimester abortions illegal. In the *Webster* decision, several justices said that the state's legitimate interest in protecting human life is more powerful than Blackmun recognized, and justifies more sweeping regulation of abortion than he allowed.

Nevertheless, in spite of the crucial part that the idea of a legitimate state interest in preserving all human life now plays in constitutional law, there has been remarkably little attention, either in Supreme Court opinons or in the legal literature, to the question of what that supposed interest is or why it is legitimate for a state to pursue it. It is particularly unclear how the supposed state interest bears on the questions that were at stake in the *Cruzan* case. Of course government is properly concerned with the welfare and well-being of its citizens, and it has the right, for that reason, to try to prevent them from being killed or put at risk of death from disease or accident. But the state's obvious and general concern with its citizens' well-being does not give it a reason to preserve someone's life when his or her welfare would be better served by being permitted to die in dignity. So the state interest that Rehnquist has in mind, as justifying Missouri's otherwise unreasonable evidentiary rule, must be a different, less familiar, one: it must supply a reason for forcing people to accept medical treatment when they or their guardians plausibly think they would be better off dead.

Scalia's Concurrence

Scalia, in his concurring opinion, said that we must assume that states are constitutionally entitled to preserve people's lives, even against their own interests, because otherwise familiar laws making either suicide or aiding suicide a crime, which no one doubts are valid, would be unconstitutional. As I said, he disagreed with Rehnquist's hypothetical assumption that, at least, competent people have a constitutional right to refuse lifesaving medical treatment. But Scalia's argument is doubly suspect.

First, his assumption that states have the constitutional power to prevent suicide in all circumstances is too broad, and it is premature. It is true that both suicide and assisting suicide were crimes according to common law, and Scalia relies heavily on the views of William Blackstone, the famous and influential eighteenth-century legal commentator, who declared that it was a crime even for someone suffering a terminal illness and in terrible pain to take his own life. But there are many examples in constitutional history of constraints on liberty that were unquestioned for long periods of history but were then reexamined and found unconstitutional because lawyers and the public as a whole had developed a more sophisticated understanding of the underlying ethical and moral issues.[3] That is particularly likely when the historical support for the constraint has been mainly religious. It was long unquestioned that states have the power to outlaw contraception, for example, before the Supreme Court held otherwise in 1965 in *Griswold v. Connecticut*.

Longstanding practice is an even worse guide to constitutional law when technological change has created entirely new problems or exacerbated old ones. Doctors can now keep people alive in terminal illness for long periods that would have seemed incredible in the recent past, and their new abilities have made the position of people who would rather die than continue living in pain both more tragic and more common. So when the Supreme Court is next asked to rule on whether states can constitutionally forbid someone in that position from taking his own life, or can make it criminal for a doctor to assist him, even if the doctor takes every precaution to be sure that the person has freely decided to commit suicide, the Court will face a very different situation from that in which the common-law principles about suicide developed. It seems premature for Scalia simply to declare that the power of states to forbid suicide has no exceptions at all. Government is entitled to try to prevent people from killing themselves in many circumstances—in periods of severe but transient depression, for example. But it does not follow that it has the power to prolong the suffering of someone in terrible and pointless pain.

In any case, it is bizarre to classify as suicide someone's decision to reject treatment that would keep him alive but at a cost he and many other people think too great. Many people whose lives could be lengthened through severe amputations or incapacitating operations decide to die instead, and they are not thought to have taken their own lives for that reason. It seems plain that states have no constitutional power to direct doctors to perform such operations without the consent and against the wishes of the patient. People imagining themselves as permanently comatose are in the same position: their biological lives could then be prolonged only through medical treatment they would think degrading, and only in a form they would think worse than death. So it is a mistake, for that reason, to describe someone who signs a living will as committing hypothetical suicide. It seems a mistake for another reason as well.

Even if Scalia were right, that a conscious and competent patient who refuses an amputation that would prolong his life should be treated as a suicide, it would still not follow that someone who decides to die if he becomes a permanent vegetable is in fact taking his own life, because it is at least a reasonable view that a permanently comatose person is, for all that matters, dead already.

Scalia's argument is therefore a red herring, and in spite of Rehnquist's confident remark that no one can "gainsay" Missouri's inter-

est in protecting and preserving life, we still lack an explanation of
what that interest is and why it is proper for Missouri to pursue it.
It might be said that keeping people alive, even when they would be
better off dead, helps to protect the community's sense of the importance of life. I agree that society is better and more secure when
its members share a sense that human life is sacred, and that no effort
should be spared to save lives. People who lack that sense may
themselves be more ready to kill, and will be less anxious to make
sacrifices to protect the lives of others. That seems to me the most
powerful available argument why states should be permitted to outlaw elective abortion of very late-stage fetuses, for example. But it is
extremely implausible that allowing a permanently comatose patient
to die, after a solemn proceeding devoted only to her wishes and
interests, will in any way erode a community's sense of the importance of life.

Life for the Sake of Life

So a state cannot justify keeping comatose people alive on the
instrumental ground that this is necessary to prevent murder or to
encourage people to vote for famine relief. If Rehnquist is right that
a state has a legitimate interest in preserving all human life, then this
must be in virtue not of any instrumental argument but of the
intrinsic value of such life, its importance for its own sake. Most
people do believe that human life has intrinsic importance, and
perhaps Rehnquist thinks it unnecessary either to clarify or to justify
that idea.[4] It is unclear, however, that they accept the idea on any
ground, or in any sense, that supports his case. For some people, for
example, life has intrinsic value because it is a gift of God; they
believe, as I said, that it is wrong not to struggle to prolong life,
because this is an insult to Him who alone should decide when life
ends. But the Constitution does not allow states to justify policy on
grounds of religious doctrine; some more secular account of the
intrinsic value of life would be needed to support Rehnquist's second
argument.

It will be helpful to distinguish two forms that a more secular
version of the claim might take. The first supposes that a human life,
in any form or circumstance, is a unique and valuable addition to the

universe, so that the stock of value is needlessly diminished when any life is shorter than it might be. That does not seem a convincing view. Even if we think that a conscious, reflective, engaged human life is inherently valuable, we might well doubt that an insensate, vegetative life has any value at all.

The view that all forms of life are inherently valuable is also disqualified for a different reason. On that view we would have as much reason to bring new lives into being, increasing the population, as for prolonging lives already in progress. After all, people who think that great art is inherently valuable have the same reason for encouraging the production of more masterpieces as for preserving art that now exists. But most people who think life has intrinsic significance do not think that they therefore have any general duty to procreate or to encourage procreation. In any case, the Supreme Court's decision in *Griswold,* which is now accepted by almost everyone, holds that the states have no power to prohibit contraception.

People who think that life has intrinsic value or importance, but do not think that this fact offers any reason for increasing the population, understand life's value in a second and more conditional way. They mean, I think, that once a human life has begun it is terribly important that it go well, that it be a good rather than a bad life, a successful rather than a wasted one. Most people accept that human life has inherent importance in that sense. That explains why they try not just to make their lives pleasant but to give them worth, and also why it seems a tragedy when people decide, late in life, that they can take neither pride nor satisfaction in the way they have lived.[5] Of course nothing in the idea that life has intrinsic importance in this second sense can justify a policy of keeping permanently comatose people alive. The worth of their lives—the character of the lives they have led—cannot be improved just by keeping the bodies they used to inhabit technically alive. On the contrary, that makes their lives worse, because it is a bad thing, for all the reasons I described earlier, to have one's body medicated, fed, and groomed, as an object of pointless and degrading solicitude, after one's mind is dead. Rehnquist's second argument is therefore a dramatic failure: Missouri's policy is not supported but condemned by the idea that human life is important for its own sake, on the only understanding of that idea that is available in our constitutional system.

What Is at Stake

It is a relatively new question how the medical technology that now allows doctors to keep wholly incompetent people alive for decades should be used. Of course the Constitution leaves considerable latitude to the state legislatures in fixing detailed schemes for regulating how and what doctors and guardians decide. But the Constitution does limit a state's power in certain ways, as it must in order to protect the autonomy and the most fundamental interests of the patient.

In the *Cruzan* case the Supreme Court recognized, even if only hypothetically, an important part of that constitutional protection: that in principle a state has no right to keep a comatose patient alive against his previously expressed wish that he be allowed to die in the circumstances he has now reached. But the Court undercut the full value of that principle by allowing Missouri to impose an evidentiary rule that substantially decreases the chance that a patient will receive only the treatment he or she would have wanted. Even worse, the justification the Chief Justice offered for the Court's decision put forward two principles that, unless they are soon rejected, will damage the rest of the law as it develops. It is therefore worth summarizing the argument I have made against these principles.

Rehnquist assumed that it is in the best interests of at least most people who become permanent vegetables to remain alive in that condition. But there is no way in which continued life can be good for such people, and several ways in which it might well be thought bad. He also assumed that a state can have its own legitimate reasons for keeping such people alive even when it concedes that this is against their best interests. But that judgment rests on a dangerous misunderstanding of the irresistible idea that human life has intrinsic moral significance. We do not honor that idea—on the contrary we insult it—when we waste resources in prolonging a bare, technical, insensate form of life.

More than just the right to die, or even the right to abortion, is at stake in these issues. In the next decades the question of why and how human life has intrinsic value is likely to be debated, by philosophers, lawyers, and the public, with respect not just to those issues but to others as well, including genetic engineering, for example. Constitutional law will both encourage and reflect the debate, and though it is far too early to anticipate what form that law will take, Rehnquist's unreasoned opinion was a poor beginning.

An Addendum

A lawsuit decided on May 3, 1994, in Seattle might well become the *Roe v. Wade* of euthanasia. In *Compassion in Dying v. State of Washington,* Federal District Court Judge Barbara Rothstein struck down Washington state's 140-year-old anti-assisted-suicide law, and declared that competent terminal patients have a constitutional right to a willing doctor's help in killing themselves.

She decided, that is, that the laws of almost all the states that make assisting suicide a crime are unconstitutional. Once again the courts are at the center of a bitter moral and religious controversy.

Americans have been arguing about euthanasia for decades. Two states, Washington and California, recently rejected voluntary euthanasia schemes in fairly close votes; another such measure will be on the ballot in Oregon later this year [1994]. In Michigan, a special statute was passed to stop Dr. Jack Kevorkian from helping patients to die, but a jury, expressing the depth of the public's sympathy for patients dying in pain, refused to convict him of violating that statute even though he admitted he had. The Michigan supreme court then invalidated the special statute on technical grounds. But it also reinstated murder charges against him.

If Judge Rothstein's decision (or a similar one) is upheld in the Supreme Court, the Constitution will have preempted part of this sprawling debate: every state will have to recognize that, though it can regulate doctor-assisted suicide, it may not prohibit it altogether. That result will outrage millions of conscientious citizens who think euthanasia an abomination in any form. Great constitutional cases, in the United States, are also great public arguments, and it is crucial that we all begin to think about the issues Judge Rothstein has raised.

She said that the Supreme Court's 1992 decision in *Planned Parenthood v. Casey,* which reaffirmed *Roe v. Wade,* "almost" compelled her own decision. *Casey*'s central opinion declared that "matters involving the most intimate and personal choices a person may make in a lifetime . . . are central to the liberty protected by the Fourteenth Amendment. At the heart of liberty is the right to define one's own concept of existence, of meaning, of the universe, and of the mystery of human life." Judge Rothstein observed, correctly, that the freedom of a competent dying person to hasten his own death falls under that description at least as clearly as does the right of a pregnant woman to choose abortion.

The "Slippery Slope"

Many opponents of euthanasia try to distinguish the two issues, however, by appealing to a "slippery slope" argument. They say, for example, that voluntary euthanasia will so habituate doctors to killing that they will begin executing sick, old, unwanted people whose care is expensive but who plainly want to live. That contradicts common sense: doctors know the moral difference between helping people who beg to die and killing those who want to live. If anything, ignoring the pain of terminal patients pleading for death seems more likely to dull a doctor's humane instincts than trying to help.

Some critics worry about the practice in Holland, where doctors have given lethal injections to unconscious or incompetent terminal patients who had not explicitly asked to die. But Judge Rothstein's opinion applies only to assisted suicide, which demands a contemporary request, and even if a legislature were to allow for such injection, for patients incapable of taking pills or killing themselves in any other humane way, it could stipulate that a contemporary request was still essential.

A more plausible version of the slippery-slope argument supposes that if euthanasia is legalized, dying people whose treatment is expensive or burdensome may ask help in suicide only because they feel guilty, and that family members may perhaps try to coax or shame them into that decision. But states plainly have the power to guard against requests influenced by guilt, depression, poor care, or economic worries. (The main plaintiff in the case, the organization Compassion in Dying, helps only terminal patients who have repeated their request three times and have expressed no ambivalence or uncertainty.) States also have the power to discourage distasteful, near-assembly-line suicides like those orchestrated by Dr. Kevorkian.

Patients go to him—and juries acquit him—only because there is no better alternative.

No set of regulations can be perfect. But it would be perverse to force competent people to die in great pain or drugged stupor for that reason, accepting a great and known evil to avoid the risk of a speculative one. In the *Cruzan* decision discussed above, the Supreme Court held that states must respect some form of "living will" that allows people to specify in advance that certain procedures not be used to keep them alive, in spite of the fact that patients can also be coaxed or shamed into signing such documents. No one thinks, moreover, that the fact that doctors sometimes deliberately give dying patients large enough doses of pain-killing drugs to kill them—a covert decision much more open to abuse than a scheme of voluntary euthanasia would be—is a good reason for withholding all dangerous pain-killers from terminal patients in torment.

These slippery-slope arguments, then, are very weak ones; they seem only disguises for the deeper convictions that actually move most opponents of all euthanasia. Fr. Matthew Habiger, president of Human Life International, described as the largest "pro-life" organization in the world, denounced the *Compassion in Dying* decision in terms that made those deeper convictions explicit. "The march toward a complete anti-life philosophy," he said, "can now be easily mapped: from contraception to abortion to euthanasia. Once life is no longer treated as a sacred gift from God, a society inevitably embraces death in all its forms."

In this view, all euthanasia—even when fully voluntary and rational —is wrong because human life has an objective, intrinsic value as well as a subjective value for the person whose life it is, and euthanasia dishonors that intrinsic value. That conviction underlies most opposition to abortion as well. Many people, particularly those who agree with Fr. Habiger that human life is a divine gift, believe that ending it deliberately (except, perhaps, as punishment) is always, at any stage, the most profound insult to life's objective value.

It would be wrong to think, however, that those who are more permissive about abortion and euthanasia are indifferent to the value of life. Rather, they disagree about what respecting that value means. They think that in some circumstances—when a fetus is terribly deformed, for example—abortion shows more respect for life than childbirth would. And they think dying with dignity shows more respect for their own lives—better fits their sense of what is really important in and about human existence—than ending their lives in long agony or senseless sedation.

Our constitution takes no sides in these ancient disputes about life's "meaning." But it does protect people's right to die as well as to live, so far as possible, in the light of their own intensely personal convictions about "the mystery of human life." It insists that these values are too central to personality, too much at the core of liberty, to allow a majority to decide what everyone must believe. Of course the law must protect people who think it would be appalling to be killed, even if they had only painful months or minutes to live anyway. But the law must also protect those with the opposite conviction: that it would be appalling not to be offered an easier, calmer death with the help of doctors they trust. Making someone die in a way that others approve, but that he believes contradicts his own dignity, is a serious, unjustified, unnecessary form of tyranny.

4

The Right to Die—Again

Hadley V. Arkes

I live in one of those rare enclaves, an academic town, a place that is in America but not quite of it. It is in places of this kind that one is more likely to encounter the macabre spectacle that took place in my own town of Amherst shortly after the military action began in the Persian Gulf. A young man, near thirty, apparently distressed by a war that was understood and supported widely in the country, decided to make his own response by engaging in an act of self-immolation on the town common. That evening the charred ground was marked off in a perimeter of lights, and two days later students planned to assemble on that spot to mark the death of this young man and express their opposition to the war. Before the meeting, as the sentiment was building, I addressed some stern words of warning to my own students, who were collected in a large class. For what seemed to be building was a movement to consecrate this ground, and in consecrating it, to honor an act of self-murder.

A year earlier a promising student, nineteen years old, had hanged himself, apparently in a seizure of depression, and no one had sought

Hadley V. Arkes is the Edward Ney Professor of Jurisprudence and American Institutions at Amherst College. He is the author of *First Things* (1986) and *Beyond the Constitution* (1990). This essay is reprinted by permission of the publisher from *Issues in Law and Medicine* 8, no. 3 (Winter 1992; © 1992 by the National Legal Center for the Medically Dependent and Disabled).

to make a shrine of his place of suicide. In this later case, the act of self-immolation drew on a precedent of distinctly political acts, and it was assumed that the suicide was connected with the war. And yet, we still had no inkling of the reasons that moved this young man to make a victim of himself; and without knowing the reasons, we could not possibly know whether his act was animated by an understanding we could honor. Before the Christian era, Plato had taught us, in the *Laches,* that we could not regard as courageous, or commendable, just any act that showed a striking disregard for one's own life. A captain who squandered the lives of his men in battle, with reckless abandon, could not be counted as courageous. Nor could a soldier who charged up hills merely because he loved the excitement of battle. Lions were aggressive, but they couldn't be regarded as "courageous" because they could not reflect on the ends that justified aggressiveness. In a similar way, we could find soldiers in the Wehrmacht who risked their lives for their country, but they were willing to risk their lives for a regime that was despicable in its character and its ends. As Plato taught in the *Laches,* we could call someone courageous only if his act of sacrifice proceeded from an understanding of the kinds of ends that truly justified the risk of his life.

It mattered profoundly, then, what the reasons were that moved the young man in Amherst to set fire to himself. If he killed himself out of a despair that Israel would survive the war, that not enough Jews would be killed, then we would probably be reluctant to commend his act or even to describe it as an act of sacrifice. If he were Jewish, and he killed himself out of a despair about the killing of Jews, we might wonder about the coherence of his act: how could he protest the killing of Jews by killing another innocent Jew (himself), or by having Jews act as their own executioners? The young man in Amherst protested the war in the Gulf, but if we found that his reasons were muddled, wrong, or incoherent, we would not be in a position to say that his act was "justified," in any strict sense, and we would be hesitant, once again, to celebrate his act.

I raised the question with my students of just which tradition of reflection was informing their reactions as they were about to participate in a meeting to consecrate an act of suicide. Most of them had not read the *Laches* or reflected on the teachings of Plato. Most of them had been raised in families that were nominally Christian or

Jewish, but most of them were not instructed in the teachings of their religion on the matter of suicide: namely, that we are not "self-made," nor are we the "owners" of our bodies, and we do not have a despotic license to destroy our own bodies, in an act of willfulness, for reasons that are sufficient simply to us. The Jewish and Christian traditions do not accept the current notions of personal "autonomy" and privacy that are guiding the American courts. But then, neither does the tradition of moral reflection that gave rise to the notions of autonomy and government by consent. In the understanding of Kant[1] and the American Founders, the claims of autonomy attached only to moral agents, to beings who could give and understand reasons over matters of right and wrong. And if they could understand the principles of moral judgment, they would understand the things that are wrong to do, even to themselves.

In the tradition of the American Founders, this understanding came to us in the logic of what were called "unalienable rights." That term has been repeated often in our own day, but many lawyers, judges, and doctors have detached the term from the logic that imparted its meaning. "Unalienable rights" referred to the rights that we were not competent to alienate or waive, even for ourselves, because their goodness or badness was grounded in principle, quite independent of our will. And, therefore, the Founders could understand that we may not properly alienate our freedom, or contract ourselves into slavery. And if we could not alienate our freedom, it went without saying that we could not alienate our right, or obligation, to preserve our own lives. In other words, the Founders understood, as all philosophers through the ages had understood, that it was possible to treat oneself unjustly. Not all killing was unjustified, and hence murder. But every unjustified killing was a murder, and the person who killed himself unjustly engaged in an act of self-murder. That point was understood by Kant and the American Founders, by the people who taught us the notions of autonomy and consent.

And so I put the problem again: The students were not instructed in the understanding of the Founders, of the men who framed the American Constitution and articulated the principles of this regime. Nor were the students apparently guided by the teachings of their religion. Nor were they aware of the best reflection that has come to us from the pagan philosophers. They were going off to celebrate an act of self-killing, but they were marching off, apparently, untethered to any of the serious traditions of moral reflection that could have shaped their motives and supplied principles for their judgments.

What, then, *constituted* them as they prepared to march in this wave of sentiment? They did not march as Christians or Jews, as children of the American regime, or as students of the classics. We might say that they were simply the children of modernity: they professed no grounds of moral judgment on which they could cast judgments on others. They were willing to honor an act if it seemed "authentic" and deeply felt. They could not judge the rightness or wrongness of the reason underlying the act, but they were willing to credit the seriousness of the actor if he showed a willingness to act emphatically, in visiting lasting injuries upon himself. Of course, they knew that they would not lend their endorsement if this man in Amherst had sought to protest the destruction of life in war by setting fire to an innocent bystander in town. That he had set fire to himself should not have distracted anyone from the fact that he had set fire to just another innocent person. Anything that established the wrong of torching an innocent person for the war in the Gulf should have been quite as compelling in establishing the wrong of the self-killing in this case. But the audience was now composed of the children of modernity, and they were willing to make a decisive distinction, in moral questions, between the harms inflicted on others and the harms inflicted on oneself.

The Claim of a "Right" to Die

This distinction was unknown to traditional moral philosophy. It became part of our vocabularies, and our understanding, in the nineteenth century, with John Stuart Mill's writing *On Liberty*. But that doctrine, that distinction, depends on a critical act of forgetting, and what it forgets is the logic of a moral principle, which cannot be affected by any such distinction between oneself and others. And yet, as far as I can see, the claim of a "right to die" depends on the acceptance of this doctrine, or this distinction, as nothing less than an axiom of moral reasoning: namely, that the principles that restrain killing in relation to all other persons do not necessarily bind the individual when he is acting solely on himself; that in matters concerning only himself, the individual bears the sovereign authority to dispose of his own body for reasons that are sufficient to himself, without the need to render a justification to anyone else.

This doctrine has now acquired a hold on some of our people that quite blocks from memory, and shields from our comprehension, anything in the traditions of moral philosophy that would point out its vacuity, its utter inability to give an account of itself. If we ask what supports it, what renders it intelligible as a claim to a "right," we are simply met with a baffled expression and a restatement of the right to dispose of our own bodies for reasons sufficient to ourselves. The claim to a right to die, or a right to destroy ourselves, is simply posited as an axiom, or a self-evident truth. It is simply asserted, stipulated, as though asserting it were enough to establish its truth. But as Bertrand Russell remarked, presupposing has all of the advantages over demonstrating that theft has over honest labor. And the labor not undertaken by the partisans of a right to die is the labor of explaining just what there is about this claim that can render it "rightful."

In a conference a few years ago, a doctor from Los Angeles posed the problem to me of one of his patients, a woman in her twenties who was a paraplegic and quite distressed. She had come to the melancholy judgment that she simply did not wish to go on with her life. As the doctor pointed out, she was *free* to take her life; she had the means to do it—and therefore how could we deny that she had the *right* to do it? Now to say that she was "free" to take her life is simply to say that she had the means and that we may not be able, practicably, to prevent her from committing suicide. But of course, even people who reflect only dimly on moral matters will usually understand that a statement of capabilities does not supply a statement of moral justification. I may be free to take the life of my neighbor, in the sense that I have the means of doing it; but this report on the state of my capabilities could not possibly establish that I would be *justified* in taking the life of my neighbor. To say that I *can* kill Jones is patently different from saying that I would be morally right or justified in killing Jones. That much would be evident to any child, new to moral reasoning.

But it should be equally evident that my capacity to take my own life could not establish that I have a right to take my life, or a right to die. The question then is: What needs to be added to the sentence?

What would we need to establish as the ground of our judgment before we could be warranted in drawing the conclusion that I would be justified in killing Jones, or that I have a right to kill myself? The answer, simply put, is that we would have to explain what is rightful or justified about these acts. But that is to say we would have to go back to the ground of logic that would have to underlie any statements we could make about the things that are rightful or wrongful.

Since the stakes here are grave, this is not a matter on which we can afford to be casual; and so we can be warranted in being very clinical and demanding about this question as moral philosophers. The claim to a right is a moral claim about the things that are right and justified, and therefore it must attach itself to all of the properties and functions of a "justification." The motive to claim a right is often driven by the desire to fend off the interference of other people. I claim a right, or a rightful freedom, to do something, because I wish to block the inclination of other people to interfere and deny me that freedom. And so I move beyond merely personal statements about the things that I merely like or dislike, according to my own irreducible feelings, for those kinds of statements are met, quite sufficiently, by comparable statements on the other side. I may say to the assailant, "I don't like being assaulted; it does not give me pleasure." But that protest is countered by his own claim that he *does* happen to like it; the act *does* give him pleasure and profit. If the matter turned entirely on matters of personal feeling, we could not adjudicate between these two claims. We would have to move to the level of considering whether the assault was provoked or justified.

When we move to that level, when we speak about the things that are justified or right, we speak about the things that are right or wrong, just or unjust, more generally or universally, which is to say, right or wrong, just or unjust, for others as well as ourselves. If we can say that someone is unjustified in interfering with us, that it is wrong for him to interfere with us, then we are establishing the point that it would be wrong for him to interfere even if the act gave him pleasure or benefit. We would then say that we have a right to our freedom, that it would be wrong for anyone to restrain us from our rightful freedom.

But again, I note that this movement to the level of a moral claim involves a movement away from standards that are entirely personal and subjective; it must involve a move to standards, principles, truths that are accessible to others as well as ourselves. When we say that something is wrong for others, we can be obliged now to give reasons, to cite principles of judgment that can be shown to be true for others as well as ourselves. We can do that only by drawing on the standards of proof, or the laws of logic, that underlie any claim to truth. And so Kant would have taught us, in an earlier day, that what we call the moral laws are laws that find their ground eventually in the laws of reason, or the laws of logic. For that reason, any claim to a right that is based on a logical mistake, or any claim that is founded on an incoherent proposition, simply cannot claim the name of a "right" in any literal sense.

The "Right" to Do a Wrong

Now, anyone with experience in the colleges these days is surrounded by beings who seem to have a limitless capacity to invent incoherent rights-claims. For example, we might encounter the primate who claims that there is no truth and that "I have a right to believe I don't exist." And we ask, who is the bearer of that right? The one who does not exist? In the famous debate between Lincoln and Douglas, Lincoln found himself reworking a line of Thomas Aquinas and explaining to Douglas that he could not claim a "right to do a wrong." But now, in our own day, we have philosophers who have sought to claim a right to do a wrong, for the sake of insulating certain personal choices from the moral judgments cast by others. That is, they try to establish an argument of this kind: Even if there is something wrong with the reason for my act, you may not judge it to be wrong, for I must have the freedom to engage in certain personal acts, supremely important to myself, without a judgment cast by others. And so, even if it is wrong, I may have a right to do it.

But none of these clever efforts can rescue this claim from the incoherence that Lincoln rightly found in it. After all, the claim of a right to do a wrong comes into play only when someone is suffering resistance — someone else is interfering with our freedom to do as we like (perhaps our freedom to torture animals, or perhaps even torture ourselves, in the privacy of our homes). The claim of a right is made to fend off that resistance: to say that we have a right to have our freedom respected is to say that anyone who interferes with us is doing a "wrong"; and by a wrong we mean something that person ought not to do, something he is not justified in doing, even if it suits his interests or his pleasure. But of course, the apt response on the part of the intervenor is that he too has "a right to do a wrong."

The claim cannot escape its incoherence, and the example merely draws us back to the ground of all of our claims to rights. We are drawn back to recognize, again, that all of our moral claims must find their ground within the laws of logic. And that is why it cannot matter, finally, whether we are visiting a wrong on others or on ourselves—whether we are selling others into slavery or only ourselves, whether we are taking the lives of others or only ourselves. If the ground of the act is incoherent or indefensible, the wrong of the act is utterly unaffected by the question of whether the act is performed on others or on ourselves.

I've put the problem to my students in this way: Let us imagine that we have a judge who says to the defendant, "Smith, you've been acquitted; therefore I sentence you to twenty years." The judge has violated the law of contradiction—he has declared Smith innocent, not deserving of punishment, and yet he has gone on to order up punishment anyway. He is mistaken or wrong, and on the basis of this wrong he has inflicted a harm on Smith. Now, imagine that the judge says, "Smith, you've been acquitted; therefore I sentence myself to twenty years!" The basis of the wrong remains precisely the same. The judge has violated the law of contradiction and inflicted a harm. The nature of the wrong has not been effaced in any degree by the fact that he visits the punishment solely on himself. The point is that the ground of his judgment simply cannot supply a coherent reason for his act, regardless of whether he inflicts the punishment on others or on himself.

And that is precisely the point in the claim and estimate of "rights" —a point that manages to elude even some of the most seasoned writers. If anyone is merely offering us a report that he has the *means* of taking his own life, or the life of his neighbor, he may be wholly correct. But if he moves beyond that and claims that he has a *right* to take his own life or the life of his neighbor, then he is obliged to show that the maxim behind his act can be reconciled with the laws of reason. And the modest, but telling, point I am making is this: If the reason behind his action happens to be radically mistaken or incoherent as a reason, then that reason cannot supply a justification. If he cannot supply a justification, he cannot plausibly claim that what he is doing is rightful or justified; and therefore he cannot plausibly claim that he has a right to do it.

A Free-Floating "Autonomy"

What we have seen, on the part of so-called ethicists, is a tendency to solve the problem by steering around it. The right to die, the right to dispose of our bodies, is simply stipulated, as I say, as though it were an axiom of our reasoning; or the right is declared simply in the name of the "autonomy" that marks the character of human beings. The decisions of the courts have leaned importantly, even decisively, on this claim of autonomy and privacy. And yet what we find here, once again, is a notion of autonomy that is utterly detached from the moral ground that imparted to autonomy its very meaning—and is defined, at the same time, by the limits of what we can claim in the name of our autonomy.

Immanuel Kant once made clear to us that the idea of autonomy was indeed central to the notion of a moral agent, who has the freedom to choose his own course, to will his own acts. But apart from his freedom, it is also critical to the character of a moral agent that he have access to the laws of reason in judging whether his choices are right or wrong, justified or unjustified. Animals may be free, but they cannot claim the standing of moral agents because they do not have access to the moral understanding that could govern their acts of choice. That may be why even today, in the era of "animal rights," we hear no insistence that we obtain the informed consent of dogs and cats before we operate upon them. We cannot expect the dogs and cats to weigh the reasons or consider the justification for the surgery. In that respect, we do not recognize any claims to autonomy on the part of animals. We respect the claims of autonomy only in creatures who are able to deliberate on the question of whether the choices they make are good or bad, right or wrong. I reminded the doctor from Los Angeles that we are inclined to consider the opinions of his patient—to give them our respectful attention—precisely because we assume that we are dealing with a moral agent. But at the same time, we come to this paradox: The right to autonomy, the freedom to make a choice, is a right that arises only for a moral being; but it is the nature of a moral being that she is capable of reflecting about the moral ground of her choice. She can make judgments about the things that are right and wrong, and therefore *she can understand the things she is not free to choose in the name of her own autonomy*.

She could not have a "right" to kill herself on the strength of her conviction that she does not exist. Nor would it be coherent for her to kill herself because she is willing to hold herself blameworthy and responsible for an act she was powerless to effect. She may regard herself as deeply guilty of a crime that was committed before she was born. But she could not possibly offer a coherent justification if she killed herself for this reason, and therefore it would be a corruption of reasoning to say that she has a right to kill as a punishment for a crime she had been powerless to effect. In a similar way, we could show that the wrong of racial discrimination finds its ground in the laws of reason, and we could make a similar argument on that basis as well. If it is wrong for the racialist to kill people because of their race, it would be equally wrong for the racialist to kill himself on account of his race if he discovered that he had a black ancestor. In these instances, we could show that the wrong behind these killings is rooted in the laws of reason. They are wrong, then, as a matter of logical necessity, and for that reason, as I say, their wrongness must be unaffected by the question of whether the killing is inflicted on oneself or other people.

The incoherence is revealed to us far more readily in these examples, but if we had the space here we could show that the same incoherence affects most of the other reasons that are offered to us, quite commonly today, as a ground for ending life. For example, do we think that people generally lose the claim to live when they lose their hearing, their sight, or their speech, when they suffer pain, or when they fall into a prolonged sleep? In none of these cases would we cite any condition of moral relevance that could establish why anyone might deserve to die. In none of these cases could people be justified in taking the lives of persons who are not their relatives because they suffer these infirmities. If that is the case, neither can they claim the right to do in their own relatives for these reasons. And if they cannot claim that authority, it is because the individual himself cannot claim the license to take his own life—and make other people accomplices in the taking of his life—for reasons that could not be justified.

I once gave my students the problem of a celebrated conductor who loses his hearing and concludes that a life without music is not, for him, a life worth living. But my students quickly came to understand that nothing in his deafness could be the mark of wrongdoing; nor would this infirmity disarm him from leading a moral and creditable life. It could not be claimed, then, in any strictness, that a life of deafness was bound to be a useless or unsatisfying life if it were a life that still retained the possibilities for acting morally, acting sensitively, acting for good ends. My students recognized that it would be wrong to take the life of any other person because of his deafness, and therefore it would be quite as wrong to destroy one's own life for the same, indefensible reason.

But if that is the case, then I submit that the next step follows: If we do not have the right to do a wrong, even in the name of our personal autonomy, if we do not have a right of privacy that permits us to destroy ourselves when, say, we are deaf, then it follows that we cannot delegate to other people a right of "substitute judgment" and permit them to order, in the name of our autonomy, a withdrawal of treatment that we would not be warranted in ordering even for ourselves, even in the name of our own autonomy.

From Decision to Doctrine

When I offered these remarks at the law school of the University of Illinois in 1989, a nurse from the state of Washington, who was in the audience, came up to say that this account finally illuminated for her a vexing problem she had encountered. She had been ministering to patients afflicted with AIDS. But some of those patients were demanding a "right," in the name of their "privacy," to withdraw the medical treatment that might prolong their lives in a comatose state. What finally fell into place for the nurse was this chain of propositions: In order to justify the removal of medical care from a live patient with AIDS, one would have to explain, in effect, that something about the condition of AIDS made it "justified" or "right" to end the life of a patient. With the logic of a moral justification, what made it right to remove medical aid from a patient with AIDS made it universally or impersonally right: it was a rightful thing that might be ordered for *anyone in this situation,* by *anyone* with the legitimate authority to decide. Through these steps, a "personal" decision is transformed into a doctrine or a license that may be employed now by people other than the patient: by relatives, perhaps, or even by administrators in a hospital, when the patient could not make decisions for himself. For after all, the administrators would now have been taught, as a point of doctrine, that patients with AIDS may rightfully be allowed to die. If a choice had to be made in the assignment of facilities, who could blame administrators if they assigned a lesser priority to the patients who had sought to establish, as a matter of right, that they bore a condition that made it rightful to end their lives?

Of course, the perverse problem in these cases of the "right to die" is that the patients are not dying. Or they are not dying with a decorous speed. If they were, there would be no need for the cases to be in court. The cases are in court precisely because the patients are not dying, though their relatives wish they were. It may now be hard to believe that, as recently as five years ago, we were still debating the question of removing food and water from a patient in a "cognitive and sapient" state. But now the courts have swept past that dubious standard of a cognitive and sapient state; the judges have moved rapidly from the implausible to the indefensible, without showing much awareness that they have been crossing thresholds worth mentioning. In the *Bouvia* case in California, Justice Beach on the appellate court thought it was rank prejudice on the part of the trial judge that he would not permit a withdrawal of medical care as long as there was some potential that the patient could be restored to a "cognitive, sapient life."[2] In this cramped notion of rights, the right to refuse to consent to medical treatment was extended only to patients who were terminally ill. But that right was denied initially to patients, like Elizabeth Bouvia, who were quadriplegic but not in a terminal condition, and certainly not in a comatose state.

I have already sought to show at length, in another place, that the judges themselves have been notably wanting in a cognitive state about the very meaning of a cognitive and sapient state.[3] From the want of wakefulness, or apparent consciousness, there is no ground on which to conclude that the patient is unaware, incapable of understanding, or even incapable of learning new things. To this original ignorance, the judges have added a willingness to suspend even a minimal respect for the canons of evidence and logic. In the celebrated case of Nancy Jobes, there was testimony about the responsiveness of the patient and one report, from two doctors, that Nancy was able to respond to their instructions when they asked her to pick up her head.[4] Still, a court that was determined to remove the hindrances to the dispatching of patients was willing to sweep casually past this testimony. Justice Garibaldi, in the supreme court of New Jersey, was willing to treat these reports as simply fragments of evidence that were at odds with the conclusions drawn by other doctors. Other doctors had not seen the same reactions on the part of Nancy Jobes, and yet there was no mention of any rebuttal or denial of the responses noted by Doctors Victor and Ropper. If the doctors had described accurately what they had seen, there were ample grounds for doubting the conclusion of the court that Nancy Jobes was in a comatose state.

Then what are those deficits that remove these patients from the protections of the law? In the case of Barbara Grant in Washington, Judge Callow explained that the patient was "suffering severe and permanent mental and physical deterioration"[5]—a condition that is commonly reported by every person I know who has touched his forty-ninth year. As Justice Beach sought to explain the precise medical deficits that made Elizabeth Bouvia's life not worth preserving, he observed that her life was "terribly diminished"—a term that is defined in no medical dictionary—and he went on to report that "the quality of her life has been diminished to the point of hopelessness, uselessness, unenjoyability, and frustration."[6]

A Wider View of Life

Now it is curious that when we measure these kinds of labels with the stringency of moral reasoning, we are often accused of flying to abstraction and neglecting the real person with real hurts before us. But if we remind ourselves just why these arguments fail the test of a moral argument, we may be alerted to a wider view of life than the view contained in the briefs, and we may even notice parts of the record that had not come into sight. I pointed out earlier that infirmities such as deafness have no moral significance: from the fact of a person's deafness, we could not infer that he deserves to die, and therefore we would not be justified in killing anyone on account of deafness. When we say that deafness has no moral significance, we say that it does not determine the moral quality of a person's life. His life may be diminished by the absence of music, but he has a wide range in which to act honorably, to minister to others, to act for good ends in a host of decisions that fill out his daily life.

Elizabeth Bouvia was no doubt "terribly diminished" in her life, but did her disabilities remove from her the possibility of engaging this world actively and having an effect, even a moral effect, on people around her? The appellate court in California offered the most un-equivocal answer to that question: Elizabeth Bouvia could move a few fingers of one hand, and she could manage slight movements with her head and face. As the court remarked, she was wholly dependent on other people for her "feeding, washing, . . . toileting, turning, and helping her with elimination and other bodily functions." The court allowed that she was quite intelligent, and she had earned a college degree. In fact, that disparity deepened the tragedy of the case: Justice Beach remarked that Elizabeth Bouvia was "alert, bright, sensitive, perhaps even brave and feisty," and yet her life was now, as the judge said, devoid of "dignity and purpose."

But how did Justice Beach know that Elizabeth Bouvia was "feisty" and "brave"? Might it have had something to do with the fact that through her own decision to starve herself she forced a test case in the courts on her right to deny her own treatment and, through her own willfulness, compelled that case to advance through appeals? And while her appetite for food and life had professedly vanished, her appetite for litigation seemed to be unappeasable. After she had won her case on the right to deny her treatment, she launched yet another case for the recovery of lawyers' fees—a case that had to be based explicitly on the claim that her litigation had offered a "significant benefit" to the public.[7] Presumably, the business of the courts is the vindication of rights, and therefore we would be obliged to say that Elizabeth Bouvia had engaged in a strenuous project to articulate or confirm certain claims of personal rights.

By any reckoning, this kind of project would have to count as an activity animated by "purpose" and the claim of "dignity." In few cases have the judges produced a higher density of non sequiturs than

Justice Beach managed to produce in the *Bouvia* case; but in an opinion rich in fallacies, this one must stand as preeminent: The court conceded to Bouvia the "right to die" on the predicate that her life was empty of the possibility of purpose and dignity, while at the same time it commended her for her strength of purpose in forcing this issue through the engines of justice. One concurring judge said that no one could blame Elizabeth Bouvia for reaching the decision to "fold her cards and say, 'I am out.'"[8] Perhaps he was the only one surprised by the fact that she did not fold her cards and take the exit she had pestered the courts to arrange for her. Apparently, her success in this project awakened her to the possibility of other projects and other victories. Or to put it plainly, if she had enough force to push a lawsuit, why would we think that she was not quite as capable of pursuing many other projects in this life, modest or momentous, projects affected with purpose, the kinds of projects that fill out lives for most people in this country?

I am not the first to suggest that the jurists of our own day suffer an embarrassment when they are measured against the first generation of our jurists in this country. The judges of our own day are far less tutored in the traditional canons of philosophy and jurisprudence; they are simply more credulous and less resistant to the rationales served up to them under the authority of medical science. They could be helped immeasurably if doctors could preserve a more demanding sense of the kinds of evidence and measures that would be required in an authentic medical judgment. But when they play at philosophy, they become a band of affable utilitarians, winging it, hardly distinguishable any longer from judges or accountants or anyone else these days who is inspired to say something philosophic.

Edmund Burke once remarked on the deranged political men who were trying to reshape the life of France according to the maxims of the French Revolution. They were counting, he said, on "bungling practice [to correct] absurd theory."[9] In our recent jurisprudence on euthanasia, we seem to find a medical profession permitting its practice to become bungling and vaudevillian as it is reshaped by a moral sensibility that is skewed and a moral theory that must be regarded as sophomoric. The late Alexander King once offered some choice words about doctors who deserved to die of their own specialty. My own prayer for the profession is that one day soon, some of our doctors may be faced, not with a family claiming to vindicate the right of their uncle to die, but with a litigant claiming to act as the guardian for the patient—and to vindicate the right of the patient not to have his life ended by doctors joined to the service of bungling philosophy.

5

Ethical Issues in
Physician-Assisted Suicide

Margaret Pabst Battin

In June 1990 a woman named Janet Adkins lay down on a cot in the back of a Volkswagen van, watched as Dr. Jack Kevorkian worked to insert an intravenous line into a vein in her arm, and then pushed a lever on a three-chambered device, the "suicide machine," rigged up by Dr. Kevorkian to deliver first saline solution, then the sedative thiopental, and finally potassium chloride to stop her heart.[1] Mrs. Adkins had been diagnosed with early Alzheimer's disease, and —after extended conversations with her husband, her sons, her minister, and her local doctor—had decided that she did not want to undergo the sustained mental deterioration that this disease would involve: loss of memory, confusion, increasing inability to recognize others or to know members of her own family, and finally a loss of virtually all cognitive function.[2] While she could then still beat her

Margaret Pabst Battin is a professor of philosophy and an adjunct professor of internal medicine in the Division of Medical Ethics at the University of Utah. Among her books are *Ethics in the Sanctuary* and *The Least Worst Death*. This essay is reprinted by permission from *Ethical Issues in Suicide* (Upper Saddle River, N.J.: Prentice-Hall, 1995), chapter 7. Most of the author's references to other chapters in that book have been deleted here without ellipses.

son at tennis—though she couldn't keep score—she could no longer play bridge, and she knew the further deterioration that was coming. She approached Dr. Kevorkian, a retired pathologist whom she had read about, traveled to Michigan, and pushed the fatal lever in what was to become a highly controversial case of physician-assisted suicide, the first of twenty "Dr. Death" would perform before agreeing to desist while his case was argued before Michigan courts.

Just a year or so later Timothy Quill, M.D., provided his patient Diane with a prescription for a lethal dose of barbiturates. Diane, who had been his patient for eight years, had been diagnosed with acute myelomocytic leukemia, and rather than endure an extremely difficult course of chemotherapy and bone marrow transplant, estimated to give her about a 25 per cent chance of survival, she asked Dr. Quill for help in dying. He talked with her extensively, hoping to dissuade her, but in the end was persuaded that her choice was genuine. Diane took the barbiturates several months later, and Dr. Quill published an account of his assistance in her suicide in the august *New England Journal of Medicine,* regretting only that legal concerns had prevented him from being at her side when she actually died.[3] [Dr. Quill's account is reprinted in this volume.]

In the United States, these two cases have served to frame the public discussion of physician-assisted suicide, as volatile an issue as has erupted in medicine for many years. . . . Physician-assisted suicide and the twin issue of euthanasia have become the flashpoints for issues across the board about the end of life, and the challenge this poses to traditional medical practice, cultural norms, and other values is enormous. Although there are other end-of-life issues concerning suicide—especially suicide assisted by someone other than a physician, and suicide in circumstances other than terminal illness—it is the issue of physician-assisted suicide in terminal illness that is at the center of the political debate. . . .

THE PUBLIC DEBATE

As committed and extensive as they are, however, the debates over physician-assisted suicide and euthanasia are often conducted at a comparatively superficial level, directed largely to the policy issue of whether these practices should be legalized. In this final chapter [of her book *Ethical Issues in Suicide*] I'd like to use our earlier explorations of the underlying philosophical issues in suicide to see what genuinely basic matters are at issue in the current ferment, and what sorts of issues can be expected to arise if—or when—legalization occurs. . . .

The Legal Issues

The legal situation concerning physician-assisted suicide is so rapidly changing, as [her 1995] book goes to press, that no definitive account can be offered.[4] Some things are clear: For example, it is not a crime to attempt suicide, and virtually all U.S. states have decriminalized suicide attempts in order to make psychiatric treatment more available to suicide attempters who survive. However, while slightly more than half of the U.S. states have had statutes criminalizing assisted suicide, twelve states that do not have such statutes have adopted English common law, making assisted suicide a criminal matter; two other states prohibit assisted suicide on the basis of case law, and one protects citizens from euthanasia under constitutional law. Three states do not have explicit statutes, do not recognize common law, and have no holding or court case in the matter. Since the emergence of Dr. Kevorkian, another handful of states, including Michigan, have attempted to pass statutes criminalizing assisted suicide.

Meanwhile, ballot measures that would legalize physician-assisted suicide, are being introduced by initiative in several other states. . . . A variety of rulings have been issued in the Kevorkian case, challenging the constitutionality of the new Michigan statute. While some states are drafting "anti-Kevorkian" statutes of their own, others are considering legalization. And some have appointed advisory commissions to study the issue—two of which, Michigan's and New York's, have yielded flatly opposite recommendations about legalization. Some proposals would legalize only physician-assisted suicide; others would legalize voluntary active euthanasia as well. And while legal activity has been occurring largely on a state-by-state basis, in May 1994 a federal judge for the Western District of Washington, where a Seattle-based organization that provides assistance in suicide to the terminally ill, Compassion in Dying, is located, has ruled—basing the argument on the *Casey* [*Planned Parenthood v. Casey,* 1992, affirming a constitutional right to abortion] and *Cruzan* [*Cruzan v. Director, Missouri Department of Health,* 1990] cases—that the state's 140-year-old ban on assisted suicide is unconstitutional and that "a competent, terminally ill adult has a constitutionally guaranteed right under the Fourteenth Amendment to commit physician assisted suicide."[5] Virtually all observers, for and against legalization, believe that the issue will soon be brought before the U.S. Supreme Court, and all agree that the constitutional issues raised in the case will be of extraordinary importance.

Why the Issue Has Emerged

It is important to see why the twin issues of physician-assisted suicide and voluntary active euthanasia are coming into focus so rapidly, not only in the United States but in Canada, Australia, the Netherlands, England, the Scandinavian countries, and many other developed nations. A number of distinct factors have contributed. . . .

Crucial among these factors is what is often called the new epidemiology: the new pattern of the way in which we die. For virtually the entire course of human history, up until about the middle of the nineteenth century, human beings died primarily of infectious and parasitic diseases, often exacerbated by famine or epidemics of specific pestilences or plagues. Maternal and infant mortality was high. This "Age of Pestilence and Famine," as it was named by Abdel Omran, the originator of the theory describing the pattern of epidemiologic transition, lasted from the beginning of human existence until about 1850.[6] As new developments occurred in public sanitation, immunization, and antiseptic techniques in surgery and childbirth, it gave way to the "Age of Receding Pandemics," in which life expectancy rose substantially. This in turn gave way around 1920 to the "Age of Degenerative and Man-Made Diseases," during which developments such as antibiotics, improved surgical techniques, techniques for intravenous administration of fluids and drugs, respiratory support, and improved diagnostic and therapeutic techniques not only have continued to raise life expectancy but have changed the causes of death. Most people were now likely to die later in life of degenerative diseases rather than parasitic and infectious ones. More recent investigators[7] have described a fourth stage of epidemiologic transition: the "Age of Delayed Degenerative Diseases," in which this transition is even more pronounced as mortality rates decline even further and people die of the major degenerative diseases—cancer, heart disease, stroke, pulmonary disease, diabetes, neurological diseases, and so forth—at still later ages. The average life expectancy in the United States has increased from just under 50 in 1900 to its current level, 72, in what is regarded as middle old age.

These transitions have occurred primarily in the rich, developed nations, partly as a result of their advanced health-care systems, while poor third-world populations remain in the first or second stages of epidemiological transition. Of course in many countries, especially those undergoing rapid economic development, middle-income and rich segments of the population inhabit different epidemiological worlds, partly as a function of access to different levels of public sanitation, immunization, and modern health care. It is in the advanced industrial nations—including the United States—that the majority of the population faces death of diseases with extended deteriorative declines. Today AIDS is virtually the only visible example of the category of diseases that, in earlier periods of human history, virtually everyone died of, and the diseases that did kill then—typhoid, tetanus, smallpox, diarrhea, measles, tuberculosis, puerperal sepsis, and many others—no longer pose widespread risk in the developed world. But these transitions in the epidemiology of causes of death contribute to the emergence of issues about dying in a direct way. For the first time, most people in the developed world—informal estimates range as high as 70-80 per cent—face death at a comparatively predictable time, later in life, and they face death from diseases with long, generally predictable deteriorative declines. Except for specific high-risk subgroups within the population, death is very much less likely to occur suddenly or at earlier points in the normal lifespan.

Second, issues about dying—and about physician-assisted suicide —are emerging as a continuation of new attention to patient autonomy. Since the early right-to-die laws, pioneered by California's 1976 "Natural Death Act," all of the U.S. states have passed some form of legislation expanding patients' rights to control not only what medical treatment they receive while they are still competent to choose but also what is done to them after they have become incompetent in the later stages of a terminal illness. These extensions of rights of autonomous choice, taking the form of advanced directives such as the living will and the durable power of attorney, have led naturally to a new question: If the patient is entitled to refuse life-prolonging treatment while he or she is still competent and so die, or to direct in advance that treatment be withheld after he or she is no longer competent and so die, why isn't the patient entitled to choose to die by more direct, immediate means? . . .

Further factors . . . include a more general challenge to traditional religious and cultural assumptions . . . [and] the sensitive matter of the cost of medical care, rooted perhaps in the increased perception that it is a "waste" to spend money on dying while other medical needs are unserved. (About both I shall have more to say shortly.) These factors—the new epidemiology, the extension of patient autonomy, the challenge to traditional values, and the perception of costs —all contribute in important ways to the very rapid emergence of the issue of physician-assisted suicide.

Despite the many contexts in which dispute over the legalization of physician-assisted suicide occurs, the public debate tends to be played out with just a handful of basic arguments. Much of the same argumentation is also used in the associated debates about euthanasia, though since it is suicide that is our focus here, and since it is, I believe, physician-assisted suicide rather than voluntary active euthanasia that is more likely to be legalized or legally tolerated in the United States, I will attend just to arguments about it here. . . . Each argument is met by objections, counterobjections, and in [in some cases] counter-counterobjections and counter-counter-counterobjections, and of course each of the principal lines of argument appears in a variety of different guises.

ARGUMENTS FAVORING PHYSICIAN-ASSISTED SUICIDE

The principal arguments here are (1) the argument from autonomy and (2) the argument from mercy.

1. The argument from autonomy

Just as a person has the right to determine as much as possible the course of his or her own life, a person also has the right to determine as much as possible the course of his or her own dying. If a terminally ill person seeks assistance in suicide from a physician, the physician ought to provide it, provided the request is made freely and rationally.

Objection: True autonomy is rarely possible, especially for someone who is dying, since not only are most choices socially formed, but in terminal illness depression and other psychiatric disturbances are likely to be a factor. **Counterobjection 1**: Even if many choices are socially shaped, they must be respected as autonomous. **Counterobjection 2**: Rational suicide is possible, and it is possible for patients to make choices about dying without distortion by depression.

Objection: One cannot obligate another to do what is morally wrong, even if one's choice is made freely and rationally. Since suicide is wrong, the physician can have no obligation to assist in it. **Counterobjection**: No adequate moral argument shows that suicide in circumstances of terminal illness is morally wrong.

2. The argument from mercy

No person should have to endure pointless terminal suffering. If the physician is unable to relieve the patient's suffering in other ways and the only way to avoid such suffering is by death, then the physician ought to bring death about.

Objection: Thanks to techniques of pain management developed by Hospice and others, it is possible to treat virtually all pain and to relieve virtually all suffering. Thus the dying process can be valuable as a positive, transformative experience of new intimacy and spiritual growth. **Counterobjection 1**: "Virtually all" is not "all"; if some pain or suffering cannot be treated, there will still sometimes be a need to avoid them by death. **Counter-counterobjection**: Complete sedation can be used where pain cannot be controlled. **Counter-counter-counterobjection**: Complete sedation means complete obtundation, and because the patient can no longer communicate or perceive, is equivalent to causing death. If these are permitted, why not more direct methods of bringing about death? **Counterobjection 2**: There can be no guarantee of a positive, transformative experience.

ARGUMENTS OPPOSING PHYSICIAN-ASSISTED SUICIDE

The principal arguments here are (1) the argument from the intrinsic wrongness of killing, (2) the slippery-slope argument, and (3) the argument concerning the physician's role.

1. The argument from the intrinsic wrongness of killing

The taking of a human life is simply wrong; this is evident in the commandment "Thou shall not kill." **Objection**: But killing is socially and legally accepted in self-defense, war, capital punishment, and other situations, and so it should be socially and legally accepted when it is the choice of the person who would be killed. **Counterobjection**:In self-defense, war, and capital punishment, the person killed is guilty; in assisted suicide the person killed is innocent.

2. The slippery-slope argument

Permitting physicians to assist in suicide, even in sympathetic cases, would lead to situations in which patients were killed against their will. **Objection**: A basis for these predictions must be demonstrated before they can be used to suppress personal choices and individual rights. **Counterobjection**: The basis for these predictions is increasing cost pressures, as well as greed, laziness, insensitivity, and other factors affecting physicians and their institutions. **Counter-counterobjection**: It is possible, with careful design, to erect effective protections against abuse by doctors or institutions.

3. The argument concerning the physician's role

Doctors should not kill; this is prohibited by the Hippocratic Oath. The physician is bound to save life, not take it. **Objection**: In its original version the Hippocratic Oath also prohibits doctors from performing surgery, providing abortifacients, or taking fees for teaching medicine. If these can be permitted within the physician's role, why not assistance in suicide, where the patient is dying anyway and seeks the physician's help? **Counterobjection**: To permit physicians to kill patients would undermine the patient's trust in the physician. **Counter-counterobjection**: Patients trust their physicians more when they know that their physicians will help them, not desert them as they die.

None of the formulations presented here is canonical, and they occur in an enormous range of varieties. . . . In the public arena these debates are often conducted at a comparatively superficial level—often simply by reciting the above arguments in equally schematic form, or by pitting cases like Janet Adkins and Dr. Kevorkian against others like Dr. Quill and Diane, when in fact such cases exhibit both similarities and differences. It is important for this reason to look more closely at the underlying philosophical issues.

ETHICAL ISSUES BEFORE LEGALIZATION

Following the first three chapters of this book [the author's *Ethical Issues in Suicide*], we can explore the basic ethical issues underlying the current public discussion of physician-assisted suicide. Though ethical theory is not their primary concern, these three chapters, on (1) religious, (2) social, and (3) value-of-life arguments, reflect three types of background normative positions, based in divine-command, utilitarian, and deontological ethical theories respectively. I shall be making a central assumption in exploring these issues: Physician-assisted suicide is a practice the purpose of which is to help a patient in need avoid what he or she perceives as a far worse death, or avoid continued existence in a state he or she perceives as worse than death.

1. Religious Arguments

Christian religious arguments, almost always employed to oppose both the legalization and the practice of physician-assisted suicide, variously insist that it would violate the biblical commandment "Thou shalt not kill"; that it would violate the gratitude one owes God for the "gift of life," the obligation one has to "remain at one's post," or the trust one ought to have in one's heavenly father; and that it would run contrary to natural law. The variety of religiously based argumentation against physician-assisted suicide is enormous. To be sure, there have been some religious voices on the other side of the public debate: for example, some liberal Protestant churches have supported legalization initiatives in Washington, California, and Oregon. But most religious groups—especially the Catholic Church—have been opposed to legalization and would no doubt be opposed to the practice even if it were legalized.

In this political dispute, however, a number of much more basic issues are often overlooked. The first group are those associated with the fact that, as we've seen, Western religious views of an individual's role in his or her own dying developed during historical periods when death was likely to occur of infectious or parasitic disease, often comparatively suddenly, and at any age. Thus these religious views may not be appropriate for late-twentieth-century medical circumstances in the developed world, where the vast majority of people no longer die young or suddenly but die predictably later in life of diseases with long deteriorative declines. The major religious traditions all developed during the "Age of Pestilence and Famine," which lasted from the beginning of human existence to about 1850; but the developed nations have all now passed through the various stages of the epidemiological transition in the "Age of Delayed Degenerative Diseases." Modern life in these nations presents an entirely different environment for dying.

This new epidemiological pattern may affect a number of the common religiously based arguments. For example, the argument from mercy, concerning the role of pain, may require modification to take account of the fact that the new pattern of death from degenerative diseases may lengthen and intensify the degree of suffering a dying person undergoes, even with modern pain-control techniques. The late-twentieth-century first-world trajectories of death, with their extensive medicalization and long downhill courses, have the capacity even with modern pain-control techniques to prolong terminal suffering far beyond what would have been likely in any earlier historical period. After all, prior to the development of antibiotics in the 1940s, a person who became bedridden was likely to succumb to pneumonia not long afterward, and the prospect of an extended period of medical deterioration, with or without high-tech medical treatment such as intravenous feeding or machine-assisted respiration, did not arise. Nor did people with severe disabilities or illnesses, such as quadriplegia or amyotrophic lateral sclerosis (ALS), survive very long, and issues about the quality of life in these conditions could not arise. It is sometimes even rather crudely remarked that, in terms of physical pain alone, the contemporary terminally ill patient may endure more sustained pain over a longer period of time than the central figure of sacrifice in the Christian tradition, a first-century crucifixion victim, so that exhortations to emulate that central occasion of voluntary suffering cannot require the contemporary patient to continue on to the end.

This new picture may also affect some of the other traditional religiously based arguments. For instance, the argument that "life is a gift from God and therefore wrong to destroy" may have looked quite different in eras during which the average life expectancy was around thirty or thirty-five than when it is seventy-two. Throughout almost the entire history of humankind, people died—on average—

in early or middle adulthood; in the advanced industrial nations it is now the norm that people die in old age. In the latter circumstances, it may be tempting to argue, to take just one of the traditional religious arguments against suicide, that the gift of life has already been welcomed—a full life has already been lived—so that ending it in suicide would not be to reject the gift in the same way that ending a life only half complete might represent. Then, too, since physician-assisted suicide would be occurring primarily in the context of terminal illness, it might plausibly be claimed that bringing about death somewhat earlier cannot violate natural law for someone who is already in the process of dying: if the human being's natural end would be subverted by death, that will occur in any case, and if not, then there can be little objection to suicide on these grounds.

Most conspicuous, though, in current religious argumentation about physician-assisted suicide is the absence of attention to what I have called the religious "invitation" to suicide. The Christian tradition . . . incorporates five major inducements to suicide; two of them may be particularly relevant in the terminal-illness situations associated with physician-assisted suicide.

One of these is *the promise of reunion with the deceased.* In the traditional Christian belief system, although the person facing death will be separated from loved ones who are now alive, he or she may hope for reunion with those who have already died. For the person dying of terminal illness, it may be particularly important that these loved ones who have already died are likely to be parents or older family members—persons who might provide comfort—since in terminal illness the dying person may slip into increasingly childlike, dependent conditions where care by a loved, long-missed elder would be especially desired. The pull of an invitation can hardly be underestimated when the belief in a personal afterlife is strong.

The other premise within the Christian tradition perhaps constituting the strongest invitation to suicide in conditions of terminal illness is that of *release of the soul.* Given a traditional metaphysic in which the perishable body is viewed as distinct from the immortal soul, the prospect of release of the soul may seem especially alluring when the body is undergoing the deteriorative, degenerative processes associated with terminal illness. The body fails, in this view, but the soul lives on; and when the body's failing is prolonged and painful, it may seem especially inviting to liberate the soul earlier and more easily in this long downhill course. After all, death in this view is not really dying; it is a transition to another, better state in the afterlife to come.

These two invitations to suicide within the Christian tradition may seem, thus, much stronger when death is approaching in any case, and may be particularly inviting for a person undergoing a period of extended terminal decline accompanied by sustained, untreatable suffering or continuous pain—that is, in the very circumstances that would make physician-assisted suicide seem most plausible. The challenge for the traditional religious view is to come to full grips with the realities of modern dying, and to reexamine traditional claims about the purpose of suffering in the face of extended deteriorative illness.

To be sure, much of this has already been accomplished in the context of withdrawing or withholding treatment. As early as 1958, Pope Pius XII held that it is not obligatory to use "extraordinary means" to prolong the lives of the dying, if it is "such a burden for the family that one cannot in conscience impose it on them."[8] But many of the same arguments apply in self-caused or self-authorized death as well; facing this parallel is what the traditional religious groups —perhaps because of the stigma attached to the word "suicide"— have often avoided. By and large, traditional religious groups have not really explored the issues of suicide or physician-assisted suicide in terminal illness, and have tended to reject it virtually unexplored.[9]

Finally, of course, exploration of these issues will direct attention to a question arising from the epidemiological shift as well as from the notion of invitation to death: Does the fact that contemporary medical treatment is now able to prolong life beyond the point at which the patient would earlier have died—beyond, some might like to say, its formerly "natural" endpoint—mean that views about the termination of life must be revised? If it is not wrong for a patient to decline further treatment, how can it be wrong to wish a more directly caused death for the same reasons and at the same time? If the traditional religious groups do explore these issues more carefully, they may see a way to play a major supportive role in aiding terminally ill persons who seek to bring their lives to a close in a responsible, dignified way.

Of course, traditional Christianity's two implicit invitations to suicide especially relevant in terminal illness are not now generally explicitly recognized by those committed to the Christian view. A more conventional account of traditional religious attitudes would no doubt emphasize the centrality of obedience, submission to God's will, the voluntary acceptance of suffering, and hope in an afterlife. But it is important to recognize all the ways—explicit and submerged—in which religious considerations bear on the issue of physician-assisted suicide in terminal illness.

2. Social Arguments

The social arguments so frequently used to oppose suicide—that the suicide of a person would harm his or her family, community, or society, or that the suicide would deprive society of his or her contribution to it—backfire whenever the suicide of a person would benefit rather than harm these other parties. Suicide can mean the removal of social burdens, including the psychological, emotional, and/or financial burdens imposed by a person who is abusive, criminal, sociopathic, or chronically or terminally ill. This is an argument first associated with Plato, but because it runs so strongly counter to the traditional taboo against suicide, and because it would yield such profoundly unsettling consequences for accepted social policies concerning suicide and suicide prevention, it is very, very rarely raised in contemporary discussion.

The social-burdens argument is particularly problematic in the circumstances associated with physician-assisted suicide—terminal illness, and perhaps severe chronic illness, severe disability, and extreme old age—since the costs of medical treatment, hospitalization, palliation, rehabilitative treatment, domestic assistance, and other terminal and chronic care can be enormous. This is the root of the slippery-slope argument, that permitting some cases of physician-assisted suicide would lead to a situation in which patients are killed against their will. The social-burdens argument against suicide invites an argument about cost savings that is extremely sensitive and problematic, but it cannot be avoided if we are to look more closely at the underlying philosophical issues.

Almost no one involved in the current debate over the legalization of physician-assisted suicide and euthanasia dares to raise such issues publicly, and especially not the issue of cost savings in medical care. Yet I think there is a widespread assumption operative in these debates: permitting physician-assisted suicide and euthanasia would mean huge savings at the end of life. This is not a partisan assumption; it is shared, I believe, by those favoring legalization and those opposed to it. Those supporting legalization assume, I suspect, that the projected end savings from euthanasia and assisted suicide are an additional reason favoring legalization, and consequently that in this special case, patients' rights of autonomous choice coincide with the demands of justice by permitting fairer distribution of health-care resources. This is a view compatible with the utilitarian background of these arguments: even though some losses might be borne by a few, the imposition of these losses would produce the greater good for the greater number. On this argument, however, when the talk is of voluntary suicide in terminal illness, the case is even stronger, since we cannot assume that the person who chooses death in preference to deteriorative terminal illness regards it as a loss.

Those opposing legalization seem to accept the same underlying assumption, that the practice of assisted suicide in terminal illness would mean huge cost savings, but draw from it a different conclusion: they fear that the prospect of huge savings, both in financial costs for institutions and in other psychological and emotional costs for family members, would lead physicians and the cost managers who influence them, as well as family members who bear the burdens of care, to manipulate or force terminally ill patients into such choices, thus effectively greasing the slippery slope.

Thus, although the social arguments concerning suicide are, as we have seen, almost always explicitly employed only in their negative form—that is, as slippery-slope arguments against suicide on the grounds that it would harm family, community, and society—I think that the corresponding positive version of these arguments concerning potential benefits to society, especially in the form of cost savings, plays an extraordinary covert role in contemporary thinking about physician-assisted suicide.

In view of this, I think both sides in the public debate over physician-assisted suicide are obligated to identify the roles that these covert arguments play, examine them critically, and minimize the covert and unexamined influence they currently have. A preliminary calculation suggests that the actual cost savings of euthanasia and physician-assisted suicide, if practiced in the United States at the same rate and in the same conditions as in the one country in which they are effectively legal, the Netherlands, would be very much smaller than what is usually tacitly assumed. While euthanasia and physician-assisted suicide are widely approved in the Netherlands (by about 80 per cent of the population) and universally known to be an option in terminal care, only a small fraction of Dutch actually choose these forms of dying, and when they do so they typically forgo only a few weeks of life. Two-thirds of all requests for assisted suicide or euthanasia are turned down, and less than 3 per cent of all Dutch patients who die in a given year do so in this way.[10] Thus, although the majority of these Dutch patients have cancer and cancer is the most expensive terminal condition to treat, savings from this practice cannot be assumed to be great, and do not play a role in Dutch policy or practice at all.

While in the United States it is sometimes assumed that permitting physician-assisted suicide or euthanasia would save a huge proportion of health-care costs—as much, one sometimes hears, as a third or a fourth of all costs—more careful calculations suggest that the actual savings would be at most 1/100th, perhaps as little as 1/900th, of the U.S. health-care budget.[11] The smallness of this figure ought to silence talk of costs in discussions of the morality of physician-assisted suicide and euthanasia and return discussion to the ethical issues at hand, but it is important to recognize that tacit unfounded assumptions concerning costs are very widely made.

But the matter is not that simple. Under the social-burdens arguments we are considering here, all benefits and burdens must be accounted for. The cost of medical treatment in a terminal illness does not reflect ancillary financial expenses like home assistance or lost income of family members who serve as caretakers; and it does not include emotional or psychological costs at all. A true computation of all of the costs saved by a terminally or chronically ill person's suicide might be enormous (one need only consider the burden sustained by a spouse caring for a person with Alzheimer's over a period of up to ten years or even more, and remember that in the age group 85 and older, the risks of Alzheimer's are as high as 1:4 or higher), even if this computation were somehow adjusted to compensate for the emotional and psychological gains of, say, greater family intimacy and understanding.

This is a very problematic fact, of course. Calculating such costs has in the past invited the involuntary killing of the terminally ill, along with the chronically ill and the developmentally disabled; Nazi Germany's early T4 euthanasia program is no doubt the most horrifying example. But the discussion here is not about *involuntary* killing, or the kinds of practices that would not only produce endemic fear in a society but also impose the incalculable cost of depriving people of their lives who wished to continue them; the issue in physician-assisted suicide concerns *voluntary* self-killing, consentingly performed by one's physician and accepted by one's family, community, and society. Under the sort of calculus that the social arguments concerning suicide invites, physician-assisted suicide may seem to produce, on balance, benefits rather than harms. That is what makes these arguments so particularly problematic in these contexts, and makes the slippery-slope objection to accepting physician-assisted suicide such a powerful one.

Social-burdens arguments, covert or explicit, ought also to be examined in relation to classical utilitarian theory. It will be evident, I believe, that like the justice objection, these social-burdens arguments concerning suicide constitute another major objection to utilitarian theory across the board. Utilitarian theory in its classical form appears to welcome the exit not only of any person whose care represents a cost to others, but also of any person whose misery reduces the average or aggregate level of happiness or utility. Thus, even apart from costs, the earlier exit of those suffering in terminal illnesses is to be encouraged—or, rather, on this theory, is morally required rather than acknowledged as an option open to the voluntary request or refusal of those who are terminally ill. Only if the degree of distress to people under such expectations were greater than the burdens lifted from others would this not be the case, but—given the enormous objective burdens that an extended deteriorative illness like Alzheimer's, Huntington's, or ALS can constitute—this is hardly likely. Yet this result—that utilitarian theory would encourage or require suicide, perhaps socially urged or recommended by the physician—is difficult to accept. Indeed, this result is so difficult to accept that it should be explored as a potential counterobjection to classical utilitarian theory as a whole and to the kinds of computations of losses and gains that give the arguments considered here such problematic pull. It would be irresponsible not to acknowledge that these arguments work covertly in the background of the public discussions; but it would be equally irresponsible not to examine them with a severely critical eye.

3. Value-of-Life Arguments

In the current ferment over physician-assisted suicide, appeal is often made—almost always by those opposed to legalization—to the concept of the value of life. Life is of absolute, intrinsic value, it is often asserted, and hence it is always wrong to put it to an end. The principle of the value of life is usually modified to apply only or primarily to human life and to permit certain exceptions, such as killing in self-defense, war, and capital punishment. but it is not usually held to permit suicide.

Indeed, it might seem that physician-assisted suicide in terminal illness would not be licensed by any of these limitations on the principle of the value of life. Physician-assisted suicide involves the killing of a human being; except in an extended sense, it cannot be said to be killing in self-defense, war, or capital punishment. Of course, it is sometimes argued that suicide in circumstances of terminal illness is analogous to killing in self-defense, but if so, it is clearly not any ordinary form of self-defense: there is no aggressor against whom one defends oneself (though some have argued that the disease plays this role), and in any case one does not kill the aggressor but oneself, the person presumably to be defended.

Furthermore, although the notion of "quality of life" is often substituted for that of "value of life" in discussions of end-of-life practices and when it would be appropriate to withdraw life-sustaining support—such as a respirator or artificial nutrition and hydration—from a patient, physician-assisted suicide cannot involve ending a life that has fallen below a certain minimum quality. The standards for withdrawing life support are sometimes fixed quite narrowly at irreversible coma or at brain death; sometimes they are set at intermediate levels to include capacity for reflex response or minimal EEG activity; and sometimes they are set comparatively high, to require some degree of emotional response, reaction, and reasoning activity. But *suicide* would seem to presuppose life that meets or exceeds the highest minimum standards, since anyone capable of making a decision to commit suicide—and to ask the physician for assistance in doing so —must be able to think, intend, at least to some extent, foresee the future otherwise in store, and, in general, reason in a deliberative way. All recent and current legislative proposals put forward in the United States would permit physician-assisted suicide only for mentally competent persons, and, since these proposals have covered only voluntary active euthanasia, have made the same requirement for physician-performed euthanasia as well.

Of course this conclusion—that under the principle of the value of life, physician-assisted suicide could not be permitted, since it would mean the self-killing of a life of sufficient quality to meet standards of mental competency and voluntariness in making this choice—is open to further challenges. For example, a person foreseeing that his or her life is about to drop below a specified level—that is, that he or she is about to slip below an acceptable quality of life— might use an advance directive to instruct the physician to perform the termination of life after it drops below a specified level (though it would then be counted as euthanasia). Alternatively, this person might choose to commit suicide in a preemptive way, by ending his or her life before the foreseen deterioration begins.

This latter notion poses a substantial challenge to the value-of-life position against physician-assisted suicide. It has been a crucial ingredient in many of the most conspicuous physician-assisted suicide cases, including Jack Kevorkian's use of his "suicide machine" for Janet Adkins, and Timothy Quill's writing a prescription for a lethal dose of barbiturates for his patient Diane. Janet Adkins sought Dr. Kevorkian's assistance very early in the downhill course of Alzheimer's disease, while she still possessed nearly her full mental skills as well as her physical abilities, while she could still see clearly what lay ahead, and while she could discuss her choice with her husband, her physician, and Dr. Kevorkian. Similarly, Dr. Quill's patient Diane preferred suicide to undertaking the very difficult treatment for her leukemia, recognizing that it had only a low chance of success, but remained quite functional virtually up until the time she took the lethal drug. To be sure, Janet Adkins's suicide was timed further in advance than

Diane's of the onset of the condition each wished to avoid; indeed, Adkins understood that she would have to plan her suicide and carry it out well in advance, since there would be no chance of doing so later on, while Diane could wait until symptoms of her illness began to be pronounced. Yet in neither case did the patient's current quality of life fall below any reasonable threshold.

The underlying issue here is what C. G. Prado has introduced as the question of *preemptive* suicide: suicide undertaken not out of current suffering, illness, or extreme old age, but to avoid what is otherwise predictably a part of terminal decline—"a sensible alternative to demeaning deterioration and stultifying dependency."[12] Preemptive suicide is not the same as surcease suicide, an escape from current suffering; it is suicide that takes place before the predictable suffering or deterioration begins, as with Janet Adkins, or at least, as with Diane, before it has progressed very far. Some legislative proposals, however, appear to have addressed only what would be surcease suicide: they permit such choices only when the patient is already enduring, in the language of the Dutch guidelines, "intolerable suffering," though, like the Dutch, they may permit the patient to determine what counts as intolerable.

Other proposals, including most of those in the United States, require that the patient be terminally ill, usually defined as within six months of death. If the terminal course is likely to be longer, these proposals would nevertheless prohibit assistance in suicide even if the terminal course is likely to involve more suffering over a longer period of time. A 1994 proposal published in the *New England Journal of Medicine* by Dr. Quill and others would not limit physician-assisted suicide to terminally ill persons—and so would include "incurable and debilitating" conditions like ALS—but insists that lethal treatment be made available "only as a last resort for unrelievable suffering."[13] None of these proposals would clearly permit doctors to honor the choice of a person who has been diagnosed with a terminal illness but is still comparatively healthy to avoid the whole course of terminal decline. Preemptive suicide of this sort does involve trading the good time left for the certainty of avoiding an extended decline and a bad death; it is this choice, Prado says, that our present culture largely denies us.[14]

Preemptive choices will become, I suspect, an increasingly central issue as physician-assisted suicide is legalized or grows increasingly widely accepted in practice. How great a tradeoff is to be permitted between current still-good life, and the certainty of avoiding a very much worse future? This, of course, is a prudential problem for anyone considering suicide to avoid any feared future; but it is a particular problem in physician-assisted suicide. After all, in cases where physician-assisted suicide is relevant, it is typically the physician who provides information about the future to be expected, and it is typically the physician who answers patients' questions about what lies ahead for them: what it will be like to have Alzheimer's, whether it will be possible to control cancer pain, whether communication will be at all possible in advanced ALS. It is also the physician who would play a large role in mitigating the worst effects of that feared future, whether it is a future of Alzheimer's, cancer, or ALS, or perhaps in exacerbating them.

The underlying question here is one about the value of life—not just about assessing it, but about comparing the value of life now and the value or disvalue of life in the future, as the patient sees it, where the difficulty of making this comparison is exacerbated by the physician's role both in predicting what the characteristics of life in the future will be and in treating and altering them. The issue of the value of life is difficult enough in suicide issues generally; it is made far more complex by the physician's role in mediating perceptions in the context of treatment or medically assisted suicide.

ETHICAL ISSUES AFTER LEGALIZATION

Suicide can be rational, we saw [earlier in the author's book], if it meets five criteria: (1) ability to reason, (2) realistic world view, (3) adequacy of information, (4) avoidance of harm, and (5) accordance with fundamental interests. We also saw that paternalist considerations may speak against or, much more problematically, in favor of suicide. And we saw how suicide can be considered a matter of fundamental right, though only when it conduces to human dignity, and that it is roughly—though not perfectly—possible to distinguish between these sorts of cases. But these results do not yet yield a practical policy covering physician-assisted suicide, and it to this need that we must now turn.

Two distinct questions must be kept clearly in mind: the practical issue of whether physician-assisted suicide, and perhaps voluntary active euthanasia as well, *should* be legalized, and the more sustained issue of what ethical dilemmas would arise if physician-assisted suicide *were* legalized, or at least widely available. To be sure, it is already effectively legal in some places—the Netherlands, for instance[15]—and so widely accepted that it is virtually legal in some other places, for example, among people with AIDS in the gay communities of the U.S. west coast. But whatever one's views may be about the propriety of legalization, we are, I believe, currently witnessing the fairly rapid *de facto* transition to a climate in which such assistance is freely available.[16] Thus it is crucial to pay heed to the second of these questions, concerning what ethical issues we should be alert to after it has become legalized or freely available. I shall attend to the most central: How is it possible to protect against abuse? How strong is a person's claim to a physician's assistance in suicide? What does the long-term future hold?

The Problem of Abuse

If an initial case can be made in favor of accepting physician-assisted suicide as an option in terminal illness and also, perhaps, in severe chronic illness, severe disability, and extreme old age, then the immediate question arises: How is it possible to prevent the development of pressures, manipulation, cavalier attitudes, financial motivations, and other malevolent factors that, especially in the presence of personal agendas or cost controls, would lead to the killing of patients against their will? How is it possible to prevent a slide down the slippery slope, from an acceptance of physician-assisted suicide in clearly voluntary, well-grounded cases to the involuntary killing of the weak, helpless, and infirm, then those whose care is particularly expensive, and then the culturally misunderstood, the politically undesirable, the racially despised, and other vulnerable persons? How is it possible to keep a permissive policy from leading to moral holocaust?

Most versions of the slippery-slope argument trade on simple assumptions about human venality or greed: they simply assume that if some practices were allowed, these factors would lead to others much less ethically defensible, and that permitting (voluntary) suicide would lead to (involuntary) killing. The quick reply is that abuse can be prevented by erecting or reinforcing clear legal barriers to involuntary killing—legal barriers already on the books. To legalize physician-assisted suicide would not be to legalize involuntary physician-performed murder, and the line could be clearly and effectively drawn by requiring incontrovertible evidence of the patient's informed, uncoerced choice.

This slippery-slope argument is not the same as the claim, ubiquitous in conservative circles, that equal-rights law would require the extension of any right of suicide to disabled persons, incompetent persons, comatose persons, children, or others not in a position to exercise choice.[17] That misleading argument can be met by pointing out that the right in question is understood as a right of *voluntary* choice and hence cannot be extended to those not capable of choice. Just as we do not extend the right to marry to those not capable of voluntary choice by arranging for them to marry anyhow, so a right to voluntary, physician-assisted suicide simply could not be extended to those not capable of voluntary choice by "arranging" for them to commit suicide. Were a physician to end the life of such a person, this would not be assisted suicide but non-voluntary euthanasia, homicide, or murder. To be sure, non-voluntary euthanasia might be held defensible on other grounds—for instance, the avoidance of suffering —but such a practice would require separate defense and justification.

But there is a troubling version of the slippery-slope argument that points to the possibility of manipulation: manipulation in such a way that patients are brought to seek what they would not have chosen otherwise. It is not possible to prevent completely this sort of manipulation, I believe, any more than it is possible to prevent some people from pushing others into contracts, marriages, financial sacrifices, and so on. But it is possible to make it far more difficult by erecting various mechanisms to protect against abuse, including waiting periods, reporting requirements, optional or mandatory counseling, and various legal restrictions designed to provide evidence of voluntary choice.

However, this counterargument, common in the literature and rhetoric supporting legalization, that it is possible to erect or reinforce protections against abuse, becomes more complex if we recall our discussion [in an earlier chapter] of paternalism, and the ways in which circumstantial and ideological manipulation can lead a person to make voluntary choices that he or she would not otherwise have made. A manipulative party—perhaps an impatient family member or an over-worked nursing-home attendant—can "arrange things" so that circum-stances a dying person would not have found it rational to avoid now become worse than the alternative of death, especially since death is coming in any case. We also saw that the continuing redefinition of what counts as a rational basis for suicide can lead to quite difficult choices. We can already detect an ideological change in contemporary society: it is moving away from the view that there is *no* good reason for suicide to the view that there is at least one adequate reason for it, extreme and irremediable pain in terminal illness. We can also see the beginnings of further movement toward accepting other conditions as good reasons for suicide: extreme physical dependence, "low quality of life," financial burdens to oneself or one's family, the conserving of scarce resources, and perhaps certain religious beliefs.

We can also distinguish among various types of abuse by observing the different circumstances in which it might occur. *Interpersonal* abuse characteristically involves family members or other domestic or close personal associates, whose message may simply be to communicate to the terminally or chronically ill patient not only that there is no reason to hang on, but that it is "time to go." *Professional* abuse employs in addition the weight of professional authority, especially that of physicians, to shape the ways a patient sees his or her future and thus to structure the patient's choices. *Institutional* abuse incorporates some of the features of both interpersonal and professional abuse, but may also objectively constrict the patient's choices, for example by con-trolling the patient's circumstances, by declining to cover some types of care, and by making the financial consequences of extended termi-nal or chronic illness so devastating to the patient's family that he or she sees no alternative to choosing death.[18]

Beneath these discussions about abuse, two related elements are particularly central. The first involves the treacherous notion that there are "indications" for physician-assisted suicide or euthanasia—that is, circumstances in which it is the procedure the physician ought to perform, or in which the physician ought to "see to it" that it occurs —other than the voluntary request of the patient. This is a particular risk in developing notions of rational suicide, since although suicide could be rationally chosen and, given the patient's circumstances, could be the rational thing to do, it might nevertheless not be what the patient actually wants. This is just to say that, as a matter of policy, the patient's irrational choice to stay alive must be respected as well, whether or not paternalist considerations would require urging the patient to depart. To be sure, there may be negative indications for suicide, conditions in which it ought not to be done or assisted, such as when the patient's illness is readily reversible or when the choice is the product of treatable depression. Nevertheless, if choices of suicide in terminal illness or other conditions are to remain an option, not an obligation, and so are to remain crucially voluntary, it cannot be the case that positive indications are recognized that would encourage physicians to promote such a choice. Scrupulous alertness to professional and institutional policies and guidelines governing the practice of physician-assisted suicide, as well as in the training of physicians, is what is required here.

Second, and related, it is imperative not to confuse *request* with *consent*. As is widely acknowledged, it is easy for others, especially physicians, to shape patient choices by presenting information in varying ways; this is the familiar "half empty, half full" problem. A 50-50 outcome prediction in surgery, for example, can be presented as "a good chance of surviving" or as "a good chance of dying," depending on how the physician wishes to influence patient choice. Dr. Quill presented Diane's likelihood of survival in acute leukemia as a 25 per cent chance of success, but she clearly saw it as a 75 per cent chance of failure. While Dr. Quill went to considerable lengths to avoid shaping Diane's choice, it is sometimes said of Dr. Kevorkian—though perhaps falsely—that he has sought to reinforce choices that patients had made only ambivalently. In any case, for many physicians the opportunity to mold the patient's choice in matters of assisted suicide may be viewed as particularly great. While there is no guarantee that abuse can be wholly prevented and that physicians or others can be kept from inadvertently or intentionally shaping patient choice, the best bulwark is to insist on request: that physician-assisted suicide occur must be the patient's idea, as it was with Diane, not something the physician proposes and the patient accepts or rejects. The entire rhetoric of "informed consent" is out of place here; we may legitimately speak only of "informed request."

The Patient's Claim to Assistance

What rights does a terminally ill person have, if any, to his or her physician's assistance in suicide? In [a previous chapter] we discussed the issue of whether suicide is a matter of rights, and I've argued at some length that it must be regarded not just as a simple right or as a claim-right, but as a natural, fundamental right in virtue of its capacity to protect and promote human dignity. In ordinary situations usually labeled suicide, I hastened to add, most cases can hardly be said to protect or promote human dignity—for example, the suicides of lovesick teenagers or middle-aged business failures, or dyadic suicides where the aim is to make someone else suffer. But the sort of example we adduced of a situation in which suicide might protect or enhance human dignity included not only terminal-illness suicides—for instance, that of a terminal cancer patient who must save up her pain pills for weeks in order to avoid what she perceives as final medical indignities—but also those of principle. . . . But if the terminally ill patient has a right to assistance from her physician in suicide, though it is not acknowledged, wouldn't the [person who intends to commit suicide out of honor or principle], for whom it is equally a matter of natural or fundamental right to end his life, have such a claim too?

Who, then, has a claim to the assistance of a physician in suicide, and under what circumstances? Anyone whose suicide would be a matter of fundamental right? Or only some persons, and if so, which ones? What sort of help may the patient legitimately expect? Or does no one in any situation have a claim to the physician's help (if the physician does not wish to volunteer it) such that the physician would be obligated to comply? Are there limits to what the physician can be asked to do?

If we understand the underlying rationale for physician-assisted suicide as based in the moral obligation to provide help to those in need, the physician's obligation to provide help in suicide will be a function of the patient's degree of medical impairment. Thus this obligation will increase in strength along a sliding scale, and will be strongest when the patient's medical impairment is greatest, when the patient is profoundly ill and incapable of recovery, or when the patient is so severely physically handicapped as to be unable to accomplish this goal on his or her own. (Of course, if removal of the impairing condition is possible, then that is the physician's obligation instead.) The physician's obligation to provide assistance in suicide is less strong where the patient's condition is not so severely impaired, and still less strong in the preemptive suicide, where the patient will become impaired in the future but at the moment retains something close to normal function. The physician has no obligation to assist in the suicide of a person who is, medically speaking, fully healthy, even if, for example, this person's reasons for suicide involve matters of principle and the preservation of dignity, and he or she has a natural, fundamental right to suicide. Thus in cases at one end of the scale the physician has a fully compelling obligation to assist a patient in suicide, while at the other end of the scale he or she has no obligation to assist at all. Many of the issues, of course, concern the broad range of cases in between.

This view of the physician's obligation—a graduated obligation of varying degree, depending on the patient's medical need—still raises certain problems. For instance, it leaves unresolved the question of whether untreatable mental illness, as in the highly controversial Chabot case argued in the Netherlands in the spring of 1994 [see Herbert Hendin's essay in this volume],[19] should count as the kind of medical impairment that lays claim to a physician's help, even though the patient is physically healthy. Nor does it make clear what a physician's role should be in deviations from normal neurobiology. It does not make clear whether extreme old age counts as medical impairment, though of course if that age results in a limitation of function equivalent to severe illness or handicap, it would. It treats chronic illness where there is extreme impairment on a par with terminal illness, and so does not coincide with most of the current legal proposals, which would permit physician-assisted suicide only if the patient is terminally ill.

But this sense of graduated obligation on the part of the physician is, I think, most consistent with our intuitions. It imposes no obligation to some persons (no obligation, for instance, to just any healthy person who might walk in from the street), but at the same time imposes growing obligation to patients as they grow more seriously ill or disabled. It imposes a fully compelling obligation, subject only to the restricted limitation to be discussed shortly in the case of physician scruple, to patients fully disabled or in severe, untreatable, terminal pain.

Social Differences and the Physician's Role

But the issue of whether the physician has an obligation to assist in suicide, if that is what the patient in need seeks, is also a matter that can only be raised within various social contexts. What, exactly, does it mean for the physician to "assist" in suicide? In the Netherlands, for example, where both voluntary active euthanasia and physician-assisted suicide are openly practiced and broadly accepted, assistance in either suicide or euthanasia involves the physician in a direct, immediate role in helping the patient bring about his or her own death. The physician is almost always present, along with the family; the physician provides the drugs and the IV equipment or other supplies; and even if the patient drinks the lethal drug or administers it himself or herself, the physician remains available to intervene if the drug should produce unwanted side effects like vomiting or convulsions, willing to perform euthanasia if need be. In this culture, physician assistance means the physician's emotional and moral support, the continuous presence or at least availability of the physician, and the physician's willingness to provide still more direct means of producing death should the means used by the patient fail.

Germany provides a sharp contrast. Assisting suicide is not illegal in Germany, provided the person aided is competent and in control of his or her will; yet a contentious point of German law has been interpreted widely to put the physician who administers a lethal dose to a patient at substantial legal risk for failure to rescue. Thus while assistance in suicide may be openly practiced by family or friends, physicians are only very rarely involved. It is often said that in an authoritarian medical system, given the facts of physician cooperation in Nazi experimentation schemes, this arrangement is appropriate: doctors cannot be trusted in bringing about the end of life. . . .

In the United States, it is often assumed that physician-assisted suicide would in practice be like Timothy Quill's assistance with Diane: the physician makes the lethal drug available, but the patient decides the time to use it and takes the drug in the privacy of his or her home, alone or in the company of family members. This arm's-length role appears to be the model incorporated in the 1994 proposed Oregon statute that would legalize physician-assisted suicide: physicians would be permitted to write prescriptions for lethal drugs, but there is no explicit authorization of any more direct, involved role.

The distanced arrangement between Dr. Quill and Diane is one possibility; but the United States is also familiar with the practice of Dr. Kevorkian. Here, although the physician assisting in the suicide is a stranger and not the patient's familiar physician, and although the physician who assists in the suicide relies on the diagnoses and prognoses of other physicians to determine whether it is appropriate to do so, he or she is present during the administration of the lethal drugs to assist with the control of unwanted side effects and to ensure that the procedure goes smoothly. In this model, the physician is not at arm's length but is present throughout the process of dying.

Which of these models, or which other model, if any, would a patient's fundamental right to suicide underwrite? This question is closely related to that concerning the strength of the physician's obligation to assist a patient at all. An initial answer, drawing on the principle that the strength of the physician's obligation is a function of the patient's medical need, holds that for those patients in greatest medical need—those most severely and irreversibly ill, or most completely disabled and hence unable to act on their own wishes—the physician must be most available, not at arm's length but present at the bedside, if the patient wishes, during the entire process of dying. The more distanced, arm's-length form of assistance in suicide, in which the physician provides a prescription for the lethal drug together perhaps with advice about how to take it but is not present at the time, would be more appropriate where the physician's obligation is less strong, as for example in preemptive cases like that of Janet Adkins and perhaps Diane.

But it is not quite this simple. After all, the physician's role must also serve, under the basic justification for regarding suicide as a natural or fundamental right, to protect or enhance the patient's dignity, and so must conform to whatever model will best serve this purpose. In a social climate in which choices of physician-aided death are respected, the closer physician-patient model may enhance dignity more, by enabling the physician to provide emotional as well as technical support and protection against unwanted side effects. This is perhaps what Dr. Quill had in mind when he said that he regretted that legal risk had made it impossible for him to be with Diane when she took the drugs she had asked him to prescribe. On the other hand, in a social climate in which physician assistance in suicide remains illegal or in which the comparatively commercial nature of the health-care system means that financial pressures are more likely to compromise both the professional integrity of the physician and the dignity of the patient, a more distanced relationship may be the more justified. The more distanced relationship may place a greater burden on the patient and subject him or her to greater risk of suffering during the period of dying, but it may also protect more greatly against abuse. Thus the policy question of what shall be permitted in "assistance" in suicide is not one that can be answered easily or without reference to cultural circumstances, but remains centrally tied to its underlying justification.

Physician Scruples

In most proposals and discussions of physician-assisted suicide, it is assumed that the physician who has scruples against assisting the patient in suicide or euthanasia has no obligation to do so; while the patient is free to request assistance, the physician is free to decline to participate. In the Netherlands, for example, only about a third of all requests for assistance in dying, whether by euthanasia or physician-assisted suicide, are honored. All twenty of Dr. Kevorkian's patients presumably were people whose own physicians had refused to help. And a new survey of physicians in Washington state, where awareness of the issue has been high in the wake of the defeat of Initiative 119, which would have legalized physician-assisted suicide and euthanasia, shows that while many physicians now think both practices should be legal, a substantially smaller proportion of these physicians say they would be willing to participate in these practices themselves.[20]

I think it is right, on both moral and prudential grounds, that physicians be able to refuse to help—even if the intended suicide would be a matter of natural right. But there are limitations. First, moral scruples are not the same as objections on grounds other than principle—such as inconvenience, unprofitableness, or simple distaste; these objections carry no moral weight. Second, if all physicians were to decline to participate, this would render the patient's right to assistance nil, and while the likelihood of this may not be great in general, in any situation in which a particular physician is the only physician available, the obligation to help remains. Third, and most important because of its probable frequency, there is a specific situation that requires attention: that of the physician who has scruples about assistance in suicide, but does not let the patient know that until quite late in the downhill course of the disease. By this time the patient is often seriously incapacitated and in substantial need of ongoing medical care, and it is extremely difficult for the patient to transfer to the care of another physician—with whom, in any case, there would be no longstanding relationship or pattern of mutual understanding. Thus, although the individual physician may not have an obligation to assist in the suicide of a patient, even in circumstances that would enhance the patient's dignity, and even when that patient is his or her own patient, the physician does have an obligation not to compromise the dignity of the patient by announcing his or her principled objection only when it is too late for the patient to switch to another doctor. Thus physicians who fail to make clear their scruples early on acquire positive obligations to help.

This does not mean that the physician who does not entertain a scrupled objection to assisted dying is required to honor any patient request; it is still up to the physician to assess as carefully as possible whether the request is stable, genuine, freely made, fully informed, and reflective of the patient's most basic values (in short, whether it is a rational request, rationally made). It does mean that the physician is obligated not to entrap the patient into compliance with the physician's rather than the patient's values.

A LOOK INTO THE FUTURE

Our intuitions about the moral permissibility of physician-assisted suicide and about matters of practical policy like the appropriate role of the physician are most clear in the case of severely painful or disabling terminal physical illness: while these are not *indications* for suicide, the patient may request assistance in suicide, and the physician should be prepared to provide it if that is what the patient genuinely wants. However, as our intuitions about suicide—and thus, we may expect, our intuitions about physician-assisted suicide—are in an extreme state of flux, and while we have advanced here the principle that the physician's obligations are a function of the patient's degree of medical impairment or need, our views about specific cases may well undergo change.

Furthermore, not only are our intuitions in rapid flux; so is our cultural situation. The legal climate is increasingly unstable, as constitutional issues are raised in challenge to traditional laws. Our strategies for preventing abuse rest on rapidly changing institutional structures. Ideological commitments are evolving on nearly every front—religious, medical, social—as the societies of the developed world rethink their traditional views about suicide in the context of the new epidemiology of dying and the medical issues that raises. In other words, our reflections here about suicide and physician-assisted suicide are taking place at an extremely volatile moment, and we can be sure that our current views will change. Will physician assistance in suicide be legalized in the United States? . . . Will this issue reach the U.S. Supreme Court? That seems certain, though the outcome is not; the Canadian supreme court's physician-assisted-suicide case, *Rodriguez v. British Columbia,* decided in September 1991, ended in a 5-4 decision.[21] Nevertheless, I think it inevitable that the practice of physician-assisted suicide will become more widespread, whether technically legal or not, and I think it is important to turn our attention to the characteristics such a practice must have if it is to remain morally defensible. . . .

First, the defensible practice of physician-assisted suicide *must make available opportunities for counseling*—non-directive, non-paternalist counseling, not designed to dissuade the patient but to help the patient contemplating suicide to explore what his or her real wishes are. Much current counseling is antecedently committed to suicide prevention, thus making it impossible for patients whose claim to assistance is greatest (i.e., those with the most severe medical impairments) to make use of these services, for fear that if they reveal that they are considering suicide, prevention measures will be put in place and they will be left still more in need than before. What is required here is counseling that is able to explore not only the patient's feelings and background values but issues of the accuracy of diagnostic and prognostic information, long-shot hopes for cure, possibilities for palliative care, the timing of a suicide, its impact on others, experiences of suffering and pain, and—most important—any perceptions the patient may have of being pushed or manipulated into this choice by family members, physicians, institutional policies, or any other factor. The patient considering suicide because of terminal illness or extreme disability must have access to someone to talk with about it, without fear of preventive intervention, so that the rationality and genuineness of choice can be explored. This is one way of protecting and promoting human dignity and, in the bargain, preventing abuse.

Although such counseling would presumably be secular, the provision of non-directive end-of-life counseling may also open a major role for the churches. In addition to current support for the dying, such as encouraging life review, planning one's own funeral, or making amends with those from whom one is estranged, one can imagine religious groups providing pastoral counseling intended not to prevent the choice of physician-assisted suicide but to explore whether it is a genuine choice and whether it is experienced by the person making the choice as respectful of both self and others in a religious as well as social sense. Not only could such counseling be especially vigilant about abuse, since the counselor would in most cases have access to the entire family, but it would also be the occasion for exploring the pull of implicit invitations to suicide within the religious tradition, to see to what degree they are a factor in the patient's choice. Religious groups are well suited for this task; after all, they have traditionally been the arbiters of end-of-life solemnities, and this would continue their traditional role. This is not to say that all suicide counseling should be done by religious groups; it is only to conjecture that religious groups might adopt a supportive rather than prohibitive role in recognizing responsible, rational choice in matters of dying.

In addition to the expectation that non-directive, non-paternalist counseling, secular or pastoral, be available, the defensible practice of physician-assisted suicide must also erect regulatory mechanisms for the control of abuse. Many such safeguards are or could be incorporated into proposals for legalization, such as waiting times or requirements documenting the continuity and non-ambivalence of the patient's choice, prohibitions of charging fees for assistance in suicide, reporting requirements, review by independent medical, pain-control, and psychiatric consultants, retroactive auditing, and the development of objective indices of abuse.[22] It must also be the case that patients considering suicide are offered all available care that would relieve their conditions, at least to the extent that a patient in similar circumstances not considering suicide would be offered such care. And it must be the case that patients considering suicide have full information about their diagnosis, prognosis, and the various forms of treatment available; a defensible practice of physician-assisted suicide would not permit cornering patients into choices of suicide because appropriate alternative treatments—including extended comfort care —were not offered them. Adequate protection against abuse, whether personal, professional, or institutional, is crucial to the protection of human dignity.

The defensible practice of physician-assisted suicide would also necessitate widespread reflection on the physician's role accompanied by radically altered instruction in how to assist patients in suicide. First, to be sure, the training of physicians would need to include instruction in non-directive counseling, so that the patient's choice remains genuinely free. It would need to teach physicians how to avoid either unrealistic expectations for the patient's recovery or unduly grim assessments of the prognosis. It would need to prepare physicians for the emotionally difficult task of ending the life of a patient.

But physicians would also need explicit training in the pharmacology of assisting in suicide: what drugs to provide, in what dosages, what ancillary drugs to use to control vomiting, and so on. As information comes to light about the underground practice of assisted suicide, a particularly disturbing feature is the frequency of bungled attempts, failures that often increase the patient's suffering when the aim is to alleviate it. For example, a study of "back alley" assisted suicides among people with AIDS in Vancouver between 1980 and 1993 revealed that half were botched: victims were unsuccessfully suffocated, assisters resorted to slitting the victim's wrists with a razor blade or shooting him, and so on.[23] An empirical study of euthanasia and physician-assisted suicide in the Netherlands revealed that complications or unintended effects occurred in 12 per cent of physician-assisted or physician-performed procedures.[24] It took Jack Kevorkian five tries to insert the intravenous line in Janet Adkins's arm, and four tries for the next patient.[25] Even Timothy Quill wondered whether Diane had struggled during her final hour, after she took the drugs, since legal risk prevented him and her family from being at her side.

Thus appropriate training serves to ensure that physicians perform competently that function which the patient in greatest need may expect from them, barring only principled objections where the patient is informed well in advance and an alternative, more accommodating physician is available. The obligation to secure appropriate training in how to provide assistance in suicide for patients in need is an obligation not just of individual physicians but of the medical profession as a whole, so that it can assure its clients—patients generally—of the help that they request in facing death in a way that protects or promotes their dignity.

But the real issue about the future of physician-assisted suicide concerns the role it will play, if any, in our future practices surrounding dying. Some think that there should be no role for assisted suicide at all, though many who oppose legalization say that they do not object to the practice being conducted "quietly" or "privately" between physician and patient—that is, under the table, without legal protection for either. On the other hand, if physician-assisted suicide is legalized or becomes legally tolerated, will it remain a comparatively infrequent choice, hovering somewhere around the figure of 3 per cent of all deaths, as is now the case in the Netherlands? Or will it be viewed as a nearly universal choice, at least for the vast majority of people in the developed world, who can expect after all to die of degenerative diseases late in life, diseases with long downhill courses? There is some reason to think that preferences will increase in this direction. For example, a 1994 Australian study of cancer patients found that those who anticipated a role for the more active options of suicide and/or euthanasia in their own futures were less fatalistic and did not report a reduced quality of life, compared to those who anticipated a future possible role for the more passive options of wishing death to come early or ceasing all treatment—that is, patients who saw suicide or euthanasia as real options were more hopeful and reported a higher qualify of life than patients who regarded them as out of the question.[26] These issues, too, are clearly relevant to questions of dignity not just in life but in death.

The real issue is cultural shaping: what will come to be seen as the normal way to die? Until within the last two decades or so, it was considered normal for a terminally ill person to try—heroically—to hang on until the very end, to stave off death as long as possible. More recently, we have begun to see as normal a terminal course in which life-prolonging treatment is withheld or withdrawn when it is thought pointless to go on; this usually occurs only toward the end of the downhill terminal course. Often the issue of withholding or withdrawing is raised by the physician or by the family after the patient is no longer competent, and a do-not-resuscitate order is signed; perhaps a respirator is discontinued or artificial nutrition and hydration withdrawn.

But we may be witnessing a transition into an era in which personal choice in the matter of dying is given a much larger role, in which preemptive as well as surcease choices are honored, and in which self-chosen death, with the skilled and sensitive assistance of one's physician, becomes a much more normal, ordinary, respected thing to do. We may actually begin to think in advance, realistically and responsibly, about how we want our lives to end. Inasmuch as some 70-80 per cent of people in the developed world can expect to face death in circumstances in which such issues may arise, this is no small or trivial matter.

6

Always to Care, Never to Kill:
A Declaration on Euthanasia

The Ramsey Colloquium

W e are grateful that the citizens of Washington State have turned back a measure that would have extended the permission to kill [November 1991], but we know that this is not the end of the matter. The American people must now prepare themselves to meet similar proposals for legally sanctioned euthanasia. Toward that end we offer this explanation of why euthanasia is contrary to our faith as Jews and Christians, is based upon a grave moral error, does violence to our political tradition, and undermines the integrity of the medical profession.

In relating to the sick, the suffering, the incompetent, the disabled, and the dying, we must learn again the wisdom that teaches us *always to care, never to kill.* Although it may sometimes appear to be an act of compassion, killing is never a means of caring.

The well-organized campaign for legalized euthanasia cruelly ex-

The **Ramsey Colloquium**, named for the late Princeton ethicist Paul Ramsey, is a group of Jewish and Christian theologians, ethicists, philosophers, legal scholars, and others that meets occasionally to consider questions of ethics, religion, and public life. This declaration was issued on November 27, 1991, and is reprinted by permission of the Ramsey Colloquium of the Institute on Religion and Public Life, New York.

ploits the fear of suffering and frustration felt when we cannot restore to health those whom we love. Such fear and frustration is genuine and deeply felt, especially with respect to the aging. But to deal with suffering by eliminating those who suffer is an evasion of moral duty and a great wrong.

Deeply embedded in our moral and medical traditions is the distinction between *allowing to die,* on the one hand, and *killing,* on the other. That distinction is now under attack and must be defended with all the force available to us. It is permitted to refuse or withhold medical treatment in accepting death while we continue to care for the dying. It is never permitted, it is always prohibited, to take any action that is aimed at the death of ourselves or others.

Medical treatments can be refused or withheld if they are either useless or excessively burdensome. No one should be subjected to useless treatment; no one need accept any and all lifesaving treatments, no matter how burdensome. In making such decisions, the judgment is about the worth of treatments, *not* about the worth of lives. When we ask whether a treatment is useless, the question is: "Will this treatment be useful for this patient, will it benefit the life he or she has?" When we ask whether a treatment is burdensome, the question is: "Is this treatment excessively burdensome to the life of this patient?" The question is *not* whether this life is useless or burdensome. Our decisions, whether for or against a specific treatment, are to be always in the service of life. We can and should allow the dying to die; we must never intend the death of the living. We may reject a treatment; we must never reject a life.

Once we cross the boundary between killing and allowing to die, there will be no turning back. Current proposals would legalize euthanasia only for the terminally ill. But the logic of the argument —and its practical consequences—will inevitably push us further. Arguments for euthanasia usually appeal to our supposed right of self-determination and to the desirability of relieving suffering. If a right to euthanasia is grounded in self-determination, it cannot reasonably be limited to the terminally ill. If people have a right to die, why must they wait until they are actually dying before they are permitted to exercise that right? Similarly, if the warrant for euthanasia is to relieve suffering, why should we be able to relieve the suffering only of those who are self-determining and competent to give their consent? Why not euthanasia for the suffering who can no longer speak for themselves? To ask such a question is to expose the logical incoherence and the fragile arbitrariness of suggested "limits" in proposals for legalized euthanasia.

We must not delude ourselves. Euthanasia is an extension of the license to kill. Once we have transgressed and blurred the line between killing and allowing to die, it will be exceedingly difficult—in logic, law, and practice—to effectively limit the license to kill. Once the judgment is not about the worth of specific treatments but about the worth of specific lives, our nursing homes and other institutions will present us with countless candidates for elimination who would "be better off dead."

In the face of such mortal danger, we would direct public attention to four interwoven sources of wisdom in our cultural heritage that can teach us again always to care, never to kill.

1. Religious Wisdom

As Christians and Jews, we have learned to think of human life— our own and that of others—as both gift and trust. We have been entrusted to one another and are to care for one another. We have not been authorized to make comparative judgments about the worth of lives or to cut short the years that God gives to us or others. We are to relieve suffering when we can, and to bear with those who suffer, helping them to bear their suffering, when we cannot. We are never to "solve" the problem of suffering by eliminating those who suffer. Euthanasia, once established as an option, will inevitably tempt us to abandon those who suffer. This is especially the case when we permit ourselves to be persuaded that their lives are a burden to us or them. The biblical tradition compels us to seek and exercise better ways to care. We may think that we care when we kill, but killing is never caring. Whatever good intentions we might invoke to excuse it, killing is the rejection of God's command to care and of his help in caring.

2. Moral Wisdom

We may possess many good things in life. Although we benefit from such goods, they do not constitute our very being. We can, if we wish, renounce such goods or give them into the control of another. Life, however, is not simply a "good" that we possess. We *are* living beings. Our life *is* our person. To treat our life as a "thing" that we can authorize another to terminate is profoundly dehumanizing. Euthanasia, even when requested by the competent, can never be a humanitarian act, for it attacks the distinctiveness and limitations of being human. Persons—ourselves and others—are not things to be discarded when they are no longer deemed useful.

We can give our life *for* another, but we cannot give ultimate authority over our life *to* another. The painfully learned moral wisdom of our heritage is that persons cannot "own" persons. The decision for euthanasia is not an exercise of human freedom but the abandonment of human freedom. To attempt to turn one's life into an object that is at the final disposition of another is to become less than human, while it places the other in a position of being more than human—a lord of life and death, a possessor of the personhood of others.

Human community and the entirety of civilization is premised upon a relationship of moral claims and duties between persons. Personhood has no meaning apart from life. If life is a thing that can be renounced or taken at will, the moral structure of human community, understood as a community of persons, is shattered. Whatever the intentions of their proponents, proposals for legalizing euthanasia must be seen not as a solution to discrete problems but as an assault upon the fundamental ideas undergirding the possibility of moral order. The alternative to that moral order is the lethal disorder of a brave new world in which killing is defined as caring, life is viewed as the enemy, and death is counted as a benefit to be bestowed.

3. Political Wisdom

"We hold these truths," the founders of our political community declared, and among the truths that our community has held is that the right to life is "unalienable." All human beings have an equal right to life bestowed by "Nature and Nature's God." Government is to recognize and respect that right; it does not bestow that right.

This unalienable right places a clear limit on the power of the state. Except when government exercises its duty to protect citizens against force and injustice, or when it punishes evildoers, it may not presume for itself an authority over human life. To claim that—apart from these exceptions—the state may authorize the killing of even consenting persons is to give state authority an ultimacy it has never had in our political tradition. Again, legalized euthanasia is an unprecedented extension of the license to kill. In the name of individual rights it undercuts the foundation of individual rights. An unalienable right cannot be alienated, it cannot be given away. Our political tradition has wisely recognized that government cannot authorize the alienation of a right it did not first bestow.

4. Institutional Wisdom

Legalized euthanasia would inevitably require the complicity of physicians. Members of the healing profession are asked to blur or erase the distinction between healing and killing. In our tradition, medical caregivers have understood this to be their calling: to cure when possible, to care always, never to kill. Legalized euthanasia would require a sweeping transformation of the meaning of medicine.

In a time when the medical profession is subjected to increasing criticism, when many people feel vulnerable before medical technology and practice, it would be foolhardy for our society to authorize physicians to kill. Euthanasia is not the way to respond to legitimate fears about medical technology and practice. It is unconscionable that the proponents of euthanasia exploit such fears. Such fears can be met and overcome by strongly reaffirming the distinction between killing and allowing to die—by making clear that useless and excessively burdensome treatment *can* be refused, while at the same time leaving no doubt that this society will neither authorize physicians to kill nor look the other way if they do.

Conclusion

This fourfold wisdom can be rejected only at our moral peril. By attending to these sources of wisdom, we can find our way back to a firmer understanding of the limits of human responsibility, and of the imperative to embrace compassionately those who suffer from illness and the fears associated with the end of life. Guided by this wisdom, we will not presume to eliminate a fellow human being, nor need we fear being abandoned in our suffering. The compact of rights, duties, and mutual trust that makes community possible depends upon our continuing adherence to the precept, *Always to care, never to kill.*

7

Jewish Views on Euthanasia

Byron L. Sherwin

Scripture says: "You should love your neighbor as yourself" (Lev. 19:18); therefore, choose an easy death for him.

— FROM THE TALMUD[1]

The "miracles" of modern medicine have made moral decision-making in medical settings ever more complex. In this realm, one of the most compelling issues is euthanasia, literally (in Greek) "a good death." Modern philosophers often distinguish between two kinds of euthanasia, active and passive. *Active euthanasia* refers to the taking of an action that causes or accelerates death, while *passive euthanasia* refers to the withdrawal of life support. In addition, a distinction is also often made between voluntary and involuntary euthanasia. In *voluntary euthanasia,* the individual makes or accedes to the decision to bring his or her life to an end. In *involuntary euthanasia,* an action to end the patient's life is taken without his or her explicit

---

Rabbi Dr. **Byron L. Sherwin** is vice president and Distinguished Service Professor of Jewish Philosophy and Mysticism at Spertus Institute of Jewish Studies, Chicago. He is the author of eighteen books. This essay is abridged and reprinted by permission from his book *In Partnership With God: Contemporary Jewish Law and Ethics* (Syracuse, N.Y.: Syracuse University Press, 1990). Many of the notes have been omitted or substantially abridged.

consent. Thus euthanasia may take a variety of forms: active-voluntary, passive-voluntary, active-involuntary, and passive-involuntary. . . .

How does Jewish tradition deal with euthanasia? Though as a rule Judaism condemns both murder and suicide, there are exceptions to the rule. For example, martyrdom—i.e., killing oneself or allowing oneself to be killed—for "the sanctification of God's Name" is not considered murder or suicide by Talmudic and subsequent Jewish tradition. (The Talmud is a compendium of Jewish law, lore, religion, and culture produced over roughly a thousand years ending about the seventh century.) Moreover, killing in self-defense and other forms of "justified homicide" have been sanctioned as "necessary evils" by rabbinic tradition. Neither were all examples of manslaughter considered murder: rabbinic tradition required conditions such as premeditation and malicious intent before defining an act as murder.

Since martyrdom is one of the exceptions to the prohibition against suicide and murder, it is interesting that post-Talmudic Jewish sources found a precedent for euthanasia in a Talmudic text that discusses martyrdom:

It was said that within but few days Rabbi Jose ben Kisma died, and all the great men of Rome went to his burial and made a great lamentation for him. On their return, they found Rabbi Hanina ben Teradion sitting and occupying himself with the Torah, publicly gathering assemblies, and keeping a scroll of the Torah in his bosom. Straightaway they took hold of him, wrapt him in the scroll of the Torah, placed bundles of branches around him and set them on fire. They then brought tufts of wool, which they had soaked in water, and placed them over his heart, so that he should not expire quickly.

His daughter exclaimed, "Father, that I should see you in this state!" He replied, "If it were I alone being burnt it would have been a thing hard to bear; but now I am burning together with the scroll of the Torah. He who will have regard for the plight of the Torah will also have regard for my plight." His disciples called out, "Rabbi, what seest thou?" He answered them, "The parchments are being burnt but the letters are soaring high." "Open then thy mouth" [said they] "so that the fire enter into thee." He replied: "Let Him who gave me [my soul] take it away, but no one should injure oneself."

The executioner then said to him, "Rabbi, if I raise the flame and take away the tufts of wool from over thy heart, will thou cause me to enter into the life to come?" "Yes," he replied. "Then swear unto me" [he urged]. He swore unto him. He thereupon raised the flame and removed the tufts of wool from over his heart, and his soul departed speedily. The executioner then jumped and threw himself into the fire. And a *bath kol* [a heavenly voice] exclaimed: "Rabbi Hanina ben Teradion and the executioner have been assigned to the World to Come." When Rabbi heard it he wept and said: "One may acquire eternal life in a single hour, another after many years."[2]

This Talmudic text was interpreted by later authorities as having established the following principles:

1. Martyrdom is not to be considered self-murder or suicide.
2. An individual's life belongs not to himself or herself but to God.
3. Active-voluntary euthanasia is prohibited, but passive-voluntary euthanasia may be permitted. When the rabbi is encouraged to open his mouth so that the fire may enter and end his agony (i.e., active-voluntary euthanasia), he refuses. But when the executioner offers to remove the soaked tufts of wool artificially prolonging his life (i.e., a life-support system), the rabbi gives him permission (i.e., passive-voluntary euthanasia).

As we shall see, the views on euthanasia that are drawn from this Talmudic text are reiterated in subsequent Jewish literature.

ACTIVE EUTHANASIA: PROHIBITED

The *Sefer Hasidim* (a medieval compendium of Jewish law, lore, and mysticism) states: "If a person is suffering from extreme pain and he says to another: 'You see that I shall not live [long]; [therefore,] kill me because I cannot bear the pain,' one is forbidden to touch him [the terminal patient]." The text goes on to proscribe the terminal patient from taking his or her own life: "If a person is suffering great pain and he knows that he will not live [long], he cannot kill himself. And this principle we learn from Rabbi Hanina ben Teradion, who refused to open his mouth [to allow the fire to enter and take his life]."[3]

In one of the "minor tractates" of the Talmud, we read:

A dying man [*goses*] is regarded as a living entity in respect to all matters in the world. Whosoever touches or moves him is a murderer [if by so doing his death is accelerated]. Rabbi Meir used to say: He may be compared to a lamp which is dripping [going out]; should one touch it, one extinguishes it. Similarly, whoever closes the eyes of a dying man [thereby accelerating his death] is considered as if he had taken his life.[4]

This prohibition against practicing active euthanasia is reiterated by the medieval codes of Jewish law. It extends to the patient, the attending physician, the family and friends of the patient, and to all other individuals. In his twelfth-century legal code, the *Mishneh Torah*, Maimonides wrote:

One who is in a dying condition is regarded as a living person in all respects. . . . He who touches him [thereby accelerating his death] is guilty of shedding blood. To what may he [the dying person] be compared? To a flickering flame, which is extinguished as soon as one touches it. Whoever closes the eyes of a dying person while the soul is about to depart is shedding blood. One should wait a while; perhaps he is just in a swoon.[5]

The fourteenth-century code of Jacob ben Asher, the *Arba'ah Turim*, in many ways served as the model for Joseph Karo's sixteenth-century code, the *Shulhan Arukh*. Echoing earlier texts, Jacob ben Asher wrote: "A dying man is to be considered a living person in all respects. . . . [Therefore] anyone who hastens the exiting of the person's soul is a shedder of blood."[6] Karo's *Shulhan Arukh* reads, "A patient on his deathbed is considered a living person in every respect . . . and it is forbidden to cause him to die quickly . . . and whosoever closes his eyes with the onset of death is regarded as shedding blood."[7]

The nineteenth-century *Kitzur Shulhan Arukh* by Solomon Ganzfried embellishes a bit on the earlier sources: "Even if one has been dying for a long time, which causes agony to the patient and his family, it is still forbidden to accelerate his death."[8]

The premises upon which classical Jewish views prohibiting active euthanasia are based include the following:

1. An individual's life is not his or her own "property" but God's, and therefore God has the final disposition over it. In other words,

each person serves as God's steward for the life given into his or her care. As Hanina ben Teradion put it, "Let Him who gave me my soul take it away."[9]

2. Jewish law does not dwell on the issue of quality of life. Rather, Jewish law maintains that each moment of life is inherently valuable in and of itself, independent of its quality. Life being sacred—each moment of life being intrinsically valuable—every effort must be made to preserve each moment of life, even to the moment of death. For example, according to Jewish law, "even if they find a person crushed [under a fallen building] so that he can live only for a short time, they must continue to dig," and if this has occurred on the Sabbath, the rescuers are required to violate the Sabbath even if it means granting the victim only "momentary life."[10]

3. An individual is prohibited from inflicting self-injury, particularly the ultimate self-injury—suicide, which is generally defined as self-homicide.[11]

4. Since "there is no agency for wrongful acts," and since murder is a wrongful act, one cannot act as the agent of a person who desires death and bring about or accelerate that person's death, even at his or her explicit request.[12] In this regard, the physician is explicitly enjoined from employing medical intervention for the intention of accelerating death.[13]

PASSIVE EUTHANASIA: MAY BE PERMITTED

As noted, the Talmudic case of Hanina ben Teradion is used by some post-Talmudic sources as a precedent for the permissibility (but not necessarily a requirement) of passive euthanasia. The rabbi allowed the removal of the tufts of wool that were "artificially" sustaining his life. This would seem to permit both voluntary and involuntary passive euthanasia, either on the part of the patient (voluntary) or on the part of another party (voluntary or involuntary), such as a physician. To be sure, Jewish law would not permit the removal of all life-support mechanisms; for example, it generally would not permit the withholding of insulin from a diabetic. The story of Hanina ben Teradion clearly relates to a person who has no chance of survival in any case.

In many of the same sources noted above proscribing *active* euthanasia, one finds material that permits passive euthanasia. The *Sefer Hasidim* observes,

> One may not [artificially] prolong the act of dying. If, for example, someone is dying and nearby a woodcutter insists on chopping wood, thereby disturbing the dying person so that he cannot die, we remove the woodcutter from the vicinity of the dying person. Also, one must not place salt in the mouth of a dying person in order to prevent death from overtaking him.[14]

This view is adapted and is quoted almost verbatim in subsequent codes of Jewish law. In his gloss to the *Shulhan Arukh,* the sixteenth-century Polish rabbi Moses Isserles observed,

> It is forbidden to cause one's death to be accelerated, even in the case of one who has been terminally ill for a long time. . . . *however,* if there is some factor which is preventing the exit of the soul such as a nearby woodchopper or salt placed under his tongue—and these things are impeding his death—it is permissible to remove them because in so doing one actively does nothing but remove an obstacle [preventing his natural death].[15]

Again, echoing the *Sefer Hasidim* the *Shulhan Arukh* states,

> One must not scream at the moment at which the soul [of another] departs, lest the soul return and the person suffer great pain. That is to say, it is not simply permitted to remove an obstacle to one's [natural] death, but one cannot lengthen the pain and suffering of the patient.[16]

In this regard, Isserles interpreted the view of the *Sefer Hasidim* as meaning that "it is certain that for one to do anything that stifles the [natural] process of dying [in a dying person] is forbidden."[17] Similarly, the sixteenth-century Italian rabbi Joshua Boaz referred to the *Sefer Hasidim* as being the basis of his own view that "it is permissible to remove any obstacle preventing [death] because so doing is not an action in and of itself."[18] Furthermore, in a seventeenth-century responsum (i.e., a decision of Jewish case law) by Jacob ben Samuel, the author takes the controversial view that any medical or pharmacological intervention that impedes the natural process of dying should not be introduced.[19]

Commenting on the phrase in Ecclesiastes 3:2, "There is a time to die," the *Sefer Hasidim* observes that Ecclesiastes does *not* also state that "there is a time to live." The reason for this, according to the *Sefer Hasidim*, is that, when the "time to die" arrives, it is not the time to extend life. Consequently, the *Sefer Hasidim* prohibits efforts to resuscitate a terminal patient, on the grounds that extending the process of dying by resuscitation would cause the patient continued unnecessary anguish.[20] This text might serve as the basis for justifying a "do not resuscitate" (DNR) order for terminal patients whose condition has reached the point of death: to resuscitate them through heroic measures would only prolong their dying and extend their agony. Just as some sources consider active euthanasia to be a presumption of God's authority over life and death, the *Sefer Hasidim* insists that extending the process of dying, when the terminal patient is in severe pain, is also a presumption of God's authority over life and death and a presumptive rejection of the scriptural view that "there is a time to die."

It should be noted, though, that the removal of natural hydration and food from a terminal patient to hasten death is specifically proscribed, probably because such withdrawal is considered cruel.[21] According to a text in the *Sefer Hasidim*, however, the removal of food and water is required in two kinds of cases: first, when nutrition or hydration would harm or cause pain to the patient, and second, with a terminal patient where death is imminent. Such a patient must be made comfortable by, for example, the moistening of his lips and mouth, but he must not be fed, lest the process of dying be prolonged and agony be unduly lengthened.[22]

So far, it would appear that passive euthanasia may be permissible and even desirable; for while classical Jewish sources place great value on saving and prolonging human life, they put no premium on needlessly prolonging the act of dying. However, the sources seem uncompromising in the view that active euthanasia, under any circumstances, is a form of suicide or murder and is therefore prohibited. The former chief rabbi of England, Lord Immanuel Jakobovits, in his significant work *Jewish Medical Ethics*, summarizes the Jewish position on euthanasia as follows:

It is clear, then, even when the patient is already known to be on his deathbed and close to the end, any form of active euthanasia is strictly prohibited. In fact, it is condemned as plain murder. In purely legal terms, this is borne out by the ruling that anyone who kills a dying person is liable to the death penalty as a common murderer. At the same time, Jewish law sanctions, and perhaps even demands, the withdrawal of any factor—whether extraneous to the patient himself or not—which may artificially delay his demise in the final phase.[23]

Despite this apparent consensus, a number of contemporary scholars have attempted to discover and to formulate a basis for active euthanasia under certain circumstances. This reevaluation of the sources has been prompted by certain medical and pharmacological developments and by the proliferation of terminal cancer cases owing to the lengthening of the average human life span, as well as by the proliferation of other degenerative diseases such as AIDS.

ACTIVE EUTHANASIA RECONSIDERED

The unanimity of opinion in Jewish tradition that life, even "momentary life," is intrinsically precious makes moot any discussion regarding the quantity of life versus the quality of life. This claim also serves as a foundation for the condemnation of murder and suicide, of killing and self-killing. However, as noted above, exceptions to the prohibition against killing and self-killing were condoned by classical Jewish tradition, such as in cases of martyrdom and "justifiable homicide." These exceptions lead one to conclude that the preservation of life is not always an absolute moral imperative.

There exists in Jewish tradition an alternative view that relates both to cases of martyrdom and to cases of pain and anguish. For example, one Talmudic text maintains that a life of unbearable pain, a life coming to an inevitable and excruciating end, is not a life worth continuing, that such a life is like having no life at all. A Talmudic passage describes a person who is overcome with a severe physical affliction as one "whose life is no life."[24] Similarly, a nineteenth-century commentary on the Mishnah (the early stratum of the Talmud, codified in the third century) observes that "great pain is worse than death." And while "a dying person [*goses*] is like a living person in all respects," the Mishnah in effect "devalued" the monetary worth of a dying person who wished to vow the equivalent of his monetary worth as a donation to the sanctuary.[25] The Mishnah reads, "One at the point of death [*goses*] . . . cannot have his worth vowed, nor be subject to valuation." On this text, the Talmud comments, "It is quite right that one at the point of death cannot have his worth vowed, because he has no monetary value; nor can he be made the subject of a valuation, because he is not fit to be made subject of a valuation."[26] Thus the imperative "Choose life" (Deut. 30:19) is not as absolute as is often assumed.

An Exception for Martyrdom

A further examination of classical Jewish sources related to martyrdom reveals that life in and of itself was not always considered of ultimate value. Such an examination also reveals precedents for taking one's own life or allowing oneself to be killed rather than to endure the physical torture that was frequently a martyr's fate. In such cases, taking one's own life was often not considered suicide. Instances in which martyrs chose accelerated death over prolonged physical suffering may have pertinence to the problem of euthanasia in general, and active euthanasia in particular.

Talmudic literature records many instances of martyrdom. One, noted above, was the case of Rabbi Hanina ben Teradion. Another text describes how four hundred Jewish children drowned themselves at sea to avoid submitting to rape at the hands of Romans. In a medieval commentary on the tale of the children, a reference is made to the case of Hanina ben Teradion. The two cases taken together are interpreted by Jacob Tam as meaning that, to avoid sufferings certain to result in death, it is permitted to take one's own life, that is, to injure oneself by choosing death.

While suicide is proscribed by Jewish law, the prohibition against suicide was clearly set aside in the aforementioned cases of martyrdom. In other sources, suicide was redefined so that killing oneself was not always defined as suicide. One such source is a controversial nineteenth-century responsum by Saul Berlin in which he maintains that a person who takes his or her own life because of mental or physical anguish is not to be considered a suicide. According to Berlin, the earlier prohibitions of suicide were primarily intended for cases where the act resulted from a pessimistic view of life. However, Berlin asserted, a person who takes his or her own life to avoid continued pain and anguish is not to be considered a suicide.[27]

Berlin's responsum and the possibly tenuous analogy between cases of martyrdom and cases of euthanasia, while suggestive, still do not adequately defend an option for active euthanasia within Jewish tradition. It is necessary to look further.

A Rabbinic Precedent

In a late midrash (i.e., an ancient interpretation of Scripture) on Proverbs, the text tells us,

It happened that a woman who had aged considerably appeared before Rabbi Yose ben Halafta. She said: "Rabbi, I am much too old, life has become a burden for me. I can no longer taste food or drink, and I wish to die." Rabbi Yose answered her: "To what do you ascribe your longevity?" She answered that it was her habit to pray in the synagogue every morning, and despite occasional more pressing needs she never had missed a service. Rabbi Yose advised her to refrain from attending services for three consecutive days. She heeded his advice, and on the third day she took ill and died.[28]

This text may be interpreted as a reinforcement of the view that passive euthanasia is permitted by Jewish law under certain conditions. The woman's withholding of her prayers removed the cause of the extension of her life. Similarly, the removal of life-support systems from a patient to whom—as for this woman—life has become a burden would be permissible.[29] Nevertheless, it may be argued that this case underscores the fact that it is not always possible to make a clear-cut distinction between passive and active euthanasia. Her discontinuance of her prayers or a physician's or nurse's "pulling the plug" may be considered a deliberate action aimed at accelerating death. Once the line between passive and active euthanasia becomes so blurred, one may attempt only with great caution to cross the line. For if the woman's withholding of her prayers is a sanctioned action deliberately designed to accelerate her own death, then other actions designed to hasten the death of those to whom life has become an unbearable burden might also be eligible for the sanction of Jewish tradition.

The underlying assumption of this midrashic text is the efficacy of prayer in attaining particular results. Here, the woman effected those results (her own death) by withholding prayer. But what about a case in which one actively prays for death to avoid further pain and suffering? And what about a case in which prayer is aimed at bringing about the death of another in order to end his or her suffering? It would seem to reason that if the rabbis permitted one actively to pray for one's own death and even for the death of another, in order to avoid further pain and suffering, then a basis of an argument could be made for a rabbinic precedent for both voluntary and involuntary active euthanasia. In the Talmud one finds such a precedent:

> On the day that Rabbi Judah was dying, the rabbis deemed a public fast and offered prayers for heavenly mercy [so that he would not die]. . . . Rabbi Judah's handmaid ascended to the roof and prayed: "The immortals [the angels] desire him [to join them] and the mortals desire him [to remain with them]; may it be the will [of God] that the mortals may overpower the immortals [i.e., that he would not die]." When, however, she saw how often he resorted to the privy, painfully removing and replacing his *tefillin* [in terrible agony], she prayed: "May it be the will [of God] that the immortals may overpower the mortals." The rabbis meanwhile continued their prayers for heavenly mercy. She took a jar and threw it down from the roof to the ground. [For a moment,] they stopped praying, and the soul of Rabbi Judah departed.[30]

Some interpret this text to mean that the death of Rabbi Judah was caused by the rabbis' cessation of their prayers when they were startled by the noise of the shattering jar. Others think it means that his death was caused by the handmaiden's active prayer aimed at bringing about death in order to end his suffering. It is in this latter sense that the text was interpreted by the fourteenth-century Talmudic commentator Rabbenu Nissim (Ran): "Sometimes one must request mercy on behalf of the ill so that he might die, as in the case of a patient who is terminal and who is in great pain."[31]

On Praying for Death

The question of whether one may pray for the death of a patient in pain is discussed in a lengthy responsum by the nineteenth-century Turkish rabbi Hayyim Palaggi. In this case, a woman has been suffering for many years with a degenerative terminal disease. She has been afforded the best available medical treatment, and her family has provided constant and loving care. Hope for a remission has been abandoned by the patient, the family, and the attending physicians. Her condition has progressively deteriorated, and her pain has become constant and unbearable. Preferring death to life as a liberation from pain, she has prayed to God to let her die. She has also asked her family to pray for her death, but they have refused. Rabbi Palaggi has been asked whether there are any grounds for prohibiting prayers that she might find rest in death.

In a long and complicated argument, Palaggi ruled that, while family members may not pray for her death, others may do so. In reaching this conclusion, Palaggi quoted a number of earlier sources, including the previously cited statement of Rabbenu Nissim. Thus Palaggi reaffirmed the earlier view that active prayer for the death of a terminal patient in pain, whose life has become a self-burden, is permissible and even desirable. It is noteworthy that Palaggi did not even question the woman's right to pray for death on her own behalf.

Among Palaggi's reasons for refusing the patient's family permission to pray for her death was the possibility that their actions were motivated by less than honorable motives. Palaggi specifically considered the possibility of the patient's spouse wishing her death so he could remarry someone already in mind. Palaggi also reflected on the possibility that the members of the patient's family may have desired her death—consciously or subconsciously—to free themselves from the burden of her care and support. This insightful psychological observation should be considered in cases of involuntary euthanasia, where the patient's family is confronted with the decision whether to hasten the patient's death, either by active or by passive euthanasia. As Palaggi noted, consideration for the patient is the only consideration. The financial or psychological condition of family members must not be the determining factor. The establishment of ethics committees in many hospitals has helped to relieve patients' families of the anguish of such decisions and of the guilt they may feel if they later realize that the decision to accelerate death might have been a product of conscious or subconscious ulterior motives. As Palaggi noted, "strangers" cannot be held under suspicion of ulterior motives.

What is also significant about Palaggi's responsum is the manner in which he dealt with the endemic conflict of principles—preserving life and relieving agony—embodied in any examination of euthanasia from a Jewish perspective. Palaggi attempted to get around this by reframing the question. According to him the question is, To what point is one morally obligated to continue life? By stating the question in this manner, Palaggi found a loophole in the categorical imperative to continue preserving life. He was therefore able to conclude that, in certain instances, such as the one at hand, it is permissible and even desirable to take positive action that will liberate a terminal patient from agony by accelerating his or her death.

To be sure, Palaggi did not explicitly advocate active euthanasia in the sense of performing medical or other intervention other than prayer to accelerate the death of a terminal patient in agony. Nevertheless, he established the viability of an *attitude* that would recommend active euthanasia in particular instances. And, while it was not his intention, Palaggi's view might be extended a step further to serve as the basis for advocating active euthanasia in cases similar to that of the woman described in his responsum.[32]

The Light and the Weighty

A further basis for a possible justification for active euthanasia from classical Jewish sources may be posited by the combining of related precedent with a form of argument characteristic of Jewish legal discourse. The precedent is the Talmudic text in which the term "euthanasia"—an easy, good, or quick death (Hebrew: *mitah yafah*)—occurs. The form of argument is *a fortiori* (Hebrew: *kal va-homer;* literally, "the light and the weighty"). An example of this form of inference would be, "Here is a teetotaler who does not touch cider; he will certainly refuse whiskey." The acceptability of applying this form of argument is stated in the Talmud.[33]

The term *mitah yafah* is used in the course of Talmudic discussion concerning the execution of criminals convicted of capital offenses.

In one text, the verse "You should love your neighbor as yourself" (Lev. 19:18) is interpreted to mean that the criminal is to be given a *mitah yafah:* the pain usually inflicted by the various types of death sentences is to be reduced both in time and in degree by the administration of a pain-killing drug.[34] At this point, one may argue either from one comparable case to another or from the "weighty" to the "light" case.

1. The terminal patient is compared by the Talmud to a criminal condemned to death in that his or her case is hopeless.[35] From this equation one might argue that the terminal patient ought to be given at least the same consideration as a criminal about to be executed for having committed a capital offense.

2. One may also argue that if a criminal, guilty of a capital offense, is shown such consideration, how much more should be shown the terminal patient, innocent of any capital offense.

3. One may extend these lines of argument to a further consideration of how cases of martyrdom, that is, cases of "justified" self-homicide, might be extended to cases of active euthanasia. As noted earlier, some sources maintain that it is permissible in cases of martyrdom to allow oneself to be killed quickly or to take one's own life rather than endure prolonged suffering and anguish. One may maintain that, if such cases of martyrdom are not to be considered suicide or self-homicide, so cases in which a person suffering agony takes his or her own life are similarly not to be condemned as suicide, and that certain cases of accelerating one's own death in order to be free of excruciating pain may be justifiable.

4. Jewish law forbids self-harm. Jewish law further prohibits an individual from intentionally placing himself or herself in a harmful or potentially harmful situation. Yet, even though Jewish legal authorities recognize the potentially hazardous nature of various types of medical, pharmacological, and surgical intervention, they nevertheless sanction such intervention. Therefore, the rule against potential danger may be set aside where such treatment is concerned.

According to some Jewish legal authorities, when conventional therapies have been exhausted, experimental therapy may be introduced by a competent physician. This approach is sanctioned even if death might result from such experimental therapy, especially where a terminal patient is involved. As long as even the most remote possibility of remission exists, hazardous therapy, even life-threatening therapy, may be employed. Using such therapy, even if it is known in advance that it might immediately end the patient's life, would be a form of active euthanasia not prohibited by Jewish law.

The prohibition against placing oneself in danger may also be set aside when a medical or surgical procedure potentially endangers the life of a patient whose life is not clearly endangered by his or her medical condition. Specifically, if the purpose of the procedure is to reduce or eliminate substantial pain, the procedure is permitted, despite its potential threat to the life of the patient. From this perspective, as from that of Palaggi, the imperative to reduce or to eliminate pain is given precedence over the obligation to sustain life at all costs. One may extend this argument to a conclusion that would sanction the administering of pain-killing drugs or procedures, even if it is known in advance that the patient might die as a result. Hence, active euthanasia employed with the specific primary intention of alleviating unbearable pain would be an acceptable moral option.

In this case, as in those previously discussed, an *a fortiori* argument can be made: If administering a pain-killing drug or undertaking a pain-alleviating procedure that may accelerate the patient's death can be done in cases in which death is not imminent, then it should be permissible to do so in cases in which death is certainly imminent. From this basis, one may argue that, where death seems imminent and certain, if there is a choice between prolonging the process of dying and taking action that will alleviate pain but will also accelerate death, then the latter option is both morally viable and legally permissible.

Not only may one make a case for active euthanasia in Jewish law, but one may also argue that in certain circumstances the killer is not to be considered a murderer. To consider an act as murder, according to Jewish law two of the conditions that must be satisfied are premeditation and malice (see Exod. 21:14). Rabbinic literature specifically exonerates a physician who kills his patient, even if he acted with willfulness, when malice is not also present. Though the medieval codes link premeditation with malice, there is no logical or psychological reason to do so. The rabbinic precedent may stand on its own.[36] Thus, under certain circumstances, according to this minority view, the physician may be legally (but not necessarily morally) blameless for practicing active euthanasia.

One specific case in which active euthanasia by patient, agent, or physician may be more justifiable than others, according to some of the literature, would be that in which the terminally ill person has sustained irreparable damage to vital organs. Talmudic law distinguishes between *goses*, one terminally ill, and *tereifah* (literally, "torn"), one with substantial and irreparable vital-organ damage (e.g., as the result of liver cancer, or of an automobile crash). Apparently, in the former case, recovery is at least theoretically possible, whereas in the latter it is altogether impossible. One who kills a *goses* is considered a murderer by the Talmud and the codes. But one who kills a *tereifah* may not be guilty of murder.[37]

So, while the majority view found in classical and contemporary Jewish literature condemns active euthanasia, it is possible to defend a minority view supporting voluntary euthanasia when the primary motive is to alleviate pain and suffering. Indeed, a number of contemporary rabbinic decisions and views affirm this position. For example, David Shohet, writing in *Conservative Judaism* in 1952, concluded after a review of the classical Jewish sources that an adequate defense can be made to "support the contention that to bring a merciful end to intolerable suffering to a patient who has no longer any hope of recovery and whose death is imminent, is an act which may be considered lawful and ethical in Jewish law."[38] . . .

Concluding Observations

Jewish tradition puts a high premium on extending life but recognizes that prolonging the process of painful death is not necessarily desirable. Therefore, the tradition endorses *passive euthanasia* in most cases where death is imminent and inevitable and where the process of dying is accompanied by unbearable anguish. This attitude also relates to the introduction of heroic measures. When death is near and certain and where considerable pain will ensue, such measures are not encouraged; indeed, according to some authorities, they are proscribed.

The dominant view in Jewish sources prohibits *active euthanasia* of any kind. However, in view of contemporary realities I have felt it necessary to defend, within the framework of classical Jewish sources, a position that would justify active euthanasia in certain circumstances.

I believe that in the case of terminally ill persons with no hope of recovery, with irreparable vital-organ damage, who have exhausted all medical remedies, and whose last days are overwhelmed with unbearable agony, the patients, their families, physicians, health-care workers, and social-service professionals should be able to advocate and to practice active euthanasia without feeling that they have transgressed divine and human laws, without being burdened with great guilt for actions that they sincerely consider merciful.

To be sure, Judaism instructs us to "choose life" (Deut. 30:19). But Judaism also recognizes that "there is a time to die" (Eccles. 3:2). Whenever the problem of euthanasia presents itself, each person involved must decide which verse applies and how the principle therein may best be implemented.

8

Rethinking Life and Death:
A New Ethical Approach

Peter Singer

Four hundred years ago our views about our place in the universe underwent a crisis. The ancients used a model of the solar system devised by Ptolemy, according to which the earth was the center of the universe and all the heavenly bodies revolved around it. Even the ancients knew, however, that this model did not work very well. It did not predict the positions of the planets with sufficient accuracy. So it was assumed that, as the planets moved in great circles around the earth, they also moved in smaller circles around their own orbits. This helped to patch up the model, but it didn't fix all the problems, and further adjustments were required. These adjustments were again an improvement but still did not quite get it right.

It would have been possible to add yet another modification to the basic geocentric model—but then Copernicus proposed a radically new approach. He suggested that the planets, including the earth,

Peter Singer is the director of the Centre for Human Bioethics at Monash University in Victoria, Australia, and president of the International Society for Bioethics. Among his books are *Should the Baby Live?* (co-authored with Helga Kuhse) and *Embryo Experimentation.* This essay is reprinted by permission from his book *Rethinking Life and Death: The Collapse of Our Traditional Ethics* (New York: St. Martin's Press; © 1955 by Peter Singer).

revolve around the sun. This terrible new view met stiff resistance, because it required us to give up our cherished idea that we are the center of the universe. It also clashed with the Judeo-Christian view of human beings as the pinnacle of creation. If we are the reason why everything else was made, why do we have such an undistinguished address? The resistance to the Copernican theory was not, however, simply due to human pride, hidebound conservatism, or religious prejudice. The truth is that, in predicting the movements of the planets, Copernicus was not really any more accurate than the latest patched-up version of Ptolemy's old system. For Copernicus too had made a mistake. He clung to the idea that the heavenly bodies move in perfect circles, when really, as Kepler was later to show, the orbits of the planets are slightly elliptical. So there were some who continued to believe in the ancient model of the universe, and looked for better ways of making it fit the facts. The Copernican theory nevertheless triumphed, not because it was more accurate than the old one, but because it was a fresh approach, full of promise.[1]

Like cosmology before Copernicus, the traditional doctrine of the sanctity of human life is today in deep trouble. Its defenders have responded, naturally enough, by trying to patch up the holes that keep appearing in it. They have redefined death so that they can remove beating hearts from warm, breathing bodies and give them to others with better prospects, while telling themselves that they are only taking organs from a corpse. They have drawn a distinction between "ordinary" and "extraordinary" means of treatment, which allows them to persuade themselves that their decision to withdraw a respirator from a person in an irreversible coma has nothing to do with the patient's poor quality of life. They give terminally ill patients huge doses of morphine that they know will shorten their lives, but say that this is not euthanasia, because their declared intention is to relieve pain. They select severely disabled infants for "non-treatment" and make sure that they die, without thinking of themselves as killing them. By denying that an individual human being comes into existence before birth, the more flexible adherents of the sanctity-of-life doctrine are able to put the life, health, and well-being of a woman ahead of that of a fetus. Finally, by putting a taboo on comparisons between intellectually disabled human beings and non-human animals, they have preserved the species boundary as the boundary of the sanctity-of-life ethic, despite overwhelming evidence that the differences between us and other species are differences of degree rather than kind.

The patching could go on, but it is hard to see a long and beneficial future for an ethic as paradoxical, incoherent, and dependent on pretense as our conventional ethic of life and death has become. New medical techniques, decisions in landmark legal cases, and shifts of public opinion are constantly threatening to bring the whole edifice crashing down. All I have done is to draw together and put on display the fatal weaknesses that have become apparent over the last two or three decades. For anyone who thinks clearly about the whole range of questions I have raised, modern medical practice has become incompatible with belief in the equal value of all human life.

It is time for another Copernican revolution. It will be, once again, a revolution against a set of ideas we have inherited from the period in which the intellectual world was dominated by a religious outlook. Because it will change our tendency to see human beings as the center of the *ethical* universe, it will meet with fierce resistance from those who do not want to accept such a blow to our human pride. At first, it will have its own problems, and will need to tread carefully over new ground. For many the ideas will be too shocking to take seriously. Yet eventually the change will come. The traditional view that all human life is sacrosanct is simply not able to cope with the array of issues that we face. The new view will offer a fresh and more promising approach.

REWRITING THE COMMANDMENTS

What will the new ethical outlook be like? I shall take five commandments of the old ethic that we have seen to be false, and show how they need to be rewritten for a new ethical approach to life and death. But I do not want the five new commandments to be taken as something carved in stone. I do not really approve of ethics carved in stone anyway. There may be better ways of remedying the weaknesses of the traditional ethic. The title of this book [*Rethinking Life and Death*] suggests an ongoing activity: we can rethink something more than once. The point is to start, and to do so with a clear understanding of how fundamental our rethinking must be.

First Old Commandment:
Treat all human life as of equal worth.

Hardly anyone really believes that all human life is of equal worth. The rhetoric that flow so easily from the pens and mouths of popes, theologians, ethicists, and some doctors is belied every time these same people accept that we need not go all out to save a severely malformed baby; that we may allow an elderly man with advanced Alzheimer's disease to die from pneumonia, untreated by antibiotics; or that we can withdraw food and water from a patient in a persistent vegetative state. . . . The new approach is able to deal with these situations in the obvious way, without struggling to reconcile them with any lofty claims that all human life is of equal worth, irrespective of its potential for gaining or regaining consciousness.

First New Commandment:
Recognize that the worth of human life varies.

This new commandment allows us frankly to acknowledge . . . that life without consciousness is of no worth at all. We can reach the same view . . . about a life that has no possibility of mental, social, or physical interaction with other human beings. Where life is not one of total or near total deprivation, the new ethic will judge the worth of continued life by taking into account both predictable suffering and possible compensations.

Consistent with the first new commandment, we should treat human beings in accordance with their ethically relevant characteristics. Some of these are inherent in the nature of the being. They include consciousness, the capacity for physical, social, and mental interaction with other beings, having conscious preferences for continued life, and having enjoyable experiences. Other relevant aspects depend on the relationship of the being to others—having relatives, for example, who will grieve over your death, or being so situated in a group that if you are killed, others will fear for their own lives. All of these things make a difference to the regard and respect we should have for a being.

The best argument for the new commandment is the sheer absurdity of the old one. If we were to take seriously the idea that all human life, irrespective of its capacity for consciousness, is equally worthy of our care and support, we would have to root out of medicine not only open quality-of-life judgments, but also the disguised ones. We would then be left trying to do our best to prolong indefinitely the lives of anencephalics, cortically dead infants, and patients in a persistent vegetative state. Ultimately, if we were really honest with ourselves, we would have to try to prolong the lives of those we now classify as dead because their brains have entirely ceased to function. For if human life is of equal worth whether it has the capacity for consciousness or not, why focus on the death of the brain, rather than on the death of the body as a whole?

On the other hand, if we do accept the first new commandment, we overcome the problems that arise for a sanctity-of-life ethic in making decisions about anencephalics, cortically dead infants, patients in a persistent vegetative state, and those who are declared to be brain-dead by current medical criteria. In none of these cases is the really important issue one of how we define death. That question has had so much attention only because we are still trying to live with an ethical and legal framework formed by the old commandment. When we reject that commandment, we will instead focus on ethically relevant characteristics like the capacity for enjoyable experiences, for interacting with others, or for having preferences about continued life. Without consciousness, none of these are possible; therefore, once we are certain that consciousness has been irrevocably lost, it is not ethically relevant that there is still some hormonal brain function, for hormonal brain function without consciousness cannot benefit the patient. Nor can brain-stem function alone benefit a patient, in the absence of a cortex.

So our decisions about how to treat such patients should depend, not on lofty rhetoric about the equal worth of all human life, but on the views of families and partners, who deserve consideration at a time of tragic loss. If a patient in a persistent vegetative state has previously expressed wishes about what should happen to her or him in such circumstances, those wishes should also be taken into account. (We may do this purely out of respect for the wishes of the dead, or we may do it in order to reassure others, still alive, that their wishes will not be ignored.) At the same time, in a public health-care system, we cannot ignore the limits set by the finite nature of our medical resources, nor the needs of others whose lives may be saved by an organ transplant.

Second Old Commandment:
Never intentionally take innocent human life.

The second commandment should be rejected because it is too absolutist to deal with all the circumstances that can arise. We have already seen how far this can be taken, in the Roman Catholic Church's teaching that it is wrong to kill a fetus, *even if that would be the only way to prevent both the pregnant woman and the fetus dying.*) For those who take responsibility for the consequence of their decisions, this doctrine is absurd. It is horrifying to think that in the nineteenth and early twentieth century it was probably responsible for the preventable and agonizing death of an unknown number of women in Roman Catholic hospitals or at the hands of devout Roman Catholic doctors and midwives. This could occur if, for example, the head of the fetus became stuck during labor, and could not be dislodged. Then the only way of saving the woman was to perform an operation known as a craniotomy, which involves inserting a surgical implement through the vagina and crushing the cranium, or skull, of the fetus. If this was not done, the woman and fetus would die in childbirth.

Such an operation is obviously a last resort. Nevertheless, in those difficult circumstances, it seems appalling that any well-intentioned health-care professional could stand by while both woman and fetus died. For an ethic that combines an exceptionless prohibition on taking innocent human life with the doctrine that the fetus is an innocent human being, however, there could be no other course of action. If the Roman Catholic Church had said that performing a craniotomy is permissible, it would have had to give up either the absolute nature of its prohibition on taking innocent human life, or its view that the fetus is an innocent human being. Obviously, it was —and remains—willing to do neither. The teaching still stands. It is only because the development of obstetric techniques now allows the fetus to be dislodged and removed alive that the doctrine is no longer causing women to die pointlessly.

Another circumstance in which the second old commandment needs to be abandoned is—as the British law lords pointed out in deciding the Bland case [Tony Bland lived on life support for four years after his brain cortex was destroyed in a football-game stampede in 1989]—when life is of no benefit to the person living it. But the only modification to the absolute prohibition on taking human life that their lordships felt able to justify in that case—to allow a life to be taken intentionally by withholding or omitting treatment—still leaves the problem of cases in which it is better to use active means to take innocent human life. The law found Dr. Nigel Cox guilty of the attempted murder of Mrs. Lillian Boyes [a 70-year-old woman who for twenty years had suffered greatly from rheumatoid arthritis, which led to abscesses, gangrene, and other complications], despite the fact that she begged for death, and knew that she had nothing ahead of her but a few more hours of agony. Needless to say, no law, no court, and no code of medical ethics would have required Dr. Cox to do everything in his power to prolong Mrs. Boyes's life. Had she suddenly become unable to breathe on her own, for instance, it would have been quite in accordance with the law and the traditional ethical view not to put her on a respirator—or if she was already on one, to take it away.

The very thought of drawing out the kind of suffering that Mrs. Boyes had to endure is repugnant, and would have been regarded as wrong under the traditional ethic as well as the new one. But this only shows how much weight the traditional ethic places on the fine line between ending life by withdrawing treatment, and ending it by a lethal injection. The attitude of the traditional ethic is summed up in the famous couplet:

> *Thou shalt not kill; but need'st not strive*
> *Officiously to keep alive.*

These lines are sometimes uttered in revered tones, as if they were the wisdom of some ancient sage. One doctor, writing in the *Lancet* to defend the non-treatment of infants with spina bifida, referred to the lines as "the old dictum we were taught as medical students."[2] This is ironic, for a glance at the poem from which the couplet comes—Arthur Hugh Clough's "The Latest Decalogue"—leaves no doubt that the intention of this verse, as of each couplet in the poem, is to point out how we have failed to heed the spirit of the original ten commandments. In some of the other couplets, this is unmistakable. For example:

> *No graven images may be*
> *Worshipped, except the currency.*

Clough would therefore have supported an extended view of responsibility. Not killing is not enough. We are also responsible for the consequences of our decision not to strive to keep alive.[3]

Second New Commandment:

Take responsibility for the consequences of your decisions.

Instead of focusing on whether doctors do or do not intend to end their patients' lives, or on whether they end their patients' lives by withdrawing feeding tubes rather than giving lethal injections, the new commandment insists that doctors must ask whether a decision that they foresee will end a patient's life is the right one, all things considered.

By insisting that we are responsible for our omissions as well as for our acts—for what we deliberately don't do, as well as for what we do—we can neatly explain why the doctors were wrong to follow the Roman Catholic teaching when a craniotomy was the only way to prevent the deaths of both mother and fetus. But there is a price to pay for this solution to the dilemma, too: unless our responsibility is limited in some way, the new ethical approach could be extremely demanding. In a world with modern means of communication and transport, in which some people live on the edge of starvation while others enjoy great affluence, there is always something that we could do, somewhere, to keep another sick or malnourished person alive. That all of us living in affluent nations, with disposable incomes far in excess of what is required to meet our needs, should be doing much more to help those in poorer countries achieve a standard of living that can meet their basic needs is a point on which most thoughtful people will agree; but the worrying aspect of this view of responsibility is that there seems to be no limit on how much we must do. If we are as responsible for what we fail to do as for what we do, is it wrong to buy fashionable clothes, or to dine at expensive restaurants, when the money could have saved the life of a stranger dying for want of enough to eat? Is failing to give to aid organizations really a form of killing or as bad as killing?

The new approach need not regard failing to save as equivalent to killing. Without some form of prohibition on killing people, society itself could not survive. Society can survive if people do not save others in need—though it will be a colder, less cohesive society. Normally there is more to fear from people who would kill you than there is from people who would allow you to die. So in everyday life there are good grounds for having a stricter prohibition on killing than on allowing to die. In addition, while we can demand of everyone that he or she refrain from killing people who want to go on living, to demand too much in the way of self-sacrifice in order to provide assistance to strangers is to confront head-on some powerful and near-universal aspects of human nature. Perhaps a viable ethic must allow us to show a moderate degree of partiality for ourselves, our family, and our friends. These are the grains of truth within the misleading view that we are responsible only for what we do, and not for what we fail to do.

To pursue these questions about our responsibility to come to the aid of strangers would take us beyond the scope of this book—but two conclusions are already apparent. First, the distinction between killing and allowing to die is less clear-cut than we commonly think. Rethinking our ethic of life and death may lead us to take more seriously our failure to do enough for those whose lives we could save at no great sacrifice to our own. Second, whatever reasons there may be for preserving at least a part of the traditional distinction between killing and allowing to die—for example, maintaining that it is worse to kill strangers than to fail to give them the food they need to survive—these reasons do not apply when, like Lillian Boyes, a person wants to die, and death would come more swiftly and with less suffering if brought about by an act (for example, giving a lethal injection) than by an omission (for example, waiting until the patient develops an infection, and then not giving antibiotics).

Third Old Commandment:
Never take your own life, and always try to prevent others' taking theirs.

For nearly two thousand years, Christian writers have condemned suicide as a sin. When we should die, said Thomas Aquinas, is God's decision, not ours.[4] That view became so deeply embedded in Christian nations that to attempt suicide was a crime, in some cases punished—ideologues lack a sense of irony—by death. The prohibition on suicide was one element of a general view that the state should enforce morality and act paternalistically towards its citizens.

This view of the proper role of the state was first powerfully challenged by the nineteenth-century British philosopher John Stuart

Mill, who wrote in his classic *On Liberty:* "The only purpose for which power can be rightfully exercised over any member of a civilized community, against his will, is to prevent harm to others. His own good, either physical or moral, is not a sufficient warrant."[5]

Incurably ill people who ask their doctors to help them die at a time of their own choosing are not harming others. (There could be rare exceptions, for example if they have young children who need them; but people who are so ill as to want to die are generally in no position to care adequately for their children.) The state has no grounds for interfering, once it is satisfied that others are not harmed, and the decision is an enduring one that has been freely made, on the basis of relevant information, by a competent adult person. Hence the new version of the third commandment is the direct opposite of the original version.

Third New Commandment:
Respect a person's desire to live or die.

John Locke defined a "person" as a being with reason and reflection that can "consider itself as itself, the same thinking thing in different times and places." This concept of a person is at the center of the third new commandment. Only a person can *want* to go on living, or have plans for the future, because only a person can even understand the possibility of a future existence for herself or himself. This means that to end the lives of people, against their will, is different from ending the lives of beings who are not people. Indeed, strictly speaking, in the case of those who are not people, we cannot talk of ending their lives against or in accordance with their will, because they are not capable of having a will on such a matter. To have a sense of self, and of one's continued existence over time, makes possible an entirely different kind of life. For a person, who can see her life as a whole, the end of life takes on an entirely different significance. Think about how much of what we do is oriented towards the future—our education, our developing personal relationships, our family life, our career paths, our savings, our holiday plans. Because of this, to end a person's life prematurely may render fruitless much of her past striving.

For all these reasons, killing a person against her or his will is a much more serious wrong than killing a being that is not a person. If we want to put this in the language of rights, then it is reasonable to say that only a person has a right to life.[6]

Fourth Old Commandment:
Be fruitful and multiply.

This biblical injunction has been a central feature of Judeo-Christian ethics for thousands of years. The Jewish outlook regarded large families as a blessing. Augustine said that sexual intercourse without procreative intent is a sin, and to try actively to prevent procreation "turns the bridal chamber into a brothel." Luther and Calvin were equally forceful in their encouragement of procreation, with Calvin even referring to Onan's act of "spilling his seed on the ground" as "to kill before he is born the son who was hoped for." As late as 1877, the British government prosecuted Annie Besant and Charles Bradlagh for distributing a book on contraception, and around the same time in America the Comstock law prohibited the mailing or importation of contraceptives. In the twentieth century, until World War II, several European powers, among them France and Germany, continued to have national policies of increasing population in order to be able to support large armies. In some American states, old laws against the use of contraceptives survived until 1965, when the Supreme Court struck them down on the grounds that they were an invasion of privacy.[7]

Restrictions on abortion should be seen against this background view that more people are a good thing. The biblical injunction may have been apt for its time, but with world population having risen from two billion in 1930 to over five billion today, and projected to go to eleven billion by the middle of the next century, it is unethical to encourage more births. It may seem that in developed countries with low population densities, like Australia, Canada, or the United States, there is ample room for a much larger population; but all nations put their wastes down the same atmospheric and oceanic sinks, and the average Australian or North American uses several times his or her share of these sinks.

If this situation continues, it will either mean that people in developing countries cannot achieve a life-style like ours, with similar outputs of carbon dioxide and other wastes; or, if they do, then each of us will share responsibility for global warming that will speed up the melting of the polar icecaps, and so lead to a rise in sea levels. This will cause devastating floods in low-lying coastal areas, including the delta areas of Bangladesh and Egypt where forty-six million people live. Entire island nations like Tuvalu, the Marshall Islands, and the Maldives could disappear beneath the waves.[8] Global warming may also mean devastating droughts in areas that now feed millions. Irrespective of how few people there may be per square kilometer, additional people living in developed countries add to the strain we are placing on the ecosystems of our planet.

The new version of the fourth commandment therefore takes a different perspective.

Fourth New Commandment:

Bring children into the world only if they are wanted.

What do the original and new versions of the fourth commandment have to do with the questions discussed in this book? The two versions underpin very different views of how we should treat human life before a person comes into existence.

Consider, for example, an embryo in a laboratory. The crucial characteristic that makes it wrong to kill such an embryo, some would say, is that it has the potential to become a person, with all the characteristics that mature humans usually possess, including a degree of rationality and self-awareness that will far surpass that of a rat or a fish. But the fact that the embryo could become a person does not mean that the embryo is now capable of being harmed. The embryo does not have, and never has had, any wants or desires, so we cannot harm it by doing something contrary to its desires. Nor can we cause it to suffer. In other words, the embryo is not, now, the kind of being that can be harmed, any more than the egg is before fertilization. In the absence of any meaningful sense in which the embryo can be harmed, the argument from potential seems to presuppose that it is good to promote the existence of new human beings. Otherwise, why would the fact that the embryo has a certain potential require us to realize that potential?

There are (or soon will be) as many people on this planet as it can reasonably be expected to support. If it is not wrong to kill an embryo because of the wrong it does to an existing being, then the fact that killing it will mean that one fewer person comes into existence does not make it wrong either. Those who use the potential of the embryo as an argument against abortion are rather like Calvin, who, as we saw, objected to Onan's practice of spilling his seed on the ground because this killed "the son who was hoped for." Suppose that we really were hoping for a son. Suppose, too, that if we did not conceive a son now, then it would become impossible for us to conceive one at all. Then Calvin's objection would be sound. But if we are not hoping for another son, then the argument will pass us by.

Fifth Old Commandment:
Treat all human life as always more precious than any non-human life.
The fifth and last of the traditional commandments that make up the sanctity-of-life ethic is so deeply embedded in the Western mind that even to compare human and non-human animals is to risk causing offense. At the time of the controversy over the Reagan administration's "Baby Doe" rules, I wrote a commentary on the issue for *Pediatrics,* the journal of the American Academy of Pediatrics. My commentary contained this sentence: "If we compare a severely defective human infant with a non-human animal, a dog or a pig, for example, we will often find the non-human to have superior capacities, both actual and potential, for rationality, self-consciousness, communication, and anything else that can plausibly be considered morally significant."

The editor received more than fifty letters protesting against my views in this commentary, several condemning the editor for allowing it to be published. Many of the correspondents protested particularly against the comparison of the intellectual ability of a human being and a dog or a pig. Yet the sentence that so disturbed them is not only true, but *obviously* true.[9]

Opposition to comparisons between humans and animals has been even stronger in Germany. In 1989 an organization called "Lebenshilfe" invited me to speak at a European symposium on "Bioengineering, Ethics, and Disability." Lebenshilfe is the major German organization for parents of intellectually disabled infants. When my invitation became more widely known, a number of groups began to campaign against my participation, citing passages from my book *Practical Ethics* (which had been translated into German) as evidence for the fact that I held views so shocking that they ought not even to be discussed. Among the passages often cited during this campaign was one similar to the sentence just quoted from my *Pediatrics* article. Astonishingly, the campaign succeeded: Lebenshilfe withdrew its invitation to me, only a few days before the symposium was due to open. Then, when that was not enough to appease the protesters, Lebenshilfe canceled the entire symposium. Evidently shaken by these events, the following year Lebenshilfe adopted a set of "Ethical Foundational Statements" that included the following: "The uniqueness of human life forbids any comparison—or, more specifically, equation —of human existence with other living beings, with their forms of life or interests."[10]

This prohibition is simply a last-ditch defense of the human-centered view of the universe that, as we saw, was severely battered by Copernicus and Galileo, and to which Darwin gave what ought to have been its final blow. We like to think of ourselves as the darlings of the universe. We do not like to think of ourselves as a species of animal. But the truth is that there is no unbridgeable gulf between us. Instead there is an overlap. The more intellectually sophisticated non-human animals have a mental and emotional life that in every significant respect equals or surpasses that of some of the most profoundly intellectually disabled human beings. This is not my subjective value judgment. It is a statement of fact that can be tested and verified over and over again. Only human arrogance can prevent us from seeing it.

Fifth New Commandment:
Do not discriminate on the basis of species.

Some people will be happy to accept the previous four new commandments but will have doubts about this one, because they associate the rejection of a bias in favor of our own species with an extreme form of species-egalitarianism that treats every living thing as of equal worth.[11] Obviously, since the new ethical outlook I have been defending rejects even the view that all *human* lives are of equal worth, I am not going to hold that *all* life is of equal worth, irrespective of its quality or characteristics.

These two claims—the rejection of speciesism, and the rejection of *any* difference in the value of different living things—are quite distinct. Belief in the equal value of all life suggests that it is as wrong to uproot a cabbage as it would be to shoot dead the next person who rings your doorbell. We can reject speciesism, however, and still find many good reasons for holding that there is nothing wrong with pulling up a cabbage, while shooting the next person to ring your doorbell is utterly dreadful. For example, we can point out that cabbages lack the kind of nervous system and brain associated with consciousness, and so are not capable of experiencing anything. To uproot the cabbage therefore does not frustrate its conscious preferences for continuing to live, deprive it of enjoyable experiences, bring grief to its relatives, nor cause alarm to others who fear that they too may be uprooted. To shoot the next person to ring your doorbell is likely to do all of these things.

In listing the possible reasons why it is wrong to shoot the next person to ring your doorbell, I never mentioned species. Perhaps a flying saucer has just landed in your front garden, and a friendly alien has rung the bell. If the alien is capable of having conscious preferences for continuing to live, that is a reason for not killing it. The same applies if the living alien will have enjoyable experiences, or if the alien has relatives who will grieve for its death, or other companions who will fear that they too may now be shot. So the four possible reasons I mentioned for regarding it as wrong to kill the person ringing your doorbell will apply to the alien just as they would apply to the girl from next door who wants to retrieve her ball. The rejection of speciesism implies only that the *species* of the doorbell ringer is irrelevant.

Why isn't species a legitimate reason? For essentially the same reason as we now exclude race or sex. The racist, sexist, and speciesist are all saying that the boundary of my group also marks a difference of value. If you are a member of my group, you are more valuable than if you are not—no matter what other characteristics you may lack. Each of these positions is a form of group protectiveness, or group selfishness. Throughout human history, we have broadened the circle of those whose interests we take into account, from the tribe to the nation, from the nation to the race, and from the race to the species. We now take for granted the inadequacy of having made the circle narrower than our entire species; but we do not notice that the circle remains an arbitrarily exclusionary one. It still leaves beings outside who are very like us in morally important respects.

For instance, in the very respects that British judges have recently said are relevant to deciding whether there is a duty to preserve life, some non-human animals are more like normal humans than are some seriously damaged members of our own species. Dogs are conscious beings. They can feel pain, and they evidently enjoy many aspects of their lives. In that respect they are like you and me, and unlike Tony Bland after the tragedy at the Hillsborough Stadium. Or to take another example: If the ability to interact with others is an essential part of what it is to be us, then a normal chimpanzee is more like us than was Baby C, who was described by the Court of Appeal as "permanently unable to interact mentally, socially and physically."

Many people will want to cling to the superior status of the *human* being. We are so used to talk of *human* rights, *human* dignity, and the infinite value of *human* life, that we will not easily abandon the idea that to be *human* is in itself to be very special. In part, the problem is that the very word "human" is not a purely descriptive term. It can mean simply a member of the species *Homo sapiens,* but it can also have built into it the very qualities that we think make human beings special. This is the sense listed by the *Oxford English Dictionary* as "having or showing the qualities or attributes proper to or distinctive of man." As an illustration of this usage, the dictionary offers the following quotation from Harriet Martineau's *Society in America,* published in 1837: "Every prison visitor has been conscious, on first conversing privately with a criminal, of a feeling of surprise at finding him so human."

Clearly there would be no surprise at finding the prisoner to be a member of the species *Homo sapiens!* Martineau meant, and her readers will immediately have understood, that she was referring to the discovery that criminals have wants, feelings, desires, and other characteristics very like our own. Henry Longfellow put the two senses of the word together in one line from his popular poem "The Song of Hiawatha": "Every human heart is human."[12]

Pedantic as it may be to correct a poetic utterance, the ethical significance of distinguishing between the two senses could be put by saying that *not* every human heart is human, whereas some nonhuman hearts *are* human. The heart of the anencephalic Baby Valentina [born in Sicily in 1992] was the heart of a member of the species *Homo sapiens,* but, no matter how long Valentina had lived, her heart would never have beaten faster when her mother came into the room, because Valentina could never feel emotions of love or concern for anyone. The heart of the gorilla Koko, on the other hand, is not the heart of a member of the species *Homo sapiens,* but it is a heart capable of relating to others, and of showing love and concern for them. In the second sense of the term "human," Koko's heart is more human than Valentina's.

If, as I hope, this lengthy discussion has put to rest possible doubts about the new fifth commandment, it remains only to say what its implications are for the issues discussed in this book. Because membership of the species *Homo sapiens* is not ethically relevant, any characteristic or combination of characteristics that we regard as giving human beings a right to life, or as making it generally wrong to end a human life, may be possessed by some non-human animals. If they are, then we must grant those non-human animals the same right to life as we grant to human beings, or consider it as seriously wrong to end the lives of those non-human animals as we consider it wrong to end the life of a human being with the same characteristic or combination of characteristics. Likewise, we cannot justifiably give more protection to the life of a human being than we give to a non-human animal if the human being clearly ranks lower on any possible scale of relevant characteristics than the animal. Baby Valentina clearly ranks lower on any possible scale of relevant characteristics than Koko. Yet as the law now stands, a surgeon could kill Koko in order to take her heart and transplant it into a human being, while to take Valentina's heart would have been murder. In terms of the revised ethical outlook, that is wrong.

The right to life is not a right of members of the species *Homo sapiens;* it is—as we saw in discussing the third new commandment —a right that properly belongs to persons. Not all members of the species *Homo sapiens* are persons, and not all persons are members of the species *Homo sapiens*.

SOME ANSWERS FROM THE NEW ETHIC

All we have so far is a rough sketch of how the five crumbling pillars of the old ethic might be replaced with solid new material, better able to support a structure that will guide our decisions about life and death into the next century. More thought and discussion are needed to develop these broad proposals into a working ethic. But we have to keep living in the house we are rebuilding. We cannot move out during the renovations, because decisions about life and death need to be made all the time. We cannot live without an ethic, and we cannot buy a new one ready-made. So despite the preliminary nature of our sketch of the new ethic, it is not premature to see what answers it gives to some of the issues I have discussed.

Brain Death, Anencephaly, a Persistent Vegetative State

The decision to regard people as dead whose brains have irreversibly ceased to function is an ethical judgment. To cease to support the bodily functions of such people is normally a justifiable ethical decision, in accordance with the first and fifth new commandments, for the most significant ethically relevant characteristic of human beings whose brains have irreversibly ceased to function is not that they are members of our species, but that they have no prospect of regaining consciousness. Without consciousness, continued life cannot benefit them. There may, of course, be other issues: the need for the family to have time to adjust to a tragic loss, the preservation of organs that could save the lives of others, and occasionally . . . a pregnancy. Exactly the same holds for patients in a persistent vegetative state, once we can be certain that there is no possibility of restoring consciousness. It holds, too—apart from the impossibility of pregnancy—for anencephalics and cortically dead infants.

This does not mean that the decision to end the life of an irreversibly unconscious patient is simple or automatic. The considerations of family feelings are both subtle and important, particularly if the patient is an infant or young person, and the loss of consciousness was unexpected. But the new approach does make the decision more manageable. There are some situations in which all the considerations point in the same direction. . . . When the parents of an anencephalic baby would like their child to be used as a source of organs to save the life of another infant, the fact that the anencephalic baby is alive should not stop us from doing the obvious thing: taking the heart from the baby who cannot benefit from continued life, and giving it to the one who can. . . .

Abortion and the Brain-dead Pregnant Woman

The first, fourth, and fifth new commandments have implications for the abortion controversy. What ethically relevant characteristics does the fetus have? The fact that it is a member of the species *Homo sapiens* does not answer this question. The argument from the potential of the embryo has already been examined and found wanting. In terms of the actual capacities of the fetus, there is little to suggest that it would be wrong to end its life. Probably at some point in its development in the womb the fetus does become conscious. This may happen around the tenth week of gestation, when brain activity can first be detected. Even then, brain-wave activity measurable by an EEG does not become continuous until the thirty-second week, so it may be that the fetus is only intermittently conscious until that stage, which is well past the date when it becomes viable.[13]

Suppose, though, that the fetus is capable of feeling pain at the earliest possible date, ten weeks. Is the capacity to feel pain a sufficient reason to grant a being a right to life? If we think that it is, we will have to grant the same right to (at least) every normal vertebrate animal, since there is more evidence for brain activity and a capacity to feel pain even in vertebrates with relatively small brains, like frogs and fish, than there is in the fetus at ten weeks of gestation. If we balk at so radical a change in our attitudes to non-human animals, we shall have to hold that the fetus may be killed for relatively trivial reasons, like those that we now consider justify us in killing rats (say, to test new food colorings) or fish (because some people prefer tuna to tofu).

An intermediate position would be that we may kill both fetuses and non-human animals at a similar level of awareness, if we can do so in a way that does not cause pain or distress, or if, despite the fact that some pain or distress is caused, the need to kill the fetus or non-human animal is sufficiently serious to outweigh the pain or distress caused. This would mean that we would have to stop the routine product-safety tests now carried out on rats and other animals, because these cause the animals to become ill, and often to die in considerable distress, and the products generally do not serve any need that could not be served by an existing product. (It may not be a popular comparison to make, but rats are indisputably more aware of their surroundings, and more able to respond in purposeful and complex ways to things they like or dislike, than a fetus at ten or even at thirty-two weeks' gestation.) Fishing, too, would have to stop, except when practiced by those who have no other way of getting enough to eat. Most commercially caught fish die slowly of suffocation, as they lie gasping in the air. Recreational anglers inflict pain and distress by inducing fish to bite on a barbed metal hook. In the case of abortion, whether pain and distress is caused to the fetus would depend not only on how developed the fetus is, but also on the method used. This intermediate position would allow unrestricted early abortions, and would not entirely exclude late abortions, if a method of abortion that killed the fetus painlessly were used, or if the reason for the abortion were sufficiently serious to outweigh the pain that might be caused.

It follows that there are no grounds for opposing abortion before the fetus is conscious, and only very tenuous grounds for opposing it at any stage of pregnancy. In fact, since a woman's reasons for having an abortion are invariably far more serious than the reasons most people in developed countries have for eating fish rather than tofu, and there is no reason to think that a fish suffers less when dying in a net than a fetus suffers during an abortion, the argument for not eating fish is much stronger than the argument against abortion that can be derived from the possible consciousness of the fetus after ten weeks. What has been said here of fish would also be true, in different ways, of the commercially reared and killed animals we commonly eat—apart from any ethically relevant characteristics that animals like cows and pigs may have in addition to their capacity to suffer. So while one may consistently be an ethical vegetarian and still accept even late abortions, those who oppose late abortions on the grounds of fetal distress will need to be ethical vegetarians if their position is to be consistent and non-speciesist.

Resolving the issue of abortion in this way has direct implications for the dilemma of the brain-dead woman who is pregnant. Since neither the actual characteristics of the fetus, nor its potential, is a reason for keeping it alive, such women can normally be allowed to become dead in every sense. The only ground for not doing so would be the strong desire of the father of the child, or of other close relatives of the pregnant woman, that the child should live. The issue then ceases to be one of a life-or-death decision for the fetus, and becomes a question of whether the medical resources required should be used to satisfy this desire rather than others.

Infants

In the modern era of liberal abortion laws, most of those not opposed to abortion have drawn a sharp line at birth. If, as I have argued, that line does not mark a sudden change in the status of the fetus, then there appear to be only two possibilities: oppose abortion, or allow infanticide. I have already given reasons why the fetus is not the kind of being whose life must be protected in the way that the life of a person should be. Although the fetus may, after a certain point, be capable of feeling pain, there is no basis for thinking it rational or self-aware, let alone capable of seeing itself as existing in different times and places. But the same can be said of the newborn infant. Human babies are not born self-aware, or capable of grasping that they exist over time. They are not persons. Hence their lives would seem to be no more worthy of protection than the life of a fetus.

Must we accept this shocking conclusion? Or does birth somehow make a difference, in some way that has so far been overlooked? Perhaps our focus on the status of the fetus and the infant has led us to neglect other aspects of the situation. Here are two ways in which birth may make a difference, not so much to the fetus/infant and its claim to life, but to others who are affected by it.

First, after birth the pregnant woman is no longer pregnant. The baby is outside her body. Thus her claim to control her own body and her own reproductive system is no longer enough to determine the life or death of the newborn baby. This right in itself was never enough to resolve the abortion issue. Still, that does not mean that it was without any weight at all, and so the fact that at birth it no longer applies will make some difference in how we think of the newborn infant.

The second difference birth makes is that if the baby's mother does not want to keep her child, it can be cared for by someone else who does. This reason for preserving infant life is strong in a society in which there are more couples wanting to adopt a baby than there are babies needing adoption. It is no reason at all for preserving infant life if there are babies in need of adoption, and no one willing to adopt them. The coming of effective contraception and of safe legal abortion has moved most developed nations sharply into the former status (though not, unfortunately, if we focus on babies with major disabilities, whom very few couples are willing to adopt). In these societies there is an important reason to protect the lives of babies, even those unwanted by their parents. In other societies that have difficulty coping with unwanted children and so have traditionally accepted infanticide, this is not a reason for preserving infant life.

So birth does make a difference to the status of the infant. But the difference is one of degree, and it remains true that the new approach, drawing on the third new commandment and the idea of a person on which that commandment is based, will not consider the newborn infant entitled to the same degree of protection as a person. There are other issues at stake as well. . . . The future prospects of life may be so bleak that it is kinder to the baby, both now and in the future, to "treat it to die." That decision must depend crucially on the wishes of the parents. Their desire to keep and cherish the child can make an enormous difference to its prospects; conversely, the quality of life of a child abandoned to an institution, without loving parents, can be much less acceptable. The views of the parents, as the people most closely concerned with the infant, should also be given great weight simply because of the effects, both good and bad, that the continued life of their child will have on them and any other children they may have. In general, therefore, decisions about the future of severely disabled newborn infants should be made, not by judges who will have nothing to do with the child after their judgment is delivered, but by the parents, in consultation with their doctor.[14]

It must be extraordinarily difficult to cut oneself off from one's own child, and prefer it to die, so that another child with better prospects can be born. Yet many women think like this when they discover that they are pregnant with an abnormal child. There was broad public support for Sherri Finkbane's efforts to abort a fetus after she had taken thalidomide during pregnancy [after being refused an abortion in several states in the mid-sixties, this American woman obtained one in Sweden; the fetus proved to be deformed]. Today, prenatal diagnosis is routine for older women, who are more at risk of having a baby with Down syndrome. It is premised on the assumption that if the test shows a fetus with Down syndrome or other abnormalities, an abortion will follow. When the pregnancy was a wanted one, the couple will usually then try to conceive another child.

In our culture, it is only before the baby is born that we openly accept this idea of saying no to a new life that does not have good prospects. But many other cultures say no shortly after birth as well. Kung women who give birth when they still have a child too young to walk probably do not find it easy to go to the bushes and smother the newborn infant, but doing this does not prevent them from being loving mothers to the children that they do choose to bring up. Japanese mothers are renowned for their devotion to their children, and this was compatible with the tradition of "mabiki," or "thinning" of infants. Japanese midwives who attended births did not assume that the baby was to live; instead they always asked if the baby was "to be left" or "to be returned" to wherever it was thought to have come from. Needless to say, in Japan as in all these cultures, a baby born with an obvious disability would almost always be "returned."[15]

The official Western reaction to these practices is that they are shocking examples of the barbaric standards of non-Christian morality. I do not share this view. My dissent has nothing to do with cultural relativism. Some non-Western practices—for example, female circumcision—are wrong and should, if possible, be stopped. But, in the case of infanticide, it is our culture that has something to learn from others, especially now that we, like them, are in a situation where we must limit family size. I do not mean, of course, that infanticide should become a means of limiting family size. Contraception is obviously the best way to do this, since there is no point in going through an unwanted pregnancy and birth; and, for the same reason, abortion is much better than infanticide. But, for reasons we have already discussed, in regarding a newborn infant as not having the same right to life as a person, the cultures that practiced infanticide were on solid ground. . . .

. . . The seriousness of taking life increases gradually, parallel with the gradual development of the child's capacities that culminate in its life as a full person. On this view, birth marks the beginning of the next stage of development, but important changes continue to happen in the weeks and months after birth as well. These changes are not only in the capacities of the baby, but also in the attachment of the parents and the acceptance of the infant into the family and the wider moral community. Many cultures have a ceremony to mark this acceptance. In ancient Greece, the infant could only be exposed on the mountainside before it had been named. (Christening may be a relic of such ceremonies.)

All of this may help to show that the ethical approach towards newborn infants proposed here is consonant with some strands of our thought about the wrongness of killing, although certainly not with all of them. Neither the first nor the second new commandment condemns Molly Pearson and her husband, or the parents of Baby Doe, for wanting their newborn Down-syndrome infants to die. There is no sharp ethical distinction between what they did [both sets of parents instructed the hospital to let the newborn die], and what most pregnant women do when they are offered an abortion because the fetus they are carrying has Down syndrome. In both cases, the decision is not primarily the concern of the state, nor of the doctors—it chiefly concerns the family into which the baby is born.

There remains, however, the problem of the lack of any clear boundary between the newborn infant, who is clearly not a person in the ethically relevant sense, and the young child, who is. In our book, Should the Baby Live?, my colleague Helga Kuhse and I suggested that a period of twenty-eight days after birth might be allowed before an infant is accepted as having the same right to life as others. This is clearly well before the infant could have a sense of its own existence over time, and would allow a couple to decide that it is better not to continue with a life that has begun very badly.

The boundary is, admittedly, an arbitrary one, and this makes it problematic. We accept other arbitrary boundaries based on age, like eligibility for voting or for holding a driving license—but a right to life is a more serious matter. Could we return to a view of infants more like that of ancient Greece, in which a public ceremony a short time after birth marked not only the parents' decision to accept the child but also society's conferral on it of the status of a person? The strongest argument for treating infants as having a right to life from the moment of birth is simply that no other line has the visibility and self-evidence required to mark the beginning of a socially recognized right to life. This is a powerful consideration; maybe in the end it is even enough to tilt the balance against a change in the law in this area. On that I remain unsure.[16]

Persons and the Right to Life

The third new commandment recognizes that every person has a right to life. We have seen that the basic reason for taking this view derives from what it is to be a person, a being with awareness of her or his own existence over time, and the capacity to have wants and plans for the future. There is also a powerful social and political reason for protecting the lives of those who are capable of fearing their own death. Universal acceptance and secure protection of the right to life of every person is the most important good that a society can bestow upon its members. Without it there is, as the seventeenth-century English philosopher Thomas Hobbes said, "continual fear and danger of violent death, and the life of man solitary, poor, nasty, brutish, and short."[17] Only a being able to see herself as existing over time can fear death and can know that, if people may be killed with impunity, her own life could be in jeopardy. Neither infants nor those non-human animals incapable of seeing themselves as existing over time can fear their own deaths (although they may be frightened by threatening or unfamiliar circumstances, as a fish in a net may be frightened). It is reasonable to regard more seriously crimes that cause fear in others, and threaten the peaceful coexistence on which society depends. This provides another reason for recognizing that every person has a right to life, or in other words, that it is a greater wrong to take the life of a person than to take the life of any other being.

A right is something one can choose to exercise or not to exercise. I have a right to a percentage of the money my publisher earns by selling this book, because I wrote it and then made an agreement with my publisher for it to be published on this basis. But I can waive this right, if I wish to do so. I could pass the royalties on to an overseas aid organization, or to the next homeless person I meet, or even tell my publisher to keep them. Similarly, the most important aspect of having a right to life is that one can choose whether or not to invoke it. We value the protection given by a right to life only when we want to go on living. No one can fear being killed at his or her own persistent, informed, and autonomous request. On the contrary, the evidence shows that many people approaching the end of their lives fear suffering much more than death. Hence the very argument that so powerfully supports recognition and protection of every person's right to life also supports the right to medical assistance in dying when this is in accordance with a person's persistent, informed, and autonomous request.

The right to medical assistance in dying has been accepted as legitimate in the Netherlands, and those who want to exercise it in other countries are increasingly finding ways around existing laws. But respect for a person's right to live or die also suggests that, where a person is capable of expressing a view about continuing to live, life-sustaining treatment should not be withdrawn without the patient's consent. The second new commandment indicates that doctors cannot take refuge in the idea that in withdrawing treatment, they are only "letting nature take its course." On the contrary, they are responsible for the decision taken, which was to let the patient die rather than to postpone death.

THE BASIS OF THE NEW APPROACH

The new approach to life-and-death decisions is very different from the old one. But it is important to realize that the ethics of decision-making about life and death are only one part of ethics, important as they are. In particular, before leaving the sketch of the new ethic I have drawn, I want to emphasize that to deny that a being has a right to life is not to put it altogether outside the sphere of moral concern. A being that is not a person does not have the same interest in continuing to live into the future that a person usually has, but it will still have interests in not suffering, and in experiencing pleasure from the satisfaction of its wants. Since neither a newborn human infant nor a fish is a person, the wrongness of killing such beings is not as great as the wrongness of killing a person. But this does not mean that we should disregard the needs of an infant to be fed, and kept warm and comfortable and free of pain, for as long as it lives. Except where life is at stake, these needs should be given the weight they would be given if they were the needs of an older person. The same is true, with the necessary changes for its different needs, of the fish. Fish can surely feel pain. Their pain matters just as much, in so far as rough comparisons can be made, as similar pains experienced by a person. We do both infants and fish wrong if we cause them pain or allow them to suffer, unless to do so is the only way of preventing greater suffering.

Even when these limits to the scope of the changes I propose are understood, many will be skeptical about the need for so great a change in our ethics. There is a common view that reason and argument play no role in ethics, and therefore we have no need to defend our ethical views when they are challenged. Some people are more ready to reason about the merits of football players or chocolate cake recipes than they are about their belief in the sanctity of human life. This is a force for conservatism in ethics. It allows people to listen to a criticism of their own views, and then say: "Oh yes, well, that is your opinion, but I think differently"—as if that is the end of the discussion. I hope I have shown that it is not so easy to ignore the fact that our standard view of the ethics of life and death is incoherent.

As we have just seen, the differences between the old and the new approach arise from just five key ethical commandments. In fact, the case for a drastic change in the old ethic is even simpler and more rationally compelling than that. Just as changing one or two lines of a complex computer program can completely alter the image that appears on your screen, so changing two central assumptions is enough to bring about a complete transformation of the old ethic. The first of these assumptions is that we are responsible for what we intentionally do in a way that we are not responsible for what we deliberately fail to prevent. The second is that the lives of all and only members of our species are more worthy of protection than the lives of any other being. These are the assumptions behind the second and fifth of the commandments that we discussed earlier.

Each of these assumptions has a religious origin. The roots of the first lie in the Judeo-Christian idea of the moral law as set down in simple rules that allow for no exceptions, and the second springs from the same tradition's idea that God created man in his own image, granted him dominion over the other animals, and bestowed an immortal soul on human beings alone of all creatures. Taken independently of their religious origins, both of the crucial assumptions are on very weak ground. Can doctors who remove the feeding tubes from patients in a persistent vegetative state really believe that there is a huge gulf between this, and giving the same patients an injection that will stop their hearts beating? Doctors may be trained in such a way that it is psychologically easier for them to do the one and not the other, but both are equally certain ways of bringing about the death of the patient. As for the second assumption, what I have already said should be sufficient to show that it is not rationally defensible.

If we did nothing to the old ethic apart from abandoning these two assumptions, we would still have to construct an entirely new ethic. We could construct it differently from the ethic I have sketched out. We could, for instance, insist that, just as it is always wrong intentionally to take human life, so it is always wrong deliberately to refrain from saving human life. This would be a consistent position, but not an attractive one. It would force us to do whatever we could to keep people alive, whether they wanted to be kept alive or not, and irrespective of whether they could ever recover consciousness. That would surely be a pointless and often cruel exercise of our medical powers. There would be other, even more far-reaching but on the whole much more desirable consequences for our responsibilities towards those in other countries who need food and other forms of aid that we can spare. In a similar manner, having abandoned the distinction between humans and non-human animals, we could refuse to adopt a distinction between persons and those who are not persons, and instead insist that every living thing or, perhaps more plausibly, every being capable of experiencing pleasure or pain, has an equal right to life.

So a new ethical approach can take many different forms. But without its two crucial but shaky assumptions, the old ethic cannot survive. The question is not whether it will be replaced, but what the shape of its successor will be.

9

Death With Dignity
and the Sanctity of Life

Leon R. Kass

Call no man happy until he is dead." With these deliberately
paradoxical words, the ancient Athenian sage Solon reminds
the self-satisfied Croesus of the perils of fortune and the need to see
the end of a life before pronouncing on its happiness. Even the
richest man on earth has little control over his own fate. The un-
predictability of human life is an old story; many a once-flourishing
life has ended in years of debility, dependence, and disgrace. But
today, it seems, the problems of the ends of lives are more acute, a
consequence, ironically, of successful—or partly successful—human
efforts to do battle with fortune and, in particular, to roll back
medically the causes of death. While many look forward to further
triumphs in the war against mortality, others here and now want to
exercise greater control over the end of life, by electing death to avoid
the burdens of lingering on. The failures resulting from the fight

Leon R. Kass, a medical doctor, teaches in the Committee on Social
Thought and at The College of the University of Chicago. He has written
and lectured widely on questions of biomedical ethics. Among his books are
Toward a More Natural Science: Biology and Human Affairs and *The Hungry Soul.*
This essay is reprinted by permission from *Commentary* 89, no. 3 (March
1990; all rights reserved).

against fate are to be resolved by taking fate still further into our own hands.

This is no joking matter. Nor are the questions it raises academic. They emerge, insistently and urgently, from poignant human situations, occurring daily in hospitals and nursing homes, as patients and families and physicians are compelled to decide matters of life and death, often in the face of only unattractive, even horrible, alternatives. Shall I allow doctors to put a feeding tube into my 85-year-old mother, who is unable to swallow as a result of a stroke? Now that it is inserted and she is not recovering, may I have it removed? When would it be right to remove a respirator, forgo renal dialysis, bypass lifesaving surgery, or omit giving antibiotics for pneumonia? When in the course of my own progressive dementia will it be right for my children to put me into a home or for me to ask my doctor or my wife or my daughter for a lethal injection? When, if ever, should I as a physician or husband or son accede to—or be forgiven for acceding to—such a request?

These dilemmas can be multiplied indefinitely, and their human significance is hard to capture in words. For one thing, posing them as well-defined problems to be solved abstracts from the full human picture, and ignores such matters as the relations between the generations, the meaning of old age, attitudes toward mortality, religious faith, and economic resources. Also, speech does not begin to convey the anguish and heartache felt by those who concretely confront such terrible decisions, nor can it do much to aid and comfort them. No amount of philosophizing is going to substitute for discernment, compassion, courage, sobriety, tact, thoughtfulness, or prudence, all needed on the spot.

Yet the attitudes, sentiments, and judgments of human agents on the spot are influenced, often unwittingly, by speech and opinion, and by the terms in which we formulate our concerns. Some speech may illuminate, other speech may distort; some terms may be more or less appropriate to the matter at hand. About death and dying, once subjects treated with decorous or superstitious silence, there is today an abundance of talk—not to say indecorous chatter. Moreover, this talk frequently proceeds under the aegis of certain increasingly accepted terminologies, which are, in my view, both questionable in themselves and dangerous in their influence. As a result, we are producing a recipe for disaster: urgent difficulties, great human anguish, and high emotions, stirred up with inadequate thinking. We have no choice but to reflect on our speech and our terminologies.

The Language of Rights and Duties

Let me illustrate the power—and possible mischief—of one notion currently in vogue: the notion of rights. It is now fashionable, in many aspects of public life, to demand what one wants or needs as a matter of rights. How to do the right thing gets translated into a right to get or do your own thing. Thus, roughly two decades ago, faced with the unwelcome fact of excessive medical efforts to forestall death, people asserted and won a right to refuse life-prolonging treatment found to be useless or burdensome. This was, in fact, a reaffirmation of the right to life, liberty, and the pursuit of happiness, even in the face of imminent death. It enabled dying patients to live as they wished, free from unwelcome intrusions, and to let death come when it would.

Today, the demand has been raised: we find people asserting a "right to die," grounded not in objective conditions regarding prognosis or the uselessness of treatment but in the supremacy of choice itself. In the name of choice, people claim the right to choose to cease to be choosing beings. From such a right to refuse not only treatment but life itself—from a right to become dead—it is then a small step to the right to be *made* dead: from my right to die will follow your duty to assist me in dying, i.e., to become the agent of my death, if I am not able, or do not wish, to kill myself. And, thanks to our egalitarian tendencies, it will continue to be an easy step to extend all these rights even to those who are incapable of claiming or exercising them for themselves, with proxies empowered to exercise a right to demand death for the comatose.[1] No one bothers very much about where these putative rights come from or what makes them right, and simple reflection will show that many of them are incoherent.

Comparable mischief can, of course, be done beginning with the notion of duty. From the acknowledged human duty not to shed innocent blood follows the public duty to protect life against those who would threaten it. This gets extended to a duty to preserve life in the face of disease or other non-human dangers to life. This gets extended to a duty to prolong life whenever possible, regardless of the condition of that life or the wishes of its bearer. This gets extended to an unconditional duty never to let death happen, if it is in one's power to do so. This position, sometimes alleged—I think mistakenly —to be entailed by belief in the "sanctity of life," could even make obligatory a search for the conquest of death altogether, through research on aging. Do we have such duties? On what do they rest? And can such a duty to prevent death—or a right to life—be squared with a right to be made dead? Is not this intransigent language of rights and duties unsuitable for finding the best course of action, in these terribly ambiguous and weighty matters? We must try to become more thoughtful about the terms we use and the questions we pose.

"Dignity" and "Sanctity": Not Either/Or

Toward this end I wish to explore here the relation between two other powerful notions, both prominent in the discussions regarding the end of life: death with dignity, and the sanctity of life. Both convey elevated, indeed lofty, ideas: what, after all, could be higher than human dignity, unless it were something sacred? As a result, each phrase often functions as a slogan or a rallying cry, though seldom with any regard for its meaning or ground. In the current debates about euthanasia, we are often told that these notions pull in opposite directions. Upholding death with dignity might mean taking actions that would seem to deny the sanctity of life. Conversely, unswervingly upholding the sanctity of life might mean denying to some a dignified death. This implied opposition is, for many of us, very disquieting. The dilemmas themselves are bad enough. Much worse is it to contemplate that human dignity and sanctity might be opposed, and that we may be forced to choose between them.[2]

The confrontation between upholders of death with dignity and upholders of the sanctity of life is nothing new. Two decades ago, the contest was over termination of treatment and letting die. Today and tomorrow, the issue is and will be assisted suicide, mercy killing, so-called active euthanasia. On the extremes stand the same opponents, many of whom—I think mistakenly—think the issues are the same. Many who now oppose mercy killing or voluntary euthanasia then opposed termination of treatment, thinking it equivalent to killing. Those who today back mercy killing in fact agree: if it is permissible to choose death by letting die, they argue, why not also by active steps to hasten, humanely, the desired death? Failing to distinguish between letting die and making dead (by failing to distinguish between intentions and deeds, causes and results, goals and outcomes), both sides polarize the debate, opposing not only one another but also those in the uncomfortable middle. It is *either* sanctity of life *or* death with dignity: one must choose.

I do not accept this polarization. Indeed, in the rest of this essay I mean to suggest the following. First, human dignity and the sanctity of life not only are compatible but, if rightly understood, go hand in hand. Second, death with dignity, rightly understood, has largely to do with exercising the humanity that life makes possible, often to the very end, and very little to do with medical procedures or the causes of death. Third, the sanctity-and-dignity of life is entirely compatible with letting die but not with deliberately killing. Finally, the practice of euthanasia will not promote human dignity, and our rush to embrace it will in fact only accelerate the various tendencies in our society that undermine not only dignified conduct but even decent human relations.

THE SANCTITY OF LIFE AND HUMAN DIGNITY

What exactly is meant by the sanctity of life? This turns out to be difficult to say. In the strictest sense, sanctity of life would mean that life is *in itself* something holy or sacred, transcendent, set apart—like God himself. Or, again, focusing on our responses to the sacred, it would mean that life is something before which we stand (or should stand) with reverence, awe, and grave respect—because it is beyond us and unfathomable. In more modest but also more practical terms, to regard life as sacred means that it should not be opposed, violated, or destroyed, and, positively, that it should be protected, defended, and preserved. Despite their differences, these various formulations agree on this: that "sacredness," whatever it is, inheres in life itself, and that life, *by its very being,* calls forth an appropriate human response, whether veneration or restraint. To say that sacredness is something that can be conferred or ascribed—or removed—by solely human agreement or decision is to miss the point entirely.

I have made a modest and so far unsuccessful effort to trace the origin of the sanctity-of-life doctrine to our own Judeo-Christian traditions. To the best of my knowledge, the phrase "sanctity of life" does not occur either in the Hebrew Bible or in the New Testament. Life as such is not said to be holy (qâdosh), as is, for example, the Sabbath. The Jewish people are said to be a holy people, and they are enjoined to be holy as God is holy. True, traditional Judaism places great emphasis on preserving human life—even the holy Sabbath may be violated to save a life, implying to some that a human life is more to be revered than the Sabbath—yet the duty to preserve one's life is not unconditional: to cite only one example, a Jew should accept martyrdom rather than commit idolatry, adultery, or murder.

Why Is Murder Wrong?

As murder is the most direct assault on human life and the most explicit denial of its sanctity, perhaps we gain some access to the meaning of the sanctity of life by thinking about why murder is proscribed. If we could uncover the ground of restraint against murder, perhaps we could learn something of the nature of the sanctity of human life, and, perhaps, of its relation to human dignity. As a result, we might be in a better position to consider the propriety of letting die, of euthanasia, and of other activities advocated by the adherents of "death with dignity."

Why is killing another human being wrong? Can the prospective victim's request to be killed nullify the wrongness of such killing, or, what is more, make such killing right? Alternatively, are there specifiable states or conditions of a human being's life that would justify—or excuse—someone else's directly and intentionally making him dead, even *without* request? The first question asks about murder, the second and third ask whether assisting suicide and mercy killing (so-called active euthanasia) can and should be morally distinguished from murder. The answers regarding assisting suicide and euthanasia will depend on the answer regarding murder, that is, on the *reasons* why it is wrong.[3]

Why is murder wrong? The laws against murder are, of course, socially useful. Though murders still occur, despite the proscriptive law and the threat of punishment, civil society is possible only because people generally accept and abide by the reasonableness of this rule. In exchange for society's protection of one's own life against those who might otherwise take it away, each member of society sacrifices, in principle, his (natural) right to the lives of all others. Civil society requires peace, and civil peace depends absolutely on the widespread adherence to the maxim, "Thou shalt not murder." This usefulness of the taboo against murder is sometimes offered as the basis of its goodness: killing is bad because it makes life unsafe and society impossible.

But this alone cannot account for the taboo against murder. In fact, the goodness of civil society is itself predicated upon the goodness of human life, which society is instituted to defend and foster. Civil society exists to defend the goods implicit in the taboo against murder, at least as much as the taboo against murder is useful in preserving civil society.

However valuable any life may be to society, each life is primarily and preeminently valued by the person whose life it is. Individuals strive to stay alive, both consciously and unconsciously. The living body, quite on its own, bends every effort to maintain its living existence. The built-in impulses toward self-preservation and individual well-being that penetrate our consciousness—say, as hunger or fear of death—are manifestations of a deep-seated and powerful will-to-live. These thoughts might suggest that murder is wrong because it opposes this will-to-live, because it deprives another of life against his will, because it kills someone who does not *want* to die. This sort of reason would explain why suicide—self-willed self-killing—might be right, while murder—killing an innocent person against his will—would always be wrong.

Is Consent an Excuse?

Let us consider this view more closely. Certainly, there are some invasions or "violations" of another's body that are made innocent by consent. Blows struck in a boxing match or on the football field do not constitute assault; conversely, an unwelcome kiss by a stranger, because it is unconsented touching, constitutes a battery, actionable at law. In these cases, the willingness or unwillingness of the "victim" alone determines the rightness or wrongness of the bodily blows.

Similar arguments are today used to explain the wrongness of rape: it is "against our wills," a violation not (as we once thought) of womanliness or chastity or nature but of freedom, autonomy, personal self-determination. If consent excuses—or even justifies—these "attacks" on the body of another, might not consent excuse—or justify—the ultimate, i.e., lethal, attack, turning murder into mere (unwrongful) homicide? A person can be murdered only if he personally does not want to be dead.

There is something obviously troublesome about this way of thinking about crimes against persons. Indeed, the most abominable practices, proscribed in virtually all societies, are *not* excused by consent. Incest, even between consenting adults, is still incest; cannibalism would not become merely *delicatessen* if the victim freely gave permission; ownership of human beings, voluntarily accepted, would still be slavery. The violation of the other is independent of the state of the will (in fact, both of victim and of perpetrator).

The question can be put this way: Is the life of another human being to be respected only because that person (or society) *deems* or *wills* it respectable, or is it to be respected because it *is in itself* respectable? If the former, then human worth depends solely on agreement or human will; since will confers dignity, will can take it away, and a permission to violate nullifies the violation. If the latter, then one can never be freed from the obligation to respect human life by a request to do so, say, from someone who no longer values his own life.

This latter view squares best with our intuitions. We are not entitled to dismember the corpse of a suicide, nor may we kill innocently those consumed by self-hatred. According to our law, killing the willing, killing the unwilling, and killing the non-willing (e.g., infants, the comatose) are all equally murder. Beneath the human will, indeed, the *ground* of human will, is something that commands respect and restraint, willy-nilly. We are to abstain from killing because of something respectable about human beings as such. But what is it?

In Western societies, moral notions trace back to biblical religion. The bedrock of Jewish and Christian morality is the Ten Commandments. "Thou shalt not murder"—the Sixth Commandment—heads up the so-called second table, which enunciates (negatively) duties toward one's fellow man. From this fact, some people have argued that murder is wrong solely because God said so. After all, that he had to legislate against it might imply that human beings on their own did not know that it was bad or wrong. And even if they were to intuit *that* murder is wrong, they might never be able to answer, if challenged, *why* it is wrong; this human inability to supply the reason would threaten the power of the taboo. Thus, so the argument goes, God's will supplies the missing reason for the human rule.

This argument is not satisfactory. True, divine authority elevates the standing and force of the commandments. But it does not follow that they "make sense" only because God willed them. Pagans yesterday believed and atheists today still believe that murder is wrong. In fact, the entire second table of the Decalogue is said to propound not so much divine law but natural law, law suited for man as man, not only for Jew or Christian.

The Bible itself provides evidence in support of this interpretation, at least about murder. In its report of the first murder, committed by Cain upon his brother Abel before there was any given or known law against it, Abel's blood is said to cry out from the earth in protest against his brother's deed. (The crime, it seems, was a crime against blood and life, not against will, human or divine.) And Cain's denial of knowledge ("Am I my brother's keeper?") seems a clear indication of guilt: if there were nothing wrong with murder, why hide one's responsibility? A "proto-religious" dread accompanies the encounter with death, especially violent death.

But the best evidence comes shortly afterward, in the story of the covenant with Noah: the first law against murder is explicitly promulgated for all mankind united, well before there are Jews or Christians or Muslims. This passage is worth looking at in some detail because, unlike the enunciation of the Sixth Commandment, it offers a specific reason why murder is wrong.[4]

After the Flood: A New Order

The prohibition of murder is part of the new order following the Flood. Before the Flood, human beings lived in the absence of law and civil society. The result appears to be something like what Hobbes called the state of nature, characterized as a condition of war of each against all. Might alone makes right, and no one is safe. The Flood washes out human life in its natural state; immediately after the Flood, some form of law and justice is instituted, and nascent civil society is founded.

At the forefront of the new order is a newly articulated respect for human life,[5] expressed in the announcement of the punishment for homicide: "Whoso sheddeth man's blood, by man shall his blood be shed; for in the image of God made he man" (Gen. 9:6). Like the law in general, this cardinal law combines speech and force. The threat of capital punishment stands as a deterrent to murder and hence provides a motive for obedience. But the measure of the punishment is instructive. By equating a life for a life—*no more* than a life for a life, and the life only of the murderer, not also of his wife and children—the threatened punishment implicitly teaches the equal worth of each human life. Such equality can be grounded only in the equal humanity of each human being. Against our own native self-preference, and against our tendency to overvalue what is our own, blood-for-blood conveys the message of universality and equality.

But we are not to refrain from murder only to avoid the punishment. That may be a reason, one that speaks to our fears; but there is also a reason that speaks to our minds and our loftier sentiments. The fundamental reason why murder is wrong—the reason that even justifies punishing it homicidally!—is man's divine-like status.[6] Not the other fellow's unwillingness to be killed, not even (or only) our desire to avoid sharing his fate, but *his*—any man's—*very being* requires that we respect his life. Human life is to be respected more than animal life, because man is more than an animal: man is said to be god-like. Please note that the truth of the Bible's assertion does not rest on biblical authority. Man's more-than-animal status is in fact performatively proved whenever human beings quit the state of nature and set up life under such a law. The law that establishes that men are to be law-abiding both insists on, and thereby demonstrates the truth of, the superiority of man.

How is man God-like? Genesis 1—where it is first said that man is created in God's image—introduces us to the divine *activities* and *powers:* (1) God speaks, commands, names, and blesses; (2) God makes and makes freely; (3) God looks at and beholds the world; (4) God is concerned with the goodness or perfection of things; (5) God addresses solicitously other living creatures. In short: God exercises speech and reason, freedom in doing and making, and the powers of contemplation, judgment, and care.

Doubters may wonder whether this is truly the case about God—after all, it is only on biblical authority that we regard God as possessing these powers and activities. But it is certain that we human beings have them, and that they lift us above the plane of a merely animal existence. Human beings, alone among earthly creatures, can think about the whole, marvel at its articulated order, and feel awe in beholding its grandeur and in pondering the mystery of its source.

A complementary, preeminently moral gloss on the "image of God" is provided—quite explicitly—in Genesis 3, at the end of the so-called second creation story: "Now the man is become *like one of us,* knowing good and bad . . ." (3:22; emphasis added).[7] Human beings, unlike the other animals, distinguish good and bad, have opinions and care about their difference, and constitute their whole life in the light of this distinction. Animals may suffer good and bad, but they have no notion of either. Indeed, the very pronouncement "Murder is bad" constitutes proof of *this* god-like quality of human beings.

In sum, man has special standing because he shares in reason, freedom, judgment, and moral concern, and, as a result, lives a life freighted with moral self-consciousness. Speech and freedom are used, among other things, to promulgate moral rules and to pass moral judgments, first among which is that murder is to be punished in kind because it violates the dignity of such a moral being. We note a crucial implication. To put it simply: the *sanctity* of life rests absolutely on the *dignity*—the god-like-ness—of human beings.

God's Image: Tied to Blood

Yet man is, at most, only god*ly;* he is not God or a god. To be an image is also to be *different* from that of which one is an image. Man is, at most, a mere likeness of God. With us, the seemingly godly powers and concerns described above occur conjoined with our animality. We are also flesh and blood—no less than the other animals. God's image is tied to blood, which is the life.

The point is crucial, and stands apart from the text that teaches it: everything high about human life—thinking, judging, loving, willing, acting—depends absolutely on everything low—metabolism, digestion, respiration, circulation, excretion. In the case of human beings, "divinity" needs blood—or "mere" life—to sustain itself. And because of what it holds up, human blood—that is, human life—deserves special respect, beyond what is owed to life as such: the low ceases to be the low. (Modern physiological evidence could be adduced in support of this thesis: in human beings, posture, gestalt, respiration, sexuality, and fetal and infant development, among other things, all show the marks of the co-presence of rationality.) The biblical text elegantly mirrors this truth about its subject, subtly merging high and low: though the reason given for punishing murder is man's *godliness,* the injunction itself concerns man's *blood.* Respect the god-like; do not shed its blood! Respect for anything human requires respecting *everything* human, requires respecting *human being* as such.

We have found, I believe, what we were searching for: a reason immanent in the nature of things for finding fault with taking human life, apart from the needs of society or the will of the victim. The wanton spilling of human blood is a violation and a desecration, not only of our laws and wills but of being itself. We have also found the ground for repudiating the opposition between the sanctity of life and human dignity. Each rests on the other. Or, rather, they are mutually implicated, as inseparable as the concave and the convex. Those who seek to pull them apart are, I submit, also engaged in wanton, albeit intellectual, violence.

Human Dignity and Blood-Shedding

Unfortunately, the matter cannot simply rest here. Though the principle seems well established, there is a difficulty, raised by the text itself. How can one assert the inviolability of human life and, in the same breath, insist that human beings deliberately *take* human life to punish those who shed human blood?[8] There are, it seems, sometimes good reasons for shedding human blood, even though man is in God's image. We have admitted the dangerous principle: humanity, to uphold the dignity of the human, must sometimes shed human blood.

Bringing this new principle to the case of euthanasia, we face the following challenge to the prior and more fundamental principle, shed no human blood: What are we to think when the continuing circulation of human blood no longer holds up anything very high, when it holds up little more—or even *no* more—than metabolism, digestion, respiration, circulation, and excretion? What if human godliness appears to be humiliated by the degradation of Alzheimer's disease or paraplegia or rampant malignancy? And what if it is the well-considered aspiration of the "god-like" to put an end to the humiliation of that very godliness, to halt the mockery that various severe debilities make of a *human* life? Are there here to be found other exceptions to our rule against murder, exceptions in which the dignity of a human life can (only!) be respected by ending it?

The first thing to observe, of course, is that the cases of euthanasia (or suicide) and capital punishment are vastly different. One cannot by an act of euthanasia deter or correct or obtain justice from the "violator" of human dignity; senility and terminal illness are of natural origin and cannot be blamed on any human agent. To be precise, these evils may in their result undermine human dignity, but, lacking malevolent intention, cannot be said to insult it or deny it. They are reasons for sadness, not in*dign*ation, unless one believes, as the tyrant does, that the cosmos owes him good and not evil and exists to satisfy his every wish. Moreover, one does not come to the defense of diminished human dignity by finishing the job, by annihilating the victims. Human dignity would be no more vindicated by euthanizing patients with Alzheimer's disease than it would be by executing as polluted the victims of rape.

Nevertheless, the question persists, and an affirmative answer remains the point of departure for the active euthanasia movement. Many who fly the banner of "death with dignity" insist that it centrally includes the option of active euthanasia, especially when requested. In order to respond more adequately to this challenge, we need first a more careful inquiry into "death with dignity."

DEATH WITH DIGNITY: AN EXERCISE OF HUMANITY

The phrase "death with dignity," whatever it means precisely, certainly implies that there more and less dignified ways to die. The demand for death with dignity arises only because more and more people are encountering in others and fearing for themselves or their loved ones death of the less dignified sort. This point is indisputable. The possibility of dying with dignity can be diminished or undermined by many things; for example, by coma or senility or madness, by unbearable

pain or extensive paralysis, by isolation, by institutionalization or desti-
tution, by sudden death, as well as by excessive or impersonal medical
interventions directed toward the postponement of death. It is the
impediments connected with modern medicine that increasingly
arouse indignation, and the demand for death with dignity pleads for
the removal of these "unwanted" obstacles.

More generally, the demand for autonomy and the cry for dignity
are asserted against a medicalization and institutionalization of the end
of life that robs the old and the incurable of most of their autonomy
and dignity: intubated and electrified, with bizarre mechanical companions, confined and immobile, helpless and regimented, once proud
and independent people find themselves cast in the roles of passive,
obedient children. Death with dignity means, in the first instance, the
removal of these added indignities and dehumanizations of the end
of life.

One can only sympathize with this concern. Yet even if successful,
efforts to remove these obstacles would not yet produce a death with
dignity. For one thing, not all obstacles to dignity are artificial and
externally imposed. Infirmity and incompetence, dementia and im-
mobility—all of them of natural origins—greatly limit human possibility, and for many of us they will be sooner or later unavoidable, the
products of inevitable bodily or mental decay. Second, there is nothing
of human dignity in the process of dying itself—only in the way we
face it: at its best, death with complete dignity will always be compromised by the extinction of dignified humanity. It is, I suspect, a
death-denying culture's anger about dying and mortality that expresses
itself in the partly oxymoronic and unreasonable demand for dignity
in death. Third, insofar as we seek better health and longer life, insofar
as we turn to doctors to help us get better, we necessarily and voluntarily compromise our dignity: being a patient rather than an agent is,
humanly speaking, undignified. All people, especially the old, accept
a whole stable of indignities simply by seeking medical assistance. The
really proud people refuse altogether to submit to doctors and hospitals. It is well to be reminded of these limits on our ability to roll back
the indignities that assault the dying, so that we might acquire more
realistic expectations about just how much dignity a "death-with-
dignity" campaign can provide.

A death with positive dignity—which may turn out to be something rare, like a life with dignity—entails more than the absence of external indignities. Dignity in the face of death cannot be given or conferred from the outside but requires a dignity of soul in the human being who faces it. To understand the meaning of and prospects for death with dignity, we need first to think more about dignity itself, what it is.

Defining Dignity

Dignity is, to begin with, an undemocratic idea. The central notion, etymologically, both in English and in its Latin root *(dignitas),* is that of worthiness, elevation, honor, nobility, height—in short, of excellence or virtue. In all its meanings it is a term of distinction; dignity is not something that, like a nose or a navel, is to be expected or found in every living human being. Dignity is, in principle, aristocratic.

It follows that dignity, thus understood, cannot be demanded or claimed; for it cannot be provided and it is not owed. One has no more right to dignity—and hence to dignity in death—than one has to beauty or courage or wisdom, desirable though these all may be.

One can, of course, seek to democratize the principle; one can argue that "excellence," "being worthy," is a property of all human beings, say, in comparison with animals or plants, or with machines. This, I take it, is what is often meant by *"human* dignity." This is also what is implied when one asserts that much of the terminal treatment of dying patients is dehumanizing, or that attachments to catheters, respirators, and suction tubes hide the human countenance and thereby insult the dignity of the dying. I myself earlier argued that the special dignity of the human species, thus understood, is the ground of the sanctity of human life. Yet on further examination I have come to think that this universal attribution of dignity to human beings pays tribute more to human potentiality, to the *possibilities* for human excellence. *Full* dignity, or dignity properly so-called, would depend on the *realization* of these possibilities.

There would still be, on any such material principle, distinctions to be made among human beings. If universal human dignity is grounded, for example, in the moral life, in that everyone faces and makes moral choices, dignity would seem to depend mainly on having a *good* moral life, that is, on choosing well. Is there not more dignity in the courageous than in the cowardly, in the moderate than in the self-indulgent, in the righteous than in the wicked?[9] But courage, moderation, righteousness, and the other human virtues are not confined to the few. Many of us strive for them, with partial success, and still more of us do ourselves honor when we recognize and honor those people nobler and finer than ourselves. With proper models, proper rearing, and proper encouragement, many of us can be and act more in accord with our higher natures. In these ways, the openness to dignity can perhaps be democratized still further.

In truth, if we know how to look, we find evidence of human dignity all around us, in the valiant efforts ordinary people make to meet necessity, to combat adversity and disappointment, to provide for their children, to care for their parents, to help their neighbors, to serve their country. Life provides numerous hard occasions that call for endurance and equanimity, generosity and kindness, courage and self-command. Adversity sometimes brings out the best in a person, and often shows best what he is made of. Confronting our own death —or the deaths of our beloved ones—provides an opportunity for great and small alike to exercise our humanity. Death with dignity, in its most important sense, would mean a dignified attitude and virtuous conduct in the face of death.

Defining Dignity in Death

What would such a dignified facing of death require? First of all, it would require knowing that one is dying. One cannot attempt to settle accounts, make arrangements, complete projects, keep promises, or say farewell if one does not know the score. Second, it requires that one remain to some degree an agent rather than (just) a patient. One cannot make a good end to one's life if one is buffeted about by forces beyond one's control, if one is denied a decisive share in decisions about medical treatments, institutionalization, and the way to spend one's remaining time. Third, it requires the upkeep—as much as possible—of one's familial, social, and professional relationships and activities. One cannot function as an actor if one has been swept off the stage and abandoned by the rest of the cast. It would also seem to require some direct, self-conscious confrontation, in the loneliness of one's soul, with the brute fact and meaning of nearing one's end.

Even, or especially, as he must be passive to the forces of decay, the dignified human being can preserve and reaffirm his humanity by seeing clearly and without illusion.[10] (It is for this reason, among others, that sudden and unexpected death, however painless, robs a person of the opportunity to have a dignified end.)

But as a dignified human life is not just a lonely project against an inevitable death but a life whose meaning is entwined in human relationships, we must stress again the importance for a death with dignity—as for a life with dignity—of dignified human intercourse with all those around us. Who we are to ourselves is largely inseparable from who we are to and for others; thus, our own exercise of dignified humanity will depend crucially on continuing to receive respectful treatment from others. The manner in which we are addressed, what is said to us or in our presence, how our bodies are attended or our feelings regarded—in all these ways, our dignity in dying can be nourished and sustained. Dying people are all too easily reduced ahead of time to "thinghood" by those who cannot bear to deal with the suffering or disability of those they love. Objectification and detachment are understandable defenses. Yet this withdrawal of contact, affection, and care is probably the greatest single cause of the dehumanization of dying. Death with dignity requires absolutely that the survivors treat the human being at all times as if full god-like-ness remains, right up to the very end.

It will, I hope, now be perfectly clear that death with dignity, understood as living dignifiedly in the face of death, is not a matter of pulling plugs or taking poison. To speak this way—and it is unfortunately common to speak this way[11]—is to shrink still further the notion of human dignity, and thus heap still greater indignity upon the dying, beyond all the insults of illness and the medicalized bureaucratization of the end of life. If it really is death with dignity we are after, we must think in human and not technical terms. With these thoughts firmly in mind, we can turn in closing back to the matter of euthanasia.

EUTHANASIA AND HUMAN DIGNITY

Having followed the argument to this point, even a friendly reader might chide me as follows: "Well and good to think humanistically, but tough practical dilemmas arise, precisely about the use of techniques, and they must be addressed. Not everyone is so fortunate as to be able to die at home, in the company of a loving family, beyond the long reach of the medical-industrial complex. How should these technical decisions—about respirators and antibiotics and feeding tubes and, yes, even poison—be made, precisely in order to uphold human dignity and the sanctity of life that you say are so intermingled?" A fair question: I offer the following outline of an answer.

About treatment for the actually dying, there is in principle no difficulty. In my book *Toward a More Natural Science,* I have argued for the primacy of easing pain and suffering, along with using supportive and comforting speech, and, more to the point, the need to draw back from some efforts at prolongation of life that prolong or increase only the patient's pain, discomfort, and suffering. Although I am mindful of the dangers and aware of the impossibility of writing explicit rules for ceasing treatment—hence the need for prudence —considerations of the individual's health, activity, and state of mind must enter into decisions of *whether* and *how vigorously* to treat if the decision is indeed to be for the patient's good. Ceasing treatment and allowing death to occur when (and if) it will can, under some circumstances, be quite compatible with the respect that life itself commands for itself. For life can be revered not only in its preservation but also in the manner in which we allow a given life to reach its terminus.

What about so-called active euthanasia, the direct making dead of someone who is not yet dying or not dying "fast enough"? Elsewhere I have argued at great length against the practice of euthanasia *by physicians,* partly on the grounds of bad social consequences, but mainly on the grounds that killing patients—even those who ask for death—violates the inner meaning of the art of healing.[12] [See "Why Doctors Must Not Kill," elsewhere in this volume.] Powerful prudential arguments—unanswerable, in my view—have been advanced as to why legalized mercy killing would be a disastrous social policy, at least for the United States. But some will insist that social policy cannot remain deaf to cries for human dignity, and that dangers must be run to preserve a dignified death through euthanasia, at least where it is requested. As our theme here is dignity and sanctity, I will confine my answer to the question of euthanasia and human dignity.

Choosing Death Freely

Let us begin with voluntary euthanasia—the request for assistance in dying. To repeat: the claim here is that the choice for death, because a free act, affirms the dignity of free will against dumb necessity. Or, using my earlier formulation, is it not precisely dignified for the "god-like" to put a voluntary end to the humiliation of that very godliness?

In response, let me start with the following questions. Do the people who are actually contemplating euthanasia *for themselves*—as opposed to their proxies who lead the euthanasia movement—generally put their requests in these terms? Or are they not rather looking for a way to end their troubles and pains? One can sympathize with such a motive, out of compassion, but can one admire it, out of respect? Is it really *dignified* to seek escape from troubles for oneself? Is there, to repeat, not more dignity in courage than in absence?

Euthanasia for one's own dignity is, at best, paradoxical, even self-contradictory: how can I honor myself by making myself nothing? Even if dignity were to consist solely in autonomy, is it not an embarrassment to claim that autonomy reaches its zenith precisely as it disappears? Voluntary euthanasia, in the name of *positive* dignity, does not make sense.

Acknowledging the paradox, some will still argue the cause of freedom on a more narrow ground: the process of euthanasia increases human freedom by increasing options. It is, of course, a long theoretical question whether human freedom is best understood—and best served—through the increase of possibilities. But as a practical matter, in the *present* case, I am certain that this view is mistaken. On the contrary, the opening up of this "option" of assisted suicide will greatly constrain human choice. For the choice for death is not one option among many, but an option to end all options. Socially, there will be great pressure on the aged and the vulnerable to exercise this option. Once there looms the legal alternative of euthanasia, it will burden every decision made by any seriously ill elderly person—not to speak of his or her more powerful caretakers—even without the subtle hints and pressures applied by others.

And, thinking about others, is it dignified to ask or demand that someone else become my killer? It may be sad that one is unable to end one's own life, but can it conduce to either party's dignity to make the request? Consider its double meaning if made to a son or daughter: Do you love me so little as to force me to live on? Do you love me so little as to want me dead? What person in full possession of his own dignity would inflict such a duty on anyone he loved?

Of course, the whole thing could be made impersonal. No requests to family members, only to physicians. But precisely the same point applies: how can one demand care and humanity from one's physician and, at the same time, demand that he play the role of technical dispenser of death? To turn the matter over to non-physicians—that is, to technically competent professional euthanizers—is, of course, to dehumanize the matter completely.[13]

Proponents of euthanasia do not understand human dignity, which, at best, they confuse with humaneness. One of their favorite arguments proves this point. Why, they say, do we put animals out of their misery but insist on compelling fellow human beings to suffer to the bitter end? Why, if it is not a contradiction for the veterinarian, does the medical ethic absolutely rule out mercy killing? Is this not simply inhumane?

Perhaps inhumane, but not thereby inhuman. On the contrary, it is precisely because animals are not human that we must treat them (merely) humanely. We put dumb animals to sleep because they do not know that they are dying, because they can make nothing of their misery or mortality, and, therefore, because they cannot live deliberately—i.e., humanly—in the face of their own suffering or dying. They cannot live out a fitting end. Compassion for their weakness and dumbness is our only appropriate emotion, and given our responsibility for their care and well-being, we do the only humane thing we can. But when a conscious human being asks us for death, by that very action he displays the presence of something that precludes our regarding him as a dumb animal. Humanity is owed humanity, not humaneness. Humanity is owed the bolstering of the human, even or especially in its dying moments, in resistance to the temptation to ignore its presence at the scene of suffering.

Courage in Dying

What humanity needs most in the face of evils is courage, the ability to stand against fear and pain and thoughts of nothingness. The deaths we most admire are those of people who, knowing that they are dying, face the fact frontally and act accordingly: they set their affairs in order, they arrange what could be final meetings with their loved ones, and yet, with strength of soul and a small reservoir of hope, they continue to live and work and love as much as they can for as long as they can. Because such conclusions of life require courage, they call for our encouragement—and for the many small speeches and deeds that shore up the human spirit against despair and defeat.

And what of non-voluntary euthanasia, for those too disabled to request it for themselves—the comatose, the senile, the psychotic: can this be said to be in the service of *their* human dignity? If dignity is, as the autonomy people say, tied crucially to consciousness and will, then non-voluntary or "proxy-voluntary" euthanasia can never be a dignified act for the one euthanized. Indeed, it is precisely the absence of dignified humanity that invites the thought of active euthanasia in the first place.

Is it really true that such people are beneath all human dignity? I suppose it depends on the particulars. Many people in greatly reduced states still retain clear, even if partial, participation in human relations. They may respond to kind words or familiar music; they may keep up pride in their appearance or in achievements of the grandchildren; they may take pleasure in reminiscences or simply in having someone who cares enough to be present; conversely, they may be irritated or hurt or sad, even appropriately so; and, even nearer bottom, they may be able to return a smile or glance in response to a drink of water or a change of bedding or a bath. Because we really do not know their inner life—what they feel and understand—we run the risk of robbing them of opportunities for dignity by treating them as if they had none. It does not follow from the fact that *we* would never willingly trade places with them that *they* have *nothing* left worth respecting.

But what, finally, about the very bottom of the line, say, people in a "persistent vegetative state," unresponsive, contorted, with no evident ability to interact with the environment? What human dignity remains here? Why should we not treat such human beings as we (properly) treat dumb animals, and put them out of "their misery"?[14]

I grant that one faces here the hardest case for the argument I am advancing. Yet one probably cannot be absolutely sure, even here,

about the complete absence of inner life or awareness of their surroundings. In some cases, admittedly extremely rare, persons recover
from profound coma (even with flat EEG); and they sometimes report
having had partial yet vivid awareness of what was said and done to
them, though they had given no external evidence of that. But beyond
any restraint owing to ignorance, I would also myself be restrained by
the human form, by *human blood,* and by what I owe to the full human
life that this particular instance of humanity once lived. I would gladly
stand aside and let die, say in the advent of pneumonia; I would do
little beyond the minimum to sustain life; but I would not countenance the giving of lethal injections or the taking of other actions
deliberately intending the patient's death. Between only undignified
courses of action, this strikes me as the least dignified—especially for
myself.

I have no illusions that it is easy to live with a Karen Ann Quinlan
or a Nancy Cruzan or the baby Linares [who was in a coma after an
accident for eight months, until his father unplugged the respirator].
I think I sufficiently appreciate the anguish of their parents or their
children, and the distortion of their lives and the lives of their families.
I also know that, when hearts break and people can stand it no longer,
mercy killing will happen, and I think we should be prepared to excuse
it—as we generally do—when it occurs this way. But an excuse is not
yet a justification, and very far from dignity.

Concluding Observations

What then should we conclude, as a matter of social policy? We
should reject the counsel of those who, seeking to drive a wedge
between human dignity and the sanctity of life, argue the need for
active euthanasia, especially in the name of death with dignity. For it
is precisely the setting of fixed limits on violating human life that
makes possible our efforts at dignified relations with our fellow men,
especially when their neediness and disability try our patience. We
will never be able to relate even decently to people if we are entitled
always to consider that one option before us is to make them dead.
Thus, when the advocates for euthanasia press us with the most
heart-rending cases, we should be sympathetic but firm. Our response
should be neither "Yes, for mercy's sake," nor "Murder! Unthinka-

ble!" but "Sorry. No." Above all we must not allow ourselves to become self-deceived: we must never seek to relieve *our own* frustrations and bitterness over the lingering deaths of others by pretending that we can kill them to sustain *their dignity*.

The ancient Greeks knew about hubris and its tragic fate. We modern rationalists do not. We do not yet understand that the project for the conquest of death leads only to dehumanization, that any attempt to gain the tree of life by means of the tree of knowledge leads inevitably also to the hemlock, and that the utter rationalization of life under the banner of the will gives rise to a world in which the victors live long enough to finish life demented and without choice. The human curse is to discover only too late the evils latent in acquiring the goods we wish for.

Against the background of enormous medical success, terminal illness and incurable disease appear as failures and as affronts to human pride. We refuse to be caught resourceless. Thus, having adopted a largely technical approach to human life and having medicalized so much the end of life, we now are willing to contemplate a final technical solution for the evil of human finitude and for our own technical (but unavoidable) "failure," as well as for the degradations of life that are the unintended consequences of our technical successes. This is dangerous folly. People who care for autonomy and human dignity should try to reverse this dehumanization of the last stages of life, instead of giving dehumanization its final triumph by welcoming the desperate goodbye-to-all-that contained in one final plea for poison.

The present crisis that leads some to press for active euthanasia is really an opportunity to learn the limits of the medicalization of life and death and to recover an appreciation of living with and against mortality. It is an opportunity to remember and affirm that there remains a residual human wholeness—however precarious—that can be cared for even in the face of incurable and terminal illness. Should we cave in, should we choose to become technical dispensers of death, we will not only be abandoning our loved ones and our duty to care, but we will also exacerbate the worst tendencies of modern life, embracing technicism and so-called humaneness where encouragement and humanity are both required and sorely lacking.

On the other hand, should we hold fast, should we decline "the ethics of choice" and its deadly options, should we learn that finitude is no disgrace and that human dignity can be cared for to the very end, we may yet be able to stem the rising tide that threatens permanently to submerge the best hopes for human dignity.

1 0

The Gospel of Life

John Paul II

1. THE GOSPEL OF LIFE is at the heart of Jesus' message. Lovingly received day after day by the Church, it is to be preached with dauntless fidelity as "good news" to the people of every age and culture.

At the dawn of salvation, it is the Birth of a Child which is proclaimed as joyful news: "I bring you good news of a great joy which will come to all the people; for to you is born this day in the city of David a Saviour, who is Christ the Lord" (Luke 2:10-11). The source of this "great joy" is the Birth of the Saviour, but Christmas also reveals the full meaning of every human birth, and the joy which accompanies the Birth of the Messiah is thus seen to be the foundation and fulfillment of joy at every child born into the world (cf. John 16:21).

When he presents the heart of his redemptive mission, Jesus says: "I came that they may have life, and have it abundantly" (John 10:10). In truth, he is referring to that "new" and "eternal" life which consists in communion with the Father, to which every person is freely called

---

John Paul II was elected to the papacy in 1978 after a distinguished career as a pastor, bishop, and philosopher. This is an excerpt from his eleventh encyclical, *Evangelium Vitae* (The Gospel of Life), released March 25, 1995. Sections 1 through 4 are from the Introduction, and sections 64 through 71, 75, and 76 are from the third of the four chapters. The notes have been slightly abridged and newly numbered.

in the Son by the power of the Sanctifying Spirit. It is precisely in this "life" that all the aspects and stages of human life achieve their full significance.

The Incomparable Worth of the Human Person

2. Man is called to a fullness of life which far exceeds the dimensions of his earthly existence, because it consists in sharing the very life of God. The loftiness of this supernatural vocation reveals the *greatness* and the *inestimable value* of human life even in its temporal phase. Life in time, in fact, is the fundamental condition, the initial stage, and an integral part of the entire unified process of human existence. It is a process which, unexpectedly and undeservedly, is enlightened by the promise and renewed by the gift of divine life, which will reach its full realization in eternity (cf. I John 3:1-2). At the same time, it is precisely this supernatural calling which highlights the *relative character* of each individual's earthly life. After all, life on earth is not an "ultimate" but a "penultimate" reality; even so, it remains a *sacred reality* entrusted to us, to be preserved with a sense of responsibility and brought to perfection in love and in the gift of ourselves to God and to our brothers and sisters.

The Church knows that this *Gospel of life,* which she has received from her Lord,[1] has a profound and persuasive echo in the heart of every person believer and non-believer alike — because it marvelously fulfills all the heart's expectations while infinitely surpassing them. Even in the midst of difficulties and uncertainties, every person sincerely open to truth and goodness can, by the light of reason and the hidden action of grace, come to recognize in the natural law written in the heart (cf. Rom. 2:14-15) the sacred value of human life from its very beginning until its end, and can affirm the right of every human being to have this primary good respected to the highest degree. Upon the recognition of this right, every human community and the political community itself are founded.

In a special way, believers in Christ must defend and promote this right, aware as they are of the wonderful truth recalled by the Second Vatican Council: "By his incarnation the Son of God has united himself in some fashion with every human being."[2] This saving event reveals to humanity not only the boundless love of God, who "so loved the world that he gave his only Son" (John 3:16), but also the *incomparable value of every human person.*

The Church, faithfully contemplating the mystery of the Redemption, acknowledges this value with ever new wonder.[3] She feels called to proclaim to the people of all times this "Gospel," the source of invincible hope and true joy for every period of history. *The Gospel of God's love for man, the Gospel of the dignity of the person, and the Gospel of life are a single and indivisible Gospel.*

For this reason, man—living man—represents the primary and fundamental way for the Church.[4]

New Threats to Human Life

3. Every individual, precisely by reason of the mystery of the Word of God who was made flesh (cf. John 1:14), is entrusted to the maternal care of the Church. Therefore every threat to human dignity and life must necessarily be felt in the Church's very heart; it cannot but affect her at the core of her faith in the Redemptive Incarnation of the Son of God, and engage her in her mission of proclaiming the *Gospel of life* in all the world and to every creature (cf. Mark 16:15).

Today this proclamation is especially pressing because of the extraordinary increase and gravity of threats to the life of individuals and peoples, especially where life is weak and defenseless. In addition to the ancient scourges of poverty, hunger, endemic diseases, violence, and war, new threats are emerging on an alarmingly vast scale.

The Second Vatican Council, in a passage which retains all its relevance today, forcefully condemned a number of crimes and attacks against human life. Thirty years later, taking up the words of the Council and with the same forcefulness I repeat that condemnation in the name of the whole Church, certain that I am interpreting the genuine sentiment of every upright conscience: "Whatever is opposed to life itself, such as any type of murder, genocide, abortion, euthanasia, or willful self-destruction; whatever violates the integrity of the human person, such as mutilation, torments inflicted on body or mind, attempts to coerce the will itself; whatever insults human dignity, such as subhuman living conditions, arbitrary imprisonment, deportation, slavery, prostitution, the selling of women and children, as well as disgraceful working conditions, where people are treated as mere instruments of gain rather than as free and responsible persons: all these things and others like them are infamies indeed. They poison human society, and they do more harm to those who practice them than to those who suffer from the injury. Moreover, they are a supreme dishonor to the Creator."5

4. Unfortunately, this disturbing state of affairs, far from decreasing, is expanding: with the new prospects opened up by scientific and technological progress there arise new forms of attacks on the dignity of the human being. At the same time a new cultural climate is developing and taking hold, which gives crimes against life a *new and —if possible—even more sinister character,* giving rise to further grave concern: broad sectors of public opinion justify certain crimes against life in the name of the rights of individual freedom, and on this basis they claim not only exemption from punishment but even authorization by the State, so that these things can be done with total freedom and indeed with the free assistance of health-care systems.

All this is causing a profound change in the way in which life and relationships between people are considered. The fact that legislation in many countries, perhaps even departing from basic principles of their constitutions, has determined not to punish these practices against life, and even to make them altogether legal, is both a disturbing symptom and a significant cause of grave moral decline. Choices once unanimously considered criminal and rejected by the common moral sense are gradually becoming socially acceptable. Even certain sectors of the medical profession, which by its calling is directed to the defense and care of human life, are increasingly willing to carry out these acts against the person. In this way the very nature of the medical profession is distorted and contradicted, and the dignity of those who practice it is degraded. In such a cultural and legislative situation, the serious demographic, social, and family problems which weigh upon many of the world's peoples, and which require responsible and effective attention from national and international bodies, are left open to false and deceptive solutions, opposed to the truth and the good of persons and nations.

The end result of this is tragic: not only is the fact of the destruction of so many human lives still to be born or in their final stage extremely grave and disturbing, but no less grave and disturbing is the fact that conscience itself, darkened as it were by such widespread conditioning, is finding it increasingly difficult to distinguish between good and evil in what concerns the basic value of human life. . . .

THE TRAGEDY OF EUTHANASIA

"It is I who bring both death and life" (Dt. 32:39).

From chapter 3, "'You Shall Not Kill': God's Holy Law":

64. At the other end of life's spectrum, men and women find themselves facing the mystery of death. Today, as a result of advances in medicine and in a cultural context frequently closed to the transcendent, the experience of dying is marked by new features. When the prevailing tendency is to value life only to the extent that it brings pleasure and well-being, suffering seems like an unbearable setback, something from which one must be freed at all costs. Death is considered "senseless" if it suddenly interrupts a life still open to a future of new and interesting experiences. But it becomes a "rightful liberation" once life is held to be no longer meaningful because it is filled with pain and inexorably doomed to even greater suffering.

Furthermore, when he denies or neglects his fundamental relationship to God, man thinks he is his own rule and measure, with the right to demand that society should guarantee him the ways and means of deciding what to do with his life in full and complete autonomy. It is especially people in the developed countries who act in this way: they feel encouraged to do so also by the constant progress of medicine and its ever more advanced techniques. By using highly sophisticated systems and equipment, science and medical practice today are able not only to attend to cases formerly considered untreatable and to reduce or eliminate pain, but also to sustain and prolong life even in situations of extreme frailty, to resuscitate artificially patients whose basic biological functions have undergone sudden collapse, and to use special procedures to make organs available for transplanting.

In this context the temptation grows to have recourse to *euthanasia,* that is, *to take control of death and bring it about before its time,* "gently" ending one's own life or the life of others. In reality, what might seem logical and humane, when looked at more closely is seen to be *senseless and inhumane.* Here we are faced with one of the more alarming symptoms of the "culture of death," which is advancing above all in prosperous societies marked by an attitude of excessive preoccupation with efficiency, and which sees the growing number of elderly and disabled people as intolerable and too burdensome. These people are very often isolated by their families and by society, which are organized almost exclusively on the basis of criteria of productive efficiency, according to which a hopelessly impaired life no longer has any value.

65. For a correct moral judgment on euthanasia, in the first place a clear definition is required. *Euthanasia in the strict sense* is understood to be an action or omission which of itself and by intention causes death, with the purpose of eliminating all suffering. "Euthanasia's terms of reference, therefore, are to be found in the intention of the will and in the methods used."[6]

Euthanasia must be distinguished from the decision to forgo so-called "aggressive medical treatment," in other words, medical procedures which no longer correspond to the real situation of the patient, either because they are by now disproportionate to any expected results or because they impose an excessive burden on the patient and his family. In such situations, when death is clearly imminent and inevitable, one can in conscience "refuse forms of treatment that would only secure a precarious and burdensome prolongation of life, so long as the normal care due to the sick person in similar cases is not interrupted."[7] Certainly there is a moral obligation to care for oneself and to allow oneself to be cared for, but this duty must take account of concrete circumstances. It needs to be determined whether the means of treatment available are objectively proportionate to the prospects for improvement. To forgo extraordinary or disproportionate means is not the equivalent of suicide or euthanasia; it rather expresses acceptance of the human condition in the face of death.[8]

In modern medicine, increased attention is being given to what are called "methods of palliative care," which seek to make suffering more bearable in the final stages of illness and to ensure that the patient is supported and accompanied in his or her ordeal. Among the questions which arise in this context is that of the licitness of using various types of painkillers and sedatives for relieving the patient's pain when this involves the risk of shortening life. While praise may be due to the person who voluntarily accepts suffering by forgoing treatment with pain-killers in order to remain fully lucid and, if a believer, to share consciously in the Lord's Passion, such "heroic" behavior cannot be considered the duty of everyone. Pius XII affirmed that it is licit to relieve pain by narcotics, even when the result is decreased consciousness and a shortening of life, "if no other means exist, and if, in the given circumstances, this does not prevent the carrying out of other religious and moral duties."[9] In such a case death is not willed or sought, even though for reasonable motives one runs the risk of it: there is simply a desire to ease pain effectively by using the analgesics which medicine provides. All the same, "it is not right to deprive the dying person of consciousness without a serious reason"[10]: as they approach death people ought to be able to satisfy their moral and family duties, and above all they ought to be able to prepare in a fully conscious way for their definitive meeting with God.

Taking into account these distinctions, in harmony with the Magisterium of my Predecessors[11] and in communion with the Bishops of the Catholic Church, *I confirm that euthanasia is a grave violation of the law of God,* since it is the deliberate and morally unacceptable killing of a human person. This doctrine is based upon the natural law and upon the written word of God, is transmitted by the Church's Tradition and taught by the ordinary and universal Magisterium.[12]

Depending on the circumstances, this practice involves the malice proper to suicide or murder.

66. Suicide is always as morally objectionable as murder. The Church's tradition has always rejected it as a gravely evil choice.[13] Even though a certain psychological, cultural, and social conditioning may induce a person to carry out an action which so radically contradicts the innate inclination to life, thus lessening or removing subjective responsibility, *suicide,* when viewed objectively, is a gravely immoral act. In fact, it involves the rejection of love of self and the renunciation of the obligation of justice and charity towards one's neighbor, towards the communities to which one belongs, and towards society as a whole.[14] In its deepest reality, suicide represents a rejection of God's absolute sovereignty over life and death, as proclaimed in the prayer of the ancient sage of Israel: "You have power

over life and death; you lead men down to the gates of Hades and back again" (Wis. 16:13; cf. Tob. 13:2).

To concur with the intention of another person to commit suicide and to help in carrying it out through so-called "assisted suicide" means to cooperate in, and at times to be the actual perpetrator of, an injustice which can never be excused, even if it is requested. In a remarkably relevant passage Saint Augustine writes that "it is never licit to kill another: even if he should wish it, indeed if he request it because, hanging between life and death, he begs for help in freeing the soul struggling against the bonds of the body and longing to be released; nor is it licit even when a sick person is no longer able to live."[15]

Even when not motivated by a selfish refusal to be burdened with the life of someone who is suffering, euthanasia must be called a *false mercy,* and indeed a disturbing "perversion" of mercy. True "compassion" leads to sharing another's pain; it does not kill the person whose suffering we cannot bear. Moreover, the act of euthanasia appears all the more perverse if it is carried out by those, like relatives, who are supposed to treat a family member with patience and love, or by those, such as doctors, who by virtue of their specific profession are supposed to care for the sick person even in the most painful terminal stages.

The choice of euthanasia becomes more serious when it takes the form of a *murder* committed by others on a person who has in no way requested it and who has never consented to it. The height of arbitrariness and injustice is reached when certain people, such as physicians or legislators, arrogate to themselves the power to decide who ought to live and who ought to die. Once again we find ourselves before the temptation of Eden: to become like God, who "knows good and evil" (cf. Gen. 3:5). God alone has the power over life and death: "It is I who bring both death and life" (Dt. 32:39; cf. II Kg. 5:7; I Sam. 2:6). But he only exercises this power in accordance with a plan of wisdom and love. When man usurps this power, being enslaved by a foolish and selfish way of thinking, he inevitably uses it for injustice and death. Thus the life of the person who is weak is put into the hands of the one who is strong; in society the sense of justice is lost, and mutual trust, the basis of every authentic interpersonal relationship, is undermined at its root.

67. Quite different from this is the *way of love and true mercy,* which our common humanity calls for, and upon which faith in Christ the Redeemer, who died and rose again, sheds ever new light. The request which arises from the human heart in the supreme confrontation with suffering and death, especially when faced with the temptation to give up in utter desperation, is above all a request for companionship, sympathy, and support in the time of trial. It is a plea for help to keep on hoping when all human hopes fail. As the Second Vatican Council reminds us: "It is in the face of death that the riddle of human existence becomes most acute" and yet "man rightly follows the intuition of his heart when he abhors and repudiates the absolute ruin and total disappearance of his own person. Man rebels against death because he bears in himself an eternal seed which cannot be reduced to mere matter."[16]

This natural aversion to death and this incipient hope of immortality are illumined and brought to fulfillment by Christian faith, which both promises and offers a share in the victory of the Risen Christ: it is the victory of the One who, by his redemptive death, has set man free from death, "the wages of sin" (Rom. 6:23), and has given him the Spirit, the pledge of resurrection and of life (cf. Rom. 8:11). The certainty of future immortality and *hope in the promised resurrection* cast new light on the mystery of suffering and death, and fill the believer with an extraordinary capacity to trust fully in the plan of God.

The Apostle Paul expressed this newness in terms of belonging completely to the Lord who embraces every human condition: "None of us lives to himself, and none of us dies to himself. If we live, we live to the Lord, and if we die, we die to the Lord; so then, whether we live or whether we die, we are the Lord's" (Rom. 14:7-8). *Dying to the Lord* means experiencing one's death as the supreme act of obedience to the Father (cf. Phil. 2:8), being ready to meet death at the "hour" willed and chosen by him (cf. John 13:1), which can only mean when one's earthly pilgrimage is completed. *Living to the Lord* also means recognizing that suffering, while still an evil and a trial in itself, can always become a source of good. It becomes such if it is experienced for love and with love through sharing, by God's gracious gift and one's own personal and free choice, in the suffering of Christ Crucified. In this way, the person who lives his suffering in the Lord grows more fully conformed to him (cf. Phil. 3:10; I Pet. 2:21) and more closely associated with his redemptive work on behalf of the Church and humanity.[17] This was the experience of Saint Paul, which every person who suffers is called to relive: "I rejoice in my sufferings for your sake, and in my flesh I complete what is lacking in Christ's afflictions for the sake of his Body, that is, the Church" (Col. 1:24).

CIVIL LAW AND THE MORAL LAW

"We must obey God rather than men" (Acts 5:29).

68. One of the specific characteristics of present-day attacks on human life—as has already been said several times—consists in the trend to demand a *legal justification* for them, as if they were rights which the State, at least under certain conditions, must acknowledge as belonging to citizens. Consequently, there is a tendency to claim that it should be possible to exercise these rights with the safe and free assistance of doctors and medical personnel.

It is often claimed that the life of an unborn child or a seriously disabled person is only a relative good: according to a proportionalist approach, or one of sheer calculation, this good should be compared with and balanced against other goods. It is even maintained that only someone present and personally involved in a concrete situation can correctly judge the goods at stake: consequently, only that person would be able to decide on the morality of his choice. The State therefore, in the interest of civil coexistence and social harmony, should respect this choice, even to the point of permitting abortion and euthanasia.

At other times, it is claimed that civil law cannot demand that all citizens should live according to moral standards higher than what all citizens themselves acknowledge and share. Hence the law should always express the opinion and will of the majority of citizens and recognize that they have, at least in certain extreme cases, the right even to abortion and euthanasia. Moreover the prohibition and the punishment of abortion and euthanasia in these cases would inevitably lead—so it is said—to an increase of illegal practices: and these would not be subject to necessary control by society and would be carried out in a medically unsafe way. The question is also raised whether supporting a law which in practice cannot be enforced would not ultimately undermine the authority of all laws.

Finally, the more radical views go so far as to maintain that in a modern and pluralistic society people should be allowed complete freedom to dispose of their own lives as well as of the lives of the unborn: it is asserted that it is not the task of the law to choose between different moral opinions, and still less can the law claim to impose one particular opinion to the detriment of others.

69. In any case, in the democratic culture of our time it is commonly held that the legal system of any society should limit itself to taking account of and accepting the convictions of the majority. It should therefore be based solely upon what the majority itself considers moral and actually practices. Furthermore, if it is believed that an objective truth shared by all is *de facto* unattainable, then respect for the freedom of the citizens—who in a democratic system are considered the true rulers—would require that on the legislative level the autonomy of individual consciences be acknowledged. Consequently, when establishing those norms which are absolutely necessary for social coexistence, the only determining factor should be the will of the majority, whatever this may be. Hence every politician, in his or her activity, should clearly separate the realm of private conscience from that of public conduct.

As a result we have what appear to be two diametrically opposed tendencies. On the one hand, individuals claim for themselves in the moral sphere the most complete freedom of choice and demand that the State should not adopt or impose any ethical position but limit itself to guaranteeing maximum space for the freedom of each individual, with the sole limitation of not infringing on the freedom and rights of any other citizen. On the other hand, it is held that, in the exercise of public and professional duties, respect for other people's freedom of choice requires that each one should set aside his or her own convictions in order to satisfy every demand of the citizens which is recognized and guaranteed by law; in carrying out one's duties the only moral criterion should be what is laid down by the law itself. Individual responsibility is thus turned over to the civil law, with a renouncing of personal conscience, at least in the public sphere.

70. At the basis of all these tendencies lies the *ethical relativism* which characterizes much of present-day culture. There are those who consider such relativism an essential condition of democracy, inasmuch as it alone is held to guarantee tolerance, mutual respect between people, and acceptance of the decisions of the majority, whereas moral norms considered to be objective and binding are held to lead to authoritarianism and intolerance.

But it is precisely the issue of respect for life which shows what misunderstandings and contradictions, accompanied by terrible practical consequences, are concealed in this position. It is true that history has known cases where crimes have been committed in the name of "truth." But equally grave crimes and radical denials of freedom have also been committed and are still being committed in the name of "ethical relativism." When a parliamentary or social majority decrees that it is legal, at least under certain conditions, to kill unborn human life, is it not really making a "tyrannical" decision with regard to the weakest and most defenseless of human beings? Everyone's conscience rightly rejects those crimes against humanity of which our century has had such sad experience. But would these crimes cease to be crimes if, instead of being committed by unscrupulous tyrants, they were legitimated by popular consensus?

Democracy cannot be idolized to the point of making it a substitute for morality or a panacea for immorality. Fundamentally, democracy is a "system" and as such is a means and not an end. Its "moral" value is not automatic, but depends on conformity to the moral law to which it, like every other form of human behavior, must be subject: in other words, its morality depends on the morality of the ends which it pursues and of the means which it employs. If today we see an almost universal consensus with regard to the value of democracy, this is to be considered a positive "sign of the times," as the Church's Magisterium has frequently noted.[18] But the value of democracy stands or falls with the values which it embodies and promotes. Of course, values such as the dignity of every human person, respect for inviolable and undeniable human rights, and the adoption of the "common good" as the end and criterion regulating political life are certainly fundamental and not to be ignored.

The basis of these values cannot be provisional and changeable "majority" opinions, but only the acknowledgment of an objective moral law which, as the "natural law" written in the human heart, is the obligatory point of reference for civil law itself. If, as a result of a tragic obscuring of the collective conscience, an attitude of skepticism were to succeed in bringing into question even the fundamental principles of the moral law, the democratic system itself would be shaken in its foundations, and would be reduced to a mere mechanism for regulating different and opposing interests on a purely empirical basis.[19]

Some might think that even this function, in the absence of anything better, should be valued for the sake of peace in society. While one acknowledges some element of truth in this point of view, it is easy to see that without an objective moral grounding not even democracy is capable of ensuring a stable peace, especially since peace which is not built upon the values of the dignity of every individual and of solidarity between all people frequently proves to be illusory. Even in participatory systems of government, the regulation of interests often occurs to the advantage of the most powerful, since they are the ones most capable not only of maneuvering the levers of power but also of shaping the formation of consensus. In such a situation, "democracy" easily becomes an empty word.

71. It is therefore urgently necessary, for the future of society and the development of a sound democracy, to rediscover those essential and innate human and moral values which flow from the very truth of the human being and express and safeguard the dignity of the person: values which no individual, no majority, and no State can ever create, modify, or destroy, but must only acknowledge, respect, and promote. . . .

"PROMOTE" LIFE

"You shall love your neighbor as yourself" (Luke 10:27).

75. God's commandments teach us the way of life. The *negative moral precepts,* which declare that the choice of certain actions is morally unacceptable, have an absolute value for human freedom: they are valid always and everywhere, without exception. They make it clear that the choice of certain ways of acting is radically incompatible with

the love of God and with the dignity of the person created in his image. Such choices cannot be redeemed by the goodness of any intention or of any consequence; they are irrevocably opposed to the bond between persons; they contradict the fundamental decision to direct one's life to God.[20]

In this sense, the negative moral precepts have an extremely important positive function. The "no" which they unconditionally require makes clear the absolute limit beneath which free individuals cannot lower themselves. At the same time they indicate the minimum which they must respect and from which they must start out in order to say "yes" over and over again, a "yes" which will gradually embrace *the entire horizon of the good* (cf. Mt. 5:48). The commandments, in particular the negative moral precepts, are the beginning and the first necessary stage of the journey towards freedom. As Saint Augustine writes, "the beginning of freedom is to be free from crimes . . . like murder, adultery, fornication, theft, fraud, sacrilege, and so forth. Only when one stops committing these crimes (and no Christian should commit them), one begins to lift up one's head towards freedom. But this is only the beginning of freedom, not perfect freedom."[21]

76. The commandment "You shall not kill" thus establishes the point of departure for the start of true freedom. It leads us to promote life actively, and to develop particular ways of thinking and acting which serve life. In this way we exercise our responsibility towards the persons entrusted to us and we show, in deeds and in truth, our gratitude to God for the great gift of life. . . .

Euthanasia and Christian Vision

Gilbert Meilaender

Every teacher has probably experienced, along with countless frustrations, moments in the classroom when something was said with perfect lucidity. I recall one such moment during a seminar I was teaching on ethical issues in death and dying. Knowing how difficult it can be to get students to consider these problems from within a religious perspective, I decided to force the issue at the outset by assigning as the first reading parts of those magnificent sections in the third volume of Karl Barth's *Church Dogmatics* in which he discusses "Respect for Life" and "The Protection of Life." I gave the students little warning, preferring to let the vigor and bombast of Barth's style have whatever effect it might.

The students, I must say in retrospect, probably thought more kindly of Barth—who had, after all, only *written* these sections—than of the teacher who had assigned them to be read. But they did the assignment, and we had a worthwhile discussion, with students criticizing Barth and also, sometimes, defending him.

But neither criticism nor defense was really my goal. What I sought

---

Gilbert Meilaender, formerly at Oberlin College, now holds a chair in theological ethics at Valparaiso University. Among his books are *Body, Soul, and Bioethics* (1995) and *Bioethics: A Primer for Christians* (1996). This essay is reprinted by permission of the author from the journal *Thought* (now defunct), December 1982.

was understanding—understanding of death and dying within a perspective steeped in centuries of Christian life and thought—and at one point we achieved that understanding. One young woman in the class, seeking to explain why Barth puzzled her so, put it quite simply: "What I really don't like about him is that he seems to think our lives are not our own." To which I could only respond: "If you begin to see that about Barth, even if it offends you deeply, then indeed you have begun to understand what he is saying."

In his discussion of "The Protection of Life" Barth notes some difficult questions that seem to nudge us in the direction of approving euthanasia in certain tormenting cases. And then, rejecting these "tempting questions," he responds with typical flair: "All honor to the well-meaning humanitarianism of underlying motive! But the derivation is obviously from another book than that which we have thus far consulted."[1] In this brief essay I want to think about euthanasia not from the perspective of any "well-meaning humanitarianism" but from within the parameters of Christian belief—though, as we will see, one of the most important things to note is that, within those parameters, only what is consonant with Christian belief can be truly humane.[2]

The Paradigm Case

Determining what really qualifies as euthanasia is no easy matter. Need the person "euthanized" be suffering terribly? Or, at least, be near death? Suppose the person simply feels life is no longer worth living in a particular condition that may be deeply dissatisfying even though it is not filled with suffering? Suppose the person's life is filled with suffering or seemingly devoid of meaning but he is unable to request euthanasia (because of, for instance, a comatose condition, or senile dementia)? Or suppose the person is suffering greatly but steadfastly says he does not want to die? Suppose the motive of the "euthanizer" is not mercy but despair at the continued burden of caring for the person—will that qualify?

Once we start down this path, the list of questions needing clarification is endless. But I intend to get off the path at once by taking as our focus of attention a kind of paradigm case of what must surely count as euthanasia. If we see that *this* is morally wrong, much else will fall into place.

James Rachels has suggested that "the clearest possible case of euthanasia" would be one having the following five features: The person (1) is deliberately killed, (2) would have died soon anyway, (3) was suffering terrible pain, and (4) asked to be killed, and (5) the motive of the killing was mercy—to provide the person with as a good a death as possible under the circumstances.[3] Such a case is not simply "assisted suicide," since the case requires the presence of great suffering, the imminence of death in any case, and a motive of mercy. Furthermore, considering this sort of case sets aside arguments about non-voluntary and involuntary euthanasia and gives focus to our discussion.[4] If this case of voluntary euthanasia is permissible, other cases may also be. If this case is itself morally wrong, we are less likely to be able to argue for euthanasia in non-voluntary and involuntary circumstances.

Distinguishing Aim From Result

One way of arguing that the paradigm case of euthanasia is morally permissible (perhaps even obligatory) is to claim that it does not differ in morally relevant ways from other acts that most of us approve. Consider a patient whose death is imminent, who is suffering terribly, and who may suddenly stop breathing and require resuscitation. We may think it best not to resuscitate such a person but simply to let him die. What could be the morally significant difference between such a "letting die" and simply giving this person a lethal injection that would end his life (and suffering) just as quickly? If it is morally right not to prolong his dying when he ceases breathing for a few moments, why is it morally wrong to kill him quickly and painlessly? Each act responds to the fact that death is imminent and recognizes that terrible suffering calls for relief. And the result in each case is the same: death.

To appreciate the important difference between these possibilities we must distinguish what we *aim* at in our action from the *result* of the action. Or, to paraphrase Charles Fried, we must distinguish between those actions that we invest with the personal involvement of purpose and those that merely "run through" our person.[5] This is a distinction that moral reflection can scarcely get along without. For example, if we fail to distinguish between aim and result we will be unable to see any difference between the self-sacrifice of a martyr and the suicide of a person weary of life. The *result* is the same: death. But whereas the suicide *aims* at his death, the martyr aims at faithfulness to God (or loyalty of some other sort). Both martyr and suicide know that the result of their choice and act will be death. But the martyr does not aim at death.

This distinction between aim and result helps explain the moral difference between euthanizing a suffering person near death and simply letting such a person die. Suppose this patient were to stop breathing, we were to reject the possibility of resuscitation, and then he were suddenly to begin breathing again. Would we, simply because we had been willing to let this patient die, now proceed to smother him so that he would indeed die? Hardly. And the fact that we would not indicates that in rejecting resuscitation we did not *aim* at his death, though his death could have been one *result* of what we did aim at, namely, proper care for him in his dying. By contrast, if we euthanatized such a person by giving him a lethal injection, we would indeed aim at his death; we would invest the act of aiming at his death with the personal involvement of our purpose.

But someone might say: It is possible to grant the distinction between aim and result while still claiming that euthanasia in our paradigm case would be permissible (or obligatory). It may be that there is a difference between allowing a patient to die and aiming at someone's death. But if the suffering of the dying person is truly intense and the person requests death, on what grounds could we refuse to assist him? If we refuse on the grounds that it would be wrong for us to aim at his death (which will certainly result soon anyway after more terrible suffering), are we not saying that we are unwilling to do him a great good if doing it requires that we dirty our hands in any way? Is our real concern with our own moral rectitude, rather than with the needs of the sufferer? In our eagerness to narrow the scope of our moral responsibility, have we lost sight of the need and imperative to offer care?

The Appeal of Consequentialism

This is what ethicists call a *consequentialist* rejoinder. It suggests that the good results (relieving the suffering) are sufficiently weighty to make the aim (killing) morally permissible or obligatory. And, as far as I can tell, this rejoinder has become increasingly persuasive to large numbers of people.

The moral theory of consequentialism holds that when that some state of affairs *ought to be,* it follows that we *ought to do* whatever is necessary to bring about that state of affairs. Although teleological theories of morality are ancient, consequentialism as a full-blown moral theory is traceable largely to Bentham and Mill in the late eighteenth and early nineteenth century. To remember this is instructive, since it is not implausible to suggest that such a moral theory would be most persuasive when Christendom had, in large measure, ceased to be Christian. Those who know themselves as creatures, not Creator, will recognize limits even upon their obligation to do good. As creatures, we are to do all the good we can, but this means all the good we *morally* can, all the good we can do within certain limits. It may be that the Creator *ought to do* whatever is necessary to bring about states of affairs that *ought to be,* but we stand under no such God-like imperative.[6]

One of the best ways to understand the remarkable appeal today of consequentialism as a moral theory is to see it as an ethic for those who (a) remain morally serious but (b) have ceased to believe in a God whose providential care will ultimately bring about whatever ought to be. If God is not there to accomplish whatever ought to be, we are the most likely candidates to shoulder that responsibility.[7] Conversely, it may be that we can distinguish between two acts whose result is the same but whose aim is different only if we believe that our responsibilities as creatures are limited—that the responsibility for achieving certain results has been taken out of our hands, or, better, never given to us in the first place. It ought to be the case that dying people do not suffer terribly (indeed, that they do not die). But, at least for Christians, it does not follow from that "ought to be" that we "ought to do" whatever is necessary—even to engage in euthanasia —to relieve them of that suffering.[8]

We are now in a position to see something important about the argument that in the paradigm case euthanasia is permissible because it does not differ morally from cases of "letting die" that most of us approve. This argument often begins in a failure to distinguish between aim and result. However, it is difficult, as we have seen, for moral theory to get along without this distinction. Seeing this, we realize that the argument really becomes a claim that if the results are sufficiently good, any aim necessary to achieve them is permissible. And precisely at this turn in the argument it may be difficult to keep "religion" and "morality" in those neat and separate compartments we have fashioned for them. At this point, one steeped in Christian thought and committed to Christian life may wish to say with Barth: All honor to the well-meaning humanitarianism—and it *is* well-meaning. But it is "derived from another book" and is only for those who would, even if reluctantly, be "like God."

Distinguishing Aim From Motive

If the distinction between aim and result makes it difficult to justify euthanasia in the paradigm case, another distinction may be more useful. We might suggest that the act of euthanizing be redescribed in terms of the motive of mercy. We could portray the act not as killing but as relieving suffering. Or, rather than engage in a wholesale redescription, we might simply argue that our moral evaluation of the act cannot depend solely on its *aim* but must also consider its *motive*.

Consider this situation.[9] A condemned prisoner is in his cell only minutes before his scheduled execution. As he sits in fear and anguish, certain of his doom, another man who has managed to sneak into the prison shoots and kills him. This man is either (a) the father of children murdered by the prisoner, or (b) a close friend of the prisoner. In case *a* he shoots because he will not be satisfied simply to have the man executed; he desires that his own hand should bring about the prisoner's death. In case *b* the man shoots because he wishes to spare his friend the terror and anguish of those last minutes.

Would it be proper to describe the father's act as an act of killing and the friend's as an act of relieving suffering? Although we may be tempted to do so, it muddies rather than clarifies our analysis. If anything is clear in these cases, it is that both the vengeful father and the compassionate friend *aim* to kill, though their *motives* are very different. Only by refusing to redescribe the aim of the act in terms of its motive do we keep the moral issue clearly before us. That issue is whether our moral evaluation of the act should depend solely on the agent's aim or whether that evaluation must also include the motive.

That the motive makes *some* difference almost everyone would agree. Few of us would be content to analyze the two cases simply as instances of "aiming to kill" without considering the quite different motives. The important question, however, is whether the praiseworthy motive of relieving suffering should so dominate our moral reflection that it leads us to judge the act "right." I want to suggest that it should not, at least not within the parameters of Christian belief.

One might think that the Christian emphasis on the overriding importance of love as a motive would suggest that whatever was done out of love was right, and Christians do often talk this way. Such talk, however, must be done against the background assumptions of Christian anthropology. Apart from that background of meaning we may doubt whether we have really understood the motive of love correctly. We need therefore to sketch in the background against which we can properly understand what loving care for a suffering person should be.[10]

A Larger View of Life and Death

Barth writes that human life "must always be regarded as a divine act of trust."[11] This means that all human life is "surrounded by a particular solemnity" that, if recognized, will lead us to "treat it with respect." At the same time, however, "life is no second God, and therefore the respect due to it cannot rival the reverence owed to God." One who knows this will seek to live life "within its appointed limits." Recognizing our life as a trust, we will be moved not by an "absolute will to live" but by a will to live within these limits. Hence, when we understand ourselves as creatures, we will both value God's gift of life and realize that the Giver himself constitutes the limit beyond which we ought not to value the gift. "Temporal life is certainly not the highest of all goods. Just because it belongs to God, man may be forbidden to will its continuation at all costs." And at the same time, "if life is not the highest possession, then it is at least the highest . . . price" that human beings can pay. In short, life is a great good but not the greatest, which is fidelity to God.

Death, the final enemy of life, must also be understood dialectically. The human mind has quite naturally taken two equally plausible attitudes toward death.[12] We can regard death as of no consequence, heeding the Epicurean maxim that while we are alive death is not yet here, and when death is here we are no more. Thus the human being, in a majestic transcendence of the limits of earthly life, might seek to soar beyond the limits of finitude and find his good elsewhere. If death is of no consequence, we may seek it in exchange for some important good. Equally natural to the human mind is a seemingly opposite view: that death is the *summum malum,* the greatest evil, to be avoided at all costs. Such a view, finding good only in earthly life, can find none in suffering and death.

The Christian mind, however, transcending what is "natural" and correcting it in light of the book it is accustomed to consult, has refused to take either of these quite plausible directions. Understood within the biblical narrative, death is an ambivalent phenomenon—too ambivalent to be seen only as the greatest of all evils, or as indifferent. Since the world narrated by the Bible begins in God and moves toward God, earthly life is his trust to be sustained faithfully, his gift to be valued and cared for. When life is seen from this perspective, we cannot say that death and suffering are of no consequence; on the contrary, we can even say with Barth that the human task in the face of suffering and death is not to accept but to offer "final resistance."[13] It is just as true, however, that death could never be the greatest evil. That title must be reserved for disobedience to and disbelief in God—a refusal to live within our appointed limits. So we can also repeat with Barth that "life is no second God."[14] We remember, after all, that Jesus goes to the cross in the name of obedience to his Father. We need not glorify or seek suffering, but we must be struck by the fact that a human being who is a willing sufferer stands squarely in the center of Christian piety. Jesus bears his suffering not because it is desirable but because the Father allots it to him within the limits of his earthly life.

Death is—there is no way to put the matter simply—a great evil that God can turn to his good purposes. It is an evil that must ordinarily be resisted but must also at some point be acknowledged. We can and ought to acknowledge what we do not and ought not to seek. George Orwell, himself an "outsider," nicely summarized the background assumptions of Christian anthropology:

The Christian attitude towards death is not that it is something to be welcomed, or that it is something to be met with stoical indifference, or that it is something to be avoided as long as possible; but that it is something profoundly tragic which has to be gone through with. A Christian, I suppose, if he were offered the chance of everlasting life on this earth would refuse it, but he would still feel that death is profoundly sad.[15]

This vision of the world, and of the meaning of life and death, has within Christendom given guidance to those reflecting on human suffering and dying. That moral guidance has amounted to the twofold proposition that, though we might properly cease to oppose death while aiming at other choiceworthy goods in life (hence, the possibility of martyrdom), we ought never to aim at death as our end or our means.

The Meaning of Love and Care

Against this background of belief we can better understand what *love* and *care* must be within a world construed in Christian terms. In such a world, no action that deliberately hastens death can be called "love." It is not that the death-hastener need have an evil motive; he may, like the compassionate friend, seem to have a praiseworthy motive. Rather, such an action cannot be loving because it cannot be part of the meaning of commitment to the well-being of another human being within the appointed limits of earthly life. The benevolence of the euthanizer is enough like love to give us pause, to tempt us to call it love. Perhaps it may be the closest to love that those who feel they bear full responsibility for relieving suffering and producing good can come. But it is not the creaturely love that Christians praise, a love that can sometimes require that we do no more than suffer as best we can with the sufferer.

Against this background—a background that pours meaning into words like "love" and "care"—we can contemplate the kind of case often considered in discussions of euthanasia.[16] A person may be in severe pain, certain to die within a few days. Most of us would agree that further lifesaving treatments were not in order, that they would do no more than prolong his dying. Why, someone may ask, do we not subject such a patient to useless treatments? Because, we reply, he is in agony, and it would be wrong to prolong that agony needlessly.

But now, if we face the facts honestly, we will admit that it takes this patient longer to die—and therefore prolongs his suffering—if we simply withhold treatment than if we euthanize him. There seems to be a contradiction within our reasoning. The motive for withholding treatment was a humanitarian one: relief of suffering. But in refusing to take the next step and euthanize the patient, we prolong his suffering and thereby belie our original motive. Hence the conclusion follows, quite contrary to the moral guidance embedded in the Christian vision of the world: Either we should keep this person alive as long as possible and not pretend that our motive is the relief of suffering, or we should be willing to euthanize him.

The argument gets much of its force from the seeming simplicity of the dilemma, but that simplicity is misleading. For, at least for Christian vision, the fundamental imperative is not "minimize suffering" but "maximize love and care." In that Christian world, in which death and suffering are great evils but not the greatest evil, love can never include in its meaning hastening a fellow human being toward the evil of death, nor can it mean a refusal to acknowledge death, when it comes, as an evil (but not the greatest evil). We can know what the imperative "maximize love" means only if we understand it against the background assumptions that make intelligible for Christians words like "love" and "care." The Christian mind has certainly not recommended that we seek suffering or call it an unqualified good, but it is an evil that, if endured faithfully, can be redemptive.

William May has noted how parents in our time think that love for their children means, above all else, protecting those children from suffering. "As conscientious parents, they operate as though the powers that are decisive in the universe could not possibly do anything in and through the suffering of their children. . . . They take upon themselves the responsibilities of a savior-figure."[17] May sees clearly that "minimize suffering" and "maximize love" are not identical imperatives and do not offer the same direction for human action. Perhaps the direction that they give may often be the same, but at times —especially when we consider what is proper to do for the irretrievably dying—we will discover how sharply they may differ.

I suggested above that we should not redescribe the *aim* of an act in terms of its *motive*. (We should not say that an act of killing a suffering person was simply an act of relieving suffering. We should say rather that we aimed at the death of the person in order to relieve his suffering. This keeps the moral issue more clearly before us.) But by now it will be evident that I have in fact gone some way toward redescribing the *motive* of the act in terms of its *aim:* If the act is aimed at hastening the death of the suffering person, we should not see it as motivated by love. Is this any better?

The answer, I think, is, it depends. It would not be better, it might even be worse, if my purpose were to deny any humanitarian motive to the person tempted to euthanize a sufferer. Few people would find such a denial persuasive, and because we would not, we are tempted to turn in the opposite direction and describe the act's aim in terms of its motive. We *do* recognize the difference between the vengeful father and the compassionate friend even though both aim to kill the condemned prisoner, and we want our moral judgments to be sufficiently nuanced to take account of these differences. The simple truth is that our evaluation of the act described in terms of aim and our evaluation of the act described in terms of motive often fall apart. In a world broken by sin and its consequences, this should perhaps come as no surprise. Christians believe that we sinners—all of us—are not whole, and many of the stubborn problems of systematic ethical reflection testify to the truth of that belief. Our lack of wholeness is displayed in our inability to arrive at one judgment (or even one description) "whole and entire" of a single act. We find ourselves in a world in which people may sometimes seem to aim at doing evil from the best of motives (and think they must do so). And then we are tempted to elide aim and motive and call that evil at which they aim "good."

No amount of ethical reflection can heal this rift in our nature. For escape from that predicament we will have to look for a deliverance greater than ethics can offer. However, here and now, in our broken world, we do better to take the aim of an act as our guiding light in describing and evaluating the act—and then to evaluate the motive in light of this aim. This is better because moral reflection is not primarily a tool for fixing guilt and responsibility (in which case motive comes to the fore). It is, first and foremost, one of the ways in which we train ourselves and others to see the world rightly. We would be wrong to assert that no euthanizer has a humanitarian motive. But if we want not so much to fix praise or blame as to teach the meaning of the word "love," we are not wrong to say that love could never euthanize. In the Christian world this is true. And in that world we know the right name for our own tendency to call those other, seemingly humanitarian motives "love." The name for that tendency is *temptation*. We are being tempted to be "like God" when we toy with the possibility of defining our love—and the meaning of humanity—apart from the appointed limits of human life.

To redescribe the motive in terms of the act's aim, to attempt to inculcate a vision of the world in which love could never euthanatize, is therefore not only permissible but necessary for Christians. It is the only proper way to respond to the supposed dilemmas presented by reasoning that sets aside Christian assumptions from the outset. The Christian moral stance that emerges here is not a club for beating over the head those who disagree. It does not provide a superior vantage point from which to deny them any humanitarian motive in the ordinary sense. But it *is* a vision of what "humanity" and "humanitarian motives" should be. We may therefore say of those who disagree: "All honor to the well-meaning humanitarianism of underlying motive! But the derivation is obviously from another book than that which we have thus far consulted."

PART THREE

Medical Perspectives

Medical Perspectives:
An Introduction

For two millennia or more, medical ethics has been guided by the moral principles embodied in the Hippocratic Oath. Although it originated in ancient Greece, the Hippocratic tradition was decisively shaped by Judeo-Christian thought and has enjoyed dominion in Western thought and culture ever since. Under its aegis, medicine was directed toward the good of the patient: first, to do no harm, and, where possible, to cure his afflictions. Recognizing the unequal power of physicians and patients, the Hippocratic Oath also contained a number of specific prohibitions: for example, the doctor must maintain the confidentiality of patients, refrain from sexual relations with them, and refuse, even upon request, to perform abortions or take a patient's life. The Oath thus served the good of the patient not only by defining the purpose of the medical art but also by imposing particular restrictions on the behavior of physicians.

The philosophical and moral assumptions of the Hippocratic tradition are today being challenged as never before. Physician-patient relationships now occur in the shadow cast by moral skepticism, the economics of health care, and revolutionary changes in medical technology. These developments, it is said, create a host of ethical dilemmas that earlier eras never had to confront. Some argue that the moral foundations of the Hippocratic tradition are inadequate to an age that places almost supreme value on personal autonomy. Just as the Oath's stricture against abortion has given way to the demand for reproductive freedom, so its strictures against physician-assisted suicide and euthanasia should be revised or eliminated. The moral judgments of a pre-scientific and religious era, it is said,

251

should not bind a highly technological age premised on religious and ethical pluralism.

Contemporary medicine is caught in the swirl of these conflicting opinions, and as the following essays make clear, nowhere is the tension greater than in the debate over assisted suicide and euthanasia. This section opens with the reflections of **Edmund D. Pellegrino** on the history of the Hippocratic tradition and the arguments for and against its principles. He points out that the debate within medicine mirrors the debate within society at large about the nature of moral truth: are our opinions culture-bound, or is it possible to know truths that transcend our particular time and place? While acknowledging that the Hippocratic tradition needs to be rearticulated for modern times, Pellegrino is dubious about the claims of more radical revisionists. It is all well and good, he says, to talk about the need for change, but how will patients fare under a new dispensation?

One answer is provided by **Jack Kevorkian**, the Michigan pathologist who has "assisted" in the deaths of more than fifty persons and calls himself a pioneer of a modern medical ethic. The crudeness of Kevorkian's techniques, his penchant for publicity, and his sometimes bizarre behavior clearly embarrass the medical profession. Among the medical critics of Kevorkian, however, it is not always clear whether they object to his philosophical and moral assumptions, or only to his methods and abrasive style.

Kevorkian is remarkably candid in his assault upon the religious and ethical foundations of the Hippocratic tradition. In his view, the prohibition against physician-assisted suicide is a punitive taboo foisted upon society by religious zealots who want to commit medicine to, as he puts it, the preservation of life "at all costs." In the name of protecting life, he says, the taboo tyrannizes patients and exacerbates their suffering. Kevorkian believes that licensed "medicide" should be permitted not only for the terminally ill but also for those who suffer an "excruciating and severely incapacitating" illness. In his essay in this section he proposes a new medical specialty, "obitiatry," that will train physicians to administer death upon request, and he gives a detailed description (along with a hypothetical case study) of how "obitiatrists" would function. What he offers, he says, is a "fail-safe model" for medically assisted suicide in the United States.

Physician and philosopher **Leon R. Kass** is among the most eloquent defenders of the traditional medical ethic. In his view, the prohibition of medical killing is anything but outmoded religious prejudice or irrational taboo. To the contrary, it expresses in compressed form a profound wisdom not only about the medical art but also about the human condition in general. Allowing doctors to kill will destroy the trust upon which the doctor-patient relationship rests and radically alter the physician's understanding of himself. Moreover, it would be foolish to think that once killing by doctors is made licit, their new power will be confined to patients who request assistance. We do not lack ostensibly compassionate or utilitarian reasons for killing, says Kass, and what we do not contrive on our own, lawyers will be sure to invent in the name of expanding human freedom. The experience of the Netherlands, where medical killing has been legal for nearly two decades, suggests to Kass that once licensed killing starts, it becomes very hard to stop.

By paying close attention to the philosophy embodied in the Hippocratic tradition, Kass argues, we may be able to stop before we start. The key to the Hippocratic Oath is that it limits the power of doctors precisely at those points where the physician is most powerful and the patient most vulnerable. Behind these prohibitions lies not some arbitrary, culture-bound prejudice but a universally applicable understanding of "the dignity and mysterious power of human life itself." By recognizing that neither compassion nor a good intention is a sufficient restraint against the abuse of power, the Oath instructs physicians about the true purpose of their art and the difference between serving a patient's will and serving his good.

The founder of the Hemlock Society and author of a best-selling how-to manual on suicide, **Derek Humphry**, believes that once certain conditions are met, people should be free to take their own lives and doctors should be free to help them. Not all suicides are the consequence of mental instability, he says, and when a patient is terminally ill or suffering greatly, a truly humane medicine will come to his assistance. Many members of the medical profession would agree with Humphry's premises, if not always with his particular recommendations. The anonymous author of **"It's Over, Debbie,"** for example, occasioned a heated debate within medical circles when he acknowledged that (as a resident) he had administered a lethal injection to a dying young patient whose only words to him were,

"Let's get this over with." His brief account presents in capsule form the kind of dilemma that doctors frequently face. Some of them, like **Timothy E. Quill**, believe that current restrictions operate to the disadvantage of patients suffering from incurable illnesses or "unrelenting, intolerable suffering." Dr. Quill, a noted and ardent advocate of physician-assisted suicide, argues that as long as doctors stay within carefully confined criteria, the risk of abuse can be kept within socially and morally tolerable limits. He describes these criteria in some detail and by applying them to one of his patients, undertakes to demonstrate their general applicability.

No matter whose criteria are employed, **D. Alan Shewmon** believes that once we abandon the distinction between killing and letting die, we will inevitably set foot upon a "two-dimensional slippery slope"—from killing terminally ill patients to killing on demand, and from voluntary to involuntary euthanasia. In Shewmon's view, the most commonly advanced justifications for assisted suicide (personal autonomy and the prospect of great suffering) contain no inherent limiting principles. And even if they did, courts would inevitably enlarge the categories of eligibility, much as abortion rights were expanded from the availability of abortion in hardship cases to abortion on demand. Anyone seeking further evidence, he argues, need look no further than Holland.

Herbert Hendin, a leading authority on the psychology of suicide, also believes that the experience of the Netherlands bodes ill as a model for the United States: despite a highly detailed regulatory scheme, Dutch physicians are performing both voluntary and involuntary euthanasia with relative impunity. In a 1991 study, over 40 per cent of the doctors surveyed admitted to killing patients without their knowledge or request. Significantly, Hendin points out, more requests for euthanasia came from patients' families than from patients themselves. From his own clinical observations and study, Hendin reports that most patient requests are a plea for attention and affection or a symptom of depression. More than 90 per cent of those who commit suicide exhibit a diagnosable psychiatric illness in the months prior to death, and the overwhelming majority are profoundly ambivalent about their intentions in any case. Surprisingly, terminally ill patients constitute only a small percentage of all suicides. Advocates like Humphry and Kevorkian, Hendin believes, feed upon people's understandable anxiety about dying in painful circumstances. Medicine, he argues, has far more humane ways to address anxiety than by killing the patient.

While Kass, Shewmon, and Hendin argue against yielding to patient autonomy in requests for deliverance by death, **H. Tristram Englehardt, Jr.**, would be much more lenient in that respect. He assumes that mature adults possess a right to suicide and that certain conditions justify its exercise as a rational act. He then takes the logic of that assumption to its next step and asks, What shall we do about those who are unable to exercise such a right?

Englehardt examines the case of severely disabled infants. Because children are not persons "in a strict sense," he says, decisions concerning their continued existence must be made by responsible adults, typically their parents. When very young children are gravely compromised by disease or handicap and unlikely to achieve "a developed personal life," Englehart argues that we do them no favor by keeping them alive. Life is not always a gift to be treasured, he says, and for those condemned to "a painful and compromised existence," it is closer to a curse than a blessing. Under such circumstances, he argues for the moral legitimacy of euthanasia and asserts that, when properly circumscribed by procedural safeguards, the practice can be shielded from abuse by both parents and doctors. Englehardt's suggestions are troubling, but if his premises are correct, it is inevitable that surrogate decision-makers will exercise the right of suicide for those who cannot do so on their own.

The **American Medical Association** bestrides these disagreements within the profession somewhat gingerly but remains resolute in its commitment to the Hippocratic tradition. In April 1996 its president, Lonnie R. Bristow, testifying before a subcommittee of the House Judiciary Committee, reiterated the AMA's long-standing position that doctors must not be allowed to cross the line between killing and letting die. Subsequent to that testimony, which is reprinted here along with an excerpt from the Code of Medical Ethics, the AMA House of Delegates overwhelmingly defeated proposals to soften the stand against physician-assisted suicide.

12

Rethinking the Hippocratic Oath

Edmund D. Pellegrino

Thirty years ago, at the inception of the era of contemporary bioethics, the Hippocratic Oath and the moral precepts it embodies were the immutable bedrock of medical ethics. They bound physicians in a moral community that reached across temporal, cultural, and national barriers. They seemed impervious even to the powerful scientific and societal forces then emerging.

Today, those forces have made the oath and each of its precepts the subject of critical challenge. Revisionists judge them anachronistic and in need of radical revision or total abandonment. Traditionalists, as urgently, insist on their timelessness, restoration, and reaffirmation. On the eve of the twenty-first century, the future shape and the viability of the centuries-old tradition of medical ethics are seriously in question.

What is at issue is the credibility and authority of the moral covenants that are at the heart of the oath, i.e., the promises to act primarily for the benefit and not for the harm of patients, to protect their confidences, to refrain from performing abortion and euthanasia

Edmund D. Pellegrino is the John Carroll Professor of Medicine and Medical Ethics at the Center of Clinical Bioethics, Georgetown University, Washington, D.C. This essay is reprinted by permission from *Journal of the American Medical Association* 275, no. 23 (June 19, 1996; © 1996 by the American Medical Association). The notes have been omitted.

and from having sexual relations with patients or their families, and to lead a life of moral integrity. Do these precepts retain their moral validity? Should they be revised to conform to contemporary mores? How free are physicians, society, and the profession to reinterpret and revise them?

These questions transcend academic and professional interest. How we answer them will determine the moral conduct, commitments, and trust patients may rightfully expect when they enter a therapeutic relationship. The nature of the physician's moral and social role in the next century is in the balance. All of us as present or future patients have a stake in the debate and, therefore, need to examine its opposing positions.

What the Critics Say

Critics of the oath and its moral content point to historical doubts about the date, authorship, and philosophical origins of the oath. They cite evidence that the oath was the work of a small group of reformist Pythagorean physicians and never of the whole profession. They deny the existence of a continuous moral tradition with wide acceptance among pagans, Christians, Jews, or Muslims. They also contend that the many violations of the oath in practice argue against any real influence on physician behavior.

Another criticism is that the oath is now morally irrelevant. Its authoritarianism and fixed moral rules are inconsistent with contemporary mores. Modern skepticism and pluralism in morals, together with the preeminence of privacy, autonomy, and free choice, make the oath a cultural irrelevancy and an impediment to social progress. Critics also denounce the sexism and elitism of the oath, which they perceive as instruments of professional privilege, power, and oppression.

For still other critics, the Hippocratic Oath expresses an independent ethic internal to the practice of medicine that they take to be an obstruction to the popular will. Where assisted suicide, euthanasia, abortion, or state-ordered executions are given social or legal sanction, the Hippocratic ethic has been set aside or reinterpreted to satisfy legislative fiat. In less democratic countries, the oath has been refashioned specifically to suit political purposes.

Perhaps the most disturbing criticism is the perceived insensitivity of the Hippocratic ethic to contemporary economic exigencies. For these critics, the primary emphasis on beneficence toward individual patients frustrates the physician's obligatory role as gatekeeper in managed-care plans. Beneficence is an impediment to the operation of competition and market forces, which, the critics argue, should determine the quality, price, and distribution of health care as of any other commodity. For these critics, medical ethics must be tailored to economic realities, rather than economics to ethics.

Finally, the Hippocratic ethic has been faulted for its lacunae, i.e., its failure to mention such important issues as human experimentation, the societal and communal obligations of physicians, and the relationships of physicians with other health professionals.

These criticisms are advanced by influential jurists, ethicists, and physicians. They merit serious consideration because their acceptance would definitely reshape the ethical profile of the profession. To evaluate these criticisms properly, the countervailing arguments of the defenders of the tradition also must be examined.

What Defenders Say

Defenders of the Hippocratic Oath readily admit that certain emendations are in order without compromise of its moral force, e.g., the invocation of pagan gods, the sexism, and the guild mentality. These have no morally valid defense. Likewise, the ethics of human experimentation, social obligation, and team care should be included. If the vague proscription against "cutting for the stone" is interpreted to mean practicing within the confines of one's expertise, it should be retained; if it is to forbid all surgery, it should be excluded.

For defenders of the oath, neither its omissions nor doubts about its authorship, date, place, or philosophical origins constitutes sufficient reason to jettison its ethical precepts. These have an independent moral grounding in the covenantal realities of the patient-physician relationship.

Defenders hold that even if the oath had not been widely accepted in ancient times, it did become almost universal subsequently. They point to the historical evidence for the continuity of a set of moral precepts dating at least to the first century A.D./C.E. with acceptance by

Jewish, Christian, and Muslim physicians. Through the English physicians of the eighteenth century, that same tradition shaped American medical ethics until just a decade or so ago.

Defenders deny the relevance of the charge of anachronism. Medical ethics, they hold, is not a matter of social convention, alterable by political, social, or economic exigency or by public referendum. Critics are required to counter the moral precepts with moral, not historical, arguments. Beneficence, for example, is central to medicine and not necessarily in conflict with autonomy. Sexual relations with patients are a violation of trust and always have been. Many of us still hold abortion and euthanasia to be intrinsically wrong and not redeemable by changes in public opinion. Any ethic changeable by fortuitous social, economic, political, or legal fiat ultimately ceases to be a viable ethic.

Options for Response

As a result of the debate, several options are emerging: restoration of the oath without change, restoration with minor, non-substantive changes or with substantial changes, replacement by a thoroughly modern version, or abandonment of all oaths.

A reasoned choice among these options requires engagement of the more fundamental questions of normative ethics: What is the moral justification for each of the norms of the oath? Which of the precepts are morally sound, and which are not? Why? What must be added to fill the lacunae? Is there something common to the ethics of medical praxis that transcends culture, economics, politics, or history? If so, what is it?

The difficulties of resolving such questions in our culturally, religiously, and morally diverse societies are obviously enormous. They extend well beyond the perimeters of medical ethics. Some philosophical ethicists are highly skeptical of the existence of any moral truths. Others deny there is anything ethically unique about medicine. The rift between traditionalists and revisionists is deep and wide. Yet the difficulties do not obviate the need for reasoned choices. This is no mere academic skirmish. Its practical consequences affect all of society and all of us as physicians and citizens.

No human being can escape the reality of being sick and being cared for. All must seriously contemplate what a divided profession without a common set of moral commitments would mean. Most important, we are obligated to ask how patients might fare in the hands of a profession with its moral fabric in tatters.

13

A Fail-safe Model for Justifiable Medically Assisted Suicide

Jack Kevorkian

The decriminalization and rehabilitation, as an honorable medical service, of the justifiable act of causing (euthanasia) or facilitating (assisted suicide) the death of hopelessly suffering patients is long overdue. It is the mores of society which should determine the ethics of any society;[1] and the latter, in turn, is the only reliable and practicable basis of law.[2] Unfortunately, most of the Western world over the last two millennia has reversed the process by enacting arbitrary laws to foist rules of conduct dictated by religion. These laws often and tragically cause unspeakable pain and suffering and result in irreparable harm to society as a whole. Unfortunately, in the context of relieving the torture of the irremediably suffering, "the law is a ass—a idiot."[3]

As medical services, euthanasia and assisted suicide were always ethical, widely practiced by physicians, and endorsed by almost all

Jack Kevorkian received his M.D. from the University of Michigan and was chief of pathology at a hospital in Detroit 1970-76. His book *Prescription: Medicide—The Goodness of Planned Death* was published by Prometheus Books in 1991. This essay is reprinted by permission from the *American Journal of Forensic Psychiatry* 13, no. 1 (1992), a publication of the American College of Forensic Psychiatry (P.O. Box 5870, Balboa Island, CA 92662).

263

segments of society in Hippocratic Greece.[4] The only opposition came from the tiny pagan religious sect called Pythagoreanism (which is said to have concocted the oath erroneously ascribed to Hippocrates). Despite their opposition, the Pythagoreans acknowledged that their contrary tenets could not be imposed on all of Greek society without seriously impairing its functional integrity. Later on there was none of that blunt honesty and respect for mores when the Western Judeo-Christian principles, which coincided almost exactly with those of extremely puritanical Pythagoreanism, dictated harshly punitive laws against euthanasia for all of society. Such laws cannot change but can only abuse and subvert ethics by paralyzing humans through brutal intimidation and fear. Eventually, in spite of all the fearful acquiescence and repressive atrocities born of such transgression, the mores will prevail and ethics will be disabused.

We are now witnessing that transition; and it behooves us, especially physicians, to guide it responsibly and correctly—in the true Hippocratic spirit. The latter embodies a dual medical mandate which has always been out of balance, especially in our highly technological age: to ameliorate or end pain and suffering as well as to preserve life. Any rational physician knows that in some cases the balancing of these two aims requires exquisite ratiocination. In many cases, these objectives can be mutually exclusive. Almost fanatically committed to preserving life at all costs (which have just about reached their limit today), physicians sometimes override patient autonomy and not only cause pain and suffering but also magnify it to horrendous proportions. It is easy to rationalize this terrible imbalance as obedience to laws which threaten harsh punishment for any physician who, in suitable cases, would want and try to restore the balance by mercifully helping to end a hopelessly tortured life.

The lessons of history are too easily and conveniently ignored or forgotten. We should always bear in mind the tragic mistakes of the recent past from which emanated the mandate of the Nuremberg Tribunal after World War II—to ask first about the ethical status of any law before dutifully obeying it. The "ethical" doctors in Nazi Germany were guilty of obeying obviously immoral laws, dictated by their own peculiar National Socialist "religion," which compelled them to do to or for patients what they should not even have thought about doing.

Medicine: A Secular Profession

Any religion ought to be irrelevant to the strictly secular doctor-patient relationship. After all, it is a medical problem that brings the patient to a doctor. If the patient has any religious qualms or constraints, he has consulted the wrong professional. If the same is true of the doctor, then he is not a complete professional and should probably change occupations, as should also all those "ethical" physicians who refuse to deal with AIDS patients. The religious or philosophical orientation of either the patient or the doctor is absolutely irrelevant to the latter's professional duty to the patient's health problem. It shouldn't matter to a Protestant doctor that a patient complaining of bodily signs and symptoms practices voodoo; or to a Muslim doctor that a patient is Buddhist or Shinto; or to a Catholic doctor that an atheistic woman wants an abortion; or to a Jewish doctor that the patient's name is Adolf Hitler. In each instance the truly ethical doctor's action is clear. Were he alive today, Hippocrates surely would say that to deny these four hypothetical patients the benefits of help, from those solely in a position to best render it, on the basis of incongruence of arbitrarily contrived and medically irrelevant ideation manifests unethical conduct of the highest order.

Medicine is a purely secular profession, like engineering and many others. It deals with health, disease, life, and death in this empirical world. Religion has as its centerpiece the uninvestigable "world." The two worlds should co-exist but without the intrusion of one on the other. It is as absurd for a theologian to dictate medical ethics as it is for a doctor to dictate religious ethics. For example, is it not ludicrous for a minister, priest, or rabbi to tell a doctor how, when, or where to excise a gall bladder or to treat myocardial infarction—or to help a suffering and pleading patient die—and equally ludicrous for a physician to tell the religious professional how, when, or where to perform a baptism, a mass, a bar mitzvah, or funeral rites?

Every profession should have its own unique code of ethics, which is best created by those most knowledgeable and able to do so: its own well-trained and experienced practitioners. And as society evolves, the components of each code must change to accommodate the inexorable and irresistible flux of nature. To resort to arcane and contrived "eternal truths" in that accommodation is certainly futile and doomed to engender crippling ethical crises for individuals and society alike. Euthanasia and medically assisted suicide can never be new practices but only resurrected from deplorable dormancy; hence, as mentioned in the opening paragraph, "decriminalized and rehabilitated."

The Fear of Abuse

That is only part of the problem. The overriding concern of most critics is the fear of potential abuse, or society going down the so-called slippery slope. Any attempt to allay such fears will necessitate more than a simple approach; but that need not imply an overly cumbersome system. Surely the collective intelligence of the medical profession is equal to this task, provided there is the will to do so. To that end, the following is proposed as a foolproof or fail-safe model which would guarantee maximal efficiency with minimal or no potential for abuse or corruption.

Medicine is a worldwide activity and its ethics the same everywhere. The following model is proposed also to serve that broad scope.

It should be pointed out that the neologism "medicide" is introduced and being used for the purpose of linguistic convenience, which is the case in most of science. Even though the Latin equivalents imply "killing a physician," it is appropriate as a shorthand label using the first and last syllables of the phrase "medically assisted suicide." Nominal inaccuracy is not uncommon: whereas "orthopedics" originally meant "straightening the child" afflicted with bony deformations, today it denotes a specialty encompassing far more than its original intention. Also, surgery—the Anglicized corruption of the Greek term "cheirergy"—literally means "working with the hands," which certainly doesn't adequately describe modern surgery and does not differentiate the activities of others who work with their hands, such as physiotherapists, masseurs, and other craftsmen.

THE THEORETICAL MODEL

Not every physician can participate in euthanasia or medicide either by choice or by temperament. It would be unreasonable to expect this to be within the legitimate duty of every physician, just as such expectation is unreasonable when it comes to very sophisticated and extremely demanding specialties such as neurosurgery or psychiatry. It is easy to imagine that the abuse, tragedy, and chaos which would result if every physician were allowed to practice neurosurgery or psychiatry would be no less horrifying if every physician—no matter what his or her talents, experience, and attitude—were allowed to practice euthanasia and assisted suicide. An assisted-suicide specialist is just as essential as a neurosurgeon or psychiatrist, because the current system of specialization and referrals guarantees a consistently uniform quality and a complete spectrum of medical practice for all physicians, as well as universal accessibility to all services for all patients.

It stands to reason, therefore, that medicide calls for the creation of a new group of specialists having impeccable credentials and reputations, sincere dedication and commitment, proper orientation, and the necessary skill and thorough training. At first glance the name for such a specialty would seem to include the Greek term "thanatos." However, the word "thanatologist" is already being used by other paraprofessionals, such as psychologists and sociologists who deal with human death. Therefore, a suitable new term would be a combination of Greek and Latin roots to form "obitiatry," and its practitioner, "obitiatrist"—literally "doctor of death."

At the beginning of this rehabilitated specialty, obitiatrists must be evolved through experience and certified by reason of their being pioneers ("grandfather clause"). With further development, obitiatry should follow the course of all other specialties with official postgraduate training programs (residencies) promulgated and administered by such pioneers, and a certifying board to conduct examinations and to certify competence. Furthermore, the specialty must have its own journal to document all of its activities through reports of cases and of theoretical and practical research. This would serve as a superb wellspring for sensible and workable laws for the benefit of medically untutored legislators.

At this early stage the proposed model must be confined geographically to demonstrate its practicability. That can best be done in a state in the United States, and Michigan has been chosen as an example. The state has been arbitrarily divided into eleven zones, each of which encompasses multiple counties according to size and population density in such a way as to minimize geographic burdens for obitiatrists concerned. For the obitiatrist's convenience and ease of control, zone headquarters will be located in a city as close as possible to the center of each zone. The administrative staff of each headquarters will of necessity be small at the outset, consisting of one secretary or assistant. At least one obitiatrist must reside in or very close to the headquarters office. All requests for medicide must be forwarded to the headquarters in writing by patients' personal physicians—never by patients themselves. All telephone inquiries must be followed up immediately by written confirmation before any action can be taken.

An official request will set in motion a comprehensive process entailing thorough written documentation. Please note in Document G (fig. 11) that there must be five obitiatrists in each zone. [Figures 1-12 appear on pages 284-95.] Because every case requires the involvement of at least five obitiatrists, it follows that there should be more obitiatrists available to cover unforeseen circumstances, such as personal illnesses or absences of any of the primary five.

The Case of Wanda Endittal

A hypothetical case based on my experience will illustrate the entire procedure in detail and will demonstrate the indispensability of foolproof documentation entailing the cross-checking safeguards of multiple forms, labeled Documents A through H and Z. The latter are designated with bold alphabetic letters, the sequence of which dictates the proper order of action. (The names in the following hypothetical scenario have been devised not out of flippancy but rather to facilitate and understand the various roles involved.)

The hypothetical patient is Wanda Endittal, a 45-year-old female afflicted with multiple sclerosis, whose residence is in Wayne County, Michigan. She has requested of her physician, neurologist Frieda Blaime, M.D., aid in ending her life. Dr. Blaime immediately conveys the patient's request in writing to Zone One headquarters in Pontiac, Michigan. Any request emanating from Zone One must be referred only to Zone One headquarters; every obitiatrist-patient relationship must entail individuals residing and practicing in the same zone.

At headquarters is posted a duty roster of available obitiatrists in the order of availability. On receipt of Dr. Blaime's request, the secretary immediately telephones the next available obitiatrist, Will B. Reddy, M.D. Dr. Reddy obtains Documents A, B and C (figs. 1-A, 2, 3, pp. 284-86) and visits the patient (in this case, in the hospital where the patient is undergoing physiotherapy). After the therapy session, Dr. Reddy meets with the patient, her parents, and Dr. Blaime in Dr. Blaime's office at the hospital. Because of her personal opposition to assisted suicide, Dr. Blaime has reservations about Wanda's decision. Nevertheless, in this meeting Dr. Blaime listens attentively and contributes information to the discussion as needed. When the meeting has ended, the patient signs the initial request for medicide, duly witnessed and verified by Dr. Reddy (fig. 1-A). At the same time, he obtains the information about all the family members and puts a few personal questions to the patient. These are recorded by Dr. Reddy on Document B (fig. 2). If time permitted and he were so inclined, Dr. Reddy could also compile all the information required for Document C (fig. 3), or he could postpone that for a day or two for convenience. This brief but concise document includes Dr. Reddy's entire initial clinical assessment based on current and past hospital records, the history he himself takes, and the physical examination he performs.

The stage is now set for the first joint consultation of the obitiatrist with Wanda and her nearest relatives. In situations where there is no next of kin, the patient's best friend and/or a confidante must be present. Wanda's next of kin are listed in Document D (fig. 4). It is Dr. Reddy's duty to summarize the discussion where indicated on Document D to the satisfaction of all participants, who have the privilege of reviewing it and Dr. Reddy's conclusions as written. Dr. Reddy then signs Document D, duly witnessed.

It is important at this time for essential consultants to be involved, all of whom report on Document E (figs. 5-9). The first such step is to certify the patient's primary diagnosis, which calls for a neurology consult (fig. 7). Wanda's mental state is also of paramount importance, so a psychiatric evaluation is necessary (fig. 5). Because of the gravity of the responsibility of Dr. Reddy and other obitiatrists, at least one psychiatrist must serve in this evaluation process.

Of the panel of five obitiatrists, three will be designated as advisory, having but one responsibility: to decide whether or not medicide is justifiable in Wanda's case at the time of consideration. The other two panel members compose the action group: they cannot decide but can only perform medicide. Any obitiatrist can serve on either panel at any time; however, one of the advisory group must be a psychiatrist.

In Wanda's case, the obitiatric psychiatrist is Dr. Lotte Goode, who is part of the advisory panel. If a significant amount of time (several months or more) elapses between the first joint consultation and the final obitiatric decision (as recorded in Documents D and G), a second independent psychiatrist must reevaluate the patient immediately after the final obitiatric decision has been made to detect any possible change in mental competency. Because in Wanda's case the interim was more than eight months, Dr. Goode called in her classmate, Dr. Sy Keyes, whose evaluation is also reported in a separate Document E (fig. 9).

It is obvious that consultation by a competent sociologist is necessary to detect personal or family disputes or irregularities, to clarify financial problems among family members, to cover the matter of a will, and to determine if funeral arrangements have been considered (fig. 6).

Another crucial adjunct is the matter of religion, about which Dr. Reddy must inquire. Wanda professes to be Episcopal and names I. Ammon Abbott, D.D., as her minister (fig. 8). If a patient denies any religious affiliation or preference, such a consultation is out of the question. If a patient is religious but has no preference or no specific minister in mind, the obitiatrist is obligated to make sure that a theologian of the denomination or sect concerned meets personally with the patient.

All consultation forms must emanate from zone headquarters. In Wanda's case, Dr. Reddy will supply the following information at the top of the document: the appropriate discipline concerned, the specific points to be covered by the request, and the patient's name and address. The remaining information will be supplied by Doctors Keyes and Abbott and Ms. Tydings on the documents mailed to them from zone headquarters. Each consultant will return his or her completed document to zone headquarters to be included in Wanda's file. Dr. Reddy will take them to Wanda for review and approval. This cross-check maximizes honesty and objectivity, instills confidence in the patient, and serves as control against oversight or abuse. If in any of her reviews Wanda manifests *any degree* of ambivalence, hesitancy, or outright doubt with regard to her original decision, the entire process is stopped immediately, and Wanda is no longer—and can never again be—a candidate for medicide in the state of Michigan.

The various Documents E (figs. 5-9) may be presented for Wanda's review when she and her family meet with Dr. Reddy for joint consultation. In some cases of a less chronic nature, this may be the final meeting. For Wanda, the final consultation will take place at the home of her parents. This will begin with a private meeting between doctors and Wanda during which time she may be permitted to review and comment on prior consultant reports. Following this, Dr. Reddy will meet in private only with family members for an open and frank exchange. It would be advisable to have all joint sessions videotaped. Finally, all parties will meet in a joint session. These three sessions are summarized in Document F, duly witnessed (fig. 10).

The Action Obitiatrists

Dr. Reddy now returns to headquarters with Documents E and F in hand, and from the headquarters duty roster selects a panel of the next four available obitiatrists. Three obiatrists will serve as advisory, and two (Dr. Reddy and another) as action.

Please note that the three advisory obitiatrists must agree. If not, the process reverts to Document E for repetition of consultations, evaluations, and recommendations for as long as the request of the patient is still valid. If one of the *action* obitiatrists hesitates because of doubt, no matter how inconsequential, the case is referred back to the same advisory panel for thorough review. This may take place at the same time or may necessitate further consultation with medical colleagues and specialists, other paraprofessionals, further examination of the patient, and more laboratory tests, followed by another attempt at coming to a final decision at a later time. Advisory unanimity then unconditionally mandates obitiatric action. In Wanda's case, this was certified under "Action Response" by Dr. Dunne in Document G (fig. 11) with simple terms, such as "agreed" or "acknowledged."

This marks the only joint meeting of all obitiatrists, preferably but not necessarily at zone headquarters. Henceforth, the advisory panel is not involved in the case. Responsibility now passes to the action obitiatrists, one of whom will continue. In Wanda's case, Dr. Dewey Ledder had the shortest task—to evaluate Wanda's file and to vote. It is up to Dr. Shelby Dunne to continue by having Wanda review her original request (Document A, fig. 1-A) and verify final informed consent (Document Z, fig. 1-B). For the sake of convenience, the patient's request and final consent are on the same sheet, which in effect summarizes the entire procedure from A to Z.

The practice of medicide is so serious and profound as to require recording the times of all machinations documented in the various forms. However, such a notation on Document Z is most important, because the actual procedure must be accomplished within twenty-four hours of the patient's signing of the final consent. If more than twenty-four hours elapses, the chain of events must be repeated beginning with Document F.

It will be noted from Document A that two medicide procedures will be made available to all patients. The optimal choice is lethal injection as described, activated by the patient. This can be accomplished by anyone no matter how incapacitated physically. All that is required is extremely light pressure on a hair-trigger switch. If a patient is quadriplegic, it would be simple to attach a small item to the head of the patient by some sort of band, which on slight turning of the head could activate the switch. Or, a tiny item such as a stick or wire held between the teeth, or even the lips, could do it. The limiting factor is the status of the patient's veins. Excessive scarring or fragility would militate against this optimal choice. In such a case, the second option of lethal gas—which is equally painless, humane, and almost as fast—would be no less desirable.

It is the responsibility of Dr. Dunne, the action obitiatrist, to arrange for the site of medicide according to Wanda's preference. This may be at Wanda's home, the home of a family member or friend, in the hospital or nursing home if necessary and permitted. In the future a small clinic should be provided in each zone headquarters for those patients who have no access to the above sites.

The action obitiatrist must also prepare and make available and arrange all necessary materials and devices, and instruct the patient in minute detail how the procedure is to be carried out. When everything is ready, because Wanda has suitable veins, it will be her free choice to decide when and if she will activate her chosen lethal injection method. Dr. Dunne will indicate this at the space marked "Start Time" on Document H (fig. 12). He will also list, as indicated in the document, all persons present.

The crucial distinction should be pointed out with regard to euthanasia as conventionally understood and assisted suicide, and the equally critical distinction of the ethics of the physician's role in each procedure. On the one hand (euthanasia), the physician is obligated to be the direct agent of killing, and on the other hand, is merely the indirect agent abetting the killers—the patients themselves—and consequently less vulnerable to moral censure.

The final action for Wanda cannot proceed without the presence of an official designated by law or some other legally empowered authority. The name of the official observer must be printed where indicated in Document H, followed by a signature.

When medicide is completed, Dr. Dunne will note the end time in the space provided in Document H (which will be the official time of death), will summarize details of the procedure in the space provided, print his name, and sign Document H. He will also fill out and sign the death certificate, listing the primary cause of death truthfully as "medicide"; contributory cause: "multiple sclerosis."

Impressions of the official observer will be noted where indicated together with his or her evaluation of the entire procedure. This observer's duty does not affect medicide in any way; it is to serve only as witness for the political jurisdiction as stipulated by federal or state law to guarantee propriety.

THE IMPLEMENTATION

The above theoretical model, if diligently and honestly put into practice by qualified individuals who are steadfastly committed to the enhancement of human welfare, individually and collectively, in the true Hippocratic tradition, represents a rational and compassionate resolution of the conflicting duties to alleviate pain and suffering on the one hand, and to prolong life on the other.

Let us now consider in more detail the envisioned components and mechanism of such a practice.

The Personnel

Obviously, physicians are the best qualified to perform medicide. In fact, because of their training, experience, and legitimate access to all kinds of drugs, they are the only ones who should. This fact is underscored by the inevitable sense of serenity and confidence that would be imparted to patients by the mere presence of such superbly qualified individuals.

As already stated, the pioneers serving as obitiatrists must be physicians of various general and specialized practices and qualifications. Normally, every physician is obligated by ethical and regulatory dicta to confine his or her activities within certain professional limits in dealing with the diagnosis and treatment of living patients. Moreover, all physicians, because of their basic training and mandatory clinical experience, have intimate knowledge about the dying process through daily contact with terminal and chronically agonized or hopelessly incapacitated patients. Therefore, no matter what ordinary practice or specialty is involved, any physician can justifiably serve as a pioneer obitiatrist. Of course, many attributes other than strictly professional acumen are desirable and indeed necessary. Provided the so-called pioneers are carefully selected, such deficiencies could be diminished and even eradicated among pioneers themselves by concurrent voluntary teaching sessions.

The deficiencies might include lack of psychological insight, religious insensitivity or intolerance, legal ignorance, and poor interpersonal skills. As the practice of obitiatry develops and the pioneers participate in the establishment of their own specialty board, this kind of makeshift program will be institutionalized as an honorable, legitimate, and indispensable specialty. Like all other specialties, this too will require that candidates complete perhaps two years of routine general practice following internship before applying for residency training. The latter must consist of not less than four years of postgraduate work involving a uniform mix of philosophical, religious, psychological, and legal training interspersed with rotation through routine surgical and medical duties in hospitals or clinics as well as through selected facilities on the frontiers of medical research.

Where possible, the non-medical activities will involve more than mere didactics; for example, training in all religious faiths will also entail at least infrequent personal participation in the actual rites involved. In addition, theoretical exposure to various relevant aspects of law mandates personal participation in the judicial process involved, such as accompanying attorneys, judges, and legislators in the performance of their own professional duties. In other words, hands-on experience is equal to, or more important than, theoretical training.

Upon completion of four years of residency, candidates must pass stringent written and oral examinations; and when certified by the board, must pass re-certifying examinations—perhaps every five years.

Finally, the specialty will have its own journal; and because obitiatry should and probably will be a uniform medical activity throughout the world, the journal should be international in scope. It will embody only communications concerned with obitiatric practice.

This proposal may sound overblown, overly grandiose, or impractical. However, any activity aimed at trying to regulate and affect medical circumstances during the dying process and at the actual moment of death can never be overblown, too grandiose, or impractical. Even more important, the aim of obitiatry for the future goes far beyond the mere termination of human life. As I have already outlined elsewhere in detail,[5] obitiatry alone is capable of making death positively meaningful to human life—of extracting from inevitable and justifiable medicide incalculable benefit for all of humanity.

In most instances, an obitiatrist will need competent assistance in the performance of medicide. Although not essential, such an assistant —preferably a para-medical person (nurse or technologist)—could help by preparing apparatus and handling materials. Here, too, "pioneers" will be necessary, and in the future, assistants may also have to go through official para-obitiatric training programs.

The Patients

Finally, the most important personnel are patients themselves, who may be suffering from other than imminently terminal diseases. Whereas in the United States discussion of euthanasia seems to center solely on acutely terminal diseases, such as cancer, physicians in the Netherlands have wisely expanded their perspective also to include patients facing many years of excruciating and severely incapacitating illnesses, such as crippling arthritis or emphysema, severe pneumonia and bronchitis, progressive degenerative necrologic diseases, and stroke.

From personal experience I know that the Dutch scope is the best approach. In at least three cases of terminal cancer I have consulted with the patients, their families, their medical records, and their personal physicians, and in all three the patients proceeded to die with surprising serenity and calm resignation before medicide could be performed. There are several reasons for this. In the first place, the stigma of taboo impeded cooperation of colleagues and caused subtle and unavoidable apprehension and reticence among everyone made aware of the situation. Secondly, the patients' mental outlook was so relieved of panic after my initial consultation with them that they contentedly made plans to fulfill certain personal obligations which had previously seemed inconsequential or burdensome. In this tranquil frame of mind each of the three patients died naturally within a period of from two to four weeks.

A long letter of gratitude from the wife of one of the three, a 55-year-old successful businessman dying of liver cancer widely metastatic to the brain, began:

> I am sorry the law (politics) doesn't understand what you do for those who need your service and compassion. My husband . . . was in severe pain. . . . After your talking to (him) . . . that night he agreed to get more radiation . . . (but) was never strong enough to get in for treatment. And after your visit he never talked about taking his life again. . . . We never know what's in store for us. Thank you for caring.

One needs no more evidence that the mere availability of competent medicide will reduce the need, desire, and incidence of suicide among ill patients and elderly healthy individuals by relieving the sense of hopelessness in their panic-stricken minds. Rather than increasing the incidence of suicide, the practice of medicide will reduce it substantially and at the same time immeasurably enhance human welfare.

An equally urgent reason for the practice of medicide is to offer an alternative to the inevitably violent methods now used by suffering patients to end their own lives. This is substantiated by an extensive report of one week's toll of suicide by gunshot alone, 10 per cent of which were for medical reasons (not psychiatric). The report verifies more than 2,000 cases a year.[6] These patients, too, deserve the less bloody and less violent, more humane and more painless option of medicide. In view of this neglect, inertia on the part of the medical profession denotes barbarity, which is only magnified by real or feigned unawareness of being so barbaric.

For emphasis, I cite a couple of examples in two different states from my own experience. The first concerned a man dying of mesothelioma apparently induced by asbestos. In September 1990 he wrote to me: "Presently I am taking morphine pills. But they do not help much. You probably know better ways by which to take the final step. . . . People suffering from terminal illnesses should be allowed to die without more suffering." Of course, I was unable to do anything for the patient because of insuperable restraints imposed by the authorities. A month later I received a letter from his wife:

> He was in great pain and . . . was searching for a way out of that misery. . . . Somehow during another sleepless night he must have thought about it all and come to a decision. . . . While I was in the kitchen, he locked the garage and shot himself. What a miserable way to end an otherwise loving and successful life. . . . He had left a note for me and also to the authorities: ". . . There should be a legal way with narcotics and poison." . . . This I believe is not an isolated case, and I hope you press on with your fight to help people in misery and so desperate.

The second case was similar, involving a man dying of lung cancer with massive cerebral metastases. A month after his initial letter to me, I received word from his wife that she "experienced the shock" of accidentally finding him dead at home of a gunshot wound to the head.

A third case is just as dramatic and convincing. In a letter to me shortly after the Janet Adkins suicide, a woman afflicted with multiple sclerosis wrote the following:

> I am unable to move my lower limbs . . . to change position while lying in bed, someone has to move my legs, bend my knees and help me turn. To get . . . any place I have to be carried. I also am having some difficulty with speech. I only have minimum use of

the upper limbs and body. On [date given] I shot myself in the chest. Not knowing exactly where the heart was, I aimed about two inches too far to the left. I had to do something while I was still able. I am tired of fighting the MS. I just want it over. I do not look forward to becoming a vegetable. Please help me if you can.

It should be pointed out that exactly the same sentiments were expressed by another, even more incapacitated MS patient here in Michigan before her assisted suicide.

Finally, the pleas from several patients have informed me of a unique psychiatric condition of which I was not aware. About half a dozen patients, ranging in age from late teens to early forties, complained of a perpetual desire to have their lives ended even though they denied any sort of significant depression or specific illness. In one typical letter, a woman wrote:

I am twenty years old and have always wanted to die my whole life. I am not a bad person. I am not sick or depressed. I have just about everything that anyone could ever have. I have never been in trouble with the law, never taken drugs or anything like that. I don't have any problems. I just feel this way and always will until someone helps me accomplish what I want. . . . I have tried to take my life twice now by taking pills, and neither time it worked. . . . I have been to see psychologists, been through counseling, and have been admitted to an institute. I still feel the same way. They didn't help me. I suffer every day by being here. This place is just not meant for me. . . . I have talked to my mother about you, and she said that you won't help me because you only help the ones that are suffering from a dying disease.

She is right, of course. Here is where I draw the line. And here is where it should be drawn—until this kind of fail-safe model has been finely honed by years of experience. Only then might medicide be expanded for the benefit of patients apparently tortured by other than organic diseases; and that expansion will be the sole prerogative and duty of psychiatrists. In the future if such a case is ever to be considered, the obitiatric advisory panel must consist only of psychiatrists. The action obitiatrists need not be psychiatric experts. I emphasize: such an expansion can be fraught with immense potential uncertainty, and therefore will be contingent upon exhaustive and penetrating research and experimentation into the human mind and psyche while medicide dealing with organic diseases is carefully implemented, expanded, and refined. Only then might the line of medicide be justifiably redrawn.

The Facilities

A zone headquarters should consist of a small office (rented or purchased) for administrative purposes employing a secretary-receptionist. All patients' records dealing with obitiatry will be kept at this office. There should also be an adjoining small room to serve as a clinic or modified operating room where medicide procedures can be carried out by patients who are homeless or otherwise prefer it. Final decision by obitiatrists can be made anywhere, but preferably arrived at in a joint meeting at headquarters. The office will always be accessible by telephone, directly during business hours, and by telephone answering service at all other times without interruption.

In all likelihood there will not be enough pioneers to initiate this idealized model on the basis of multiple zones as depicted and described. The few available pioneers will have to treat the entire state as one massive zone having its headquarters where population is concentrated. Of necessity and unfortunately, that will mean limited service which would therefore be unavailable to some deserving patients. In time this situation will be rectified as increasing numbers of obitiatrists justify the delineation of zones and consequent expansion of the service for all patients according to the model proposed herein.

The Materials and Documents

Everything needed for the performance of medicide will be stored in abundance at headquarters and taken by the action obitiatrist to the site of the procedure on the designated day. Included will be drugs and pre-prepared solutions in bottles, intravenous infusion sets, plastic tubes, syringes, needles, and everything necessary for venipuncture. With the help of an assistant, the obitiatrist will make ready a special suicide device, which may be activated electrically or mechanically. If lethal gas inhalation is to be the method, a canister of appropriate carbon-monoxide–air mixture, with attached regulatory valve and gauge, plastic tube, and mask (or tent) will be supplied and set up by the obitiatrist and his or her assistant. The patient and/or family will pay only for expendable materials used, if able to do so. All other unused materials together with the lethal devices used will be returned to headquarters by the obitiatrist personally as soon as possible. The returned items will have been inventoried briefly in a review of the procedure as recorded in Document H (fig. 12). This will be verified at headquarters on return of the materials.

A copy of every document from A through H and Z will be filed confidentially at headquarters with every case. In some instances, when death is imminent or the disease fulminating, there may be time enough for only one joint consultation. Therefore, at the top of Document D the word "final" will be inserted by the obitiatrist concerned with the consultation. Nevertheless, Document F must be filed in such a case with some sort of notation in a space marked "conclusions" to the effect that there was not sufficient time for more than one joint consultation. This Document F, too, must be filed by the obitiatrist concerned. Such an "acute" case would also mean a limited number of professional consultants, as reported in Document E.

As previously stated, it is advisable to have all joint sessions videotaped, and all videotapes filed at headquarters.

Financial Considerations

There will be no fee for service charged to patients or their families. From experience I know that in many cases patients and family members would be eager to donate an amount of money out of gratitude. This will never be solicited but will be accepted and placed in a special non-profit fund to be administered jointly by certain designated obitiatrists together with an independent banker and an independent accountant. All three parties will be required to sign checks of disbursement for materials and suitable salaries for obitiatrists. A salary limits the potential of abuse by eliminating the incentive for inordinate pecuniary gain which might occur with remuneration on a per-case basis. Salaries will be the same for all members of the advisory and action panels despite variations in responsibilities and time expended.

Additional sources of potential income for the non-profit fund are unsolicited private donations from uninvolved parties, charitable foundations and groups, and special fund-raising events. Government grants are acceptable only if absolutely unconditional, and will never be solicited.

Assistants also will be paid from the non-profit fund on a per-case basis. However, the administrative secretary will be a salaried position. All office expenses will be paid from the fund in the usual manner of check disbursement.

Financial accounts will be audited on an annual basis by an independent certified accountant not involved with disbursements, and all annual statements will be open to public review. It should be emphasized that annual reports will be totally itemized as to receipts—actual sources of receipts by name—and disbursements by name.

In the beginning pioneers will undoubtedly work altruistically with donated time, expertise, and even materials. This is a practicable approach, because some (even most) of the so-called pioneers will be either retired physicians with more than satisfactory income or highly motivated, altruistic, practicing physicians who likewise would not expect remuneration. As the system develops and funds begin to pour in, the foregoing system of payment will be set in operation. In any event, obitiatrists will not be, and should not expect to be, highly paid. This most likely will not be an overriding concern because, contrary to some opinions, there will be diminished demand for medicide among patients whose mental panic will certainly be dissipated by the existence of this option.

Legal Controls

The only state law needed for the proposed practice is one which makes assisting any suicide a felony for everybody except obitiatrists. Like any medical specialty, the rules and regulations governing the practice are the responsibility of the medical profession—in particular, the physicians with the expertise and training to practice it. As it is now, the law stipulates only that a physician act competently and honestly; and that is all the law can say with regard to medicide and obitiatry.

The matter of an official observer may be stipulated by law, or could be an official state regulation, or part of the drafted medical code.

For the sake of certainty of control, it would be advisable to make infringement of the law or code a felony with maximum punishment. To help avoid such a catastrophe, there will be kept at headquarters and in the action obitiatrist's possession a detailed procedural checklist; and it is his or her responsibility alone to make sure that it is scrupulously adhered to.

All activities in each zone in each state will be subjected to an annual review seminar, open to the public, at a meeting hall (not zone headquarters). All obitiatrists and official observers in a particular state must attend the annual convention, which is organized to inform and to educate specialists and the public alike.

A similar national conclave will be held biennially to review the experiences of all states for the same purposes. The national meeting will be rotated among the states just as the annual meetings will be rotated among the various state zones.

Accusation of professional misconduct will be addressed by a board having jurisdiction over the same.

Miscellaneous Points

Witnesses at medicide procedures can be anyone designated by the patient, the number kept within a reasonable limit depending on the size of the site. At every procedure the obitiatrist, assenting physicians concerned with the patient, an assistant, and the official observer must be present.

An autopsy is not mandatory, because without a doubt the cause of death and the pathologic process concerned will be beyond question. If an autopsy is desired by the patient or family members, they must arrange and pay for it. When death is pronounced, the patient's body is handled in the ordinary way with regard to morticians and funerals, none of which concerns obitiatry.

The legitimized and routine practice of obitiatry as outlined above eliminates the current situation in which an assisted suicide is accompanied by sensationalized and frantic responses and investigations by governmental police agencies and judicial inquiries. An instance of justifiable medicide as described should arouse no more special concern or attention than any other routine medical service.

Concluding Observations

Most physicians would agree that birth and death are the two most important events in the existence of any human being. But in reality, their importance is not equal, simply because once having been unconsciously experienced, a person's birth is no longer part of his or her life. Therefore, death, which is not yet experienced, becomes paramount, because everything in life is terminated by it. No other experience in life has such a devastatingly total effect. Herein lies one of medicine's greatest and most subtle inconsistencies, which too easily escapes attention.

Not too long ago the important event of birth was not a part of honorable or acceptable medical practice. The "demeaning" activity of obstetrics was left to abject midwives and was deemed far beneath the exalted status of noble physicians. In time, with increasing maturity and honesty of a grudging medical profession, the practice of helping to ease the entrance of human life into the world became completely honorable and ethical. And this is proper, because issues concerning the health and illness of any living human are in the domain of medicine. The same is true of birth control, yet it took decades of further struggle before this legitimate medical obligation was grudgingly acknowledged.

The time has come to do the same, but less grudgingly, in easing the exit of human beings from this world. After all, a dying patient is still alive, and his or her concerns are still in the domain of medicine. Currently, we blaspheme the process of exiting—the most important event—by not according it even the indignity of comparable "midwifery." Such brazen inconsistency is inexcusable. But even that degree of indignity would not do. The medical profession must take the lead immediately to shorten the deplorable evolution of this last unjustified taboo by elevating the most important life event called death to the place of honor in the hierarchy of ethics it has always deserved.

[*Note:* The documents begin on the following page.]

FIGURE 1-A

MICHIGAN OBITIATRY—ZONE 1

A   No. _92-1_

Request for Medically Assisted Suicide   CONFIDENTIAL   A

I, _WANDA ENDITTAL_, the undersigned, hereby request, of my own free will and without any reservations or extrinsic persuasion or duress, that my life of intolerable and interminable pain and/or suffering be ended in the most humane, rapid, and painless manner with the help of a competent medical professional. It is my understanding that if the status of my veins permits, I will have access to, and myself activate, a special device which will introduce into my vein a fast-acting barbiturate type drug to put me to sleep in several seconds, followed within 30 to 60 seconds by a lethal mixture of drugs to stop heart action and to paralyze all muscles. I further understand that the medical professional will perform the necessary venipuncture which will be kept operational with a slow drip of physiological saline solution until the time I choose to activate the lethal flows.

If my veins are not suitable for intravenous manipulations, I will end my life by breathing through a routine facial mask or plastic tent a lethal mixture of carbon monoxide in air.

All details of both procedures have been explained to me by the undersigned medical professional, and I am fully aware of the implications and consequences of my voluntarily carrying them out.

Patient _Wanda Endittal_   Obitiatrist WILL B. REDDY, M.D.
Witness _Vera Feier, RN_   (Signature) _Will B. Reddy, M.D._
Site CITY GEN. HOSP., SUMTOWN, MI   Date 8 JAN. 1992

FIGURE 1-B

Z   Z

Final Consent for Assistance
(To be completed immediately after action is authorized in Document G)

I, _Wanda Endittal_, the undersigned, have once again read the above request and had all aspects explained to me in detail, which I understand fully. The procedure deemed to be the most appropriate for me is _lethal injection with a special device_, with which I agree and which I wish to be implemented without delay.

Patient X _(her mark)_   Obitiatrist _Shelby Dunne, MD._
Witness _Sheila Byde_   (Signature) _Shelby Dunne, MD._
Site _1234 Main St, Sumtown, MI_   Date _15 Sept. 1992_ Time _7:00 pm_

(IMPORTANT: FINAL CONSENT VALID ONLY FOR 24 HOURS!)

FIGURE 2

B No. 92-1   MICHIGAN OBITIATRY—ZONE 1   **CONFIDENTIAL** **B**

Patient Data

PERSONAL

Patient's Name WANDA ENDITTAL   Age 45 Sex F

Address 1234 MAIN ST., SUMTOWN, MI 48000   Phone (313) 200-1992

Patient's Doctor FRIEDA BLAIME, MD   Diagnosis MULTIPLE SCLEROSIS

Patient's Religion EPISCOPAL   Religious Advisor I. AMMON ABBOTT, DD

FAMILY	(Name)	(Address)	(Phone)	(Age)
Spouse	FRANK LEE ENDITTAL,	1234 MAIN ST., SUMTOWN	(313) 200-1992	52
Mother	FLO N. TIERS	4231 FIRST ST., SUMTOWN	(313) 202-2991	69
Father	JUSTIN TIERS	" " " "	"	74
Siblings	SHEILA BYDE	567 N ST., ANYVILLE, MI	(313) 300-9291	38
	BARRY GRIEPH	100 RHODE AVE, OTHERBURG IL	(312) 444-0011	51
Other	DAWN ENDITTAL	1234 MAIN ST., SUMTOWN, MI	(313) 200-1992	19

ADDITIONAL

Have you discussed your wishes with any of the persons listed above? YES

If "yes", please write their names here Husband Parents Dawn

Do you have any family or financial problems or disputes? NO   If "yes", please explain:

(DICTATED) "MY DAUGHTER, DAWN, DOES NOT AGREE WITH MY DECISION. SHE REFUSES TO DISCUSS IT."

Witness Ben Luken, M.T.   Patient's Signature *[signature]*

Witness Monica Marker, R.N.   Date 8 JAN. 1992

FIGURE 3

C

MICHIGAN OBITIATRY—ZONE 1

No. _92-1_   **CONFIDENTIAL** C

Initial Clinical Assessment

PATIENT _WANDA ENDITTAL_

HOSPITAL RECORDS

Site _CITY GEN. HOSP., SUMTOWN, MI_   Date _8 JAN. 1992_ Time _10:45am_

History: _8 years ago onset of weakness & tingling in legs. Lasted a few weeks, better but no complete remission. Since then progressively worse, paralyzed with only slight movement L. arm. Muscle atrophy._

Physical: _Paralysis as noted. Coarse movements L. arm, hand, fingers. Confined to wheelchair. Mod. to marked atrophy, generalized. Mild nystagmus. Pain in back & neck. Urinary incontinence._

Laboratory: _CSF protein normal, IgG elevated._

Special Tests: _CT & NMR: Scattered lesions in cerebral white matter, mainly periventricular; also in cord. EMG: Delayed evoked potentials._

Diagnosis: _Multiple sclerosis._

Therapy: _Supportive. O.T. Intermittent antibiotics for urinary tract infect. Indwelling urinary catheter. Diazepam prn. Home visits by nurse._

Recorded Consults: ① _Urology for urinary problems._
② _Neurosurgery for poss. intrathecal R for spasticity (not recommended)._
③ _Physiotherapy for R in hosp, occasionally at home._

OBITIATRIST'S EXAMINATION:

Site _CITY GEN. HOSP, SUMTOWN, MI_   Date _8 JAN. 1992_ Time _11:15am_

History: _As noted above. Pt. claims that she is deteriorating more rapidly during last 2 months. Progressive course since onset 8 years ago._

Physical: _Paralyzed neck down, except slight movement L. arm. Fingers rigid & flexed. Can't raise arm past shoulder. Weak neck muscles, pain on flexion. Flexor spasms c̄ passive motion, esp. legs. Mild nystagmus. Mentally intact._

Additional (If any): _Pt. mildly depressed, consistent with normal reaction to physical condition. She is reluctant but agrees to a trial of azathioprine. Will request neurology consult about starting the R regimen._

Obitiatrist (Print) _WILL B. REDDY, M.D._   (Signature) _Will B. Reddy, M.D._

FIGURE 4

D **D**

MICHIGAN OBITIATRY—ZONE 1

No. 92-1   CONFIDENTIAL

First _Joint Consultation_

Patient WANDA ENDITTAL   Date 15 JAN 1992   Start Time 2:00 pm

Site 1234 MAIN ST., SUMTOWN, MI

PARTICIPANTS:

(Name)	(Relationship)	(Signature)
FRANK LEE ENDITTAL	HUSBAND	Frank Lee Endittal
FLO N. TIERS	MOTHER	Flo N. Tiers
JUSTIN TIERS	FATHER	Justin Tiers
SHEILA BYDE	SISTER	Sheila Byde
BARRY GRIEPH	STEPBROTHER	Barry Grieph
FRIEDA BLAIME, MD	PHYSICIAN	Frieda Blaime, M.D.
DAWN ENDITTAL	DAUGHTER	Dawn Endittal

SUMMARY OF DISCUSSION: Everyone joined in with free expression of feelings and opinions. In general the mood was subdued, even somewhat sad; but there was much understanding and almost unanimous agreement. The only opposition to Wanda's decision came from her daughter, Dawn, who tearfully begged her mother to change her mind.

The planned procedures were explained in detail. Wanda's choice is lethal injection, at home. Husband concurred. Necessary consultations explained. Will request them in a week or two.

She agreed to a trial Rx with azathioprine. Will arrange.

CONCLUSIONS: ① Patient must begin the Rx regimen (azathioprine).

② Will request neurology, psychiatry, religious, sociological consultations.

Patient's Signature Wanda Endittal   Obitiatrist Will B. Reddy, MD

                    (Signature) Will B. Reddy, M.D.

Witness' Signature Sheila Byde   End Time 2:40 pm

FIGURE 5

E

No. ___92-1___

MICHIGAN OBITIATRY—ZONE 1

Consultant Report

CONFIDENTIAL

E

Patient's Name ___WANDA ENDITTAL___   Age __45__ Sex __F__

Address ___1234 Main St., Sumtown, MI 48000___   Phone __(313) 200-1992__

| Request | To: Lotte Goode, MD, Psychiatrist | Obitiatrist ___Will B. Reddy, MD___ |

For: Evaluation of mental state and capability for rational decisions.

(Signature) ___Will B. Reddy, MD.___

Date __21 JAN. 1992__   Time __9:00 am__

Patient ___Wanda Endittal___   Date __1/16/92__   Start Time __1:00 pm__

Site of Consultation ___Neuropsychiatric Clinic, City Gen. Hospital, Sumtown, MI___

Consultant's Report:

   Appropriately dressed, middle-aged, severely crippled woman, appears to be mentally alert. Fully oriented as to time, place, person. No concentration deficit. Reasoning and judgment intact (10 out of 10 on Goldfarb Mental Status Exam). No evidence of aphasia. No deficit on Revised Wechsler Memory Scale.
   No evidence of morbid depression, but patient's keen insight into the implications of her progressive neurologic deterioration and incapacity leaves her vulnerable to more severe adjustment reaction with deepening depression.

Conclusion: *Patient is mentally competent and able to come to a rational decision. Mild reactive depression.*

Consultant (Print) ___Lotte Goode, MD___   (Signature) ___Lotte Goode, MD.___

End Time __3:00 pm__

Review by Patient

Patient's Comments: (DICTATED)

   "I DON'T FEEL DEPRESSED AT ALL."

Site _1234 MAIN ST., SUMTOWN, MI_   Date _6 FEB. 1992_   Time _5:10 pm_

Witness' Signature _Frank Lee Endittal_   Patient's Signature _Wanda Endittal_

FIGURE 6

MICHIGAN OBITIATRY—ZONE 1

E

No. _92-1_

Consultant Report

CONFIDENTIAL

E

Patient's Name _WANDA ENDITTAL_   Age _45_   Sex _F_

Address _1234 Main St., Sumtown, MI 48000_   Phone _(313) 200-1992_

Request	To: Sharon Tydings, MA, Sociologist For: Evaluation of family relation- ships, funeral arrangements, possible financial irregularities. Does she have a will prepared?	Obitiatrist _Will B. Reddy, MD_ (Signature) _Will B. Reddy, M.D._ Date _21 JAN. 1992_ Time _9:00 am_

Patient _Wanda Endittal_   Date _1-24-92_   Start Time _9:00 am_

Site of Consultation _4321 First Street, Sumtown, MI 48000_

Consultant's Report:

No obvious or serious disputes among family members (2 brothers live out of state, but those present deny disagreements). However, Wanda's daughter, Dawn, is not fully in agreement with her mother's wish. Dawn is to graduate from college next year, is very close to her mother, and the absence of the latter, she feels, will impair her ability to complete her course of study. Although not violently opposed, Dawn is not yet reconciled to the idea.

The patient has made out and filed her will. There are no detectable family disputes or complications. Family members are not at all concerned about finances. Funeral arrangements have been made with the Cary DeBiers Funeral Home. Wanda prefers cremation.

Conclusion: _NO APPARENT FAMILY DISAGREEMENTS OR FINANCIAL IRREGULARITIES._

Consultant (Print) _Sharon Tydings, MA_   (Signature) _Sharon Tydings, MA_

End Time _10:40 am_

Review by Patient

Patient's Comments: (DICTATED) "WE'VE NEVER ARGUED ABOUT MONEY. MY SISTER AND BROTHER ARE MARRIED AND WELL OFF. MY WILL TAKES CARE OF MY HUSBAND AND PARENTS. AND WE'VE PROVIDED FOR DAWN'S FUTURE. HER OPINION DOESN'T BOTHER ME. IT'S MY LIFE AND MY CHOICE!"

Site _1234 MAIN ST., SUMTOWN, MI_   Date _6 FEB. 1992_   Time _6:00 pm_

Witness' Signature _Will B. Reddy, MD._   Patient's Signature _Wanda Endittal_

FIGURE 7

E No. ___92-1___

MICHIGAN OBITIATRY—ZONE 1

Consultant Report

CONFIDENTIAL **E**

Patient's Name ___WANDA ENDITTAL___   Age __45__ Sex __F__

Address ___1234 Main St., Sumtown, MI 48000___   Phone __(313) 200-1992__

Request	To:	Sarah Brumm, MD, Neurologist	Obitiatrist ___Will B. Reddy, MD___

For: Evaluation with regard to trial
course of

(Signature) _Will B. Reddy, M.D._

Date __21 JAN. 1992__ Time __9:00 am__

Patient ___Wanda Endittal___   Date __May 4, 1992__ Start Time __10:30 am__

Site of Consultation ___Neurology Clinic, City General Hospital, Sumtown, MI___

Consultant's Report:

    Course of trial azathioprine therapy started on Feb. 25, 1992. No apparent improvement in patient's condition. In fact, the paralysis has gotten worse, with loss of what little movement there was in the left arm and hand. Now completely immobile from neck down, with urinary incontinence. Confined to wheelchair.

    Azathioprine discontinued on May 5. Patient refused further physiotherapy, which probably would have been of little or no use.

    No further recommendations other than continuing prescribed medication for pain.

Conclusion: ___Trial of Imuran was not helpful, discontinued.___
___Rapidly progressive neurological deterioration.___

Consultant (Print) ___Sarah Brumm, MD___   (Signature) _Sarah Brumm, M.D._

End Time __N/A__

Review by Patient

Patient's Comments: (DICTATED)

    "I WANT TO DIE—NOW! PLEASE, PLEASE. THIS IS NO LIFE—IT'S JUST EXISTING."

Site __1234 MAIN ST., SUMTOWN, MI__   Date __8 MAY 1992__   Time __8:00 pm__

Witness' Signature _Will B. Reddy, MD_ Patient's Signature X (HER MARK)

FIGURE 8

MICHIGAN OBITIATRY—ZONE 1

E No. _____92-1_____ *Consultant Report*   **CONFIDENTIAL** **E**

Patient's Name ___WANDA ENDITTAL___   Age __45__ Sex __F__

Address __1234 Main St., Sumtown, MI 48000__   Phone __(313) 200-1992__

Request	To: I. Ammon Abbott, DD	Obitiatrist ___Will B. Reddy, MD___
	For: Counseling patient about her wish for assisted suicide.	(Signature) _Will B. Reddy, M.D._
		Date _21 JAN. 1992_ Time _9:00 am_

Patient ___Wanda Endittal___   Date _1-23-92_   Start Time _10:30 am_

Site of Consultation ___Patient's home___

Consultant's Report:

A long conversation with Mrs. Wanda Endittal, who seemed quite cheerful and very willing to discuss the matter openly. I stressed the importance of respect for life, that it is a God-given gift to be respected and lovingly cared for; that He decides when to live and when to die. Wanda listened courteously and attentively, but her calm demeanor belied the strain of disagreement restricted by a desire to show politeness and respect toward me. I don't believe my attempt to convince succeeded, although she didn't voice outright disapproval.

Conclusion: Wanda's religious orientation apparently is not strong enough to override her decision to act in a way which many would consider to be sinful.

Consultant (Print) ___I. Ammon Abbott, DD___   (Signature) _I. Ammon Abbott, DD_

End Time _11:45 am_

Review by Patient

Patient's Comments: (DICTATED) "IF THERE'S A GOD, HE'LL UNDERSTAND. HE WOULDN'T WANT ME TO KEEP SUFFERING LIKE THIS IN THIS WORLD. I STILL WANT TO END IT. IT'S NOT A SIN TO END TERRIBLE SUFFERING."

Site _1234 MAIN ST., SUMTOWN, MI_   Date _6 FEB 1992_   Time _6:20 pm_

Witness' Signature _Frank Lee Endittal_   Patient's Signature _Wanda Endittal_

FIGURE 9

E **MICHIGAN OBITIATRY—ZONE 1** **E**

No. 92-1

Consultant Report **CONFIDENTIAL**

Patient's Name ___WANDA ENDITTAL___ Age ___45___ Sex ___F___

Address ___1234 Main St., Sumtown, MI 48000___ Phone ___(313) 200-1992___

Request	To: Sy Keyes, MD, Psychiatrist

For: Final assessment of mental competency for rational decisions.

Obitiatrist ___Will B. Reddy, MD___

(Signature) ___Will B. Reddy, M.D.___

Date ___28 AUG. 1992___ Time ___9:00 am___

Patient ___Wanda Endittal___ Date ___31 Aug. 92___ Start Time ___1:45 pm___

Site of Consultation ___1234 Main St. Sumtown, MI___

Consultant's Report: Psych. Consult of 18 Jan. reviewed. Essentially no change in interim. Pt's depression slightly more pronounced, accompanied by understandable frustration & resultant anger. Mentally well oriented. No evidence of deficiency or incompetence.

Conclusion: Pt. is mentally competent & able to reach rational decisions.

Consultant (Print) ___Sy Keyes, MD___ (Signature) _____

End Time ___2:20 pm___

Review by Patient

Patient's Comments:

(NO COMMENTS)

Site ___1234 MAIN ST, SUMTOWN, MI___ Date ___2 SEPT. 1992___ Time ___7:00 pm___

Witness' Signature ___Sheila Byde___ Patient's Signature _____ (her mark)

FIGURE 10

MICHIGAN OBITIATRY—ZONE 1

F No. ___92-1___   *Final Joint Consultation*   **CONFIDENTIAL** **F**

PATIENT ___WANDA ENDITTAL___   Date _25 JUN 1992_ Start Time _9:00 am_

Also Present: (Name)   (Relationship)   (Signature)

FRIEDA BLAIME, MD   PHYSICIAN   *Frieda Blaime, M.D.*

SHELBY DUNNE, MD   OBITIATRIST   *Shelly Dunne, MD*

Conclusions: PATIENT FIRM IN DECISION. SHE REJECTED THE SUGGESTION TO CONTINUE A MORE INTENSIVE O.T. PROGRAM.

Site _4321 FIRST ST., SUMTOWN, MI_   End Time _9:35 am_

FAMILY ONLY: (Name)   (Relationship)   (Signature)

FRANK LEE ENDITTAL   HUSBAND   *Frank Lee Endittal*

FLO N. TIERS   MOTHER   *Flo N. Tiers*

JUSTIN TIERS   FATHER   *Justin Tiers*

SHEILA BYDE   SISTER   *Sheila Byde*

DAWN ENDITTAL   DAUGHTER   *Dawn Endittal*

Conclusions: MUCH EMOTIONAL DISCUSSION. UNANIMOUS APPROVAL OF WANDA's PLANNED ACTION, ESPECIALLY IN VIEW OF HER RAPID DETERIORATION. DAWN NOW TEARFULLY AGREES FULLY WITH HER MOTHER'S WISH.

Start Time _9:40 am_   End Time _10:00 am_

PATIENT & FAMILY

Start Time _10:00 am_   End Time _10:45 am_

Conclusions: NO REASON TO DENY MEDICIDE.
NO OPPOSITION FROM FAMILY MEMBERS
DATE AND TIME TO BE SET BY PATIENT. SHE WANTS INJECTION.

Signatures:
Patient _X_ (HER MARK)   Obitiatrist *Will B. Reddy, M.D.*
Witness *Sheila Byde*
Witness *Dawn Endittal*

FIGURE 11

G   No. _92-1_   MICHIGAN OBITIATRY—ZONE 1   **CONFIDENTIAL** **G**

PATIENT _WANDA ENDITTAL_   Date _14 SEPT. 1992_   Start Time _6:30 pm_

ADVISORY: (Unanimity Mandatory)

Obitiatrist	Vote	Signature	Date	Comments
Les Payne, MD	YES	Les Payne MD	9-11-92	—
Hugh R. Luckey, MD	YES	Hugh R. Luckey MD	9-10-92	None
Lotte Goode, MD	YES	Lotte Goode M.D.	9-10-92	None

Recommend:

     ACTION.

ACTION:

Obitiatrist	Vote	Signature	Date	Comments
Dewey Ledder, MD	YES	Dewey Ledder, MD	9-10-92	None
Shelby Dunne, MD	YES	Shelby Dunne MD	Sep.10 '92	—

Recommend:

     ACTION — BY DR. DUNNE.

REVIEW ADVISORY: (Unanimity Mandatory)

Obitiatrist	Vote	Signature	Date	Comments

Recommend:

ACTION RESPONSE:

     ADVISORY ACKNOWLEDGED.

Action Obitiatrist _SHELBY DUNNE, MD_   (Signature) _Shelby Dunne MD._
Date _14 SEPT, 1992_   Time _7:10 pm_

FIGURE 12

H   MICHIGAN OBITIATRY—ZONE 1   **H**

No. ___92-1___   **CONFIDENTIAL**

Final Action

Patient ___WANDA ENDITTAL___   Date _16 SEPT. 1992_ Start Time _9:00 am_

Site _1234 MAIN ST., SUMTOWN, MI_

Persons Present: (Name)   (Relationship)   (Signature)

FLO N. TIERS   MOTHER   *Flo N. Tiers*

SHEILA BYDE   SISTER   *Sheila Byde*

FRANK LEE ENDITTAL   HUSBAND   *Frank Lee Endittal*

M. D. HELPERN   OBIT. TECH.   *M.D. Helpern*

Official Observer: ___POLLY TISHEN___   (Signature) *Polly Tishen*

Procedure: PATIENT GIVEN 0.25 mg OF XANAX AT 8:30 am. GROUP DISCUSSION AND CONVERSATION FOLLOWED UNTIL PATIENT DECIDED TO ACTIVATE THE DEVICE'S SWITCH FOR LETHAL INJECTION AT 9:00 am. NO COMPLICATIONS. FULL FLOW OF 250 cc OF 1% BREVITAL FOR 30 SECONDS; THEN CONCOMMITANT FLOW OF MIXTURE (200 mEq KCL + ANECTINE). PATIENT LOST CONSCIOUSNESS IN 12 SECONDS, RESPIRATION NOT DETECTABLE 15 SECONDS LATER. NO MUSCULAR ACTIVITY. ECG MONITORING: CARDIAC STANDSTILL AT 9:06 am. NO AUTOPSY REQUESTED.

UNUSED: CO-CANISTER, MASK, TENT, TUBES. 2.5 g OF BREVITAL POWDER. 10 cc ANECTINE. 240 mEq KCL. 2-50cc SYRINGES, 5-10 cc SYRINGES, 10-18 GAUGE NEEDLES, 9-20 GA. NEEDLES.

Observer's Remarks:

No irregularities noted.

End Time _9:06 am_

Obitiatrist   Shelby Dunne, MD

(Signature) *Shelby Dunne, M.D.*

14

Why Doctors Must Not Kill

Leon R. Kass

D o you want your doctor licensed to kill? Should he or she be
permitted or encouraged to inject or prescribe poison? Shall the
mantle of privacy that protects the doctor-patient relationship, in the
service of life and wholeness, now also cloak decisions for death? Do
you want *your* doctor deciding, on the basis of his own private views,
when you still deserve to live and when you now deserve to die? And
what about the other fellow's doctor—that shallow technician, that
insensitive boor who neither asks nor listens, that unprincipled
money-grubber, that doctor you used to go to before you got up the
nerve to switch: do you want *him* licensed to kill? Speaking generally,
shall the healing profession become also the euthanizing profession?

Common sense has always answered, "No." For more than two
millennia, the reigning medical ethic, mindful that the power to cure
is also the power to kill, has held as an inviolable rule, "Doctors must
not kill." Yet this venerable taboo is now under attack. Proponents of
euthanasia and physician-assisted suicide would have us believe that
it is but an irrational vestige of religious prejudice, alien to a true ethic

---

Leon R. Kass, a medical doctor, teaches in the Committee on Social
Thought and at The College of the University of Chicago. He is the author
of *Toward a More Natural Science: Biology and Human Affairs* (1985) and other
works. This essay is reprinted by permission from the September 1992 issue
of *Commonweal* (© 1992 by the Commonweal Foundation).

of medicine, that stands in the way of a rational and humane approach to suffering at the end of life. Nothing could be further from the truth. The taboo against doctors killing patients (even on request) is the very embodiment of reason and wisdom. Without it, medicine will have trouble doing its proper work; without it, medicine will have lost its claim to be an ethical and trustworthy profession; without it, all of us will suffer—yes, more than we now suffer because some of us are not soon enough released from life.

Consider first the damaging consequences for the doctor-patient relationship. The patient's trust in the doctor's wholehearted devotion to the patient's best interests will be hard to sustain once doctors are licensed to kill. Imagine the scene: you are old, poor, in failing health, and alone in the world; you are brought to the city hospital with fractured ribs and pneumonia. The nurse or intern enters late at night with a syringe full of yellow stuff for your intravenous drip. How soundly will you sleep? It will not matter that your doctor has never yet put anyone to death; that he is legally entitled to do so will make a world of difference.

And it will make a world of psychic difference to conscientious physicians. How easily will they be able to care wholeheartedly for patients when it is always possible to think of killing them as a "therapeutic option"? Shall it be penicillin and a respirator one more time, or, perhaps, this time just an overdose of morphine? Physicians get tired of treating patients who are hard to cure, who resist their best efforts, who are on their way down—"gorks," "gomers," and "vegetables" are only some of the less than affectionate names they receive from the house officers. Won't it be tempting to think that death is the best "treatment" for the little old lady "dumped" again on the emergency room by the nearby nursing home?

It is naïve and foolish to take comfort in the fact that the currently proposed change in the law provides "aid-in-dying" only to those who request it. For we know from long experience how difficult it is to discover what we truly want when we are suffering. Verbal "requests" made under duress rarely reveal the whole story. Often a demand for euthanasia is, in fact, an angry or anxious plea for help, born of fear of rejection or abandonment, or made in ignorance of available alternatives that could alleviate pain and suffering. Everyone knows how easy it is for those who control the information to engineer requests and manipulate choices, especially in the vulnerable. Paint vividly a horrible prognosis, and contrast it with that "gentle, quick release": which will the depressed or frightened patient choose, especially in the face of a spiraling hospital bill or children who visit grudgingly? . . .

Consent by Proxy

Euthanasia, once legalized, will not remain confined to those who freely and knowingly elect it—and the most energetic backers of euthanasia do not really want it restricted. Why? Because the vast majority of candidates who merit mercy killing cannot request it for themselves: adults with persistent vegetative state or severe depression or senility or aphasia or mental illness or Alzheimer's disease; infants who are deformed; and children who are retarded or dying. All incapable of requesting death, they will thus be denied our new humane "assistance-in-dying." But not to worry. The lawyers and the doctors (and the cost-containers) will soon rectify this injustice. The enactment of a law legalizing mercy killing (or assisted suicide) on voluntary request will certainly be challenged in the courts under the Equal Protection clause of the Fourteenth Amendment. Why, it will be argued, should the comatose or the demented be denied the right to such a "dignified death" or such a "treatment" just because they cannot claim it for themselves? With the aid of court-appointed proxy consenters, we will quickly erase the distinction between the right to choose one's own death and the right to request someone else's—as we have already done in the termination-of-treatment cases.

Clever doctors and relatives will not need to wait for such changes in the law. Who will be around to notice when the elderly, poor, crippled, weak, powerless, retarded, uneducated, demented, or gullible are mercifully released from the lives their doctors, nurses, and next-of-kin deem no longer worth living? In Holland, for example, a 1989 survey of 300 physicians (conducted by an author who supports euthanasia) disclosed that over 40 per cent had performed euthanasia *without the patient's request,* and over 10 per cent had done so in more than five cases. According to the 1991 "Report of the Dutch Government," over one thousand patients were directly killed by doctors in the previous year *without their knowledge or consent,* including more than one hundred persons who were mentally fully competent.

Is there any reason to believe that the average American physician is, in his private heart, more committed than his Dutch counterpart to the equal worth and dignity of every life under his care? Do we really want to find out what he is like, once the taboo is broken?

Even the most humane and conscientious physician psychologically needs protection against himself and his weaknesses, if he is to care fully for those who entrust themselves to him. A physician friend who worked many years in a hospice caring for dying patients explained it to me most convincingly: "Only because I knew that I could not and would not kill my patients was I able to enter most fully and intimately into caring for them as they lay dying." The psychological burden of the license to kill (not to speak of the brutalization of the doctor/killer) could very well be an intolerably high price to pay for physician-administered euthanasia.

The point, however, is not merely psychological: it is also moral and essential. My friend's horror at the thought that he might be tempted to kill dying patients, were he not enjoined from doing so, embodies a deep understanding of the medical ethic and its intrinsic limits.

The Outer Limits of Power

The beginning of ethics regarding the use of power generally lies in nay-saying. The wise setting of limits on the use of power is based on discerning the excesses to which the power, unrestrained, is prone. Applied to the professions, this principle would establish strict outer boundaries—indeed, inviolable taboos—against those "occupational hazards" to which each profession is especially prone. *Within* these outer limits, no fixed rules of conduct apply; instead, prudence—the wise judgment of the man-on-the-spot—finds and adopts the best course of action in light of the circumstances. But the outer limits themselves are fixed, firm, and non-negotiable.

What are those limits for medicine? At least three are set forth in the venerable Hippocratic Oath: no breach of confidentiality; no sexual relations with patients; no dispensing of deadly drugs. These unqualified, self-imposed restrictions are readily understood in terms of the temptations to which the physician is most vulnerable, temptations in each case regarding an area of vulnerability and exposure that the practice of medicine requires of patients. Patients necessarily divulge and reveal private and intimate details of their personal lives; patients necessarily expose their naked bodies to the physician's objectifying gaze and investigating hands; patients necessarily expose and entrust their very lives to the physician's skill, technique, and judgment. The exposure is, in all cases, one-sided and asymmetric: the doctor does not reveal his intimacies, display his nakedness, offer up his embodied life to the patient. Mindful of the meaning of such non-mutual exposure, the physician voluntarily sets limits on his own conduct, pledging not to take advantage of or to violate the patient's intimacies, naked sexuality, or life itself.

The prohibition against killing patients, the first negative promise of self-restraint sworn to in the Hippocratic Oath, stands as medicine's first and most abiding taboo: "I will neither give a deadly drug to anybody if asked for it, nor will I make a suggestion to this effect. . . . In purity and holiness I will guard my life and my art." In forswearing the giving of poison, the physician recognizes and restrains a god-like power he wields over patients, mindful that his drugs can both cure and kill. But in forswearing the giving of poison *if asked for it,* the Hippocratic physician rejects the view that the patient's choice for death can make killing him—or assisting his suicide—right. For the physician, at least, human life in living bodies commands respect and reverence—*by its very nature.* As its respectability does not depend upon human agreement or patient consent, revocation of one's consent to live does not deprive one's living body of respectability. The deepest ethical principle restraining the physician's power is not the autonomy or freedom of the patient; neither is it his own compassion or good intention. Rather, it is the dignity and mysterious power of human life itself, and, therefore, also what the oath calls the purity and holiness of the life and art to which he has sworn devotion. A person can choose to be a physician, but he cannot simply choose what physicianship means.

The central meaning of physicianship derives not from medicine's powers but from its goal, not from its means but from its end: to benefit the sick by the activity of healing. The physician as physician serves only the sick. He does not serve the relatives or the hospital or the national debt inflated by Medicare costs. Thus he will never sacrifice the well-being of the sick to convenience the pocketbook or feelings of the relatives or society. Moreover, the physician serves the sick not because they have rights or wants or claims, but because they are sick. The healer works with and for those who need to be healed, in order to help make them whole. Despite enormous changes in medical technique and institutional practice, despite enormous changes in nosology and therapeutics, the center of medicine has not changed: it is as true today as it was in the days of Hippocrates that the ill desire to be whole; that wholeness means a certain well-working of the enlivened body and its unimpaired powers to sense, think, feel, desire, move, and maintain itself; and that the relationship between the healer and the ill is constituted, essentially even if only tacitly, around the desire of both to promote the wholeness of the one who is ailing.

No Benefit Without a Beneficiary

Can wholeness and healing ever be compatible with intentionally killing the patient? Can one benefit the patient as a whole by making him dead? There is, of course, a logical difficulty: how can any good exist for a being that is not? But the error is more than logical: to intend and to act for someone's good requires his continued existence to receive the benefit.

To be sure, certain attempts may in fact turn out, unintentionally, to be lethal. Giving adequate morphine to control pain might induce respiratory depression leading to death. But the intent to relieve the pain of the living presupposes that the living still live to be relieved. This must be the starting point in discussing all medical benefits: no benefit without a beneficiary.

Against this view, someone will surely bring forth the hard cases, patients so ill served by their bodies that they can no longer bear to live, bodies riddled with cancer and racked with pain, against which their "owners" protest in horror and from which they insist on being released. Cannot the person "in the body" speak up against the rest, and request death for "personal" reasons?

However sympathetically we listen to such requests, we must see them as incoherent. Such person-body dualism cannot be sustained. "Personhood" is manifest on earth only in living bodies; our highest mental functions are held up by, and are inseparable from, lowly metabolism, respiration, circulation, excretion. There may be blood without consciousness, but there is never consciousness without blood. Thus one who calls for death in the service of personhood is like a tree seeking to cut its roots for the sake of growing its highest fruit. No physician, devoted to the benefit of the sick, can serve the patient as person by denying and thwarting his personal embodiment.

To say it plainly, to bring nothingness is incompatible with serving wholeness: one cannot heal—or comfort—by making nil. The healer cannot annihilate if he is truly to heal. The physician-euthanizer is a deadly self-contradiction.

When Medicine Fails

But we must acknowledge a difficulty. The central goal of medicine —health—is, in each case, a perishable good: inevitably, patients get irreversibly sick, patients degenerate, patients die. Healing the sick is *in principle* a project that must at some point fail. And here is where all the trouble begins: How does one deal with "medical failure"? What does one seek when restoration of wholeness—or "much" wholeness—is by and large out of the question?

Contrary to the propaganda of the euthanasia movement, there is, in fact, much that can be done. Indeed, by recognizing finitude yet knowing that we will not kill, we are empowered to focus on easing and enhancing the *lives* of those who are dying. First of all, medicine can follow the lead of the hospice movement and—abandoning decades of shameful mismanagement—provide truly adequate (and now technically feasible) relief of pain and discomfort. Second, physicians (and patients and families) can continue to learn how to withhold or withdraw those technical interventions that are, in truth, merely burdensome or degrading medical additions to the unhappy end of a life —including, frequently, hospitalization itself. Ceasing treatment and allowing death to occur when (and if) it will seem to be quite compatible with the respect life itself commands for itself. Doctors may and must allow to die, even if they must not intentionally kill.

Ceasing medical intervention, allowing nature to take its course, differs fundamentally from mercy killing. For one thing, death does not necessarily follow the discontinuance of treatment; Karen Ann Quinlan lived more than ten years after the court allowed the "life-sustaining" respirator to be removed. Not the physician but the underlying fatal illness becomes the true cause of death. More important morally, in ceasing treatment the physician need not *intend* the death of the patient, even when death follows as a result of his omission. His intention should be to avoid useless and degrading medical *additions* to the already sad end of a life. In contrast, in active, direct mercy killing the physician must, necessarily and indubitably, intend *primarily* that the patient be made dead. And he must knowingly and indubitably cast himself in the role of the agent of death. This remains true even if he is merely an assistant in suicide. A physician who provides the pills or lets the patient plunge the syringe after he leaves the room is *morally* no different from the one who does the deed himself. "I will neither give a deadly drug to anybody if asked for it, nor will I make a suggestion to this effect."

Once we refuse the technical fix, physicians and the rest of us can also rise to the occasion: we can learn to act humanly in the presence of finitude. Far more than adequate morphine and the removal of burdensome machinery, the dying need our presence and our encouragement. Dying people are all too easily reduced ahead of time to "thinghood" by those who cannot bear to deal with the suffering or disability of those they love. Withdrawal of contact, affection, and care is the greatest single cause of the dehumanization of the dying. Not the alleged humaneness of an elixir of death, but the humanness of connected living-while-dying is what medicine—and the rest of us—most owe the dying. The treatment of choice is company and care.

Humanity Is Owed Humanity

The euthanasia movement would have us believe that the physician's refusal to assist in suicide or perform euthanasia constitutes an affront to human dignity. Yet one of their favorite arguments seems to me rather to prove the reverse. Why, it is argued, do we put animals out of their misery but insist on compelling fellow human beings to suffer to the bitter end? Why, if it is not a contradiction for the veterinarian, does the medical ethic absolutely rule out mercy killing? Is this not simply inhumane?

Perhaps *inhumane,* but not thereby *inhuman.* On the contrary, it is precisely because animals are not human that we must treat them merely humanely. We put dumb animals to sleep because they do not know that they are dying, because they can make nothing of their misery or mortality, and, therefore, because they cannot live deliberately—i.e., humanly—in the face of their own suffering and dying. They cannot live out a fitting end. Compassion for their weakness and dumbness is our only appropriate emotion, and given our responsibility for their care and well-being, we do the only humane thing we can. But when a conscious human being asks us for death, by that very action he displays the presence of something that precludes our regarding him as a dumb animal. Humanity is owed humanity, not humaneness. Humanity is owed the bolstering of the human, even or especially in its dying moments, in resistance to the temptation to ignore its presence in the sight of suffering.

What humanity needs most in the face of evil is courage, the ability to stand against fear and pain and thoughts of nothingness. The deaths we most admire are those of people who, knowing that they are dying, face the fact frontally and act accordingly: they set their affairs in order, they arrange what could be final meetings with their loved ones, and yet, with strength of soul and a small reservoir of hope, they continue to live and work and love as much as they can for as long as they can. Because such conclusions of life require courage, they call for our encouragement—and for the many small speeches and deeds that shore up the human spirit against despair and defeat.

Many doctors are in fact rather poor at this sort of encouragement. They tend to regard every dying or incurable patient as a failure, as if an earlier diagnosis or a more vigorous intervention might have avoided what is, in truth, an inevitable collapse. The enormous successes of medicine these past fifty years have made both doctors and laymen less prepared than ever to accept the fact of finitude. Doctors behave, not without some reason, as if they have god-like powers to revive the moribund; laymen expect an endless string of medical miracles. Physicians today are not likely to be agents of encouragement once their technique begins to fail.

It is, of course, partly for these reasons that doctors will be pressed to kill—and many of them will, alas, be willing. Having adopted a largely technical approach to healing, having medicalized so much of the end of life, doctors are being asked—often with thinly veiled anger—to provide a final technical solution for the evil of human finitude and for their own technical failure: If you cannot cure me, kill me. The last gasp of autonomy or cry for dignity is asserted against a medicalization and institutionalization of the end of life that robs the old and the incurable of most of their autonomy and dignity: intubated and electrified, with bizarre mechanical companions, once proud and independent people find themselves cast in the roles of passive, obedient, highly disciplined children. People who care for autonomy and dignity should try to reverse this dehumanization of the last stages of life, instead of giving dehumanization its final triumph by welcoming the desperate, goodbye-to-all-that contained in one final plea for poison.

The present crisis that leads some to press for active euthanasia is really an opportunity to learn the limits of the medicalization of life and death and to recover an appreciation of living with and against mortality. It is an opportunity for physicians to recover an understanding that there remains a residual human wholeness—however precarious—that can be cared for even in the face of incurable and terminal illness. Should doctors cave in, should doctors become technical dispensers of death, they will not only be abandoning their posts, their patients, and their duty to care; they will also be setting the worst sort of example for the community at large—teaching technicism and so-called humaneness where encouragement and humanity are both required and sorely lacking. On the other hand, should physicians hold fast, should doctors learn that finitude is no disgrace and that human wholeness can be cared for to the very end, medicine may serve not only the good of its patients but also, by example, the failing moral health of modern times.

15

The Case for Rational Suicide

Derek Humphry

The Hemlock Society is dedicated to the view that there are at least two forms of suicide. One is "emotional suicide," or irrational self-murder in all its complexities. Let me emphasize that the Hemlock Society's view on this form of suicide is approximately the same as that of the American Association of Suicidology and the rest of society, which is to prevent it whenever possible. We do not encourage any form of suicide for mental health or emotional reasons.

We say that there is a second form of suicide, "justifiable suicide" —that is, rational and planned self-deliverance. Put another way, this is autoeuthanasia, using suicide as the means. I don't think the word "suicide" really sits well in this context, but we are stuck with it.

What the Hemlock Society and its supporters are talking about is autoeuthanasia. But we also have to face up to the fact that it is called "suicide" by the law. (Suicide is not a crime in the English-speaking

Derek Humphry is the co-founder of the Hemlock Society and subsequently of ERGO! (Euthanasia Research and Guidance Organization). Among his books are *Final Exit: The Practicalities of Self-Deliverance* and *Dying With Dignity: Understanding Euthanasia.* This two-section essay is reprinted by permission from two issues of *Suicide and Life-Threatening Behavior:* vol. 17, no. 4 ("The Case for Rational Suicide"), and vol. 22, no. 1 ("Rational Suicide Among the Elderly") (© 1987 and 1992 by the American Association of Suicidology).

world, and neither is attempted suicide, but giving *assistance* in suicide for any reason remains a crime. Even if the person is requesting it on the grounds of compassion and the helper is acting from the best of motives, it remains a crime in the Anglo-American world.)

The word "euthanasia" comes from the Greek—*eu,* "good," and *thanatos,* "death." But it has acquired a more complex meaning in recent times. The word "euthanasia" has now come to mean doing something, either positive or negative, about achieving a good death.

Suicide can be justified ethically by the average Hemlock Society supporter for the following reasons:

1. *Advanced terminal illness that is causing unbearable suffering to the individual.* This is the most common reason for self-deliverance.

2. *Grave physical handicap so restricting that the individual cannot, even after due consideration and training, tolerate such a limited existence.* This is fairly rare as a reason for suicide, despite the publicity surrounding Elizabeth Bouvia's court cases.

What are the ethical parameters for autoeuthanasia?

1. *The person is a mature adult.* This is essential. The exact age will depend on the individual.

2. *The person has clearly made a considered decision.* The individual has to indicate this by such indirect ways as belonging to a right-to-die society, signing a "living will," or signing a "durable power of attorney for health care." These documents do not give anybody freedom from criminality in assistance in suicide, but they do indicate clearly and in an authoritative way what the intention was, and especially the fact that this was not a hasty act.

3. *The decision has not been made at the first knowledge of the life-threatening illness, and reasonable medical help has been sought.* We certainly do not believe in giving up the minute a person is informed that he or she has a terminal illness, which is a common misconception of our critics.

4. *The treating physician has been informed, and his or her response has been taken into account.* What the physician's response will be depends on the circumstances, of course, but we advise our members that as autoeuthanasia (or rational suicide) is not a crime, there is nothing a doctor can do about it. But it is best to inform the doctor and hear his or her response. The patient may well be mistaken—perhaps the diagnosis has been misheard or misunderstood. Usually the patient will meet a discreet silence.

5. *The person has made a will disposing of his or her worldly effects.* This shows evidence of a tidy mind and an orderly life—again, something that is paramount in rational suicide.

6. *The person has made plans to exit this life that do not involve others in criminal liability.* As I have mentioned earlier, assistance in suicide is a crime. (However, it is a rarely punished crime, and certainly the most compassionate of all crimes. Very few cases ever come before the courts—perhaps one apiece every four or five years in Britain, Canada, and the United States.)

7. *The person leaves a note saying exactly why he or she is committing suicide.* Also, as an act of politeness, if the deed of self-destruction is done in a hotel, one should leave a note of apology to the staff for inconvenience and embarrassment caused. Some people, because of the criminality of assistance in suicide, do not want to put their loved ones at any risk; such people will leave home, go down the road, check into a hotel, and take their lives.

Many cases of autoeuthanasia through the use of drugs go absolutely undetected by the doctors, especially now that autopsies in this country have become the exception rather than the rule. Autopsies are performed on only 12 per cent of patients today, compared to 60 per cent in 1965, because of the high cost and the pointlessness of most autopsies. Also, of course, autopsies often catch doctors' misdiagnoses. One study showed that 29 per cent of death certificates did not correlate to the autopsy finding. Many doctors these days prefer not to have an autopsy unless there is good scientific reason or foul play is suspected.

We in the Hemlock Society find that police, paramedics, and coroners put a very low priority on investigation of suicide when evidence comes before them that the person was dying anyway. Detectives and coroners' officers will walk away from the scene, once they are satisfied that the person who has committed suicide was terminally ill.

Countervailing Considerations

But, having considered the logic in favor of autoeuthanasia, the person should also address the countervailing arguments.

First, should the person instead go into a hospice? Put bluntly, hospices make the best of a bad job, and they do so with great skill and love. The euthanasia movement supports their work. But not everyone wants a beneficent lingering; not everyone wants that form of treatment and care. Hospices cannot make dying into a beautiful experience, although they do try hard. At best, hospices provide appropriate medicine and care, which everybody deserves. A major study has recently shown that most hospitals have adopted hospice standards, so the hospice movement has done a marvelous educative job. We do not feel there is any conflict of interests between euthanasia and hospices; both are appropriate to different people, with different values.

The other consideration is this question: Does suffering ennoble? Is suffering a part of life and a preparation for death? If that is a person's firm belief, then that person is not a candidate for voluntary euthanasia; it is not an ethical option. But it should be remembered that in America there are millions of agnostics, atheists, and people of varying religions and denominations, and they have rights, too. We know that a good 50 per cent of the Hemlock Society's members are strong Christians and churchgoers, and that the God they worship is a God of love and understanding. As long as their autoeuthanasia is justifiable and meets the conditions of not hurting other people, then they feel that their God will accept them into heaven.

Another consideration is whether, by checking out before the Grim Reaper calls, one is depriving oneself of a valuable period of good life, and also depriving family and friends of love and companionship. Here again, there is a great deal of misunderatanding about our point of view and what actually happens. Practitioners of active voluntary euthanasia almost always wait to a late stage in the dying process; some even wait too long, go into a coma, and are thus frustrated in self-deliverance.

For example, one man who was probably this country's greatest enthusiast for autoeuthanasia, Morgan Sibbett, had lung cancer. He not only intended at some point to take his life but was going to have an "educational" movie made about his technique. I thought the plan was in poor taste myself and would have nothing to do with it, but it shows the level of his enthusiasm. As it happened, Morgan Sibbett died naturally. He had a strong feeling for life, and he hung on, not realizing how sick he was; then he suddenly passed out and died within a couple of hours. Obviously, he didn't need autoeuthanasia.

My first wife told me of her intention to end her life deliberately nine months before she actually did so. When she died by her own hand, with drugs that I had secured from a physician and brought to her, she was in a pitiful physical state; I estimate that she was between one and three weeks from certain death. Her doctor, by the way, when he came to see her body, assumed that she had died naturally—it was that late.

From my years since then in the Hemlock Society, hearing the feedback of hundreds, maybe thousands, of cases, I can assure you that most euthanasists do enjoy life and love living, and their feeling of the sanctity of life is as strong as anybody's. Yet they are willing, if their dying is distressing to them, to forgo a few weeks of the end and leave under their own control. What is also not generally realized in the field of euthanasia is that, for many people, just knowing how to kill themselves is in itself of great comfort and often extends their lives. Once such people know how to make an exit and have the means to do so, they will often renegotiate with themselves the conditions of their dying.

An example quite recently was a Hemlock member in his nineties who called up and told me his health was so bad he was ready to terminate his life. He ordered and purchased the latest edition of *Let Me Die Before I Wake,* Hemlock's book on how to kill oneself, and called back a week or so later to say that he had gotten a friend in Europe to provide him with the lethal overdose. So everything was in position. "Where do you stand now?" I asked cautiously. "Oh, I'm not ready to go yet," he replied. Now that he had the means to make his exit, he was convinced that he could hold on longer. Thus, with control and choice in his grasp, he had negotiated new terms concerning his fate. Surely, for those who want it this way, this is commendable and is in fact an extension rather than a curtailment of life.

Rational Suicide Among the Elderly

Not long ago I was invited to speak on the subject of voluntary euthanasia to a senior citizens' club in Los Angeles. As I walked into the club headquarters in the basement of a high-rise building, I wondered why they had asked me. I soon found out when the clergyman who was chairing the meeting said: "We've asked the head of the Hemlock Society to come and talk to us because, as you all know, we've lost two members recently who jumped from the roof."

Although an avid follower of local news, I had not heard about this. Apparently the two deaths had gone unreported. Suicide in Los Angeles obviously cannot compete with the city's other momentous events.

Momentarily, this cause for my presence threw me off guard. The Hemlock Society does not advocate suicide per se: it believes suicide and assisted suicide carried out in the face of terminal illness causing unbearable suffering should be ethically and legally acceptable.

Old age, in and of itself, should never be a cause for self-destruction. But whether we like it or not, the effects of aging are, for some people, sufficient cause to give up. I have come to realize that a great many of the Hemlock Society's 40,000 members believe that the organization does not go far enough in its objectives. They tolerate our limited aims but would prefer that we also fought for the right of the elderly to choose a dignified and assisted exit.

Some of these people are my friends and acquaintances, and it is fatuous for psychologists and psychiatrists to claim, as most do, that they are temporarily mentally ill or depressed. These are solid, thinking, planning people. They could be your parents!

Some of the elderly people I have met since I became executive director of the Hemlock Society in 1980 have taken their lives. In a few cases I knew them right up to within days of their suicide and saw nothing exceptional about the daily conduct of their lives. In fact, it may be the case that the more lucid and rational the person, the more likely the suicide, for they can assess the balance sheet of their situation more coolly.

I recall the various aftereffects of the suicide of one Hemlock member I knew who, at 85 and widowed the previous year, took an overdose and died. There was no terminal illness, but her horror of having a stroke and spending her final years in the hospital was unbearable now that her beloved husband was gone and her children grown and scattered. She could see no point in going on and risking a prolonged dying.

Two days later the man who rented the upper part of her house called in great distress. "She was such a lovely person," he wailed.

"Why did she do it? Why didn't she tell us? I saw her walking in the garden the previous evening and she seemed her usual self." I told him that I too admired the intelligence and poise of this woman. I reminded him that she had been a regular attender of Hemlock conferences for years and had clearly thought the matter through very thoroughly. "She was entitled to the privacy of her own decision-making," I added. We chatted for a while and he felt better.

Two years later when I was addressing a public meeting in Honolulu, Hawaii, a young man in the audience asked my view on elder suicide. Afterwards, he came up to me and said that he was the grandson of this woman. Then, in 1990, a woman approached me at the end of a meeting in Dallas, Texas, and introduced herself as the daughter of this woman. Both told me that they had come to the Hemlock meeting to hear more about the organization to which their relative had belonged, and that it was cathartic for them to share the experience. They were still coming to terms with the manner of the death.

How Euthanasia Can Extend Life

Sometimes I hear of elderly people who, on seeing the early signs of a breakdown in physical health, or what they think is the onset of senility, proceed to end their lives by overdose. Quietly, unceremoniously, with tremendous care not to inconvenience or shock others, they will self-destruct. Their fear of losing control and choice is so great that they will willingly shorten their lives. And I am saddened. We may have lost a valuable life too soon. I believe that if we were able to offer them the option of lawful medical euthanasia, they would in most cases hang on to life for a bit longer. If they could make a firm deal with their physician that he or she would provide the means for a certain exit at the point of serious deterioration, they would clutch at it. The prospect of euthanasia can extend, rather than shorten, life.

In the Netherlands, as well as physician aid-in-dying for the terminally ill, there is also lawful assisted suicide for the elderly. It is not a procedure that the Dutch take lightly. The decision of the doctor to help is arrived at—if it is appropriate—after time and reflection by everyone concerned. The family is closely involved with the consideration of the request to die. Those most likely to get medical help to die are (a) elderly, (b) in poor health, (c) making a persistent and consistent request for help with death. It doesn't happen extensively —in fact, no more than 4 per cent of all deaths in the Netherlands are attributed to euthanasia.

It is the consolation of the *availability* of euthanasia that is the boon to Dutch senior citizens, and a benefit as well for the rest of the public, which is spared the prospect of bodies mangled by guns and jumping.

Besides avoiding violence, the Dutch seniors do not need to end their lives in a lonely and covert manner. Because it is lawful and acceptable to be helped to die, the family is usually present or nearby when the doctor administers the lethal dose. Many, many American seniors tell me that they dearly wish such an option were available to them. They believe that it is a basic civil liberty to be able to end their lives at a point they choose. They are offended by the thought of having to make their exit in a secretive and ultimately violent manner.

Not a Slippery Slope

While the Hemlock Society's principal mission is to achieve physician aid-in-dying (through assisted suicide or direct euthanasia) for the terminally ill, there is huge pressure amongst our membership to go one step further and obtain this service for the ailing elder. The very fact that there is an entire book devoted to the subject—not to mention numerous other articles—authenticates their concern.

Our critics will call it the "slippery slope," but I predict that after the problems of helping the terminally ill are solved, the question of aid to the elderly in dying will, by sheer force of public opinion, have to be addressed ethically and legally. Ex-governor Richard Lamm of Colorado, who made a shattering speech about the rationing of health care costs in the 1980s, suggesting that the elderly were taking more than their fair share, now says that the elderly people were his most ardent supporters. Let's not forget that the elderly have considerable financial and political clout. More of them take the trouble to vote than the younger section of the population.

How can it be a slippery slope if it is what a certain section of the public is democratically asking for? A slippery slope is when government moves in and insists on euthanasia for nefarious reasons. We must never allow that to happen. I do not think the older generations will let it occur—they are too independently minded!

A Hemlock member wrote me this letter which typifies, I think, a great many of the attitudes of the elderly:

Your emphasis is, of course, on deliverance from terminal illness and excessive pain, but there are two kinds of pain: physical, which we can all understand, and emotional, which one must experience to understand. It can be as fierce as the physical and probably less acceptable as it is less visual and could be taken advantage of.

I am 81 years old, a good span of years. I have always had exceptionally good health. I had a happy marriage. I have a kind family and am financially secure. I have an attractive and convenient home and a pretty garden.

But the future is crowding me. I have lost a most beloved husband and a splendid son. The suffering doesn't diminish but in fact is augmented as my need of them increases and I grow older and more vulnerable.

I have already lost favorite neighbors, and most of my close friends were in an in-between age bracket, about five years younger than my husband and about five years older than I. They are now, those left, moving into their upper eighties and dropping by the wayside.

My two sons, who are exceedingly good to me, live some distance away. They have busy lives of their own, families to care for, and move in a different generation. Life will become more difficult for me and for them as I age.

I see a man I admired becoming senile; I see oldsters beset with all kinds of ailments physical and emotional; I see a multitude in wheelchairs and in rest homes just waiting to die, all suffering from the pain of loneliness!

We really do not belong to anyone. As children we were first with our parents; first then with our spouses; later, first with our own young; but then the mate dies and the children have homes of their own, and we oldsters are not first with anyone anymore. We are fifth wheels, forgetful, awkward, and then a burden to someone.

In thinking about deliverance, have you ever addressed yourselves to the proposition that there are many who would like to be on their way before that troublesome, heartbreaking deterioration destroys us?

After a full life, should we not be able to choose to terminate it? So our children could remember us as a whole person, not a vegetable? A declaration of intent, then a span of time, like six months to be sure, and then a return to the hospital or clinic where this kind of thing could be set up to ask for a lethal pill or shot in the arm. Don't you think this idea has merit?

Recently a Hemlock member wrote in the newsletter, *Hemlock Quarterly,* about the suicide of her father, saying that she was happy for him. She explained her attitude this way:

How can a daughter who loves her father be happy that her father committed suicide? He was not ill; in fact, he had been swimming that morning. But for my father life was over. He was healthy, but he was 88 years old. He could still see but not well enough to sustain long periods of reading; he could hear, but the sounds of music or words from a television show were blurred; he could walk but not long enough to play golf; he loved to talk about the past, but his friends were all gone. He was bored.

Suicide is a process. It creeps slowly into a person's mind, and if the person expresses his feelings, those feelings engulf the whole family. My father was open with his thoughts for over a over a year, but we didn't listen. He was particularly concerned with the idea that he was going to become a burden to us. He was afraid of losing his independence.

This man, comfortably off, living in the warmth of Florida, still married, Jewish, put a plastic bag over his head as he lay in bed, and died.

I think society now needs to come to terms with elder suicide. The subject requires our tolerance and understanding of what it is like to be hovering at the point of a living death without the release that death brings to some. There should be regular, local, open forums held for seniors to discuss the pros and cons of their suicides. Only with honesty and frankness of a caliber not yet practiced, by all of us, will elder suicide be kept to the bare minimum.

16

It's Over, Debbie

Anonymous

The call came in the middle of the night. As a gynecology resident rotating through a large, private hospital, I had come to detest telephone calls, because invariably I would be up for several hours and not feel good the next day. However, duty called, so I answered the phone. A nurse informed me that a patient was having difficulty getting rest, could I please see her. She was on 3 North. That was the gynecologic-oncology unit, not my usual duty station. As I trudged along, bumping sleepily against the walls and corners and not believing I was up again, I tried to imagine what I might find at the end of my walk. Maybe an elderly woman with an anxiety reaction, or perhaps something particularly horrible.

I grabbed the chart from the nurses' station on my way to the patient's room, and the nurse gave me some hurried details: a 20-year-old girl named Debbie was dying of ovarian cancer. She was having unrelenting vomiting apparently as the result of an alcohol drip administered for sedation. Hmmm, I thought. Very sad.

As I approached the room I could hear loud, labored breathing. I entered and saw an emaciated, dark-haired woman who appeared

---

much older than 20. She was receiving nasal oxygen, had an IV, and was sitting in bed suffering from what was obviously severe air hunger. The chart noted her weight at eighty pounds. A second woman, also dark-haired but of middle age, stood at her right, holding her hand. Both looked up as I entered.

The room seemed filled with the patient's desperate effort to survive. Her eyes were hollow, and she had suprasternal and intercostal retractions with her rapid inspirations. She had not eaten or slept in two days. She had not responded to chemotherapy and was being given supportive care only. It was a gallows scene, a cruel mockery of her youth and unfulfilled potential. Her only words to me were, "Let's get this over with."

I retreated with my thoughts to the nurses' station. The patient was tired and needed rest. I could not give her health, but I could give her rest. I asked the nurse to draw 20 mg of morphine sulfate into a syringe. Enough, I thought, to do the job. I took the syringe into the room and told the two women I was going to give Debbie something that would let her rest and to say good-bye.

Debbie looked at the syringe, then laid her head on the pillow with her eyes open, watching what was left of the world. I injected the morphine intravenously and watched to see if my calculations on its effects would be correct. Within seconds her breathing slowed to a normal rate, her eyes closed, and her features softened as she seemed restful at last. The older woman stroked the hair of the now-sleeping patient. I waited for the inevitable next effect of depressing the respiratory drive. With clocklike certainty, within four minutes the breathing rate slowed even more, then became irregular, then ceased. The dark-haired woman stood erect and seemed relieved.

It's over, Debbie.

17

Death and Dignity:
A. The Case of Diane

Timothy E. Quill

Diane was feeling tired and had a rash. A common scenario, though there was something subliminally worrisome that prompted me to check her blood count. Her hematocrit was 22, and the white-cell count was 4.3 with some metamyelocytes and unusual white cells. I wanted it to be viral, trying to deny what was staring me in the face. Perhaps in a repeated count it would disappear. I called Diane and told her it might be more serious than I had initially thought—that the test needed to be repeated and that if she felt worse, we might have to move quickly. When she pressed for the possibilities, I reluctantly opened the door to leukemia. Hearing the word seemed to make it exist. "Oh, shit!" she said. "Don't tell me that." Oh, shit! I thought, I wish I didn't have to.

Diane was no ordinary person (although no one I have ever come

Timothy E. Quill is a professor of medicine and psychiatry at the University of Rochester (N.Y.) School of Medicine and the associate chief of medicine at Genesee Hospital, Rochester. This three-part essay is excerpted by permission of W. W. Norton and Company from his *Death and Dignity: Making Choices and Taking Charge* (New York: Norton, 1993; © 1993 by Timothy E. Quill). It consists of the preface (an essay originally published in the *New England Journal of Medicine*) and the two-part chapter 8.

to know has been really ordinary). She was raised in an alcoholic family and had felt alone for much of her life. She had vaginal cancer as a young woman. Through much of her adult life, she had struggled with depression and her own alcoholism. I had come to know, respect, and admire her over the previous eight years as she confronted these problems and gradually overcame them. She was an incredibly clear, at times brutally honest, thinker and communicator. As she took control of her life, she developed a strong sense of independence and confidence. In the previous 3½ years, her hard work had paid off. She was completely abstinent from alcohol, she had established much deeper connections with her husband, college-age son, and several friends, and her business and her artistic work were blossoming. She felt she was really living fully for the first time.

Not surprisingly, the repeated blood count was abnormal, and detailed examination of the peripheral-blood smear showed myelo-cyte. I advised her to come into the hospital, explaining that we needed to do a bone-marrow biopsy and make some decisions relatively rapidly. She came to the hospital knowing what we would find. She was terrified, angry, and sad. Although we knew the odds, we both clung to the thread of possibility that it might be something else.

The bone marrow confirmed the worst: acute myelomonocytic leukemia. In the face of this tragedy, we looked for signs of hope. This is an area of medicine in which technological intervention has been successful, with cures 25 per cent of the time—long-term cures. As I probed the costs of these cures, I heard about induction chemother-apy (three weeks in the hospital, prolonged neutropenia, probable infectious complications, and hair loss; 75 per cent of patients respond, 25 per cent do not). For the survivors, this is followed by consolidation chemotherapy (with similar side effects; another 25 per cent die, for a net survival of 50 per cent). Those still alive, to have a reasonable chance of long-term survival, then need bone-marrow transplantation (hospitalization for two months and whole-body irradiation, with complete killing of the bone marrow, infectious complications, and the possibility for graft-versus-host disease—with a survival of ap-proximately 50 per cent, or 25 per cent of the original group). Though hematologists may argue over the exact percentages, they don't argue about the outcome of no treatment—certain death in days, weeks, or at most a few months.

Believing that delay was dangerous, our oncologist broke the news to Diane and began making plans to insert a Hickman catheter and begin induction chemotherapy that afternoon. When I saw her shortly thereafter, she was enraged at his presumption that she would want treatment, and devastated by the finality of the diagnosis. All she wanted to do was go home and be with her family. She had no further questions about treatment and in fact had decided that she wanted none. Together we lamented her tragedy and the unfairness of life. Before she left, I felt the need to be sure she and her husband understood that there was some risk in delay, that the problem was not going to go away, and that we needed to keep considering the options over the next several days. We agreed to meet in two days.

Diane's Choice

She returned in two days with her husband and son. They had talked extensively about the problem and the options. She remained very clear about her wish not to undergo chemotherapy and to live whatever time she had left outside the hospital. As we explored her thinking further, it became clear that she was convinced she would die during the period of treatment and would suffer unspeakably in the process (from hospitalization, from lack of control over her body, from the side effects of chemotherapy, and from pain and anguish). Although I could offer support and my best effort to minimize her suffering if she chose treatment, there was no way I could say any of this would not occur. In fact, the last four patients with acute leukemia at our hospital had died very painful deaths in the hospital during various stages of treatment (a fact I did not share with her). Her family wished she would choose treatment but sadly accepted her decision. She articulated very clearly that it was she who would be experiencing all the side effects of treatment and that odds of 25 per cent were not good enough for her to undergo so toxic a course of therapy, given her expectations of chemotherapy and hospitalization and the absence of a closely matched bone-marrow donor. I had her repeat her understanding of the treatment, the odds, and what to expect if there were no treatment. I clarified a few misunderstandings, but she had a remarkable grasp of the options and implications.

I have been a longtime advocate of active, informed patient choice of treatment or non-treatment, and of a patient's right to die with as much control and dignity as possible. Yet there was something about her giving up a 25 per cent chance of long-term survival in favor of almost certain death that disturbed me. I had seen Diane fight and use her considerable inner resources to overcome alcoholism and depression, and I half expected her to change her mind over the next week. Since the window of time in which effective treatment can be initiated is rather narrow, we met several times that week. We obtained a second hematology consultation and talked at length about the meaning and implications of treatment and non-treatment. She talked to a psychologist she had seen in the past. I gradually understood the decision from her perspective and became convinced that it was the right decision for her. We arranged for home hospice care (although at that time Diane felt reasonably well, was active, and looked healthy), left the door open for her to change her mind, and tried to anticipate how to keep her comfortable in the time she had left.

Just as I was adjusting to her decision, she opened up another area that would stretch me profoundly. It was extraordinarily important to Diane to maintain control of herself and her own dignity during the time remaining to her. When this was no longer possible, she clearly wanted to die. As a former director of a hospice program, I know how to use pain medicines to keep patients comfortable and lessen suffering. I explained the philosophy of comfort care, which I strongly believe in.

Although Diane understood and appreciated this, she had known of people lingering in what was called relative comfort, and she wanted no part of it. When the time came, she wanted to take her life in the least painful way possible. Knowing of her desire for independence and her decision to stay in control, I thought this request made perfect sense. I acknowledged and explored this wish but also thought that it was out of the realm of currently accepted medical practice and that it was more than I could offer or promise. In our discussion, it became clear that preoccupation with her fear of a lingering death would interfere with Diane's getting the most out of the time she had left until she found a safe way to ensure her death. I feared the effects of a violent death on her family, the consequences of an ineffective suicide that would leave her lingering in precisely the state she dreaded so much, and the possibility that a family member would be forced to assist her, with all the legal and personal repercussions that would follow. She discussed this at length with her family. They believed that they should respect her choice. With this in mind, I told Diane that information was available from the Hemlock Society that might be helpful to her.

A week later she phoned me with a request for barbiturates for sleep. Since I knew that this was an essential ingredient in a Hemlock Society suicide, I asked her to come to the office to talk things over. She was more than willing to protect me by participating in a superficial conversation about her insomnia, but it was important to me to know how she planned to use the drugs and to be sure that she was not in despair or overwhelmed in a way that might color her judgment.

In our discussion, it was apparent that she was having trouble sleeping, but it was also evident that the security of having enough barbiturates available to commit suicide when and if the time came would leave her secure enough to live fully and concentrate on the present. It was clear that she was not despondent and that in fact she was making deep, personal connections with her family and close friends. I made sure that she knew how to use the barbiturates for sleep, and also that she knew the amount needed to commit suicide. We agreed to meet regularly, and she promised to meet with me before taking her life, to ensure that all other avenues had been exhausted. I wrote the prescription with an uneasy feeling about the boundaries I was exploring—spiritual, legal, professional, and personal. Yet I also felt strongly that I was setting her free to get the most out of the time she had left, and to maintain dignity and control on her own terms until her death.

Diane's Last Months

The next several months were very intense and important for Diane. Her husband did his work at home and her son stayed home from college, and they were able to be together and say much that had not been said earlier. She spent time with her closest friends. I had her come into the hospital for a conference with our residents, at which she illustrated in a most profound and personal way the importance of informed decision-making, the right to refuse treatment, and the extraordinarily personal effects of illness and interaction with the medical system. There were emotional and physical hardships as well. She had periods of intense sadness and anger. Several times she became very weak, but she received transfusions as an outpatient and responded with marked improvement of symptoms. She had two serious infections that responded surprisingly well to empirical courses of oral antibiotics. After three tumultuous months, there were two weeks of relative calm and well-being, and fantasies of a miracle began to surface.

Unfortunately, we had no miracle. Bone pain, weakness, fatigue, and fevers began to dominate her life. Although the hospice workers, family members, and I tried our best to minimize the suffering and promote comfort, it was clear that the end was approaching. Diane's immediate future held what she feared the most—increasing discomfort, dependence, and hard choices between pain and sedation. She called up her closest friends and asked them to come over to say goodbye, telling them that she would be leaving soon. As we had agreed, she let me know as well. When we met, it was clear that she knew what she was doing, that she was sad and frightened to be leaving, but that she would be even more terrified to stay and suffer. In our tearful goodbye, she promised a reunion in the future at her favorite spot on the edge of Lake Geneva, with dragons swimming in the sunset.

Two days later her husband called to say that Diane had died. She had said her final goodbyes to her husband and son that morning, and asked them to leave her alone for an hour. After an hour, which must have seemed an eternity, they found her on the couch, lying very still and covered by her favorite shawl. There was no sign of struggle. She seemed to be at peace. They called me for advice about how to proceed. When I arrived at their house, Diane indeed seemed peaceful. Her husband and son were quiet. We talked about what a remarkable person she had been. They seemed to have no doubts about the course she had chosen or about their cooperation, although the unfairness of her illness and the finality of her death were overwhelming to us all.

I called the medical examiner to inform him that a hospice patient had died. When asked about the cause of death, I said, "acute leukemia." He said that was fine and that we should call a funeral director. Although acute leukemia was the truth, it was not the whole story. Yet any mention of suicide would have given rise to a police investigation and probably brought the arrival of an ambulance crew for resuscitation. Diane would have become a "coroner's case," and the decision to perform an autopsy would have been made at the discretion of the medical examiner. The family or I could have been subject to criminal prosecution, and I to professional review, for our roles in support of Diane's choices. Although I firmly believe that the family and I gave her the best care possible, allowing her to define her limits and directions as much as possible, I am not sure that the law, society, or the medical profession would agree. So I said "acute leukemia" to protect all of us, to protect Diane from an invasion into her past and her body, and to continue to shield society from the knowledge of the degree of suffering that people often undergo in the process of dying. Suffering can be lessened to some extent, but in no way eliminated, by the careful intervention of a competent, caring physician, given current social constraints.

Diane taught me about the range of help I can provide if I know people well and if I allow them to say what they really want. She taught me about life, death, and honesty and about taking charge and facing tragedy squarely when it strikes. She taught me that I can take small risks for people that I really know and care about. Although I did not assist in her suicide directly, I helped indirectly to make it possible, successful, and relatively painless. Although I know we have measures to help control pain and lessen suffering, to think that people do not suffer in the process of dying is an illusion. Prolonged dying can occasionally be peaceful, but more often the role of the physician and family is limited to lessening but not eliminating severe suffering.

I wonder how many families and physicians secretly help patients over the edge into death in the face of such severe suffering. I wonder how many severely ill or dying patients secretly take their lives, dying alone in despair. I wonder whether the image of Diane's final alone-ness will persist in the minds of her family, or if they will remember more the intense, meaningful months they had together before she died. I wonder whether Diane struggled in that last hour, and whether the Hemlock Society's way of death by suicide is the most benign. I wonder why Diane, who gave so much to so many of us, had to be alone for the last hour of her life. I wonder whether I will see Diane again, on the shore of Lake Geneva at sunset, with dragons swimming on the horizon.

B. *Potential Clinical Criteria for Physician-Assisted Suicide*

One of medicine's highest missions is to allow hopelessly ill persons to die with as much comfort, control, and dignity as possible. The philosophy and techniques of comfort care provide a humane alternative to more traditional, curative medical approaches that can help patients to achieve this end. Yet there remain troubling instances where incurably ill patients suffer intolerably prior to death in spite of comprehensive efforts to provide comfort care. Some of these patients reach a point where they would rather die than continue living under the conditions imposed by their illness, and a few request assistance from their physicians.

The patients who ask us to face their tragic dilemma do not fall into simple diagnostic categories. Until recently, their problem has been relatively unacknowledged and unexplored by the medical profession, so there is little objectively known about its spectrum and prevalence, or about the range of physician responses. Yet each unique request can be compelling:

■ A former athlete, weighing eighty pounds after an eight-year struggle with acquired immunodeficiency syndrome (AIDS), who is losing his sight and his memory and is terrified of AIDS dementia.

■ A mother of seven children, continually exhausted and bedbound at home with a gaping, foul-smelling, open wound in her abdomen, who can no longer eat, and who no longer finds any meaning in her fight against ovarian cancer.

■ A fiercely independent retired factory worker, quadriplegic from amyotrophic lateral sclerosis, who no longer wants to linger in a hapless, dependent state, waiting and hoping for death.

■ A writer with extensive bony metastases from lung cancer, whose condition did not respond to chemotherapy or radiation, and who cannot accept the daily choice he must make between sedation or severe pain.

326

■ A physician colleague, dying of respiratory failure from progressive pulmonary fibrosis, who doesn't want to go onto a ventilator but is also terrified of suffocation.

Like the case of "Diane," which has been told in more depth, there are personal stories of courage and grief behind each of these images that force us to take their requests for a physician's assistance very seriously. It is for competent, incurably ill patients such as these who have no escape other than death that this discussion is being opened.

The purpose of this paper is to present potential clinical criteria that, if met, would allow physicians to respond openly and safely to requests from their competent, incurably ill patients for assisted suicide. We support legalization of physician-assisted suicide, but not active euthanasia, as the correct balance of humane response to the requests of patients like those outlined above, and protection of other vulnerable populations. We strongly advocate the principles and practices of intensive, unrestrained comfort care for all incurably ill persons. When properly applied, comfort care should result in meaningful, tolerable, and relatively symptom-controlled deaths for most patients. Physician-assisted suicide should never be contemplated as a substitute for comprehensive comfort care, or for joining with patients to find unique solutions for the physical, personal, and social challenges posed by the difficult process of dying.

Yet it is neither idiosyncratic, selfish, nor emblematic of a psychiatric disorder for a person with an incurable illness to want to have some control over how he leaves this world. A noble, dignified death is exalted in great literature, poetry, art, and music, and its meaning is deeply personal and unique. When an incurably ill patient asks for help achieving a dignified death, we believe that physicians have an obligation to fully explore the request, and, under specified circumstances, to carefully consider making an exception to the prohibition against assisting suicide.

Physician-Assisted Suicide vs. Euthanasia

Physician-assisted suicide is defined as the act of making a means of suicide (such as a prescription for barbiturates) available to a patient who is otherwise physically capable of suicide, and who subsequently acts on his or her own. It is distinguished from voluntary euthanasia, where the physician not only makes the means available but is the actual agent of death upon the patient's request. Whereas active euthanasia is uniformly illegal in the United States, only thirty-six states have laws explicitly prohibiting assisted suicide. In every situation where a physician has compassionately assisted a terminally ill person to commit suicide, criminal charges have been dismissed or a verdict of not guilty found. But though the reality of successful prosecution may be remote, the risk of an expensive, publicized professional and legal inquiry will be prohibitive for most physicians, and will certainly keep the practice covert and isolating for those who participate.

It is not known how widespread the secret practice of physician-assisted suicide is currently in the United States, nor how frequently patients' requests to physicians are turned down. Approximately 6,000 deaths per day are in some way planned or indirectly assisted in the United States, probably confined to the "double effect" of pain-relieving medications, and to discontinuing or not starting potentially life-prolonging treatments. Survey data that are flawed by low response rates and poor design suggest that from 3 to 37 per cent of anonymously responding physicians admitted secretly taking active steps to hasten a patient's death. Every public opinion survey taken over the past forty years asking questions about physician-assisted dying for the terminally ill has shown that a majority of Americans support the idea. . . .

A Policy Proposal

While both physician-assisted suicide and voluntary euthanasia have as their common intent the active facilitation of a wished-for death, there are several important distinctions between them. In assisted suicide, the final act is solely the patient's, thus greatly reducing the risk of suicide coercion from doctors, family members, institutions, or other social forces. The balance of power between doctor and patient is more nearly equal in physician-assisted suicide. The physician is counselor and witness, and makes the means available, but ultimately the patient must act or not act on his or her own.

With voluntary euthanasia, the physician must provide both the means and the actual conduct of the final act, greatly amplifying the physician's power over the patient and increasing the risk of error, coercion, or abuse.

In view of these distinctions, we have concluded that legalization of physician-assisted suicide, but not voluntary euthanasia, is the policy option best able to both respond to and protect this vulnerable population. From this perspective, physician-assisted suicide would be part of a continuum of comfort-care options, beginning with forgoing life-sustaining therapy, coupled with aggressive symptom-relieving measures, and permitting physician-assisted suicide only if all other alternatives have failed and all criteria are met.

Active voluntary euthanasia would be excluded from this continuum because of the risk of abuse. We recognize that this exclusion occurs at a cost to those competent, incurably ill patients who are unable to swallow or to move, and who therefore could not be helped to die by assisted suicide. Such persons who otherwise meet agreed-upon criteria must not be abandoned to their suffering: an opportunity to forgo life-sustaining treatments (including food and fluids) and be given aggressive comfort measures (such as analgesics and sedatives) could be offered, along with a commitment to search for creative alternatives. We acknowledge that this is a less than ideal solution, but also recognize that access to medical care in the United States currently is too inequitable and many doctor-patient relationships too impersonal to tolerate the risks of condoning active voluntary euthanasia. We must study and monitor any change in public policy in this domain to evaluate both its benefits and its burdens.

We propose the following clinical guidelines to stimulate serious discussion about permitting physician-assisted suicide. Though we favor a reconsideration of the legal and professional prohibitions for patients who clearly meet carefully defined criteria, we do not wish to promote an easy or impersonal process. If we are to consider allowing incurably ill patients more control over their deaths, it must be as an expression of our compassion and concern about the ultimate fate of those who have exhausted all other alternatives. Such patients should not be held hostage to our reluctance or inability to forge policies in this difficult terrain.

The Proposed Criteria

Because assisted suicide is extraordinary and irreversible treatment, the patient's primary physician must ensure that the conditions set forth below are clearly satisfied before proceeding:

1. *The patient must, of his own free will and at his own initiative, clearly and repeatedly request to die rather than continue suffering.* The physician should have a thorough understanding of what continued life would mean to the patient and on what basis the patient deems death preferable. A physician's too-ready acceptance of a patient's request could be perceived as encouragement to commit suicide, yet we also don't want to be so prohibitive or reticent that the patient is forced to "beg" for assistance. Understanding the patient's desire to die and ensuring that the request is enduring are critical in evaluating the patient's rationality, and in assuring that all alternative means of relieving suffering have been adequately explored. Any sign of patient ambivalence or uncertainty should abort the process, as a clear, convincing, and continuous desire for an end of suffering through death is a strict requirement to proceed. Requests for assisted suicide by advance directive or by health-care surrogate should not be honored.

2. *The patient's judgment must not be distorted.* The patient must be capable of understanding the decision and its implications and consequences. The presence of depression is relevant if it is distorting rational decision-making and is reversible in a way that would substantially alter the situation. Expert psychiatric evaluation should be sought when the primary physician is inexperienced in the diagnosis and treatment of depression, or when there is any uncertainty about the rationality of the request or the presence of a reversible mental disorder that would substantially change the patient's perception of his condition once treated.

3. *The patient must have a condition that is incurable, and associated with severe, unrelenting, intolerable suffering.* The patient must understand his condition, his prognosis, and the comfort-care alternatives available. Though we anticipate that most patients making this request will be imminently terminal, we acknowledge the inexactness of such prognostications, and do not want to arbitrarily exclude persons with incurable, but not imminently terminal, progressive illnesses such as ALS or multiple sclerosis. When there is considerable uncertainty

about the patient's medical condition or prognosis, second opinions should be sought and the uncertainty clarified as much as possible before a final response to the patient's request is made.

4. *The physician must ensure that the patient's suffering and the request are not the result of inadequate comfort care.* All reasonable comfort-oriented measures must have been at least considered, and preferably tried, before the means are provided for a physician-assisted suicide. Physician-assisted suicide must never be used to circumvent the struggle to provide comprehensive comfort care, or find acceptable alternatives. The physician's willingness to provide assisted suicide in the future is legitimate and important to discuss if raised by the patient, since many will probably find the potential of an escape more important than the reality.

5. *Physician-assisted suicide should be carried out only in the context of a meaningful doctor-patient relationship.* This relationship should not be based solely on the patient's request for assisted suicide. Ideally, the physician should have witnessed the patient's prior illness and suffering. Though a preexisting relationship may not always be possible, the aiding physician must get to know the patient personally, so that the reasons for the request are fully understood. The physician must understand why, from the patient's perspective, death is the best of a limited number of very unfortunate options. The primary physician must personally confirm each of the criteria. The patient should have no doubt about the physician's commitment to find alternative solutions with him if at any moment he changes his mind. Rather than creating a new death subspecialty, assisted suicide should be provided by the same physician who is struggling with the patient to find comfort-care alternatives, and who will stand by the patient and provide care for him until his death no matter what path is taken.

No physician should be forced to assist a patient in suicide if it violates her fundamental values, though the patient's personal physician should think deeply before turning down the patient's request. Should transfer of care be necessary, the patient's personal physician should help the patient find another more receptive primary physician.

6. *Consultation with another experienced physician is required* to ensure the voluntariness and rationality of the patient's request, the accuracy of the diagnosis and prognosis, and the full exploration of comfort-oriented alternatives. The consulting physician should review the

supporting materials, and personally interview and examine the patient.

7. *Clear documentation to support each condition above is required.* A system must be developed for reporting, reviewing, studying, and clearly distinguishing such deaths from other forms of suicide. The patient, the primary physican, and the consultant must each sign a consent form. A physician-assisted suicide must neither invalidate insurance policies nor lead to an investigation by a medical examiner or an unwanted autopsy. The primary physician, the medical consultant, and the involved family must have assurance that, if the agreed-upon conditions are satisfied in good faith, they will be free from criminal prosecution for their role in assisting the patient to die.

Informing family members is strongly recommended, but final control over whom to involve and inform is left to the discretion and control of the patient. Similarly, spiritual counseling should be offered, depending on the patient's background and beliefs. Ideally, close family members are integrally involved in the decision-making process, and should understand and support the patient's decision. If there is an unresolvable dispute about how to proceed between the family and patient, such matters may need involvement of an ethics committee, or even the courts. However, it is hoped that most of these painful decisions can be worked through directly between the patient, family, and health-care providers. Under no circumstances should the wishes and requests of the family override those of a competent patient.

The Method

The main method used in physician-assisted suicide is the prescription of a lethal amount of medication, which the patient then ingests on his own. Since assisted suicide has been a covert, largely unstudied process, little is known about the most humane and effective methods. If there is a change in policy, there must be an open sharing of information about methods within the profession, and a careful analysis of effectiveness. The methods selected should be 100 per cent effective, and should not contribute to further patient suffering. We must also provide support systems and careful monitoring for the patients, physicians, and families who participate, since the emotional and social effects are largely unknown, but undoubtedly far-reaching.

Physician-assisted suicide is one of the most profound and meaningful acts that a patient can ask of his physician. If both the patient and the physician agree that there are no acceptable alternatives and that all the required conditions are met, the lethal medication should ideally be taken in the presence of the patient's physician. Unless the patient specifically requests it, he should not be left alone at the time of death. In addition to the personal physician, other health-care providers and family members whom the patient wishes should be encouraged to be present.

The principle of not abandoning the patient is of utmost importance at this critical moment. The time before a controlled death can provide an opportunity for a rich and meaningful goodbye between family members, health-care providers, and the patient. In this context, we must be sure that any policies and laws enacted to allow assisted suicide do not require that the patient be alone at the moment of death in order for the assisters to be safe from prosecution.

Balancing Risks and Benefits

There is an intensifying debate within and outside of the medical profession about the physician's appropriate role in assisting dying. While most will agree that there are exceptional circumstances where death would be preferable to intolerable suffering, the case against physician-assisted suicide (and voluntary euthanasia) is based mainly on its implications for public policy and its potential impact on the moral integrity of the medical profession. The "slippery slope" argument suggests that permissive policies would inevitably lead to subtle coercion of the powerless to choose death rather than become a burden on society or their family. Access to health care in the United States is extraordinarily variable, often impersonal, and subject to intense cost-containment pressures. It may be dangerous to license physicians to take life in this unstable environment. It is also suggested that skillfully applied comfort care could provide a tolerable and dignified death for most persons, and that the incentive for the physician to become more proficient at comfort care would be less if the option of a quick, controlled death were too readily available. Finally, some believe that physician-assisted death, no matter how noble and pure its intentions, could destroy the identity of the medical profession and its central ethos of protecting the sanctity of life. The question before policy-makers, physicians, and voters is whether criteria such as those we have outlined in this paper adequately safeguard patients against these risks.

The risks and burdens of continuing with current prohibitions have been less clearly articulated in the literature. The most pressing problem is the potential abandonment of those competent, incurably ill patients who yearn for death rather than the continuance of a life without meaning or hope, in spite of comprehensively applied comfort care. These patients have sometimes used medical treatments to extend their lives to the point that they are both physically and emotionally falling apart, but not imminently dying. Those who have witnessed difficult deaths of patients on hospice programs are not reassured by the glib assertion that we always know how to make death tolerable, and they fear that physicians will abandon them if their course becomes difficult or overwhelming in the face of comfort care. In fact, there is no empirical evidence that all physical suffering associated with incurable illness can be effectively relieved. In addition, for many the most frightening aspect of death is not physical pain, but the prospect of losing control and independence, and dying in an undignified, unesthetic, absurd, and existentially unacceptable condition.

Physicians who respond to the requests for assisted suicide by these patients do so at substantial professional and legal peril, often acting in secret out of compassion without the benefit of consultation or support from colleagues. This covert practice discourages open and honest communication between physicians, their colleagues, and their dying patients. Decisions are often dependent more on the physician's values and willingness to take risk than the compelling nature of the patient's request. There may be more risk for abuse and idiosyncratic decision-making with such secret practices than with a more open, carefully defined practice. Finally, those terminally ill patients who do choose to take their life often die alone so as not to legally jeopardize their families or care-givers.

Given current professional and legal prohibitions, physicians find themselves in a difficult position when faced with requests for assisted suicide by suffering patients who have exhausted comfort-care measures. To adhere to the letter of the law, they must turn down their patients' requests even if they find them reasonable and personally acceptable. To accede to their patients' requests, they must risk violating legal and professional standards, and therefore act in isolation and secret collaboration with their patients. It is our opinion that there is more risk for vulnerable patients and for the integrity of the profession in such hidden practices, however well intended, than there would be in a more open process restricted to competent patients who met carefully defined criteria. The professions of medicine and law must collaborate if we are to create public policy that fully acknowledges irreversible end-of-life suffering, and offers dying patients a broader range of options for exploration with their physicians.

C. The Case of Diane Revisited

How would Diane's illness or death have been altered if physician-assisted suicide according to strict clinical guidelines were legal? We can first determine if she would have met all seven conditions, and then speculate about how she, her family, and I as her physician would have been helped by a more open process. If a change in public policy is seriously contemplated, it is vital to explore its effects on actual patients such as Diane who would clearly seem to benefit from this option. Only by exploring a policy's effect on real people can we realistically determine whether the benefits of a change outweigh the burdens.

All seven criteria for physician-assisted suicide must be clearly satisfied before it would be sanctioned under the proposed guidelines. I will now consider the implications of each criterion on Diane's case.

1. *The patient must, of her own free will and at her own initiative, clearly and repeatedly request to die rather than continue suffering.* Diane was a person of strong will and clear opinions who was not about to be controlled or overly influenced by others. The initial idea was hers alone, and I as her physician was reluctant and skeptical. Yet her request to die was consistent with her longstanding values and beliefs, and her motivation to avoid lingering near death at the end in a state that she would have found meaningless was clearly stated and unambiguous. She was clear and consistent about the circumstances under which she would want to end her life, and when she came to that point, her commitment was unwavering. As we reviewed what comfort care could be offered at the end, she remained clear that death was now far preferable to lingering for hours, days, or weeks in relative "comfort."

2. *The patient's judgment must not be distorted.* Earlier I described Diane as an "incredibly clear, brutally honest" thinker. There was no doubt in the minds of any of the professional or lay people who were fortunate enough to spend time with Diane over her last three months that her judgment was intact. Diane faced death directly and openly, and could explore the implications of each of her decisions with a

336

clarity and sophistication that impressed everyone she met. This is not to say that she was not sad or discouraged at times in her illness, for she was not at all eager to leave this life. But her fear of lingering and dependence at the end outweighed her fear of death. She believed in her own way in an afterlife, and the imagery of Lake Geneva at sunset gave her great solace.

Diane's resolve remained consistent for the three months that she lived after her diagnosis, and she fulfilled her part of our agreement to meet with me prior to taking her life to ensure that all alternatives had been explored. In that sad visit, as Diane faced death and I faced my inability to change the inevitable, it was tragically dear that there were no good alternatives. Superficial solutions seemed trivial, and the mandate not to abandon my patient became paramount. What this meant to me was to give her as much choice and control as possible, given the severe limits of the options available.

3. *The patient must have a condition that is incurable, and associated with severe, unrelenting, intolerable suffering.* There could conceivably be some debate about whether Diane would meet this criterion. Acute leukemia is potentially curable, but only if one is willing to undertake very severe medical treatment with relatively poor odds. Since patients have the unequivocal right to refuse medical treatment, even if that treatment might be lifesaving, we cannot then punish those who do so by not offering them treatments intended to humanize their dying. At the time of her diagnosis, Diane had seen several independent oncologists. There was no question in each consultant's mind that she had a full understanding of the options and their implications. Three months later, when she took her life, her acute leukemia was incurable and her suffering had become intolerable to her. Not only was acute medical treatment unacceptable, but at the end, traditional comfort-care measures offered little of value to her. In her eyes, since death was inevitable, why subject herself to the humiliation of total physical and emotional dependence on others for her last moments?

4. *The physician must ensure that the patient's suffering and the request are not the result of inadequate comfort care.* Diane spent three months in a hospice program, from the time she was diagnosed to her death. During much of that time she had enough medication to take her life, but she had made a personal commitment not to use it for that purpose without meeting with me first to ensure that all other comfort-

oriented options had been exhausted. She had several life-prolonging and comfort-enhancing medical interventions during that period. Several of her severe infections responded surprisingly well to oral antibiotics. When she became severely fatigued from anemia, she was briefly admitted to the inpatient hospice unit for transfusions, which gave her a short boost in energy. Her bone pain from the leukemia was well controlled by an oral narcotic medication. She was wonderfully supported by her husband, who began doing much of his work from home, and her son, who took a semester off from school in order to be close to his mother. She was regularly seen by her hospice nurse and by her closest friends.

Diane and her family grew closer during her time on the hospice program. In those three months she experienced the best that comfort care has to offer—good control of her physical symptoms, excellent emotional and social support, and intimate, healing contact with family and friends. Toward the end of the three months, however, the quality of her life began to decline. High fevers persisted despite antibiotics, weakness progressed in the face of repeated transfusions, the increased narcotic pain medications needed to control her pain made her sleepy, and the leukemia progressively invaded her skin, which became sore, red, and swollen. She became so weak that walking even a few steps was an ordeal. . . .

Though Diane clearly benefited from comfort care for three months, toward the end it was not enough to ensure a dignified death. I believe that if she had not had the assurance of a controlled death when her suffering became intolerable, much of the quality of the three months that she did have would have been contaminated by fear and by searching for a potential way out. She might even have taken an earlier escape through suicide, since she would have had to fear becoming too weak to act on her own if she waited too long.

5. *Physician-assisted suicide should only be carried out in the context of a meaningful doctor-patient relationship.* Diane and I had an eight-year relationship that had weathered other storms. Though a preexisting relationship is not a requirement, in-depth knowledge of the patient's request and the motivation behind it is extremely important. Our relationship was in no way contingent on her decision about suicide. We were committed to working together until her death, no matter which course she chose and which direction her illness took us.

Diane's family was fully informed and involved in the decision-making. . . .

Diane's request was also not inconsistent with my own personal values. I have seen considerable end-of-life suffering, both in my work as a hospice medical director and as a primary-care physician, which could have been lessened by a wider range of physician options to ease the passage into death. If, as a patient, I personally faced increasing haplessness and indignity that could only end with my death, I would seriously consider putting an end to my life. . . . After several discussions with Diane and her family, I elected to remain true to my personal values and to take a professional risk. I want to emphasize that I did this out of my own free will, under no pressure from Diane. However, had I been unwilling to help her, she would have had to consider other methods to act on her own.

6. *Consultation with another experienced physician is required.* Shortly after her initial diagnosis, Diane saw two oncologists from two different institutions to ensure that she understood her disease and the implications of her refusal of treatment. She also discussed her situation briefly with a psychologist whom she had worked with extensively in the past. In addition, the medical director of the home hospice program (the job I held in the past) was informally consulted, as she is on all hospice cases to ensure that every measure that might enhance patient comfort is being considered. There was no doubt that Diane fully understood her situation, and no questions were raised by any health-care providers about her judgment or rationality. She clearly received the best that comfort care had to offer.

Because of the potential illegality of assisted suicide, the consultations that I obtained pertaining to Diane's request for a controlled death were more informal and confidential, but extremely helpful nonetheless. As I contemplated crossing a frightening boundary that I had never crossed before, it was important for me to ensure that my own thinking was rational, and that I had fully considered all other options and alternatives. Ideally, such consultants would confirm adherence to the prestated criteria by reviewing data recorded by the primary physician, and also by meeting directly with the patient and even the family to independently confirm the key elements. Such a direct consultation would be much more valuable than the indirect consultations that I received, though the support and consultation I received were far preferable to the situation of a doctor and a patient acting in complete secrecy and isolation.

7. *Clear documentation to support each condition above is required.* Just as it is difficult to get an in-depth second opinion about a practice that is potentially illegal and on the ethical edge of appropriate physician behavior, clearly documenting the data supporting the decisions is also dangerous. Thus, Diane's medical record contains a detailed account of the reasoning behind her refusal of medical treatment for acute leukemia (an accepted though controversial decision, given current medical standards), but no mention of her considerations about suicide, or my thinking about my potential role in indirectly assisting her. Requiring careful, systematic documentation to show that the criteria were met prior to allowing physician-assisted suicide would clearly bring the decision-making more out in the open, and allow the supporting data to be reviewed by outside observers. Diane would have been more than willing to sign a consent form. . . .

In addition to more open documentation in the patient's medical record and a formal consent form, a mechanism for recording such deaths on a death certificate, and for distinguishing them from suicides stemming from depression and other mental illnesses, would also be needed. Patients and their families would need reassurance that life insurance policies would not be invalidated by such acts, and that the stigma associated with other suicide deaths would be minimized.

I was severely criticized for recording "acute leukemia" as the cause of death on Diane's death certificate, yet suicide would not have even been a remote question to her had she not been dying of leukemia. Any mention of suicide to the medical examiner or the funeral director would have led to an immediate call to an ambulance crew to try cardiopulmonary resuscitation, in spite of the fact Diane had already been dead for several hours. This unwarranted and unwanted assault would then have been followed by an interrogation of the family by the medical examiner to determine their possible role in the death, and an unwanted autopsy to establish with certainty if medication had contributed to her death.

Such an invasion of Diane's body and of her family's potential role in her death would have violated fundamental principles of humane care of the dying, as well as all that we were working together to achieve in terms of allowing Diane a dignified, partially controlled death. My obligation to Diane and her family seemed to outweigh my obligation to share the full complexity of her death with the medical examiner. Designation of the immediate cause of death is notoriously inaccurate under the best of circumstances. Whether or not the medical examiner would have differentiated between Diane's death and a suicide stemming from mental illness, in my opinion her death resulted much more from her leukemia. The overdose of medication that she took probably shortened her life by at most a few days to a week.

Ironically, under media pressure to determine exactly who Diane was in the wake of my article describing her illness and death, her full name was identified by an anonymous tip. Her body, which she had generously given to science for medical education and research, was eventually located by the district attorney. Without the family's permission, it was confiscated, and an unwanted autopsy was performed that "proved" that the immediate cause of her death was an overdose of medication. I was told that, had Diane been buried when she died, she would have been exhumed without the family's permission as part of the medical examiner's inquiry. Unfortunately, Diane's family went through a very public interrogation because of the article—the exact processes that I had tried to protect them from. Though Diane's family and I jointly reached the original decision that Diane would have wanted her story to be told, none of us had anticipated the seemingly absurd lengths to which the legal inquiry would go.

The notion that we can allow such violations of dying patients and their families who dare to take some small measure of control over death still mystifies and infuriates me. I feel angry and sad that Diane's family had to suffer through this added humiliation after already losing so much. I just hope that we all can learn from that experience.

The most tragic aspect of the story for Diane herself is that she died alone. Diane was correct in her assumption that the grand jury would find my role too ambiguous to prosecute if she were alone at her death. Yet, as physicians, we make a commitment to our dying patients not to abandon them no matter how difficult or overwhelming their situation may become. Patients would not feel they would have to put their doctor and family at risk to be with them at the time of death if assisted suicide were more open and legalized. Family members, friends, and the doctor could all say goodbye to the patient, and then freely remain together during the patient's waning moments.

Enhancing patient choice and control while minimizing abandonment and isolation are probably the most compelling reasons for considering a change in public policy. The costs of the current prohibitions—uncontrolled suffering, increased dependence on the physician's values rather than the patient's, idiosyncratic, secretive behavior on the part of the physician, and abandonment of the patient —are so high that serious consideration of a change in policy is imperative.

18

Active Voluntary Euthanasia: Opening Pandora's Box

D. Alan Shewmon

"Whatever proportions these crimes finally assumed . . . the beginnings at first were merely a subtle shift in emphasis in the basic attitude of the physicians . . . toward the non-rehabilitable sick." — LEO ALEXANDER, M.D., U.S. medical consultant at the Nuremberg Trials[1]

Many physicians remain unaware of the growing general interest in active euthanasia. It was approved by the Rotterdam Criminal Court in 1981, and there is heavy lobbying for its statutory legalization across Europe. Various U.S. "right to die" societies have been doing everything possible to create popularity for the issue, and their efforts have not gone entirely unrewarded. A California appellate court, in its [1986] *Bouvia* decision, not only asserted the right of an adult with severe disabilities to starve herself to death in a hospital, but went so far as to require the medical staff to assist her against their

D. Alan Shewmon is an assistant clinical professor in the division of pediatric neurology at the University of California, Los Angeles. This essay is reprinted by permission from *Issues in Law and Medicine* 3, no. 3 (Winter 1987; © 1987 by the National Legal Center for the Medically Dependent and Disabled). About half of the notes have been omitted.

own consciences.[2] Justice Compton's separate concurring opinion explicitly endorsed active euthanasia on general principles. In January 1987, lawyers for the American Civil Liberties Union petitioned a Colorado court for a lethal injection for Hector Rodas, claiming that he had a "constitutional right . . . to be provided with medicine and medicinal agents that would cause his death."[3]

The reasons advanced in favor of euthanasia vary according to the audience. On TV talk shows and in newspaper articles, advocates usually emphasize extreme cases of terminally ill patients in great pain, who are kept alive against their wills by means of oppressive and invasive tubes and other technology. The President's Commission for the Study of Ethical Problems in Medicine and Biomedical and Behavioral Research (hereinafter President's Commission), however, emphasized in its 1983 report that excessive pain, discomfort, and anxiety are nearly always examples of inadequate treatment, not inadequate ethics.[4] The experience of hospices also bears this out. In fact, even the euthanasia advocates themselves admit elsewhere that terminal pain is not the real reason for their efforts. In the words of Derek Humphry, co-founder of the Hemlock Society, "pain is by no means the only reason, if at all, why people contemplate self-deliverance, with or without assistance. Control and choice of when, where and how, plus personal dignity and a wish to avoid distress, physical and emotional, during the dying process are the key considerations."[5]

Self-determination is indeed the only issue of any real substance in the controversy over euthanasia. But the legal and medical professions have always recognized the right of competent patients to refuse any and all medical treatment, or to discharge themselves from a hospital at any time (an option Bouvia refused), even if so doing would hasten or directly cause death. What they then do with their lives is their own responsibility.

Taken literally, the catch phrase "right to die" is meaningless. There can be no such thing as a right to something inevitable and unavoidable. But in common parlance it is an unfortunate ambiguity, meaning sometimes the "right to be allowed to die" from one's terminal illness and other times a supposed "right to be killed." The former has always been recognized by traditional medical ethics. But can there be a "right to be killed"? The cumulative wisdom of centuries has consistently answered in the negative. Although self-determination is an important right, like all other rights it is not absolute; it can be qualified if it conflicts with the rights of others (e.g., no one has a right to self-determine to be a thief or a murderer). If put into practice consistently, the principle that death is an acceptable solution to human problems would ultimately destroy the very fabric of society, and with it all individual rights. Therefore, a "right to be killed" cannot derive from the right of self-determination.

This is why legal sanctions against aiding and abetting suicide remain, even though suicide and attempted suicide have been decriminalized in most states. The reason for the decriminalization is not any implicit recognition of a "right to suicide," as is often claimed by euthanasia advocates, but rather "that there is no form of criminal punishment that is acceptable for a completed suicide and that criminal punishment is singularly inefficacious to deter attempts to commit suicide."[6] Furthermore, the drafters of the Model Penal Code stated explicitly that "the interests in the sanctity of life that are represented by the criminal homicide laws are threatened by one who expresses a willingness to participate in taking the life of another, even though the act may be accomplished with the consent, or at the request, of the suicide victim."[7] The President's Commission reiterated this:

> An individual who seeks death at the hands of another, regardless of the reason, does not confer immunity from prosecution on the one who takes the life, because the taking of innocent human life is seen as a wrong to the entire society, not just to the dead person. . . . Policies prohibiting direct killing may also conflict with the important value of patient self-determination. . . . The Commission finds this limitation on individual self-determination to be an acceptable cost of securing the general protection of human life afforded by the prohibition of direct killing.[8]

Such statements represent a nearly unanimous consensus based on the combined experience, reflection, and wisdom of a great number of people over many centuries. They should not be lightly disregarded.

Legalized euthanasia would also infringe on the rights and consciences of many physicians. Proponents argue that, to ensure patients' "right" to euthanasia, the law should establish a corresponding duty on the part of physicians either to comply or to refer the patient to a willing physician. But even a duty of referral would infringe upon a physician's conscience. No patient, in the name of self-determination, can oblige a physician to render treatment that he or she considers inappropriate or unethical, or to find a replacement who will necessarily fulfill such wishes.

The Two-Dimensional "Slippery Slope"

One of the main reasons why the legal and medical professions have always opposed active euthanasia is that such societal issues are never static; they necessarily evolve according to the dynamics of their underlying philosophy, with the laws forever being revised to accommodate it. Because the logical endpoint of that evolution is considered undesirable, so is its initiation. Euthanasia advocates dismiss the "slippery-slope" argument by reference to other societies in which the practice of suicide for specific indications has not evolved into a horror of abuses—for example, the voluntary freezing to death of elderly Eskimos. But such societies are not valid testing grounds for voluntary euthanasia in our own society, because of the differences in basic philosophy and the radically different levels of social complexity. The Netherlands would serve this purpose well, except for the fact that insufficient time has passed, since that country's acceptance of active euthanasia, to observe any long-term effects. Our similarities with pre-Nazi Germany, however, are compelling, and will be discussed later. Thus, the President's Commission stated: "Obviously, slippery-slope arguments must be very carefully employed lest they serve merely as an unthinking defense of the status quo. . . . Nevertheless, the Commission has found that in [this] area . . . valid concerns warrant being especially cautious before adopting any policy that weakens the protections against taking human life."[9]

In what follows, it will be shown that this particular "slippery slope" is not merely a theoretical possibility; it is a present reality. The practice of euthanasia will necessarily facilitate this ongoing evolution along at least two dimensions simultaneously: the scope of indications (beginning with terminal illnesses and ending with euthanasia "on demand") and the degree of voluntariness (beginning with voluntary euthanasia and ending with involuntary "euthanasia" for the benefit of others).

Dimension 1: Scope of Indications

The inherent ambiguity of "terminal illness." According to the "Hemlock Manifesto," formulated in 1982, one of the guiding principles for the practice of active voluntary euthanasia ought to be that the recipient have a "terminal illness," meaning that "the person is likely, in the judgment of two examining physicians, to die of that condition within six months."[10] But prognoses for survival are never that accurate; about 10 per cent of patients admitted to hospices to die end up being discharged home because of either remission or inappropriate diagnosis.

The inherent unenforceability of the proposed criteria. Moreover, the six month cut-off is arbitrary. Proponents argue that arbitrary line-drawing is unavoidable in many areas that are nonetheless beneficial (e.g., highway speed limits), but statutory arbitrariness in this area will certainly encourage judicial discretion far beyond the literal interpretation of any such requirement. If one receives a speeding ticket and defends oneself in court on the basis that speed limits are inherently arbitrary, one will most likely end up paying the fine. But if a doctor were to administer euthanasia to someone projected to die within seven months who kept pleading for "deliverance," it is not likely that he would be charged with murder, or even for aiding and abetting suicide, if active euthanasia at six months were recognized not only as legal but as good. This is especially true given that the present cut-off of zero months is already not enforced (most defendants in mercy killings or assisted suicides are acquitted). Regardless of where the time limit is placed, there will be patients just beyond it who will demand their "right" to euthanasia; then the advocacy groups will seek to abolish the manifest hypocrisy of the already liberalized law. Once set in motion, this positive feedback cannot halt until its logical culmination in euthanasia on demand.

Expanding criteria within the euthanasia movement itself. The reality of this slippery slope is evident within the euthanasia movement itself. Much of what follows pertains to the Hemlock Society as a specific example, only because, of all the "right to die" societies, it is the most forthright about its goal to promote active euthanasia. It began as an advocate of active voluntary euthanasia for the terminally ill. Hemlock's "Manifesto" declares that "[i]ncurable distress is a legally insufficient basis for justification [of euthanasia] unless it is a product of terminal illness."[11]

Nevertheless, with the passage of time, Hemlock began to refer to itself as "a society supporting the option of voluntary euthanasia . . . for the terminally ill, or the seriously incurably physically ill."[12] Nowhere in any of its literature is the concept "incurably physically ill" defined, but it is obviously intended to be distinct from "terminally ill." In fact, the *Hemlock Quarterly* has many articles and letters approving suicide and euthanasia for a wide variety of non-terminal conditions. In a poll of its members, 61 per cent disagreed with the statement, "Life is worth living in extreme loneliness or in the absence of loved ones and close friends."[13] Hemlock officials explain that such things are printed in a spirit of open communication and do not necessarily reflect Hemlock's formal stance. Even so, they are usually not accompanied by editorial commentary in keeping with Hemlock's stated principles.

The more recent writings of Hemlock's co-founder, Derek Humphry, reveal that the concept of terminal illness has now expanded to embrace such conditions as Alzheimer's disease and even osteoporosis.[14] In an article by Humphry entitled "Mrs. Bouvia's Sad Mistakes Are Lessons," the sad mistakes were that she undermined her plan by admitting herself to a hospital and attracting publicity.[15] Elsewhere, Humphry also advocates a "right" of quadriplegics to receive euthanasia.[16]

Concerning double suicide pacts, Humphry maintains that "[t]here can be no firm rules in this subject. No two sets of circumstances are alike. When all is said and done, it is an extremely personal decision. There must, we think, be a tolerance for those people who have been partners for many years and now cannot bear the thought of life without their spouse."[17] Along similar lines, Ann Wickett (Humphry's present wife and the editor of the *Hemlock Quarterly*) wrote concerning Cynthia Koestler, 55, who was in perfect health at the time she killed herself following her husband's suicide: "For a man in grave and failing health, self-deliverance was the final right. For Cynthia, it was the final act of devotion. That too was her right. One regrets, however, less the nature of her death, than the nature of her life."[18]

The above statements clearly illustrate a gravitation within Hemlock toward "euthanasia on demand." As Humphry succinctly wrote:

"When should it be done? We are only here once (or so I believe) and it is folly to leave too soon. Decide what is [sic] the criteria for an acceptable quality of life for you."[19]

Although Concern for Dying cultivates a considerably more moderate public image than Hemlock, the difference seems to be more one of tactic than of goal. A letter, written in 1978 by Executive Director A.-J. Rock-Levinson (now A.-J. Levinson) in response to an inquiry, revealed the wedge principle in action:

> You are right when you say that our people believe rational suicide to be acceptable. . . . We also know from experience that if we try to foist our ideas too strongly and too soon on a society not yet ready to consider them, we will damage if not destroy our effectiveness. By moving cautiously and without stridency . . . we gain a larger audience for our views. On the subject of crisis centers for potential suicides, or the granting of access to lethal substances, we feel that the time is not yet right to take a public position.[20]

That euthanasia on demand is the unstated goal of the euthanasia movement should not be surprising, because (1) emotional pain is as real as, and can be worse than, physical pain, and (2) self-determination and "situation ethics" are the guiding principles. Joseph Fletcher stated that "[e]very one of these pragmatic objections [to suicide] proves . . . to be false in a great many cases. . . . [I]f our ethics is humane, . . . we'll look at every case on its own merits and refuse to be bound indiscriminately by universal rules of right and wrong, whether they claim to rest on religious or pragmatic grounds."[21] This obviously includes any rule that would restrict self-determination arbitrarily to cases of terminal illness, to say nothing of restricting "terminal illness" arbitrarily to death within six months.

The Dutch understand this perfectly well. When the Rotterdam Criminal Court legalized active voluntary euthanasia in 1981, it stipulated that the recipient need not be terminally ill; in Holland, "paraplegics can request and get aid-in-dying."[22] In fact, in the very first issue of the *Hemlock Quarterly,* under the boldfaced caption **"Euthanasia on Demand,"** it is reported that at the World Voluntary Euthanasia Conference in 1980, "[r]epresentatives from the three Dutch voluntary euthanasia groups surprised the conference by saying that euthanasia was available virtually 'on demand' in Holland," a situation described by the *Hemlock Quarterly* as "advanced."[23]

A historical analogue—the expanding indications for abortion. Euthanasia advocates frequently allude to a close relationship between euthanasia and abortion. If the analogy is valid, then it ironically undermines their claim that the scope of indications for legalized euthanasia would not expand beyond terminal illness. Regardless of one's views on the ethics of abortion, it is an evident historical fact that the scope of indications for it has expanded tremendously since its legalization one and a half decades ago. Although the main indications stressed by legalization proponents in the early 1970s were rape, incest, or danger to the mother's health, now as many as 99 per cent of the 1.5 million annual abortions in the United States are performed for reasons of economics or convenience.[24] Moreover, the upper limit of gestational age has crept well beyond "viability," and abortion on demand at any time up to term is effectively legal in many states.[25]

The tendency of indications for legalized killing to expand is nowhere better evidenced than in the disillusionment of Chief Justice Warren Burger, who had cast a favorable vote in *Roe v. Wade,* yet strongly dissented in the most recent U.S. Supreme Court abortion decision. On July 11, 1986, the Court struck down a Pennsylvania statute requiring that women seeking abortions be informed about the relative risks of the procedure and about available support agencies if they decided to give birth. The Chief Justice stated that "every member of the *Roe* Court rejected the idea of abortion on demand":

> The Court's opinion today, however, plainly undermines that important principle, and I regretfully conclude that some of the concerns of the dissenting Justices in *Roe,* as well as the concerns I expressed in my separate concurrence, have now been realized. . . . We have apparently already passed the point at which abortion is available merely on demand. If the statute at issue here is to be invalidated, the "demand" will not even have to be the result of an informed choice.[26]

The experience with legalized abortion, therefore, indicates it is naïve to suggest that the indications for legalized euthanasia would remain forever restricted only to cases of terminal illness with great suffering.

A further historical analogue—the Nazi "euthanasia" program. Euthanasia advocates reject the Nazi analogy on the basis that the Nazi "euthanasia" program was neither benevolent nor voluntary on the part of the recipient, and thus it was anything but euthanasia in the true sense. Moreover, they contend that the excesses of a genocide program could not possibly occur in a democracy. But the meaningful analogy lies rather with the approach to medical care for Germany's own Aryan patients. Many do not realize that the first gas chambers were set up, not in concentration camps, but in hospitals, and were first used, not on Jews, but on sick Aryans. In fact, in the beginning sick Jews were considered unworthy to receive the "benefit" of "euthanasia."[27] Of course, this "euthanasia" was entirely involuntary, but for the moment the focus is on the dimension of "indications for candidacy."

It is important to realize that euthanasia (in what the right-to-die organizations would consider the true, benevolent sense) had gained acceptance in substantial sectors of the German society and medical profession long before Hitler's assumption of power in 1933. As early as 1920, jurist Karl Binding and psychiatrist Alfred Hoche had published a highly influential book entitled *The Permission to Destroy Life Not Worth Living,* in which euthanasia was advocated for those suffering from incurable physical and mental illnesses, and for severely retarded and defective children. Emphasis was placed on "death assistance," patient consent (either explicit or by proxy), compassion, quality of life, and cost containment, concepts not unfamiliar in modern health care. The book was so popular that a second printing was required only two years later, and its concept of "life not worth living" became the philosophical basis for future developments in German medical/ethical thinking.

Euthanasia was increasingly discussed in academic circles during the 1920s, particularly in medical and law schools, and considerable public sympathy for it developed. Even prior to Hitler's authorization of euthanasia in 1939, some parents of infants with severe disabilities had been seeking "mercy deaths" for their children and were pleased by the Führer's personal interest in their cases. Significantly, Hitler's authorization was not so much a command but an extension of "the authority of physicians . . . so that a mercy death may be granted to patients who according to human judgment are incurably ill according to the most critical evaluation of the state of their disease."[28] Even as late as 1944, severely malformed adults were being brought for "euthanasia" at the request of their families.

The euthanasia propaganda then was essentially no different from what it is now. One of the movies popular then featured a woman with multiple sclerosis whose physician husband "finally kills her to the accompaniment of soft piano music rendered by a sympathetic colleague in an adjoining room." There was a continuing reference to the costs of caring for the handicapped, retarded, and insane. The purpose behind such propaganda was to facilitate the ongoing program of involuntary "euthanasia." But the point here is that—whether voluntary or involuntary—the indications for legalized killing naturally expand. Eventually patients with minor deformities, the mildly senile, amputee war veterans, "problem children," bed-wetters, and the like were being selected by physicians on their own initiative for "mercy deaths."

This expansion of criteria was not forced upon the doctors by the Nazi regime, but evolved according to its own dynamic within the medical profession, as evidenced by several facts. First, doctors who did not want to participate in the "euthanasia" program were able to continue their own practice of medicine undisturbed. Second, although the regime had a perverse interest in ridding German society of "useless eaters," it would hardly have perceived the lives of basically healthy patients as detrimental either to the war effort or to its mystical quest for genetic purification. Third, the liberalization of indications actually became most wanton after Hitler had officially ended the "euthanasia" project in 1941 (in fact, the selection and killing by doctors of such minimally sick patients, for neither racial nor ideological reasons, continued in full swing right up to the end of the war, and in some places even a few days thereafter).

A contemporary case in point—legalized euthanasia in the Netherlands. The claim that legalized euthanasia in this country will go no further than voluntary euthanasia for competent adults destined to die within six months ignores not only the lessons of history but also what is currently taking place in Holland. Since its inception there at the beginning of this decade [1980s], legalized euthanasia has evolved with surprising rapidity. "Dutch courts have steadily expanded the circumstances in which a doctor may avoid prosecution if he kills— with case law now permitting euthanasia for patients with such non-terminal afflictions as multiple sclerosis or simply the physical ravages of old age." There has been infighting between radical and moderate factions within the euthanasia movement itself, with the radicals recently prevailing. The Royal Dutch Medical Association has endorsed euthanasia on demand not only for competent adults, but also even for minors without parental consent. Advocates are now reasoning that patients with incurable psychiatric illnesses ought to be able to receive euthanasia upon request, in spite of their lack of mental competence.[29]

The situation has evolved so far in such a short period of time that even some of Holland's most prominent euthanasists are beginning to express fears for the future, given the obvious impotence of the legal system to deal with the already existing abuses. After performing euthanasia, most Dutch physicians falsify the death certificate to reflect a "natural death," so as to minimize the likelihood of an investigation of the case. The number of complaints of suggested abuse reported to authorities rose from twelve in 1986 to twenty-four during the first half of 1987, and this is undoubtedly only the tip of an iceberg. One Dutch physician has reported that involuntary euthanasia has become so rampant and is so overlooked by the courts that elderly patients are afraid to be hospitalized or even to consult doctors.[30] The Netherlands is, therefore, demonstrating the reality, the steepness, and the slipperiness of the "slippery slope" of legalized euthanasia. It would be advisable to await the final outcome of this drastic social experiment before embarking along the same irreversible path.

Dimension 2: Degree of Voluntariness

The fringes of mental competence. We now turn to that other dimension of the evolution of legalized euthanasia—the degree of voluntariness. The Hemlock Society believes that active euthanasia should be available, in the context of a terminal illness, to requesting adults "of sound mind," and that it is not "evidence of mental instability or incompetence . . . for anyone to plan to or attempt to terminate his/her own life."[31] But how is mental competence for such a momentous decision to be determined in practice? The proponents of euthanasia do not provide criteria for distinguishing between a rationally suicidal patient, whom the doctor will have the supposed "duty" to kill, and a pathologically suicidal patient, whom the doctor has the duty to restrain. Even psychiatric experts cannot provide clear criteria here, because the conditions obviously represent but two ends of a continuum. The distinction is particularly fuzzy in patients with chronic illness or disabilities, or borderline mental retardation.

In clinical settings, it is often difficult to determine the true wishes of supposedly competent patients. They sometimes say one thing but communicate the opposite non-verbally. Their desire to live or die may fluctuate, the *Bouvia* case being a prime example. The fact that Elizabeth Bouvia had obtained a college degree and managed to get married indicated that she must have habitually found life meaningful and worth living in spite of her quadriplegia and arthritis. Her decision to die came after her divorce, which must have been a cause of despondency, even though the appellate court considered her decision to be rational and competently made. Nevertheless, by the time Bouvia finally won her legal battle to receive hospital assistance in starving to death, she had changed her mind and opted to go on with life after all. Had euthanasia already been acceptable, she would never have survived to discover the transience of her death wish.

Similarly, cancer patients admitted to hospices sometimes gain a new lease on life once their pain has been appropriately treated, and discharge themselves in order to seek more aggressive medical therapy. When a patient is depressed about a chronic or terminal illness, it is really quite impossible to determine whether he or she is mentally competent to make such a monumental, irreversible, once-in-a-lifetime decision as suicide. This is why the law has traditionally erred on the side of regarding attempted suicide as an intrinsically irrational decision, constituting *prima facie* evidence of psychiatric incompetence.

Voluntary euthanasia by proxy. The rights of incompetent patients are ordinarily exercised by their legal proxies, according to the principle of substituted judgment (by which the proxy attempts to choose for the patient what the patient would choose for him/herself if competent). As of 1986, thirteen states had living-will laws with proxy provisions. Although proxy decision-making for voluntary euthanasia could be precluded, to do so would be inconsistent with the philosophy that regards euthanasia as both a benefit and a right. In fact, a sample legal document for euthanasia by proxy was contained in the first version of the "Hemlock Manifesto."

From substituted judgment to best interests of the patient. Although substituted judgment could be the ideal basis for proxy decision-making, its application is often problematic. In practice, there will always be some admixture of the paternalistic best-interests criterion. Of course, for young children or persons with mental retardation, best interests is the only possible criterion. As of 1985, four states had living-will laws with proxy provisions for minors, and there is no reason to believe that minors would be excluded from active euthanasia, were it to become legal. Euthanasic paternalism is sometimes presented even as a moral obligation to kill, as evidenced by "wrongful life" suits and by statements such as Joseph Fletcher's: "If we are morally obliged to put an end to a pregnancy when an amniocentesis reveals a terribly defective fetus, we are equally obliged to put an end to a [cancer] patient's hopeless misery when a brain scan reveals advanced brain metastases."[32]

From best interests of the patient to best interests of the proxy. But it is hard for proxies to be entirely objective in determining a patient's best interests, particularly if the patient's illness or handicap places a burden on the proxy. Objectivity is even more elusive if the patient is too senile or retarded to generate much emotional return or is downright disagreeable. Such circumstances can try the patience of even the most selfless individuals. When proxies say things like "I just couldn't bear to see him suffer," the end of *whose* suffering is the primary object of the killing? Still further conflict of interest can arise if the proxy happens to be a potential heir.

Of course, a potential for abuse exists in all types of proxy decision-making, and that does not justify abolishing the very institution of legal proxies. Nevertheless, the abuses that would derive from legalized euthanasia by proxy would be neither theoretical nor rare. As will be seen, substantial subsegments of the medical and legal professions have already demonstrated their propensity to replace, in effect, the "best interests" of the patient with the "best interests" of others as a criterion for a patient's death, all the while maintaining a façade of the former.

Newborns with disabilities. Parents of newborns with disabilities often have great difficulty in distinguishing what the infant would want if competent from what they would want if they were the infant. Normal adults, with their experiences of the fullness of life, tend to view any serious disability as dreadful; but children who grow up never having experienced another lifestyle usually adjust remarkably well.

Involuntary "euthanasia" is not in the best interests of children with physical and mental disabilities and would surely flourish upon legalization of voluntary euthanasia, because it is something that has been practiced all along, usually under the guise of "letting die" or "selective non-treatment." Of course the issue of non-treatment is complex, and the author is not advocating that all newborns with severe malformations incompatible with survival should receive maximal therapeutic intervention. Nevertheless, the past two decades have clearly shown how far the views of some in our society and in our medical profession diverge from the best interests of certain categories of patients. One survey found that as many as 63 per cent of pediatricians considered parental willingness to care for a child with disabilities to be relevant to decisions on the aggressiveness of treatment.[33]

The famous "Baby Doe" case, in which an infant with Down syndrome was denied a life-saving routine surgical procedure purely on the basis of mental retardation, spawned not only the famous "Baby Doe regulations" but also policy statements by the President's Commission and the American Academy of Pediatrics (AAP), all of which were in unanimous agreement that "[c]onsiderations such as anticipated or actual limited potential of an individual and present or future lack of available community resources are irrelevant and must not determine the decisions concerning medical care. . . . In cases where it is uncertain whether medical treatment will be beneficial, a person's disability must not be the basis for a decision to withhold treatment."[34] As specific examples of conditions in which future disability should not influence the decision-making process, the President's Commission cited spina bifida, and both the President's Commission and the AAP cited Down syndrome. Individuals with these conditions generally find life enjoyable and fulfilling; nevertheless, non-treatment continues to be practiced.

The most outspoken advocate of selective non-treatment of spina bifida has been the British pediatrician Dr. John Lorber. Publicly, he has advocated compassion for the untreated infants, who "should be protected against all pain and discomfort"[35] and "should be fed on demand."[36] Although he agrees that "[a]ctive euthanasia is not only illegal, but also could be an extremely dangerous weapon in the hands of unscrupulous individuals,"[37] he has never published the circumstances of death of his untreated infants, which would be of interest in light of the common experience that many such untreated infants do not die, but survive with severe hydrocephalus. It remains little known outside of Britain that a common practice there, at least during the late seventies, was to place those infants selected for non-treatment in a special room where they were so heavily sedated that they never "demanded" to be fed.

With improved methods of rehabilitation, the outcome in several recent series of unselected patients is as good as that of Lorber's highly selected group. In McLone's series of nearly one thousand unselected patients, for example, 75 per cent had normal intelligence, more than 80 per cent were ambulatory by school age, and almost 90 per cent had achieved bowel and bladder continence by school age.[38] Parental satisfaction with the decision to operate in the newborn period was 99 per cent. Similarly positive outcomes have been reported by others. Of the families reachable for a follow-up survey (the majority) in Peacock's series of one hundred fifty unselected patients, all were satisfied with their decision to have the operation, and the parental divorce rate was one-fifth the national average.[39] The older children themselves were also surveyed as to whether their various disabilities made life not worth living, and whether they would rather have been "allowed" to die in infancy. The response was immediate and unanimous; in fact, they considered the question ridiculous.

This is all highly relevant to the issue of best interests when it comes to euthanasia by proxy, because the victims of tomorrow's euthanasia will surely be the same as the victims of today's non-treatment. Even at the peak of the medico-legal caution engendered by the Baby Doe regulations, a group in Oklahoma reported that as many as 48 per cent of babies with spina bifida at their hospital were selected for "supportive care only," and in some of those cases, the family's motivation was clearly not the best interests of the child: "[t]hey felt vigorous, long-term care of this baby would have added undue stress to their family unit."[40] The reason why all the untreated infants died unusually early was not stated, but is at least suspicious. There are still sophisticated medical centers outside the United States where spina bifida infants are starved to death under therapeutic euphemisms. The only reason the latter is not done here would seem to be fear of criminal prosecution, which would obviously be relieved were euthanasia accepted. Regardless of how much these patients may value their own lives, the fact that California has introduced a mandatory program of prenatal screening for spina bifida sends a strong message to these individuals and their families as to how much the state and society value their lives.

As regards Down syndrome, it is well known that these children are generally affectionate and happy, have varying degrees of retardation (often mild), and have not been known to commit suicide. Nevertheless, 50 per cent of pediatricians in one survey favored nontreatment if there was duodenal obstruction, and 22 per cent favored "withholding all treatment" for *un*complicated Down syndrome.[41] Given that the latter patients have no condition to "not treat," it is evident that modern physicians, like those of Nazi Germany, can get caught up in medical euphemisms for what is, by law, murder by starvation, which in spite of its cruelty (only partially mitigated by sedation) has the appearance of "naturalness" (no one feels as though he or she is performing a killing *act*).

A method even more brutal, also used by Nazi physicians, is intracardiac injection. A few years ago, the *New England Journal of Medicine* featured an article about the selective *in utero* killing of a twin with Down syndrome by means of ultrasonically guided cardiac puncture and exsanguination.[42] The motivation was explicit: "The mother desperately wanted to have the normal child but could not face the burden of caring for an abnormal child for the rest of her life." In a follow-up letter to the editor, another group reported a case of a twin with Tay-Sachs disease who survived two separate exsanguination procedures and was finally killed by intracardiac air embolization.

These were not abortions (defined as "the expulsion or removal of an embryo or fetus from the womb at a stage of pregnancy when it is incapable of independent survival"), much less were they "terminations of pregnancy," "removal of products of conception," or any of the other tiresome euphemisms. They were direct, intentional killings, the only differences from those on the German pediatric wards of the 1940s being age, location in space, and the injection of air instead of phenol. Given that some in our society and in the

medical profession seem to find nothing anomalous about such practices, all the while paying lip service to the best-interest principle, how
can anyone doubt the relevance of the Nazi precedent to legalized
euthanasia?

There are also ethicists who quite openly advocate infanticide for
the best interests of others than the child. Mary Anne Warren, for
example, argues that "[s]ome human beings are not people."[43] She
includes all fetuses and young infants, as well as those with serious
mental impairment. Therefore, "when an unwanted or defective infant is born into a society which cannot afford and/or is not willing
to care for it, then its destruction is permissible."[44] Similarly, the
British philosopher Jonathan Glover believes that "[w]here the handicap is sufficiently serious, the killing of a baby may benefit the family
to an extent that is sufficient to outweigh the unpleasantness of the
killing."[45] That individuals with similar views can become official
ethicists for hospital ethics committees exemplifies how great an impact philosophy can have on everyday life and how real the slippery
slope is.

*The right-to-die movement and child "euthanasia" in the best interests of
proxies.* This phenomenon of involuntary child "euthanasia" for the
benefit of others is not irrelevant to the present argument for voluntary
euthanasia. How can the slippery slope connecting the two be denied,
when some of the chief promoters of both are the same individuals?
Consider the following statement of Florence Clothier, M.D., then
member of the board of directors of the Euthanasia Educational
Council (also vice president emeritus of the Society for the Right to
Die and current member of the advisory board of Concern for Dying):

> [T]oday I am discussing voluntary, negative or passive
> Euthanasia. . . . Eventually [the physician] will have to confront
> the greater dilemmas inherent in active Euthanasia for the hope-
> lessly malformed and handicapped infants doomed to a bestial
> subhuman existence in our state institutions. Active Euthanasia on
> a voluntary basis may also have its place for patients suffering from
> incurable, intractable pain.[46]

Although the Hemlock Society claims to have no official position on
euthanasia for children, its esteemed member and ethicist Joseph
Fletcher (also president emeritus of the Society for the Right to Die)

does. According to him, infanticide is perfectly legitimate if the infant is determined to be not a "person" but only a "human life." His fifteen "indicators of humanhood" include such attributes as self-control, sense of time, concern for others, and curiosity, to name some of the more interesting ones. Minimal intelligence is also an important prerequisite: "Any individual of the species *homo sapiens* who falls below the I.Q. 40-mark in a standard Stanford-Binet test . . . is questionably a person; below the 20-mark, not a person. . . . This has bearing, obviously, on decision-making in . . . pediatrics, as well as in general surgery and medicine."[47] But even if an infant does qualify as a person according to this checklist, killing it may still be justified in some situations, taking into account not only the good of the child in question, but also "the economic resources of the family, . . . the welfare of other children involved, as well as the parents' physical and emotional capacity to cope."[48] Therefore, physicians should have only a "*qualified* respect for human life."[49] Once a decision has been made that a child should not live, the means are ethically indifferent: starvation, withholding treatment, or direct killing are all equally legitimate.[50]

The elderly. There is also an increasingly evident movement toward involuntary euthanasia at the other end of the life cycle. A 1984 article in the *New England Journal of Medicine,* entitled "The Physician's Responsibility Toward Hopelessly Ill Patients," co-authored by ten physicians prominent in the field of bioethics, was the fruit of a project sponsored by the Society for the Right to Die.[51] Toward the end of the article, guidelines are offered concerning the appropriate level of care for a series of graded conditions, beginning with "brain death" and ending with "permanent mild impairment of competence." What the latter has to do with the stated subject matter of the article is unclear; but what is said about these patients, who are in no way "hopelessly ill," is significant in terms of the article's sponsorship and the issue of voluntarism in euthanasia:

> Many elderly patients are described as "pleasantly senile." Although somewhat limited in their ability to initiate activities and communicate, they often appear to be enjoying their moderately restricted lives. . . . If emergency resuscitation and intensive care are required, the physician should provide these measures sparingly, guided by

the patient's prior wishes, if known, by the wishes of the patient's family, and by an assessment of the patient's prospects for improvement.[52]

Even with a progressive disease such as Alzheimer's, the burdens of the disease are generally less for the patient than for the caregivers. Thus, Humphry undermines his own insistence on patient voluntarism in euthanasia by maintaining that, "in the final years" of that disease, euthanasia "can be a valid release from insupportable suffering, including that of the caregiver."[53] The following chilling advice was given at a special workshop on Alzheimer's at the second National Voluntary Euthanasia Conference, held in 1985: "With Alzheimer's Disease the problem of euthanasia is further complicated because of a lack of participation in decision-making on the part of the patient. . . . Do not share plans for this action with anyone because of the risk of criminal prosecution."[54]

Quality-of-life messianism and physician integrity. Nor should it be imagined that physicians are incapable of subterfuge in order to circumvent sanctions against involuntary euthanasia. One example by analogy is the sham of "mental health" indications for abortion in the years just prior to its legalization. In Canada, abortion is still illegal except for health reasons; yet, in effect, abortion on demand is available there through the same loophole of danger to the mother's "mental health," certification of which is essentially rubber-stamped by hospital therapeutic-abortion committees. Such deceit is not essentially different from the falsification of records and bureaucratic mass-processing of patient-selection questionnaires by committees of "expert" physicians in Nazi Germany. Once euthanasia is legalized, there will be no way to stem the tide of involuntary "euthanasia" by proxy for the benefit of the proxy carried out by a minority of families in collusion with a minority of equally clever socially messianic physicians.

As C. Everett Koop, [then] surgeon general, put it [in 1982],

Semantics have made infanticide palatable by never referring to the practice by that word, but by using such euphemisms as "selection." "Starving a child to death" becomes "allowing him to die." Although infanticide is not talked about even in professional circles, the euphemisms are. It is all illegal, but the law has turned its back. The day will come when the argument will be as it was for abortion:

"Let's legalize what is already happening." Then what is legal is right. Attention will then be turned to the next class of individuals that might be exterminated without too loud an outcry.[55]

This tendency to "legalize what is already happening" is precisely the dynamic underlying the evolution of euthanasia policy in Holland, rendering the legal system intrinsically incapable of keeping what is already happening within any predetermined bounds.

Disturbing previews of physician subterfuge are the widespread practice of falsification of death certificates in Holland and the recent phenomenon of "negotiated deaths" in the United States: "Carried out quietly and with a deliberate minimum of legal fuss or public attention, a patient's death is planned by the hospital, initiated either by the patient or by his physician and family." Parties in the negotiation typically include "the patient, his physician, his family, the hospital ethics committee (if there is one), hospital administrators, and some-times lawyers."[56] Humphry proposes such "negotiated death" as an appropriate way of dealing with end-stage Alzheimer's disease.[57]

Economic and social pressure to opt for voluntary euthanasia. For the elderly as for infants with disabilities, efforts at cost containment have the potential for creating serious conflicts of interest and for effectively eliminating all but one alternative for ostensibly "free" decisions. California's mandatory prenatal screening program for spina bifida and Down syndrome is projected to save the state $11.9 million per year, and the state-produced waiting-room brochures are clearly worded to sway parents toward the abortion option. The brochures emphasize the negative aspects of the physical and/or mental disability, do not provide information concerning the improved prognosis brought about by recent medical advances, and omit mention of support groups for these families. Considering the older person, it has been suggested that "living wills" should be systematically distributed in Veterans Administration hospitals, so that the "no-hope veterans" could be permitted to die, saving the government two billion dollars annually and eliminating overcrowding. Politicians have advocated that the institutionalized severely retarded should be "allowed to die" on account of the annual cost to taxpayers of around one hundred million dollars in the state of Florida and two billion dollars nation-wide.[58] A former head of the Health Care Financing Administration pointed out that "[o]ver one-fifth of Medicare expenditures are for persons in their last year of life," and that a national system of "living wills" could have saved the country $1.2 billion in fiscal year 1978.[59] He went so far as to suggest that states could be motivated to comply by means of threatened cutoff of federal funding. A prominent physician has advocated in effect that the proper response to reduced federal funding for child health care, and the paucity of social supports for persons with disabilities, should be to allow more newborns with spina bifida to die.[60] Similar statements abound, and if one did not know their sources, one might think he was reading an English translation of Binding and Hoche or a medical/economic report from Germany in the 1920s or 1930s, except for our more diplomatic avoidance of the phrase "useless eaters."

The free-market health-insurance industry (to say nothing of profit-oriented health maintenance organizations) can hardly be expected not to take advantage of a climate of legalized voluntary euthanasia. Is there anything to prevent them from offering lower premiums to parents who agree to legal euthanasia of children with major chronic illnesses or handicaps, or to adults who sign a document requesting euthanasia if certain medical conditions befall them?

This is not to say that efforts to reduce medical costs are inappropriate. But lest we be overwhelmed with the magnitude of social burden implied by the enormous figures constantly cited, we should place them in the context of our national expenditures for various superfluities, such as an annual $2-10 billion on pornography, $10 billion on pets, $176.3 billion on recreation, $53.5 billion on alcoholic drinks, $31.8 billion on tobacco products, $21.3 billion on jewelry and watches, $38.6 billion on personal care, $100 billion on illegal drugs. . . .

Our consumeristic, egocentric values system cannot but affect the self-image of debilitated elderly adults as regards their burdensomeness on their family and uselessness to society. Witness the following pathetic letter printed in the *Hemlock Quarterly*, written by a 91-year-old woman in reaction to Colorado Governor Lamm's famous "duty to die" speech on March 27, 1984:

I am certain [it] found many advocates. . . . There are countless numbers of the chronically ill elderly who wish to die, but no means is furnished them. To die and "get out of the way," some try ineffective methods. . . . Isn't it about time someone (including the doctors) did something for those who need to die to fulfill their duty to the kids of the other society?[61]

Hemlock, of course, does not officially endorse this view, but neither did it hesitate to create the unmistakable overtones of the boldfaced caption, **"Gov. Lamm Right—Now Supply Ways."** If some elderly are already made to feel that they have a duty to die, what will become of the "voluntary" concept in a society where the benefits of "voluntary euthanasia" are inculcated?

Commercialization. Any "good thing" quickly becomes commercialized in this country. Even euthanasia advocates are concerned about the possible abuses from that direction:

These [suicide] manuals should not be aggressively marketed and hustled to make a commerical profit from human misery. For example, the French manual made a substantial profit. Instead, they should be available only upon request and after satisfying the age restrictions and cooling off period proposed earlier.[62]

Does the writer believe that this admonition will be heeded by the entrepreneurs? Our country already witnessed how quickly legalized abortion became transformed into a lucrative commercial venture of assembly-line clinics specializing in nothing but that, even to the point of advertisements offering door-to-door limousine service. Is there any reason to believe that, if euthanasia were legally recognized as a good to which everyone had a right, analogous euthanasia centers would not also spring up, marketing their services as aggressively and attractively as possible?

Why Involve Doctors?

Even if the acceptance of euthanasia did not entail all the above problems and were desirable for society, there would still be no reason to involve physicians in it, and many reasons not to. To kill someone (even gently) does not require any medical knowledge. The main reason that physicians are supposedly needed is that the "best" drugs are all prescription drugs. But what about the case of Dr. Julius

Hackethal, a German oncologist and contemporary hero of the euthanasia movement, who provided one of his terminal patients with an appropriately lethal amount of potassium cyanide? Cyanide is hardly a prescription drug, even in Germany, and anyone can look up its lethal dose in a toxicology book. The Hemlock Society discourages this method, however, because a cyanide death, though quick, is somewhat unpleasant. It therefore recommends sedative drugs as first choice. Still, it could just as well argue that these drugs be made non-prescription, or that specially certified euthanasists be allowed to establish their own clinics, without having to involve the medical profession at all. Any patient would then have the right to transfer himself from a hospital to the nearest euthanasia center.

It would seem, therefore, that the real reason for Hemlock's insistence on *physician*-assisted suicide is to lend an air of respectability and credibility to its cause. Lifton, in his book on the Nazi doctors,[63] emphasizes that the maintenance of a façade of respectability was precisely the reason that the Nazi regime insisted so much on having *doctors* "select" the recipients for "special treatment," operate the gas chambers, falsify death certificates to resemble natural causes, and in general maintain an aura of medicalization in every aspect of the genocide program.

The advocates of euthanasia attempt to use the medical profession for their own purposes, without regard to the irreparable harm that would be done to society by transforming the public image of physician from healer to killer, which could only undermine the covenant of trust at the very heart of the doctor-patient relationship. If this were not the case, there would be no need for the existing strong policies against physician participation in other legal forms of killing, such as capital punishment. . . .

Concluding Observations

For all these reasons, efforts to promote death with dignity would be more appropriately channeled in the direction of physician education with regard to care of the dying, research to improve methods of symptomatic relief, and provision by society of improved resources for the persons who are disabled, chronically ill, or dying—particularly the establishment of hospices. It is unnecessary to kill these people in order to provide them with comfort and compassion; much less should physicians be the ones to kill them.

Most proponents of euthanasia are well intentioned, but all are short-sighted. The slippery slope of euthanasia is no mere pro-life bogeyman; it is a present reality. Dr. Leo Alexander, U.S. medical consultant to the Nuremberg Trials, was concerned as far back as 1949 about the direction American medicine was heading:

> To be sure, American physicians are still far from the point of thinking of killing centers, but they have arrived at a danger point in thinking, at which likelihood of full rehabilitation is considered a factor that should determine the amount of time, effort, and cost to be devoted to a particular type of patient. . . . Americans should remember that the enormity of a euthanasia movement is present in their own midst.[64]

Thirty-six years later, upon reading in the above-cited *New England Journal of Medicine* article about the policy of selective starvation of certain "hopelessly ill" patients,[65] the same Dr. Alexander sadly remarked: "It is much like Germany in the twenties and thirties. The barriers against killing are coming down."[66]

They need not. History does not have to repeat itself. Those few terminal patients who may desire to be "helped to die" must rather be helped to realize that their acceptance of the natural process is "an acceptable cost of securing the general protection of human life afforded by the prohibition of direct killing."[67]

19

Assisted Suicide and Euthanasia: The Dutch Experience

Herbert Hendin

For two decades the discussion over assisted suicide and euthanasia has been dominated by philosophers, theologians, and physicians who are often uninformed about the psychiatric and psychosocial dimensions of the problem. They deferentially quote Camus's view that the question of suicide—that is, "judging whether life is or is not worth living"—is the fundamental question in life and for philosophy.[1] It is not the central question for most people nor has it been for most philosophers, but it is the central question for suicidally depressed patients and for a few twentieth-century existential philosophers. For those who are suicidal, control over whether they live or die provides the illusion of control over many of life's existential anxieties, including those of dying.[2]

Many people have experienced situations where hastening the death

---

Herbert Hendin is a professor of psychiatry at New York Medical College and a practicing psychiatrist treating suicidal patients. He is also the executive director of the American Suicide Foundation and has written five books. This essay is reprinted by permission of W. W. Norton and Company from his *Suicide in America* (New York: Norton, expanded edition, 1995; © 1995, 1989 by Herbert Hendin, M.D.). The opening six pages of the chapter have been omitted.

of a terminally ill relative or friend who has not been suicidal may be humane and where a physician may be justified in providing such help. For reasons that I will try to make clear, legalizing physician-assisted suicide and euthanasia would be one of the worst possible answers to a problem that needs to be addressed. Since the movement toward legalization represents such a drastic departure from established social policy and medical tradition, it is helpful to look first at current psychiatric knowledge about suicide and terminal illness.

We know that 95 per cent of those who kill themselves have been shown to have a diagnosable psychiatric illness in the months preceding suicide.[3] The majority suffer from depression, which can be treated. This is particularly true of the elderly, who are more prone than younger people to take their lives during the type of acute depressive episode that responds most effectively to treatment.[4] Other diagnoses among the suicides include alcoholism, substance abuse, schizophrenia, and panic disorder; treatments are available for all of these illnesses.

Advocates of physician-assisted suicide and euthanasia maintain that in terminally ill patients the wish to die is completely different from that of other suicidal patients. Although the terminally ill constitute only 3 per cent of the total number of suicides,[5] like other suicidal individuals, patients who desire an early death during a terminal illness are usually suffering from a treatable mental illness, most commonly a depressive condition.[6] Strikingly, the overwhelming majority of the terminally ill fight for life to the end. Some may voice suicidal thoughts in response to transient depression or severe pain, but these patients usually respond well to treatment for depressive illness and pain medication and are grateful to be alive.

Studies of those who have died by suicide underscore the nonrational elements of the wish to die in reaction to serious illness. More individuals, particularly elderly individuals, killed themselves because they feared or *mistakenly* believed they had cancer than killed themselves bcause they knew that they actually had cancer.[7] Similarly, preoccupation with suicide is higher for those awaiting the results of tests for HIV antibodies than for those who know they are HIV positive.[8]

Given the advances in our medical knowledge and treatment ability, a thorough psychiatric evaluation for the presence of a treatable disorder may literally make a life-or-death difference for patients who say they wish to die or to have a physician help them to do so. This is not an evaluation that can be made by the average physician who does not have extensive experience with depression and suicide.[9]

In studies of assisted suicide and euthanasia, most of which have been done in the Netherlands, physicians reported that loss of dignity, pain, not wishing to die in an "unworthy way," being dependent on others, and being tired of living were the reasons patients have for requesting euthanasia.[10] The fear of death itself is not mentioned.

My own experience has been that many patients and physicians displace anxieties about death onto the circumstances of dying: pain, dependence, loss of dignity, and the unpleasant side effects resulting from medical treatment, or, for the physician, frustration at not being able to offer a sure cure. Focusing on or becoming enraged at the process of dying distracts from the fear of death itself. . . . If life were so structured that we all knew we would die on the day of our eighty-fifth birthday, but live in good health up to that time, it is likely that many people would kill themselves in the months or years prior to their eighty-fifth birthday so as to avoid anxiety over the inevitability of their fate and their lack of control over it.

Potential for Abuse

If euthanasia were to be legalized, certain groups would be at a higher risk for abuse than others: the elderly, those particularly frightened by illness, and the depressed of all ages. The elderly often feel that their families would prefer that they were gone. Societal sanction for physician-assisted suicide for the terminally ill is likely to encourage family members so inclined to pressure the infirm and the elderly, and to collude with uninformed or unscrupulous physicians to provide such deaths. According to philosophers Karen Lebacqz and N. Tristan Englehardt, that an individual might choose to die rather than burden the family is socially affirming.[11] Just as love-pact suicides rarely turn out to be affirmations of love, so the self-sacrificial suicide may lend itself to becoming the instrument of tyranny of the healthy over the aged and infirm.

Margaret Battin, an advocate of euthanasia, admits that social acceptance of euthanasia would undoubtedly lead to situations in which families that wish to be free of the burden of caring for the elderly pressure them to end their lives. She recognizes that this pressure could be expressed through an appeal to the older person that suicide would be for the good of all concerned; but such an appeal would be effective only in a climate that sanctioned suicide for infirm older people. Battin warns of the dangers of institutional abuse of euthanasizing the elderly in a health-care system in which coverage is inequitable, costs are out of control, a high proportion of these costs are associated with terminal illness, and patients who choose death would provide the cheapest alternative. Although she is conscious of the "moral quicksand" into which the right to suicide "threatens to lead us," she believe it must be accepted on moral grounds.[12] [An essay by Margaret Pabst Battin appears in this volume.] . . .

Publicists Kevorkian and Humphry

The general public has encountered the question of assisted suicide and euthanasia mainly through the publicity afforded Dr. Jack Kevorkian and Derek Humphry. Many of the patients who have been drawn to Kevorkian have been people whose terror of illness persuades them that quick death is the best solution. Janet Adkins, a woman in the early stages of Alzheimer's who was fearful of the progress of the disease, was seen by Kevorkian, a retired pathologist in Michigan with a passionate commitment to promoting assisted suicide and the use of his "suicide machine." After a brief conversation he decided she was a suitable candidate. He used the machine to help her kill herself. Clearly, his lack of knowledge of her and his investment in promoting assisted suicide disqualified him from making such a determination.

No Michigan law then prohibited assisted suicide (most states have such laws), but he was admonished by the court not to engage in the practice. Disregarding the admonition, Kevorkian subsequently helped to end the lives of many others, some of whom were seriously ill but not near death.[13] Dr. Kevorkian's license to practice medicine has since been summarily suspended, but a Michigan judge ruled that he could not be prosecuted for murder in the absence of a state law prohibiting assisting a suicide. In 1993, Michigan passed such a law, which Kevorkian violated with the avowed intention of testing its constitutionality.

Kevorkian advocates creation of a board-certified medical specialty, "obitiatry," based on a four-year medical residency that would train physicians in the practice of "medicide." A grandfather clause would permit pioneers like Dr. Kevorkian to be certified to develop the program. Kevorkian presents a detailed model plan for the state of Michigan, dividing it into eleven geographically mapped zones, each with its own headquarters and death clinic. [See Kevorkian's article elsewhere in this volume.] He talks the reader through the process by which Wanda Endittal, a hypothetical patient with multiple sclerosis, seeks help to end her life. Her physician, Dr. Frieda Blame, refers her to an obitiatrist, Dr. Will B. Reddy. After an elaborate consultation process with other obitiatrists including Dr. Lotte Goode, a psychiatrist, Wanda's case is referred to the "action obitiatrists." One of them, Dr. Dewey Ledder, makes a last review of her file, and the other, Dr. Shelby Donne, performs the medicide. Kevorkian's account reads much like a Swiftian satire on the world we would create if Kevorkian's vision were followed. Kevorkian recognizes that his plan "may sound overblown, overly grandiose, or impractical."[14]

Derek Humphry, like Kevorkian, was tapping into deeply felt anxieties concerning dying in intolerable circumstances that led some to support his efforts without regard for their consequences. Initially, Humphry and the Hemlock Society would not send instructions on how to commit suicide to the public at large, presumably because the information might get into the wrong hands.[15] At some point Humphry changed his mind; he published a how-to-kill-yourself book and promoted its sale to the general public.[16] Since the publication of his book, however, there has been a significant increase in the number of people—some of them young people found dead with the book nearby—who have asphyxiated themselves with plastic bags, one of the methods recommended by Humphry.[17]

Humphry's participation in the suicide pact of his former wife's parents also raised questions. Ann Wickett, the former wife of Derek Humphry, and a co-founder of the Hemlock Society, made clear in her book, letters, conversations with friends, and her own taped suicide note that she was tormented by having actively participated with Humphry in the suicide pact of her parents.[18] Although her 92-year-old father may have been ready to die, she was aware that her 78-year-old mother was not. Such pacts have been romanticized and considered rational suicides, but published case reports confirm my own clinical experience that in most such pacts a man who wishes to end his life coerces a woman into joining him to prove her love.[19]

Today, proponents of what is called "rational suicide" draw on the concept of *bilanz selbstmord* or "balance-sheet suicide," developed by German philosophers in the early part of this century.[20] Individuals assumed to be mentally unimpaired dispassionately took stock of their life situation and, having found it unacceptable or untenable and foreseeing no significant change for the better, decided to end their lives. Contemporary advocates see a close analogy between a rational decision for suicide and the decision of the directors of a firm to declare bankruptcy and go out of business.[21]

The idea that life can be measured by balancing assets and liabilities is itself a characteristic of suicidal people. Some of the most depressed suicidal patients spend years making elaborate lists of reasons why they should go on living to counter the many reasons they can think of for dying. They are prone to make conditions on life: I won't live "if I can't be in control," "without my husband," "if I lose my looks, power, prestige, or health," or "if I am going to die soon." Depression, often precipitated by discovering a serious illness, exaggerates the tendency toward seeing problems in black-and-white terms. If society sanctions the view that life is worth living only if certain conditions are met, the patient's rigidity is reinforced.[22]

THE DUTCH EXPERIENCE

Anyone interested in the consequences of social sanction of euthanasia is inevitably led to the Netherlands, a Western democracy with a distinguished medical tradition, where doctors, provided they follow certain guidelines, can practice euthanasia and assisted suicide with impunity and public acceptance. That acceptance has now been extended to suicidal patients who are not physically ill.

In the spring of 1993 in the city of Assen, a court of three judges acquitted a psychiatrist who had assisted in the suicide of his patient, a 50-year-old woman who had lost her two sons and was recently divorced from her husband. The Assen case is joining the handful of internationally known Dutch cases of assisted suicide and euthanasia, each referred to by the name of the city where it was tried.[23] Before

I left for the Netherlands on a trip to study euthanasia and assisted suicide in medical and psychiatric cases and the subject of involuntary euthanasia, Dr. Boudewijn Chabot, the psychiatrist in the Assen case, responded positively to my letter asking to discuss the case with him.

Is the Netherlands the place where Jack Kevorkian's vision has come to pass? How much can the Dutch experience with euthanasia help to guide or caution us?

De facto legalization of euthanasia and assisted suicide exists in the Netherlands. Although the criminal law provides punishment for euthanasia and a lesser punishment for assisted suicide, the same code stipulates that there can be exceptions to the law in special circumstances. The Dutch courts, in a series of cases tried during the past twenty years, have ruled that euthanasia is such a special circumstance. It is permitted by a doctor driven by *force majeure,* an overpowering conflict between the law—which makes euthanasia illegal—and his responsibility to help a patient, which makes euthanasia necessary and overrides a conflict with the law.

The Dutch courts and the Royal Dutch Medical Association (KNMG) separately established the same guidelines for physicians to follow whether practicing assisted suicide or euthanasia: (1) voluntariness—the patient's request must be made freely, persistently, and consciously; (2) there must exist unbearable suffering that cannot be relieved by other means; and (3) consultation—the attending physician should consult with a colleague. Doctors are expected to report cases of euthanasia as death due to "unnatural causes" with the understanding that they will not be prosecuted if the guidelines were followed.

Few cases have been brought to trial. The recommended guidelines are not fixed conditions, so even when they were not followed, judges have consistently exonerated physicians on the grounds of *force majeure.* Only one doctor, the physician in the infamous De Terp nursing-home case, who pled guilty to putting to death without their consent patients under his care, has been sent to prison.

The Remmelink Report

Despite their acceptance of euthanasia, prior to 1991 the Dutch did not have hard facts about the practice. Estimates of the number of euthanasia cases had ranged from 5,000 to 20,000 of the 130,000 deaths in the Netherlands each year. Charges by doctors and others that involuntary euthanasia was widespread were made.

To ascertain actual Dutch medical practice regarding euthanasia, a government commission, headed by Professor Jan Remmelink, arranged a study by investigators at Erasmus University in which physicians were granted anonymity and immunity from prosecution for information revealed in the study. The investigators found that 49,000 deaths in the Netherlands each year involve a medical decision at the end of life (MDEL). Ninety-five per cent of these MDEL cases involve, in equal numbers, either withholding or discontinuing life support, or the alleviation of pain and symptoms through potentially lethal narcotic injections. Outright euthanasia was the cause of death in 2,300 (2 per cent) of all Dutch deaths. Assisted suicide was relatively uncommon, occurring some four hundred times per year. Over 50 per cent of Dutch physicians admitted to practicing euthanasia, with cancer patients being the majority of their cases. Only 60 per cent of doctors kept a written record of their cases, and only 29 per cent of doctors filled out the death certificates honestly in euthanasia cases.[24]

The Dutch were hoping the Remmelink Report would put to rest concerns about euthanasia. Indeed, many have tried to put such a spin on it. Instead, and largely because of the integrity of the study, the report opened up a Pandora's box of questions that need to be addressed. Moreover, the more serious side of the problem turned out to be so-called involuntary euthanasia, a term that is disturbing to the Dutch.

Of obvious concern to Dutch and foreign observers of euthanasia in the Netherlands was the revelation that in over one thousand cases, physicians admitted they had actively caused or hastened death without the request of the patient. The impossibility of treating pain effectively was given as the reason for killing the patient in about 30 per cent of these cases. The remaining 70 per cent were killed with a variety of justifications ranging from "low quality of life" to "all treatment was withdrawn but the patient did not die." The Remmelink Commission considered that these cases were not morally troublesome, because the suffering of those patients had become unbearable and they would usually have died soon anyhow. Twenty-seven per cent of physicians indicated that they had terminated the lives of patient without a request from the patient to do so; another 32 per cent could conceive of doing so.

According to the report, other forms of hastening death without the patient's consent are common practice in the Netherlands. In more than 4,000 cases the doctor's explicit intention in administering pain medication or withdrawing or withholding treatment was to shorten life; in over 11,000 cases this was a "secondary goal." In half of the 49,000 MDEL cases, apart from the euthanasia cases, decisions that might or were intended to end the life of the patient were made without consulting the patient. In about 80 per cent of these cases, physicians gave the patient's impaired ability to communicate as their justification. This left about 5,000 cases in which physicians made decisions that might, or were intended to, take the lives of competent patients without consulting them.

Involuntary euthanasia rasied such large questions that only the report's principal investigator seemed able to address them. Dr. Paul van der Maas, chair of the Department of Public Health and Social Medicine of Erasmus University in Rotterdam, had led the investigative effort. I asked van der Maas about the decision to include all medical decisions at the end of life and not just euthanasia in his study. He said people claim that termination of life without request does not occur, but every doctor knows it does and it should be looked at as well.

Van der Maas followed the Dutch practice of never using the term "involuntary euthanasia." The Dutch define euthanasia as the ending of the life of one person by another at the first person's request. If a life is terminated without explicit request, it is not considered to be euthanasia. For me, "involuntary euthanasia" has a far less Orwellian and sinister connotation than "termination of the patient without explicit request."

Van der Maas and I talked about a boundary area where it is not clear if the death is the result of medicine given to alleviate pain and symptoms, or the result of either euthanasia or the termination of life without explicit request. It seemed that a case could be classified as euthanasia when the doctor is giving medication with the explicit intention of shortening life, and the patient knows and consents. The only real difference, van der Maas pointed out, is that in ordinary euthanasia cases death is immediate, whereas in the borderline cases death may take a day or two. If the patient is given medication to end his life and does not know it, the case would seem to fall into the "termination of life without request" category. Because of these and other problems defining the exact category of a death, van der Maas would not be surprised if the actual number of euthanasia cases were higher than the official figure.

More alarming were the statistics in the report indicating that there were thousands of cases in which decisions that might or were intended to end a fully competent patient's life were made without consulting the patient. It was therefore surprising that the report did not include a recommendation for doctors to discuss their plans with competent patients. Van der Maas said he would make such a point in other contexts but, in order to secure the cooperation of the KNMG and the participating doctors, it was understood that the report would make as few recommendations as possible.

Unanswered Questions

In the interests of maintaining harmony, virtually all of the explanations of the physicians in the study appear to have been accepted at face value, even when follow-up questions seemed necessary. For example, in 13 per cent of the cases, physicians who did not communicate with competent patients concerning MDELs that might or were intended to end their lives gave as a reason for not doing so some previous discussion of the subject with the patient. Yet it seemed incomprehensible that the physician would terminate the life of a competent patient on the basis of prior discussion without checking to see if the patient still felt the same way. One could only conjecture that the physician, actually knowing that the patient would not agree or had changed his mind, did not want to hear the answer because he felt it appropriate to end the patient's life, and to do so after a negative reply would amount to murder. Another possibility was that the physician was justifying the death by stretching the patient's words, which may, according to the study, have been no more than an urgent request for the relief of pain. Challenging such explanations could have clarified the doctors' rationale for ending some patients' lives without ascertaining their wishes.

Other areas warranted further inquiry. Failure to obtain consultation, not providing alternative treatment plans, the claim that in almost all cases life was shortened by only a few hours or days—all these were accepted without challenge. Van der Maas seemed concerned that to do otherwise would compromise the investigation's neutrality. I had the impression that the interviewers—who were primarily physicians—were questioning their colleagues in a somewhat collegial manner.

The Remmelink Commission accepted the report with one major addition. They felt that even if it was appropriate to terminate cases without explicit request, such cases should also be reported to the authorities. In November 1993 legislation was passed putting into law what had previously been case law: if *force majeure* applied, the physician would not be prosecuted for assisted suicide and euthanasia (although both still remained illegal), but physicians would be required to report all cases in which life was terminated without explicit request. The KNMG is opposed to this broadening of the notification procedure, particularly since the new legislative protection of doctors does not include cases terminated without request, which would have to be decided on a case-by-case basis. The new law, however, also includes the physician's "mental duress" as an exceptional circumstance that could exempt a doctor from prosecution; conceivably, it could be used in a defense of involuntary euthanasia, since the consent of the patient killed is irrelevant in such a defense.

If in his private comments van der Maas seemed concerned about terminations of life without request, in his public utterances he was more restrained. Following publication of the report, he wrote an article demonstrating that in many of the cases in which patients' lives were ended without their consent, doctors had been required to make emergency decisions about patients who were not competent or fully competent.[25] However, when I asked how he felt about broadening the notification procedure to include such cases, he said it was right to do so. That seemed to say more than anything else that he regards the problem as serious.

In an earlier study of euthanasia in Dutch hospitals, doctors explained to H. W. Hilhorst that they resorted to active euthanasia of sick people without their patients' knowledge when they did not have either the courage or the cruelty to talk openly to the patient and offer the option of death.[26] From a psychological point of view, cowardice, cruelty, and guilt are probably involved in equal measure. The frequency of this practice in the Netherlands suggests that Dutch doctors are no more comfortable than their American counterparts in dealing with the terminally ill as people.

Doctors and nurses told Hilhorst that more requests for euthanasia came from the patient's family than from the patient; he concluded that the family, the doctors, and the nurses often pressured the patient to request euthanasia. Others have reported such pressure outside of the hospital environment. A Dutch medical journal noted an example of a wife who no longer wished to care for her sick husband; she gave him a choice between euthanasia and admission to a home for the chronically ill. The man, afraid of being with strangers in an unfamiliar place, chose to be killed. His doctor, although aware of the coercion, ended the man's life.[27] The Remmelink Report provided little information about such pressure apart from the finding that more than half of Dutch physicians considered it appropriate to introduce the subject of euthanasia with their patients. Virtually all the euthanasia advocates I spoke to in the Netherlands saw this as enabling the patient to consider an option that he or she may have felt inhibited about bringing up and not as a form of coercion. . . .

Dr. Chabot and "Netty"

Most recently the Dutch have begun to accept psychological distress as justification for assisted suicide or euthanasia whether or not physical illness is present. Although assisted suicide for a small number of psychiatric patients who are suicidal has been practiced for some time, the trial in 1993 of Dr. Boudewijn Chabot, a psychiatrist, established a legal basis for assisting in such suicides and brought the issue to international attention.[28] . . .

[The author here relates the story of Dr. Chabot's patient "Netty Boomsma." Netty, 50, had an unhappy marriage but loved her two sons deeply. Her first son committed suicide at the age of 20, and the second died of cancer at the age of 20. Netty attempted suicide on the day of the second son's death. Having been referred to her by the Dutch Voluntary Euthanasia Society, Dr. Chabot saw her, sometimes along with her sister and brother-in-law, for a total of about thirty hours over a period of a month. He made a written summary of her case and asked several experts for their opinion; most agreed that Chabot should go ahead—"seemingly," says the author, "because Netty's suffering was unbearable and there was little chance that therapy would help." Being unable to persuade Netty to change or postpone her decision, Chabot agreed to help her with her suicide, and he subsequently got her the pills needed. On the appointed day in September 1991, Chabot, a colleague of his, and a friend of Netty's gathered in Netty's home, where she sat on her son's bed and, to the accompaniment of a Bach flute sonata that had been played at his funeral, took the pills and died. Chabot followed the prescribed procedure for reporting an unnatural death. There was a police investigation, and in April 1993 Chabot was tried and acquitted. The ministry of justice appealed.]

At the end of September 1993 Chabot learned that he had been exonerated by the appeals court. As is common in the Netherlands, the Leeuwaarden court slightly modified the Assen court's opinion in the matter. The Leeuwaarden court ruled that since the source of the suffering was not somatic, it was relevant to look into psychiatric pathology; the competence of the person was at stake. Since all the experts agreed the patient was competent, the court upheld the decision, adding to the case law that now constitutes the *de facto* legalization of assisted suicide and euthanasia the idea that a patient a physician claims is not suffering from either psychiatric or physical illness can receive assisted suicide simply because he or she is unhappy.

The Dutch supreme court, which ruled on the Assen case in June 1994, agreed with the lower courts in affirming that mental suffering can be grounds for euthanasia, but found Chabot guilty of not having had a psychiatric consultant see the patient. Although the court expressed the belief that such consultation was necessary in the absence of physical illness, it imposed no punishment, because it felt that in all other regards Chabot had behaved responsibly. The case was seen as a triumph by euthanasia advocates since it legally established mental suffering as a basis for euthanasia.[29] It was clear that Chabot could have persuaded a consultant who agreed with him to see the patient had he known that would be necessary. . . .

The Opposition

Opposition to assisted suicide and euthanasia is limited in the Netherlands and estimated in polls at 20 to 25 per cent of the population. Most of the opposition, both medical and in the community at large, is dismissed by advocates as coming from religious conservatives and those people, mainly Jewish, who lost families in Nazi concentration camps and are said by some advocates to be unable to be objective about euthanasia.

Karl Gunning is a now retired physician who helped found the Dutch Physicians' Association, a small group of doctors that split off from the KNMG because of disagreements on abortion and euthanasia. He told me the association's membership has dwindled from 1,200 to 600 members, approximately 2 per cent of the KNMG's total of 30,000. Gunning believes that if more people were aware of the extent of involuntary euthanasia, the situation might change.

Some people, concerned that their lives might be ended without their consent, have joined the Dutch Patients Association (60,000 members), a group organized by Protestants opposed to both euthanasia and abortion. The association receives inquiries from people wanting to know if a particular hospital is "safe," and, together with the Stichting Schuilplaats (Sanctuary Foundation), a religious group also opposed to euthanasia, it distributes a "passport for life" indicating that, in medical emergencies, a patient does not want his or her life terminated without his or her consent.

Dutch euthanasia advocates are dismissive of or defensive about any criticism of assisted suicide or euthanasia in the Netherlands. I was not entirely reassured to find that the most knowledgeable supporters of euthanasia are privately willing to discuss the abuses in their system even if they publicly deny that there are problems. The Dutch overreactions to criticism of their euthanasia policies, and their many published articles that deny their problems, lead one to fear that they might never address the need for reform.

Most opponents of euthanasia are willing to concede that no one is going to undo *de facto* legalization of euthanasia in the Netherlands. The Dutch have accomplished something they wanted: giving their citizens the reassurance that they will not have to endure an unnecessarily prolonged, painful ending to their lives. Even if the Dutch public were fully aware of the contents of the difficult-to-read Rem-melink Report or its implications, they would probably not want to undo what they consider their right to euthanasia, although they might insist on some better control.

The Need for More Control

The issue for the Netherlands is whether or not the Dutch can gain better control of euthanasia and also the process by which patients' lives are ended without their consent. There is no consensus on removing the criminal penalties against euthanasia and assisted suicide, penalties that the public has the impression serve as a form of control over the doctors' behavior. In euthanasia court cases, with prosecutors, consultants, experts, attorneys, and probably judges concerned that any legal decision must protect euthanasia—and hence the doctor—from its opponents, with public sympathies on the side of the doctor, who in most instances would not be on trial if he had not reported the case, and with what is known about the case being primarily what the doctor chooses to reveal, the Dutch judicial system presents a ritualized drama that allows for some subtle, minor improvisation before admonishment or acquittal. If our adversarial judicial system could be said at times to sacrifice justice on the altar of victory, in the Netherlands the sacrifice seems to have been for the sake of what the Dutch would regard as the higher goal of social harmony.

American, British, and some Dutch jurists do not like the way in which *force majeure,* a concept ordinarily invoked to justify extreme actions taken when necessary to defend, not to take, life, has been used as the legal underpinning for the support and medicalization of euthanasia and assisted suicide. Originally the Dutch courts interpreted *force majeure* as applying if virtually anyone in the doctor's situation would have acted as he did. Subsequently, the courts have interpreted it as applying if any other member of the medical profession would have acted as the doctor did. Joseph Welie, an ethicist at the University of Nijmegen, points out that this ruling elevates physicians to a superior moral status whose judgments on life and death are always just. When combined with Dutch acceptance of the use of a sympathetic colleague as a consultant, there is an increasing tendency to free the physician from legal control.[30] Moreover, considering the unexpected frequency with which physicians end the lives of patients without their consent, several Dutch euthanasia advocates have conceded privately that the general acceptance of euthanasia has probably encouraged doctors to feel they can decide for patients what is an acceptable quality of life.

Euthanasia, fought for on the basis of the principle of autonomy and self-determination of patients, has actually increased the paternalistic power of the medical profession in the Netherlands. Doctors' organizations behave like groups or unions everywhere—they protect the interests of their members. Doctors are especially unaccustomed to explaining their decisions to non-physicians. American medicine has reluctantly accepted that in matters of what we call "quality assurance," the different perspectives of nurses, social workers, psychologists, and even lay administrators can be invaluable even if the initial impulse is to resent it.

The acceptance of euthanasia for psychiatric patients who are suicidal is simply bad psychiatry. It seems the inevitable consequence of allowing such criteria as "competence" and "intolerable suffering" to determine the outcome rather than sound clinical judgment. The idea that a depressed patient can make a decision for suicide uninfluenced by his pathology only demonstrates how limited "competence" is as a criterion for evaluating those who are suicidal. In these cases, the psychiatrist is in the position of working to prevent suicide until the patient asks for his assistance in committing suicide; then, the rules of the game change and the psychiatrist negotiates with the patient as to whose approach is best.

Seriously suicidal patients want suicide. In a society that makes euthanasia accessible for them they will be harder to treat, not easier. Many of them fantasize closeness in death with a person who kills them, and given that some psychiatrists and general practitioners have complementary fantasies, euthanasia fulfills their needs as much as the patient's.

The Assen case has given psychiatrists and psychologists in the Netherlands reason to question where they are going. Unless one is prepared to declare that in euthanasia the Dutch have found a cure for suicide, one can only hope the Dutch will take a second look at their current policies. Even patients who desire an early death during a terminal illness are usually suffering from a depression that is treatable; they are likely to be different from those who seek to avoid pain in the last days of terminal illness. The vast majority of the terminally ill fight for life to the end. Those who voice suicidal thoughts in response to transient depression or severe pain usually respond well to treatment for depressive illness and pain medication. Those who need to bring suicide and death into the relationship with their physician and use it coercively may be expressing a more severe depression than their doctors recognize.

Evaluation of the prospective euthanasia patient by psychiatrists knowledgeable about suicide, depression, and terminal illness cannot provide us with a simple solution to a complex social problem. Nor should psychiatrists be sanguine at being reduced to the role, suggested by some, of simply determining if a patient is competent to make a decision regarding euthanasia. . . .

Psychological issues play an equally important role in cases that are medical in origin. Doctors in both the Netherlands and the United States are insufficiently sensitive to the influence a doctor has on a patient's decision in these matters. Those doctors who are most emotionally involved in euthanasia and most interested in actually performing it may be those whose own needs in the matter should disqualify them.

The American Difference

Virtually all Dutch advocates of euthanasia familiar with the United States see our legalizing assisted suicide and/or euthanasia as unwise for a variety of reasons. From their perspective, the United States is not characterized by either a legal or a medical system that fosters social harmony; instead, it pits one profession against the other. They believe the tendency of American patients in general to undertake litigation would make euthanasia a nightmare for physicians. They cite social and economic disparities in health care as another source of contention and recognize that without comprehensive care for the sickly poor and the elderly, assisted suicide and euthanasia will tend to become their only options. The Dutch believe their hospitals are not subject to the economic pressure to get rid of the terminally ill that would be present in this country. The relative absence of the family doctor, the core of medical practice in the Netherlands, eliminates what the Dutch perceive as a major source of patient protection. Further contaminating the process in the United States would be the difficulty of preventing the profit motive from making euthanasia and assisted suicide a lucrative business.

If assisted suicide and euthanasia were legalized in this country, it would be likely to encourage involuntary euthanasia, as has happened in the Netherlands. If involuntary euthanasia with competent patients alone were to take place in the United States at the same frequency as it does in the Netherlands, at the most conservative estimate it would lead to 75,000 such deaths a year—more than the current number of suicides and homicides combined.

The Dutch have had twenty years of experience, court cases, and KNMG deliberation to help them reach a social consensus on euthanasia. In contrast, in our country, proposals for legalization of assisted suicide and euthanasia have been hastily introduced without a sufficient body of case law or procedures to define acceptable parameters for all.

Nor would a social consensus be simply the answer to the question, "Are you in favor of euthanasia?" A majority of people are, by which they mean little more than that they would rather die painlessly than painfully. If the question were asked, "If terminally ill, would you rather be given treatment to make you comfortable or have your life ended by a physician?" responses might be different. The question "If terminally ill, should you (or someone you delegate) or your doctor decide when you should die?" is also likely to evoke a different set of responses.

Kevorkian and other doctors are testing the American judicial system in the same way that some Dutch doctors tested their system. It has been suggested that prosecutors would feel freer to exercise their own discretion as to where to prosecute if they could consult with an arbitration panel representing diverse perspectives. This would permit us to deal with euthanasia and assisted suicide on a case-by-case basis without giving it legal sanction.[31]

Kevorkian's acquittal in the case in which he assisted in the suicide of a patient dying painfully of amyotrophic lateral sclerosis does not open the floodgates for such cases, as feared by opponents of assisted suicide, nor does it suggest the need for legalization of assisted suicide, as hoped for by its advocates.[32] There have been many comparable cases where a suffering, dying patient's life has been ended by a doctor, and in no case so far has an American jury convicted a physician. Some of Kevorkian's cases who were not terminally ill but were fearful of becoming so might arouse a less sympathetic response from a jury.

More is needed than case-by-case testing in the courts. We need a national commission to develop a consensus on the care and treatment of the terminally ill in the United States—a scientific commission similar to the President's Commission that in 1983 gave us guidelines about forgoing life-sustaining treatment with dying patients.[33] Work of a wider scope needs to be done now. There is a great deal of evidence that in the United States, as in the Netherlands, doctors are not sufficiently trained in the relief of pain and other symptoms in the terminally ill. Hospice care is in its infancy in both countries. We have not yet educated the public as to the choices they have in refusing or terminating treatment that prolongs a painful process of dying. Nor have we devoted enough time in our medical schools to educating future physicians about coming to terms with the painful truth that there will be patients they will not be able to save but whose needs they must address.

The relationship between doctor and patient and the attitude of each in facing serious or terminal illness is at the heart of the matter. Dr. C. Everett Koop captured this in discussing "the intent of the heart" in treating a hypothetical older woman with a powerful painkiller. "The intent behind the gradual administration of drugs is to be her ally in her remaining hours or days of her life and to keep her comfortable as she slips away. The intent behind . . . drug overdose is to get her 'out of her misery' and 'off our hands' as quickly as possible."[34]

It will not always be possible to know the "intent of the heart" or to uncover the intense ambivalence that illness, treatment, and imminent death inflame in both doctors and patients. There are now, and will continue to be, abuses. But as long as producing death with the intent of doing so is illegal, as long as physicians know that in case of a complaint they will have to be able to justify their actions to their peers and to the legal system, the amount of such abuse will be limited. If a doctor chooses to break the law, he should do so with full knowledge of the seriousness of his action. The protection of the honorable physician does not now warrant legalizing physician-assisted suicide or euthanasia in a society where the public is relatively uninformed of present abuses and where there exists the potential for much greater abuses if legalization occurs. . . .

20

Aiding the Death of Young Children: Ethical Issues

H. Tristram Engelhardt, Jr.

E uthanasia in the pediatric age group involves a constellation of issues that are materially different from those of adult euthanasia.[1] The difference lies in the somewhat obvious fact that infants and young children are not able to decide about their own futures and thus are not persons in the same sense that normal adults are. While adults usually decide their own fate, others decide on behalf of young children. Although one can argue that euthanasia is or should be a personal right, the sense of such an argument is obscure with respect to children. Young children do not have any personal rights, at least none that they can exercise on their own behalf with regard to the manner of their life and death. As a result, euthanasia of young children raises special questions concerning the standing of the rights of children, the status of parental rights, the obligations of adults to prevent the suffering of children, and the

---

H. Tristram Engelhardt, Jr., is a professor in the departments of medicine and community medicine at Baylor College of Medicine, Houston, Texas, and a member of the Center for Medical Ethics and Health Policy. He is co-editor of a series of books, "Philosophy and Medicine." This essay is reprinted by permission from *Beneficent Euthanasia,* Prometheus Books (Amherst, N.Y.: © Prometheus Books 1975).

possible effects on society of allowing or expediting the death of seriously defective infants.

What I will refer to as the euthanasia of infants and young children might be termed by others infanticide, while some cases might be termed the withholding of extraordinary life-prolonging treatment.[2] One needs a term that will encompass both death that results from active intervention and death that ensues when one simply ceases further therapy.[3] In using such a term, one must recognize that death is often not directly but only obliquely intended. That is, one often intends only to treat no further, not actually to have death follow, even though one knows death will follow.[4] Finally, one must realize that deaths as the result of withholding treatment constitute a significant proportion of neonatal deaths. For example, as high as 14 per cent of children in one hospital have been identified as dying after a decision was made not to treat further, the presumption being that the children would have lived longer had treatment been offered.[5]

Even popular magazines have presented accounts of parental decisions not to pursue treatment.[6] These decisions often involve a choice between expensive treatment with little chance of achieving a full, normal life for the child and "letting nature take its course," with the child dying as a result of its defects. As this suggests, many of these problems are products of medical progress. Such children in the past would have died. The quandaries are in a sense an embarrassment of riches: now that one *can* treat such defective children, *must* one treat them? And, if one need not treat such defective children, may one expedite their death?

I will here briefly examine some of these issues. First, I will review differences that contrast the euthanasia of adults to euthanasia of children. Second, I will review the issue of the rights of parents and the status of children. Third, I will suggest a new notion, the concept of the "injury of continued existence," and draw out some of its implications with respect to a duty to prevent suffering. Finally, I will outline some important questions that remain unanswered even if the foregoing issues can be settled. In all, I hope more to display the issues involved in a difficult question than to advance a particular set of answers to particular dilemmas.

Adult Euthanasia: The Freedom to Choose

For the purpose of this paper, I will presume that adult euthanasia can be justified by an appeal to freedom. In the face of imminent death, one is usually choosing between a more painful and more protracted dying and a less painful or less protracted dying, in circumstances where either choice makes little difference with regard to the discharge of social duties and responsibilities. In the case of suicide, we might argue that, in general, social duties (for example, the duty to support one's family) restrain one from taking one's own life. But in the face of imminent death and in the presence of the pain and deterioration of a fatal disease, such duties are usually impossible to discharge and are thus rendered moot. One can, for example, picture an extreme case of an adult with a widely disseminated carcinoma, including metastases to the brain, who because of severe pain and debilitation is no longer capable of discharging any social duties. In these and similar circumstances, euthanasia becomes the issue of the right to control one's own body, even to the point of seeking assistance in suicide. Euthanasia is, as such, the issue of assisted suicide, the universalization of a maxim that all persons should be free, *in extremis,* to decide with regard to the circumstances of their death.

Further, the choice of positive euthanasia could be defended as the more rational choice: the choice of a less painful death and the affirmation of the value of a rational life. In so choosing, one would be acting to set limits to one's life in order not to live when pain and physical and mental deterioration make further rational life impossible. The choice to end one's life can be understood as a non-contradictory willing of a smaller set of states of existence for oneself, a set that would not include a painful death. As such, it would not involve a desire to destroy oneself. That is, adult euthanasia can be construed as an affirmation of the rationality and autonomy of the self.[7]

The remarks above focus on the active or positive euthanasia of adults. But they hold as well concerning what is often called passive or negative euthanasia, the refusal of life-prolonging therapy. In such cases, the patient's refusal of life-prolonging therapy is seen to be a right that derives from personal freedom, or at least from a zone of privacy into which there are no good grounds for social intervention.[8]

Again, none of these considerations apply directly to the euthanasia of young children, because they cannot participate in such decisions. Whatever else pediatric—in particular neonatal—euthanasia involves, it surely involves issues different from those of adult euthanasia. Since infants and small children cannot commit suicide, their right to assisted suicide is difficult to pose. The difference between the euthanasia of young children and that of adults resides in the difference between children and adults. The difference, in fact, raises the troublesome question of whether young children are persons, or at least whether they are persons in the sense in which adults are. Answering that question will resolve in part at least the right of others to decide whether a young child should live or die and whether he should receive life-prolonging treatment.

The Status of Children

Adults belong to themselves in the sense that they are rational and free and therefore responsible for their actions. Adults are *sui juris*. Young children, though, are neither self-possessed nor responsible. While adults exist in and for themselves, as self-directive and self-conscious beings, young children, especially newborn infants, exist for their families and those who love them. They are not, nor can they in any sense be, responsible for themselves. If being a person is to be a responsible agent, a bearer of rights and duties, children are not persons in a strict sense. They are, rather, persons in a social sense: others must act on their behalf and bear responsibility for them. They are, as it were, entities defined by their place in social roles (for example, mother-child, family-child) rather than beings that define themselves as persons, that is, in and through themselves. Young children live as persons in and through the care of those who are responsible for them, and those responsible for them exercise the children's rights on their behalf. In this sense children belong to families in ways that most adults do not. They exist in and through their family and society.

Treating young children with respect has, then, a sense different from treating adults with respect. One can respect neither a newborn infant's or very young child's wishes nor its freedom. In fact, a newborn infant or young child is more an entity that is valued highly because it will grow to be a person and because it plays a social role as if it were a person.[9] That is, a small child is treated as if it were a person in social roles such as mother-child and family-child relationships, though strictly speaking the child is in no way capable of claiming or being responsible for the rights imputed to it. All the rights and duties of the child are exercised and "held in trust" by others for a future time and for a person yet to develop.

Medical decisions to treat or not to treat a neonate or small child often turn on the probability and cost of achieving that future status —a developed personal life. The usual practice of letting anencephalic children (who congenitally lack all or most of the brain) die can be understood as a decision based on the absence of the possibility of achieving a personal life. The practice of refusing treatment to at least some children born with meningomyelocele can be justified through a similar, but more utilitarian, calculus. In the case of anencephalic children, one might argue that care for them as persons is futile since they will never be persons. In the case of a child with meningomyelocele, one might argue that when the cost of cure would be likely to be very high and the probable lifestyle open to attainment very truncated, there is not a positive duty to make a large investment of money and suffering. One should note that the cost here must include not only financial costs but also the anxiety and suffering that prolonged and uncertain treatment of the child would cause the parents.

Who Decides?

This further raises the issue of the scope of positive duties not only when there is no person present in a strict sense, but when the likelihood of a full human life is also very uncertain. Clinical and parental judgment may and should be guided by the expected lifestyle and the cost (in parental and societal pain and money) of its attainment. The decision about treatment, however, belongs properly to the parents, because the child belongs to them in a sense that it does not belong to anyone else, even to itself. The care and raising of the child falls to the parents, and when considerable cost and little prospect of reasonable success are present, the parents may properly decide against life-prolonging treatment.

The physician's role is to present sufficient information in a usable form to the parents to aid them in making a decision. The accent is on the absence of a positive duty to treat in the presence of severe inconvenience (costs) to the parents; treatment that is very costly is not obligatory. What is suggested here is a general notion that there is never a duty to engage in extraordinary treatment and that "extraordinary" can be defined in terms of costs. This argument concerns children (1) whose future quality of life is likely to be seriously compromised and (2) whose present treatment would be very costly. The issue is that of the circumstances under which parents would not be obliged to take on severe burdens on behalf of their children or those circumstances under which society would not be so obliged.

The argument should hold as well for those cases where the expected future life *would* surely be of normal quality, though its attainment would be extremely costly. The fact of little likelihood of success in attaining a normal life for the child makes decisions to do without treatment more plausible, because the hope of success is even more remote and therefore the burden borne by parents or society becomes in that sense more extraordinary. But very high costs themselves could be a sufficient criterion, though in actual cases judgments in that regard would be very difficult when a normal life could be expected.[10]

The decisions in these matters correctly lie in the hands of the parents, because it is primarily in terms of the family that children exist and develop—until children become persons strictly, they are persons in virtue of their social roles. As long as parents do not unjustifiably neglect the humans in those roles so that the value and purpose of that role (that is, child) stands to be eroded (thus endangering other children), society need not intervene. In short, parents may decide for or against the treatment of their severely deformed children.

However, society has a right to intervene and protect children for whom parents refuse care (including treatment) when such care does not constitute a severe burden and when it is likely that the child could be brought to a good quality of life. Obviously, "severe burden" and "good quality of life" will be difficult to define and their meanings will vary, just as it is difficult to say when grains of sand dropped on a table constitute a heap. At most, though, society need intervene only when the grains clearly do not constitute a heap, that is, when it is clear that the burden is light and the chance of a good quality of life for the child is high. A small child's dependence on his parents is so essential that society need intervene only when the absence of intervention would lead to the role "child" being undermined. Society must value mother-child and family-child relationships and should intervene only in cases where (1) neglect is unreasonable and therefore would undermine respect and care for children, or (2) societal intervention would prevent children from suffering unnecessary pain.[11]

The Injury of Continued Existence

But there is another viewpoint that must be considered: that of the child or even the person that the child might become. It might be argued that the child has a right not to have its life prolonged. The idea that forcing existence on a child could be wrong is a difficult notion, which, if true, would serve to amplify the foregoing argument. Such an argument would allow the construal of the issue in terms of the perspective of the child, that is, in terms of a duty not to treat in circumstances where treatment would only prolong suffering. In particular, it would at least give a framework for a decision to stop treatment in cases where, though the costs of treatment are not high, the child's existence would be characterized by severe pain and deprivation.

A basis for speaking of continuing existence as an injury to the child is suggested by the proposed legal concept of "wrongful life." A number of suits have been initiated in the United States and in other countries on the grounds that life or existence itself is, under certain circumstances, a tort or injury to the living person.[12] Although thus far all such suits have ultimately failed, some have succeeded in their initial stages. Two examples may be instructive. In each case the ability to receive recompense for the injury (the tort) presupposed the existence of the individual whose existence was itself the injury. In one case a suit was initiated on behalf of a child against his father alleging that his father's siring him out of wedlock was an injury to the child.[13] In another case a suit on behalf of a child born to an inmate of a state mental hospital impregnated by rape in that institution was brought against the state of New York.[14] The suit was brought on the grounds that being born with such historical antecedents was itself an injury for which recovery was due. Both cases presupposed that non-existence would have been preferable to the conditions under which the person born was forced to live.

The suits for tort for wrongful life raise the issue not only of when it would be preferable not to have been born but also of when it would be *wrong* to cause a person to be born. This implies that someone should have judged that it would have been preferable for the child never to have had existence, never to have been in the position to judge that the particular circumstances of life were intolerable.[15] Further, it implies that the person's existence under those circumstances should have been prevented and that, not having been prevented, life was not a gift but an injury.

The concept of tort for wrongful life raises an issue concerning the responsibility for giving another person existence, namely, the notion that giving life is not always necessarily a good and justifiable action. Instead, in certain circumstances, so it has been argued, one may have a duty *not* to give existence to another person. This concept involves the claim that certain qualities of life have a negative value, making life an injury, not a gift; it involves, in short, a concept of human accountability and responsibility for human life. It contrasts with the notion that life is a gift of God and thus similar to other "acts of God" (that is, events for which no human being is accountable). The concept thus signals the fact that humans can now control reproduction and that where rational control is possible, humans are accountable. That is, the expansion of human capabilities has resulted in an expansion of human responsibilities such that one must now decide when and under what circumstances persons will come into existence.

The concept of tort for wrongful life is transferable in part to the painfully compromised existence of children who can have their life prolonged only for a short, painful, and marginal existence. The concept suggests that allowing life to be prolonged under such circumstances would itself be an injury of the person whose painful and severely compromised existence would be made to continue. In fact, it suggests that there is a duty not to prolong life if it can be determined to have a substantial negative value for the person involved.[16] Such issues are moot in the case of adults, who can and should decide for themselves. But small children cannot make such a choice. For them it is an issue of justifying prolonging life under circumstances of painful and compromised existence. Or, put differently, such cases indicate the need to develop social canons to allow a decent death for children for whom the only possibility is protracted, painful suffering.

I do not mean to imply that one should develop a new basis for civil damages. In the field of medicine, the need is to recognize an ethical category, a concept of wrongful continuance of existence, not a new legal right. The concept of injury for continuance of existence, the proposed analogue of the concept of tort for wrongful life, presupposes that life can be of a negative value such that the medical maxim *primum non nocere* ("first do no harm") would require not sustaining life.[17]

The idea of responsibility for acts that sustain or prolong life is cardinal to the notion that one should not under certain circumstances further prolong the life of a child. Unlike adults, children cannot decide with regard to euthanasia (positive or negative), and if more than a utilitarian justification is sought, it must be sought in a duty not to inflict life on another person in circumstances where that life would be painful and futile. This position must rest on the facts that (1) medicine now can cause the prolongation of the life of seriously deformed children who in the past would have died young and (2) it is not clear that life so prolonged is a good for the child. Further, the choice is made not on the basis of costs to the parents or to society but on the basis of the child's suffering and compromised existence.

What Makes Life Not Worth Living

The difficulty lies in determining what makes life not worth living for a child. Answers could never be clear. It seems reasonable, however, that the life of children with diseases that involve pain and no hope of survival should not be prolonged. In the case of Tay-Sachs disease (a disease marked by a progressive increase in spasticity and dementia, usually leading to death at age three or four), one can hardly imagine that the terminal stages of spastic reaction to stimuli and great difficulty in swallowing are at all pleasant to the child (even insofar as it can only minimally perceive its circumstances). If such a child develops aspiration pneumonia and is treated, it can reasonably be said that to prolong its life is to inflict suffering. Other diseases give fairly clear portraits of lives not worth living: for example, Lesch-Nyhan disease, which is marked by mental retardation and compulsive self-mutilation.

The issue is more difficult in the case of children with diseases for whom the prospects for normal intelligence and a fair lifestyle do exist, but where these chances are remote and their realization expensive. Children born with meningomyelocele present this dilemma. Imagine, for example, a child that falls within Lorber's fifth category (an IQ of sixty or less, sometimes blind, subject to fits, and always incontinent). Such a child has little prospect of anything approaching a normal life, and there is a good chance of its dying even with treatment.[18] But such judgments are statistical. And if one does not treat such children, some will still survive and, as John Freeman indicates, be worse off if not treated.[19]

In such cases one is in a dilemma. If one always treats, one must justify extending the life of those who will ultimately die anyway and in the process subjecting them to the morbidity of multiple surgical procedures. How remote does the prospect of a good life have to be in order not to be worth great pain and expense?[20] It is probably best to decide, in the absence of a positive duty to treat, on the basis of the cost and suffering to parents and society. But, as Freeman argues, the prospect of prolonged or even increased suffering raises the issue of active euthanasia.[21]

If the child is not a person strictly, and if death is inevitable and expediting it would diminish the child's pain prior to death, then it would seem to follow that, all else being equal, a decision for active euthanasia would be permissible, even obligatory.[22] The difficulty lies with "all else being equal," for it is doubtful that active euthanasia could be established as a practice without eroding and endangering children generally, since, as John Lorber has pointed out, children cannot speak in their own behalf.[23] Thus, although there is no argument in principle against the active euthanasia of small children, there could be an argument against such practices based on questions of prudence. To put it another way, even though one might have a duty to hasten the death of a particular child, one's duty to protect children in general could override that first duty.

The issue of active euthanasia turns in the end on whether it would have social consequences that refraining would not, on whether (1) it is possible to establish procedural safeguards for limited active euthanasia and (2) whether such practices would have a significant adverse effect on the treatment of small children in general. But since these are procedural issues dependent on sociological facts, they are not open to an answer within the confines of this article. In any event, the concept of the injury of continued existence provides a basis for the justification of passive euthanasia of small children—a practice already widespread and somewhat established in our society—beyond the mere absence of a positive duty to treat.[24]

Concluding Observations

Though the lack of certainty concerning questions such as the prognosis of particular patients and the social consequence of active euthanasia of children prevents a clear answer to all the issues raised by the euthanasia of infants, it would seem that this much can be maintained:

1. Since children are not persons strictly but exist in and through their families, parents are the appropriate ones to decide whether or not to treat a deformed child when (a) there is not only little likelihood of full human life but also great likelihood of suffering if the life is prolonged, or (b) the cost of prolonging life is very great. Such decisions must be made in consort with a physician who can accurately give estimates of cost and prognosis and who will be able to help the parents with the consequences of their decision.

2. It is reasonable to speak of a duty not to treat a small child when such treatment will only prolong a painful life or would in any event lead to a painful death.

Though this does not by any means answer all the questions, it does point out an important fact—that medicine's duty is not always to prolong life doggedly but sometimes is quite the contrary.

21

A Statement on
Physician-Assisted Suicide

American Medical Association

For nearly 2,500 years, physicians have vowed to "give no deadly drug if asked for it, [nor] make a suggestion to this effect." What has changed, that there should be this attempt to make "assisted suicide" an accepted practice of medicine? Certainly the experience of physical pain has not changed over time. Yet the blessings of medical research and technology present their own new challenges, as our ability to delay or draw out the dying process alters our perceptions and needs. Our efforts in this new paradigm must recognize the importance of care that relieves pain, supports family and relationships, enhances functioning, and respects spiritual needs. Calls for legalization of physician-assisted suicide point to a public perception that these needs are not being met by the current health-care system. In addition, society has not met its responsibility to plan adequately for end-of-life care. It is this issue—how to provide quality care at

This statement was given before the U.S. House of Representatives' Committee on the Judiciary, Subcommittee on the Constitution, by Lonnie R. Bristow, president of the American Medical Association, on April 29, 1996. Following the statement is the position on physician-assisted suicide from the AMA's Code of Medical Ethics (Council on Legal and Judicial Affairs, *Code of Medical Ethics: Current Opinions with Annotations,* © 1994, AMA).

the end of life—which the AMA believes should be our legitimate focus.

The AMA believes that physician-assisted suicide is unethical and fundamentally inconsistent with the pledge physicians make to devote themselves to healing and to life. Laws that sanction physician-assisted suicide undermine the foundation of the patient-physician relationship that is grounded in the patient's trust that the physician is working wholeheartedly for the patient's health and welfare. The multidisciplinary members of the New York State Task Force on Life and the Law concur in this belief, writing that "physician-assisted suicide and euthanasia violate values that are fundamental to the practice of medicine and the patient-physician relationship."

Yet physicians also have an ethical responsibility to relieve pain and to respect their patient's wishes regarding care, and it is when these duties converge at the bedside of a seriously or terminally ill patient that physicians are torn.

The AMA believes that these additional ethical duties require physicians to respond aggressively to the needs of the patients at the end of life with adequate pain control, emotional support, comfort care, respect for patient autonomy, and good communications. Further efforts are necessary to better educate physicians in the areas of pain management and effective end-of-life care. Patient education is the other essential component of an effective outreach to minimize the circumstances which might lead to a patient's request for physician-assisted suicide: inadequate social support; the perceived burden to family and friends; clinical depression; hopelessness; loss of self-esteem; and the fear of living with chronic, unrelieved pain.

ETHICAL CONSIDERATIONS

Physicians' Fundamental Obligation: The physician's primary obligation is to advocate for the individual patient. At the end of life, this means the physician must strive to understand the various existential, psychological, and physiological factors that play out over the course of terminal illness and must help the patient cope with each of them. Patients who are understandably apprehensive or afraid of their own mortality need support and comforting, not a prescription to help them avoid the issues of death. Patients who believe sudden and "controlled" death would protect them from the perceived indignities of prolonged deterioration and terminal illness must receive social support as well as the support of the profession to work through these issues. Providing assisted suicide would breach the ethical means of medicine to safeguard patients' dignity and independence.

Pain Management and the Doctrine of Double Effect: Many proponents of assisted suicide cite a fear of prolonged suffering and unmanageable pain as support for their position. For most patients, advancements in palliative care can adequately control pain through oral medications, nerve blocks, or radiotherapy. We all recognize, however, that there are patients whose intractable pain cannot be relieved by treating the area, organ, or system perceived as the source of the pain. For patients for whom pain cannot be controlled by other means, it is ethically permissible for physicians to administer sufficient levels of controlled substances to ease pain, even if the patient's risk of addiction or death is increased.

The failure of most states to expressly permit this practice has generated reluctance among physicians to prescribe adequate pain medication. Additional uncertainty is produced by the potential for legal action against the physician when controlled substances are prescribed in large amounts to treat patients with intractable pain. This uncertainty chills physicians' ability to effectively control their terminally ill patients' pain and suffering through the appropriate prescription and administration of opiates and other controlled substances. In this area, states such as California and Texas have developed clear legislative guidance that resolves these concerns for most physicians. The AMA is developing similarly structured model legislation for state medical societies to pursue with their state legislatures and medical licensing boards.

In some instances, administration of adequate pain medication will have the secondary effect of suppressing the respiration of the patient, thereby hastening death. This is commonly referred to as the "double effect." The distinction between this action and assisted suicide is crucial. The physician has an obligation to provide for the comfort of the patient. If there are no alternatives but to increase the risk of death in order to provide that comfort, the physician is ethically permitted to exercise that option. In this circumstance, the physician's clinical decision is guided by the intent to provide pain relief, rather than an intent to cause death. This distinguishes the ethical use of palliative care medications from the unethical application of medical skills to cause death.

Distinction Between Withholding or Withdrawing Treatment and Assisted Suicide: Some participants in the debate about assisted suicide see no meaningful distinction between withholding or withdrawing treatment and providing assistance in suicide. They argue that the results of each action are the same and therefore the acts themselves carry equal moral status. This argument largely ignores the distinction between act and omission in the circumstances of terminal care and does not address many of the principles that underlie the right of patients to refuse the continuation of medical care and the duty of physicians to exercise their best clinical judgment.

Specifically, proponents who voice this line of reasoning fail to recognize the crucial difference between a patient's right to refuse unwanted medical treatment and any proposed right to receive medical intervention which would cause death. Withholding or withdrawing treatment allows death to proceed naturally, with the underlying disease being the cause of death. Assisted suicide, on the other hand, requires action to cause death, independent from the disease process.

The "Slippery Slope": Physician-assisted suicide raises troubling and insurmountable "slippery slope" problems. Despite attempts by some, it is difficult to imagine adequate safeguards which could effectively guarantee that patients' decisions to request assisted suicide were unambivalent, informed, and free of coercion.

A policy allowing assisted suicide could also result in the victimization of poor and disenfranchised populations who may have greater financial burdens and social burdens which could be "relieved" by hastening death. As reported two years ago by the New York State Task Force on Life and the Law (composed of bioethicists, lawyers, clergy, and state health officials), "[a]ssisted suicide and euthanasia will be practiced through the prism of social inequality and prejudice that characterizes the delivery of services in all segments of society, including health care."

Recent studies documenting reasons for patient requests for physician-assisted suicide speak to our "slippery slope" concerns. Patients were rarely suffering intractable pain. Rather, they cited fears of losing control, being a burden, being dependent on others for personal care, and loss of dignity often associated with end-stage disease.

The Case of the Netherlands: While euthanasia and assisted suicide are not legal in the Netherlands, comprehensive guidelines have been established which allow physicians to avoid prosecution for the practice. Despite this environment, Dutch physicians have become uneasy about their active role in euthanasia, prompting the Royal Dutch Medical Association to revise its recommendations on the practice.

Findings of more than 1,000 cases of involuntary euthanasia in the Netherlands should raise hackles in the United States, particularly given the stark societal differences between the two countries. Health coverage is universal in the Netherlands, the prevalence of long-term patient-physician relationships is greater, and social supports are more comprehensive. The inequities in the American health-care system, where the majority of patients who request physician-assisted suicide cite financial burden as a motive, make the practice of physician-assisted suicide all the more unjustifiable. No other country in the world, including the Netherlands, has legalized assisted suicide or euthanasia. This is one movement in which the United States should not be a "leader." . . .

[Omitted here are brief sections on "Educating Physicians and Patients" and "Medicare and Medicaid Coverage."]

SIGNIFICANT JUDICIAL DECISIONS

Troubling decisions in the Ninth and Second Circuits have held that state laws in Washington and New York prohibiting physician-assisted suicide could not be upheld. Notably, while both decisions were based on constitutional arguments, the constitutional bases cited were *different* in each case.

In the Ninth Circuit Court of Appeals in California, the panel overruled an earlier finding in the case *Compassion in Dying v. Washington,* finding a constitutional right to physician-assisted suicide for terminally ill, competent adults who wish to hasten their death. The ruling concluded that the Washington state law prohibiting assisted suicide was in violation of the Due Process clause of the U.S. Constitution, as it found a liberty interest in controlling the time and manner of one's death. The AMA had filed an *amicus curiae* brief in this case and its arguments were discussed in the decision. The Court summarily dismissed the important ethical and practice principles of double effect in pain management as well as the critical distinction between the withholding or withdrawing of life-sustaining treatment versus physician-assisted suicide.

While the majority opinion dismisses "slippery slope" arguments, a dissenting judge writes that "[i]f physician-assisted suicide for mentally competent, terminally ill patients is made a constitutional right, voluntary euthanasia for weaker patients, unable to self-terminate, will soon follow. After voluntary euthanasia, it is but a short step to a 'substituted judgment' or 'best interests' analysis for terminally ill patients who have not expressed their constitutionally sanctioned desire to be dispatched from this world." The Washington State Attorney General has indicated that it will appeal the decision to the U.S. Supreme Court, a plan fully supported by the AMA.

In the Second Circuit, the Court overturned a decision by a District Court and found New York State laws criminalizing physician-assisted suicide to be unconstitutional. This ruling is more narrowly drawn than the Ninth Circuit decision, as it did not find a constitutional right to assisted suicide. Rather, the Second Circuit found the laws in violation of the Equal Protection clause of the Fourteenth Amendment. The Court's opinion stated that a physician's ability to withdraw life-sustaining treatment and the ability to administer life-ending measures should be considered as equivalent acts. Any distinction between the two, argued the Court, would deny competent, terminally ill patients who are not on life support the opportunity to end their lives. The AMA is pleased that the New York State Attorney General has announced plans to appeal this decision.

Both decisions are disturbing as they articulate constitutional support for the practice of physician-assisted suicide. Neither decision recognizes the vital clinical distinctions involved in end-of-life care, particularly the administration of pain medication and the use of life-sustaining treatment. Additionally, the decisions counter the ethical requirements of the medical profession, asserting a necessary role for physicians in assisted suicide. The Courts also fail to bring some definition to the concept of a disease's "final stages" or the state of being "terminally ill." Ultimately, these definitions would be crucial in preventing abuse. The Courts also dismissed arguments about the potential social threats of assisted suicide to vulnerable patients in our current health-care climate. The Ninth Circuit case is particularly disconcerting in its treatment of medical ethics as a simple matter for the courts to decide.

CONCLUSION

The movement for legally sanctioning physician-assisted suicide is a sign of society's failure to address the complex issues raised at the end of life. It is not a victory for personal rights. We are equipped with the tools to effectively manage end-of-life pain and to offer terminally ill patients dignity and to add value to their remaining time. As the voice of the medical profession, the AMA offers its capability to coordinate multidisciplinary discourse on end-of-life issues, for it is essential to coordinate medical educators, patients, advocacy organizations, allied health professionals and the counseling and pastoral professions to reach a comprehensive solution to these challenging issues. Our response should be a better informed medical profession and public, working together to preserve fundamental human values at the end of life.

[The relevant passage from the AMA's Code of Medical Ethics is on the following page.]

From the American Medical Association's 'Code of Medical Ethics'

2.211 Physician Assisted Suicide. Physician assisted suicide occurs when a physician facilitates a patient's death by providing the necessary means and/or information to enable the patient to perform the life-ending act (e.g., the physician provides sleeping pills and information about the lethal dose, while aware that the patient may commit suicide).

It is understandable, though tragic, that some patients in extreme duress—such as those suffering from a terminal, painful, debilitating illness—may come to decide that death is preferable to life. However, allowing physicians to participate in assisted suicide would cause more harm than good. Physician assisted suicide is fundamentally incompatible with the physician's role as healer, would be difficult or impossible to control, and would pose serious societal risks.

Instead of participating in assisted suicide, physicians must aggressively respond to the needs of patients at the end of life. Patients should not be abandoned once it is determined that cure is impossible. Patients near the end of life must continue to receive emotional support, comfort care, adequate pain control, respect for patient autonomy, and good communication.

PART FOUR

Legal Perspectives

Legal Perspectives:
An Introduction

Americans are prone to equate legal and moral rights. The United States was, after all, the first political society in history founded on the basis of *universal* principles of right, i.e., principles deemed to be true not just for Americans but for all persons at all times, everywhere. The source of these principles is not the positive law but, as the Preamble to the Declaration of Independence states, the laws of "Nature and Nature's God." The rights enumerated in the Constitution, and those reasonably inferred therefrom, rest on that vital moral predicate of the Declaration, which is why Americans tend to identify constitutional rights with those we possess by our nature as human beings.

Judges and legal commentators frequently criticize the simplicity of that equation, pointing out that legal right and moral right are not necessarily the same thing. That is certainly true, though one cannot help remarking the irony that many of these same judges and commentators are in the forefront of those who wish to align the Constitution with what they believe to be morally right. Laymen, it would seem, are not the only ones who believe that constitutional litigation should be concerned not only with what the law says in some narrow sense, but with what kind of people we wish to be.

Nowhere is this desire more apparent than in the great controversies in American history: almost without exception, our most serious political and moral debates have become *constitutional* debates. That was true of the controversies over the establishment of a national bank, over slavery, over the growth of industrial power in the late nineteenth century, and over the expansion of federal power in the twentieth.

Closer to our own time, it has been true also of the struggle for civil rights, of the effort to define the role of religion in contemporary society, and of the controversy over abortion. In these and similar disputes, constitutional argument almost invariably proceeds from statements about what the law is to statements about what the law ought to be.

As the American people wrestle with the issues raised in this volume, the courts are sure to be in the thick of it, and in the process of adjudicating particular cases they will inevitably give instructions concerning how we *ought* to think about questions of life and death. Indeed, the greatest power of courts may lie precisely in their ability to form public opinion, and judges seem to understand that fact better than many elected officials. Prior to the 1990s, the debate over euthanasia and assisted suicide had been largely confined to academic and professional circles, but by mid-decade it had crossed over dramatically into the public arena. The most conspicuous figure thus far has been Jack Kevorkian, the retired Michigan pathologist who has contemptuously flouted state laws embodying the traditional medical ethic. Three times he has been criminally charged, and three times acquitted by juries. This suggests a certain public sympathy for Kevorkian's goals, if not always for his methods. But jury verdicts are not always a sound measure of the public mood. Oregon is still the only state whose citizens have voted (in a 1994 plebiscite) to approve physician-assisted suicide. Voters in California and Washington defeated similar ballot propositions in 1992 by larger margins than that by which Oregon's carried.

Alan Meisel points out in the opening essay of this section that a consensus has been building for some years in state legislatures and courts on the question of forgoing medical treatment. That consensus is built upon two premises: (1) that patients have a right, deriving from both common and constitutional law, to refuse medical treatment, which includes the right, under certain circumstances, to refuse artificial nutrition and hydration; and (2) that refusal of medical treatment is legally and morally distinguishable from assisted suicide and euthanasia, which continue to be proscribed. Although, as Meisel says, this consensus is now widely accepted, it is being severely challenged, especially in federal courts, by litigants who assert a constitutional "right to die."

The next author, **Yale Kamisar**, finds unpersuasive the arguments made on behalf of such a right. Not only is there no precedent for it in our laws and customs, he points out, but precedent, if anything, cuts the other way. The *Cruzan* case, often cited by proponents as establishing the foundation for a right to die, did no such thing: the states remain constitutionally free to prohibit suicide and assisted suicide. Kamisar argues that it would be all but impossible to circumscribe even a narrowly framed right to physician-assisted suicide; such a right, once declared, would inexorably expand to include ever-broader categories of medical killing. The elderly, the gravely ill, and the severely disabled or depressed, Kamisar argues, need the protection of the law, not the empowerment of doctors to kill them.

Professor Kamisar has it all wrong, says **Robert A. Sedler**, who represented a group of patients and doctors in a 1993 challenge to Michigan's law prohibiting assisted suicide. The question is not the right to die, or even a right to physician-assisted suicide, he argues, but whether a state should be able to ban doctors from prescribing medications that "hasten inevitable death" in terminally ill patients. Sedler argues for a constitutional right of personal autonomy, which, he says, has already been recognized by the Supreme Court's abortion decisions. The hastening of inevitable death is for him but a logical extension of that right. The Michigan prohibition places an "undue burden" on the exercise of a patient's right to "bodily integrity": just as a state may not place "substantial obstacles" in the path of women who seek abortions, so it may not do so with terminally ill patients who wish to die sooner rather than later. "There can be no valid [state] interest in preserving life when there is no life left to preserve." As for Kamisar's fears about the slippery slope, Sedler is prepared to let the issues evolve case by case but says the state must carry the burden of demonstrating a "valid justification for the particular interference" with personal autonomy.

Professor Sedler's hopes for an expansive understanding of rights based on personal autonomy were vindicated in May 1994, when Judge Barbara Rothstein of the Federal District Court for the Western District of Washington ruled that the U.S. Constitution guaranteed a right to assisted suicide and that the state's 146-year-old ban against the practice must fall. (*Compassion in Dying v. Washington*, 850 F. Supp. 1454 W.D. Wa. 1994.) On appeal, Judge Rothstein's ruling was reversed by a divided three-judge panel of the Ninth Circuit Court of Appeals (49 F. 3d 586 [1995]), and Judge **John Noonan**'s opinion for the majority opens our three-part set of court decisions. Noonan writes that nothing in the Constitution, in Supreme Court rulings, in common law, or in customary practice gives sanction to a "right to die." To the contrary, says Noonan, the legal tradition (including the Supreme Court's decision in *Cruzan*) is virtually unanimous in its *rejection* of any such right. The invention of the right by the trial court was not only unfounded as a matter of law but dangerous as a matter of policy, particularly for the poor, the elderly, and the severely handicapped. "Unless the federal judiciary is to be a floating constitutional convention," Noonan concludes, "a federal court should not invent a constitutional right unknown in the past and antithetical to the defense of human life that has been a chief responsibility of our constitutional government."

Noonan's decision was reversed after an *en banc* appeal by an eleven-judge panel of the Ninth Circuit. (79 F. 3d 790 [1996].) Judge **Stephen Reinhardt**, writing for an 8-3 majority, rests his argument primarily on the logic of the Supreme Court's 1993 *Casey* decision, which rejected a challenge against *Roe v. Wade*. In reframing the constitutional jurisprudence justifying the right to abortion, a plurality opinion of the high court in *Casey* stated that "the heart of liberty is the right to define one's own concept of existence, of meaning, of the universe, and of the mystery of human life." Reinhardt takes that language as controlling and concludes (1) that the liberty protected by the Fourteenth Amendment includes a generic right to bodily integrity, and (2) that this liberty encompasses a right "to determine the time and manner" of one's own death. Accordingly, he ruled that Washington's prohibition against assisted suicide violated the Due Process clause of the Fourteenth Amendment.

Judge Reinhardt dismisses the distinction between killing and letting die: the fact that patients can decline or instruct their doctors to terminate treatment makes "the line between commission and omission" a "distinction without a difference." Whatever the morals and customs of bygone eras, Reinhardt adds, a pluralistic society that celebrates the right of personal autonomy should be entitled to make new moral rules for itself. Although Reinhardt's opinion focuses primarily on assisted suicide for competent, terminally ill adults, he makes it clear that the logic of the case may extend to involuntary euthanasia of comatose patients who are unable to speak for themselves.

A few weeks after the Ninth Circuit decision, the Second Circuit Court of Appeals handed down its opinion in *Quill v. Vacco* (80 F. 3d 716 [1996]), ruling that New York's statute prohibiting assisted suicide violated the Equal Protection clause of the Fourteenth Amendment. (The named plaintiff in the case was Dr. Timothy Quill, whose essay appears in the medical section of this volume.) A unanimous three-judge panel headed by **John Miner** specifically rejected Judge Reinhardt's rationale as constitutionally unfounded: there is simply no "right to die" to be found in the Constitution itself, or in Supreme Court or common-law precedent. Nevertheless, Judge Miner found that New York had failed to provide a rational basis for distinguishing between terminally ill patients who wish to end medical treatment and those who wish to end their lives by means of physician-assisted suicide. That failure constituted an unlawful discrimination against "competent persons who are in the final stages of fatal illness and wish to hasten their deaths." In a lengthy concurrence from which we give a brief excerpt, Judge **Guido Calabresi** stated that New York might be able to craft a new law against assisted suicide that passed constitutional muster, but that such a statute would have to be narrowly tailored to meet rationally defensible and well-articulated public-policy criteria. (The *Compassion* and *Quill* cases were appealed to the U.S. Supreme Court, which overturned the decisions of Judge Reinhardt and Judge Miner in June 1997. Opinions of the justices are presented in the final chapter of this book.)

Victor G. Rosenblum finds little to admire and much to worry about in the Ninth and Second Circuit rulings. Both courts, he says, took liberties with Supreme Court precedent and ignored the philosophical rationale supporting long-standing state policies against assisted suicide. Legal custom and clinical practice have long recognized the crucial difference between killing and letting die; yet both courts treated it as either capricious or trivial and, by so doing, opened the gate to the slippery slope: "They introduce a bias in favor of death . . . that will corrupt the delivery of health care to every patient with a life-threatening illness." Although Judges Reinhardt and Miner claimed that the states, through reasonable regulation, could restrict the exercise of the newly created right, Rosenblum believes that the "elasticity" of their decisions precludes effective regulation.

Nine doctors and academics from Boston think otherwise. In 1996 they proposed a **model state statute** to authorize and regulate physician-assisted suicide, believing such a step to be the logical outgrowth of the already recognized right to refuse treatment. A properly structured statutory scheme, they contend, would remove the legal liability of physicians under specified circumstances, eliminate secrecy, produce greater accountability, and bring needed relief to terminally ill or severely distressed persons who wish to end their lives. Although the authors were divided on how broadly the right to assisted suicide should be extended, they concluded that their proposed statute, reprinted here, would assuage public fears about the inevitability of the slippery slope.

Daniel Callahan and Margot White conclude that it is impossible both in principle and in practice to place physician-assisted suicide within tolerable limits. Those who advocate the liberalization of current law frequently contend that present restrictions are widely ignored. If that is so, Callahan and White ask, why should we believe that more lenient rules will be taken seriously? The central difficulty with all regulatory schemes in this area, they argue, is their necessary dependence upon subjective evaluations of patients and doctors. Although the proposed regulations speak in ostensibly objective terms — "terminally ill," "competent," and "voluntary," for example — there are in fact no objective standards to determine whether the regulations have been violated. Callahan and White examine the criteria proposed by Dr. Quill (printed in the medical section of this volume), a set of guidelines published in the *New England Journal of Medicine,* and the model statute put forth by the Boston group. All three, they argue, would do little more than ratify medical decisions already made, while laying the groundwork for euthanasia generally. Such fears are hardly academic, say Callahan and White: we have a test laboratory in the Netherlands, where legal restrictions are routinely ignored by both doctors and prosecutors, and multiple thousands of patients have been killed without their knowledge or consent.

The justices of the Supreme Court join the debate in the final chapter. In June 1997 a unanimous Court overturned the rulings of the Ninth and Second Circuits set forth in chapter 25, thereby affirming the right of states to prohibit assisted suicide. Five members of the Court limited their concurrence to the litigation before them, however, and indicated a willingness to revisit the subject in the future. In his opinion deciding *Glucksberg v. Washington,* Chief Justice **William H. Rehnquist** finds no precedent in American law or custom for recognizing a constitutional right to assisted suicide, nor does he believe the judiciary is empowered to deduce such a right "from abstract concepts of personal autonomy." Accordingly, Washington's prohibition against causing or aiding suicide does not violate the Due Process clause of the Constitution. In *Vacco v. Quill,* Rehnquist argues that New York's long established distinction between killing and letting die is both widely recognized and rationally grounded and that, accordingly, the state's prohibition against assisting suicide does not violate the Equal Protection clause.

In their concurrences, Justices **Sandra Day O'Connor** (whose opinion was joined by Ruth Bader Ginsburg), **John Paul Stevens**, **David Souter**, and **Stephen Breyer** argue, with varying degrees of intensity, that circumstances may arise in which a state prohibition against assisted suicide will run afoul of the Constitution, especially in the case of mentally competent, terminally ill patients who seek to end their suffering.

22

Forgoing Life-Sustaining Treatment: The Legal Consensus

Alan Meisel

In 1976 the name Karen Quinlan made headlines as lawyers debated whether she had a "right to die." Since the *Quinlan* case ushered in this era of right-to-die litigation, close to seventy-five similar cases—the precise number depends on what one considers a "right-to-die case" to be—have been decided in the state appellate courts or the federal district courts in twenty-one states and the District of Columbia.[1] From these cases, from an even larger body of unreported trial-court cases, and from legislation enacted in almost every state, a consensus has gradually emerged in law, medicine, and public opinion that termination of life support is legitimate under certain circumstances.

This consensus has developed primarily through a gradual, non-linear process of litigation and judicial decision. There have been any number of false starts; some courts have departed from the consensus on one or more issues, some of them fundamental and highly controversial issues; and there have been some strongly worded dissenting

Alan Meisel is the director of the Center for Medical Ethics at the University of Pittsburgh and a professor of law at the university's law school. This essay is reprinted by permission from the *Kennedy Institute of Ethics Journal*, vol. 2, no. 4 (December 1992; © 1993 by the Johns Hopkins University Press). Most of the notes and case citations have been omitted.

opinions. Thus no single, monolithic statement can be made about what "the law" is governing the termination of life support. Qualifications are needed about a particular jurisdiction, kind of illness or injury, kind of patient, kind of treatment, treatment setting, and the degree of unanimity on the court that wrote the decision.

In the American legal system, law is a product of many factors. The most important historically is the body of published opinions of *state and federal appellate courts.* Although these opinions remain an exceedingly important source of law—especially the law governing the termination of life support—the statutory enactments of *legislatures* and the regulations promulgated by *governmental administrative agencies* are also an essential ingredient of law today. However, legislation plays a much smaller role in the law governing the termination of life support than it does in, for example, contemporary environmental law, and administrative regulation is an even more insignificant component in right-to-die law.

Although litigation is the central component of the law governing the termination of life support, it is essential that it be understood what kind of litigation this is. It has predominantly involved *actions for declaratory and injunctive relief* in which litigants have sought a declaration from courts of the right to have life-sustaining treatment withdrawn or withheld. Litigants have predominantly been competent patients and the families of incompetent patients bringing suit against physicians and health-care institutions. Rarely has anyone sought to impose criminal penalties or collect monetary damages. Indeed, one of the important functions of a declaratory judgment is to obtain an adjudication of rights so that action can be taken free from the fear of criminal or civil liability. It is somewhat ironic, given physicians' fears of liability for allowing a patient to die, that there have been more reported lawsuits for damages for keeping a patient alive who had expressed a wish to have treatment terminated, or whose family had done so, than lawsuits for withholding or prematurely terminating life support.

How Consensus Evolves

In general, unanimity is not necessary for there to be a legal consensus, and this is true about the termination of life support. There are several reasons why unanimity is difficult to achieve. First, most states have not had an appellate right-to-die case. Second, there are more than fifty distinct American jurisdictions: besides the states, there is the District of Columbia, a commonwealth, and territories. Superimposed on state law is the federal legal system, and different federal courts can disagree on various points of law unless the conflict is resolved by the Supreme Court, which often does not occur.

Another ingredient in the legal consensus is advance-directive legislation, that is, legislation dealing with living wills and health-care power of attorney. Statutory law nicely illustrates the notion of consensus and distinguishes it from some more monolithic and positivistic, but idealized, notion of law. For example, although most states have a living-will statute, a few do not. Even more have a health-care power-of-attorney statute, but again not all do, and further, not all health-care power-of-attorney statutes explicitly apply to decisions about life-sustaining treatment. Further, these state advance-directive statutes vary widely. But most important, none of the statutes purport to specify the full range of rights and obligations concerning the termination of life support. They merely deal with decision-making for that (currently small) portion of the population who make the effort to plan in advance, and they leave it to the courts or to clinical practice to fill in the interstices.

The consensus about the law governing the termination of life support has not arisen only from appellate cases and statutes—what is called formal law. Less formal kinds of law-making, such as (1) the impact of law-making in one state on the law of another, (2) trial-court decisions, and (3) the interplay between law and clinical practice, have also substantially influenced it.

1. Extra-territorial Effect of Law
The judicial opinions of the highest court of a jurisdiction are binding on lower courts within that same jurisdiction and only on courts within that jurisdiction. Thus, for example, the New Jersey supreme court's *Quinlan* decision is "the law" in New Jersey; it is a legal precedent that lower courts in New Jersey must follow. (But even this is a simplification. Lower courts can, without formal penalty, choose to ignore precedent by "distinguishing it away"—i.e., by claiming that the facts in the case before it are sufficiently different

from those in the precedential case that the latter should not govern. They may even explicitly ignore precedent without incurring more than reversal by an appellate court, if there is an appeal, which there usually is not.) *Quinlan* has been modified and supplemented by subsequent decisions of the New Jersey supreme court and superior court; these modifications and additions, taken together with the *Quinlan* decision, form the corpus of right-to-die case law in New Jersey.

In neighboring Pennsylvania, neither the supreme court nor the superior court has had occasion to consider a right-to-die case. There have been a handful of reported trial-court cases, but none of these are binding on any other court in Pennsylvania. But if there are no Pennsylvania appellate-court opinions—if there is no law to follow, so to speak—on what basis do the trial courts decide these cases, and how do we know what "the law" is in Pennsylvania or in any other state that has no appellate case law?

A variety of factors come into play, not the least of which are the appellate opinions of the New Jersey courts. Pennsylvania trial courts have sometimes looked to New Jersey cases not because of the geographic proximity but because the reasoning of the New Jersey cases is persuasive, and because the appellate courts of other states have been strongly influenced by and have sometimes followed the New Jersey decisions. In fact, most new right-to-die cases at the very least cite the appellate decisions in prior right-to-die cases in many other states. Occasionally they recount the fates and holdings in these cases at some length. In other words, Pennsylvania trial courts have, like so many other courts, chosen to adopt the evolving consensus, which is why we can say both that there is a consensus and that it is evolving. (This is also why New York right-to-die opinions have not been as influential in the reasoning of the Pennsylvania trial courts. New York is, in some important regards, on the fringe of the consensus.)

Thus, while the opinions of the appellate courts in one state are not binding precedent in other states, to the extent that courts—both trial courts and appellate courts—find them to be persuasive, they are highly influential and have the *effect* of law, even if, formally speaking, they are not *the law*. What emerges, then, is a web of interlocking judicial opinions, sometimes influenced by statutory enactments, but also influenced by a number of other important factors.

2. Trial-Court Litigation

There are only about fifty to seventy-five (depending on what one considers to be a right-to-die case) of these appellate-court opinions that are binding on other courts in the same jurisdiction. However, these appellate cases constitute not merely the tip of the proverbial iceberg but the tip of the tip, when one takes into account the cases that have been litigated in trial courts but have not been appealed and the total number of deaths from forgoing life-sustaining treatment.

The only known, published estimate of the number of forgoing-treatment cases heard by the judiciary is between 2,900 and 7,000 trial-court cases during the fifteen-year period between 1975 and 1989.[2] This means that only a very small proportion of all right-to-die cases commenced in trial courts is appealed. Although in a formal sense, it is only appellate-court cases that are of precedential value and legally binding on (at least some) other courts, trial-court litigation also plays an important role. It becomes part of the local lore, if not law, and becomes incorporated in people's behavior and thinking—especially, in this context, that of health-care administrators, physicians, other health-care professionals and the lawyers who counsel them, patients, and patients' families.

As small as the proportion of appealed cases is, the proportion of deaths from forgoing life-sustaining treatment that is litigated is also very small. Somewhere between 0.2 per cent and 0.5 per cent have been litigated at all, and between 37 and 55 in 10 million have been litigated to the point of yielding an appellate decision. Thus, although the proportion of deaths from forgoing life-sustaining treatment that influences the formal law-making process is exceedingly small, the fact that death from forgoing life-sustaining treatment frequently occurs without benefit of judicial blessing has probably had a substantial impact on the acceptance, the development, and the further evolution of the consensus.

3. Interplay Between Law and Clinical Practice

One thing that these numbers point out is that forgoing life-sustaining treatment is well accepted in clinical practice. Although clinical practice has been influenced by both formal law (primarily appellate judicial opinions) and less formal law (i.e., trial-court decisions), the practices of physicians who attend dying patients have also been substantially influenced by large numbers of instances in which life support is terminated or limited without benefit of judiciary, that is, by clinical practice itself. This is not a tautology; rather, the point is that accepted clinical practice gradually becomes even better accepted clinical practice as more physicians adopt it and become comfortable doing so.

At the same time, the law has been substantially influenced by the changing attitudes in clinical practice. Clinical practice exists in an iterative relationship with the law, and vice versa. In 1977, in the *Saikewicz* case, the next right-to-die case after *Quinlan,* the Massachusetts supreme judicial court, in what may well have been wishful thinking, observed that "the prevailing ethical practice seems to be to recognize that the dying are more often in need of comfort than treatment."[3] Whether true or not, the court's *expression* of this view was probably instrumental in obtaining its gradual acceptance by both the medical profession and other courts. Other courts have cited similar kinds of evidence. In the *Cruzan* case, Justice Stevens noted, quoting Justice Blackman, " 'Decisions of this kind are made daily by the patient or relatives, on the basis of medical advice and their conclusion as to what is best. Very few cases reach court, and I doubt whether this case would be before us but for the fact that Nancy lies in a state hospital.' "[4]

The practices of physicians have also been influenced by policy statements promulgated by medical associations (such as American Academy of Neurology, 1989; American Nurses' Association, 1988; American Medical Association, 1986) and by more informal groups of well-respected physicians and others at the same time that the authors of these statements have probably been influenced by the trends in the law. These, in turn, have been brought to the attention of courts in right-to-die litigation, and judges have incorporated these views into their opinions, in effect making them a part of the law. The same has occurred with academic and governmental reports. The 1983 report of the President's Commission for the Study of Ethical Problems in Medicine and Biomedical and Behavioral Research has been especially influential in shaping the legal consensus, having been relied upon and cited by numerous appellate courts since its publication.[5]

CONTENT OF THE CONSENSUS

That there is a consensus is simple to demonstrate. What the consensus consists of is also not difficult to specify. It consists of the following points:

1. Competent patients have a common-law and constitutional right to refuse treatment.

2. Incompetent patients have the same rights as competent patients; however, the manner in which these rights are exercised is, of necessity, different.

3. No right is absolute, and limitations are imposed on the right to refuse treatment by societal interests.

4. The decision-making process should generally occur in the clinical setting without recourse to the courts.

5. In making decisions for incompetent patients, surrogate decision-makers should apply, in descending order of preference, the subjective standard, the substituted-judgment standard, and the best-interests standard.

6. In ascertaining an incompetent patient's preferences, the attending physician and the surrogate may rely on a patient's "advance directive."

7. Artificial nutrition and hydration is a medical treatment and may be withheld or withdrawn under the same conditions as any other form of medical treatment.

8. Active euthanasia and assisted suicide are morally and legally distinct from forgoing life-sustaining treatment.

Again, it is important to emphasize that this is a consensus, not a monolithic body of law. There are important dissenting voices on each of the above points, but they are a distinct minority insofar as appellate cases are concerned.

Competent Patients: Right to Refuse

1. Competent patients have a common-law and constitutional right to refuse treatment.

The cornerstone of the legal consensus about forgoing life-sustaining treatment is that competent patients have a right to refuse treatment, including life-sustaining treatment. This right is firmly rooted in the protection given to bodily integrity by the common law through the civil and criminal protections against assault and battery and, more recently, in the protection given to autonomy in medical matters through the requirement of informed consent to treatment. These rights of bodily integrity and autonomy are so well accepted in law that even in those jurisdictions that have not had an appellate right-to-die case, there can be no doubt, at least as a point of departure for analysis, that there is a legally recognized and protected common-law right to refuse treatment. Even the single American jurisdiction (Georgia) that rejects the requirement of informed consent to medical treatment (though it does require "simple" consent) has strongly affirmed the right of a competent person to refuse life-saving medical treatment.

Many right-to-die decisions are predicated on a constitutional right as well as, or instead of, a common-law right. Many courts have cited a federal constitutional right of privacy as the basis for the right to control one's body. However, decisions of the United States Supreme Court in recent years have been increasingly less receptive to the right of privacy in general and in medical decision-making in particular, especially in the context of the termination of a pregnancy. Thus, when the first right-to-die case reached the Supreme Court in 1990, some proponents of a right to refuse treatment attempted to plant the right not in a right of privacy but in the constitutional protection accorded to individual "liberty." And the Supreme Court agreed that "this issue is more properly analyzed in terms of a Fourteenth Amendment liberty interest."[6]

Some state courts have also predicated the right to die on *state* constitutional grounds. This basis is virtually immune to challenge from United States Supreme Court decisions and is also, unlike the common-law basis, relatively free from challenge by the actions of state legislatures that might seek to restrict the right to refuse treatment. For example, only a few months after the Supreme Court's *Cruzan* decision, the Florida supreme court strongly reiterated the support it had previously accorded to the right to die on state constitutional-law grounds, evading a Florida living-will statute in the process.

Incompetent Patients: Right to Refuse

2. Incompetent patients have the same rights as competent patients; however, the manner in which these rights are exercised is, of necessity, different.

Virtually all courts agree that "[a]n incompetent's right to refuse treatment should be equal to a competent's right to do so"[7] because "the right of privacy would be an empty right were it not to extend to competent and incompetent persons alike."[8] However, because incompetent patients, by definition, are unable to participate directly and contemporaneously in the decision-making process,[9] the manner in which decisions about continuing, limiting, or terminating their treatment are to be made is, of necessity, different from decision-making for competent patients. Simply put, competent patients make their own decisions by giving or withholding informed consent; in the case of incompetent patients, someone else must make decisions for them. As a consequence, a constellation of questions arises concerning such decision-making: By whom should it be done? By what standards? And with what protections, if any?

Limitations on the Right to Refuse Treatment

3. No right is absolute, and limitations are imposed on the right to refuse treatment by societal interests.

In catechismic fashion, courts in right-to-die cases have consistently intoned several interests that society has in not letting patients die from the refusal of medical treatment, which must be "balanced" against the individual's right to refuse treatment. Although others have been enumerated, the main interests are: (1) preserving life, (2) preventing suicide, (3) protecting third parties, and (4) protecting the ethical integrity of the health-care professions. Most courts begin with a presumption that individual interests must be accorded a higher degree of importance than societal interests and that these societal interests may override a patient's right to refuse treatment only if they are "compelling." In actually striking this balance, the courts have uniformly found that societal interests pale in comparison.

Incompetent Patients. Following the reasoning of *Quinlan,* courts recognize that although societal interests might predominate in a case in which treatment could save the patient's life, "the State's interest *contra* [forgoing treatment] weakens and the individual's right to privacy grows as the degree of bodily invasion increases and the prognosis dims."[10] Consequently, when a patient is terminally ill or irreversibly critically ill, the state interest in administering treatment has been held not to be compelling, and the termination of life support permitted.

Competent Patients. The manner in which courts have treated the weighing of societal interests for competent patients is more complicated. When the patient's prognosis has been "dim," honoring the patient's refusal of treatment has posed no difficulty. However, when a competent patient has declined treatment, the administration of which almost certainly would save the patient's life at the same quality-of-life level as existed before the need for treatment arose, the courts have been presented with their most serious dilemma.

In the decade or so before the *Quinlan* decision, when faced with these kinds of cases, courts gave lip-service to the right to refuse treatment, albeit in strong tones, but often found a way to ensure that the patient received treatment. Sometimes this was done by finding the patient incompetent in whole or in part because the patient refused treatment rather than because of the patient's actual decision-making capacity; sometimes by finding that societal interests in the well-being of the patient's minor children demanded that the patient not be allowed to die; and sometimes by finding that the ethical integrity of the health-care professions demanded that the patient not be allowed to die. In most cases, some combination of these factors was invoked.

Perhaps the most interesting case of circumvention of a patient's objection to treatment was *United States v. George,* which is worth quoting at length to illustrate:

> [Mr.] George's first remarks [to the judge who visited him in the hospital] were that he would not agree to be transfused but would in no way resist a court order permitting it, because it would be the Court's will and not his own. His "conscience was clear," and the responsibility for the act was "upon the Court's conscience." He stated he would rather die than agree to a transfusion. The Court advised George it had no power to force a transfusion upon him, and he was free to resist the transfusion, even by the rather simple physical maneuver of placing his hand over the area to be injected by the needle. . . .
>
> In the present case the patient voluntarily submitted himself to and insisted upon medical care. Simultaneously he sought to dictate to treating physicians a course of treatment amounting to medical

malpractice. To require these doctors to ignore the mandates of their own conscience, even in the name of free religious exercise, cannot be justified under these circumstances. The patient may knowingly decline treatment, but he may not demand mistreatment. Therefore, this Court . . . "determined to act on the side of life" in the pending emergency.[11]

Although the patient's behavior was certainly equivocal as to the manifestation of consent, if the court had truly believed that the patient had consented to treatment, it would not have needed to issue an order permitting treatment unless the patient was incompetent. However, the patient was competent, and yet the judge ordered treatment.

Since 1985, there has been a small and slowly growing number of cases in a small number of states (California, Florida, Georgia, Maryland, Massachusetts, Nevada, and New York) involving the refusal of treatment by competent patients that almost certainly would result in their death, though they were not terminally ill. Most of these patients, as in the classic pre-*Quinlan* cases, needed a blood transfusion but were prohibited from consenting to it by their religious beliefs. Two, however, involved mentally intact quadriplegic patients being kept alive by ventilators, and one was a patient with cerebral palsy being force-fed.

A decade or two earlier, the courts would probably have tried diligently to find some way to circumvent these patients' refusals of treatment. However, there is no evidence of that in any of these cases. Judicial thinking in cases of this sort has been strongly influenced by fifteen years of decisions in which courts have permitted the termination of life support because—implicitly at least—terminally ill competent patients judged their life not worth living, or the families of incompetent patients determined that the patient would not have wanted to live in this condition. Consequently, when a competent patient refuses treatment, societal interests in circumventing or overriding the refusal and compelling the administration of treatment have become increasingly less weighty, so that it is not far from the mark to say, as the New Jersey supreme court did in the *Jobes* case (1987), that "a competent patient's right to make that decision [to forgo life support] generally will outweigh any countervailing state interests."[12]

In other words, the right of a competent person to refuse medical treatment is virtually absolute.[13]

The Forum for Decision-Making

4. The decision-making process should generally occur in the clinical setting without recourse to the courts.

After some debate among various courts in early right-to-die cases, a judicial consensus has emerged—reflecting a strongly held view in the medical profession—that decisions about life-sustaining treatment are best made in the clinical setting and that ordinarily the courts should not be involved. This consensus is strongest with respect to competent patients where decision-making takes place through informed consent, which is traditionally not monitored prospectively by any entity outside the doctor-patient relationship. Apart from the imposition of a legal requirement on physicians to disclose information to patients that is material to making a decision about the matter in question, the law is content to assume that competent individuals are able to safeguard their own interests, for example to avoid undue pressure from the doctor or from third parties (such as family and friends).

Decision-making for incompetent patients poses more serious concerns because the assumption in the case of competent patients that they can look out for their own interests is, by definition, not valid in the case of incompetent patients. Nonetheless, there is still a strong consensus that routine recourse to the courts is unwarranted.

There are at least three points in the process of decision-making about life-sustaining treatment at which one might consider seeking judicial guidance. The first is to determine whether or not the patient possesses or lacks decision-making capacity. Courts are available to adjudicate incompetency, but does that mean that there must be a judicial determination of incompetency before a physician can feel comfortable in turning to a surrogate decision-maker? A closely related question has to do with the designation of a surrogate decision-maker. May the physician rely on the patient's close family (or even unrelated persons) to make decisions for a patient who lacks decision-making capacity, or must there be a judicial appointment of a guardian? Finally, regardless of the answers to the previous two questions, once a decision is made to forgo life-sustaining treatment, does this decision require judicial approval?

In resolving these issues, courts have been strongly influenced by clinical practice. In effect, they have adopted clinical practice and clothed it with the force of law. Specifically, the courts to which these questions have been posed have almost unanimously held that there is a strong presumption in favor of not seeking a judicial blessing for determinations about decision-making capacity, for the designation of a surrogate, or for forgoing life-sustaining treatment.

Decision-making capacity. The consensus is that it is the role of the attending physician to determine whether the patient lacks decision-making capacity, with the assistance of consultants if necessary. In cases in which a patient clearly lacks decision-making capacity—for example, an unconscious patient—a judicial determination is, equally clearly, unnecessary. When it is a closer question, the attending physician should seek the assistance of psychiatric, neurological, or psychological consultants. Only when no agreement can be reached is recourse to a court necessity (or even advisable) for an adjudication of incompetency.

Surrogates. Courts acknowledge and approve of the long-standing practice among physicians of regarding the patient's family as surrogates and involving them in decision-making when the patient is unable to play this role. Rather than seeking the judicial appointment of a guardian, doctors should continue to counsel, and seek counsel from, the patient's family about treatment decision-making. The basis for presuming that family members speak for patients is not the degree of relationship per se but the assumption that family members know the wishes of the patient. In an increasing number of states, this long-standing practice and the judicial approval accorded it are embodied in surrogate decision-making statutes, which specifically set forth the order of priority for surrogate designation. If the patient has no family, it is best to seek judicial appointment of a guardian, although there is some support for the proposition that a close friend of the patient should be considered the patient's surrogate.

Termination of life support. Assuming that there is no need to seek judicial guidance about the patient's decision-making capacity or about who is to serve as the patient's surrogate, most courts have expressed a preference for keeping the decision-making process per se in the clinical setting; that is, the consensus is to allow decisions to terminate life support to be made and implemented without judicial review.

The overwhelming consensus is that only in exceptional circumstances should there be recourse to the courts for any facet of the decision-making process. There are two general kinds of "exceptional circumstances." One occurs when there is intractable disagreement among participants in the decision-making process—members of the health-care team, the family, possibly close friends of the patient—about whether the patient lacks decision-making capacity, about who should act as the surrogate, or about whether life-sustaining treatment should be administered or forgone. The other kind of situation in which recourse to the courts may be desirable occurs when there is a serious conflict of interest between the surrogate decision-maker and the patient, such that it is clear that the surrogate decision-maker lacks the capacity to act primarily out of regard for the patient's best interests.

In addition, there are some departures, small in number but significant in nature, from this facet of the consensus. The Illinois supreme court requires approval of a decision to forgo artificial nutrition and hydration and to permit the forgoing of life-sustaining treatment if the patient is a minor. The Nevada supreme court requires judicial approval to forgo life-sustaining treatment if the patient is not terminally ill. Originally, the Massachusetts supreme judicial court seemed to require judicial review of all decisions to forgo life-sustaining treatment, but it has substantially backed away from, if not entirely abandoned, this position in later cases.

Incompetent Patients: Decision-making Standards

5. In making decisions for incompetent patients, surrogate decision-makers should apply, in descending order of preference, the subjective standard, the substituted-judgment standard, and the best-interests standard.

It is an accepted part of the legal consensus that the same moral and legal principles—respect for individual self-determination and bodily integrity—requiring physicians to honor the treatment choices of competent patients should also, insofar as possible, govern decision-making for patients who lack decision-making capacity. Just as with competent patients, decision-making for incompetent patients must seek to learn what the patient's treatment preferences are.

In practice, this has come to mean that the goal in decision-making for incompetent patients is to approximate as closely as possible the decision about treatment the patient would make if able to do so. This is necessarily a hypothetical exercise. The primary point of divergence among courts subscribing to the consensus is how hypothetical an exercise they will permit it to be. Only two or three courts reject the consensus position itself. The consensus view is that there is a hierarchy of standards to be applied in making decisions for patients lacking in decision-making capacity.

Subjective standard. All courts agree that it is best in making decisions for incompetent patients that surrogates be guided by a "subjective" standard, which requires that any instructions the patient gave before losing decision-making capacity about what kind of treatment he did or did not want should guide decision-making. Only two states, Missouri and New York, with the possible addition of Maine, require that this standard be met or else treatment cannot be terminated.[14] Other states merely view it as the preferred standard.

Substituted-judgment standard. If the subjective standard cannot be applied because such information about the patient's treatment preferences is not available or does not meet the high level of proof necessary to meet the subjective standard, the consensus holds that the surrogate should attempt to apply the "substituted judgment" standard. This requires that, through discussions with members of the patient's family and significant others, attempts should be made to ascertain what the patient would have wanted.

Although the conceptual differences between the substituted-judgment standard and the other two standards for decision-making for incompetent patients are clear, the large and varied number of factors that different courts have enjoined surrogates to consider in applying the substituted-judgment standard can, in practice, result in substantial overlap with either of the other two standards. Some of these factors would also be relevant to proof of the subjective standard, such as prior oral or written statements by the patient "even though the treatment alternatives at hand may not have been addressed,"[15] or "evidence of the patient's intent, derived either from a patient's explicit expressions of intent or from knowledge of the patient's personal value system."[16] On the other hand, some of the factors are more suggestive of a best-interests standard, such as "the probability of adverse side effects," and some, such as "the impact on the patient's family," are not relevant to any accepted standard for decision-making for incompetent patients.

Best-interests standard. If there is inadequate information about what the patient would have wanted done about continuing or terminating treatment, the path is more uncertain. Some courts have directed that a best-interests standard be applied, by which the surrogate decision-maker is guided not by the patient's preferences but by his interests. Some courts refuse to allow treatment to be terminated in the absence of actual or presumed knowledge of the patient's preferences. Nonetheless, the best-interests standard is well accepted in clinical practice, with or without judicial blessing.

There is a fair amount of inconsistency in the ways in which different courts define and apply these three standards for surrogate decision-making. In some cases, the substituted-judgment standard is applied in ways that make it seem very much like a best-interests standard—especially when it is applied to patients who never possessed decision-making capacity (such as infants and those who have been mentally retarded since birth). Other courts apply the substituted-judgment standard in such a way that it comes very close to being a subjective standard, and others, while adhering to a subjective standard and rejecting a substituted-judgment standard in name, apply the subjective standard as if it were a substituted-judgment standard.

The Role of Advance Directives

6. In ascertaining an incompetent patient's preferences, the attending physician and the surrogate may rely on the patient's "advance directive."

Unlike most other aspects of the consensus about the termination of life support, the consensus about the validity of advance directives has arisen predominantly from legislation, although there have been many voices of judicial support for advance directives and hardly any in dissent. Advance directives are instructions that persons in possession of decision-making capacity give to facilitate decision-making about treatment should they, at some future time, lose the capacity to make such decisions. Advance directives are of two main types. The best known is the living will, but possibly of greater use is the health-care power of attorney.[17] They may be combined, and they may be oral as well as written.

These two kinds of advance directives perform complementary functions. A living will addresses the question "what decision should be made for an incompetent patient?" If specific enough, it should satisfy the subjective standard and, *a fortiori,* the substituted-judgment standard. However, because of the virtual impossibility of predicting in advance precisely what kinds of treatment one might be offered and under what circumstances, a living will is often of only hortatory value when specific decisions need to be made. Consequently, even when a patient has given instructions about treatment before losing decision-making capacity, the physician will need to consult with a surrogate decision-maker, at the least, to "fine tune" the patient's instructions. A health-care power of attorney answers the question "who is to act as the patient's surrogate?" and tells the physician whom to turn to for informed consent to administer or forgo a particular treatment or course of treatment.

Because the judicial acceptance of advance directives is a corollary of the primacy of the patient's own preferences in decision-making about life-sustaining treatment, there is little doubt that advance directives should presumptively be honored even in those few states that do not have advance-directive legislation. Although advance directives have not been the subject of extensive litigation, most courts that have been presented with the issue have shown no reluctance to enforce a patient's oral instructions about future treatment decisions or a patient's oral designation of an agent for decision-making. Further legal support for advance directives is manifested by the enactment by Congress in 1990 of the Patient Self-Determination Act, which requires most institutional health-care providers to give patients information about advance directives. This has been further reinforced by the standards on advance directives issued by the Joint Commission on Accreditation of Healthcare Organizations (1992).

Forgoing Artificial Nutrition and Hydration

7. Artificial nutrition and hydration is a medical treatment and may be withheld or withdrawn under the same conditions as any other form of medical treatment. Forgoing artificial nutrition and hydration is one of the most controversial aspects of the right to die. It is also a problem of potentially great magnitude because a significant proportion of nursing-home patients are kept alive by tube-feeding. The permissibility of forgoing artificial nutrition and hydration has been repeatedly litigated and fervently discussed in professional literature. Virtually every appellate case has concluded that artificial nutrition and hydration is a medical procedure, that it may be forgone under appropriate circumstances as may any other procedure, and that the fact that it involves basic sustenance is not relevant to whether it must be administered or may be forgone. This judicial consensus is embodied in a policy statement of the American Medical Association, widely cited in judicial opinions, which classifies artificial nutrition and hydration as "life-prolonging medical treatment."[18] Similar position statements have been issued by the American Academy of Neurology (1989), the American Thoracic Society (1991), and the American Nurses' Association (1988).

Although not squarely addressing the constitutionality of the termination of artificial nutrition and hydration, the United States Supreme Court's *Cruzan* opinion assumed but did not decide that "the United States Constitution would grant a competent person a constitutionally protected right to refuse lifesaving hydration and nutrition."[19] The Court did state that "the logic of the cases [from which the principle of a competent patient's right to refuse treatment is derived] would embrace such a liberty interest. . . ."[20] However, the Court also left open the door for states to limit the forgoing of artificial nutrition and hydration, declaring that "[w]e do not think a State is required to remain neutral in the face of an informed and voluntary decision by a physically-able adult to starve to death. . . . [Because of] the dramatic consequences involved in refusal of such treatment," they would have to be weighed against the individual's liberty interest to determine whether or not "the deprivation of that interest is constitutionally permissible."[21]

Whatever the Supreme Court's position turns out to be, it will have no effect in those jurisdictions in which the basis for the forgoing of life-sustaining treatment, whether artificial nutrition and hydration or other treatment, is the common law or the state constitution. This was demonstrated in the *Browning* case in Florida only a few months after *Cruzan*. Although Mrs. Browning had executed a written living will and had made oral statements requesting that she not be kept alive by tube-feeding, these directions did not conform to the then existing Florida statute that did not permit the withdrawal of artificial nutrition and hydration.[22] Nonetheless, the state supreme court held that the Florida constitutional right of privacy permitted enforcement of the advance directive.

Active Euthanasia vs. Forgoing Treatment

8. Active euthanasia and assisted suicide are morally and legally distinct from forgoing life-sustaining treatment.

A bedrock assumption on which the consensus is grounded is that there is a fundamental distinction between a patient's death from forgoing life-sustaining treatment and active intervention to end life. The courts have manifested an unflagging insistence on establishing and maintaining a bright line between active euthanasia and passive euthanasia (or as the latter is more frequently referred to, forgoing life-sustaining treatment or termination of life support), even when it seriously strains reasoning to do so. So intent have courts been on maintaining this distinction that they have frequently eschewed the use of the term "euthanasia." Out of fear of confusing the two, or because the unmodified term "euthanasia" has for some people acquired connotations of active euthanasia, involuntary euthanasia, or both, courts ordinarily avoid the term "euthanasia" (even modified by "passive") and refer to passive euthanasia as forgoing life-sustaining treatment or terminating life support or refusing treatment, and to active euthanasia as killing or mercy killing. Although most judicial right-to-die opinions do not mention active euthanasia or mercy killing, the few that do clearly reject it, and there is an implicit rejection in most others.

Although, judging from news accounts, what is referred to as mercy killing occurs with some frequency, there are few reported prosecutions for performing it. The state legislatures have taken a similar posture. Many living-will and health-care power-of-attorney statutes also clearly draw a line between euthanasia or mercy killing on the one hand and termination of life-sustaining treatment on the other, prohibiting the former and permitting the latter. And regardless of its legal status, active euthanasia is frequently said to violate the tradition and ethics of the medical profession.

Courts have usually framed the distinction between active and passive euthanasia in terms of "killing" and "letting die." Killing is said to be morally and legally impermissible, while letting die is acceptable. Passive euthanasia consists of letting a patient die by withholding that treatment necessary to sustain life. It is what is virtually uniformly involved in litigated right-to-die cases and, despite the occasional judicial denials, is in fact the functional equivalent of the right to die as that right has been recognized by courts and legislatures.

Even as a general proposition, the distinction that the courts have established is far too facile. There is just not the clear line between killing and letting die that many courts would like there to be. Even in the simplest case—for example, when a competent, terminally ill patient dies after a ventilator is withdrawn—the courts are wont to say that the patient was permitted to die (not killed) because his medical condition was such that he could not breathe without a ventilator, and that the cause of death was that same medical condition, rather than the removal of the ventilator.

It may well be that as a matter of law, morals, and policy we do not wish to penalize the physician who honors the request of a competent patient to terminate life-sustaining treatment; indeed, we might wish to encourage such behavior as an indication of respect for patient autonomy. However, that does not, per se, make the physician's conduct into a "letting die" rather than a "killing" any more than does labeling it a killing make the conduct morally or legally wrongful. The same is true in reverse. Letting a patient die is not per se rightful conduct, any more than killing a patient is necessarily wrongful conduct. Letting a patient die is morally and legally acceptable only under certain conditions, the most general of which is that the physician has no duty to continue to try to keep the patient alive.

No one would hold for a moment that physicians are exempt from wrongdoing if they arbitrarily disconnect patients from ventilators or other forms of life support. What makes such conduct acceptable, when it is, is not the fact that it is a letting die—indeed, whether it is an instance of one or the other is itself debatable—but that the physician is under no duty to continue to treat the patient because there has been valid consent by the patient, or by one authorized to speak for the patient, to the physician's conduct, alone or in combination with other factors (such as the patient's dim prognosis). And what makes such conduct wrongful, when it is, is that the physician has not been absolved of the duty to continue treatment by the same factors. Thus, if a physician terminates life support without consent, or even if he terminates treatment with consent of the surrogate of an incompetent patient but the surrogate has not applied the proper standard for decision-making for incompetent patients, the physician's conduct is wrongful regardless of whether one labels it as killing or letting die; and neither is it self-evident what one *should* label it.

WHITHER THE CONSENSUS?

The consensus about forgoing life-sustaining treatment is now deeply rooted in American law. But as with a deeply rooted tree, adverse conditions could take a toll on it. In the absence of unfavorable conditions, the consensus is likely to spread to states in which there has been no appellate litigation, as it gradually has done over the last decade and a half. The consensus has weathered one threat in recent years, the *Cruzan* case; but two other phenomena gradually gaining momentum—the efforts to legalize mercy killing, and the authority of physicians, when they deem continued treatment to be "futile," to terminate life-sustaining treatment without the permission of the patient's surrogate—could, rather inadvertently, pose challenges to the consensus. I call these challenges inadvertent because their proponents, virtually without exception, are supporters of the consensus about forgoing life-sustaining treatment. Indeed, their efforts are not aimed at undermining the consensus, but at extending it. Nonetheless, the unintended consequence may be to undermine the consensus.

The Cruzan Case

As mentioned earlier, in 1990 the United States Supreme Court issued its decision in the first "right-to-die case" to reach the high court. Before the decision was announced, there were dire predictions about what the Court might decide, and afterwards there were equally dire alarms sounded about what it had decided and the grave consequences that would ensue. In fact, however, the Court's holding was very narrow. Even more significant is the fact that in the most significant appellate decisions handed down by state courts since *Cruzan,* not only has there not been a turning back, but there has been a reaffirmation—and possibly even an extension—of the consensus.

The holding of the *Cruzan* case is quite straightforward: a state may, without violating the federal Constitution, require the continuation of life support for an incompetent patient unless there is "clear and convincing evidence" that the patient, before losing decision-making capacity, made a decision that under such circumstances, she would not want life support continued. The critical word is "may": a state court or legislature *may* establish such a rule for the termination of life support, but the Supreme Court did not hold that the federal Constitution *requires* the application of such a rule. States are free— as the overwhelming majority of right-to-die cases have held—to allow for the termination of life support on the basis of less stringent evidence. In other words, states may allow the termination of life support on the basis of the substituted-judgment standard or the best-interests standard, and are not constitutionally bound to apply the subjective standard.

None of the handful of appellate "right-to-die" decisions issued by state courts since *Cruzan* has restricted rights. Only two months after the *Cruzan* decision, the Florida supreme court permitted the termination of tube-feeding of a patient in a persistent vegetative state on the basis of her advance directive (*Browning* 1990). The most significant aspect of this decision is that the court grounded the decision in the state constitution's right of privacy, which it held conferred a right to control one's medical decision-making broader than the state living-will statute. By basing the decision on the state constitution, the court may have been signaling that the right to die would not be constrained in Florida by possible narrow interpretations by the United States Supreme Court.

Less than three months after the Florida decision, the Nevada supreme court issued its first right-to-die decision, affirming the right of a competent patient to forgo life-sustaining treatment even if not "terminally ill" (*Bergstedt* 1990). Citations in this opinion to the *Cruzan* decision make clear that the Nevada court relied on *Cruzan* not for the diminution of rights but as the basis for their existence.

Perhaps most significant, however, are five state-court decisions involving never-competent patients (*Lawrance* 1991; *Rosebush* 1992; *Moorhouse* 1991; *Doe* 1992; *Beth* 1992). Not only do these cases reaffirm the consensus about forgoing life-sustaining treatment, but they also affirm perhaps the weakest aspect of the consensus: the permissibility of termination of life support for patients who have left no evidence about their treatment preferences and could not have done so. It is one thing to permit the forgoing of life-sustaining treatment in the absence of something less than clear and convincing evidence that the patient wanted treatment forgone. It is a much longer step beyond *Cruzan* to permit the forgoing of treatment of a patient who never expressed, nor could have expressed, a preference about the matter. Although the United States Supreme Court is unlikely to uproot the consensus, there are two other threats to it that have begun to manifest themselves: the increasing pressure for mercy killing, and "futility" cases.

Mercy Killing

The distinction between killing and letting die, although a mainstay of the consensus about forgoing life-sustaining treatment, has nonetheless always been a weak link in the chain. Increasing pressure is likely to be placed on it as efforts to accept mercy killing increase. If nothing else, there has been an increased focus in the professional and lay press about mercy killing—I use this term to include both active euthanasia and physician-assisted suicide—in recent years. Since 1988, articles have been published in two prestigious medical journals, the *Journal of the American Medical Association* and the *New England Journal of Medicine,* in which physicians have admitted that they administered or provided lethal doses of medication to terminally ill patients.[23] [Both articles are reprinted in this volume; see "It's Over, Debbie," and Timothy Quill's "Death and Dignity."] Substantial attention has been commanded by Jack Kevorkian, who has assisted the suicide of a number of patients with his "suicide machine," and Derek Humphry's self-help suicide manual for the terminally ill, *Final Exit,* has made it to the top of the *New York Times* best-seller list. Voters in Washington state narrowly rejected a citizen initiative to legalize physician-assisted suicide, and efforts are being made in California, for the second time in the last few years, to place a similar referendum on the ballot. Reports continue to appear in the lay press and in medical journals about mercy killing for terminally ill competent patients in the Netherlands, a practice that has existed for more than a decade.

The pressures for legalizing mercy killing are intended to extend the consensus about forgoing life-sustaining treatment. However, because the distinction between killing and letting die has always been a tenuous one, it could easily give way under the pressure. Even those who support decriminalizing mercy killing must acknowledge that doing so—or doing so too rapidly and too soon—risks upsetting the consensus that has developed in law, medicine, and public opinion about the termination of life support. Rather than resulting in the acceptance of mercy killing, the pressure to dissolve the distinction between killing and letting die—between active and passive euthanasia—could easily boomerang and undermine the entire consensus and not merely this one pillar of the consensus.

"Futility" Cases

Another source of pressure on the consensus about forgoing life-sustaining treatment is what are being called futility cases. These cases threaten to undermine the principle of patient autonomy and the derivative principle of the primacy of familial decision-making for incompetent patients.

Several aspects of the consensus rest on the principle of autonomy, which prescribes that competent patients have a right not to be treated without their informed consent and the corollary right to refuse treatment, and that the families may exercise these rights on behalf of incompetent patients. The paradigm right-to-die case—

indeed virtually all of the right-to-die cases from *Quinlan* to *Cruzan* —is of a physician who insists on administering treatment (either because of a belief that is the morally appropriate course of action, or because of a fear of legal liability for not doing so) against the wishes of competent patients or the families of incompetent patients who have come to believe that treatment is contrary to their goals, i.e., that continued treatment is futile. This is the stuff from which the consensus has emerged: simply put, that health-care professionals cannot enforce their preferences in favor of treatment on unwilling patients who speak this unwillingness themselves or through their families.

Slowly the tables have begun to turn, first in the form of case reports and newspaper articles, and then in the form of two litigated cases (*Wanglie* 1991; *Doe* 1992)[24]—though of course there is strong reason to suspect that there have been many more instances than appear either in case reports or in litigation. Now, in the face of families who wish for treatment to be continued, physicians have begun to seek to terminate life support on the ground that it is futile. Perhaps these efforts are evidence of just how well accepted the consensus is among health-care professionals. Karen Quinlan's physicians probably genuinely believed that it was wrong to withdraw ventilator support. But in the ensuing decade and a half, it has become so standard a practice to terminate life support when patients are in a persistent vegetative state that some (or perhaps most) physicians are confused, surprised, and even angered when their recommendation to terminate life support is rejected by the patient's family.

Whether or not efforts by physicians to terminate treatment that they, but not the patient's family, believe to be futile are justified, these efforts, like those to legalize mercy killing, place pressure on the consensus about forgoing life-sustaining treatment. However, where mercy killing attacks one of the most vulnerable aspects of the consensus (the distinction between killing and letting die), futility cases are aimed at one of the strongest: patient and family primacy in decision-making. This is why, in some respects, the threat to the consensus posed by futility cases is even greater than that posed by mercy killing. If such a fundamental proposition is under attack, can the consensus long survive? Or can it be reformulated in such a way as to assure its complete or partial survival?

Concluding Observations

It has taken roughly a decade and a half to establish a consensus about the circumstances under which the forgoing of life-sustaining treatment is a legally appropriate course of action. This consensus has weathered a most important test, a challenge in the United States Supreme Court, and has probably come out stronger for it.

There are, however, a number of weak spots in the consensus, and the fact that in slightly more than half of the states there has been no appellate right-to-die case, and thus no opportunity for the courts of those states to adhere to or dissent from the consensus, further illustrates its potential tenuousness. Nonetheless, the consensus is so well accepted in clinical practice, and there is enough momentum in the courts and legislatures, that it is reasonable to assume that, barring any unforeseeable difficulties, the consensus is likely to grow in strength and in explicit judicial acceptance in additional states.

However, consensus-building is a slow and incremental process. The consensus about the circumstances under which it is legitimate to forgo life-sustaining treatment has become as widely accepted as it is in no small part because it has found a receptive audience among judges, legislators, and the public at large, whose views lawmakers often reflect. But a consensus exists not merely when there is a majority; there must also be the absence of a significant opposition with strongly held views. The legal status of abortion is a good example. Although public opinion polls generally demonstrate that a majority favors the legalization of abortion, it would be straining the meaning of the word to say there is a consensus that abortion ought to be legal. And so it might be with the right to die. Although there has been little organized opposition, there are signs that the opposition is growing. Judging by public opinion polls, it is certainly a small minority, but judging from the intensity with which it holds its views, there is strong reason to suspect that its efforts, not merely to prevent the extension of the consensus to mercy killing and the termination of futile treatment, but to undermine the existing consensus about forgoing life-sustaining treatment, will continue to grow.

This opposition has already begun to manifest itself in right-to-die cases through the filing of *amicus curiae* briefs, intervention as a party, or representation of a party by "right to life" groups. More graphic illustrations of these efforts are a group of protectors who tried to enter the hospital room in which Nancy Cruzan was dying in order to reconnect her feeding tube, which had been disconnected with judicial permission, and the filing of lawsuits by Lawyers for Life, the Center for Christian Activism, and others seeking to have her feeding tube reconnected. There is no reason to assume that these efforts will abate. Indeed, to the extent that these efforts have come from groups that have long been connected with anti-abortion efforts, it is reasonable to assume that their efforts and strength in the right-to-die realm will grow.

Proponents of extending the consensus must be sure not to move too far too fast; they must be sure that they have a receptive audience in the court of public opinion; and they must be sure that there is not a substantial minority with strongly held views in opposition. Otherwise their efforts will do more to undermine the consensus than to perpetuate, strengthen, and augment it.

2 3

Are Laws Against Assisted Suicide Unconstitutional?

Yale Kamisar

On 15 February of this year [1993], shortly after the number of people Dr. Jack Kevorkian had helped to commit suicide swelled to fifteen, the Michigan legislature passed a law, effective that very day, making assisted suicide a felony punishable by up to four years in prison. The law, which is automatically repealed six months after a newly established commission on death and dying recommends permanent legislation, prohibits anyone with knowledge that another person intends to commit suicide from "intentionally provid[ing] the physical means" by which that other person does so or from "intentionally participat[ing] in a physical act" by which she does so.[1]

A two-thirds majority of each house was needed to give the new Michigan law immediate effect, but that requirement was easily met. The governor applauded the legislature and signed the law the same day. But this is not the end of the story. A week later, the American

Yale Kamisar is Clarence Darrow Distinguished University Professor at the University of Michigan Law School, Ann Arbor. His 1958 essay "Some Non-Religious Views Against Proposed 'Mercy-Killing' Legislation," published in the *Minnesota Law Review,* has been widely reprinted. This essay is reprinted by permission from the *Hastings Center Report* 23, no. 2 (May-June 1993).

Civil Liberties Union of Michigan brought a lawsuit on behalf of two cancer patients and several health-care professionals who specialize in the care of the terminally ill, attacking the law's constitutionality. The essence of the challenge is that insofar as the law prohibits a health professional, family member, or friend from assisting a competent, terminally ill person who wishes to hasten her death, the law violates the Due Process clauses of the state and federal constitutions and the "Right to Privacy Guarantee" of the state constitution.

If the Michigan supreme court overturns the prohibition against assisted suicide on state constitutional grounds, this particular lawsuit will come to an end. If, however, as I think likely, the state supreme court upholds the prohibition, the U.S. Supreme Court may decide to review the matter. Since approximately twenty-five states expressly prohibit assisted suicide by statute and another ten or twelve make some types of assisted suicide a form of murder or manslaughter,[2] the Supreme Court is likely to address the question in some case from some state, whether Michigan or another, in the near future.

In this article I shall discuss only *federal* constitutional arguments for invalidating laws against suicide, and why I believe these arguments will (and should) fail.

Is There a "Right" to Commit Suicide?

So far as I know, no state law makes either suicide or attempted suicide a crime. Why is this so, and what follows from this?

According to Dan Brock, who supports both physician-assisted suicide and voluntary active euthanasia, the fact "that suicide or attempted suicide is no longer a criminal offense in virtually all states indicates an *acceptance* of individual self-determination in the taking of one's own life analogous to that required for voluntary active euthanasia."[3] I am not sure what Professor Brock means by "acceptance"; it is an ambiguous term. In context, however, he seems to be viewing the fact that we no longer punish suicide or attempted suicide as *approval* of these acts, or at least as *recognition* that self-determination or autonomy extends this far—namely, that taking one's own life is a valid application or aspect of individual self-determination. If this is what he means, he is quite mistaken.

As the most comprehensive and most heavily documented law-review article ever written on the subject makes clear, abolition of such "punishments" as ignominious burial for suicide and then the decriminalization of both suicide and attempted suicide did not come about because suicide was deemed a "human right" or even because it was no longer considered reprehensible. These changes occurred, rather, because punishment was seen as unfair to innocent relatives of the suicide and because those who committed or attempted to commit the act were thought to be prompted by mental illness.[4]

Some of this thinking is reflected in the comments to the American Law Institute's Model Penal Code. The code does criminalize aiding or soliciting another to commit suicide, but not suicide itself or attempted suicide. Why not? "There is a certain moral extravagance in imposing criminal punishment on a person who has sought his own self-destruction . . . and who more properly requires medical or psychiatric attention."[5]

But sympathy and pity for the individual who attempts suicide "emphatically did not mean approval of the act," the law-review article points out. From colonial days through at least the 1970s, "the prominent attitude of society and the law has been one of opposition to suicide."[6]

The Model Penal Code's judgment that "there is no form of criminal punishment that is acceptable for a completed suicide and that criminal punishment is singularly inefficacious to deter attempts to commit suicide" does not mean that there is a "right" to commit the act. As Leon Kass has pointed out, the *capacity* to take one's life—"I have inclination, means, reasons, opportunity, and you cannot stop me, and it is not against the law"—does not establish the *right* to do so. Nor does it mean that one has "a *justified* claim against others that they act in a fitting manner."[7] As a practical matter, at least so long as they do not resort to physical violence, parents are "free" to treat their children unkindly, even cruelly. But few, if any, would say that a mother or father has a "right" to be a bad parent.

Society *can* do something about those who aid *another* to commit suicide—and it has. Throughout our history we have directed the force of the criminal law against aiding or assisting suicide. The commentary to the Model Penal Code notes that the fact that penal sanctions will not deter the suicide itself does not mean that the criminal law is equally powerless to influence the behavior of those who would aid or induce another to take his own life. Moreover, in principle it would seem that the interests in the sanctity of life that are represented by the criminal homicide laws are threatened by one who expresses a willingness to participate in taking the life of another, even though the act may be accomplished with the consent, or at the request, of the suicide victim.[8]

Another word about the Model Penal Code. In the memorable dictum of Oliver Wendell Holmes, "it is revolting to have no better reason for a rule of law than that so it was laid down in the time of Henry IV."[9] The quickest way to refute the belief not a few may hold that the reason for the criminal prohibition against assisted suicide falls into Holmes's category is to point to the position taken by the code. Its final "Official Draft" was the product of many years of research, deliberation, drafting, and revising by the most eminent criminal-law scholars of the 1950s and 1960s, led by Herbert Wechsler of Columbia University and Louis B. Schwartz of the University of Pennsylvania. To quote a leading scholar of the present day, the code "has become the principal text in criminal law teaching, the point of departure for criminal law scholarship, and the greatest single influence on the many new state codes that have followed in its wake."[10]

The Model Code's reporters considered the argument that the criminality of assisted suicide should turn upon "the presence of a selfish motive" (a position supported by one of its special consultants, England's Glanville Williams), but concluded that "the wiser course is to maintain the prohibition and rely on mitigation in the sentence when the ground for it appears."[11] With the stimulus of the Model Code, in the next decade and a half, eight states passed new laws specifically prohibiting assisted suicide and eleven other jurisdictions revised their existing statutes.[12]

Does the "Right to Die" Include Assisted Suicide?

As a rallying cry, the "right to die" is hard to beat. But it is much easier to chant a slogan than to apply it to specific situations. Most would consider the refusal of lifesaving medical procedures under certain circumstances (such as terminal illness and severe pain) an apt illustration of the right to die. But the term has also been used loosely and broadly to embrace such claims as the right to another's help in committing suicide and the right to authorize another to engage in active euthanasia.

Many proponents of the "right to die" are quick to point out that the "sanctity of life" is not an absolute or unqualified value (and they are right), but they are slow to realize that the same is true of the "right to die." There is no general or absolute right to die. The only right or liberty that the Karen Ann Quinlan case and subsequent so-called right-to-die rulings have established is the right under certain circumstances to be disconnected from artificial life-support systems or, as many have called it, the right to die *a natural death*. . . . The *Quinlan* court specifically distinguished between committing or assisting in a suicide and what it called "the ending of artificial life support systems"—the only issue presented.[13] . . .

The one "right to die" case that rivals *Quinlan* for prominence is the 1990 Nancy Beth Cruzan decision . . . by the U.S. Supreme Court. As did *Quinlan*, the *Cruzan* case involved the right to end artificial life support, and it too provides no comfort to proponents of a constitutional right to assisted suicide.

The *Cruzan* Court sustained a state's power to keep alive, over her family's objections, an incompetent patient who had not left clear instructions for ending life-sustaining treatment. In the course of rejecting the efforts of Ms. Cruzan's parents to terminate her artificial feeding, Chief Justice Rehnquist, who spoke for five members of the Court, pointed out that a state has an undeniable interest in the protection and preservation of human life—even the life of a person in a persistent vegetative state. The chief justice supported this assertion by noting that "the majority of states in this country have laws imposing criminal penalties on one who assists another to commit suicide."[14]

If a majority of the Supreme Court meant to suggest that laws against assisted suicide are constitutionally suspect, it chose a strange way of doing so. The chief justice "assumed for purposes of this case" that a competent person does have "a constitutionally protected right to refuse lifesaving hydration and nutrition." But he declined to characterize it as a "fundamental right," a designation that requires a state to offer a compelling justification for the right's restriction (a test the state can rarely satisfy). He called the right instead a Fourteenth Amendment liberty interest: "Although many state courts have held that a right to refuse treatment is encompassed by a generalized constitutional right of privacy, we have never so held. We believe this issue is more properly analyzed in terms of a Fourteenth Amendment liberty interest."

"By avoiding 'fundamental right' language," comments John Robertson, "the Court may implicitly allow states to restrict the 'liberty interest' upon a lesser showing of need than it would require if that interest were characterized as a fundamental right." Perhaps "any reasonable state interest" would justify state interference with that liberty, "or at least one which did not impose an 'undue burden.'"15

Of course, the Court did not suggest that one has even so much as "a Fourteenth Amendment liberty interest" in assisted suicide, and I cannot believe that it will do so in the foreseeable future. If I am right, the Court in assessing the constitutionality of a ban against assisted suicide would give great deference to the state legislature; if it furthered some coherent conception of the public good, that would probably suffice.

The *Cruzan* case is hardly the Court's last word on death, dying, termination of life support, assisted suicide, and euthanasia. The principles lurking in this area will be brought into sharper focus only by new prodding of the facts of new cases and by taking a fresh look, each time, at the overall problem. If *Cruzan* demonstrates anything, however, I think it signals the reluctance of the High Court to "constitutionalize" an area marked by divisive social and legal debate and its inclination to defer instead to the states' judgments in this difficult field.16 A Court that refused to "constitutionalize" a "right to die" broad enough to uphold the rights of the Cruzan family is hardly likely to "constitutionalize" a right to assisted suicide.

Justice Scalia's Opinion

We should not forget that there was one justice in the *Cruzan* case who did equate the termination of life support with "ordinary" suicide —Antonin Scalia. Although his lone concurring opinion was more or less ignored by the other justices, it should not go unnoticed.

Justice Scalia maintained that for constitutional purposes "there is nothing distinctive about accepting death through the refusal of 'medical treatment,' as opposed to accepting it through the refusal of [natural] food, or through the failure to shut off the engine and get out of the car after work." As he viewed the case, the request by Nancy Cruzan's parents to terminate their daughter's artificial feeding and hydration was, in effect, the assertion of a "right to suicide."

But Justice Scalia is well aware that "on the question you ask depends the answer you get." A principal reason, surely, why he framed the question the way he did was his confidence that there was no way a majority of the Court would recognize a constitutional right to commit suicide. And nothing any of the other eight justices said suggests that Scalia's confidence was unfounded.

In fact, the other justices did not *say* anything about a "right to suicide." None of them disputed Scalia's point "that American law has always accorded the State the power to prevent, by force if necessary, suicide." Nor did any of them disagree that "there is no significant support for the claim that a right to suicide is so rooted in our tradition that it may be deemed 'fundamental' or 'implicit in the concept of ordered liberty.'" As Louis Seidman remarks, the *Cruzan* dissenters "carefully avoid any claim that state suicide statutes are unconstitutional—a reticence that Justice Scalia powerfully exploits in his concurring opinion."[17] This is a reticence, I might add, that does not bode well for proponents of a constitutional right to assisted suicide.

Although none of Justice Scalia's colleagues responded in so many words to his argument that the termination of lifesaving medical treatment constitutes suicide, they responded nevertheless. They all framed the question in terms of a right to refuse or to be free from "unwanted medical treatment" or, more specifically, "unwanted artificial nutrition and hydration." *As a matter of logic,* I think there is a good deal to be said for analogizing a patient's termination of life-sustaining medical treatment to "ordinary" suicide. But law is not entirely a syllogism.

It may be helpful to view the *Cruzan* case as involving two competing traditions.[18] One is the common-law right to refuse medical treatment, even lifesaving surgery; in the language of the Court, "the logical corollary of the doctrine of informed consent," a doctrine "firmly entrenched in American tort law," is the right *not* to consent, that is, to reject treatment. The other tradition, which has continued to exist alongside the first one, is the anti-suicide tradition, as evidenced by society's discouragement of suicide and attempted suicide and by the many criminal laws against assisted suicide.

In *Cruzan,* a majority, perhaps as many as eight justices, evidently decided that the termination of artificial nutrition and hydration was more consistent with the rationale of the cases upholding the right to refuse treatment; so far as we can tell, only Justice Scalia believed it implicated concerns underlying the anti-suicide tradition.

Assisted Suicide vs. Active Voluntary Euthanasia

The line between doctor-assisted suicide and physician-administered voluntary euthanasia is a fine one that is often blurred. Voluntary euthanasia "has been variously described as 'assisted suicide' or 'within the knife's edge between suicide and murder,'" and suicide has sometimes been called "self-administered euthanasia."[19]

Doctor-assisted suicide is not quite active voluntary euthanasia, for the final act, the one that brings on death, is performed by the patient herself, not her doctor. But suppose the patient is not able to swallow the barbiturates that will bring about death or lacks the physical capacity to trigger a suicide machine? If the right to control the time and manner of one's death—the right to shape one's death in the most humane and dignified manner one can—is well founded, how can it be denied to someone simply because she is unable to perform the final act by herself? Although there is a "mechanical" distinction between assisted suicide and euthanasia, is it not a distinction without a difference?

Yes, answered the late Joseph Fletcher, who advocated active euthanasia for some fifty years. As he viewed the matter, "It is impossible to separate [active voluntary euthanasia] from suicide; it is, indeed, a form of suicide," and the case for active voluntary euthanasia "depends upon the case for the righteousness of suicide." James Rachels, author of a famous assault on the distinction between "killing" and "letting die," similarly maintains that "the permissibility of euthanasia follows from the permissibility of suicide—a result that will probably not surprise any thoughtful person."[20]

That may be, but it is a result some thoughtful persons have strongly resisted. Thus, in his new book [*Death and Dignity,* 1993; excerpts are included in this volume], Dr. Timothy Quill comes out in favor of physician-assisted suicide but balks at active voluntary euthanasia. He does not support euthanasia because of the "potential for abuse" and because "it puts the physician in a very powerful position," whereas in the case of doctor-assisted suicide "the balance of power between doctor and patient is more nearly equal."[21]

I find this reasoning more conclusory than explanatory. Dr. Quill would require many safeguards for doctor-assisted suicide (the patient must freely, clearly, and repeatedly ask to die; her judgment must not be distorted; the physician must make sure that the patient's suffering and request are not the product of inadequate comfort care). If, as he believes, these safeguards would greatly reduce the risk of abuse and render the balance of power between doctor and patient relatively equal, why would they not achieve the same results for voluntary euthanasia? Conversely, if, even when all the safeguards Quill proposes are in place, it would still be imprudent to legalize active voluntary euthanasia, why is it safe to sanction assisted suicide?

Quill recognizes that "access to medical care in the United States is too inequitable and many doctor-patient relationships too impersonal to tolerate the risks of condoning active voluntary euthanasia."[22] But why can't the very same thing be said about tolerating the risks of condoning assisted suicide?

I find it difficult to avoid the conclusion that Dr. Quill's position is colored by the fact, as he notes, that "unlike assisted suicide, where the legal implications have yet to be fully clarified, euthanasia is illegal in all states in the United States and likely to be vigorously prosecuted."[23] Dr. Quill and I disagree about a number of things. But I venture to say we are in agreement on one: the uniform ban against active euthanasia is not going to be struck down on the ground that it violates the "right to die." Therefore, a proponent of the right to assisted suicide is understandably likely to put as much distance as possible between that concept and euthanasia.

Although he would not legalize voluntary euthanasia, at least not at this time, Dr. Quill does consider it "an area worthy of our serious consideration, since it would allow patients who have exhausted all other reasonable options to choose death rather than continue suffering."[24] I make bold to say that voluntary euthanasia would receive *very* serious consideration once assisted suicide were legalized or as soon as the Supreme Court established a constitutional right to commit "rational" suicide.

Although I am opposed to both assisted suicide and voluntary euthanasia, I find the position of Professor Brock (who supports both practices) more coherent and more principled than Dr. Quill's:

> In both [assisted suicide and voluntary euthanasia], the choice rests fully with the patient. In both [cases] the patient acts last in the sense of the right to change his or her mind until the point at which the lethal process becomes irreversible. . . .
>
> If there is no significant, intrinsic moral difference between the two, it is difficult to see why public or legal policy should permit one but not the other; worries about abuse or about giving anyone dominion over the lives of others apply equally well to either.[25]

The fine distinction between assisted suicide and voluntary euthanasia was blurred by the hard-fought campaigns in Washington (1991) and California (1992) to legalize "aid-in-dying," a label covering *both* assisted suicide and voluntary euthanasia. I watched both campaigns very closely and came away with the distinct impression that few, if any, understood the distinction between the two practices, paid any attention to it, or cared one whit about it. . . .

Can the "Right" Be Confined to the Terminally Ill?

No doubt the ACLU, in challenging the constitutionality of the Michigan prohibition against assisted suicide, will frame the issue narrowly; it will emphasize that it is only asserting the rights of the *terminally ill* who may desire death by suicide. But is there any principled way so to limit the right?

Of course, it is good advocacy to frame the issue in terms of the rights of the "dying" or "terminally ill," but what reason (other than those of tactics) can be advanced for this position? If the merciful termination of suffering (or termination of an unendurable existence) is the basis for this right, why limit it to those who are terminally ill? . . .

It is interesting to note that, although he carefully circumscribes the right to assisted suicide in many respects, Dr. Quill would not limit it to the terminally ill. "The patient must have a condition," Quill tells us, "that is incurable, and associated with severe, unrelenting suffering." Though he anticipates that most people who desire physician-assisted suicide "will be imminently terminal," Quill does "not want to arbitrarily exclude persons with incurable, but not imminently terminal, progressive illnesses such as ALS [amyotrophic lateral sclerosis] or multiple sclerosis."[26] But is it any less arbitrary to exclude the quadriplegic? The victim of a paralytic stroke? The mangled survivor of a road accident? A person afflicted with severe arthritis?

Why stop there? If a competent person comes to the unhappy conclusion that his existence is unbearable and freely, clearly, and repeatedly requests assisted suicide, why should he be rebuffed because he does not "qualify" under somebody else's standards? Isn't *this* an arbitrary limitation of self-determination and personal autonomy? "How," asks Daniel Callahan, "can self-determination have any limits? Why are not the personal desires or motives, whatever they may be, sufficient?"[27]

As I understand the position of those advocating a constitutional right to suicide and to assisted suicide, a person who "qualifies" should have the same right to enlist the aid of others to die by suicide as one now has to withhold or withdraw life-sustaining medical treatment.[28] If so, it is fairly clear that once established, the right to suicide will not be restricted to the terminally ill. For as demonstrated by such decisions as *Elizabeth Bouvia,* a case involving a young woman with severe cerebral palsy who was not terminally ill, and *Larry McAfee,* a case involving a quadriplegic who apparently had a long life expectancy, the right to terminate life support has not been so limited. Indeed, the view that life support cannot be stopped unless a patient is terminally ill—a notion that may have originated in the pre-*Quinlan* cases involving the refusal of blood transfusions by Jehovah's Witnesses—is one of the "myths" that Professor Alan Meisel has recently dispelled.[29]

Widening the Scope

I share the view that before a state can punish its citizens for their actions, "it must do more than assert that the choice they have made is an 'abominable crime not fit to be named among Christians.'" I agree, too, that "the fact that the governing majority in a State has traditionally viewed a particular practice as immoral is not a sufficient reason for upholding a law prohibiting the practice."[30] But I believe that any state that prohibits assisted suicide can advance justifications for its legislation that go well beyond the law's conformity to religious doctrine or "morality." And I think these justifications are sufficiently strong to withstand constitutional attack.

I am well aware that the reasons I shall set forth for upholding "the new Michigan law" and similar laws were not the *original* reasons for condemning suicide and attempted suicide. But the new "good reasons" people give for old rules and policies "do influence the development of these policies," and "the 'good reasons' professed by our fathers yesterday are among the real reasons of the life of today." Assigning better reasons for the ban against assisted suicide than the old religious taboo against touching the gates of life and death may be dismissed by some as a process of rationalization, "but the seeking for good reasons . . . plays a leading role in the life of civilization."[31]

After all, that the criminal law arose to fill the need to regulate self-help and to obviate private vengeance does not render deterrence, incapacitation, and rehabilitation any less of a "real reason" for drafting new criminal codes or revising old ones.

Philosophers have spent much time and effort addressing such questions as, When, if ever, is it "rational" for a person to want to commit suicide? Is there a moral right to commit "rational" suicide? But I think a legislator considering the desirability of a law prohibiting assisted suicide and a judge determining the constitutionality of such a law could ask more relevant questions, such as: So far as we can tell, how common or rare is "rational" suicide? How often does suicide occur in the absence of a psychiatric disorder? How often do primary-care physicians fail to recognize treatable depression in their patients, especially elderly patients? How often is the failure of a primary-care physician to take an aggressive approach to pain management or to recognize or adequately treat depressive illness influenced by prejudice against and stereotypes about elderly people? How likely is it that the social sanctioning of "rational" suicide and assisted suicide will lead to an increase in "irrational" suicide and assisted suicide? In a suicide-permissive society, how often will the "right" to enlist the assistance of others in this enterprise be interpreted, especially by the most vulnerable, as the "duty" to do so? In a suicide-permissive society, how often will a burdensome, elderly relative not otherwise desirous of death be "helped along" or pressured or "manipulated" into suicide?

At one point in his argument for a constitutional right to suicide (and for the corollary right to enjoin government agents from taking steps to prevent suicide), Alan Sullivan disposes of a possible objection to his position—"that one suicide might encourage other suicides and ought, for that reason, to be proscribed"—on the ground that "it rests upon psychological assumptions about the suicidal character that are beyond the scope of this essay."[32] When writing about various subjects I too have put some issues "beyond the scope of this essay." After all, there is only so much time and space to explore a difficult problem (or a cluster of problems). So Mr. Sullivan's decision is understandable, especially when one keeps in mind that suicide is a complicated subject that cuts across many disciplines.

But a court assessing the constitutionality of a criminal prohibition against assisted suicide does not have the same luxury. It cannot put psychological assumptions and insights and "psychological autopsy" studies of persons who die by suicide "beyond the scope" of their inquiries. Such a court must do more, much more, than simply reason by analogy from the relevant precedents on the books. And such a court must keep in mind that it is doing something quite different from simply judging a debate among philosophers. As Professor Philip Devine has observed:

> If philosophers have something to say to the law, so also has the law something to say to philosophers. Attention to the working, or the possible working, of any institution or principle may well give us insight into weaknesses which remain concealed so long as it is posed in sufficiently abstract terms.[33]

Dangers of Establishing a "Right" to Assisted Suicide

Suicide is a problem of considerable magnitude. Although it once ranked twenty-second on the list of causes of death in the United States, it now ranks (depending on the particular year) eighth or ninth. Every year there are between 25,000 and 30,000 reported cases of suicide (and the number of cases is probably grossly under-reported both because of the social stigma that attaches and because of the possible loss of life-insurance benefits). Moreover, it is estimated that every year in this country several hundred thousand people *attempt* suicide and that about 10 per cent of that group go on to kill themselves within ten years. Although suicide occurs at an alarming rate among young people—adolescent suicide in this country increased 300 per cent between 1955 and 1975, while suicides in the 15-to-24 age group now constitute one-fifth of all reported suicides—the highest suicide rates and greatest number of suicides are found among people over the age of fifty. Indeed, for American white males, from childhood on, the risk of suicide rises linearly with age until the eighth decade of life. Suicides by people over the age of 60 account for about 25 per cent of all suicides.[34]

No doubt the higher rate of suicide among the elderly has led advocates of the right to "rational" suicide and to assisted suicide to focus on this age group, especially on elderly people who are terminally ill. But the problem of suicide is a good deal more complicated. Consider the views of Herbert Hendin, a professor of psychology and a leading suicidologist, who is opposed to the legalization of doctor-assisted suicide. [An essay by Hendin appears in this volume.] He concedes that it is sometimes "rational" for a person with a painful terminal illness to wish to end his life. Indeed, "that is precisely why supporters of the 'right to suicide' or 'death control' position are constantly presenting the case of a patient suffering from incurable, painful cancer as the case on which they based their argument." But Dr. Hendin is quick to add:

> In reality . . . such understandable cases form only a small percentage of all suicides, or potential suicides. The majority of suicides confront us with the problem of understanding people whose situation does not seem, from an outsider's viewpoint, hopeless or often even critical. The knowledge that there are more suicides by people who wrongly believe themselves to be suffering from cancer than there are suicides by those who actually have cancer puts the problem in some perspective.[35]

According to suicidologist David Clark, "the major studies all agree in showing that the fraction of suicide victims struggling with terminal illness at the time of their death is in the range of 2 per cent to 4 per cent." Two-thirds of those who died by suicide when they were in their late sixties, seventies, and eighties "were in relatively good physical health."[36]

To ask another relevant question, how often does suicide occur in the absence of a major psychiatric illness? It would not be surprising if the answer to this question were affected by what one thought about the "right" to commit suicide. Some believe that virtually every person who wishes to die by suicide is "mentally ill." Others maintain that such a person is simply called mentally ill so that his behavior may be controlled. Nevertheless, one cannot ignore the studies that do seem to bear on this question. And when one dips into the relevant literature one discovers considerable authority for the view that a suicide rarely occurs in the absence of a major psychiatric disorder.

Two of Timothy Quill's colleagues on the University of Rochester medical faculty, Yeates Conwell and Eric Caine, geriatric psychiatrists who "work with suicidal people every day," warn that "notably lacking" from the debate about "rational" suicide and physician-assisted suicide is "attention to the effects of psychiatric illness on rational decision making." They point to suicide study findings that "90 to 100 per cent of the victims die while they have a diagnosable psychiatric illness, an observation that is equally true in suicides among the elderly."[37] A number of other commentators use similarly high figures.

The most commonly cited disorders associated with suicide are depressive affective disorders, also called "depressive illness" or "major depression," a verifiable and diagnosable condition that is usually responsive to prompt treatment. One aspect of major depression, a feeling of hopelessness (which is transient and likely to respond to treatment), appears to be the most probable and frequent source of the impairment that often leads to suicide.

More significant for our purposes, I think, than the prevalence of depressive illness among people who die by suicide is the inability of depressed persons to recognize the severity of their own symptoms and the failure of primary physicians to detect major depression in their patients, especially elderly patients. As Conwell and Caine emphasize:

[M]any doctors on the front lines, who would be responsible for implementing any policy that allowed assisted suicide, are ill equipped to assess the presence and effect of depressive illness in older patients. In the absence of sophisticated understanding, the determination of a suicidal patient's "rationality" can be no more than speculation, subject to the influence of personal biases about aging, old age, and the psychological effects of chronic disease.[38]

"Ageism"—the prejudices and stereotypes applied to the elderly solely on the basis of their age—may manifest itself in a failure to recognize treatable depression, a refusal to take an aggressive approach to pain management, the view that an elderly person's desire to commit suicide is more "rational" than a younger patient's would be. As sociologist Menno Boldt has observed, "Suicidal persons are succumbing to what they experience as an overpowering and unrelenting coercion in their environment to cease living. This sense of coercion takes many familiar forms: fear, isolation, abuse, uselessness, and so on."[39]

Will these pressures intensify in a society that sanctions assisted suicide (and thereby suicide as well)? In a suicide-permissive society, will family members so inclined be more likely to alter or manipulate a sick, elderly person's circumstances (for example, by providing shoddy or even hostile care) so that suicide becomes a reasonable, even an attractive choice?

In a climate in which suicide is the "rational" thing to do, or at least a "reasonable" option, will it become the unreasonable thing *not* to do? The noble thing *to* do?[40] In a suicide-permissive society plagued by shortages of various kinds and a growing population of "non-productive" people, how likely is it that an old or ill person will be encouraged to spare both herself and her family the agony of a slow decline, even though she would not have considered suicide on her own?

The best discussion of both circumstantial manipulation and ideological manipulation appears in a famous essay by the philosopher Margaret Battin, who, ironically, is a proponent of rational suicide. [An essay by Battin appears in this volume.] In an all-too-rare display of open-minded, balanced scholarship, Professor Battin presents a strong case against her own ultimate position. She conscientiously spells out how acceptance of her views would open the way for both individual and societal manipulation of vulnerable people into choosing death by suicide when they would not otherwise have done so. She concludes, nevertheless, that "on moral grounds we must accept, not reject, the notion of rational suicide."[41]

A state legislature is free to agree with Professor Battin, but must it? Is it constitutionally required to do so? I hardly think so. I believe a legislature is free to give Battin's insights about "manipulated suicide" more weight than she herself seems willing to do; that is one of the risks, if one may call it that, one takes when one produces the kind of high-quality scholarship she does.

Professor Battin may be saying something else; she may be conceding that the dangers of "manipulated suicide" *are* quite substantial, but they are *trumped* by one's "fundamental right" to die by suicide. At one point she maintains that we cannot deny "individuals in intolerable and irremediable circumstances their *fundamental right* to die." Whether there *is* a "fundamental right" is the question, not the answer. I don't know how those of us who are not religious can get an authoritative ruling on whether *morally* there is a "fundamental right" to choose death by suicide. But I think I do know that *legally* there is no such right. As we have seen, a decade after Professor Battin wrote her provocative essay, the *Cruzan* Court declined to accord the much less controversial liberty to terminate life-sustaining treatment "fundamental right" status.

Although she is painfully aware of the "moral quicksand" into which the notion of rational suicide "threatens to lead us," Professor Battin hopes that if we accept that concept, "perhaps then we may discover a path around the quicksand." Perhaps. Perhaps not. In any event, I submit, the Constitution does not prevent a legislature from reaching the conclusion that there is no safe path around.

Some Final Thoughts

What has been said of voluntary active euthanasia applies as well, I believe, to assisted suicide. As Martin Marty and Ron Hamel have pointed out, "We are not merely a collection of isolated, self-determining individuals." It is unrealistic to think that we can sanction assisted suicide without having an impact upon "the various communities of which they are a part, and even society as a whole."[42]

I am willing to concede that the line between withholding or withdrawing life-sustaining medical treatment (what they call passive euthanasia) and "ordinary" suicide and assisted suicide is not a neat, logical line. But what line is? Surely not the line between assisted suicide and voluntary active euthanasia. Nor the line between the right of a terminally ill person to enlist the assistance of others in committing suicide and the right of a quadriplegic to seek similar assistance, or the right of a person who finds her inability even to shift position in her wheelchair intolerable, or the right of a person with a progressive illness.

I cannot believe that any court will recognize a constitutional right to suicide on request. But unless we carry the principle of self-determination or personal autonomy to its logical extreme—assisted suicide for any competent person who clearly and repeatedly requests it for *any* reason *she* deems appropriate—we have to find a "stopping point" somewhere along the way. Any such stopping point will be somewhat illogical, somewhat arbitrary. So why not maintain the line we have now?

Albert Alschuler, my counterpart at the University of Chicago Law School, recently declared: "[T]he strongest argument for the action-inaction line is that, despite its indeterminacy and imprecision, we need it. We have no other line, and without it we sense no limits." Professor Alschuler may have overstated the case, but not, I think, by very much. Why step across "the historic divide" only to draw another somewhat illogical, somewhat arbitrary line somewhere else? "[I]t is easier to move further down the slope than to climb back up."[43]

In this article I have been focusing on the constitutional dimensions of the right to shape one's death. Thus, I do not have to argue that a state ought not to cross the historic divide (although I would); I need only argue that it is not constitutionally compelled to do so. . . .

24

The Constitution and
Hastening Inevitable Death

Robert A. Sedler

Michigan's ban on assisted suicide imposes an "undue burden" on what I maintain is the constitutionally protected right of terminally ill patients to hasten inevitable death. In making this argument, I frame the issue differently from opponents of assisted suicide, as, for example, Professor Yale Kamisar's contention . . . [reprinted in this volume] that laws prohibiting assisted suicide do not violate the U.S. Constitution.

A distinguished constitutional scholar has observed, "Once taken into our constitutional system, the dialogue takes on a new seriousness. It is, therefore, critically important that we get the questions right and the answers right, because constitutional law is written in concrete and is not easily washed out by rain or tears."[1] As regards the challenge by the American Civil Liberties Union to Michigan's ban on assisted suicide, the "right question" is not, I would submit, whether there is a constitutional "right to assisted suicide" or a

Robert A. Sedler is a professor of law at Wayne State University, Detroit, Michigan, and a volunteer attorney for the ACLU of Michigan. He helped to formulate and litigate the ACLU's challenge to the state's ban on assisted suicide. This essay is reprinted by permission from the *Hastings Center Report* 23, no. 5 (September-October 1993).

constitutional "right to die." Rather, the right question, framed in the context of this particular constitutional challenge, is whether an absolute ban on the use of physician-prescribed medications by a terminally ill person to hasten that person's inevitable death, *if and when the person chooses to do so,* is an "undue burden" on the person's "liberty" interest protected by the Fourteenth Amendment's Due Process clause, and so is unconstitutional.

As in many constitutional cases, an understanding of the basis of the ACLU challenge must begin by looking at the people who are bringing the challenge and at how the ban affects what it is that they want to do. The ACLU did not bring the constitutional challenge to the law on behalf of Dr. Jack Kevorkian (by tacit mutual agreement the ACLU and Dr. Kevorkian have kept at some considerable distance from each other), on behalf of proponents of "voluntary euthanasia," or on behalf of non-terminally-ill persons who wish to terminate an "unbearable existence." The principal plaintiffs in the case are terminally ill cancer patients who want to have the *choice* to hasten their inevitable death by taking a lethal dose of physician-prescribed medications, and physicians who want to prescribe medications so that their patients will have this choice. The physician plaintiffs do *not* want to give lethal injections to terminally ill patients or perform voluntary euthanasia in any way whatsoever, and the patient plaintiffs do not want to have their lives ended by means of lethal injections.

What the patient and physician plaintiffs do want to provide is *patient empowerment* to hasten inevitable death. The physicians want to be permitted, when they consider this to be medically appropriate, to provide their patients with barbiturates, opiates, and other medications in sufficient quantities that the patients may, at any time of their own choosing, immediately terminate their lives by consuming a lethal dosage. In this respect, patient empowerment encompasses both pain control and the hastening of inevitable death. The patient takes the medications to relieve pain, but if the pain becomes so unbearable that he or she no longer wants to continue living with it, the patient can "take the whole bottle," so to speak, and bring the suffering to a merciful end.

Unlike Dr. Kevorkian's assisted suicides, and unlike voluntary euthanasia, patient empowerment means that there is no physician intervention at the time of death, and that the physician is not directly involved with the patient's death at all. There are no "suicide ma-chines" or television cameras. There is no appointed time at which the physician comes to the patient's home or hospital room to admin-ister the lethal injection. Everything is entirely in the patient's control. Only the patient, or family members or friends if the patient so chooses, will know of the patient's decision before it is carried out. The only sign of death is the empty bottle. The patient herself has determined the *timing* of her inevitable death and of her release from unbearable pain and suffering.

I would further submit that once the right of terminally ill patients to hasten their inevitable death by the use of physician-prescribed medications is firmly established as a matter of constitutional law, much of the controversy over assisted suicide may dissipate by its own force. At least the controversy will no longer involve the terminally ill. . . . There will no longer be any need for Dr. Kevorkian and his suicide machine. And there may not even be a need for voluntary euthanasia. A terminally ill patient will be able to obtain the necessary quantity of lethal medications from his or her physician, and if a particular physician refuses to prescribe them, the patient can simply find another physician. If I am correct in this contention, then the controversy over assisted suicide, at least as regards terminally ill patients, may well have been superseded by the constitutional recog-nition of patient empowerment to hasten inevitable death.

The Problem in Michigan

The problem for doctors and patients in Michigan, however, is that the Michigan legislature has defined "assisted suicide" to *include* the prescription of lethal medications by a physician to a terminally ill patient for the purpose of enabling the patient to use the medications to hasten inevitable death. The law states that it does not apply "to pre-scribing, dispensing, or administering medications or procedures if the intent is to relieve pain or discomfort and not to cause death, even if the medication or procedure may hasten or increase the risk of death."[2] This means that if the physician prescribes lethal medications in sufficient quantities to cause death and instructs the patient how to use the medications for that purpose, the physician will be found to have the "intent to cause death," and so will be guilty of a violation of the law.

Indeed, the ban is more sweeping still. Under the law, no terminally ill person in Michigan, no matter how excruciating his or her pain and suffering, will be able to receive any assistance whatsoever, either from a physician or from a family member or friend, in implementing the decision to hasten death. Under the law, a person is guilty of "criminal assistance to suicide" if she "has knowledge that another person intends to commit or attempt to commit suicide and intentionally (a) provides the physical means by which the other person attempts or commits suicide or (b) participates in a physical act by which the other person attempts or commits suicide."[3] The only intent necessary for a violation of the law is the intent to "[provide] the physical means" or "[participate] in a physical act" with the "knowledge that another person intends to commit or attempt to commit suicide." *There need not be any intent that the other person commit suicide.* So, if a terminally ill person has told a spouse or friend "I sometimes wish I could die," and the spouse or friend responds to a request for a glass of water that the terminally ill person uses to swallow a lethal dose of medication, the spouse or friend is guilty of violating the law. Furnishing the "physical means" with the knowledge that a person has "threatened suicide" is sufficient to subject the spouse or friend to up to four years' imprisonment.

Opponents of assisted suicide agree with this result. Professor Kamisar, for example, insists that a ban on assisted suicide should properly extend even to the terminally ill. This is because, he says, there is no principled way to distinguish for constitutional purposes between the terminally ill and others who desire "death by suicide."

Who Are the "Terminally Ill"?

I will respond to Professor Kamisar's "constitutional identity" argument shortly. But "constitutional identity" aside, in the real world we have no difficulty identifying and distinguishing the terminally ill. They are patients who will die from a specific disease within a relatively short period of time. Their medical treatment is limited to alleviating their pain, and the only thing that is not certain is the precise point in time when their death will occur. They thus constitute a distinct and identifiable class of persons, clearly separate from all other persons who might seek "death by suicide."

I find it appalling that the pejorative label "suicide" would be put on a terminally ill person's choice to hasten his or her inevitable death. . . . The term conjures up the image of a person jumping off a bridge or "blowing his brains out." The terminally ill person who is facing death is not "committing suicide" by ending a life that otherwise is of indefinite duration. That person's life is coming to an end, and the question is whether he or she must undergo unbearable suffering until death comes "naturally" or can choose to end the suffering by the use of physician-prescribed medications.

Professor Kamisar does not say very much about the terminally ill, emphasizing instead that most people who commit suicide are in fact not terminally ill.[4] He, along with most other opponents of "assisted suicide," is rather uncomfortable when talking about the terminally ill and so quickly brushes them off. Opponents of assisted suicide then start down the familiar slippery slope, suggesting that once we start allowing terminally ill people to hasten their inevitable death, we are but a few steps away from putting all "old and sick people" on the modern equivalent of an ice floe and ridding ourselves of the "inconvenience" of having to care for them.[5]

Because he wishes to ignore the terminally ill to the extent possible, Professor Kamisar says that the ACLU is simply engaging in "good advocacy" tactics when it restricts its challenge to the terminally ill. As I have explained above, the ACLU challenge to Michigan's assisted-suicide ban involves only the constitutionality of that ban as applied to terminally ill people. . . . The challenge is not to the law's general prohibition against assisted suicide—the plaintiffs do not care about a ban on Dr. Kevorkian's suicide machine or a ban on physician-administered lethal injections—but only to the ban on physician-prescribed medications that would empower terminally ill people to hasten their inevitable death.

For this reason, the constitutional issue presented in the ACLU challenge is relatively narrow and quite specific. It is also the issue that opponents of assisted suicide find the most troubling, because they cannot give any justification, moral or otherwise, for requiring terminally ill people to continue to undergo unbearable pain and suffering and for denying them the right to hasten their inevitable death. Rather than invoke the specter of the slippery slope, justification of the ban on its merits might begin with an admission that opponents of assisted suicide affirmatively do want to prohibit terminally ill people from using physician-prescribed medications to hasten their inevitable death.

Litigation in the U.S. Constitutional System

The fact that the issue presented in the ACLU challenge to Michigan's ban on assisted suicide is quite specific is not simply good advocacy tactics. Nor is it "the technique of overcoming opposition to a desired goal by proceeding step by step."[6] *It is the way that constitutional issues are supposed to be litigated in the American constitutional system.*

In the American system, constitutional law develops in a "line of growth," on a case-by-case, issue-by-issue basis. Indeed, it is a fundamental principle of constitutional adjudication that "constitutional issues will not be determined in broader terms than are required by the precise facts to which the ruling is to be applied."[7] The meaning of a constitutional provision develops incrementally, and that provision's line of growth strongly influences its application in particular cases.[8]

The line of growth of constitutional doctrine is clearly illustrated by the development of constitutional protection of a woman's right to have an abortion. This protection of abortion is part of the constitutional protection afforded to the broader interest of reproductive freedom, which in turn is a part of the even broader "liberty" interest that is textually protected by the Fourteenth Amendment's Due Process clause. The constitutional protection of reproductive freedom as a due-process liberty interest traces back to a 1942 Supreme Court decision holding unconstitutional the "discriminatory" sterilization of convicted felons.[9] The concept of reproductive freedom as a "fundamental right," first recognized by the Court in that case, was later invoked by the Court to hold unconstitutional a ban on the use of contraceptives by married couples,[10] and then a ban on access to contraceptives by unmarried persons.[11] So when, in the 1973 case of *Roe v. Wade,*[12] the Court had to confront the constitutionality of anti-abortion laws, reproductive freedom had already been established as a fundamental right, and the question before the Court was whether the state's interest in protecting potential human life was "sufficiently compelling" to justify a prohibition on a pregnant woman's entitlement to a medical abortion. The Court held that it was not "sufficiently compelling" prior to the stage of viability, and so in effect held that a woman had a "constitutional right" to an abortion.[13]

We see then how constitutional doctrine develops incrementally, case by case, issue by issue. The ACLU's constitutional challenge to Michigan's assisted-suicide ban thus does not involve a claimed "right to assisted suicide" or a claimed "right to die." It involves the specific question of whether the "liberty" protected by the Fourteenth Amendment's Due Process clause embraces the right of a terminally ill person to hasten inevitable death, and if so, whether Michigan's absolute ban on the use of physician-prescribed medications to hasten inevitable death is unconstitutional as imposing an "undue burden" on that right. In actual constitutional litigation, that issue must be confronted directly with reference to applicable constitutional doctrine and the Court's precedents, and it cannot be avoided by slippery-slope and "but what if" kinds of arguments. While such arguments may be appropriate for academic and political discourse, they have no place in constitutional litigation and cannot be relied on to avoid confronting the specific constitutional issue presented in the case before the court.

The Constitutional Argument

Let me now summarize the constitutional argument on the specific issue that is presented in the ACLU challenge. The first part of the argument is that the "liberty" protected by the Fourteenth Amendment's Due Process clause embraces the right of a terminally ill person to hasten inevitable death. Here we argue that the essence of the "liberty" protected by the Due Process clause is *personal autonomy*. This means that a person has the right to possess bodily integrity, to control his or her own body, and to define his or her own existence. As the Supreme Court stated in [*Planned Parenthood v.*] *Casey:*

It is a promise of the Constitution that there is a realm of personal liberty which the government may not enter. . . . It is settled now . . . that the Constitution places limits on a State's right to interfere with a person's most basic decisions about family and parenthood, as well as bodily integrity. . . . At the heart of liberty is the right to define one's own concept of existence, of [the] meaning of the universe, and of the mystery of human life. Beliefs about these matters could not define the attributes of personhood were they formed under compulsion of the State.[14]

A person's entitlement to bodily integrity and to control over his or her own body protects the right to refuse unwanted medical treatment, including the right of a competent adult to decide to discontinue lifesaving medical treatment.[15] It protects the right of a woman to have an abortion and the right of all persons to use contraception to prevent pregnancy. For the same reasons as people have a right to refuse unwanted medical treatment, to have an abortion, and to use contraception, we contend that a terminally ill person's right to control over his or her own body must include the right to make decisions about the voluntary termination of life. Thus, we contend that the decision of a terminally ill person to hasten inevitable death involves an important liberty interest that is protected by the Fourteenth Amendment's Due Process clause.

The second part of the argument is that an absolute ban on the use of physician-prescribed medications in poses an *undue burden* on the right of a terminally ill person to hasten inevitable death. This part of the argument is likewise based on the *Casey* decision, where the Supreme Court held that the state may not impose an undue burden on the exercise of a person's fundamental right to bodily integrity and control over his or her own body. In that case, the Court held that a law imposes an undue burden on the exercise of a woman's right to have an abortion when it places a substantial obstacle in the path of a woman seeking abortion of a non-viable fetus. Thus the government may not prohibit a woman from having an abortion prior to viability. Nor may it require notification to a married woman's husband of her intention, since the threat that her husband may commit an act of violence against her would effectively prevent a small number of women from deciding to have an abortion.

To say the least, a ban on the use of physician-prescribed medications places a substantial obstacle in the path of a terminally ill person seeking to hasten his or her inevitable death. Indeed, a more extreme burden on the exercise of that right cannot be imagined, and for this reason we contend that the ban on the use of physician-prescribed medications is unconstitutional.[16]

Self-Inflicted Deaths: All the Same?

Professor Kamisar, of course, does not address the constitutionality of a ban because he insists on the "constitutional identity" of all self-inflicted deaths; that is, he insists that for constitutional purposes there is no principled way to distinguish between terminally ill persons seeking to hasten their inevitable death and anybody else desiring "death by suicide." In arguing that any constitutional protection to a "right to die" does not include protection to a "right to assisted suicide," he says that there is a difference between the withholding or withdrawal of life-sustaining medical treatment and affirmatively committing suicide. This observation is true. But it is also completely irrelevant to resolving whether the right of terminally ill persons to hasten their inevitable death is a protected "liberty" interest under the Fourteenth Amendment's Due Process clause and whether an absolute ban on the use of physician-prescribed medications is an undue burden on the exercise of that right.

Rather, the resolution of these issues must take place with reference to constitutional doctrine relating to the right of personal autonomy. . . . Professor Kamisar does not explicate any principled difference, *in terms of the constitutional doctrine relating to the right of personal autonomy,* between the right of a competent terminally ill person to hasten inevitable death by refusing to continue life-sustaining medical treatment, and that person's right to hasten inevitable death by consuming physician-prescribed medications. No such principled difference can be found in the applicable constitutional doctrine, and Professor Kamisar does not suggest any. Just as the personal autonomy reflected in the constitutional right of reproductive freedom protects both the right of a woman to use contraception to prevent pregnancy from occurring and her right to have an abortion to terminate a pregnancy that has occurred, so the right of a terminally ill person to bodily integrity includes the right to hasten inevitable death, both by discontinuing lifesaving medical treatment and by taking a lethal dose of physician-prescribed medications.

Looking to the Supreme Court's ringing affirmation of the right of personal autonomy in *Casey,* I would submit that terminally ill persons do indeed have the right to make the "most basic decisions about bodily integrity," that they have the right to "define [their] own concept of existence" and "the attributes of [their] personhood" without the "compulsion of the state," and that they have the right to make the *choice* whether to continue to undergo unbearable suffering until death comes "naturally" or to hasten their inevitable death by the use of physician-prescribed medications. The right to make this choice is surely a right protected by the "liberty" of the Fourteenth Amendment's Due Process clause, and Michigan's ban clearly imposes an undue burden on this right.

The state cannot assert any valid interest in requiring a terminally ill person to undergo unbearable pain and suffering until death comes "naturally." The interest typically asserted to justify a ban on assisted suicide is that of "preserving life," or as Professor Kamisar puts it, in preventing the disregard for life that he sees resulting from a "suicide-permissive" society.[17] But there can be no valid interest in preserving life when there is no life left to preserve. . . .

Getting the Question Right

As stated at the outset, in constitutional litigation it is critically important that we get the questions right. The question presented in the ACLU challenge to Michigan's ban on assisted suicide is specifically whether the absolute ban on the use of physician-prescribed medications by terminally ill people to hasten their inevitable death is an "undue burden" on the liberty protected by the Fourteenth Amendment's Due Process clause. In this article, I have tried to demonstrate why the answer to this question, in terms of the constitutional doctrine applicable to the right of personal autonomy, should be resoundingly in the affirmative.

However, [such] a holding . . . [will be] a holding only on this specific and narrow issue. The holding will be a relevant precedent in a future case involving the constitutionality of a law that prohibits "suicide assistance" to a person who is not terminally ill, or that prohibits "suicide machines" or "physician euthanasia," but it will not be controlling. As a precedent, the case will have recognized that the right of terminally ill persons to hasten inevitable death is a right entitled to significant constitutional protection. Whether or not that precedent will be extended in future cases will be determined only if and when those cases arise.

In arguing that the Constitution should not protect a "right to assisted suicide," Professor Kamisar says that in certain circumstances life may be "unendurable" for one who is not terminally ill, and asks if that person should have the same "right to assisted suicide" that is being asserted for one who is terminally ill.[18] The question for the Court in such a case, as in all constitutional cases involving autonomy, would be whether the state can assert a valid *justification* for the particular interference with that autonomy. Perhaps the state's interest in preventing a "suicide-permissive" society is of sufficient importance to outweigh the interest of a non-terminally-ill person in ending a life that has become "unendurable." But perhaps it is not.[19] The question can be answered only when it arises, and must be answered in light of the constitutional doctrine applicable to the right of personal autonomy that has been promulgated by the Supreme Court. . . .

25

Three Court Decisions:
A. *Compassion in Dying v.*
State of Washington

United States Court of Appeals
for the Ninth Circuit
March 9, 1995

[A Washington state statute held that "(1) a person is guilty of promoting a suicide attempt when he knowingly causes or aids another
person to attempt suicide" and that "(2) promoting a suicide is a Class
C felony." The suit was brought by three terminally ill persons, four
doctors asserting their own rights and those of their patients, and the
non-profit organization Compassion in Dying, whose avowed purpose is to provide information, counselling, and emotional support to
persons it describes as "competent" and "terminally ill" who wish to
hasten their deaths. The plaintiffs charged that the Washington statute
was unconstitutional, and they were upheld in federal district court.
The state appealed, and in March 1995 a three-judge panel of the
Ninth Circuit Court of Appeals reversed the district-court ruling and
sustained the statute. Circuit Judge JOHN NOONAN wrote the opinion
for the court; there was also a dissenting opinion, omitted here. After
explaining the case, Noonan presented the analysis that follows.]

This case (49 F.3d 586 [1995]) is reprinted by permission of West Publishing
Company from the WESTLAW text. Most case citations and other references
have been omitted.

The conclusion of the district court that the statute deprived the plaintiffs of a liberty protected by the Fourteenth Amendment and denied them the equal protection of the laws cannot be sustained.

First. The language taken from *Casey* [*Planned Parenthood v. Casey,* 112 S.Ct. 2791, 2807 (1992): "These matters, including the most intimate and personal choices a person may make in a lifetime, choices central to personal dignity and autonomy, are central to the liberty protected by the Fourteenth Amendment. At the heart of liberty is the right to define one's own concept of existence, of meaning, of the universe, and of the mystery of human life. Beliefs about these matters could not define the attributes of personhood were they formed under compulsion of the State."], on which the district court pitched its principal argument, should not be removed from the context in which it was uttered. Any reader of judicial opinions knows they often attempt a generality of expression and a sententiousness of phrase that extend far beyond the problem addressed. It is commonly accounted an error to lift sentences or even paragraphs out of one context and insert the abstracted thought into a wholly different context. To take three sentences out of an opinion over thirty pages in length dealing with the highly charged subject of abortion and to find these sentences "almost prescriptive" in ruling on a statute proscribing the promotion of suicide is to make an enormous leap, to do violence to the context, and to ignore the differences between the regulation of reproduction and the prevention of the promotion of killing a patient at his or her request.

The inappropriateness of the language of *Casey* in the situation of assisted suicide is confirmed by considering what this language, as applied by the district court, implies. The decision to choose death, according to the district court's use of *Casey*'s terms, involves "personal dignity and autonomy" and "the right to define one's own concept of existence, of meaning, of the universe, and of the mystery of human life." The district court attempted to tie these concepts to the decision of a person terminally ill. But there is no way of doing so. The category created is inherently unstable. The depressed 21-year-old, the romantically devastated 28-year-old, the alcoholic 40-year-old who choose suicide are also expressing their views of existence, meaning, the universe, and life; they are also asserting their personal liberty. If at the heart of the liberty protected by the Fourteenth Amendment is this uncurtailable ability to believe and to act on one's deepest beliefs about life, the right to suicide and the right to assistance in suicide are the prerogative of at least every sane adult. The attempt to restrict such rights to the terminally ill is illusory. If such liberty exists in this context, as *Casey* asserted in the context of reproductive rights, every man and woman in the United States must enjoy it. The conclusion is a *reductio ad absurdum*.

Second. While *Casey* was not about suicide at all, *Cruzan* [*v. Director, Missouri Department of Health,* 497 U.S. 261 (1990)] was about the termination of life. The district court found itself unable to distinguish between a patient refusing life support and a patient seeking medical help to bring about death and therefore interpreted *Cruzan*'s limited acknowledgment of a right to refuse treatment as tantamount to an acceptance of a terminally ill patient's right to aid in self-killing. The district court ignored the far more relevant part of the opinion in *Cruzan* that "there can be no gainsaying" a state's interest "in the protection and preservation of human life" and, as evidence of that legitimate concern, the fact that "the majority of States in this country have laws imposing criminal penalties on one who assists another to commit suicide." (*Cruzan,* 497 U.S. at 280.) Whatever difficulty the district court experienced in distinguishing one situation from the other, it was not experienced by the majority in *Cruzan*.

Third. Unsupported by the gloss on "liberty" written by *Casey,* a gloss on a gloss, inasmuch as *Casey* developed an interpretation of "liberty" first elaborated in *Eisenstadt v. Baird* (405 U.S. 438, 453 [1972]), and implicitly controverted by *Cruzan,* the decision of the district court lacks foundation in recent precedent. It also lacks foundation in the traditions of our nation. In the 205 years of our existence no constitutional right to aid in killing oneself has ever been asserted and upheld by a court of final jurisdiction. Unless the federal judiciary is to be a floating constitutional convention, a federal court should not invent a constitutional right unknown to the past and antithetical to the defense of human life that has been a chief responsibility of our constitutional government.

Fourth. The district court extrapolated from *Casey* to hold the statute invalid on its face. That extrapolation, like the quotation from *Casey,* was an unwarranted extension of abortion jurisprudence, often unique, to a very different field. The normal rule—the rule that governs here—is that a facial challenge to a statute "must establish that no set of circumstances exists under which the Act would be valid." (*United States v. Salerno*, 481 U.S. 739, 745 [1987].) The district court indeed conceded that there were circumstances in which the statute could operate constitutionally, for example to deter suicide by teenagers or to prevent fraud upon the elderly. The district court did not even attempt the calculation carried out in *Casey* to show that in "a large fraction of the cases" the statute would operate unconstitutionally. From the declarations before it the district court had at most the opinion of several physicians that they "occasionally" met persons whom the statute affected detrimentally and their recitation of five case histories. There was no effort made to compare this number with the number of persons whose lives were guarded by the statute. The facial invalidation of the statute was wholly unwarranted.

Fifth. The district court declared the statute unconstitutional on its face without adequate consideration of Washington's interests that, individually and convergently, outweigh any alleged liberty of suicide. The most comprehensive study of our subject by a governmental body is *When Death Is Sought: Assisted Suicide and Euthanasia in the Medical Context* (1994). The study was conducted by the New York State Task Force, a commission appointed by Governor Cuomo in 1985, which filed its report in May 1994. The Task Force was composed of twenty-four members representing a broad spectrum of ethical and religious views and ethical, health, legal, and medical competencies. Its membership disagreed on the morality of suicide. Unanimously the members agreed against recommending a change in New York law to permit assisted suicide. Washington's interest in preventing such suicides is as strong as the interests that moved this diverse commission to its unanimous conclusion. A Michigan commission, set up in 1992, by majority vote in June 1994 recommended legislative change in the Michigan law against assisted suicide and set out a proposed new statute as a legislative option; the commission did not challenge the constitutionality of the existing Michigan legislation. (Michigan Commission on Death and Dying, *Final Report* [1994].) Neither the New York nor the Michigan reports were available to the district court. We take them into account on this appeal as we take into account the legal and medical articles cited by the parties and *amici* as representative professional judgments in this area of law. In the light of all these materials, Washington's interests are at least these:

1. The interest in not having physicians in the role of killers of their patients. "Physician-assisted suicide is fundamentally incompatible with the physician's role as healer," declares the American Medical Association's Code of Medical Ethics (1994) § 2.211. From the Hippocratic Oath with its promise "to do no harm" to the AMA's code, the ethics of the medical profession have proscribed killing. Washington has an interest in preserving the integrity of the physician's practice as understood by physicians.

Not only would the self-understanding of physicians be affected by removal of the state's support for their professional stance; the physician's constant search for ways to combat disease would be affected, if killing were as acceptable an option for the physician as curing. The physician's commitment to curing is the medical profession's commitment to medical progress. Medically assisted suicide as an acceptable alternative is a blind alley; Washington has a stake in barring it.

2. The interest in not subjecting the elderly and even the not-elderly but infirm to psychological pressure to consent to their own deaths. For all medical treatments, physicians decide which patients are the candidates. If assisted suicide was acceptable professional practice, physicians would make a judgment as to who was a good candidate for it. Physician neutrality and patient autonomy, independent of their physician's advice, are largely myths. Most patients do what their doctors recommend. As an eminent commission concluded, "Once the physician suggests suicide or euthanasia, some patients will feel that they have few, if any alternatives, but to accept the recommendation." (New York State Task Force, *When Death Is Sought,* 122.) Washington has an interest in preventing such persuasion.

3. The interest in protecting the poor and minorities from exploitation. The poor and minorities would be especially open to manipulation in a regime of assisted suicide for two reasons: Pain is a significant factor in creating a desire for assisted suicide, and the poor and minorities are notoriously less provided for in the alleviation of pain. The desire to reduce the cost of public assistance by quickly termi-

nating a prolonged illness cannot be ignored: "the cost of treatment is viewed as relevant to decisions at the bedside." (Idem at 129.) Convergently, the reduction of untreated (although treatable) pain and economic logic would make the poorest the primest candidates for physician-assisted and physician-recommended suicide.

4. The interest in protecting all of the handicapped from societal indifference and antipathy. Among the many briefs we have received from *amici curiae* there is one on behalf of numerous residents of nursing homes and long-term care facilities. The vulnerability of such persons to physician-assisted suicide is foreshadowed in the discriminatory way that a seriously disabled person's expression of a desire to die is interpreted. When the non-disabled say they want to die, they are labeled as suicidal; if they are disabled, it is treated as "natural" or "reasonable." In the climate of our achievement-oriented society, "simply offering the option of 'self-deliverance' shifts a burden of proof, so that helpless patients must ask themselves why they are not availing themselves of it." (Richard Doerflinger, "Assisted Suicide: Pro-Choice or Anti-Life?" *Hastings Center Report* 19, S. 16, S. 17 [Jan.-Feb. 1989].) An insidious bias against the handicapped—again coupled with a cost-saving mentality—makes them especially in need of Washington's statutory protection.

5. An interest in preventing abuse similar to what has occurred in the Netherlands where, since 1984, legal guidelines have tacitly allowed assisted suicide or euthanasia in response to a repeated request from a suffering, competent patient. In 1990, approximately 1.8 per cent of all deaths resulted from this practice. At least an additional .8 per cent of all deaths, and arguably more, come from direct measures taken to end the person's life without a contemporaneous request to end it. (New York State Task Force, *When Death Is Sought,* 133-34.)

Sixth. The scope of the district court's judgment is, perhaps necessarily, indefinite. The judgment of the district court was entered in favor of Jane Roe and John Doe although they were dead. This unheard-of judgment was a nullity. The judgment in favor of James Poe lapsed with his death pending appeal. The judgment in favor of Doctors Glucksberg, Halperin, Preston, and Shalit was "insofar as they raise claims on behalf of their terminally ill patients." No such patients were identified by these doctors except patients who were already deceased. Presumably, then, the judgment was [on] behalf of terminally ill patients that these doctors might encounter in the future. The term "terminally ill" was not defined by the court. No class was certified by the court. There is a good deal of uncertainty on whose behalf the judgment was entered.

It was suggested in argument that a definition of the terminally ill could be supplied from the Washington statute on the refusal of life-sustaining treatment, which does define "terminal condition." There are three difficulties: "terminal condition" and "terminally ill" are different terms; the examples given by the plaintiffs show considerable variation in whom they considered terminally ill to be; there is wide disagreement in definition of the terminally ill among the states. Life itself is a terminal condition, unless terminal condition is otherwise defined by a specific statute. A terminal illness can vary from a sickness causing death in days or weeks to cancer, which Dr. Glucksberg notes is "very slow" in its deadly impact, to a heart condition, which Dr. Preston notes can be relieved by a transplant, to AIDS, which Dr. Shalit declares is fatal once contracted. One can only guess which definition of the terminally ill would satisfy the constitutional criteria of the district court. Consequently, an amorphous class of beneficiaries has been created in this non-class action; and the district court has mandated Washington to reform its law against the promotion of suicide to safeguard the constitutional rights of persons whom the district court has not identified.

Seventh. At the heart of the district court's decision appears to be its refusal to distinguish between actions taking life and actions by which life is not supported or ceases to be supported. This refusal undergirds the district court's reading of *Cruzan* as well as its holding that the statute violates equal protection. The distinction, being drawn by the legislature not on the basis of race, gender, or religion or membership in any protected class and not infringing any fundamental constitutional right, must be upheld unless the plaintiffs can show "that the legislature's actions were irrational." (*Kadrmas v. Dickinson Public Schools,* 487 U.S. 450, 458 [1988].) The plaintiffs have not sustained this burden.

Against the broad background of moral experience that everyone acquires, the law of torts and the law of criminal offenses against the person have developed. "At common law, even the touching of one person by another without consent and without legal justification was a battery." (*Cruzan*, 497 U.S. at 269.) The physician's medical expertness is not a license to inflict medical procedures against your will. Protected by the law of torts, you can have or reject such medical treatment as you see fit. You can be left alone if you want. Privacy in the primordial sense in which it entered constitutional parlance—"the right to be let alone"—is yours. (See *Olmstead v. United States*, 277 U.S. 438, 478 [1928].)

Tort law and criminal law have never recognized a right to let others enslave you, mutilate you, or kill you. When you assert a claim that another—and especially another licensed by the state—should help you bring about your death, you ask for more than being let alone; you ask that the state, in protecting its own interest, not prevent its licensee from killing. The difference is not of degree but of kind. You no longer seek the ending of unwanted medical attention. You seek the right to have a second person collaborate in your death. To protect all the interests enumerated under *Fifth* above, the statute rightly and reasonably draws the line.

Compassion, according to the reflections of Prince Myshkin, is "the most important, perhaps the sole law of human existence." (Feodor Dostoevsky, *The Idiot* [Alan Myers, trans., 1991], 292.) In the vernacular, compassion is trumps. No one can read the accounts of the sufferings of the deceased plaintiffs supplied by their declarations, or the accounts of the sufferings of their patients supplied by the physicians, without being moved by them. No one would inflict such sufferings on another or want them inflicted on himself; and since the horrors recounted are those that could attend the end of life, anyone who reads of them must be aware that they could be attendant on his own death. The desire to have a good and kind way of forestalling them is understandably evident in the declarations of the plaintiffs and in the decision of the district court.

Compassion is a proper, desirable, even necessary component of judicial character; but compassion is not the most important, certainly not the sole law of human existence. Unrestrained by other virtues, as *The Idiot* illustrates, it leads to catastrophe. Justice, prudence, and fortitude are necessary too. Compassion cannot be the compass of a federal judge. That compass is the Constitution of the United States.

Where, as here in the case of Washington, the statute of a state comports with that compass, the validity of the statute must be upheld.

For all the foregoing reasons, the judgment appealed from is REVERSED.

B. *Compassion in Dying v. State of Washington*

United States Court of Appeals
for the Ninth Circuit
March 6, 1996

[A year after Judge Noonan's decision, this case was reheard *en banc* by an eleven-judge appeals panel. Circuit Judge STEPHEN REINHARDT wrote the opinion, which reversed the previous appeals-court ruling and affirmed the original district-court finding that the Washington statute was unconstitutional. The majority (8-3) found that the "or aids" provision of the statute—"a person is guilty of promoting a suicide attempt when he knowingly causes or aids another person to attempt suicide"—violated the Due Process clause of the Fourteenth Amendment. (The case was subsequently appealed to the United States Supreme Court, which handed down its opinion in June 1997; for this, see chapter 29.) Judge Reinhardt's opinion is abridged here, and the notes are omitted. After explaining the case in parts I and II, he continued with the following analysis.]

III. Is There a Due Process Violation?

In order to answer the question whether the Washington statute violates the Due Process Clause insofar as it prohibits the provision of certain medical assistance to terminally ill, competent adults who wish to hasten their own deaths, we first determine whether there is a liberty interest in choosing the time and manner of one's death—a

This case (1996 U.S. App. LEXIS 3944) is reprinted with the permission of LEXIS-NEXIS, a division of Reed Elsevier Inc. The opinion has been abridged, and most case citations and other references have been omitted.

question sometimes phrased in common parlance as: Is there a right to die? Because we hold that there is, we must then determine whether prohibiting physicians from prescribing life-ending medication for use by terminally ill patients who wish to die violates the patients' due process rights.

The mere recognition of a liberty interest does not mean that a state may not prohibit the exercise of that interest in particular circumstances, nor does it mean that a state may not adopt appropriate regulations governing its exercise. Rather, in cases like the one before us, the courts must apply a balancing test under which we weigh the individual's liberty interests against the relevant state interests in order to determine whether the state's actions are constitutionally permissible. As Chief Justice Rehnquist, writing for the Court, explained in *Cruzan v. Director, Missouri Department of Health* (497 U.S. 261 [1990]), the only right-to-die case that the Court has heretofore considered: "Determining that a person has a 'liberty interest' under the Due Process Clause does not end our inquiry; 'whether respondent's constitutional rights have been violated must be determined by balancing his liberty interests against the relevant state interests.'" (*Cruzan*, 497 U.S. at 279 [quoting *Youngberg v. Romeo*, 457 U.S. 307, 321 (1982)].) . . .

As Justice O'Connor explained in her concurring opinion in *Cruzan*, the ultimate question is whether sufficient justification exists for the intrusion by the government into the realm of a person's "liberty, dignity, and freedom." If the balance favors the state, then the given statute—whether it regulates the exercise of a due process liberty interest or prohibits that exercise to some degree—is constitutional. If the balance favors the individual, then the statute—whatever its justifications—violates the individual's due process liberty rights and must be declared unconstitutional, either on its face or as applied. Here, we conclude unhesitatingly that the balance favors the individual's liberty interest.

IV. IS THERE A LIBERTY INTEREST?

Before beginning our inquiry into whether a liberty interest exists, we reiterate a few fundamental precepts that guide us. The first lies in the Court's cautionary note in *Roe v. Wade:*

We forthwith acknowledge our awareness of the sensitive and emotional nature of the . . . controversy, of the vigorous opposing views, even among physicians, and of the deep and seemingly absolute convictions that the subject inspires. One's philosophy, one's experiences, one's exposure to the raw edges of human existence, one's religious training, one's attitude toward life and family and their values, and the moral standards one establishes and seeks to observe, are all likely to influence and to color one's thinking and conclusions. [410 U.S. 113, 116 (1973).]

Like the *Roe* Court, we endeavor to conduct an objective analysis of a most emotionally charged of topics. In doing so, we bear in mind the second Justice Harlan's admonition in his now-vindicated dissent in *Poe v. Ullman:*

The full scope of the liberty guaranteed by the Due Process Clause cannot be found in or limited by the precise terms of the specific guarantees elsewhere in the Constitution. This "liberty" is not a series of isolated points pricked out in terms of the taking of property; the freedom of speech, press, and religion; the right to keep and bear arms; the freedom from unreasonable searches and seizures; and so on. It is a rational continuum which, broadly speaking, includes a freedom from all substantial arbitrary impositions and purposeless restraints, . . . and which also recognizes, what a reasonable and sensitive judgment must, that certain interests require particularly careful scrutiny of the state needs asserted to justify their abridgment. [367 U.S. 497, 543 (1961).]

Applying Justice Harlan's teaching, we must strive to resist the natural judicial impulse to limit our vision to that which can plainly be observed on the face of the document before us, or even that which we have previously had the wisdom to recognize. . . .

In examining whether a liberty interest exists in determining the time and manner of one's death, we begin with the compelling similarities between right-to-die cases and abortion cases. In the former as in the latter, the relative strength of the competing interests changes as physical, medical, or related circumstances vary. In right-to-die cases the outcome of the balancing test may differ at different points along the life cycle as a person's physical or medical condition deteriorates, just as in abortion cases the permissibility of restrictive state legislation may vary with the progression of the pregnancy. Equally important, both types of cases raise issues of life and death, and both arouse similar religious and moral concerns. Both also present basic questions about an individual's right of choice. . . .

In deciding right-to-die cases, we are guided by the Court's approach to the abortion cases. [*Planned Parenthood v.*] *Casey* in particular provides a powerful precedent, for in that case the Court had the opportunity to evaluate its past decisions and to determine whether to adhere to its original judgment. Although *Casey* was influenced by the doctrine of *stare decisis,* the fundamental message of that case lies in its statements regarding the type of issue that confronts us here: "These matters, involving the most intimate and personal choices a person may make in a lifetime, choices central to personal dignity and autonomy, are central to the liberty protected by the Fourteenth Amendment." (*Casey,* 112 S. Ct. 2791, 2807 [1992].)

A. Defining the Liberty Interest and Other Relevant Terms

The majority opinion of the three-judge panel that first heard this case on appeal defined the claimed liberty interest as a "constitutional right to aid in killing oneself." However, the subject we must initially examine is not nearly so limited. Properly analyzed, the first issue to be resolved is whether there is a liberty interest in determining the time and manner of one's death. We do not ask simply whether there is a liberty interest in receiving "aid in killing oneself" because such a narrow interest could not exist in the absence of a broader and more important underlying interest—the right to die. In short, it is the end and not the means that defines the liberty interest.

The broader approach we employ in defining the liberty interest is identical to the approach used by the Supreme Court in the abortion cases. In those cases, the Court initially determined whether a general liberty interest existed (an interest in having an abortion), not whether there was an interest in implementing that general liberty interest by a particular means (with medical assistance). Specifically, in *Roe v. Wade* the Court determined that women had a liberty interest in securing an abortion, not that women had a liberty

interest in obtaining medical assistance for purpose of an abortion. . . .

While some people refer to the liberty interest implicated in right-
to-die cases as a liberty interest in committing suicide, we do not
describe it that way. We use the broader and more accurate terms,
"the right to die," "determining the time and manner of one's death,"
and "hastening one's death," for an important reason. The liberty
interest we examine encompasses a whole range of acts that are
generally not considered to constitute "suicide." Included within the
liberty interest we examine, is for example, the act of refusing or
terminating unwanted medical treatment. As we discuss later, a competent adult has a liberty interest in refusing to be connected to a
respirator or in being disconnected from one, even if he is terminally
ill and cannot live without mechanical assistance. The law does not
classify the death of a patient that results from the granting of his
wish to decline or discontinue treatment as "suicide." Nor does the
law label the acts of those who help the patient carry out that wish,
whether by physically disconnecting the respirator or by removing
an intravenous tube, as assistance in suicide. Accordingly, we believe
that the broader terms—"the right to die," "controlling the time and
manner of one's death," and "hastening one's death"—more accurately describe the liberty interest at issue here. Moreover, as we
discuss later, we have serious doubts that the terms "suicide" and
"assisted suicide" are appropriate legal descriptions of the specific
conduct at issue here.

There is one further definitional matter we should emphasize.
Following our determination regarding the existence of a liberty
interest in hastening one's death, we examine whether the Washington statute unconstitutionally infringes on that liberty interest.
Throughout that examination, we use the term "physician-assisted
suicide," a term that does not appear in the Washington statute but
is frequently employed in legal and medical discussions involving
the type of question before us. For purposes of this opinion, we use
"physician-assisted suicide" as it is used by the parties and district
court and as it is most frequently used: the prescribing of medication
by a physician for the purpose of enabling a patient to end his life.
It is only that conduct that the plaintiffs urge be held constitutionally
protected in this case.

B. *The Legal Standard*

There is no litmus test for courts to apply when deciding whether or not a liberty interest exists under the Due Process Clause. Our decisions involve difficult judgments regarding the conscience, traditions, and fundamental tenets of our nation. We must sometimes apply those basic principles in light of changing values based on shared experience. Other times we must apply them to new problems arising out of the development and use of new technologies. In all cases, our analysis of the applicability of the protections of the Constitution must be made in light of existing circumstances as well as our historic traditions.

Historically, the Court has classified "fundamental rights" as those that are "implicit in the concept of ordered liberty." (*Palko v. Connecticut,* 302 U.S. 319, 325 [1937].) The Court reasserted this historic standard, along with an alternative description, in its highly controversial *Bowers v. Hardwick* opinion. (478 U.S. 186, 191 [1986].) . . .

In recent years, the Court has spoken more frequently of substantive due process interests than of fundamental due process rights. The Court has also recently expressed a strong reluctance to find new fundamental rights.

The Court's evolving doctrinal approach to substantive due process claims is consistent with the basic truth enunciated by Justice Harlan [in *Poe v. Ullman*] and later endorsed by the Court in *Casey:* "The full scope of the liberty guaranteed by the Due Process Clause is a rational continuum which, broadly speaking, includes a freedom from all substantial arbitrary impositions and purposeless restraints. . . ." (*Casey,* 112 S. Ct. at 2806, citing *Poe,* 367 U.S. at 543.) . . .

Recent cases, including *Cruzan,* suggest that the Court may be heading towards the formal adoption of the continuum approach, along with a balancing test, in substantive due process cases generally. If so, there would no longer be a two-tier or three-tier set of tests that depends on the classification of the right or interest as fundamental, important, or marginal. Instead, the more important the individual's right or interest, the more persuasive the justifications for infringement would have to be. We see the evolution in the Court's approach more as a recognition of the artificiality of the current classification system than as a fundamental change in the Court's practical approach to specific issues. So long as the liberty interest is an important one, the state must shoulder the burden of justifying any significant limitations it seeks to impose. However, we need not predict the Court's future course in order to decide the case before us. Here, as we have said, even under the Court's traditional mode of analysis, a balancing test is applicable. . . .

Although in determining the existence of important rights or liberty interests, the Court examines our history and experience, it has stated on a number of occasions that the limits of the substantive reach of the Due Process Clause are not frozen at any point in time. . . .

In *Casey,* the Court made it clear that the fact that we have previously failed to acknowledge the existence of a particular liberty interest or even that we have previously prohibited its exercise is no barrier to recognizing its existence. In discussing a woman's liberty interest in securing an abortion, the *Casey* Court stated that pregnancy involves "suffering [that] is too intimate and personal for the State to insist, without more, upon its own vision of the woman's role, however dominant that vision has been in the course of our history and culture." (*Casey,* 112 S.Ct. at 2807.)

In contrast to *Casey,* the majority opinion of the three-judge panel in the case now before us erroneously concluded that a historical analysis alone is sufficient basis for rejecting plaintiffs' claim to a substantive liberty interest or right. As explained below, we believe that the panel's historical account is misguided, but even if it were indisputably correct, historical evidence alone is not a sufficient basis for rejecting a claimed liberty interest.

Were history our sole guide, the Virginia anti-miscegenation statute that the Court unanimously overturned in *Loving v. Virginia* (388 U.S. 1 [1967]), as violative of substantive due process and the Equal Protection Clause, would still be in force because such anti-miscegenation laws were commonplace both when the United States was founded and when the Fourteenth Amendment was adopted. . . .

Indeed, if historical evidence of accepted practices at the time the Fourteenth Amendment was enacted were dispositive, the Court would not only have decided *Loving* differently, but it would not have held that women have a right to have an abortion. As the dissent pointed out in *Roe,* more than three-quarters of the existing states (at least twenty-eight out of thirty-seven states), as well as eight territorial legislatures, restricted or prohibited abortions in 1868 when the Fourteenth Amendment was adopted.

C. Historical Attitudes Toward Suicide

[The opinion here summarizes societal attitudes toward suicide from ancient Greece to the present.]

D. Current Societal Attitudes

Clearly the absence of a criminal sanction alone does not show societal approbation of a practice. Nor is there any evidence that Americans approve of suicide in general. In recent years, however, there has been increasingly widespread support for allowing the terminally ill to hasten their deaths and avoid painful, undignified, and inhumane endings to their lives. Most Americans simply do not appear to view such acts as constituting suicide, and there is much support in reason for that conclusion. . . .

Just as the mere absence of criminal statutes prohibiting suicide or attempted suicide does not indicate societal approval, so the mere presence of statutes criminalizing assisting in a suicide does not necessarily indicate societal disapproval. That is especially true when such laws are seldom, if ever, enforced. There is no reported American case of criminal punishment being meted out to a doctor for helping a patient hasten his own death. The lack of enforcement of statutes prohibiting assisting a mentally competent, terminally ill adult to end his own life would appear to reflect widespread societal disaffection with such laws.

Our attitudes toward suicide of the type at issue in this case are better understood in light of our unwritten history and of technological developments. Running beneath the official history of legal condemnation of physician-assisted suicide is a strong undercurrent of a time-honored but hidden practice of physicians helping terminally ill patients to hasten their deaths. According to a survey by the American Society of Internal Medicine, one doctor in five said he had assisted in a patient's suicide. Accounts of doctors who have helped their patients end their lives have appeared both in professional journals and in the daily press.

The debate over whether terminally ill patients should have a right to reject medical treatment or to receive aid from their physicians in hastening their deaths has taken on a new prominence as a result of a number of developments. Two hundred years ago when America was founded and more than one hundred years ago when the Fourteenth Amendment was adopted, Americans died from a slew of illness and infirmities that killed their victims quickly but today are almost never fatal in this nation—scarlet fever, cholera, measles, diarrhea, influenza, pneumonia, gastritis, to name a few. Other diseases that have not been conquered can now often be controlled for years, if not decades—diseases such as diabetes, muscular dystrophy, Parkinson's disease, cardiovascular disease, and certain types of cancer. As a result, Americans are living longer, and when they finally succumb to illness, lingering longer, either in great pain or in a stuporous, semi-comatose condition that results from the infusion of vast amounts of pain-killing medications. Despite the marvels of technology, Americans frequently die with less dignity than they did in the days when ravaging diseases typically ended their lives quickly. AIDS, which often subjects its victims to a horrifying and drawn-out demise, has also contributed to the growing number of terminally ill patients who die protracted and painful deaths.

One result has been a growing movement to restore humanity and dignity to the process by which Americans die. The now recognized right to refuse or terminate treatment and the emergent right to receive medical assistance in hastening one's death are inevitable consequences of changes in the causes of death, advances in medical science, and the development of new technologies. Both the need and the capability to assist individuals [to] end their lives in peace and dignity have increased exponentially.

E. Prior Court Decisions

Next we examine previous Court decisions that delineate the boundaries of substantive due process. We believe that a careful examination of these decisions demonstrates that there is a strong liberty interest in determining how and when one's life shall end, and that an explicit recognition of that interest follows naturally, indeed inevitably, from their reasoning.

The essence of the substantive component of the Due Process Clause is to limit the ability of the state to intrude into the most important matters of our lives, at least without substantial justification. In a long line of cases, the Court has carved out certain key moments and decisions in individuals' lives and placed them beyond the general prohibitory authority of the state. The Court has recognized that the Fourteenth Amendment affords constitutional protection to personal decisions relating to marriage, family relationships, child rearing and education, and intercourse for purposes other than procreation. The Court has recognized the right of individuals to be free from government interference in deciding matters as personal as whether to bear or beget a child and whether to continue an unwanted pregnancy to term.

A common thread running through these cases is that they involve decisions that are highly personal and intimate, as well as of great importance to the individual. Certainly, few decisions are more personal, intimate or important than the decision to end one's life, especially when the reason for doing so is to avoid excessive and protracted pain. Accordingly, we believe the cases from *Pierce* through *Roe* [the previous paragraph in the full opinion cites *Pierce, Griswold, Eisenstadt,* and *Roe*] provide strong general support for our conclusion that a liberty interest in controlling the time and manner of one's death is protected by the Due Process Clause of the Fourteenth Amendment.

While the cases we have adverted to lend general support to our conclusion, we believe that two relatively recent decisions of the Court, *Planned Parenthood v. Casey* and *Cruzan v. Director, Missouri Department of Health,* are fully persuasive, and leave little doubt as to the proper result.

F. Liberty Interest Under "Casey"

In *Casey,* the Court surveyed its prior decisions affording "constitutional protection to personal decisions relating to marriage, procreation, contraception, family relationships, child rearing, and education" and then said:

These matters, involving the most intimate and personal choices a person may make in a lifetime, choices central to personal dignity and autonomy, are central to the liberty protected by the Fourteenth Amendment. At the heart of liberty is the right to define one's own concept of existence, of meaning, of the universe, and of the mystery of human life. Beliefs about these matters could not define the attributes of personhood were they formed under compulsion of the State. [112 S.Ct. at 2807.]

The district judge in this case found the Court's reasoning in *Casey* "highly instructive" and "almost prescriptive" for determining "what liberty interest may inhere in a terminally ill person's choice to commit suicide." We agree.

Like the decision of whether or not to have an abortion, the decision how and when to die is one of "the most intimate and personal choices a person may make in a lifetime," a choice "central to personal dignity and autonomy." A competent terminally ill adult, having lived nearly the full measure of his life, has a strong liberty interest in choosing a dignified and humane death rather than being reduced at the end of his existence to a childlike state of helplessness, diapered, sedated, incontinent. How a person dies not only determines the nature of the final period of his existence, but in many cases, the enduring memories held by those who love him. . . .

G. Liberty Interest Under "Cruzan"

In *Cruzan*, the Court considered whether or not there is a constitutionally protected, due process liberty interest in terminating unwanted medical treatment. The Court said that an affirmative answer followed almost inevitably from its prior decisions holding that patients have a liberty interest in refusing to submit to specific medical procedures. . . . Writing for a majority that included Justices O'Connor and Scalia, Chief Justice Rehnquist said that those cases helped answer the first critical question at issue in *Cruzan*, stating: "The principle that a competent person has a constitutionally protected liberty interest in refusing unwanted medical treatment may be inferred from our prior decisions." (*Cruzan*, 497 U.S. at 278.)

In her concurrence, Justice O'Connor explained that the majority opinion held (implicitly or otherwise) that a liberty interest in refusing medical treatment extends to all types of medical treatment from dialysis or artificial respirators to the provision of food and water by tube or other artificial means. As Justice O'Connor said: "I agree that a protected liberty interest in refusing unwanted medical treatment may be inferred from our prior decisions, and that the refusal of artificial delivery of food and water is encompassed in that liberty interest." (Idem at 287.)

Justice O'Connor further concluded that under the majority's opinion, "requiring a competent adult to endure such procedures against her will burdens the patient's liberty, dignity, and freedom to determine the course of her own treatment." (Idem at 289.) In the majority opinion itself, Chief Justice Rehnquist made a similar assertion, writing:

> The choice between life and death is a deeply personal decision of obvious and overwhelming finality. We believe Missouri may legitimately seek to safeguard the personal element of this choice through the imposition of heightened evidentiary requirements. It cannot be disputed that the Due Process Clause protects an interest in life as well as an interest in refusing life-sustaining medical treatment. [Idem at 281.]

These passages make it clear that *Cruzan* stands for the proposition that there is a due process liberty interest in rejecting unwanted medical treatment, including the provision of food and water by artificial means. Moreover, the Court majority clearly recognized that granting the request to remove the tubes through which Cruzan received artificial nutrition and hydration would lead inexorably to her death. Accordingly, we conclude that *Cruzan,* by recognizing a liberty interest that includes the refusal of artificial provision of life-sustaining food and water, necessarily recognizes a liberty interest in hastening one's own death.

H. Summary

Casey and *Cruzan* provide persuasive evidence that the Constitution encompasses a due process liberty interest in controlling the time and manner of one's death—that there is, in short, a constitutionally recognized "right to die." Our conclusion is strongly influenced by, but not limited to, the plight of mentally competent, terminally ill adults. We are influenced as well by the plight of others, such as those whose existence is reduced to a vegetative state or a permanent and irreversible state of unconsciousness.

Our conclusion that there is a liberty interest in determining the time and manner of one's death does not mean that there is a concomitant right to exercise that interest in all circumstances or to do so free from state regulation. To the contrary, we explicitly recognize that some prohibitory and regulatory state action is fully consistent with constitutional principles.

In short, finding a liberty interest constitutes a critical first step toward answering the question before us. The determination that must now be made is whether the state's attempt to curtail the exercise of that interest is constitutionally justified.

V. RELEVANT FACTORS AND INTERESTS

To determine whether a state action that impairs a liberty interest violates an individual's substantive due process rights we must identify the factors relevant to the case at hand, assess the state's interests and the individual's liberty interest in light of those factors, and then weigh and balance the competing interests. The relevant factors generally include: (1) the importance of the various state interests, both in general and in the factual context of the case; (2) the manner in which those interests are furthered by the state law or regulation; (3) the importance of the liberty interest, both in itself and in the context in which it is being exercised; (4) the extent to which that interest is burdened by the challenged state action; and (5) the consequences of upholding or overturning the statute or regulation.

A. The State's Interests

We analyze the factors in turn, and begin by considering the first: the importance of the state's interests. We identify six related state interests involved in the controversy before us: (1) the state's general interest in preserving life; (2) the state's more specific interest in preventing suicide; (3) the state's interest in avoiding the involvement of third parties and in precluding the use of arbitrary, unfair, or undue influence; (4) the state's interest in protecting family members and loved ones; (5) the state's interest in protecting the integrity of the medical profession; and (6) the state's interest in avoiding adverse consequences that might ensue if the statutory provision at issue is declared unconstitutional.

1. Preserving Life

The state may assert an unqualified interest in preserving life in general. As the Court said in *Cruzan*, "We think a State may properly decline to make judgments about the 'quality' of life that a particular individual may enjoy, and simply assert an unqualified interest in the preservation of human life. . . ." (497 U.S. at 282.) Thus, the state may assert its interest in preserving life in all cases, including those of terminally ill, competent adults who wish to hasten their deaths.

Although the state's interest in preserving life may be unqualified, and may be asserted regardless of the quality of the life or lives at issue, that interest is not always controlling. Nor is it of the same strength in each case. To the contrary, its strength is dependent on relevant circumstances, including the medical condition and the wishes of the person whose life is at stake.

Most tellingly, the state of Washington has already decided that its interest in preserving life should ordinarily give way—at least in the case of competent, terminally ill adults who are dependent on medical treatment—to the wishes of the patients. In its Natural Death Act, Washington permits adults to have "life-sustaining treatment withheld or withdrawn in instances of a terminal condition or permanent unconsciousness." In adopting the statute, the Washington legislature necessarily determined that the state's interest in preserving life is not so weighty that it ought to thwart the informed desire of a terminally ill, competent adult to refuse medical treatment.

Not only does Washington law acknowledge that terminally ill and permanently unconscious adults have a right to refuse life-sustaining treatment, the statute includes specific legislative findings that appear to recognize that a due process liberty interest underlies that right. The statute states:

The legislature finds that adult persons have the fundamental right to control the decisions relating to the rendering of their own medical care, including the decision to have life-sustaining procedures withheld or withdrawn in instances of terminal condition.

The legislature further finds that modern medical technology has made possible the artificial prolongation of human life beyond natural limits.

The legislature further finds that, in the interest of protecting individual autonomy, such prolongation of life for persons with a terminal condition may cause loss of patient dignity, and unnecessary pain and suffering, while providing nothing medically necessary or beneficial to the patient.

The Washington statute permits competent adults to reject life-sustaining medical treatment in advance by means of living wills and durable powers of attorney. Even in cases in which the Washington Natural Death Act does not authorize surrogate decision-making, the Washington Supreme Court has found that legal guardians may sometimes have life-sustaining treatment discontinued. . . .

2. Preventing Suicide

   a. While the state's general commitment to the preservation of life clearly encompasses the prevention of suicide, the state has an even more particular interest in deterring the taking of one's own life. The fact that neither Washington nor any other state currently bans suicide, or attempted suicide, does not mean that the state does not have a valid and important interest in preventing or discouraging that act.

During the course of this litigation, the state has relied on its interest in the prevention of suicide as its primary justification for its statute. The state points to statistics concerning the rate of suicide among various age groups, particularly the young. . . .

Although suicide by teenagers and young adults is especially tragic, the state has a clear interest in preventing anyone, no matter what age, from taking his own life in a fit of desperation, depression, or loneliness or as a result of any other problem, physical or psychological, which can be significantly ameliorated. Studies show that many suicides are committed by people who are suffering from treatable mental disorders. Most if not all states provide for the involuntary commitment of such persons if they are likely to physically harm themselves. For similar reasons, at least a dozen states allow the use of non-deadly force to prevent suicide attempts.

While the state has a legitimate interest in preventing suicides in general, that interest, like the state's interest in preserving life, is substantially diminished in the case of terminally ill, competent adults who wish to die. One of the heartaches of suicide is the senseless loss of a life ended prematurely. In the case of a terminally ill adult who ends his life in the final stages of an incurable and painful degenerative disease, in order to avoid debilitating pain and a humiliating death, the decision to commit suicide is not senseless, and death does not come too early. . . . While some people who contemplate suicide can be restored to a state of physical and mental well-being, terminally ill adults who wish to die can only be maintained in a debilitated and deteriorating state, unable to enjoy the presence of family or friends. Not only is the state's interest in preventing such individuals from hastening their deaths of comparatively little weight, but its insistence on frustrating their wishes seems cruel indeed. As Kent said in *King Lear,* when signs of life were seen in the dying monarch:

> *Vex not his ghost. O, let him pass. He hates him*
> *That would upon the rack of this tough world*
> *Stretch him out longer.* [V, iii, 289-91]

b. The state has explicitly recognized that its interests are frequently insufficient to override the wishes of competent, terminally ill adult patients who desire to bring their lives to an end with the assistance of a physician. Step by step, the state has acknowledged that terminally ill persons are entitled in a whole variety of circumstances to hasten their deaths, and that in such cases their physicians may assist in the process. Until relatively recently, while physicians routinely helped patients to hasten their deaths, they did so discreetly because almost all such assistance was illegal. However, beginning about twenty years ago a series of dramatic changes took place. Each provoked the type of division and debate that surrounds the issue before us today. Each time the state's interests were ultimately subordinated to the liberty interests of the individual, in part as a result of legal actions and in part as a result of a growing recognition by the medical community and society at large that a more enlightened approach was essential.

The first major breakthrough occurred when the terminally ill were permitted to reject medical treatment. The line was drawn initially at extraordinary medical treatment because the distinction between ordinary and extraordinary treatment appeared to some to offer the courts an objective, scientific standard that would enable them to recognize the right to refuse certain medical treatment without also recognizing a right to suicide or euthanasia. That distinction, however, quickly proved unworkable, and after a while, terminally ill patients were allowed to reject both extraordinary and ordinary treatment. For a while, rejection of treatment, often through "do not resuscitate" orders, was permitted, but termination was not. This dividing line, which rested on the illusory distinction between commission and omission (or active and passive), also appeared for a short time to offer a natural point of repose for doctors, patients, and the law. However, it, too, quickly proved untenable, and ultimately patients were allowed both to refuse and to terminate medical treatment, ordinary as well as extraordinary. Today, many states also allow the terminally ill to order their physicians to discontinue not just traditional medical treatment but the artificial provision of life-sustaining food and water, thus permitting the patients to die by self-starvation. Equally important, today, doctors are generally permitted to administer death-inducing medication, as long as they can point to a concomitant pain-relieving purpose.

In light of these drastic changes regarding acceptable medical practices, opponents of physician-assisted suicide must now explain precisely what it is about the physician's conduct in assisted suicide cases that distinguishes it from the conduct that the state has explicitly authorized. The state responds by urging that physician-assisted suicide is different in kind, not degree, from the type of physician-life-ending conduct that is now authorized, for three separate reasons. It argues that "assisted suicide": (1) requires doctors to play an active role; (2) causes deaths that would not result from the patient's underlying disease; and (3) requires doctors to provide the causal agent of patients' deaths.

The distinctions suggested by the state do not individually or collectively serve to distinguish the medical practices society currently accepts. The first distinction—the line between commission and omission—is a distinction without a difference now that patients are permitted not only to decline all medical treatment, but to instruct their doctors to terminate whatever treatment, artificial or otherwise, they are receiving. In disconnecting a respirator, or authorizing its disconnection, a doctor is unquestionably committing an act; he is taking an active role in bringing about the patient's death. In fact, there can be no doubt that in such instances the doctor intends that, as the result of his action, the patient will die an earlier death than he otherwise would.

Similarly, drawing a distinction on the basis of whether the patient's death results from an underlying disease no longer has any legitimacy. While the distinction may once have seemed tenable, at least from a metaphysical standpoint, it was not based on a valid or practical legal foundation and was therefore quickly abandoned. When Nancy Cruzan's feeding and hydration tube was removed, she did not die of an underlying disease. Rather, she was allowed to starve to death. In fact, Ms. Cruzan was not even terminally ill at the time, but had a life expectancy of thirty years. Similarly, when a doctor provides a conscious patient with medication to ease his discomfort while he starves himself to death—a practice that is not only legal but has been urged as an alternative to assisted suicide—the patient does not die of any underlying ailment. To the contrary, the doctor is helping the patient end his life by providing medication that makes it possible for the patient to achieve suicide by starvation.

Nor is the state's third and final distinction valid. Contrary to the state's assertion, given current medical practices and current medical ethics, it is not possible to distinguish prohibited from permissible medical conduct on the basis of whether the medication provided by the doctor will cause the patient's death. As part of the tradition of administering comfort care, doctors have been supplying the causal agent of patients' deaths for decades. Physicians routinely and openly provide medication to terminally ill patients with the knowledge that it will have a "double effect"—reduce the patient's pain and hasten his death. Such medical treatment is accepted by the medical profession as meeting its highest ethical standards. It commonly takes the form of putting a patient on an intravenous morphine drip, with full knowledge that, while such treatment will alleviate his pain, it will also indubitably hasten his death. There can be no doubt, therefore, that the actual cause of the patient's death is the drug administered by the physician or by a person acting under his supervision or direction. Thus, the causation argument is simply "another bridge crossed" in the journey to vindicate the liberty interests of the terminally ill, and the state's third distinction has no more force than the other two.

   c. We acknowledge that in some respects a recognition of the legitimacy of physician-assisted suicide would constitute an additional step beyond what the courts have previously approved. We also acknowledge that judicial acceptance of physician-assisted suicide would cause many sincere persons with strong moral or religious convictions great distress. Nevertheless, we do not believe that the state's interest in preventing that additional step is significantly greater than its interest in preventing the other forms of life-ending medical conduct that doctors now engage in regularly. More specifically, we see little, if any, difference for constitutional or ethical purposes between providing medication with a double effect and providing medication with a single effect, as long as one of the known effects in each case is to hasten the end of the patient's life. Similarly, we see no ethical or constitutionally cognizable difference between a doctor's pulling the plug on a respirator and his prescribing drugs which will permit a terminally ill patient to end his own life. In fact, some might argue that pulling the plug is a more culpable and aggressive act on the doctor's part and provides more reason for criminal prosecution. To us, what matters most is that the death of the patient is the intended result as surely in one case as in the other. In sum, we find the state's interests in preventing suicide do not make its interests substantially stronger here than in cases involving other forms of death-hastening medical intervention. To the extent that a difference exists, we conclude that it is one of degree and not of kind.

   d. Moreover, we are doubtful that deaths resulting from terminally ill patients taking medication prescribed by their doctors should be classified as "suicide." Certainly, we see little basis for such a classification when deaths that result from patients' decisions to terminate life support systems or to refuse life-sustaining food and water, for example, are not. We believe that there is a strong argument that a decision by a terminally ill patient to hasten by medical means a death that is already in process, should not be classified as suicide. Thus, notwithstanding the generally accepted use of the term "physician-assisted suicide," we have serious doubt that the state's interest in preventing suicide is even implicated in this case.

   e. In addition to the state's purported interest in preventing suicide, it has an additional interest in preventing deaths that occur as a result of errors in medical or legal judgment. We acknowledge that it is sometimes impossible to predict with certainty the duration of a terminally ill patient's remaining existence, just as it is sometimes impossible to say for certain whether a borderline individual is or is not mentally competent. However, we believe that sufficient safeguards can and will be developed by the state and medical profession to ensure that the possibility of error will ordinarily be remote. Finally, although life-and-death decisions are of the gravest order, should an error actually occur it is likely to benefit the individual by permitting a victim of unmanageable pain and suffering to end his life peacefully and with dignity at the time he deems most desirable.

3. Avoiding the Involvement of Third Parties, and Precluding the Use of Arbitrary, Unfair, or Undue Influence

a. A state may properly assert an interest in prohibiting even altruistic assistance to a person contemplating suicide on the grounds that allowing others to help may increase the incidence of suicide, undercut society's commitment to the sanctity of life, and adversely affect the person providing the assistance. In addition, joint action is generally considered more serious than action by a single person. While we recognize that these concerns are legitimate, the most important—the first two—diminish in importance to the same extent that the state's interest in preventing the act itself diminishes. All are at their minimums when the assistance is provided by or under the supervision or direction of a doctor and the recipient is a terminally ill patient.

In upholding Washington's statute, the majority of the three-judge panel relied heavily on the state's interest in preventing the exercise of undue, arbitrary, or unfair influences over the individual's decision to end his life. We agree that this is an important interest, but for entirely different reasons than the majority suggests. One of the majority's prime arguments is that the statute is necessary to protect "the poor and minorities from exploitation"—in other words, to protect the disadvantaged from becoming the victims of assisted suicide. This rationale simply recycles one of the more disingenuous and fallacious arguments raised in opposition to the legalization of abortion. It is equally meretricious here. In fact, as with abortion, there is far more reason to raise the opposite concern: the concern that the poor and the minorities, who have historically received the least adequate health care, will not be afforded a fair opportunity to obtain the medical assistance to which they are entitled—the assistance that would allow them to end their lives with a measure of dignity. The argument that disadvantaged persons will receive more medical services than the remainder of the population in one, and only one, area—assisted suicide—is ludicrous on its face. So, too, is the argument that the poor and the minorities will rush to volunteer for physician-assisted suicide because of their inability to secure adequate medical treatment.

Our analysis is similar regarding the argument relating to the handicapped. Again, the opponents of physician-assisted suicide urge a variation of the discredited anti-abortion argument. Despite the dire predictions, the disabled were not pressured into seeking abortions. Nor is it likely that the disabled will be pressured into committing physician-assisted suicide. Organizations representing the physically impaired are sufficiently active politically and sufficiently vigilant that they would soon put a halt to any effort to employ assisted suicide in a manner that affected their clients unfairly. There are other more subtle concerns, however, advanced by some representatives of the physically impaired, including the fear that certain physical disabilities will erroneously be deemed to make life "valueless." While we recognize the legitimacy of these concerns, we also recognize that seriously impaired individuals will, along with non-impaired individuals, be the beneficiaries of the liberty interest asserted here—and that if they are not afforded the option to control their own fate, they like many others will be compelled, against their will, to endure unusual and protracted suffering. The resolution that would be best for all, of course, would be to ensure that the practice of assisted suicide is conducted fairly and well, and that adequate safeguards sufficient to avoid the feared abuses are adopted and enforced.

b. There is a far more serious concern regarding third parties that we must consider—one not even mentioned by the majority in the panel opinion. That concern is the fear that infirm, elderly persons will come under undue pressure to end their lives from callous, financially burdened, or self-interested relatives, or others who have influence over them. The risk of undue influence is real—and it exists today. Persons with a stake in the outcome may now pressure the terminally ill to reject or decline life-saving treatment or take other steps likely to hasten their demise. Surrogates may make unfeeling life-and-death decisions for their incompetent relatives. This concern deserves serious consideration, as it did when the decision was made some time ago to permit the termination of life-support systems and the withdrawal or withholding of other forms of medical treatment, and when it was decided to recognize living wills, durable powers of attorney, and the right of courts to appoint substitute decision-makers. While we do not minimize the concern, the temptation to exert undue pressure is ordinarily tempered to a substantial degree in the case of the terminally ill by the knowledge that the person will die shortly in any event. Given the possibility of undue influence that already exists, the recognition of the right to physician-assisted suicide would not increase that risk unduly. In fact, the direct involvement of an impartial and professional third party in the decision-making process would more likely provide an important safeguard against such abuse.

We also realize that terminally ill patients may well feel pressured to hasten their deaths, not because of improper conduct by their loved ones, but rather for an opposite reason—out of concern for the economic welfare of their loved ones. Faced with the prospect of astronomical medical bills, terminally ill patients might decide that it is better for them to die before their health-care expenses consume the life savings they planned to leave for their families, or, worse yet, burden their families with debts they may never be able to satisfy. While state regulations can help ensure that patients do not make rash, uninformed, or ill-considered decisions, we are reluctant to say that, in a society in which the costs of protracted health care can be so exorbitant, it is improper for competent, terminally ill adults to take the economic welfare of their families and loved ones into consideration. . . .

c. We are also aware of the concern that doctors become hardened to the inevitability of death and to the plight of terminally ill patients, and that they will treat requests to die in a routine and impersonal manner, rather than affording the careful, thorough, individualized attention that each request deserves. The day of the family doctor who made house calls and knew the frailties and strengths of each family member is long gone. So, too, in the main, is the intense personal interest that doctors used to take in their patients' welfare and activities. Doctors like the rest of society face constantly increasing pressures, and may not always have the patience to deal with the elderly, some of whom can be both difficult and troublesome. Nevertheless, there are many doctors who specialize in geriatric care, and there are many more who are not specialists but who treat elderly patients with great compassion and sensitivity. We believe that most, if not all, doctors would not assist a terminally ill patient to hasten his death as long as there were any reasonable chance of alleviating the patient's suffering or enabling him to live under tolerable conditions. We also believe that physicians would not assist a patient to end his life if there were any significant doubt about the patient's true wishes. To do so would be contrary to the physicians' fundamental training, their conservative nature, and the ethics of their profession. In any case, since doctors are highly regulated professionals, it should not be difficult for the state or the profession itself to establish rules and procedures that will ensure that the occasional negligent or careless recommendation by a licensed physician will not result in an uninformed or erroneous decision by the patient or his family.

Having said all this, we do not dismiss the legitimate concerns that exist regarding undue influence. While steps can be taken to minimize the danger substantially, the concerns cannot be wholly eliminated. Accordingly, they are of more than minimal weight and, in balancing the competing interests, we treat them seriously.

4. [Protecting] Children, Other Family Members, and
Loved Ones

The state clearly has a legitimate interest in safeguarding the interests of innocent third parties such as minor children and other family members dependent on persons who wish to commit suicide. That state interest, however, is of almost negligible weight when the patient is terminally ill and his death is imminent and inevitable. The state cannot help a minor child or any other innocent third party by forcing a terminally ill patient to die a more protracted and painful death. In fact, witnessing a loved one suffer a slow and agonizing death as a result of state compulsion is more likely to harm than further the interests of innocent third parties.

5. Protecting the Integrity of the Medical Profession

The state has a legitimate interest in assuring the integrity of the medical profession, an interest that includes prohibiting physicians from engaging in conduct that is at odds with their role as healers.

We do not believe that the integrity of the medical profession would be threatened in any way by the vindication of the liberty interest at issue here. Rather, it is the existence of a statute that criminalizes the provision of medical assistance to patients in need that could create conflicts with the doctors' professional obligations and make covert criminals out of honorable, dedicated, and compassionate individuals.

The assertion that the legalization of physician-assisted suicide will erode the commitment of doctors to help their patients rests both on an ignorance of what numbers of doctors have been doing for a considerable time and on a misunderstanding of the proper function of a physician. As we have previously noted, doctors have been discreetly helping terminally ill patients hasten their deaths for decades and probably centuries, while acknowledging privately that there was no other medical purpose to their actions. They have done so with the tacit approval of a substantial percentage of both the public and the medical profession, and without in any way diluting their commitment to their patients.

In addition, as we also noted earlier, doctors may now openly take actions that will result in the deaths of their patients. They may terminate life-support systems, withdraw life-sustaining gastronomy tubes, otherwise terminate or withhold all other forms of medical treatment, and may even administer lethal doses of drugs with full knowledge of their "double effect." Given the similarity between what doctors are now permitted to do and what the plaintiffs assert they should be permitted to do, we see no risk at all to the integrity of the profession. This is a conclusion that is shared by a growing number of doctors who openly support physician-assisted suicide and proclaim it to be fully compatible with the physicians' calling and with their commitment and obligation to help the sick. Many more doctors support physician-assisted suicide but without openly advocating a change in the legal treatment of the practice. . . . Even among those doctors who oppose assisted suicide, medical ethics do not lie at the heart of the objections. The "most important personal characteristic" separating those doctors from their colleagues is a strong religious identification. . . .

Recognizing the right to "assisted suicide" would not require doctors to do anything contrary to their individual principles. A physician whose moral or religious beliefs would prevent him from assisting a patient to hasten his death would be free to follow the dictates of his conscience. Those doctors who believe that terminally ill, competent, adult patients should be permitted to choose the time and manner of their death would be able to help them do so. We believe that extending a choice to doctors as well as to patients would help protect the integrity of the medical profession without compromising the rights or principles of individual doctors and without sacrificing the welfare of their patients.

6. [Avoiding] Adverse Consequences

We now consider the state's final concern. Those opposed to permitting physician-assisted suicide often point to a concern that could be subsumed under the state's general interest in preserving life, but which for clarity's sake we treat separately. The argument is a purely pragmatic one that causes many people deep concern: permitting physician-assisted suicide would "open Pandora's Box."

Once we recognize a liberty interest in hastening one's death, the argument goes, that interest will sweep away all restrictions in its wake. It will only be a matter of time, the argument continues, before courts will sanction putting people to death, not because they are desperately ill and want to die, but because they are deemed to pose an unjustifiable burden on society. Known as a slippery-slope argument or what one commentator has called the "thin edge of the wedge" argument, the opponents of assisted suicide conjure up a parade of horribles and insist that the only way to halt the downward spiral is to stop it before it starts.

This same nihilistic argument can be offered against any constitutionally protected right or interest. Both before and after women were found to have a right to have an abortion, critics contended that legalizing that medical procedure would lead to its widespread use as a substitute for other forms of birth control or as a means of racial genocide. Inflammatory contentions regarding ways in which the recognition of the right would lead to the ruination of the country did not, however, deter the Supreme Court from first recognizing and then two decades later reaffirming a constitutionally protected liberty interest in terminating an unwanted pregnancy. In fact, the Court has never refused to recognize a substantive due process liberty right or interest merely because there were difficulties in determining when and how to limit its exercise or because others might someday attempt to use it improperly.

Recognition of any right creates the possibility of abuse. The slippery-slope fears of *Roe*'s opponents have, of course, not materialized. The legalization of abortion has not undermined our commitment to life generally; nor, as some predicted, has it led to widespread infanticide. Similarly, there is no reason to believe that legalizing assisted suicide will lead to the horrific consequences its opponents suggest.

The slippery-slope argument also comes in a second and closely related form. This version of the argument states that a due process interest in hastening one's death, even if the exercise of that interest is initially limited to the terminally ill, will prove infinitely expansive because it will be impossible to define the term "terminally ill."

The argument rests on two false premises. First, it presupposes a need for greater precision than is required in constitutional law. Second, it assumes that the terms "terminal illness" or "terminal condition" cannot be defined, even though those terms have in fact been defined repeatedly. They have, for example, been defined in a model statute, The Uniform Rights of the Terminally Ill Act, and in more than forty state natural-death statutes, including Washington's. The model statute and some of the state statutes have defined the term without reference to a fixed time period; others have taken the opposite approach, defining terminal to mean that death is likely to ensue within six months. As we have noted earlier, the Washington Act, like some others, includes persons who are permanently unconscious, that is, in an irreversible coma or a persistent vegetative state. While defining the term "terminally ill" is not free from difficulty, the experience of the states has proved that the class of the terminally ill is neither indefinable nor undefined. Indeed, all of the persons described in the various statutes would appear to fall within an appropriate definition of the term. In any event, it is apparent that purported definitional difficulties that have repeatedly been surmounted provide no legitimate reason for refusing to recognize a liberty interest in hastening one's death.

We do not dispute the dissent's contention that the prescription of lethal medication by physicians for use by terminally ill patients who wish to die does not constitute a clear point of demarcation between permissible and impermissible medical conduct. We agree that it may be difficult to make a principled distinction between physician-assisted suicide and the provision to terminally ill patients of other forms of life-ending medical assistance, such as the administration of drugs by a physician. We recognize that in some instances, the patient may be unable to self-administer the drugs and that administration by the physician, or a person acting under his direction or control, may be the only way the patient may be able to receive them. The question whether that type of physician conduct may be constitutionally prohibited must be answered directly in future cases, and not in this one.

We would be less than candid, however, if we did not acknowledge that for present purposes we view the critical line in right-to-die cases as the one between the voluntary and involuntary termination of an individual's life. In the first case—volitional death—the physician is aiding or assisting a patient who wishes to exercise a liberty interest, and in the other—involuntary death—another person acting on his own behalf, or in some instances society's, is determining that an individual's life should no longer continue. We consider it less important who administers the medication than who determines whether the terminally ill person's life shall end. In any event, here we decide only the issue before us—the constitutionality of prohibiting doctors from prescribing medication for use by terminally ill patients who wish to hasten their death.

B. The Means by Which the State Furthers Its Interests

In applying the balancing test, we must take into account not only the strength of the state's interests but also the means by which the state has chosen to further those interests.

1. Prohibition—A Total Ban for the Terminally Ill

Washington's statute prohibiting assisted suicide has a drastic impact on the terminally ill. By prohibiting physician assistance, it bars what for many terminally ill patients is the only palatable, and only practical, way to end their lives. Physically frail, confined to wheelchairs or beds, many terminally ill patients do not have the means or ability to kill themselves in the multitude of ways that healthy individuals can. Often, for example, they cannot even secure the medication or devices they would need to carry out their wishes.

Some terminally ill patients stockpile presciption medicine, which they can use to end their lives when they decide the time is right. The successful use of the stockpile technique generally depends, however, on the assistance of a physician, whether tacit or unknowing (although it is possible to end one's life with over-the-counter medication). Even if the terminally ill patients are able to accumulate sufficient drugs, given the pain-killers and other medication they are taking, most of them would lack the knowledge to determine what dose of any given drug or drugs they must take, or in what combination. Miscalculation can be tragic. It can lead to an even more painful and lingering death. Alternatively, if the medication reduces respiration enough to restrict the flow of oxygen to the brain but not enough to cause death, it can result in the patient's falling into a comatose or vegetative state.

Thus for many terminally ill patients, the Washington statute is effectively a prohibition. While technically it only prohibits one means of exercising a liberty interest, practically it prohibits the exercise of that interest as effectively as prohibiting doctors from performing abortions prevented women from having abortions in the days before *Roe*.

2. Regulation—A Permissible Means of Promoting
State Interests

State laws or regulations governing physician-assisted suicide are both necessary and desirable to ensure against errors and abuse, and to protect legitimate state interests. Any of several model statutes might serve as an example of how these legitimate and important concerns can be addressed effectively.

By adopting appropriate, reasonable, and properly drawn safeguards, Washington could ensure that people who choose to have their doctors prescribe lethal doses of medication are truly competent and meet all of the requisite standards. Without endorsing the constitutionality of any particular procedural safeguards, we note that the state might, for example, require: witnesses to ensure voluntariness; reasonable, though short, waiting periods to prevent rash decisions; second medical opinions to confirm a patient's terminal status and also to confirm that the patient has been receiving proper treatment, including adequate comfort care; psychological examinations to ensure that the patient is not suffering from momentary or treatable depression; reporting procedures that will aid in the avoidance of abuse. Alternatively, such safeguards could be adopted by interested medical associations and other organizations involved in the provision of health care, so long as they meet the state's needs and concerns. . . .

C. The Strength of the Liberty Interest

Earlier in the opinion we described the liberty interest at issue here and explained its importance. We also explained that the strength of that interest is dependent on a number of factors, especially the individual's physical condition. We noted that an individual's liberty interest in hastening his death is at its low point when that person is young and healthy, because forcing a robust individual to continue living does not, at least absent extraordinary circumstances, subject him to "pain . . . [and] suffering that is too intimate and personal for the State to insist on. . . ." (*Casey,* 112 S.Ct. at 2807.) As we also made clear, when a mentally competent adult is terminally ill, and wishes, free of any coercion, to hasten his death because his remaining days are an unmitigated torture, that person's liberty interest is at its height. For such a person, being forced to live is indeed being subjected to "pain . . . [and] suffering that is too intimate and personal for the State to insist on."

D. The Burden on the Liberty Interest

We have also previously discussed at some length the nature and extent of the burden that the Washington statute imposes on the liberty interest. Here, we need only mention some of the specific evidence introduced by the plaintiffs and refer to some of our earlier analysis. The plaintiffs offered considerable specific testimony involving individual patients that strongly supports their claims that the Washington statute frequently presents an insuperable obstacle to terminally ill persons who wish to hasten their deaths by peaceful means. The testimony produced by the plaintiffs shows that many terminally ill patients who wish to die with dignity are forced to resort to gruesome alternatives because of the unavailability of physician assistance. . . .

Following the approach of the Court in *Casey,* we note that there is also an extensive body of legal, medical, and sociological literature, lending support to the conclusion that a prohibition on physician assistance imposes an onerous burden on terminally ill, competent adults who wish to hasten their deaths. That conclusion is further buttressed by extensive anecdotal evidence compiled in newspapers and magazines. Although the statute at issue does not totally prohibit the exercise of the liberty interest by all who possess it, it does effectively prohibit its exercise by almost all of the terminally ill. In fact, as applied, the ban on the liberty interest is close to complete; for there are few terminally ill persons who do not obtain illicit help from someone in the course of their efforts to hasten their deaths. . . .

E. The Consequences of Upholding or Overturning the Statutory Provision

In various earlier sections of this opinion, we have discussed most of the consequences of upholding or overturning the Washington statutory provision at issue, because in this case those consequences are best considered as part of the discussion of the specific factors or interests. The one remaining consequence of significance is easy to identify: Whatever the outcome here, a host of painful and agonizing issues involving the right to die will continue to confront the courts. More important, these problems will continue to plague growing numbers of Americans of advanced age as well as their families, dependents, and loved ones. The issue is truly one which deserves the most thorough, careful, and objective attention from all segments of society.

VI. APPLICATION OF THE BALANCING TEST AND HOLDING

Weighing and then balancing a constitutionally protected interest against the state's countervailing interests, while bearing in mind the various consequences of the decision, is quintessentially a judicial role. Despite all of the efforts of generations of courts to categorize and objectify, to create multi-part tests and identify weights to be attached to the various factors, in the end balancing entails the exercise of judicial judgment rather than the application of scientific or mathematical formulae. No legislative body can perform the task for us. Nor can any computer. In the end, mindful of our constitutional obligations, including the limitations imposed on us by that document, we must rely on our judgment, guided by the facts and the law as we perceive them. . . .

The liberty interest at issue here is an important one and, in the case of the terminally ill, is at its peak. Conversely, the state interests, while equally important in the abstract, are for the most part at a low point here. We recognize that in the case of life-and-death decisions the state has a particularly strong interest in avoiding undue influence and other forms of abuse. Here, that concern is ameliorated in large measure because of the mandatory involvement in the decision-making process of physicians, who have a strong bias in favor of preserving life, and because the process itself can be carefully regulated and rigorous safeguards adopted. Under these circumstances, we believe that the possibility of abuse, even when considered along with the other state interests, does not outweigh the liberty interest at issue. . . .

We consider the state's interests in preventing assisted suicide as being different only in degree and not in kind from its interests in prohibiting a number of other medical practices that lead directly to a terminally ill patient's death. Moreover, we do not consider those interests to be significantly greater in the case of assisted suicide than they are in the case of those other medical practices, if indeed they are greater at all. However, even if the difference were one of kind and not degree, our result would be no different. For no matter now much weight we could legitimately afford the state's interest in preventing suicide, that weight, when combined with the weight we give all the other state's interests, is insufficient to outweigh the terminally ill individual's interest in deciding whether to end his agony and suffering by hastening the time of his death with medication prescribed by his physician. The individual's interest in making that vital decision is compelling indeed, for no decision is more painful, delicate, personal, important, or final than the decision how and when one's life shall end. If broad general state policies can be used to deprive a terminally ill individual of the right to make that choice, it is hard to envision where the exercise of arbitrary and intrusive power by the state can be halted. In this case, the state has wide power to regulate, but it may not ban the exercise of the liberty interest, and that is the practical effect of the program before us. Accordingly, after examining one final legal authority, we hold that the "or aids" provision of the Washington statute is unconstitutional as applied to terminally ill competent adults who wish to hasten their deaths with medication prescribed by their physicians.

A. One Possible Obstacle

[The judges here take issue briefly with the opinion in *Lee v. State of Oregon* (869 F. Supp. 1491 [1995]), in which a district court found that the Oregon Death With Dignity Act, which permitted doctors to prescribe medications that terminally ill people could use to end their lives, violated the Equal Protection clause of the Fourteenth Amendment.]

B. Is There an Equal Protection Violation?

In the case before us, Chief Judge Rothstein [of the district court] struck down the "or aids" provision of the Washington statute as it applies to the terminally ill, not only on due process grounds but also on the ground that it violates the Equal Protection clause. Because we are convinced that her first reason is correct, we need not consider the second. One constitutional violation is enough to support the judgment that we reach here.

VII. Conclusion

We hold that a liberty interest exists in the choice of how and when one dies, and that the provision of the Washington statute banning assisted suicide, as applied to competent, terminally ill adults who wish to hasten their deaths by obtaining medication prescribed by their doctors, violates the Due Process Clause. We recognize that this decision is a most difficult and controversial one, and that it leaves unresolved a large number of equally troublesome issues that will require resolution in the years ahead. We also recognize that other able and dedicated jurists, construing the Constitution as they believe it must be construed, may disagree not only with the result we reach but with our method of constitutional analysis. Given the nature of the judicial process and the complexity of the task of determining the rights and interests comprehended by the Constitution, good-faith disagreements within the judiciary should not surprise or disturb anyone who follows the development of the law. For these reasons, we express our hope that whatever debate may accompany the future exploration of the issues we have touched on today will be conducted in an objective, rational, and constructive manner that will increase, not diminish, respect for the Constitution.

There is one final point we must emphasize. Some argue strongly that decisions regarding matters affecting life or death should not be made by the courts. Essentially, we agree with that proposition. In this case, by permitting the individual to exercise the right to choose we are following the constitutional mandate to take such decisions out of the hands of the government, both state and federal, and to put them where they rightly belong, in the hands of the people. We are allowing individuals to make the decisions that so profoundly affect their very existence—and precluding the state from intruding excessively into that critical realm.

The Constitution and the courts stand as a bulwark between individual freedom and arbitrary and intrusive governmental power. Under our constitutional system, neither the state nor the majority of the people in a state can impose its will upon the individual in a matter so highly "central to personal dignity and autonomy." (*Casey,* 112 S.Ct. at 2807.) Those who believe strongly that death must come without physician assistance are free to follow that creed, be they doctors or patients. They are not free, however, to force their views, their religious convictions, or their philosophies on all the other members of a democratic society, and to compel those whose values differ with theirs to die painful, protracted, and agonizing deaths.

C. *Quill v. Vacco*

United States Court of Appeals
for the Second Circuit
April 2, 1996

[In July 1994 Timothy E. Quill (author of an essay in the medical section of this volume), two other doctors, and three terminally ill persons filed a complaint charging that New York state laws prohibiting assistance in suicide were unconstitutional. The district court rejected their challenges, which were based on the Due Process and Equal Protection clauses of the Fourteenth Amendment. On appeal by the three physicians, the judgment of the district court was reversed in part by the Second Circuit Court of Appeals. Circuit Judge JOHN MINER wrote the opinion of the three-judge panel, holding that "physicians who are willing to do so may prescribe drugs to be self-administered by mentally competent patients who seek to end their lives during the final stages of a terminal illness." (The case was subsequently appealed to the United States Supreme Court, which handed down its opinion in June 1997; for this, see chapter 29.) Judge GUIDO CALABRESI concurred in a separate opinion. Judge Miner's opinion, abridged, and some excerpts from Judge Calabresi's are given below. The Miner opinion begins with section II of the analysis, after the court's rejection of the defendants' contention that this was "not a justifiable case or controversy."]

II. SUBSTANTIVE DUE PROCESS

Plaintiffs argue for a right to assisted suicide as a fundamental liberty under the substantive component of the Due Process Clause of the

---

517

Fourteenth Amendment. This Clause assures the citizenry that any deprivation of life, liberty, or property by a state will be attended by appropriate legal processes. However,

> despite the language of the Due Process Clause[ ] of the . . . Fourteenth Amendment[ ], which appears to focus only on the processes by which life, liberty, or property is taken, the cases are legion in which th[at] Clause [ ] ha[s] been interpreted to have substantive content, subsuming rights that to a great extent are immune from . . . state regulation or proscription. Among such cases are those recognizing rights that have little or no textual support in the constitutional language. [*Bowers v. Hardwick,* 478 U.S. 186, 191 (1986).]

Rights that have no textual support in the language of the Constitution but qualify for heightened judicial protection include fundamental liberties so "implicit in the concept of ordered liberty" that "neither liberty nor justice would exist if they were sacrificed." (*Palko v. Connecticut,* 302 U.S. 319, 325-26 [1937].) Fundamental liberties also have been described as those that are "deeply rooted in this Nation's history and tradition." (*Moore v. City of East Cleveland,* 431 U.S. 494, 503 [1977].) It is well settled that the state must not infringe fundamental liberty interests unless the infringement is narrowly tailored to serve a compelling state interest. (*Reno v. Flores,* 113 S. Ct. 1439, 1447 [1993].)

The list of rights the Supreme Court has actually or impliedly identified as fundamental, and therefore qualified for heightened judicial protection, include the fundamental guarantees of the Bill of Rights as well as the following: freedom of association; the right to participate in the electoral process and to vote; the right to travel interstate; the right to fairness in the criminal process; the right to procedural fairness in regard to claims for governmental deprivations of life, liberty, or property; and the right to privacy. The right of privacy has been held to encompass personal decisions relating to marriage, procreation, family relationships, child rearing and education, contraception and abortion. While the Constitution does not, of course, include any explicit mention of the right of privacy, this right has been recognized as encompassed by the Fourteenth Amendment's Due Process Clause. Nevertheless, the Supreme Court has been reluctant to further expand this particular list of federal rights, and it would be most speculative for a lower court to do so.

In any event, the Supreme Court has drawn a line, albeit a shaky one, on the expansion of fundamental rights that are without support in the text of the Constitution. In *Bowers,* the Supreme Court framed the issue as "whether the Federal Constitution confers a fundamental right upon homosexuals to engage in sodomy and hence invalidates the laws of the many States that still make such conduct illegal and have done so for a very long time." (*Bowers v. Hardwick,* 478 U.S. at 190.) Holding that there was no fundamental right to engage in consensual sodomy, the Court noted that the statutes proscribing such conduct had "ancient roots." The Court noted that sodomy was a common law criminal offense, forbidden by the laws of the original thirteen states when they ratified the Bill of Rights, and that twenty-five states and the District of Columbia still penalize sodomy performed in private by consenting adults.

As in *Bowers,* the statutes plaintiffs seek to declare unconstitutional here cannot be said to infringe upon any fundamental right or liberty. As in *Bowers,* the right contended for here cannot be considered so implicit in our understanding of ordered liberty that neither justice nor liberty would exist if it were sacrificed. Nor can it be said that the right to assisted suicide claimed by plaintiffs is deeply rooted in the nation's traditions and history. Indeed, the very opposite is true. The Common Law of England, as received by the American colonies, prohibited suicide and attempted suicide. Although neither suicide nor attempted suicide is any longer a crime in the United States, thirty-two states, including New York, continue to make assisted suicide an offense. Clearly, no "right" to assisted suicide ever has been recognized in any state in the United States.

In rejecting the due process–fundamental rights argument of the plaintiffs, we are mindful of the admonition of the Supreme Court:

> Nor are we inclined to take a more expansive view of our authority to discover new fundamental rights imbedded in the Due Process Clause. The Court is most vulnerable and comes nearest to illegitimacy when it deals with judge-made constitutional law having little or no cognizable roots in the language or design of the Constitution. [*Bowers v. Hardwick,* 478 U.S. at 194.]

The right to assisted suicide finds no cognizable basis in the Constitution's language or design, even in the very limited cases of those competent persons who, in the final stages of terminal illness, seek the right to hasten death. We therefore decline the plaintiffs' invitation to identify a new fundamental right, in the absence of a clear direction from the Court whose precedents we are bound to follow. The limited room for expansion of substantive due process rights and the reasons therefor have been clearly stated: "As a general matter, the Court has always been reluctant to expand the concept of substantive due process because guideposts for responsible decision-making in this unchartered area are scarce and open-ended." (*Collins v. City of Harker Heights*, 503 U.S. 115, 125 [1992].) Our position in the judicial hierarchy constrains us to be even more reluctant than the Court to undertake an expansive approach in this unchartered area.

III. Equal Protection

According to the Fourteenth Amendment, the equal protection of the laws cannot be denied by any state to any person within its jurisdiction. This constitutional guarantee simply requires the states to treat in a similar manner all individuals who are similarly situated. But disparate treatment is not necessarily a denial of the equal protection guaranteed by the Constitution. The Supreme Court has described the wide discretion afforded to the states in establishing acceptable classifications:

> The Equal Protection Clause directs that "all persons similarly circumstanced shall be treated alike." But so too, "[t]he Constitution does not require things which are different in fact or opinion to be treated in law as though they were the same." The initial discretion to determine what is "different" and what is "the same" resides in the legislatures of the States. A legislature must have substantial latitude to establish classifications that roughly approximate the nature of the problem perceived, that accommodate competing concerns both public and private, and that account for limitations on the practical ability of the State to remedy every ill. In applying the Equal Protection Clause to most forms of state action,

we thus seek only the assurance that the classification at issue bears some fair relationship to a legitimate public purpose. [*Plyler v. Doe*, 457 U.S. 202, 216 (1982).]

The general rule, then, is that state legislation carries a presumption of validity if the statutory classification is "rationally related to a legitimate state interest." (*City of Cleburne v. Cleburne Living Ctr., Inc.*, 473 U.S. 432, 440 [1985].) In *Cleburne*, the equal protection issue revolved around a zoning ordinance that required a special use permit for homes for the mentally retarded but not for other multiple-dwelling and care-giving facilities. The Supreme Court resolved the issue as follows:

> Because in our view the record does not reveal any rational basis for believing that the Featherston home [for the mentally retarded] would pose any special threat to the city's legitimate interests, we affirm the judgment below insofar as it holds the ordinance invalid as applied in this case. [Idem at 448.]

In arriving at this conclusion, the Court rejected the city's claims that the disparate classification was justified by the negative attitudes of property owners in the neighborhood of the proposed facility, the location of the facility across the street from a junior high school and on a 500-year flood plain, concerns about legal responsibility for actions that might be taken by the mentally retarded, or concerns about the size of the facility and the number of occupants. The Court carefully examined each of these claims before finding that there was no acceptable reason for the disparate classification in any of them.

Also found invalid under the Equal Protection Clause for failure to survive rational-basis scrutiny was a New Mexico statute providing a partial exemption from the state's property tax for certain honorably discharged veterans. (*Hooper v. Bernalillo County Assessor*, 472 U.S. 612 [1985].) The exemption was limited to veterans who had served on active duty during the Vietnam War for at least ninety continuous days and were New Mexico residents before May 8, 1976. In finding the residence requirement invalid under the Equal Protection Clause, the Court analyzed the New Mexico statute in light of the following principles: "When a state distributes benefits unequally, the distinctions it makes are subject to scrutiny under the Equal Protection

Clause of the Fourteenth Amendment. Generally, a law will survive that scrutiny if the distinction rationally furthers a legitimate state purpose." (Idem at 618.) The Court determined that the distinction made between veterans who arrived in the state prior to May 8, 1976, and those who arrived thereafter bore no rational relationship to the state's declared objectives of encouraging veterans to settle in the state and of rewarding citizens who resided in the state prior to the cut-off date for their military service. . . .

While rational-basis scrutiny governs judicial review of the constitutionality of legislation in the areas of social welfare and economics, strict scrutiny is the standard of review where a classification "impermissibly interferes with the exercise of a fundamental right or operates to the peculiar disadvantage of a suspect class." (*Massachusetts Board of Retirement v. Murgia,* 427 U.S. 307, 312 [1976].)

Suspect classes are those identified by race, alienage, or national origin, and fundamental rights are those explicitly or implicitly derived from the Constitution itself. For the reasons described in Part II, *supra,* the New York statutes prohibiting assisted suicide during the terminal stages of illness do not impinge on any fundamental rights nor can it be said that they involve suspect classifications. Laws subject to strict scrutiny will survive such review only if they are suitably tailored to serve a compelling state interest.

An intermediate level of scrutiny has been applied in analyzing certain equal protection guarantee violations. To pass this scrutiny, the classification must be substantially related to an important governmental objective. This sort of examination has been applied to classifications based on sex or illegitimacy. A heightened level of equal protection scrutiny also was applied in *Plyler,* where the Supreme Court struck down a Texas statute withholding from local school districts funding for the education of children not legally admitted into the United States.

Applying the foregoing principles to the New York statutes criminalizing assisted suicide, it seems clear that: (1) the statutes in question fall within the category of social-welfare legislation and therefore are subject to rational-basis scrutiny upon judicial review; (2) New York law does not treat equally all competent persons who are in the final stages of fatal illness and wish to hasten their deaths; (3) the distinctions made by New York law with regard to such persons do not further any legitimate state purpose; and (4) accordingly, to the extent that the statutes in questions prohibit persons in the final stages of terminal illness from having assistance in ending their lives by the use of self-administered, prescribed drugs, the statutes lack any rational basis and are violative of the Equal Protection Clause.

The right to refuse medical treatment long has been recognized in New York. In 1914 Judge Cardozo wrote that, under New York law, "[e]very human being of adult years and sound mind has a right to determine what shall be done with his own body." *(Schloendorff v. Society of New York Hospital.)* In *In re Eichner* (decided with *In re Storar*), 1981, the New York Court of Appeals held that this right extended to the withdrawal of life-support systems. The Eichner case involved a terminally-ill, 83-year-old patient whose guardian ultimately was authorized to withdraw the patient's respirator. The Court of Appeals determined that the guardian had proved by clear and convincing evidence that the patient, prior to becoming incompetent due to illness, had consistently expressed his view that life should not be prolonged if there was no hope of recovery. In *Storar,* the companion case to *Eichner,* the Court of Appeals determined that a profoundly retarded, terminally-ill patient was incapable of making a decision to terminate blood transfusions. There, the patient was incapable of making a reasoned decision, having never been competent at any time in his life. In both these cases, the New York Court of Appeals recognized the right of a competent, terminally ill patient to hasten his death upon proper proof of his desire to do so.

The Court of Appeals revisited the issue in *Rivers v. Katz* (establishing the right of mentally incompetent persons to refuse certain drugs). In that case, the Court recognized the right to bring on death by refusing medical treatment not only as a "fundamental common-law right" but also as "coextensive with [a] patient's liberty interest protected by the due process clause of our State Constitution." The following language was included in the opinion:

> In our system of a free government, where notions of individual autonomy and free choice are cherished, it is the individual who must have the final say in respect to decisions regarding his medical treatment in order to insure that the greatest possible protection is accorded his autonomy and freedom from unwanted interference

with the furtherance of his own desires. [*Rivers v. Katz,* 67 N.Y. 2d 485, 493 (1986).]

After these cases were decided, the New York legislature placed its imprimatur upon the right of competent citizens to hasten death by refusing medical treatment and by directing physicians to remove life-support systems already in place. . . . An elaborate statutory scheme is in place, and it provides, among other things, for surrogate decision-making, revocation of consent, physician review, dispute mediation, and judicial review.

In 1990, the New York legislature enacted Article 29-C of the Public Health Law, entitled "Health Care Agents and Proxies." This statute allows for a person to sign a health care proxy, for the purpose of appointing an agent with "authority to make any and all health-care decisions on the principal's behalf that the principal could make." These decisions include those relating to the administration of artificial nutrition and hydration, provided the wishes of the principal are known to the agent. The agent's decision is made "[a]fter consultation with a licensed physician, registered nurse, licensed clinical psychologist or certified social worker." Accordingly, a patient has the right to hasten death by empowering an agent to require a physician to withdraw life-support systems. . . .

The concept that a competent person may order the removal of life-support systems found Supreme Court approval in *Cruzan v. Director, Missouri Department of Health* (497 U.S. 261 [1990]). There the Court upheld a determination of the Missouri Supreme Court that required proof by clear and convincing evidence of a patient's desire for the withdrawal of life-sustaining equipment. The patient in that case, Nancy Cruzan, was in a persistent vegetative state as the result of injuries sustained in an automobile accident. Her parents sought court approval in the State of Missouri to terminate the artificial nutrition and hydration with which she was supplied at the state hospital where she was confined. The hospital employees refused to withdraw the life-support systems, without which Cruzan would suffer certain death. The trial court authorized the withdrawal after finding that Cruzan had expressed some years before to a housemate friend some thoughts that suggested she would not wish to live on a life-support system. The trial court also found that one in Cruzan's

condition had a fundamental right to refuse death-prolonging procedures.

The Missouri Supreme Court, in reversing the trial court, refused
to find a broad right of privacy in the state constitution that would
support a right to refuse treatment. Moreover, that court doubted that
such a right existed under the United States Constitution. It did
identify a state policy in the Missouri Living Will Statute favoring the
preservation of life and concluded that, in the absence of compliance
with the statute's formalities or clear and convincing evidence of the
patient's choice, no person could order the withdrawal of medical
life-support services.

In affirming the Missouri Supreme Court, the United States Supreme Court stated: "The principle that a competent person has a
constitutionally protected liberty interest in refusing unwanted medical treatment may be inferred from our prior decisions." (Idem at
278.) The Court noted that the inquiry is not ended by the identification of a liberty interest, because there also must be a balancing of
the state interests and the individual's liberty interests before there
can be a determination that constitutional rights have been violated.
The Court all but made that determination in the course of the
following analysis:

> Petitioners insist that under the general holdings of our cases, the
> forced administration of life-sustaining medical treatment, and
> even of artificially delivered food and water essential to life, would
> implicate a competent person's liberty interest. Although we think
> the logic of the cases discussed above would embrace such a liberty
> interest, the dramatic consequences involved in refusal of such
> treatment would inform the inquiry as to whether the deprivation
> of that interest is constitutionally permissible. But for purposes of
> this case, we assume that the United States Constitution would
> grant a competent person a constitutionally protected right to refuse
> lifesaving hydration and nutrition. [Idem.]

The Court went on to find that Missouri allowed a surrogate to
"act for the patient in electing to have hydration and nutrition withdrawn in such a way as to cause death," subject to "a procedural
safeguard to assure that the action of the surrogate conforms as best
it may to the wishes expressed by the patient while competent." The

Court then held that the procedural safeguard or requirement imposed by Missouri—the heightened evidentiary requirement that the incompetent's wishes be proved by clear and convincing evidence—was not forbidden by the United States Constitution.

In view of the foregoing, it seems clear that New York does not treat similarly circumstanced persons alike: those in the final stages of terminal illness who are on life-support systems are allowed to hasten their deaths by directing the removal of such systems; but those who are similarly situated, except for the previous attachment of life-sustaining equipment, are not allowed to hasten death by self-administering prescribed drugs. The district judge has identified "a difference between allowing nature to take its course, even in the most severe situations, and intentionally using an artificial death-producing device." But Justice Scalia, for one, has remarked upon "the irrelevance of the action-inaction distinction," noting that "the cause of death in both cases is the suicide's conscious decision to 'pu[t] an end to his own existence.'" (*Cruzan,* 497 U.S. at 296-97 [citations omitted and alteration in original].)

Indeed, there is nothing "natural" about causing death by means other than the original illness or its complications. The withdrawal of nutrition brings on death by starvation, the withdrawal of hydration brings on death by dehydration, and the withdrawal of ventilation brings about respiratory failure. By ordering the discontinuance of these artificial life-sustaining processes or refusing to accept them in the first place, a patient hastens his death by means that are not natural in any sense. It certainly cannot be said that the death that immediately ensues is the natural result of the progression of the disease or condition from which the patient suffers.

Moreover, the writing of a prescription to hasten death, after consultation with a patient, involves a far less active role for the physician than is required in bringing about death through asphyxiation, starvation, and/or dehydration. Withdrawal of life support requires physicians or those acting at their direction physically to remove equipment and, often, to administer palliative drugs which may themselves contribute to death. The ending of life by these means is nothing more nor less than assisted suicide. It simply cannot be said that those mentally competent, terminally ill persons who seek to hasten death but whose treatment does not include life support are treated equally.

A finding of unequal treatment does not, of course, end the inquiry, unless it is determined that the inequality is not rationally related to some legitimate state interest. The burden is upon the plaintiffs to demonstrate irrationality. At oral argument and in its brief, the state's contention has been that its principal interest is in preserving the life of all its citizens at all times and under all conditions. But what interest can the state possibly have in requiring the prolongation of a life that is all but ended? Surely, the state's interest lessens as the potential for life diminishes. And what business is it of the state to require the continuation of agony when the result is imminent and inevitable? What concern prompts the state to interfere with a mentally competent patient's "right to define [his] own concept of existence, of meaning, of the universe, and of the mystery of human life" (*Planned Parenthood v. Casey*, 505 U.S. 833 [1992]), when the patient seeks to have drugs prescribed to end life during the final stages of a terminal illness? The greatly reduced interest of the state in preserving life compels the answer to these questions: "None."

A panel of the Ninth Circuit attempted to identify some state interests in reversing a district court decision holding unconstitutional a statute of the state of Washington criminalizing the promotion of a suicide attempt (*Compassion in Dying v. Washington*, 1995). The plaintiffs in the Washington case contended for physician-assisted suicide for the terminally ill, but the panel majority found that the statute prohibiting suicide promotion furthered the following: the interest in denying to physicians "the role of killers of their patients"; the interest in avoiding psychological pressure upon the elderly and infirm to consent to death; the interest of preventing the exploitation of the poor and minorities; the interest in protecting handicapped persons against societal indifference; the interest in preventing the sort of abuse that "has occurred in the Netherlands where . . . legal guidelines have tacitly allowed assisted suicide or euthanasia in response to a repeated request from a suffering, competent patient." The panel majority also raised a question relative to the lack of clear definition of the term "terminally ill."

The New York statutes prohibiting assisted suicide, which are similar to the Washington statute, do not serve any of the state interests noted, in view of the statutory and common law schemes allowing suicide through the withdrawal of life-sustaining treatment. Physicians do not fulfill the role of "killer" by prescribing drugs to hasten death any more than they do by disconnecting life-support systems. Likewise, "psychological pressure" can be applied just as much upon the elderly and infirm to consent to withdrawal of life-sustaining equipment as to take drugs to hasten death. There is no clear indication that there has been any problem in regard to the former, and there should be none as to the latter. In any event, the state of New York may establish rules and procedures to assure that all choices are free of such pressures. With respect to the protection of minorities, the poor and the non-mentally handicapped, it suffices to say that these classes of persons are entitled to treatment equal to that afforded to all those who now may hasten death by means of life-support withdrawal. In point of fact, these persons themselves are entitled to hasten death by requesting such withdrawal and should be free to do so by requesting appropriate medication to terminate life during the final stages of terminal illness.

As to the interest in avoiding abuse similar to that occurring in the Netherlands, it seems clear that some physicians there practice non-voluntary euthanasia, although it is not legal to do so. The plaintiffs here do not argue for euthanasia at all but for assisted suicide for terminally ill, mentally competent patients, who would self-administer the lethal drugs. It is difficult to see how the relief the plaintiffs seek would lead to the abuses found in the Netherlands. Moreover, note should be taken of the fact that the Royal Dutch Medical Association recently adopted new guidelines for those physicians who choose to accede to the wishes of patients to hasten death. Under the new guidelines, patients must self-administer drugs whenever possible, and physicians must obtain a second opinion from another physician who has no relationship with the requesting physician or his patient.

Finally, it seems clear that most physicians would agree on the definition of "terminally ill," at least for the purpose of the relief that plaintiffs seek. The plaintiffs seek to hasten death only where a patient is in the "final stages" of "terminal illness," and it seems even more certain that physicians would agree on when this condition occurs. Physicians are accustomed to advising patients and their families in this regard and frequently do so when decisions are to be made regarding the furnishing or withdrawal of life-support systems. Again,

New York may define that stage of illness with greater particularity, require the opinion of more than one physician, or impose any other obligation upon patients and physicians who collaborate in hastening death.

The New York statutes criminalizing assisted suicide violate the Equal Protection Clause because, to the extent that they prohibit a physician from prescribing medications to be self-administered by a mentally competent, terminally ill person in the final stages of his terminal illness, they are not rationally related to any legitimate state interest. . . .

Judge Calabresi, concurring in the result:

I agree with the Court that these statutes cannot stand. But I do not believe that the history of the statutes, and of New York's approach toward assisted suicide, requires us to make a final judgment under either Due Process or Equal Protection as to the validity of statutes prohibiting assisted suicide. What is not ready for decision ought not to be decided. I would therefore leave open the question of whether, if the state of New York were to enact new laws prohibiting assisted suicide (laws that either are less absolute in their application or are identical to those before us), such laws would stand or fall. . . .

. . . It cannot be denied that the laws here involved, whether tested by Due Process or by Equal Protection, are highly suspect. It is also the case, however, that neither *Cruzan,* nor *Casey,* nor the language of our Constitution, nor our constitutional tradition clearly makes these laws invalid. What, then, should be done?

I contend that when a law is neither plainly unconstitutional (because in derogation of one of the express clauses of our fundamental charter or, for that matter, of the more general clauses, as these have been interpreted in our constitutional history and traditions), nor plainly constitutional, the courts ought not to decide the ultimate validity of that law without current and clearly expressed statements, by the people or by their elected officials, of the state interests involved. . . .

. . . The rationale for the New York assisted-suicide prohibition has eroded with the passage of time. [The state's first such prohibition was enacted in 1828.] In the nineteenth century, both suicide and attempted suicide were crimes and assisting in those crimes was, derivatively, a crime as well. But suicide and attempted suicide are no longer crimes. Nevertheless, the prohibitions on assisted suicide might serve other valid ends. It is possible, for example, to imagine a state in which such statutes were part of an overall approach to the preservation of life that was so all-encompassing that the laws' validity might be upheld despite their infringement of important libertarian individual rights. Our Constitution gives us no more complete dominion over our bodies than it does over our property. . . .

. . . No court need or ought to make ultimate and immensely difficult constitutional decisions unless it knows that the state's elected representatives and executives—having been made to go, as it were, before the people—assert through their actions (not their inactions) that they really want and are prepared to defend laws that are constitutionally suspect.

It is different when the Constitution speaks clearly. When a law violates the plain mandates of the text, history, or structure of the Constitution, no second look is warranted or appropriate. That law must fall. Laws that violate the core of the First Amendment and the core of the Takings Clause are but two examples. When that is not the case, when the Constitution and its history do not clearly render a statute invalid, when its validity depends instead, in part, on the strength of the state interests at stake, then a second look is not only appropriate, it is, in my view, usually required. . . .

In the end, a constitutional remand does no more than this: It tells the legislatures and executives of the various states, and of the federal government as well, that if they wish to regulate conduct that, if not protected by our Constitution, is very close to being protected, they must do so clearly and openly. . . .

For all of the above reasons, I do not reach the merits in this case. . . . What, after all, are we to make of Margaret Mead's statement, cited in one of the amicus briefs, that we should beware of giving those who have the power to heal the right to kill, since anthropologically speaking the distinction between the two is relatively new in our cultures? It is certainly worth pondering. But how does it help us to distinguish between giving doctors the right to remove life-support systems and the right of the terminally ill to demand lethal drugs from the same doctors? And how is one to weigh petitioners' claim that if doctors are not allowed to give patients lethal drugs for self-administration, those patients will be forced to commit suicide, legally, in far more horrendous ways—by hanging, shooting, or gassing themselves? These methods, petitioners assert, are plausibly more dangerous to society and devastating to survivors. But is it really the case that terminally ill patients would take such measures? And which way would it cut, if they did not? These questions, moreover, hardly begin to approach the human tragedies, and the deeply held beliefs, that the issues we would have to decide would require us to explore. No. Unless New York forces us to face such choices head on, by asserting its interest in the prohibitions before us, we should not do so. And this New York has not done.

I would hold that, on the current legislative record, New York's prohibitions on assisted suicide violate both the Equal Protection and Due Process Clauses of the Fourteenth Amendment of the United States Constitution to the extent that these laws are interpreted to prohibit a physician from prescribing lethal drugs to be self-administered by a mentally competent, terminally ill person in the final stages of that terminal illness. I would, however, take no position on whether such prohibitions, or other more finely drawn ones, might be valid, under either or both clauses of the United States Constitution, were New York to reenact them while articulating the reasons for the distinctions it makes in the laws, and expressing the grounds for the prohibitions themselves. I therefore concur in the result reached by the Court.

26

Assisted Suicide in the United States: The 'Compassion' and 'Quill' Decisions

Victor G. Rosenblum

[In this testimony before a congressional subcommittee, Professor Rosenblum discusses the two 1996 decisions that, along with the Noonan decision, are printed in chapter 25 of this volume.]

I would like to thank [the committee] for the opportunity to testify regarding the importance of two recent and disturbing decisions on assisted suicide: *Compassion in Dying v. Washington,*[1] decided March 6 [1996] by an *en banc* panel of the U.S. Court of Appeals for the Ninth Circuit, and *Quill v. Vacco,*[2] decided April 2 [1996] by a three-judge panel of the Court of Appeals for the Second Circuit. The Ninth Circuit decision is particularly regrettable because it vacated a [1995] panel decision, written by Judge John T. Noonan, Jr., that eloquently showed why the right to assisted suicide is foreign to our legal traditions and inimical to a genuine understanding of liberty within our constitutional system. . . .

Victor G. Rosenblum is the Nathaniel L. Nathanson Professor of Law and Political Science at Northwestern University School of Law. He gave this testimony at a hearing before the Subcommittee on the Constitution of the Committee on the Judiciary, U.S. House of Representatives, on April 29, 1996. Many of the notes have been omitted.

My testimony will analyze these decisions in some depth. These are my principal conclusions:

■ First, the Ninth Circuit's holding that there is a constitutional liberty interest in assisted suicide, and the Second Circuit's holding that enforcement of laws against assisted suicide violates principles of equal protection, are contrary to relevant common law and constitutional precedent.

■ Second, both the Ninth and Second Circuit undervalued, and in some cases ignored, the compelling interests of the state in preventing physicians from taking actions to directly cause the deaths of their patients.

■ Third, the relief fashioned by the Ninth and Second Circuits is inherently elastic. It will expand in future cases to include the direct euthanasia, not only of competent terminally ill patients, but of patients who are incompetent and not terminally ill. These decisions will alter the physician-patient relationship and societal attitudes toward the terminally ill. They introduce a bias in favor of death, and against the more difficult challenge of fully caring for the weak and the vulnerable through the end of their natural lives. Such a bias threatens the inherent dignity of every human person, and will corrupt the delivery of health care to every patient with a life-threatening illness.

CONSTITUTIONAL ANALYSIS

First, to briefly summarize the essential holdings of these opinions: The Ninth Circuit [*Compassion in Dying v. Washington,* Judge Reinhardt] broadly held that under the Due Process clause of the Fourteenth Amendment, there is a "liberty interest in controlling the time and manner of one's death."[3] The court found that the Washington statute that prohibits "aid[ing] another person to attempt suicide" is unconstitutional "as applied to terminally ill competent adults who wish to hasten their deaths with medication prescribed by their physicians."[4]

In contrast, the Second Circuit [*Quill v. Vacco,* Judge Miner] expressly denied the existence of any such liberty interest. The court found that two New York statutes prohibiting assisted suicide "do not impinge on any fundamental rights nor can it be said that they involve suspect classifications."[5] However, because other aspects of New York law permit the withdrawal of life-sustaining treatment, which also may result in death, the court found the assisted-suicide prohibition to be a violation of the Equal Protection clause. "[T]o the extent that [these statutes] prohibit a physician from prescribing medication to be self-administered by a mentally competent, terminally ill person in the final stages of his terminal illness, they are not rationally related to any legitimate state interest."[6]

Assisted Suicide in History and Tradition

Our jurisprudence of substantive due process permits the federal courts to protect rights not specifically enumerated in the Constitution. Lest this power be wielded arbitrarily to frustrate the legitimate enactments of the legislature, the Supreme Court has placed clear strictures on its exercise. First among these is that any "new" rights ought to be protected only if they are "implicit in the concept of ordered liberty"[7] and "deeply rooted in this Nation's history and tradition."[8]

The Second Circuit correctly found that the asserted right to assisted suicide, even in the very limited cases of competent terminally ill persons who seek to hasten death, meets neither standard. The court abided by the Supreme Court's admonition that "[t]he Court is most vulnerable and comes nearest to illegitimacy when it deals with judge-made constitutional law having little or no cognizable roots in the language or design of the Constitution."[9]

Stating that analysis of the historical foundations is "useful," but not sufficient for rejecting a claimed liberty interest, the Ninth Circuit presented its own view of the legal history of assisted suicide. The court rejected the conclusions in Judge Noonan's opinion, which were identical to those of the Second Circuit, that a constitutional right to aid in killing oneself was "unknown to the past." The real history, Judge Reinhardt suggests, is far more "checkered."

The primary flaw of the Ninth Circuit's historical analysis, however, is that it relegates to secondary consideration the history that is most relevant—the common law and statutes that define the Anglo-American legal tradition regarding suicide and assisted suicide. The court downplays this tradition in favor of "literary" traditions regarding suicide. But evidence of acceptance of suicide among some ancient cultures, the deaths of Jewish resisters at Masada, and the practices of the Scythians or Vikings do not trump evidence of the common law as adopted by the American colonies, or the laws adopted by the states since 1789. The Ninth Circuit's rendition of the history of suicide demonstrates nothing more than what we already knew, and what Judge Noonan clearly knew when he wrote the majority opinion for the original Ninth Circuit panel: that in spite of millennia of philosophical, religious, and legal strictures on the duty to preserve life (including one's own), noteworthy examples of suicide are part of our history, and command study and reflection. They are not to be confused, however, with the Anglo-American legal tradition or American constitutional history.

The second and related flaw is that by focusing almost entirely upon the issue of suicide, the court fails to focus on the specific issue, which is the asserted right to *physician-assisted* suicide. This is a critical distinction. The "literary" suicides invoked by the Ninth Circuit were just that—suicides. They did not involve the assistance of others, in particular, the assistance of physicians. The Ninth Circuit identifies no tradition of physician involvement in assisting patients to die, other than contemporary reports of physicians who defy the law in this area. The court also ignores a welter of evidence establishing a clear legal consensus against assisted suicide.

As Judge Reinhardt acknowledges, under the English common law, suicide was a crime and subject to varying degrees of punishment from at least the thirteenth century and into the nineteenth century. His opinion emphasizes that criminal restrictions against suicide have waned. But he almost completely ignores the most relevant historical fact: that as criminal penalties against suicide were withdrawn in the nineteenth and twentieth centuries, penalties against *assisted* suicide were codified and strengthened.

For example, Judge Reinhardt claims that at the time of the passage of the Fourteenth Amendment, only nine states had statutes against assisted suicide. This ignores, first, that at least twelve additional states had adopted the common law of crimes, which treated assisted suicide as a species of homicide, and second, that due to a clear trend of states codifying prohibitions against assisted suicide (including several that have done so in recent years), virtually all states forbid assisted suicide either by express statute (Iowa just became the thirty-fourth state to do so), by judicial decision, or by adopting the common law of crimes.

Thus, the most relevant aspect of legal history at issue is virtually ignored by the Ninth Circuit. To the extent it is recognized, it is treated as a vestige of the past, not supported in contemporary jurisprudence or statutes. This also is an erroneous characterization. Since 1976, beginning with the case of Karen Quinlan, courts in a number of states have addressed whether there is a constitutional or common-law right to refuse life-sustaining medical treatment, and whether such a right may be exercised in the case of an incompetent patient by a surrogate, such as a family member. These have been controversial and difficult decisions, precisely because of concerns that they might involve the medical profession in causing the death of patients. But as the courts pointed out in these cases, the asserted right to be free of unwanted medical treatment is well established in the common law, and is not tantamount to a right to suicide or assisted suicide. . . .

Recent legislative enactments also confirm this distinction, and the current viability of sanctions against assisted suicide. In addition to the states that have recently codified specific restrictions against assisted suicide, virtually all states have in the past twenty years legislated some form of "advance directive" for health-care decisions at the end of life. Specifically, forty-five states and the District of Columbia expressly disapprove of mercy killing, suicide, or assisted suicide in "living will" and durable-power-of-attorney-for-health-care legislation. . . .

Against this evidence, the Ninth Circuit posits that current societal attitudes and public opinion support the right of the terminally ill to "die with dignity," that "most Americans simply do not appear to view such acts as constituting suicide," and that "there is much support in reason for that conclusion."[10] To the extent such attitudes are relevant at all—the Supreme Court has never relied upon "contemporary attitudes" to trump a record of consistent legislative action against a particular action for which constitutional protection is asserted—they must be considered in context. First, as previously indicated, the law in this area has been dynamic, not static, during the past generation. Scores of statutes and court opinions have defined rights to refuse life-sustaining medical treatment and the conditions under which the right may be exercised. Second, the refusal of treatment has been distinguished from the practice of assisted suicide. Third, proposals to legalize assisted suicide have consistently failed, save in a single state [Oregon]. . . .

In a representative democracy, these specific legislative enactments and judicial decisions are a far more relevant gauge of societal attitudes than the vagaries of public opinion polls, or anecdotal reports of individuals who choose to violate the law. In particular, the fact that some physicians may now provide assistance in suicide, or even direct mercy-killing, is irrelevant to the constitutional inquiry of whether such laws violate a constitutional liberty interest. "Attitudes" do not define tradition, and the "hidden practices" of a few do not define fundamental rights.

The flaws in the Ninth Circuit's historical analysis are reminiscent of those in the thoroughly repudiated historical excursus of Justice Blackmun in *Roe v. Wade.* The Ninth Circuit, apparently undeterred by the criticism leveled at *Roe,* has opened itself to the same type of attack. Its rendition of history offers no support for the claim that the Due Process clause protects a right to obtain assistance in ending one's life. Such a claim of radical autonomy is foreign to our legal traditions and constitutional history.

Assisted Suicide and the Abortion Cases

The court compounds these errors by misconstruing constitutional precedent, in particular the "privacy" decisions of *Roe v. Wade*[11] and *Planned Parenthood v. Casey,*[12] to support the proposition that the Due Process clause grants broad protection to all decisions relating to "personal dignity and autonomy." The Supreme Court has never enunciated such a broad standard. Indeed, the Court has rejected such claims on several occasions, including in *Roe v. Wade* itself. . . .

The Ninth Circuit . . . engaged in a facile analysis that reads into *Roe* and *Casey* principles that are not present in those decisions, and ignores the important doctrinal constraints that *are* present.

For example, the court declares that the decision to end one's life in order to avoid suffering "is highly personal and intimate," and thus subject to the same protection provided in *Roe* to a woman's decision to end a pregnancy. While plausible on its face, this equation overlooks several points. First, *Roe* and the cases on which it relied were concerned with procreation and childbearing, matters that are traditionally the province of the family. Suicide has no connection with this tradition of privacy in matters related to the family, and neither *Roe* nor any of the cases on which it relies suggests otherwise. Second, *Roe* specifically rejected the notion that one has an absolute right to do with one's body as one pleases, and thus rejected radical autonomy as a foundation for rights under the Due Process clause.

Third, on the critical question of the value of life, *Roe* recognized that if the unborn child were regarded as a constitutional person, there could be no right to abortion because the state would have a compelling interest in protecting the life of the child Although *Roe* declined so to treat the unborn child, it is crystal clear that persons who would be subject to assisted suicide are constitutional persons, and thus merit the protection of the state until their natural death. The entire *Roe* framework of trimesters and evolving rights and interests is entirely irrelevant to the case of assisted suicide. The unique status of *Roe* is illustrated by the Court's decision, in the same term that *Roe* was decided, in *Paris Adult Theatre I v. Slaton.*[13] There, the Court referred with approval to then-unchallenged laws banning [assisted] suicide.

The Ninth Circuit also relied on a selective reading of dicta in *Planned Parenthood v. Casey* to support its broad notions of autonomy. Admittedly, the language in *Casey* stating that "[a]t the heart of liberty is the right to define one's own concept of existence, of meaning, of the universe, and of the mystery of human life"[14] is capable of broad application. But this dictum should not be confused with constitutional doctrine, and should not be reflexively applied to matters outside the scope of the narrow issue before the Court in *Casey*.

That issue was whether the Court should overturn its earlier, controversial ruling in *Roe*—not whether a new right should be created. By the narrowest of majorities, the Court declined to do so. The Court's meditation on the extent of liberty was a defense of its prior decision, not an invitation to the declaration of other novel constitutional rights. And the specific language in question is preceded by a discussion of the constitutional protection given to marriage, procreation, contraception, and the rearing and education of children, thus closely tying the Court's more florid language directly to established precedent. . . .

Assisted Suicide and the Right to Refuse Treatment

1. *The Impact of Cruzan.* The Ninth Circuit, and the Second Circuit in *Quill v. Vacco,* equated the right to assisted suicide with the evolving right to refuse life-sustaining medical treatment. In doing so, they ignored the legislative enactments of virtually every state, and the unanimous judgment of the state courts that have ruled on this issue, that exercise of the common-law right to refuse even life-sustaining medical treatment is not tantamount to suicide. This disregard of precedent is all the more remarkable due to the vast professional literature and widespread public discussion of these issues since the decision of the New Jersey supreme court regarding Karen Quinlan, exactly twenty years ago [1976].

Both courts also misread *Cruzan v. Director, Missouri Dept. of Public Health,*[15] in which the Supreme Court presumed, but did not decide, that a competent patient has the right to refuse unwanted medical treatment, and may refuse assistance in feeding, even if this will result in death. . . .

Admittedly, there are certain circumstances in which decisions to withdraw medical treatment or to stop feeding a patient come close to assisted suicide or even euthanasia. These cases are particularly troubling when they involve severely disabled individuals who have played no part in the decision to withdraw treatment. They are far less troubling, for example, when a terminally ill patient decides to forgo care that will be futile in preserving life, and chooses to die at home or under hospice care.

However, even in the more difficult cases, there is a critical distinction: death, if it does result, occurs because of an underlying pathology, and not as the result of a lethal agent prescribed or administered by a physician. Moreover, from a jurisprudential point of view, the decision to decline treatment or to reject assistance in feeding is based on principles of informed consent and battery that are of long standing in the common law. Thus, the right to refuse medical treatment finds substantial support in our history and tradition, and holds a credible claim to recognition as a liberty interest protected by the Fourteenth Amendment. The right to assisted suicide has no such pedigree. Indeed, as illustrated above, the refinement of the right to refuse in recent decades was accompanied by an affirmation of the need for continued restrictions on assisted suicide. Thus, the claim presented in *Cruzan* was supported by the very form of tradition and history that is completely lacking in the case of assisted suicide. The Ninth Circuit and the Second Circuit attempt to leverage this traditional foundation for the right to refuse treatment into support for the right to assisted suicide. This is a fundamental error of these decisions. . . .

2. The Distinction Between Withdrawing Treatment and Suicide. As mentioned, both the Second and Ninth Circuits attempt to leverage the consensus supporting the right to refuse medical treatment into a broader "right to die" that now encompasses assisted suicide, and in the future, will likely include active euthanasia. The Ninth Circuit, in fact, explicitly holds that the right to assisted suicide may be exercised by a "duly appointed surrogate"—thus meaning that the right is *not* limited to competent patients.

This tactic, to blur the distinction between withdrawing treatment and direct assistance in killing, is favored by pro-euthanasia advocates for obvious reasons. By placing these very different practices under the all-encompassing rubric of a "right to die," they avoid having to make the case for dismantling centuries of legal precedent opposing assisted suicide, as well as millennia of ethical teaching that forbids physician participation in causing the deaths of their patients. In fact, these advocates often eschew the terms "assisted suicide" and "euthanasia" in favor of more palatable terms, such as "physician aid-in-dying."

It is one thing for social advocates to engage in such linguistic sleight-of-hand. It is quite another for our federal courts to adopt the practice, as has occurred in both opinions here.

Both courts gloss over the fundamental distinction between omission and commission, between allowing a patient to die and killing the patient. The Second Circuit used this equivocation to create an Equal Protection clause claim; the Ninth Circuit used it to create a Due Process clause claim: since there is a right to refuse unwanted life-sustaining medical treatment, the court reasoned, there must be a corollary right to enlist the assistance of a physician in directly causing one's death. The Ninth Circuit in particular attempts to make the case that the prescription of lethal medication to a terminally ill patient should not even be considered assistance in suicide, but merely as an effort to ensure that the patient's inevitable death will be humane and dignified.

As previously discussed, other legal authorities dismiss this point of view. . . . The vast body of legal and medical literature supporting this distinction makes the following points:

First, there is an ethical distinction between act and omission. Though the Ninth Circuit views this as a distinction without a difference, there is a clear analytical difference between actively causing one's death by introduction of an artificial agent and passively allowing death to occur from natural causes by refusing instrumentalities to prolong life. If this were not the case, no omission of a potentially life-sustaining treatment would be ethical, and physicians and patients would be obliged to use all possible means to sustain life in all cases.

Second, the right to refuse life-sustaining medical treatment articulated during the past two decades evolved out of the common law of battery and informed consent, and is properly classified as a negative right: the right not to be subjected to treatment, particularly treatment that is burdensome and carries an uncertain hope of benefit to the patient. The Ninth Circuit concludes that the rationale for permitting the withholding of treatment is to allow patients to hasten their deaths; however, it is clear from the dozens of judicial decisions on this subject that they are predicated on refusing burdensome medical treatment and not on a general right to hasten death.

Third, as drilled into first-year students of criminal law, criminal culpability often hinges on the concept of intent. If the rationale of the Ninth Circuit were taken to its logical conclusion, every decision by a physician not to employ a life-sustaining medical treatment, or to withdraw such a treatment with the consent of the patient or family members, could constitute a form of homicide, a deliberate hastening of death. As the courts recognized in *Quinlan* and subsequent cases, this has never been the law, and if it were, it would hopelessly confuse the application of the criminal law in such matters.

The intent involved in forgoing life-sustaining treatment is different from the intent involved in actively killing a patient or providing the means for a patient to commit suicide. In the former case, the direct intent is to forgo treatment, to omit an action that is not obligatory under law. While one may know or expect that death will ensue, that knowledge or assumption does not rise to the level of criminal intent. . . . In the latter case, such as prescribing lethal doses of medication, only one intent may be inferred—the intent to cause death. (The issue in these cases is not the right to prescribe pain medication that may have the secondary effect of causing death, but the right to prescribe medications whose sole purpose is to cause death.) The claim presented in these cases, therefore, is to establish constitutional protection for actions that have heretofore been prohibited because they exhibit a homicidal intent.

Finally, these distinctions apply even in cases where the withdrawal of treatment—i.e., the cessation of feeding—will most certainly result in death. The distinctions between omission and act, and between intending to refuse unwanted treatment and intending to directly cause death, still apply to these cases. The withdrawal or withholding of medically assisted feedings constitutes the refusal of a treatment that may sustain life but, especially for those in the last phases of a terminal illness, may appear unduly burdensome and hence non-obligatory.

Admittedly, such cases appear *close* to the actual causation of death, particularly if the patient's death is not imminent. This being the case, special concerns and safeguards often accompany such decisions, and the Supreme Court in *Cruzan* endorsed state efforts to attach the highest burden of proof to such cases where they involve incompetent patients. But as the counts also have ruled, assisted feeding remains a medical treatment, and thus remains within the ambit of the common-law right of a competent patient to consent to or to refuse. Such rulings should be seen as the factual endpoint of the jurisprudence commencing in *Quinlan,* and not as a departure point for creating a new right to assisted suicide and euthanasia. Clearly, it is constitutionally permissible for the states to draw a clear line between omissions and acts, even if some of the permitted omissions will have the same result as all of the forbidden acts.

Equal Protection and the Rational Basis for State Prohibition

The Second Circuit held that there is no rational basis for distinguishing between a death resulting from the omission of unwanted medical treatment, and a death resulting from suicide. I find the court's conclusion on these points incomprehensible and without any foundation in Supreme Court precedent.

First, as the Second Circuit acknowledged, terminally ill patients who are not dependent upon life support do not constitute a "suspect class" within the meaning of the Fourteenth Amendment. Thus, even if such patients were being treated differently from patients who are dependent upon life support, the state would merely have to show a rational basis for the distinction.

One need look no further than the decisions of the Supreme Court in *Harris v. McRae*[16] and *Williams v. Zbaraz*[17] to find a rational basis to support the distinction preserved not only by New York but, as discussed previously, by virtually every state in the union. In *Harris* and *Williams* the rational basis was clear: Congress through the Hyde Amendment and the states through their own statutes could choose to fund the expenses of childbirth, but not of abortion, in order to express "the legitimate [governmental] interest in protecting potential life."[18] The Court acknowledged that "[a]bortion is inherently different from other medical procedures because no other procedure involves the purposeful termination of human life."[19] Similarly, assisted suicide is inherently different from any other aspect of medical care, including decisions to forgo unwanted treatment. Only assisted suicide (and its logical consequence, active euthanasia) involves the deliberate and intentional taking of human life.

Second, assisted-suicide prohibitions are laws of general application. Thus there is no disparate treatment at all. The patients at issue enjoy the same right to refuse unwanted medical treatment as all other patients. Conversely, the prohibition against active assistance in suicide applies equally to those dependent on life support and those not dependent on life support. What the plaintiffs in these cases are claiming, and what the Second Circuit has unfortunately endorsed, is an unequal application of the laws against assisted suicide. Under the court's ruling, these laws will apply to some persons, and not others. The only "equality" that is achieved by this decision is an equality of results: the sought-after result being death. Nothing in the Constitution requires a state to fashion its laws to achieve such a strained equality, particularly when it places at risk fundamental competing state interests.

Third, as discussed previously, there are numerous rational grounds for distinguishing between the withdrawal of medical treatment, or even the cessation of feeding, and active assistance in death. To summarize, a state is free to give expansive protection to the common-law right to refuse medical treatment, a right that finds substantial support in our legal history and traditions, while at the same time prohibiting active assistance in death, a practice that finds no support in that history or tradition.

Fourth, a state may rationally conclude that maintaining prohibitions against assisted suicide is an essential part of the jurisprudence fashioned since *Quinlan* on the right to refuse life-sustaining treatment. A clear understanding that the law would not allow doctors to actively kill their patients made it possible to debate under what circumstances physicians could allow their patients to die without the use of invasive medical technology. Introducing the concept of physician-assisted killing would upset the entire set of assumptions upon which the rules for allowing withdrawal of treatment are based— which is evidenced by the consistent declarations in recent statutes and judicial opinions that allowing a patient to die does not constitute suicide or homicide. . . .

Finally, there are numerous specific grounds derived from the general interest in preserving life that justify a state's decision to draw the line between omission and act, and hold fast to the distinction set forth in the law of New York. Many of these grounds are discussed in the Report of the New York State Task Force. The Task Force was "particularly struck by the degree to which requests for suicide assistance by terminally ill patients are correlated with clinical depression or unmanaged [not unmanageable] pain, both of which can ordinarily be treated effectively with current medical techniques."[20] It noted studies which demonstrate that suicidal ideation is rare among terminally ill patients, unless those patients are also suffering from depression. It also observed that the elderly and terminally ill are less likely to receive appropriate diagnosis and treatment for depression. The Task Force stated that "[a]s a society, we can do far more to benefit these patients by improving pain relief and palliative care than by changing the law to make it easier to commit suicide or to obtain a lethal injection."[21] . . .

[Omitted here are four paragraphs in this section and also a brief following section, which deals with "contradictions" between the Second and Ninth Circuit opinions.]

ELASTICITY OF THE RIGHT TO ASSISTED SUICIDE

The Ninth and Second Circuits . . . [emphasized] that the right to assistance in suicide is limited to certain classes of persons, and can be subject to state regulations and even prohibitions. However, the doctrinal holdings of the decisions are likely to erode such regulations as "undue burdens" upon the rights these cases have established.

First, the right to assisted suicide recognized in these decisions is in principle illimitable. It cannot be restricted to the mentally competent terminally ill, or more specifically, to those whose deaths are imminent. The Ninth Circuit stated that there is a "liberty interest in determining the time and manner of one's death." If this is true, could this liberty be denied to a patient upon initial diagnosis of an inevitably fatal disease, or of a degenerative condition such as Alzheimer's? Such patients could claim an interest in preventing the slow process of disease and suffering. Their families and caregivers could thus be relieved of the burdens of care that often attend such conditions. The Ninth Circuit endorses such thinking: "Faced with the prospect of astronomical medical bills, terminally ill patients might decide it is better for them to die before their health-care expenses consume the life savings they planned to leave for their families, or, worse yet, burden their families with debts they may never be able to satisfy. . . . [W]e are reluctant to say that . . . it is improper for competent, terminally ill adults to take the economic welfare of their families into consideration."[22]

Second, terminal illness is itself an arbitrary boundary. Ironically, patients who are chronically ill but not terminally ill, and suffering from their illness, might well claim a denial of the equal protection of the laws if a state legalized assisted suicide only for the "benefit" of the terminally ill. If the right were extended in this fashion, it would be a small step to acceptance of assisted suicide for the handicapped, particularly those who are perceived to have a low "quality of life." The Ninth Circuit treats this concern with two responses: First, it asserted that the handicapped and disabled "are sufficiently active politically and sufficiently vigilant" to prevent actions that would pressure them into taking their own lives. Second, it suggested that "seriously impaired" individuals will be the beneficiary of the right to assisted suicide, because otherwise they will be compelled to "endure unusual and protracted suffering."[23]

This effective endorsement of assisted suicide for the severely handicapped demonstrates that the "boundaries" established by the Ninth Circuit are inherently subjective—the "terminal illness" criterion carries an implicit judgment that some lives are not worth living and hence, that it is reasonable that such lives be ended. . . .

Third, the criterion of "suffering," often used to defend the right to assistance in death for the terminally ill, is similarly subjective. The New York State Task Force discussed this problem:

> [A]s long as the policies hinge on notions of pain or suffering they are uncontainable; neither pain nor suffering can be gauged objectively or subjected to the kind of judgments needed to fashion coherent public policy. Moreover, even if the more narrow category of terminal illness is chosen at the outset, the line is unlikely to hold for the very reason that it has not been selected by advocates of assisted suicide—the logic of suicide as a compassionate choice for patients who are in pain or suffering suggests no such limit.[24]

Both the Second and Ninth Circuit explicitly cite suffering as grounds for diminishing the state interest in the lives of terminally ill patients. Neither adequately considers that the option of aggressive pain management, and not hastening death, is the reasonable response to such circumstances—or that the impetus to treat pain and suffering will diminish if the option of hastened death can be presented to the patient.

Fourth, the criteria of competency and "self-deliverance" of the means of death are not genuine limits. As mentioned, the Ninth Circuit specifically endorsed the practice of assisted suicide, with the consent of a duly appointed surrogate, in the case of an incompetent patient. The court left unanswered the question of how an incompetent patient can commit suicide. Clearly, such cases would require the direct killing of the patient by the physician. The court takes no position on this issue, but clearly indicates that the liberty interest "in controlling the manner of one's own death" would be broad enough to encompass such practices.

These points illustrate that, in the words of the report of the British House of Lords Select Committee on Medical Ethics, assisted suicide is not "a discrete step which need have no other consequences." That report emphasizes that "individual cases cannot reasonably establish the foundation of a policy which would have such serious and widespread repercussions." The committee concluded:

> [I]ssues of life and death do not lend themselves to clear definition, and without that it would not be possible to frame adequate safeguards against non-voluntary euthanasia if voluntary euthanasia were legalised. It would be next to impossible to ensure that all acts of euthanasia were truly voluntary, and that any liberalisation of the law was not abused. Moreover to create an exception to the general prohibition of intentional killing would inevitably open the way to its further erosion whether by design, by inadvertence, or by the human tendency to test the limits of any regulation. These dangers are such that we believe that any decriminalisation of voluntary euthanasia would give rise to more, and more grave, problems than those it sought to address.[25]

The seeds of such expansion are well planted in the opinions of the Second and Ninth Circuits.

ASSISTED SUICIDE AND HUMAN DIGNITY

These opinions further suggest that assisted suicide is necessary so that terminally ill patients can end their lives in a dignified and humane fashion. The Second Circuit asks: "What business is it of the state to require the continuation of agony when the result is imminent and inevitable?"[26] Aside from noting that the state does not require the prolongation of life in such circumstances, this admittedly is a difficult question to answer. But so is the following question: "What business does the state have in deciding that some lives are less worthy of the law's protection than others, and in suggesting through legalization of assisted suicide that this is a 'rational' way for people to end their lives?" This question, as noted by the earlier panel decision of the Ninth Circuit, is of greater relevance. The license for assisted suicide will inevitably affect society at large, not merely a handful of exceptional cases.

There is perhaps a universal temptation to surrender to the stress and tension of a chronic, long-term illness, and to despair of any relief, to give up hope of recovery, to abandon the family member in need, and inevitably, to hasten the death of the chronically ill patient. Technology has not alleviated these concerns, but neither should technology be viewed as the sole source for aggravating them. It is because of human nature itself that there is an enduring need for the protection embodied in the common law, and now codified in the law of most states.

Overturning this tradition on the basis of an unenumerated constitutional "liberty interest," or obliterating the historical distinction between act and omission, threatens the values that the law has long sought to protect. The House of Lords committee spoke to the importance of laws prohibiting assisted suicide and euthanasia in protecting the dignity of the person:

> The right to refuse medical treatment is far removed from the right to request assistance in dying. We spent a long time considering the very strongly held and sincerely expressed views of those witnesses who advocated voluntary euthanasia. . . . Ultimately, however, we do not believe that these arguments are sufficient reason to weaken society's prohibition of intentional killing. That prohibition is the cornerstone of law and of social relationships. It protects each one of us impartially, embodying the belief that all are equal. We do not wish that protection to be diminished and we therefore recommend that there should be no change in the law to permit euthanasia.[27]

Against such a background, there are fundamental problems with the decisions of the Second and Ninth Circuits. As a *legal* matter, the decisions ignore an unimpeachable legal tradition of protecting the most vulnerable among us. This tradition grows out of the common law and continues through the legal and medical reforms of the past twenty years. As a *factual* matter, these decisions assume that the state and medical practitioners can effectively limit the practice of physician-assisted death to those who are truly terminally ill, truly competent, and truly free of depression, duress, or other undue influences upon their decision. As a *constitutional* matter, the decisions presume that courts are the appropriate institutions to assess the wisdom of public policies on these questions, and that their judgments should trump those of the elected branches of government. The Ninth and Second Circuit decisions are profoundly wrong on all three counts. . . .

27

A Model State Act to Authorize and Regulate Physician-Assisted Suicide

Charles H. Baron and Others

In recent years, the prerogatives of competent patients to make end-of-life medical treatment decisions have been clarified, afforded legal protection, and increasingly accepted in medical practice. These prerogatives include the right of competent patients to hasten the moment of their death by refusing treatment that would otherwise prolong their suffering. Under legal regimes that afford terminal patients this prerogative, physicians and other health-care practitioners must comply with the decisions of such patients to withhold or withdraw medical treatment and may do so without fear of legal liability. As rights to forgo life-sustaining treatment have become established at law, many people have come to believe that a patient's control over

---

The authors in addition to Charles H. Baron are Clyde Bergstresser, Dan W. Brock, Garrick F. Cole, Nancy S. Dorfman, Judith A. Johnson, Lowell E. Schnipper, James Vorenberg, and Sidney H. Wanzer. Eight of the nine are professors, lawyers, and doctors in the Boston area; the other, an economist, is chairman of the Greater Boston Hemlock Society. This article and model statute are reprinted by permission from the *Harvard Journal on Legislation* 33, no. 1 (Winter 1996). The eighty-five notes that accompanied the article, mostly references to legal cases or to multiple journal articles, have been omitted.

his or her dying should be extended to permit active means to hasten death when there is no life-sustaining treatment to forgo.

The issue remains a source of ethical, religious, and legal controversy. Anecdotal reports and occasional confidential surveys of physicians reveal that some physicians occasionally assist patients with suicide, but data on the frequency with which physician-assisted suicide occurs are not reliable. Moreover, threats of criminal charges and civil litigation make even the most empathetic physicians wary of complying with a patient's request for such assistance in the absence of clear-cut legal guidance and protection.

Sharing the belief that physician-assisted suicide should be an option available to competent patients, we met together over a two-year period to draft a model statute to authorize physician-assisted suicide. Several of us were panel members at a symposium sponsored by the Massachusetts Bar Association in 1992 that focused on the state of the law in the Commonwealth concerning assistance in dying. With the addition of several others, we authors now include three attorneys who represent patients, hospitals, and physicians; two law professors with interests in medical and constitutional law; a professor of philosophy who specializes in bioethics; a patient advocate and public policy economist; and two physicians with experience in academic medicine and community practice.

Part 1 of this article explains the relationship of physician-assisted suicide to the current law and to current thinking in medicine and philosophy. Part 2 explores the difficult choices that we made in determining what form of physician-assisted suicide should be available, who should be able to receive assistance, and how simultaneously to protect privacy and prevent abuse. Part 3 examines the constitutionality of our model statute. Finally, Part 4 presents a detailed overview of the provisions of our statute.

THE MEDICAL, ETHICAL, AND LEGAL CONTEXT

The statute that we propose is designed to provide the option of physician-assisted suicide to competent patients who either have a terminal illness or are suffering from unrelievable and unbearable distress, due to bodily illness, that is so great that they prefer death.

The statute can be fully understood only in light of current medical, ethical, and legal constraints on physician-assisted suicide.

The Medical and Moral Basis

We believe that it is reasonable to provide relief from suffering for patients who are dying or whose suffering is so severe that it is beyond their capacity to bear. Some opponents of physician-assisted suicide see such a step as a radical moral departure from present medical practice, but we believe it is consistent with the fundamental values underlying the legal and ethical requirements of respect for the right of competent patients to give or withhold their consent to any treatment, including life-sustaining treatment. The most basic values that support and guide all health-care decision-making, including decisions about life-sustaining treatment, are the same values that provide the fundamental basis for physician-assisted suicide: promoting patients' well-being and respecting their self-determination or autonomy.

The legal right to decide about life-sustaining treatment has given most patients appropriate control over their own dying, and we believe strongly that this control, along with proper supportive care, meticulous attention to details, and truly adequate pain-relief measures, will meet the needs of the great majority of dying patients and usually obviate the occasion for the patient to consider the possibility of hastening death. However, for some patients who are undergoing severe suffering and confronting an unbearable or meaningless existence, either no life-sustaining treatment is available to be forgone or forgoing such treatment will result in a prolonged, unbearable, and inhumane dying process. Even when optimal care has been given, intolerable distress may remain in these patients, such that they may conclude rationally that hastening death is the only appropriate goal. For these patients, more active means of hastening death are necessary, supported by the very same values that promote patients' well-being and respect their self-determination.

Viewed in this way, making physician-assisted suicide available to patients who choose it is not a radical departure in medical practice or public policy, but a natural and appropriate extension of presently accepted practices. Physicians are uniquely able to provide this necessary assistance with a combination of expert knowledge, compassionate concern for the patient, professional responsibility to the patient and to society, and the ability to determine and prescribe the medication that the patient will usually require to achieve a humane and certain death. They should be able lawfully to provide the assistance necessary to achieve that goal. Our model statute would allow such assistance, while at the same time attempting to provide adequate protection against possible abuses.

Current Legal Obstacles

In a jurisdiction without a statute authorizing physician-assisted suicide, a physician who provided means of suicide to a patient could be convicted of manslaughter or a specific crime of aiding or assisting a suicide or an attempted suicide. Under certain circumstances, such a physician could be convicted of murder, but in many states, a murder conviction requires active participation in the death rather than merely supplying the means of death. Nevertheless, even the possibility of murder charges is likely to have a deterrent effect on a physician who would otherwise consider assisting a patient to commit suicide. Indeed, even in a jurisdiction where assisted suicide is not prohibited by statute, a physician who assisted in a patient's suicide could be convicted of a common-law felony.

Among the civil threats to physicians undertaking assisted suicide are liability for wrongful death and medical malpractice. A physician might also face professional sanctions, either as a result of specific ethical prohibitions on assisted suicide or because of the philosophical or political opposition of the reviewing disciplinary board. Finally, a physician who assisted in a suicide could lose staff privileges at a hospital that objected to the practice.

The net result of these obstacles to physician-assisted suicide is to deter physicians from considering the practice, even if they might otherwise have no objection to it. As we explain in the next section, we believe that a statute is needed to enable physicians to assist patients in suicide in appropriate circumstances.

The Need for a Specific Statute

Laws that deprive persons of access to physician-assisted suicide have been challenged recently on constitutional grounds in federal and state courts in several jurisdictions. We feel that a preferable way to establish a right to physician-assisted suicide is to make this option available to persons through explicit statutory authorization. Even if laws restricting assisted suicide are struck down, laws or regulations will be necessary to provide oversight and protection against abuse. Our statutory approach permits the careful development of procedures necessary to limit abuse. A statute also more clearly requires and establishes the public support that should exist for the practice before it is made legally available.

Commentators have argued that there is no need for legislation in states where assisted suicide is not specifically outlawed by statute, because physicians in those states may legally provide patients with means of suicide or, in any event, need not fear prosecution for doing so. Others have maintained that to legalize physician-assisted suicide would make suicide "too easy," opening the option to patients whose conditions do not warrant such an extreme measure and risking that it would be urged on patients who do not want it. Some contend that legislation would impose onerous regulations on the conduct of a procedure that already takes place when, in the judgment of the physician, the situation warrants it.

On the contrary, for the following reasons, we believe that society and the medical profession would be better served by a statute that expressly permits physician-assisted suicide under certain well-defined circumstances, rather than by no law at all:

First, in states that do not explicitly prohibit any form of assisted suicide, the law's silence leaves physicians in serious doubt concerning the legality of providing means of suicide to a patient, while in states that do outlaw assisted suicide, physicians must risk prosecution for a felony in order to assist in a patient's suicide. As a result, patients who seek means of dying are often denied assistance, and success in finding a physician who will help may be a result of luck more than of need.

Second, physicians who now provide assistance in suicide may be compelled by fear of prosecution to do so in secret without the opportunity to discuss the case fully and freely with colleagues or other professionals. In contrast, physicians have access to a variety of professional consultations, often including review by ethics committees or consultants, in connection with other profoundly serious medical-ethical decisions.

Third, physicians who now provide assistance in suicide do so without any form of accountability, procedures, requirements, or guidelines to assure that the patient's request for assistance is competent, fully informed, voluntary, and enduring and that the diagnosis and treatment options have been confirmed and fully explained to the patient.

Fourth, in the absence of assistance from a physician, many terminally ill patients now attempt to end their lives on their own, often in ignorance of and without access to the best means of doing so.

Fifth, some terminally ill patients prematurely elect to end their lives by forgoing treatment because they fear that the opportunity to end their lives will not arise later should their suffering become unendurable.

Finally, with or without assistance from a physician, many patients who end their lives may feel obliged to do so in solitude, without the professional advice of a physician or the presence and comfort of loved ones.

THREE FUNDAMENTAL ISSUES

Active Euthanasia Versus Physician-Assisted Suicide. Our proposed statute would legalize physician-assisted suicide under certain conditions, but it does not address voluntary active euthanasia. By "physician-assisted suicide," we mean providing the patient with the means, such as a drug that can be lethal in certain doses, to end his or her own life. Voluntary active euthanasia, in contrast, requires the active participation of the physician in performing the action, such as administering a lethal injection, that ends the patient's life. Members of the public and the medical community disagree, and we disagree among ourselves, as to whether there is an important difference between the two concepts.

We have chosen to allow only physician-assisted suicide for two main reasons. First, we consider the voluntariness of the patient's act to be critical. Restricting the statute to physician-assisted suicide provides in many cases a stronger assurance of the patient's voluntary resolve to die and of the central role of patient responsibility for the act. Second, we believe that there would be greater acceptance of the model statute by the public, legislators, and physicians if it were limited to physician-assisted suicide, partly because of the public perception of voluntariness and partly because of the strong ethical objections of some physicians and others to euthanasia.

Which Patients Should be Eligible?

We agreed from the outset that to be eligible for physician-assisted suicide, the patient must be an adult, aged eighteen years or older. We also agreed that anyone who is terminally ill, that is, likely to die from an illness within six months, should qualify without having to demonstrate that his or her suffering is unbearable. We continued to debate until the very end of our deliberations as to how far, if at all, to broaden this eligibility beyond the six-month limit. Our major concern was whether and how to extend the option to patients who are not likely to die from their illnesses within six months but have bodily disorders that cause intractable and unbearable suffering, such as AIDS, advanced emphysema, some forms of cancer, amyotrophic lateral sclerosis, multiple sclerosis, and many other debilitating conditions.

With respect to this issue, we faced the difficulty of defining unbearable suffering in a sufficiently objective fashion that physician-assisted suicide would not be available to everyone who had some form of physical or psychological suffering and merely requested it. In the end, a bare majority of us agreed to allow anyone to be eligible whose illness is incurable and who subjectively feels that the accompanying suffering is worse than death. We rejected a more objective definition of the patient's suffering for two principal reasons. First, we found that it was not possible to construct an objective definition that was not overly restrictive as to the patients who would meet it. Second, and more important, we realized that whether one's suffering is sufficiently unbearable to make death preferable to continued life is an inherently subjective determination on which people differ, and for which no objective standard should be imposed on everyone. Because the statute does not endow the patient with a right to physician-assisted suicide, however, the physician still retains the ability to decide whether the case warrants providing such relief. In addition, because the statute requires competency, the subjective preference for death of a clinically depressed or mentally ill patient would be insufficient to qualify that patient for assisted suicide.

Protecting Patients and Physicians, Maintaining Privacy

Procedural safeguards that adequately protect both patients and physicians unavoidably conflict with the privacy of patients and families and the privacy of the physician-patient relationship. To maximize privacy, we considered proposing a statute that would simply state in very general terms that physician-assisted suicide was legal under certain stated factual circumstances but would not prescribe procedural requirements. Under this abbreviated approach, an assisted-suicide statute might comprise only a few simple provisions to the effect that a physician would not be guilty of unlawfully assisting a patient to commit suicide, provided that: (1) the physician's assistance were limited to making available a substance used by the patient to end the patient's life; (2) the patient had an illness that was either terminal or caused the patient intractable and unbearable suffering; (3) the patient had made a decision to hasten death because of the illness; and (4) the patient's decision was fully informed as to relevant medical facts and was not the result of a mental illness or undue influence from other persons. We concluded that such an abbreviated approach would not adequately protect patients or physicians.

The procedures, conditions, and documentation requirements built into the model statute are designed to ensure that physician-assisted suicide is restricted to patients who are truly terminally ill or suffering from intractable and unbearable illnesses, and whose requests are demonstrably competent, fully informed, voluntary, and enduring. To govern the practice in accordance with these principles, it is necessary that the statute contain strong safeguards and precise procedural requirements. Such detailed requirements will counter a common objection to making physician-assisted suicide legally permissible: the so-called slippery-slope argument. While it is not possible to guarantee that abuse and unjustified extension of the practice cannot or will not take place, we believe strong and effective safeguards, together with a clear understanding of the rationale for the practice and the limits to which it applies, can reasonably meet concerns about a slippery slope.

From the physician's perspective, an abbreviated approach such as that described above would preserve the physician's autonomy, would avoid imposing burdensome regulations on the physician, and would not intrude into the physician-patient relationship. It would not, however, adequately protect physicians and could make them unwilling to provide assistance in suicide even in appropriate situations. Because the conditions under which physicians could legally assist patients in suicide would be stated so generally, physicians would not know in advance whether a particular case fit those conditions and what actions they should take to obviate any significant risk of criminal charges. Even if a physician acted on good-faith belief that the statutory conditions were met, he or she might be vulnerable to legal charges later. This possibility would almost certainly leave many physicians who might have no principled objection to physician-assisted suicide reluctant to provide it to any of their patients who might request it.

Thus, not only for the protection of patients, but also for the protection of physicians, we chose to outline specific requirements that, when followed, offer the physicians legal protection. Moreover, we concluded that extensive safeguards would both protect the integrity of the medical profession and help ensure that public trust in that integrity remains warranted. If the public is to ask the medical profession to participate in physician-assisted suicide, then strong safeguards are a reasonable cost for the public and patients to bear.

It would be a mistake, however, to think that procedural safeguards do not come at a significant cost to the patient and to the physician-patient relationship. At what will typically be an emotionally difficult time for the patient and the family, unfamiliar third-party consultants, evaluators, and witnesses must intrude into the physician-patient relationship. Patients and their families will often quite reasonably view the procedures as a profound invasion of their privacy at a point when time is short and privacy is especially important. We feel, nevertheless, that such procedures are necessary in order to ensure that in less-than-ideal relationships and conditions, misuse and abuse of the practice of physician-assisted suicide does not occur.

The detailed procedures also provide an openness to the practice of physician-assisted suicide that can give society greater assurance that the practice is operating as intended, and can provide feedback to government and professional bodies about needed refinements and revisions in the practice over time. In our final formulation of the statute, we therefore leaned in the direction of more extensive and comprehensive safeguards, acknowledging the costs to some patients and physicians.

CONSTITUTIONALITY OF THE MODEL ACT

In November 1994, Oregon voters enacted by initiative the nation's first statute explicitly permitting and regulating physician-assisted suicide. The Oregon Act, which is similar in a number of respects to our proposed statute, was promptly challenged in federal court on grounds that it violated the Fourteenth Amendment to the United States Constitution. On August 3, 1995, in *Lee v. Oregon,* District Judge Michael R. Hogan declared the statute unconstitutional under the Equal Protection clause of the Fourteenth Amendment. The case is now on appeal to the United States Court of Appeals for the Ninth Circuit.

We believe that the *Lee* case was wrongly decided and that our proposed statute will withstand appropriate constitutional scrutiny.

In 1990, the Supreme Court of the United States rendered its only decision to date on the subject of the right to die. In *Cruzan v. Director, Missouri Department of Health* (497 U.S. 261 [1990]), the Court held that, where an incompetent patient is involved, a state may constitutionally require "clear and convincing" proof that the patient would want life-prolonging treatment withdrawn. In passing, the Court recognized a patient's "constitutionally protected liberty interest" in refusing unwanted medical treatment. Four justices believed this liberty interest to be so strong in the context of a patient in a persistent vegetative state that they would have held the Missouri law restricting it unconstitutional under the Due Process clause of the Fourteenth Amendment. The other justices, with the exception of Justice Scalia, also recognized such a constitutionally based right. But they recognized as well a strong interest of the state in protecting the autonomy of an incompetent patient, and they held that a state could constitutionally advances its interests, if it chose to do so, by requiring clear and convincing evidence of the patient's wishes.

Judge Hogan's opinion in *Lee* turned *Cruzan* on its head. Whereas *Cruzan* dealt with state legislation that restricted a patient's right to be free from unwanted treatment, *Lee* dealt with state legislation advancing that right. Whereas *Cruzan* protected the right of the legislature to regulate the details of practice in this developing area, even though the regulation impinged upon a protected liberty interest, *Lee* struck down a popularly mandated measure that advanced that liberty interest.

The fault in the Oregon Act, from Judge Hogan's point of view, was that it did not advance patients' liberty interests as rationally as it might. In particular, the *Lee* court was concerned that (1) the Oregon Act permits "physicians who may not be psychiatrists, psychologists, or counselors to make an evaluation whether a condition is causing [the patient to exercise] impaired judgment"; (2) "[t]here is no requirement that the [patient] consult a certified social worker or other specialist to explore social services which might assist the person to live in greater comfort"; and (3) these and other failures in protection of the rights of patients apply only to the "terminally ill." The court's suggestion was that somehow the Oregon Act discriminated against the terminally ill as a class in violation of the Equal Protection clause. Yet in the case of the Oregon Act and other legislation classifying patients on the basis of terminal illness, it is those persons who fear that they will one day find themselves among the terminally ill who are urging the enactment of such legislation to protect themselves from a lingering, undignified death. Clearly invidious motives are not at work when such statutes use terminal illness as a basis for classification.

Because the Oregon Act does not impinge upon a fundamental right and does not establish a classification on a basis that raises suspicions of invidious discrimination, the court was required to review the measure under the most lenient of constitutional standards. It could find the Oregon Act unconstitutional only if one could conceive of no rational basis upon which the state could have used the means employed to advance a legitimate state interest. In fact, Judge Hogan appears to have applied his own version of rational review and to have struck down the Oregon Act because it was not as rational as he thought it should be. This sort of constitutional review is reminiscent of the discredited doctrine of *Lochner v. New York* (198 U.S. 45 [1905]). A proper application of the rational-basis test would find both the Oregon Act and the statute that we propose here to be constitutional under the Fourteenth Amendment.

While we believe *Lee* will be reversed by the Ninth Circuit, we should note that our proposed statute addresses several of what Judge Hogan perceived to be the shortcomings of the Oregon Act. Our statute provides for a review of the patient's competency by a licensed psychiatrist, clinical psychologist, or psychiatric social worker; allows patients the opportunity to consult with a social worker about alternatives to suicide; and refuses to relieve physicians from liability for such actions as a negligent diagnosis.

OVERVIEW OF THE MODEL ACT

Who May Provide Physician-Assisted Suicide? The model statute [the text begins on page 569] allows a "responsible physician" to practice physician-assisted suicide and places a series of responsibilities on that physician. The first question that we faced was who should be allowed to assume that role. Ideally, the physician who assists in a patient's suicide will be the one who has managed the patient's illness and who has a close professional relationship with the patient. However, the statute recognizes that because ethical constraints may prevent some physicians from assisting in suicide, a patient may need to have another physician provide him or her with the means of suicide. Section 2(h) therefore allows any physician who has assumed full or partial responsibility for a patient's care to assume the role of responsible physician, even though he or she is not the patient's primary physician.

Other Definitions

Section 2(e) defines "medical means of suicide" as a medical substance or device prescribed for or supplied to a patient by the responsible physician. The use of the term "medical" requires that the means of suicide be otherwise consistent with sound medical practice; thus, providing a patient with an unapproved drug or a firearm (to take an extreme example) would not be permissible. The definitions of "intractable and unbearable illness" and "terminal illness" are discussed above. The remaining definitions in section 2 are self-explanatory.

Conditions to be Met Before a Patient Receives Assistance

A fundamental goal of the statute is to protect patients from coercion or premature judgment. Section 3(a)(3) thus requires that four basic conditions be met before a physician may grant a patient's request for assisted suicide: the request must be competent, fully informed, voluntary, and enduring. The first three requirements are similar to those required for informed consent to ordinary medical treatment, and the fourth is designed to ensure the consistent resolve of the patient. However, because of the seriousness and finality of the patient's decision, the requirements of the statute exceed those of consent to ordinary treatment.

A competent request within the meaning of section 3(a)(3)(A) is a reasoned request for physician-assisted suicide from a patient, based on the patient's ability to understand his or her condition and prognosis, the benefits and burdens of available alternative treatments, and the consequences of suicide. A request distorted by clinical depression or other mental illness or impairment is not competent. However, the statute does not prohibit physician-assisted suicide for a patient suffering from clinical depression if the patient's judgment is not distorted —in other words, if the patient can make a reasoned decision consistent with his or her long-term values. A terminal illness is inherently depressing, and denying a patient assistance in suicide only because he or she feels sad or depressed would not be proper. Nevertheless, the statute mandates that a professional mental-health care provider evaluate the patient to determine that his or her decision is fully informed, free of undue influence, and not distorted by depression or any other form of mental illness.

A fully informed request within the meaning of section 3(a)(3)(B) means that the patient understands the medical options available and their consequences. Section 4 requires the physician to discuss all medical treatments that might improve the patient's condition or prognosis that are practicably available, including treatment for pain, and their benefits and burdens; to offer the patient the opportunity to consult with social workers about social services that may improve his or her condition; and to advise the patient of the options for ending his or her life and their benefits and burdens. For a request to be fully informed, the patient must understand all of this information and make a reasoned decision to seek suicide. Section 3(a)(3)(B) is intended to ensure active decision-making by the patient; passive acquiescence in the recommendations of others would not constitute a fully informed and reasoned decision.

Section 3(a)(3)(C) requires that the patient's request be voluntary, meaning that it is made independently, free from coercion or undue influence. The patient may consider the suggestions and recommendations of others, including the responsible physician, but the patient's choice must be his or her own decision.

Finally, section 3(a)(3)(D) requires that the patient's request be enduring. Ideally, the patient will have discussed physician-assisted suicide with a number of individuals on multiple occasions. At a minimum, however, the request must be stated to the responsible physician on at least two occasions that are at least two weeks apart, without self-contradiction during that interval. The two-week period is an attempt to balance the prevention of hasty decision-making against the prolonging of unbearable suffering.

Section 3(a) places the responsibility on the responsible physician to ensure that all of its requirements are met. In order to provide the physician with considerable advance assurance that he or she can avoid litigation attempting to second-guess his or her determinations, the statute makes the physician's standard entirely subjective: the physician need have only an "honest belief" that the elements of section 3(a) have been met in the particular case. However, to compensate for the lack of any requirement of reasonableness, the responsible physician enjoys the protection conferred by the statute only if he or she also satisfies the procedural requirements of sections 4, 5, and 6, which are designed to produce and preserve independent corroboration that the physician's belief is not merely honest or reasonable, but accurate. If the responsible physician materially complies with these requirements and there is no proof that he or she lacked the requisite honest belief, he or she is protected from liability for assisting in a suicide. As discussed below, however, the responsible physician and other participants are not relieved of any liability that they may otherwise incur as a result of any malpractice that they commit in the process of assisting in a suicide.

Procedures to be Followed Before and After

Section 4 outlines the information that the responsible physician must present to the patient in order to ensure that the patient's decision is fully informed and reasoned. Section 4(a) requires the responsible physician to offer the patient any medical care that may cure or palliate the illness or relieve its symptoms. Hospice care must be offered if available, but treatments that are inconsistent with accepted medical practice or impracticable need not be. Section 4(b) requires the responsible physician to make a social worker available to the patient to discuss non-medical options that might change the patient's decision to seek suicide.

The responsible physician must suggest to the patient under section 4(c) that he or she consult family members about the decision to request assistance in suicide, but the patient need not do so. Although mandatory family notification has been upheld against constitutional challenges in similarly sensitive situations, we believe that competent, adult patients should not be required to notify family members of their intended suicide against their will. The items required to be discussed by section 4(d) have been mentioned previously, but that section also requires a recorded or documented account of the discussion with two witnesses who are entitled to question the responsible physician and the patient.

Section 5 contains the corroboration requirements. Section 5(a) requires a second medical opinion as to the patient's diagnosis and prognosis, while section 5(b) requires a combination medical-factual opinion as to the patient's qualifications for physician-assisted suicide under section 3(a)(3). Broadly worded, unsupported opinions should be insufficient to enable the responsible physician to proceed; instead, each opinion should evidence a thorough investigation and demonstrate that the patient meets the statutory standards. An opinion that conflicts with the responsible physician's opinion should prevent the responsible physician from proceeding with an assisted suicide, at least until circumstances change substantially and a consultant then agrees with the responsible physician's opinion.

Finally, section 6 requires the responsible physician to document promptly the provision of medical means of suicide to a patient, both in the patient's records and with the state's regulatory authority.

Presence at the Patient's Death

Ending one's life in solitude can be a lonely and frightening undertaking, fraught with uncertainty, ambivalence, and opportunities for failure. We hope that the responsible physician will be present at the patient's death in order to reassure the patient and to make certain that the process is carried out effectively. Section 3(b) allows, but does not require, the physician to be present if the patient so desires, and section 7(a) also allows the presence of any other persons selected by the patient. Each section requires only that the final physical act of administering the means of suicide be the knowing, intentional, and voluntary act of the patient.

Monitoring and Enforcement

The submission of reports by responsible physicians allows the state Department of Public Health (or a similar regulatory agency) to collect the data specified in section 8(a) necessary to improve the statute's operation and to make the annual public report of its effectiveness required by section 9(d). For purposes of tracking the operation of the statute, it would be desirable to determine how often and under what circumstances medical means of suicide were actually used by patients to end their lives. However, because the responsible physician need not be present at the patient's death, and because the physician who signs the death certificate may not be the same physician who provided the deceased with the means of suicide, there appears to be no way of accurately determining the extent to which medical means of suicide are actually used.

A physician's report must not include the patient's name for reasons of privacy, but section 8(b) requires a coded link between the report and the patient's name, which may be used if legal or ethical questions should arise after the patient's death.

Section 9 requires the agency to monitor and enforce the requirements of the statute and grants the agency rule-making authority. The statute proceeds on the assumption that it is impossible in such a complex field to deal in advance with all possible problems by a legislative act. We believe that a reasonable solution is to enact the legislation and then to provide an administrative body with the power to respond to new patterns of problems through the regulatory rulemaking process.

Confidentiality, Conscientious Objection, and Discrimination

To protect the privacy and confidentiality of everyone involved in a particular physician-assisted suicide, section 10(a) declares that any information about a patient must be kept confidential. Section 10(b) further specifies that a responsible physician's report on file with the regulatory agency is also confidential and is not subject to the customary state statutes regarding public records.

Section 11 protects the decisions of physicians, hospital employees, and hospitals themselves to refuse to participate in physician-assisted suicide on grounds of conscience. A hospital or other institution may forbid physician-assisted suicide on its premises or within its jurisdiction if the institution notifies its staff in advance of the policy.

Finally, section 12 protects patients from discrimination by physicians, institutions, and insurers. No health-care provider or insurer is permitted to require any patient to request physician-assisted suicide as a condition of eligibility for services, benefits, or insurance. At the same time, section 12 protects patients from discrimination (including the voiding of life insurance policies) because they have chosen to pursue assisted suicide. Unless physicians, institutions, and insurers opt out for reasons of conscience under section 11, they must honor patients' choices to seek or avoid assistance in suicide.

Liability and Sanctions

Section 13 protects those who participate in physician-assisted suicide from the types of legal liabilities identified earlier in this article. The protection of section 13(a), however, is limited to the mere fact that a person has participated in an assisted suicide; he or she may not be convicted of homicide, for example, solely on the basis that he or she provided deadly drugs to a patient who committed suicide. On the other hand, section 13(c) notes that the statute does not limit the civil or criminal liability of any person for intentional or negligent actions merely because those actions were part of a physician-assisted suicide. Thus if a responsible physician or consulting physician commits malpractice by erroneously diagnosing a patient's condition, he or she is liable for the damages caused by that malpractice. The responsible physician is not, however, stripped of protection against liability for assisting in a suicide per se unless he or she has failed to meet the requirements of one or more sections of the statute.

Section 14 declares that a willful violation of a provision of section 3, 4, 5, 6, or 7 is a crime (the precise grade of the crime is left to the individual state). Whether an action results in the death of a patient or not is immaterial. Of course, a violation of one of these provisions may also render a person liable under another provision of law; for example, a responsible physician who does not comply in all material respects with sections 4, 5, and 6 does not enjoy the protection from liability for assisting in a suicide that section 13 otherwise affords. In appropriate cases, section 14 provides a prosecutor with a method for enforcing the statute that falls short of a prosecution for homicide or assisting in a suicide.

As for other wrongful acts, such as coercing a person to request or use medical means of suicide, section 13(c) leaves the definition of offenses and the imposition of sanctions to existing law.

Conclusion

Physician-assisted suicide has become a subject of increasingly widespread and intense public and professional debate. A growing array of efforts is also under way to make physician-assisted suicide available under the law. As noted earlier, Oregon recently adopted legislation to allow physician-assisted suicide. Constitutional challenges to laws prohibiting assisted suicide in Washington, Michigan, and New York have recently wound their way through the courts. Legislation to permit physician-assisted suicide has been introduced recently in a number of state legislatures.

As these efforts approach fruition, it becomes increasingly important that debates about physician-assisted suicide address concrete issues of morality and policy design. Supporters of physician-assisted suicide have a special responsibility to propose specific, detailed proposals for a well-regulated and suitably circumscribed practice. We intend the statute presented below to help meet that responsibility.

A Model State Act

SECTION 1. Statement of Purpose

The principal purpose of this Act is to enable an individual who requests it to receive assistance from a physician in obtaining the medical means for that individual to end his or her life when he or she suffers from a terminal illness or from a bodily illness that is intractable and unbearable. Its further purposes are (a) to ensure that the request for such assistance is complied with only when it is fully informed, reasoned, free of undue influence from any person, and not the result of a distortion of judgment due to clinical depression or any other mental illness; and (b) to establish mechanisms for continuing oversight and regulation of the process for providing such assistance. The provisions of this Act should be liberally construed to further these purposes.

SECTION 2. Definitions

As used in this Act,

(a) "Commissioner" means the Commissioner of the Department.

(b) "Department" means the Department of Public Health [or similar state agency].

(c) "Health care facility" means a hospital, hospice, nursing home, long-term residential care facility, or other institution providing medical services and licensed or operated in accordance with the law of this state or the United States.

(d) "Intractable and unbearable illness" means a bodily disorder (1) that cannot be cured or successfully palliated, and (2) that causes such severe suffering that a patient prefers death.

(e) "Medical means of suicide" means medical substances or devices that the responsible physician prescribes for or supplies to a patient for the purpose of enabling the patient to end his or her own life. "Providing medical means of suicide" includes providing a prescription therefor.

(f) "Patient's medical record" means (1) in the case of a patient who is in a health-care facility, the record of the patient's medical care that such facility is required by law or professional standards to compile and maintain, and (2) in the case of a patient who is not in such a facility, the record of the patient's medical care that the responsible physician is required by law or professional standards to compile and maintain.

(g) "Person" includes any individual, corporation, professional corporation, partnership, unincorporated association, government, government agency, or any other legal or commercial entity.

(h) "Responsible physician" means the physician, licensed to practice medicine in this state, who (1) has full or partial responsibility for treatment of a patient who is terminally ill or intractably and unbearably ill, and (2) takes responsibility for providing medical means of suicide to the patient.

(i) "Terminal illness" means a bodily disorder that is likely to cause a patient's death within six months.

SECTION 3. Authorization to Provide Assistance

(a) It is lawful for a responsible physician who complies in all material respects with Sections 4, 5, and 6 of this Act to provide a patient with medical means of suicide, provided that the responsible physician acts on the basis of an honest belief that

(1) the patient is eighteen years of age or older;

(2) the patient has a terminal illness or an intractable and unbearable illness; and

(3) the patient has made a request of the responsible physician to provide medical means of suicide, which request (A) is not the result of a distortion of the patient's judgment due to clinical depression or any other mental illness; (B) represents the patient's reasoned choice based on an understanding of the information that the responsible physician has provided to the patient pursuant to Section 4(d) of this Act concerning the patient's medical condition and medical options; (C) has been made free of undue influence by any person; and (D) has been repeated without self-contradiction by the patient on two separate occasions at least fourteen days apart, the last of which is no more than seventy-two hours before the responsible physician provides the patient with the medical means of suicide.

(b) A responsible physician who has provided a patient with medical means of suicide in accordance with the provisions of this Act may, if the patient so requests, be present and assist the patient at the time that the patient makes use of such means, provided that the actual use of such means is the knowing, intentional, and voluntary physical act of the patient.

SECTION 4. Discusion With Patient and Documentation

Before providing medical means of suicide to a patient pursuant to Section 3 of this Act, the responsible physician shall

(a) offer to the patient all medical care, including hospice care if available, that is consistent with accepted clinical practice and that can practicably be made available to the patient for the purpose of curing or palliating the patient's illness or alleviating symptoms, including pain and other discomfort;

(b) offer the patient the opportunity to consult with a social worker or other individual trained and experienced in providing social services to determine whether services are available to the patient that could improve the patient's circumstances sufficiently to cause the patient to reconsider his or her request for medical means of suicide;

(c) counsel the patient to inform the patient's family of the request if the patient has not already done so and the responsible physician believes that doing so would be in the patient's interest; and

(d) supply to and discuss with the patient all available medical information that is necessary to provide the basis for a reasoned decision concerning a request for medical means of suicide, including all such information regarding the patient's diagnosis and prognosis, the medical treatment options and the medical means of suicide that can be made available to the patient, and their benefits and burdens, all in accordance with the following procedures:

(1) at least two adult individuals must witness the discussion required by this paragraph (d), at least one of whom (A) is not affiliated with any person that is involved in the care of the patient, and (B) does not stand to benefit personally in any way from the patient's death;

(2) the responsible physician shall inform each witness that he or she may question the responsible physician and the patient to ascertain that the patient has, in fact, heard and understood all of the material information discussed pursuant to this paragraph (d); and

(3) the responsible physician shall document the discussion with the patient held pursuant to this paragraph (d), using one of the following methods: (A) an audio tape or a video tape of the discussion, during which the witnesses acknowledge their presence; or (B) a written summary of the discussion that the patient reads and signs and that the witnesses attest in writing to be accurate. The documentation required by this subparagraph (3) must be included and retained with the patient's medical record, and access to and disclosure of such records and copies of them are governed by the provisions of Section 10 of this Act.

SECTION 5. Professional Consultation and Documentation

Before providing medical means of suicide to a patient pursuant to Section 3 of this Act, the responsible physician shall

(a) secure a written opinion from a consulting physician who has examined the patient and is qualified to make such an assessment that the patient is suffering from a terminal illness or an intractable and unbearable illness;

(b) secure a written opinion from a licensed psychiatrist, clinical psychologist, or psychiatric social worker who has examined the patient and is qualified to make such an assessment that the patient has requested medical means of suicide and that the patient's request meets the criteria set forth in Sections 3(a)(3)(A), 3(a)(3)(B), and 3(a)(3)(C) of this Act to the effect that the request is not the result of a distortion of the patient's judgment due to clinical depression or any other mental illness, is reasoned, is fully informed, and is free of undue influence by any person; and

(c) place the written opinions described in paragraphs (a) and (b) of this section in the patient's medical record.

SECTION 6. Recording and Reporting by the
Responsible Physician

Promptly after providing medical means of suicide to a patient, the responsible physician shall (a) record the provision of such means in the patient's medical record, (b) submit a report to the Commissioner on such form as the Commissioner may require pursuant to Section 8(a) of this Act, and (c) place a copy of such report in the patient's medical record.

SECTION 7. Actions by Persons Other Than the
Responsible Physician

(a) An individual who acts on the basis of an honest belief that the requirements of this Act have been or are being met may, if the patient so requests, be present and assist at the time that the patient makes use of medical means of suicide, provided that the actual use of such means is the knowing, intentional, and voluntary physical act of the patient.

(b) A licensed pharmacist, acting in accordance with the laws and regulations of this state and the United States that govern the dispensing of prescription drugs and devices and controlled substances, may dispense medical means of suicide to a person who the pharmacist reasonably believes presents a valid prescription for such means.

(c) An individual who acts on the basis of an honest belief that the requirements of this Act have been or are being met may counsel or assist the responsible physician in providing medical means of suicide to a patient.

SECTION 8. Record Keeping by the Department

(a) The Commissioner shall by regulation specify a form of report to be submitted by physicians pursuant to Section 6(b) of this Act in order to provide the Department with such data regarding the provision of medical means of suicide as the Commissioner determines to be necessary or appropriate to enable effective oversight and regulation of the operation of this Act. Such report shall include, at a minimum, the following information:

(1) the patient's diagnosis, prognosis, and the alternative medical treatments, consistent with accepted clinical practice, that the responsible physician advised the patient were practicably available;

(2) the date on which and the name of the health care facility or other place where the responsible physician complied with the patient's request for medical means of suicide, the medical means of suicide that were prescribed or otherwise provided, and the method of recording the discussion required by Section 4(d) of this Act;

(3) the patient's vital statistics, including county of residence, age, sex, race, and marital status;

(4) the type of medical insurance and name of insurer of the patient, if any;

(5) the names of the responsible physician, the medical and mental health consultants who delivered opinions pursuant to Section 5 of this Act, and the witnesses required by Section 4(d) of this Act; and

(6) the location of the patient's medical record.

(b) The Commissioner shall require that the report described in paragraph (a) of this section not include the name of the patient but shall provide by regulation for an anonymous coding or reference system that enables the Commissioner or the responsible physician to associate such report with the patient's medical record.

SECTION 9. Enforcement and Reporting by the Department

(a) The Commissioner shall enforce the provisions of this Act and shall report to the Attorney General and the appropriate board of registration [or similar state agency] any violation of its provisions.

(b) The Commissioner shall promulgate such rules and regulations as the Commissioner determines to be necessary or appropriate to implement and achieve the purposes of this Act and shall, at least ninety days prior to adopting any rule or regulation affecting the conduct of a physician acting under the provisions of this Act, submit such proposed rule or regulation to the Board of Registration in Medicine [or similar state agency] for such Board's review and advice.

(c) The Board of Registration in Medicine [or similar state agency] may promulgate no rule or regulation inconsistent with the provisions of this Act or with the rules and regulations of the Department promulgated under it and shall, at least ninety days prior to adopting any rule or regulation affecting the conduct of a physician acting under the provisions of this Act, submit such proposed rule or regulation to the Commissioner for the Commissioner's review and advice.

(d) The Commissioner shall report to the Legislature annually concerning the operation of this Act and the achievement of its stated purposes. The report of the Commissioner shall be made available to the public upon its submission to the Legislature. In order to facilitate such annual reporting, the Commissioner may collect and review such information as the Commissioner determines to be helpful to the

Department, the Board of Registration in Medicine [or similar state agency], or the Legislature and may by regulation require the submission of such information to the Department.

SECTION 10. Confidentiality of Records and Reports

(a) The information that a person acting under this Act obtains from or about a patient is confidential and may not be disclosed to any other person without the patient's consent or the consent of a person with lawful authority to act on the patient's behalf, except as this Act or and other provision of law may otherwise require.

(b) The report that a responsible physician files with the Department pursuant to Section 6(b) of this Act is confidential, is not a public record, and is not subject to the provisions of [the state public records statute or freedom of information act].

SECTION 11. Provider's Freedom of Conscience

(a) No individual who is conscientiously opposed to providing a patient with medical means of suicide may be required to do so or to assist a responsible physician in doing so.

(b) A health care facility that has adopted a policy opposed to providing patients with medical means of suicide and has given reasonable notice of such policy to its staff members may prohibit such staff members from providing such means to a patient who is within its facilities or under its care.

SECTION 12. Patient's Freedom From Discrimination

(a) No physician, health care facility, health care service plan, provider of health or disability insurance, self-insured employee health care benefit plan, or hospital service plan may require any individual to request medical means of suicide as a condition of eligibility for service, benefits, or insurance. No such physician or entity may refuse to provide medical services or medical benefits to an individual because such individual has requested medical means of suicide, except as Section 11 of this Act permits.

(b) A patient's use of medical means of suicide to end such patient's life in compliance with the applicable provisions of this Act shall not be considered suicide for the purpose of voiding a policy of insurance on the life of such patient.

SECTION 13. Liability

(a) No person who has acted in compliance with the applicable provisions of this Act in providing medical means of suicide to an individual shall be subject to civil or criminal liability therefor.

(b) No individual who has acted in compliance with the applicable provisions of this Act in providing medical means of suicide to a patient shall be subject therefor to professional sanction, loss of employment, or loss of privileges, provided that such action does not violate a policy of a health care facility that complies with Section 11(b) of this Act.

(c) Except as provided in paragraphs (a) and (b) of this section, this Act does not limit the civil, criminal, or disciplinary liability of any person for intentional or negligent misconduct.

SECTION 14. Criminal Penalties

In addition to any other civil, criminal, or disciplinary liability that he or she may otherwise incur thereby, an individual who willfully violates Section 3, 4, 5, 6, or 7 of this Act is guilty of a [specify grade of offense].

28

The Legalization of Physician-Assisted Suicide: Creating a Potemkin Village

Daniel Callahan and Margot White

It is impossible in principle and in practice to regulate either euthanasia or physician-assisted suicide successfully. To say this is not to deny that carefully crafted laws and regulations might be written, although the fact that this has not been done in practice suggests that the goal may be unattainable. Yet however careful the language, the nature of the doctor-patient relationship and of the medical procedures themselves renders them resistant to the standards asked for by one article: "clear criteria, rigorous procedures, and adequate safeguards."[1] We liken the effort to devise suitable legal standards to that of erecting Potemkin villages,[2] an elaborate regulatory façade concealing a poverty of potential for actual enforcement.

In developing this argument, we should make clear at the outset that we morally oppose euthanasia and physician-assisted suicide (PAS). We would continue that opposition even if adequate legal

Daniel Callahan is the former director of the Hastings Center in Briarcliff Manor, N.Y., where he is now a senior scholar. **Margot White** is a visiting assistant professor at the University of Virginia School of Medicine and an independent ethics consultant. This essay is greatly abridged and reprinted by permission from the *University of Richmond Law Review* 30, no. 1 (January 1996). Many notes have been omitted.

safeguards could be developed, which we believe they cannot for the reasons we discuss in this article. The impossibility of devising effective safeguards simply adds one more reason to oppose euthanasia and PAS, but by no means is it the only reason. Since the legislative emphasis has of late seen a tactical shift from euthanasia to PAS, our analysis will focus primarily on the latter. We believe, however, that much of what we say would apply with at least as much force to euthanasia, and that the practice cannot be restricted to PAS. We will begin with an examination of the logical and practical problems of writing meaningful laws in this domain. . . .

THE LOGIC OF REGULATION

Although there has been a variety of moral and medical objections over the years to euthansaia and PAS, among the most prominent have been worries about the potential for abuse. Even many of those who might morally accept euthanasia and PAS, under some circumstances, have doubted that their legalization could avoid the danger of coercion or manipulation. Nonetheless, it is not difficult for most people to imagine circumstances where even the best medical and palliative care appears unable to relieve pain or suffering, and where dying is marked by prolonged misery and despair. Thus the pull toward legalization of PAS is strong, and even those firmly opposed on moral grounds can partially understand, and even sympathize with, the motivations of its proponents. . . .

Proponents of PAS have had to discharge a heavy double burden. They have had to show, first, that there are good moral and medical reasons to accept PAS, which they have most commonly attempted to do by arguing the rights to self-determination and to mercy in the relief of suffering. These arguments have been discussed amply elsewhere and will not be summarized here. Second, the proponents have had to show that laws and regulations can be formulated that provide clear criteria and sound procedures and, most importantly, obviate or radically minimize the possibility of abuse. Since there appears to be a considerable reservoir of public sympathy for PAS, meeting this second requirement has been of special importance, perhaps the key to legislative success.

Will Better Statutes Help?

Two arguments have been deployed to take on the worry about abuse: on the one hand, that careful and effective rules precluding or minimizing abuse can be written; and on the other hand, that the current situation of widespread violation of legal prohibitions and a secret, unregulated practice of PAS is itself a dangerous legal corruption, crying out for rectification. It is alleged that many doctors, at considerable professional and legal risk, are complying with their patients' pleas for relief, but with no oversight or regulation or consultation with colleagues. That state of affairs, it is argued, cannot fail to be a worse situation than one where the practice is brought out into the open and clear standards are formulated and implemented. . . .

Yet . . . if the present statutes forbidding euthanasia and PAS are widely ignored by physicians, why should we expect new statutes to be taken with greater moral and legal seriousness? There is no available survey or other evidence to indicate that new laws will bring any increased commitment to following the law. . . . Nor are there any surveys or other available evidence to suggest that prosecutors will show more zeal with new laws than with the old ones, or that juries will display less sympathy for violators of the new rules than they have for those who transgressed the old rules. It is, in short, very odd to claim that physicians who now do as they please, with complete *de facto* immunity from prosecution, will act differently with new laws, and that the new laws will be more stringently enforced.

Could it not, however, be said that laws that lead to few prosecutions or convictions ought to be removed from the books? Not necessarily. As the New York State Task Force on Life and the Law noted in its report on euthanasia and PAS, the legal prohibition carries intense symbolic and practical significance, and "shores up the notion of limits in human relationships."[3] Even laws that are not enforced can have an important place, particularly for physicians when they have the additional support of the traditional Hippocratic prohibition of PAS.

The Doctor-Patient Power Imbalance

The legal and moral reasons given in favor of PAS over euthanasia seem no less poorly based. Consider one prominent line of reasoning:

"[In] assisted suicide, the final act is solely the patient's, and the risk of subtle coercion from doctors, family members, institutions, or other social forces is greatly reduced. The balance of power between doctor and patient is more nearly equal in physician-assisted suicide than in euthanasia."[4] Notably, arguments of this kind do not cite any empirical studies to show there is less coercion and a greater balance of power. There are no such studies. The claim is pure assertion, and not a very plausible one at that. To insinuate the idea of suicide into the mind of someone already grievously suffering can surely be no more difficult than insinuating the idea of euthanasia. Indeed, it could be all the more manipulative if the insinuated hint were combined with a tacit flattery of someone's capacity to act on his or her own.

As for the power of doctors, their general prestige as professionals whose training and experience are widely thought to enable them to understand matters of life and death better than the rest of us, and their capacity to give or withhold lethal drugs, already establish the power differential between them and their patients. The fact that most of Dr. Kevorkian's patients—if that is the right word—were perfectly capable physically of committing suicide by themselves, including most obviously the one physician he helped to die, suggests that the desire to medicalize PAS already bespeaks the power and legitimation conferred by medical approval of it.

In any event, as Dr. Herbert Hendin has shown, it is easy for families and physicians to subtly guide someone toward a PAS choice.[5] In a prominent New York Times Magazine article and a PBS documentary, Hendin contended that there is easily available public evidence to show exactly how it can be, and has been, done. While strong-willed sick and suffering people may be able to resist patent and gross coercion, they may have far more difficulty contending with well-meaning manipulation and gentle, discreet suggestion. The most successful form of manipulation is to lead a person to think that someone else's idea is actually his or her own, or to nudge that person's ambivalence one way or the other.

There is an additional consideration about PAS that needs reflection. In the case of euthanasia, where a physician would commonly give a lethal injection or radically increase a dose of morphine fully and directly intending death, the equivalent of a paper trail exists, at least in the hospital. The use of the lethal pharmaceutical agents will have to be recorded somewhere, and that can be traced. In the instance of PAS, however, the physician can more easily cover his or her tracks; the necessary pills, to be consumed all at once, can be prescribed in typical doses over a long period of time, and no one would be the wiser. This possibility, we surmise, is no doubt one explanation why the alleged common practice of PAS is so difficult to detect and prosecute, even if the authorities are willing to do so.

We can hardly fail to note, moreover, that the perfect formula for combining legal obfuscation and patient seduction is when a doctor says something like the following to a patient: "I perfectly understand how much you would like to be relieved of your terrible pain and suffering, which seems so meaningless. Like other patients of mine, you may have considered suicide as a peaceful way out. I am sorry I cannot help you if you have had such thoughts. But I want to warn you that if you take more than twenty of the pills I have been prescribing to help you with your pain, you are going to die quietly and quickly in your sleep. So please be careful, doing what you know is best."

Regulating the Unregulatable

We have stressed two objections to PAS—that there is no reason to believe that new laws or regulations will bring more honesty and oversight into the practice, and that PAS is no less subject to coercion and a doctor-patient power imbalance than euthanasia. Both of those issues, however, touch on a still deeper problem, revealing the most fundamental flaw in regulatory proposals. If it is true, as it indubitably is, that "decisions about medical treatment are normally made in the privacy of the doctor-patient relationship,"[6] then how could it *ever* be possible to monitor and regulate those decisions regarding PAS that occur within the ambit of that privacy? . . .

We submit that maintaining the privacy of the physician-patient relationship and the confidentiality of these deliberations is fundamentally incompatible with meaningful oversight and adherence to any statutory regulations. What if a physician decides not to come forward? A patient might want to keep his suicide private. Or the doctor may decide that the regulatory specifications have not been met, but nonetheless be sympathetic to the patient's request. It is not difficult to imagine many circumstances in which either the physician or the patient, or both, would prefer to keep the agreement secret. How can that situation be monitored or regulated? How could abuses be detected if a physician wrongly decided to induce someone to consider, and then use, PAS? . . .

Consider once again the claim that legalizing PAS would end the secrecy that now marks its present practice. Why would that necessarily happen? Why would the impunity with which doctors now covertly practice it be lessened by the requirement that they follow new guidelines? In what respect would new guidelines give patients protection they do not already have? In what ways would subtle manipulation of suffering patients be less possible with new laws than with present laws?

The fact that, in the end, all regulation of PAS must be tantamount to physician self-regulation precludes any satisfactory answer to such questions. The behavior of physicians would still be screened from public scrutiny by doctor-patient confidentiality. And if new, more permissive laws would do nothing to change the privacy of doctor-patient agreements, then the cloaked circumstances that make abuse now possible would have a more overt effect. They would, for instance, morally and legally legitimate the practice and, no doubt, increase its prevalence. That effect, and not the protection of vulnerable patients, would probably be the real significance of more permissive laws.

Some Proposed Guidelines

We have laid the emphasis here on the *intrinsic* obstacles to effective regulation of PAS. Regardless of how carefully crafted regulations are on paper, that is all beside the point if doctors alone, or doctors and patients together, secretly decide to ignore them or to evade one or more of their requirements. Nonetheless, it is worth looking at some efforts in the literature to draft guidelines with the purpose of precluding or minimizing abuse. Even on their own terms, the actual details of the Potemkin village façade are riddled with problems.

It can never be easy, legally, to specify acts justifiable only in extraordinary circumstances. A well-drawn statute must ordinarily work with familiar and perspicuous standards of a kind that can be treated uniformly and that do not require, or open the way to, systematically ambiguous interpretation. Most of us could probably imagine some extraordinary circumstances that would justify theft and intentional killing, and in such situations prosecutors, juries, and judges often temper justice with mercy. But it is difficult for laws to be written that can carefully specify those conditions in advance; so they must be left to *ex post facto* judgment and resolution in the courts.

In any event, consider one prominent set of proposed criteria and the difficulty of interpretation posed by most of its features: severe, unrelenting suffering, not being the result of inadequate comfort care; repeated request; non-distorted judgment; good doctor-patient relationship; consultation with another physician; and clear documentation.[7] Of that list, only the requirements of a repeated request, consultation with another physician, and clear documentation are objectively ascertainable. The other conditions require difficult interpretations of verbal and physical behavior, [and] certainty as to what is truly going on in a patient's mind. . . .

Moreover, ordinary medical practice and human experience make clear that there is no obvious correlation between expressions of suffering and actual degree of suffering, and no way of verifying the latter. Nor is there a correlation between medical conditions and unbearable suffering, as considerable individual variation exists. Repeated requests for PAS do not prove suffering so much as they prove determination. Exactly this kind of determination would make *prima facie* plausible claims that comfort care has failed, and there would be no way to prove that it had not. All the cards, so to speak, are in the hands of the determined patient.

Another Set of Guidelines

Just how easy this will become for such a patient is made even clearer in a 1994 proposed set of guidelines.[8] Three features of those guidelines deserve special attention. First, despite the insistence on the need for special procedures and independent monitoring, the patient's evaluation of his or her suffering is the ultimate criterion: "physician-assisted death becomes a legitimate option only after standard measures for comfort care have been found unsatisfactory by competent patients *in the context of their own situation and values.*"9 There is an obvious tension between the radical subjectivity of this standard and the emphasis on the otherwise extraordinary circumstances for which the same guidelines call. Patients, not doctors, appear to be the ones who will determine what counts as extraordinary. The patient's views, moreover, may be colored by unduly pessimistic advice by doctors untrained in palliative care, or may be unduly influenced by the doctor's own views of pain and suffering.

Second, the proposed guidelines directly confront two difficult questions: What about those suffering patients physically unable to end their own lives, and what about those who have "unremitting suffering" but are not terminally ill? The response of the authors is to opt for a "liberal, inclusive policy with respect to these issues." In short, in the former case, it would be acceptable for the physician to perform direct euthanasia (the only way to effect a liberal policy), even though it would contradict the stand taken against euthanasia and in favor of PAS in the document. In the latter case, it will, once again, not be some reasonably objective standard but the standards of the patient that will be determinative. By definition, an individually determined standard is not a standard.

Third, the proposed guidelines state that "[t]reating physicians would be prohibited from providing lethal treatment without prior consultation and review by an independent, certified palliative-care consultant."10 These consultants are to be backed up by palliative-care committees that would review "difficult or disputed cases." The problem with this strategy is that, in the nature of the case, the independent consultant would have to be someone who has already accepted the morality of PAS, as would members of the review committees. Thus from the outset the deck would be stacked in a direction favorable to PAS by the elimination of those on the wrong side of the ethical fence as committee or consultant candidates.

In the end, the standards and procedures proposed by these guidelines accomplish a number of undesirable results: (1) they open the door very wide to expanded indications for PAS by including those who are suffering but not terminally ill; (2) they bring euthanasia in through the back door by apparently permitting it for those patients physically unable to commit suicide; (3) they make the system one not only of physician self-regulation, since the physicians must voluntarily come forward, but also of patient self-regulation by saying that, in the end, it is the patient's situation and values that define last resort and are determinative; and (4) while the intent of a palliative-care consultant and committee might be to avoid rubber-stamp decisions, the committees themselves are unlikely to include moral opponents of PAS. In short, the criteria and methods of these guidelines fail on all counts proposed by the authors themselves. The guidelines will not necessarily protect vulnerable patients, preserve physician integrity, assure the public that PAS will occur only as a last resort, or provide for the possibility of independent monitoring and regulation (which will apply only to those physicians who do not choose to keep their intentions secret).

LESSONS FROM THE NETHERLANDS

The Netherlands is the one country in the world that has had experience in attempting to regulate euthanasia and PAS. Although the Netherlands has yet to enact legislation to decriminalize euthanasia and PAS, court decisions and legislative developments since 1973 have established that doctors may lawfully perform them in certain circumstances. These developments were fueled, to a considerable degree, by the support of public opinion and of the main representative group of Dutch physicians, the Royal Dutch Medical Association (KNMG).

In 1984, the KNMG was the first to set forth the criteria that, until recently, were taken to be clearly determinative by the courts and the parliament. The criteria are (1) voluntariness, which is a patient's free-will choice; (2) a well-considered request, which is one made by a patient who has carefully thought about his or her request; (3) a durable death wish, which is a persistent request; (4) unacceptable suffering, which is suffering that is persistent, unbearable, and hopeless; and (5) consultation and reporting, which is a consultation with a colleague and another doctor and accurate reporting on the cause of death.[11]

Although often reiterated by the Dutch courts, the criteria are subject to one general exception and are open in principle to being set aside altogether. The general condition results from the acceptability of the defense of necessity or *force majeure*. By that principle, a doctor who can claim an exception to the criteria on the basis of "irresistible compulsion or necessity" [*overmacht*] is not criminally liable. Necessity means that in the doctor's judgment, the situation is one where euthanasia or PAS is called for because of a "conflict of interests" in the "light of medical ethics." The doctor's duty to alleviate suffering outweighs his or her duty not to kill.

Until recently, the medical profession and the courts had emphasized that this defense was available only in cases where the patient had freely requested death. Two recent cases, however, exceeded even that defense. In the first case, the supreme court of Holland held that the patient need not even be suffering physical, let alone terminal, illness, and that it could be lawful to assist a mother who was depressed over losing her two sons to kill herself. [See, in this volume, "Assisted Suicide: The Dutch Experience," by Herbert Hendin.] Then, in April 1995, a district court exonerated a Dutch physician who had euthanized a newborn with spinal bifida at the request of its parents. Moreover, it is a highly idiosyncratic understanding of "the norms of medical ethics" to claim that a duty to alleviate suffering outweighs a duty not to kill. There is no basis in the traditions of medical ethics to sustain such a claim.

It is not our intention here to examine either the necessity principle or the two recent court cases. We simply note that although the Dutch have supposedly established criteria, they seem perfectly willing to set the criteria aside in the name of necessity. The criteria become, in effect, dispensable guidelines rather than essential requirements. This situation is reminiscent of the kind of strategic and systematic vagueness of the proposed American statute we looked at earlier, which would set aside its criteria for those physically unable to commit suicide and for those who, though not terminal, are judged to be suffering unbearably.[12] The only point we would make is that with such criteria, it is hard to know just where a line could be drawn in theory or in practice.

The Success of Dutch Regulation

For our purposes here, the more salient information about the Dutch situation is how the judicially legitimated practice of euthanasia and PAS has been implemented. What can we learn about the success of regulation? The best information on this subject comes from a survey commissioned by the Dutch Government's Commission on Euthanasia, appointed in January 1990 and headed by Professor Remmelink.[13] The survey, directed by Professor P. J. van der Maas, encompassed a sample of 406 physicians, who were guaranteed anonymity in providing information to the researchers. Based on the physicians sampled, the official results showed that out of a total of 129,000 deaths, there were 2,300 cases of euthanasia[14] and 400 cases of assisted suicide. Additionally, and most strikingly, there were 1,000 cases of intentional termination of life without explicit request (nonvoluntary euthanasia).

Remarking that the narrow Dutch definition of euthanasia excludes both intentional life-shortening by omission and termination without the patient's request, one commentator concludes that the van der Maas survey reveals 10,558 cases in which it was the doctor's explicit purpose to shorten life, by act or by omission.[15] This commentator points out, moreover, that the majority of the cases were about nonvoluntary euthanasia: in 5,450 cases the patient made no explicit request for euthanasia. If cases in which doctors said it was *partly* their purpose to shorten life are included, the numbers of cases swell to 26,350 and 15,158, respectively.

This is a disturbing set of figures in its own right, rendered all the more distressing by the gloss put on them by the commission that had initiated the survey. While it deplored the act of euthanasia without the explicit request of competent patients, the commission was not nearly so hard on those acts carried out on the incompetent:

> The ultimate justification for the intervention is in both cases the patient's unbearable suffering. So, medically speaking, there is little difference between these situations and euthanasia, because in both cases patients are involved who suffer terribly. . . . The degrading situation the patient is in confronts the doctor with a case of *force majeure*.[16]

Therefore, the criteria set by the KMNG and the courts were not only ignored by the physicians who acted without a request but also regarded as dispensable by the commission, which attempted to justify the physicians' actions.[17] Even in those cases where the criteria were supposedly met, many cases lacked the quality of intolerable suffering, and there were many others in which euthanasia was not the last resort. The *avoidance* of suffering appears to have been as much a consideration for many physicians as the *relief of* suffering.

How much did the physicians actually report? The majority of cases were, and are still, unreported and were illegally certified as deaths from "natural causes."[18] In 1990, the year covered by the van der Maas survey, only 454 cases were reported. Therefore, even if the survey's low estimate of 2,700 cases of voluntary euthanasia and PAS is accepted as accurate, over 70 per cent of cases went unreported. The officially reported figures of late have, however, improved considerably—1,303 cases were reported in 1993 and 1,417 in 1994. Even so, that number is still barely more than half the Remmelink Report's estimated euthanasia total, and does not include the unreported non-voluntary cases.

Given such figures, it would appear that euthanasia is not at all effectively regulated in the Netherlands. As with the laws proposed in the United States, the Dutch guidelines depend upon the willingness of doctors voluntarily to report what they do. It is evident that most doctors do not—certainly not those substantial numbers who engage in non-voluntary euthanasia.

The Dutch have failed to monitor and regulate euthanasia and physician-assisted suicide. Can we expect to do any better? . . .

[A large portion of the article is omitted here. The omitted portion includes: *section 6*, a brief overview of provisions of bills pending in twelve U.S. state legislatures as of June 1995; *section 7*, in which the authors assert the importance of "using clearly defined terms" and charge that the legalization campaign has been marked by the use of "confusing terminology" and "a kind of Orwellian doublespeak"; *section 8*, a description of Oregon's Death With Dignity Act, which the authors see as the probable standard for future attempts at legalization. Also omitted here is *section 9*, the centerpiece of the article, a thirty-three-page "Tour of the Conceptual Landscape" in which the authors examine the provisions of the Oregon act and various pending state bills in seven categories: (1) consent, (2) mental competence or decision-making capacity, (3) voluntariness, (4) restrictions on eligibility, (5) witnesses, (6) definitions of abuse, and (7) reporting requirements. Next, *section 10* looks at "how abuse of other vulnerable populations [children, spouses, the elderly] is handled by the law." In *section*

11 the authors conclude, in part: "Given the documented confusion of terminology and the absence of consistency or consensus from state to state on definitions (of such concepts as terminal, for example, or decisional capacity, or even who should be permitted to avail themselves of medical death), the promise of regulation, standardization, clarity, and openness is unfulfilled. In our view, it cannot be fulfilled. . . . Most importantly, in the context of health care, laws are not intended to substitute for the professional judgment of the physician. And it is ultimate reliance on physician judgment and physician disclosure that renders the practice of PAS/euthanasia essentially unregulatable." The essay then concludes with an "Afterword," updating the legal picture from completion of the essay in mid-1995 to its publication in the spring of 1996. It resumes here several pages into the Afterword.]

The Harvard Model

A new proposal has emerged from academia that purports to strengthen the procedural aspects of Oregon's statute, correct some of the acknowledged weaknesses in that statute's regulatory features, and provide a "model" for future legislation in this area. . . .

The authors of *A Model State Act to Authorize and Regulate Physician-Assisted Suicide* [reprinted in this volume] argue that the medical and ethical basis for physician-assisted suicide is relief of suffering, and that the legal basis is the extension of the right to make decisions on life-sustaining treatment.[19] The existence of the latter right, they suggest, means that PAS does not signify a change in medical practice or public policy but is "a natural and appropriate extension of presently accepted practices."[20] For reasons already discussed, we disagree.

It is ironic that the authors of the model statute have chosen to confine their discussion to physician-assisted suicide and simply to ignore the issue of euthanasia. Framing their discussion in this way enables them to avoid noting that the distinction between passive and active euthanasia (removing artificial life support versus injecting lethal medication) is more sustainable than the distinction between physician-assisted suicide and voluntary active euthanasia. . . . To offer a "model" statute that is based on failing to deal with this issue is intellectually strange.

The authors of the Harvard model admit that they chose to avoid addressing the issue of euthanasia out of concern for public opinion: the public, in their view, would be likely to offer "greater acceptance" of a statute allowing only PAS because of the *perception* of voluntariness" and because there exist "strong ethical objections of some physicians and others to euthanasia."[21] This is hardly a principled reason for avoiding the issue; it seems the triumph of politics over ethics.

The Harvard model neither avoids nor corrects any of the regulatory problems we have pointed out in this article. The inherent impossibility of truly limiting eligibility is acknowledged at the outset. The nine authors apparently voted on this question and "a bare majority . . . agreed to allow anyone to be eligible whose illness is incurable and who subjectively feels that the accompanying suffering is worse than death."[22] There is, they admit, "no objective standard" for such a condition because it is inherently subjective. Far from wanting to restrict the practice, the drafters acknowledged that "it was not possible to construct an objective definition [of unbearable suffering] that was not overly restrictive as to the patients who would meet it."[23] Since there is no "cure" for many of the degenerative effects of old age, when is an elderly person "incurable"? The criteria for eligibility remain as indeterminate, subjective, and impossible to limit as ever.

If eligibility is wide open, does the model statute contain viable means of safeguarding the vulnerable elderly or the abandoned cancer patient? The Harvard model contains the minimal requirements that requests for medical means of suicide must be competent, voluntary, informed, and enduring (made at least twice). We have discussed at length our view that these are unworkable and unenforceable.

More to Facilitate Than to Regulate

What about procedural requirements? The procedures are facilitative, not regulatory. They are intended to ensure that anyone desirous of committing suicide because of suffering and incurable illness will be able to do so, and that the physician who helps achieve this goal will not be subject to legal sanctions. The model statute goes so far as to include a provision explicitly extending the blanket of legal immunity to anyone who "assist[s] the responsible physician in providing medical means of suicide to a patient."[24] What is meant by "assist"? These provisions are clearly not intended to protect patients or restrict the practice. They seem intended to facilitate the practice and protect the providers, apparently acting with or without supervision by a physician.

Included in the Harvard model is an interesting provision about witnesses: two witnesses must be present for the discussion between the physician and patient regarding the request for medical means of suicide. The witnesses may also question the patient and/or the physician to ascertain the level of comprehension of the information being provided. The physician must document this discussion by written, signed transcript, or by means of audio- or video-taping. Interestingly, however, of these two witnesses, it is required only that one of them not be involved in the care of the patient and not stand to benefit from the patient's death. This provision would hardly seem to qualify as a safeguard. Why not preclude both witnesses from belonging to either of these categories? As it stands, it would appear that at least one witness may either be a care provider or stand to profit from the patient's death.

The model statute would grant wide latitude to state agencies to craft their own rules and regulations for monitoring the suicide process, and to design the form on which physicians would supposedly report their compliance with suicide requests. The model statute contains no provision urging or requiring any individual, professional or lay person, to report suspected violations of the statute. While it purports to offer "strong safeguards and precise procedural requirements," the operating principle of the model statute seems clear from the following:

> Section 3(a) [of the model statute] places the responsibility on the responsible physician to ensure that all of its requirements are met. In order to provide the physician with considerable advance assurance that he or she can avoid litigation attempting to second-guess his or her determinations, *the statute makes the physician's standard entirely subjective: the physician need have only an honest belief that the elements of section 3(a) have been met in the particular case.*[25]

Thus, according to the Harvard proposal, the best that can be offered to reassure the public about adequate safeguards is that, in the event of allegations of malfeasance, the physician can avoid the scrutiny of public accountability through the legal system simply by asserting that it was his or her "honest belief" that the procedures had been appropriately followed.

Another example of the facilitative rather than protective function of the model statute is found in the provisions for consultation during the suicide decision-making process. The Harvard model appears to contain some regulatory teeth in its requirements for professional consultation prior to PAS. However, as one looks more closely at these provisions, they seem "curiouser and curiouser." Section 5(a) requires the responsible physician to "secure a written opinion from a consulting physician . . . that the patient is suffering from a terminal illness or an intractable and unbearable illness." Section 5(b) requires the physician to "secure a written opinion from a licensed psychiatrist, clinical psychologist, or psychiatric social worker . . . to the effect that the request" for suicide is not the result of distorted judgment or undue influence, and is "reasoned" and "fully informed." Section 5(c) then requires that the above opinions be placed in the patient's record.

Doesn't this provide a system of checks on the accuracy and appropriateness of the decision? Not at all: the only opinions that must be obtained and placed in the record are opinions corroborating the appropriateness of the suicide. *There is no requirement anywhere that any contradictory opinion, any opinion questioning the appropriateness of the request for suicide, be placed in the record.*

Another interesting departure from the Oregon statute occurs in the provisions regarding reporting of the incidence of PAS. Although the Oregon statute seems drastically deficient in requiring only that the state health department annually review "a sample of records maintained pursuant to this statute," the Harvard model requires no annual review of any medical records by anyone. It requires only that participating physicians submit a "report" of the process, the content and form of which is to be determined by the state health commissioner. The regulatory process is therefore open-ended and unspecified and is left to state discretion and ultimately the physician's assertion of good faith.

What happens in the event of suspected abuse? The Harvard model does not define abuse. The only person reviewing the physician's report is the Commissioner of Public Health or some equivalent state employee. The possibility of the commissioner's obtaining the physician's report of a patient in which the decision for PAS seemed questionable appears extremely remote: the Harvard model exempts the physician's report from public access under the state's public-records statute or freedom-of-information act. Anyone requesting a medical record therefore would have to overcome these formidable barriers to access by providing substantial grounds for suspicion of malfeasance. It is difficult to imagine that any participating physician would submit a report containing evidence of unethical or illegal acts.

We are thus offered a model statute in which: (1) the basic criteria for eligibility are acknowledged to be subjective and therefore impossible to define or determine by objective standards; (2) the safeguards are carried out by means of an honor system of physician self-regulation; (3) the only professional consultations required and recorded are those supportive of the request for PAS; (4) of the two individuals who witness the suicide discussion, one may be a beneficiary of the patient's will or an exhausted care-provider; and (5) any allegation of malfeasance can be defeated by the physician's assertion of good faith.

The fact that the drafters of a model statute chose to sidestep the question of euthanasia entirely speaks volumes: if it were intended that the practice be limited to PAS, then surely the drafters of model legislation would want to demonstrate how that could be achieved in order to reassure the public. Since they fail to demonstrate any such limitation, we conclude that this is not their goal and that the omission serves as implicit acknowledgment of the impossibility of limiting the practice to PAS.

We reiterate what so many have pointed out previously: that merely to *assert* the possibility of limiting this practice either to the terminally ill or to the final stages of terminal illness, or of limiting it to physician-assisted suicide, is simply not good enough. Such assertions remain exactly that: unproven, unsubstantiated, ungrounded, lacking evidence of workability in the real world of clinical medicine and in present-day society. And as we shall see, the courts also make these assertions of limitability without attempting in any way to demonstrate their validity.

The 1996 Ninth Circuit Decision

The 1996 Ninth Circuit ruling *Compassion in Dying v. State of Washington* is an eight-to-three appellate decision affirming the original district-court decision that struck down Washington state's law prohibiting assisted suicide. The 1996 decision overturned a 1995 appellate decision in which a three-judge panel of the Ninth Circuit concluded that there is no due-process liberty interest in physician-assisted suicide. [These two decisions are reprinted in this volume.]

Judge Stephen Reinhardt, writing for the majority, found a constitutional right to physician-assisted suicide for the terminally ill, based on "the compelling similarities between right-to-die cases and abortion cases."[26] Apart from the fact that both kinds of decisions involve death, and both are therefore laden with intense moral significance, we believe there is precious little similarity between them. On the contrary, it is the differences that should draw attention. One obvious and relevant distinction, among many, is that abortion has an inherently self-limiting quality: it will never be undergone by anyone outside the universe of pregnant women. Pregnancy is not a matter of opinion or perception but is a condition subject to an objective test, the results of which can be confirmed by repetition.

By contrast, the characteristics that are alleged to define the parameters of eligibility for PAS have no such objective qualities and are not self-limiting. The problem with concepts like "terminal," "competent," and "voluntary" is not that they cannot be defined, but that the definitions are not *clinically* verifiable with tests or measurements. Although proponents of legalization, including Judge Reinhardt, assure the public repeatedly that the practice can be regulated by means of these established and definable categories of people (terminally ill, competent, suffering, and so on), there is no objective, agreed-on standard in clinical medicine for evaluating these conditions. Since the movement to establish a right to assisted suicide entails establishing a clinical procedure that its proponents promise will be "carefully regulated" and subjected to "rigorous safeguards,"[27] is it too much to expect that some aspect of the clinical evaluation be accessible to objective criteria? Regulation of abortion is, on the basis of clinical criteria, realistic and feasible; the outer limits are knowable and the physical indications are observable.

There are no such qualitative or quantitative limits to the decision for PAS.

Even if one agrees that permissive attitudes towards abortion may result in more pregnant women choosing that option, the aim of the individual choosing abortion and society's ostensible goals are to protect or enhance the quality of the mother's health or life, either by removing a direct threat to her health or by enabling her to participate more fully in society. There is no comparable rationale for PAS; death does not enhance the well-being of the deceased unless non-existence is defined as enhancement.

It is entirely possible that the availability and acceptability of PAS will enhance the lives of care-givers, family members, even physicians and nurses, and that it will also enhance the economic well-being of hospitals and insurers. The Ninth Circuit seems to acknowledge that patients may well be motivated to seek suicide because they perceive themselves to be a burden, and it suggests that the concern to avoid becoming a financial burden is laudable:

> [W]e are reluctant to say that, in a society in which the costs of protracted health care can be so exorbitant, it is improper for competent, terminally ill adults to take the economic welfare of their families and loved ones into consideration.[28]

By this acknowledgment and apparent approval of the patient's perception of illness as burdensome to others, the way is paved for the medical community and society as a whole to take the same view. Indeed, Judge Reinhardt briefly addresses and then dismisses the concerns that have been raised by a number of commentators—including Yale Kamisar, the New York State Task Force on Life and the Law, and John Pickering, chair of the American Bar Association's Commission on Legal Problems of the Elderly—regarding the dangers of enacting PAS legislation in a society where gross inequities exist in health care as a result of disparate socioeconomic conditions. We share the view that "voluntariness" is an idealized concept that fails to take into account the profound effects of poverty on all aspects of a person's life, health status, access to and quality of health care, as well as manner of death. Rather than seeing these inequities in our society as a compelling reason to maintain the prohibition against PAS and euthanasia, Judge Reinhardt takes the view that the judiciary should "stand aside from that battle." It is odd, indeed, to stand aside from a struggle to provide access to decent health care for everyone in our society, regardless of income or health status, and yet to lead the charge, as it were, toward unlimited access to means of death.

Eliminating and Redefining Terms

In rendering its opinion, the Ninth Circuit avoids resolving a number of crucial concerns regarding the feasibility of regulation by simply redefining terms and declaring certain previously valued moral distinctions of no importance. First to disappear is the use of the word "terminal" in any consistent manner that enables it to be a useful criterion. The court dismisses this difficulty at the outset with a curious argument. It points out that, at present, at least forty states have enacted living-will statutes that define "terminal illness" in widely varying and inconsistent ways. However, instead of viewing this as evidence of the malleability and permeability of the concept, the court views the definitional smorgasbord as evidence that "terminal" can, indeed, be defined, and so it is simply not a problem.[29] As we have pointed out, the issue is not whether the word can be defined, but whether the definition has any basis in clinical reality such that it makes sense to define a class of people in this manner, not only in order to exercise a constitutional right, but also to undergo a medical procedure resulting in death.

Even more troubling, however, is the court's attempt to eliminate the terms "suicide" and "euthanasia" from the discussion. In addressing the state's interest in preventing suicide, Judge Reinhardt writes:

> We are doubtful that deaths resulting from terminally ill patients taking medication prescribed by their doctors should be classified as "suicide" . . . [because] deaths that result from patients' decisions to terminate life support systems or to refuse life-sustaining food and water, for example, are not.[30]

Thus, the court reasons, "we have serious doubt that the state's interest in preventing suicide is even implicated in this case." This seems an extraordinary line of reasoning.

Later, in its discussion of the dissent's arguments and concerns about potential abuse, the court tries to dismiss concerns about the inevitable extension of PAS to euthanasia by, again, redefining the terms. Euthanasia, the court insists, is euthanasia only when it is done *involuntarily*. The Ninth Circuit cites no reference for this definition: "We define euthanasia as the act or practice of painlessly putting to death persons suffering from incurable and distressing disease, as an act of mercy, but *not* at the person's request."[31] Interestingly, *Black's Law Dictionary* defines euthanasia in exactly the same words, but without a distinction between the involuntariness or voluntariness of the act. Most commentators have customarily used the term "non-voluntary euthanasia" when the patient is incompetent, "involuntary euthanasia" when it is done over the patient's protest, and "voluntary euthanasia" when the patient requests it. Now the Ninth Circuit declares that because the Washington statute at issue is concerned with requested death, "the issue of euthanasia is not implicated here."[32]

Finally, the court opens the door to surrogate decision-making in this highly complex and complicated arena by focusing all its moral and legal attention on the issue of voluntariness:

> [We] view the critical line in right-to-die cases as the one between the voluntary and involuntary termination of an individual's life. . . . We consider it less important who administers the medication than who determines whether the terminally ill person's life shall end.[33]

Having effectively eliminated all lines of distinction and demarcation between refusing and removing unwanted medical treatment on the one hand, and providing the means to suicide on the other, the court finds no significant distinction between PAS and euthanasia; what matters is simply that it be "voluntary." The Ninth Circuit has extraordinary confidence in the feasibility of regulation, the insignificant impact of poverty on health-care and medical choices, and the quality of medical decision-making by patients and surrogates in this country's hospitals. The question of "voluntariness" is the central issue for the Ninth Circuit, and active euthanasia would be permissible by proxy because "a decision of a duly appointed surrogate decision-maker is for all legal purposes the decision of the patient himself." With all due respect, the decisions of surrogates are usually legally valid only if they accord with the patient's known or ascertainable instructions. A full discussion of this issue is beyond the scope of this article, but the matter raises even more forcefully the importance of addressing the regulatory schemes in light of clinical experience in this area of medical decision-making.

The Ninth Circuit decision thus eviscerates the state's interest in preventing suicide or euthanasia by redefining both terms, and by eliminating every line of demarcation heretofore recognized in law and ethics along the continuum from refusing artificial means of life support to injecting a patient with a lethal dose of medicine. The court bypasses all concerns about the difficulty, if not impossibility, of providing clear or enforceable limits on the practice by declaring blandly that "while there is always room for error in any human endeavor, we believe that sufficient protections can and will be developed by the various states."34 Where? Which state has done so? In its 153-page opinion, not once does the Ninth Circuit attempt to show how this might be accomplished. As we have discussed, we believe that even the Harvard model fails to demonstrate that this can be done.

In conclusion, we reiterate our contention that regulation of the practice of physician-assisted suicide is inherently impossible. . . .

29

The Supreme Court Decides:
The 'Glucksberg' and 'Quill' Cases

June 26, 1997

The two cases in chapter 25 were appealed to the United States Supreme Court, which heard argument on January 8, 1997. (In the Washington state case, Dr. Harold Glucksberg had replaced Compassion in Dying as principal party.) On June 26, a unanimous Court reversed both rulings in opinions written by Chief Justice WILLIAM H. REHNQUIST, joined by Justices Sandra Day O'Connor, Antonin Scalia, Anthony M. Kennedy, and Clarence Thomas. Four justices wrote concurrences; those by Justices O'CONNOR, JOHN PAUL STEVENS, and STEPHEN BREYER apply to both cases, while Justice DAVID H. SOUTER wrote extensively about *Glucksberg* and minimally about *Quill*. Justice RUTH BADER GINSBURG concurred in the judgments.

In the following opinions, most case citations and other references and all notes have been omitted. Other omissions are indicated by ellipses. The main omissions are: in the two Rehnquist opinions, the opening summaries of the cases, and in Souter's *Glucksberg* concurrence, an extensive discussion of due process and substantive due process.

These case are reprinted by permission of West Publishing Company from the WESTLAW text. They may also be found at 117 S.Ct. 2258 (1997).

Washington v. Glucksberg

United States Supreme Court
June 26, 1997

Chief Justice Rehnquist delivered the opinion of the Court:
The question presented in this case is whether Washington's prohibition against "caus[ing]" or "aid[ing]" a suicide offends the Fourteenth Amendment to the United States Constitution. We hold that it does not. . . .

We begin, as we do in all due-process cases, by examining our nation's history, legal traditions, and practices. In almost every state—indeed, in almost every western democracy—it is a crime to assist a suicide. The states' assisted-suicide bans are not innovations. Rather, they are longstanding expressions of the states' commitment to the protection and preservation of all human life. Indeed, opposition to and condemnation of suicide—and, therefore, of assisting suicide—are consistent and enduring themes of our philosophical, legal, and cultural heritages.

More specifically, for over 700 years, the Anglo-American common-law tradition has punished or otherwise disapproved of both suicide and assisting suicide. In the thirteenth century, Henry de Bracton, one of the first legal treatise writers, observed that "[j]ust as a man may commit felony by slaying another so may he do so by slaying himself." The real and personal property of one who killed himself to avoid conviction and punishment for a crime were forfeit to the king; however, thought Bracton, "if a man slays himself in weariness of life or because he is unwilling to endure further bodily pain . . . [only] his movable goods [were] confiscated." Thus, "[t]he principle that suicide of a sane person, for whatever reason, was a punishable felony was . . . introduced into English common law." Centuries later, Sir William Blackstone, whose *Commentaries on the Laws of England* not only provided a definitive summary of the common law but was also a primary legal authority for eighteenth- and nineteenth-century American lawyers, referred to suicide as "self-murder" and "the pretended heroism, but real cowardice, of the Stoic

600

philosophers, who destroyed themselves to avoid those ills which they had not the fortitude to endure. . . ." Blackstone emphasized that "the law has . . . ranked [suicide] among the highest crimes," although, anticipating later developments, he conceded that the harsh and shameful punishments imposed for suicide "borde[r] a little upon severity."

For the most part, the early American colonies adopted the common-law approach. For example, the legislators of the Providence Plantations, which would later become Rhode Island, declared, in 1647, that "[s]elf murder is by all agreed to be the most unnatural, and it is by this present Assembly declared, to be that, wherein he that doth it, kills himself out of a premeditated hatred against his own life or other humor: . . . his goods and chattels are the king's custom, but not his debts nor lands; but in case he be an infant, a lunatic, mad or distracted man, he forfeits nothing." Virginia also required ignominious burial for suicides, and their estates were forfeit to the crown.

Over time, however, the American colonies abolished these harsh common-law penalties. William Penn abandoned the criminal forfeiture sanction in Pennsylvania in 1701, and the other colonies (and later, the other states) eventually followed this example. Zephaniah Swift, who would later become chief justice of Connecticut, wrote in 1796 that

[t]here can be no act more contemptible, than to attempt to punish an offender for a crime, by exercising a mean act of revenge upon lifeless clay, that is insensible of the punishment. There can be no greater cruelty, than the inflicting [of] a punishment, as the forfeiture of goods, which must fall solely on the innocent offspring of the offender. . . . [Suicide] is so abhorrent to the feelings of mankind, and that strong love of life which is implanted in the human heart, that it cannot be so frequently committed, as to become dangerous to society. There can of course be no necessity of any punishment.

This statement makes it clear, however, that the movement away from the common law's harsh sanctions did not represent an acceptance of suicide; rather, as Chief Justice Swift observed, this change reflected the growing consensus that it was unfair to punish the suicide's family for his wrongdoing. Nonetheless, although states moved away from Blackstone's treatment of suicide, courts continued to condemn it as a grave public wrong.

That suicide remained a grievous, though non-felonious, wrong is confirmed by the fact that colonial and early state legislatures and courts did not retreat from prohibiting assisting suicide. Swift, in his early nineteenth-century treatise on the laws of Connecticut, stated that "[i]f one counsels another to commit suicide, and the other by reason of the advice kills himself, the advisor is guilty of murder as principal." This was the well-established common-law view, as was the similar principle that the consent of a homicide victim is "wholly immaterial to the guilt of the person who cause[d] [his death]." And the prohibitions against assisting suicide never contained exceptions for those who were near death. Rather, "[t]he life of those to whom life ha[d] become a burden—of those who [were] hopelessly diseased or fatally wounded—nay, even the lives of criminals condemned to death, [were] under the protection of law, equally as the lives of those who [were] in the full tide of life's enjoyment, and anxious to continue to live." (*Blackburn* v. *State,* 23 Ohio St., at 163 [1872].)

The earliest American statute explicitly to outlaw assisting suicide was enacted in New York in 1828, and many of the new states and territories followed New York's example. Between 1857 and 1865, a New York commission led by Dudley Field drafted a criminal code that prohibited "aiding" a suicide and, specifically, "furnish[ing] another person with any deadly weapon or poisonous drug, knowing that such person intends to use such weapon or drug in taking his own life." By the time the Fourteenth Amendment was ratified, it was a crime in most states to assist a suicide. The Field Penal Code was adopted in the Dakota Territory in 1877, in New York in 1881, and its language served as a model for several other western states' statutes in the late nineteenth and early twentieth centuries. California, for example, codified its assisted-suicide prohibition in 1874, using language similar to the Field Code's. In this century, the Model Penal Code also prohibited "aiding" suicide, prompting many states to enact or revise their assisted-suicide bans. The code's drafters observed that "the interests in the sanctity of life that are represented by the criminal homicide laws are threatened by one who expresses a willingness to participate in taking the life of another, even though the act may be accomplished with the consent, or at the request, of the suicide victim."

Though deeply rooted, the states' assisted-suicide bans have in recent years been reexamined and, generally, reaffirmed. Because of advances in medicine and technology, Americans today are increasingly likely to die in institutions, from chronic illnesses. Public concern and democratic action are therefore sharply focused on how best to protect dignity and independence at the end of life, with the result that there have been many significant changes in state laws and in the attitudes these laws reflect. Many states, for example, now permit "living wills," surrogate health-care decision-making, and the withdrawal or refusal of life-sustaining medical treatment. At the same time, however, voters and legislators continue for the most part to reaffirm their states' prohibitions on assisting suicide.

The Washington statute at issue in this case was enacted in 1975 as part of a revision of that state's criminal code. Four years later, Washington passed its Natural Death Act, which specifically stated that the "withholding or withdrawal of life-sustaining treatment . . . shall not, for any purpose, constitute a suicide" and that "[n]othing in this chapter shall be construed to condone, authorize, or approve mercy killing. . . ." In 1991, Washington voters rejected a ballot initiative which, had it passed, would have permitted a form of physician-assisted suicide. Washington then added a provision to the Natural Death Act expressly excluding physician-assisted suicide.

California voters rejected an assisted-suicide initiative similar to Washington's in 1993. On the other hand, in 1994, voters in Oregon enacted, also through ballot initiative, that state's Death With Dignity Act, which legalized physician-assisted suicide for competent, terminally ill adults. Since the Oregon vote, many proposals to legalize assisted suicide have been and continue to be introduced in the states' legislatures, but none has been enacted. And just last year, Iowa and Rhode Island joined the overwhelming majority of states explicitly prohibiting assisted suicide. Also, on April 30, 1997, President Clinton signed the Federal Assisted Suicide Funding Restriction Act of 1997, which prohibits the use of federal funds in support of physician-assisted suicide.

Thus, the states are currently engaged in serious, thoughtful examinations of physician-assisted suicide and other similar issues. For example, New York State's Task Force on Life and the Law—an ongoing, blue-ribbon commission composed of doctors, ethicists, lawyers, religious leaders, and interested laymen—was convened in 1984 and commissioned with "a broad mandate to recommend public policy on issues raised by medical advances." Over the past decade, the Task Force has recommended laws relating to end-of-life decisions, surrogate pregnancy, and organ donation. After studying physician-assisted suicide, however, the Task Force unanimously concluded that "[l]egalizing assisted suicide and euthanasia would pose profound risks to many individuals who are ill and vulnerable. . . . [T]he potential dangers of this dramatic change in public policy would outweigh any benefit that might be achieved." (New York State Task Force, *When Death Is Sought: Assisted Suicide and Euthanasia in the Medical Context* [May 1994], 120.)

Attitudes toward suicide itself have changed since Bracton, but our laws have consistently condemned, and continue to prohibit, assisting suicide. Despite changes in medical technology and notwithstanding an increased emphasis on the importance of end-of-life decision-making, we have not retreated from this prohibition. Against this backdrop of history, tradition, and practice, we now turn to respondents' constitutional claim.

II

The Due Process Clause guarantees more than fair process, and the "liberty" it protects includes more than the absence of physical restraint. The clause also provides heightened protection against government interference with certain fundamental rights and liberty interests. In a long line of cases, we have held that, in addition to the specific freedoms protected by the Bill of Rights, the "liberty" specially protected by the Due Process Clause includes the rights to marry (*Loving v. Virginia* . . . [1967]); to have children (*Skinner* v. *Oklahoma ex rel. Williamson* . . . [1942]); to direct the education and upbringing of one's children (*Meyer v. Nebraska* . . . [1923]; *Pierce v. Society of Sisters* . . . [1925]); to marital privacy (*Griswold v. Connecticut* . . . [1965]); to use contraception (*ibid.; Eisenstadt v. Baird* . . . [1972]); to bodily integrity (*Rochin v. California* . . . [1952]), and to abortion (*Planned Parenthood v. Casey,* 505 U.S. 833 [1992]). We have also assumed, and strongly suggested, that the Due Process Clause protects the traditional right to refuse unwanted lifesaving medical treatment (*Cruzan v. Director, Mo. Dept. of Health,* 497 U.S. 261 [1990]).

But we "ha[ve] always been reluctant to expand the concept of substantive due process because guideposts for responsible decision-making in this unchartered area are scarce and open ended." (*Collins v. Harker Heights,* 503 U.S., at 125 [1992].) By extending constitutional protection to an asserted right or liberty interest, we, to a great extent, place the matter outside the arena of public debate and legislative action. We must therefore "exercise the utmost care whenever we are asked to break new ground in this field" *(ibid.),* lest the liberty protected by the Due Process Clause be subtly transformed into the policy preferences of the members of this Court.

Our established method of substantive-due-process analysis has two primary features: First, we have regularly observed that the Due Process Clause specially protects those fundamental rights and liberties which are, objectively, "deeply rooted in this nation's history and tradition." (*Moore v. East Cleveland,* 431 U.S., at 503 [plurality opinion] [1977].) Second, we have required in substantive-due-process cases a "careful description" of the asserted fundamental liberty interest. Our nation's history, legal traditions, and practices thus provide the crucial "guideposts for responsible decision-making" that direct and restrain our exposition of the Due Process Clause. As we stated recently in *Flores,* the Fourteenth Amendment "forbids the government to infringe . . . 'fundamental' liberty interests *at all,* no matter what process is provided, unless the infringement is narrowly tailored to serve a compelling state interest." (*Reno v. Flores,* 507 U.S., at 302 [1993].)

Justice Souter, relying on Justice Harlan's dissenting opinion in *Poe v. Ullman,* would largely abandon this restrained methodology, and instead ask "whether [Washington's] statute sets up one of those 'arbitrary impositions' or 'purposeless restraints' at odds with the Due Process Clause of the Fourteenth Amendment." In our view, however, the development of this Court's substantive-due-process jurisprudence, described briefly above, has been a process whereby the outlines of the "liberty" specially protected by the Fourteenth Amendment—never fully clarified, to be sure, and perhaps not capable of being fully clarified—have at least been carefully refined by concrete examples involving fundamental rights found to be deeply rooted in our legal tradition. This approach tends to rein in the subjective elements that are necessarily present in due-process judicial review. In addition, by establishing a threshold requirement—that a challenged state action implicate a fundamental right—before requiring more than a reasonable relation to a legitimate state interest to justify the action, it avoids the need for complex balancing of competing interests in every case.

Turning to the claim at issue here, the Court of Appeals stated that "[p]roperly analyzed, the first issue to be resolved is whether there is a liberty interest in determining the time and manner of one's death," or in other words, "[i]s there a right to die?" Similarly, respondents assert a "liberty to choose how to die" and a right to "control of one's final days," and describe the asserted liberty as "the right to choose a humane, dignified death," and "the liberty to shape death." As noted above, we have a tradition of carefully formulating the interest at stake in substantive-due-process cases. For example, although *Cruzan* is often described as a "right to die" case, we were, in fact, more precise: we assumed that the Constitution granted competent persons a "constitutionally protected right to refuse lifesaving hydration and nutrition." (*Cruzan,* at 279.) The Washington statute at issue in this case prohibits "aid[ing] another person to attempt suicide," and, thus, the question before us is whether the "liberty" specially protected by the Due Process Clause includes a right to commit suicide which itself includes a right to assistance in doing so.

We now inquire whether this asserted right has any place in our nation's traditions. Here . . . we are confronted with a consistent and almost universal tradition that has long rejected the asserted right, and continues explicitly to reject it today, even for terminally ill, mentally competent adults. To hold for respondents, we would have to reverse centuries of legal doctrine and practice, and strike down the considered policy choice of almost every state.

Respondents contend, however, that the liberty interest they assert *is* consistent with this Court's substantive-due-process line of cases, if not with this nation's history and practice. Pointing to *Casey* and *Cruzan,* respondents read our jurisprudence in this area as reflecting a general tradition of "self sovereignty," and as teaching that the "liberty" protected by the Due Process Clause includes "basic and intimate exercises of personal autonomy." According to respondents, our liberty jurisprudence, and the broad, individualistic principles it reflects, protects the "liberty of competent, terminally ill adults to make end-of-life decisions free of undue government interference." The question presented in this case, however, is whether the protections of the Due Process Clause include a right to commit suicide with another's assistance. With this "careful description" of respondents' claim in mind, we turn to *Casey* and *Cruzan*.

In *Cruzan,* we considered whether Nancy Beth Cruzan, who had been severely injured in an automobile accident and was in a persistive vegetative state, "ha[d] a right under the United States Constitution which would require the hospital to withdraw life-sustaining treatment" at her parents' request. We began with the observation that "[a]t common law, even the touching of one person by another without consent and without legal justification was a battery." We then discussed the related rule that "informed consent is generally required for medical treatment." After reviewing a long line of relevant state cases, we concluded that "the common-law doctrine of informed consent is viewed as generally encompassing the right of a competent individual to refuse medical treatment." Next, we reviewed our own cases on the subject, and stated that "[t]he principle that a competent person has a constitutionally protected liberty interest in refusing unwanted medical treatment may be inferred from our prior decisions." Therefore, "for purposes of [that] case, we assume[d] that the United States Constitution would grant a competent person a constitutionally protected right to refuse lifesaving hydration and nutrition." We concluded that, notwithstanding this right, the Constitution permitted Missouri to require clear and convincing evidence of an incompetent patient's wishes concerning the withdrawal of life-sustaining treatment.

Respondents contend that in *Cruzan* we "acknowledged that competent, dying persons have the right to direct the removal of life-sustaining medical treatment and thus hasten death," and that "the constitutional principle behind recognizing the patient's liberty to direct the withdrawal of artificial life support applies at least as strongly to the choice to hasten impending death by consuming lethal medication." Similarly, the Court of Appeals concluded that "*Cruzan,* by recognizing a liberty interest that includes the refusal of artificial provision of life-sustaining food and water, necessarily recognize[d] a liberty interest in hastening one's own death."

The right assumed in *Cruzan,* however, was not simply deduced from abstract concepts of personal autonomy. Given the common-law rule that forced medication was a battery, and the long legal tradition protecting the decision to refuse unwanted medical treatment, our assumption was entirely consistent with this nation's history and constitutional traditions. The decision to commit suicide with the assistance of another may be just as personal and profound as the decision to refuse unwanted medical treatment, but it has never enjoyed similar legal protection. Indeed, the two acts are widely and reasonably regarded as quite distinct. In *Cruzan* itself, we recognized that most states outlawed assisted suicide—and even more do today —and we certainly gave no intimation that the right to refuse unwanted medical treatment could be somehow transmuted into a right to assistance in committing suicide.

Respondents also rely on *Casey.* There, the Court's opinion concluded that "the essential holding of *Roe v. Wade* should be retained and once again reaffirmed." We held, first, that a woman has a right, before her fetus is viable, to an abortion "without undue interference from the state"; second, that states may restrict post-viability abortions, so long as exceptions are made to protect a woman's life and health; and third, that the state has legitimate interests throughout a pregnancy in protecting the health of the woman and the life of the unborn child. In reaching this conclusion, the opinion discussed in some detail this Court's substantive-due-process tradition of interpreting the Due Process Clause to protect certain fundamental rights and "personal decisions relating to marriage, procreation, contraception, family relationships, child rearing, and education," and noted that many of those rights and liberties "involv[e] the most intimate and personal choices a person may make in a lifetime."

The Court of Appeals, like the District Court, found *Casey* "'highly instructive'" and "'almost prescriptive'" for determining "'what liberty interest may inhere in a terminally ill person's choice to commit suicide'":

> Like the decision of whether or not to have an abortion, the decision how and when to die is one of "the most intimate and personal

choices a person may make in a lifetime," a choice "central to personal dignity and autonomy." [79 F. 3d, at 813.]

Similarly, respondents emphasize the statement in *Casey* that:

At the heart of liberty is the right to define one's own concept of existence, of meaning, of the universe, and of the mystery of human life. Beliefs about these matters could not define the attributes of personhood were they formed under compulsion of the State. [*Casey*, at 851.]

By choosing this language, the Court's opinion in *Casey* described, in a general way and in light of our prior cases, those personal activities and decisions that this Court has identified as so deeply rooted in our history and traditions, or so fundamental to our concept of constitutionally ordered liberty, that they are protected by the Fourteenth Amendment. The opinion moved from the recognition that liberty necessarily includes freedom of conscience and belief about ultimate considerations to the observation that "though the abortion decision may originate within the zone of conscience and belief, it is *more than a philosophic exercise*." (*Casey*, at 852 [emphasis added].) That many of the rights and liberties protected by the Due Process Clause found in personal autonomy does not warrant the sweeping conclusion that any and all important, intimate, and personal decisions are so protected, and *Casey* did not suggest otherwise.

The history of the law's treatment of assisted suicide in this country has been and continues to be one of the rejection of nearly all efforts to permit it. That being the case, our decisions lead us to conclude that the asserted "right" to assistance in committing suicide is not a fundamental liberty interest protected by the Due Process Clause. The Constitution also requires, however, that Washington's assisted-suicide ban be rationally related to legitimate government interests. This requirement is unquestionably met here. . . . Washington's assisted-suicide ban implicates a number of state interests.

First, Washington has an "unqualified interest in the preservation of human life." (*Cruzan*, at 282.) The state's prohibition on assisted suicide, like all homicide laws, both reflects and advances its commitment to this interest. This interest is symbolic and aspirational as well as practical:

While suicide is no longer prohibited or penalized, the ban against assisted suicide and euthanasia shores up the notion of limits in human relationships. It reflects the gravity with which we view the decision to take one's own life or the life of another, and our reluctance to encourage or promote these decisions. [New York Task Force, at 131-32.]

Respondents admit that "[t]he state has a real interest in preserving the lives of those who can still contribute to society and enjoy life." The Court of Appeals also recognized Washington's interest in protecting life, but held that the "weight" of this interest depends on the "medical condition and the wishes of the person whose life is at stake." Washington, however, has rejected this sliding-scale approach and, through its assisted-suicide ban, insists that all persons' lives, from beginning to end, regardless of physical or mental condition, are under the full protection of the law. As we have previously affirmed, the states "may properly decline to make judgments about the 'quality' of life that a particular individual may enjoy." (*Cruzan,* at 282.) This remains true, as *Cruzan* makes clear, even for those who are near death.

Relatedly, all admit that suicide is a serious public-health problem, especially among persons in otherwise vulnerable groups. The state has an interest in preventing suicide, and in studying, identifying, and treating its causes.

Those who attempt suicide—terminally ill or not—often suffer from depression or other mental disorders. Research indicates, however, that many people who request physician-assisted suicide withdraw that request if their depression and pain are treated. The New York Task Force, however, expressed its concern that, because depression is difficult to diagnose, physicians and medical professionals often fail to respond adequately to seriously ill patients' needs. Thus, legal physician-assisted suicide could make it more difficult for the state to protect depressed or mentally ill persons, or those who are suffering from untreated pain, from suicidal impulses.

The state also has an interest in protecting the integrity and ethics of the medical profession. In contrast to the Court of Appeals' conclusion that "the integrity of the medical profession would [not] be threatened in any way by [physician-assisted suicide]," the American Medical Association, like many other medical and physicians' groups, has concluded that "[p]hysician-assisted suicide is fundamentally incompatible with the physician's role as healer." (American Medical Association, Code of Ethics §2.211 [1994].) And physician-assisted suicide could, it is argued, undermine the trust that is essential to the doctor-patient relationship by blurring the time-honored line between healing and harming.

Next, the state has an interest in protecting vulnerable groups—including the poor, the elderly, and disabled persons—from abuse, neglect, and mistakes. The Court of Appeals dismissed the state's concern that disadvantaged persons might be pressured into physician-assisted suicide as "ludicrous on its face." We have recognized, however, the real risk of subtle coercion and undue influence in end-of-life situations. (*Cruzan*, at 281.) Similarly, the New York Task Force warned that "[l]egalizing physician-assisted suicide would pose profound risks to many individuals who are ill and vulnerable. . . . The risk of harm is greatest for the many individuals in our society whose autonomy and well being are already compromised by poverty, lack of access to good medical care, advanced age, or membership in a stigmatized social group." (New York Task Force, at 120). If physician-assisted suicide were permitted, many might resort to it to spare their families the substantial financial burden of end-of-life healthcare costs.

The state's interest here goes beyond protecting the vulnerable from coercion; it extends to protecting disabled and terminally ill people from prejudice, negative and inaccurate stereotypes, and "societal indifference." The state's assisted-suicide ban reflects and reinforces its policy that the lives of terminally ill, disabled, and elderly people must be no less valued than the lives of the young and healthy, and that a seriously disabled person's suicidal impulses should be interpreted and treated the same way as anyone else's.

Finally, the state may fear that permitting assisted suicide will start it down the path to voluntary and perhaps even involuntary euthanasia. The Court of Appeals struck down Washington's assisted-suicide ban only "as applied to competent, terminally ill adults who wish to hasten their deaths by obtaining medication prescribed by their doctors." Washington insists, however, that the impact of the court's decision will not and cannot be so limited. If suicide is protected as a matter of constitutional right, it is argued, "every man and woman in the United States must enjoy it." The Court of Appeals' decision, and its expansive reasoning, provide ample support for the state's concerns. The court noted, for example, that the "decision of a duly appointed surrogate decision-maker is for all legal purposes the decision of the patient himself"; that "in some instances, the patient may be unable to self-administer the drugs and . . . administration by the physician . . . may be the only way the patient may be able to receive them"; and that not only physicians, but also family members and loved ones, will inevitably participate in assisting suicide. Thus, it turns out that what is couched as a limited right to "physician-assisted suicide" is likely, in effect, a much broader license, which could prove extremely difficult to police and contain. Washington's ban on assisting suicide prevents such erosion.

This concern is further supported by evidence about the practice of euthanasia in the Netherlands. The Dutch government's own study revealed that in 1990, there were 2,300 cases of voluntary euthanasia (defined as "the deliberate termination of another's life at his request"), 400 cases of assisted suicide, and more than 1,000 cases of euthanasia without an explicit request. In addition to these latter 1,000 cases, the study found an additional 4,941 cases where physicians administered lethal morphine overdoses without the patients' explicit consent. This study suggests that, despite the existence of various reporting procedures, euthanasia in the Netherlands has not been limited to competent, terminally ill adults who are enduring physical suffering, and that regulation of the practice may not have prevented abuses in cases involving vulnerable persons, including severely disabled neonates and elderly persons suffering from dementia. The New York Task Force, citing the Dutch experience, observed that "assisted suicide and euthanasia are closely linked," and concluded that the "risk of . . . abuse is neither speculative nor distant." Washington, like most other states, reasonably ensures against this risk by banning, rather than regulating, assisting suicide.

We need not weigh exactly the relative strengths of these various interests. They are unquestionably important and legitimate, and Washington's ban on assisted suicide is at least reasonably related to their promotion and protection. We therefore hold that Wash. Rev. Code §9A.36.060(1) (1994) does not violate the Fourteenth Amendment, either on its face or "as applied to competent, terminally ill

adults who wish to hasten their deaths by obtaining medication prescribed by their doctors."

Throughout the nation, Americans are engaged in an earnest and
profound debate about the morality, legality, and practicality of physician-assisted suicide. Our holding permits this debate to continue,
as it should in a democratic society. The decision of the en banc Court
of Appeals is reversed, and the case is remanded for further proceedings consistent with this opinion.

It is so ordered.

Justice O'Connor, concurring:

Death will be different for each of us. For many, the last days will be
spent in physical pain and perhaps the despair that accompanies physical deterioration and a loss of control of basic bodily and mental
functions. Some will seek medication to alleviate that pain and other
symptoms.

The Court frames the issue in this case as whether the Due Process
Clause of the Constitution protects a "right to commit suicide which
itself includes a right to assistance in doing so," and concludes that our
nation's history, legal traditions, and practices do not support the existence of such a right. I join the Court's opinions because I agree that
there is no generalized right to "commit suicide." But respondents urge
us to address the narrower question whether a mentally competent
person who is experiencing great suffering has a constitutionally cognizable interest in controlling the circumstances of his or her imminent
death. I see no need to reach that question in the context of the facial
challenges to the New York and Washington laws at issue here. The
parties and amici agree that in these states a patient who is suffering from
a terminal illness and who is experiencing great pain has no legal barriers
to obtaining medication, from qualified physicians, to alleviate that
suffering, even to the point of causing unconsciousness and hastening
death. In this light, even assuming that we would recognize such an
interest, I agree that the state's interests in protecting those who are not
truly competent or facing imminent death, or those whose decisions to
hasten death would not truly be voluntary, are sufficiently weighty to
justify a prohibition against physician-assisted suicide.

Every one of us at some point may be affected by our own or a family member's terminal illness. There is no reason to think the democratic process will not strike the proper balance between the interests of terminally ill, mentally competent individuals who would seek to end their suffering and the state's interests in protecting those who might seek to end life mistakenly or under pressure. As the Court recognizes, states are presently undertaking extensive and serious evaluation of physician-assisted suicide and other related issues. In such circumstances, "the . . . challenging task of crafting appropriate procedures for safeguarding . . . liberty interests is entrusted to the 'laboratory' of the States . . . in the first instance." (*Cruzan,* at 292 [O'Connor, J., concurring].)

In sum, there is no need to address the question whether suffering patients have a constitutionally cognizable interest in obtaining relief from the suffering that they may experience in the last days of their lives. There is no dispute that dying patients in Washington and New York can obtain palliative care, even when doing so would hasten their deaths. The difficulty in defining terminal illness and the risk that a dying patient's request for assistance in ending his or her life might not be truly voluntary justifies the prohibitions on assisted suicide we uphold here.

Justice Stevens, concurring in the judgments:
The Court ends its opinion with the important observation that our holding today is fully consistent with a continuation of the vigorous debate about the "morality, legality, and practicality of physician-assisted suicide" in a democratic society. I write separately to make it clear that there is also room for further debate about the limits that the Constitution places on the power of the states to punish the practice.

I

The morality, legality, and practicality of capital punishment have been the subject of debate for many years. In 1976, this Court upheld the constitutionality of the practice in cases coming to us from Georgia, Florida, and Texas. In those cases we concluded that a state does have the power to place a lesser value on some lives than on others; there is no absolute requirement that a state treat all human life as having an equal right to preservation. Because the state legislatures had sufficiently narrowed the category of lives that the state could terminate, and had enacted special procedures to ensure that the defendant belonged in that limited category, we concluded that the statutes were not unconstitutional on their face. In later cases coming to us from each of those states, however, we found that some applications of the statutes were unconstitutional.

Today, the Court decides that Washington's statute prohibiting assisted suicide is not invalid "on its face," that is to say, in all or most cases in which it might be applied. That holding, however, does not foreclose the possibility that some applications of the statute might well be invalid.

As originally filed, this case presented a challenge to the Washington statute on its face and as it applied to three terminally ill, mentally competent patients and to four physicians who treat terminally ill patients. After the District Court issued its opinion holding that the statute placed an undue burden on the right to commit physician-assisted suicide, the three patients died. Although the Court of Appeals considered the constitutionality of the statute "as applied to the prescription of life-ending medication for use by terminally ill, competent adult patients who wish to hasten their deaths," the court did not have before it any individual plaintiff seeking to hasten her death or any doctor who was threatened with prosecution for assisting in the suicide of a particular patient; its analysis and eventual holding that the statute was unconstitutional was not limited to a particular set of plaintiffs before it. . . .

History and tradition provide ample support for refusing to recognize an open-ended constitutional right to commit suicide. Much more than the state's paternalistic interest in protecting the individual from the irrevocable consequences of an ill-advised decision motivated by temporary concerns is at stake. There is truth in John Donne's observation that "No man is an island." The state has an interest in preserving and fostering the benefits that every human being may provide to the community—a community that thrives on the exchange of ideas, expressions of affection, shared memories, and humorous incidents as well as on the material contributions that its members create and support. The value to others of a person's life is far too precious to allow the individual to claim a constitutional entitlement to complete autonomy in making a decision to end that life. Thus, I fully agree with the Court that the "liberty" protected by the Due Process Clause does not include a categorical "right to commit suicide which itself includes a right to assistance in doing so."

But just as our conclusion that capital punishment is not always unconstitutional did not preclude later decisions holding that it is sometimes impermissibly cruel, so is it equally clear that a decision upholding a general statutory prohibition of assisted suicide does not mean that every possible application of the statute would be valid. A state, like Washington, that has authorized the death penalty and thereby has concluded that the sanctity of human life does not require that it always be preserved, must acknowledge that there are situations in which an interest in hastening death is legitimate. Indeed, not only is that interest sometimes legitimate, I am also convinced that there are times when it is entitled to constitutional protection.

II

In *Cruzan,* the Court assumed that the interest in liberty protected by the Fourteenth Amendment encompassed the right of a terminally ill patient to direct the withdrawal of life-sustaining treatment. As the Court correctly observes today, that assumption "was not simply deduced from abstract concepts of personal autonomy." Instead, it was supported by the common-law tradition protecting the individual's general right to refuse unwanted medical treatment. We have recognized, however, that this common-law right to refuse treatment is neither absolute nor always sufficiently weighty to overcome valid countervailing state interests. As Justice Brennan pointed out in his *Cruzan* dissent, we have upheld legislation imposing punishment on persons refusing to be vaccinated, and as Justice Scalia pointed out in his concurrence, the state ordinarily has the right to interfere with an attempt to commit suicide by, for example, forcibly placing a bandage on a self-inflicted wound to stop the flow of blood. In most cases, the individual's constitutionally protected interest in his or her own physical autonomy, including the right to refuse unwanted medical treatment, will give way to the State's interest in preserving human life.

Cruzan, however, was not the normal case. Given the irreversible nature of her illness and the progressive character of her suffering, Nancy Cruzan's interest in refusing medical care was incidental to her more basic interest in controlling the manner and timing of her death. In finding that her best interests would be served by cutting off the nourishment that kept her alive, the trial court did more than simply vindicate Cruzan's interest in refusing medical treatment; the court, in essence, authorized affirmative conduct that would hasten her death. When this Court reviewed the case and upheld Missouri's requirement that there be clear and convincing evidence establishing Nancy Cruzan's intent to have life-sustaining nourishment withdrawn, it made two important assumptions: (1) that there was a "liberty interest" in refusing unwanted treatment protected by the Due Process Clause; and (2) that this liberty interest did not "end the inquiry" because it might be outweighed by relevant state interests. I agree with both of those assumptions, but I insist that the source of Nancy Cruzan's right to refuse treatment was not just a common-law rule. Rather, this right is an aspect of a far broader and more basic concept of freedom that is even older than the common law. This freedom embraces, not merely a person's right to refuse a particular kind of unwanted treatment, but also her interest in dignity, and in determining the character of the memories that will survive long after her death. . . .

The *Cruzan* case demonstrated that some state intrusions on the right to decide how death will be encountered are also intolerable. The now deceased plaintiffs in this action may in fact have had a liberty interest even stronger than Nancy Cruzan's because, not only were they terminally ill, they were suffering constant and severe pain. Avoiding intolerable pain and the indignity of living one's final days incapacitated and in agony is certainly "[a]t the heart of [the] liberty . . . to define one's own concept of existence, of meaning, of the universe, and of the mystery of human life." (*Casey,* at 851.)

While I agree with the Court that *Cruzan* does not decide the issue presented by these cases, *Cruzan* did give recognition, not just to vague, unbridled notions of autonomy, but to the more specific interest in making decisions about how to confront an imminent death. Although there is no absolute right to physician-assisted suicide, *Cruzan* makes it clear that some individuals who no longer have the option of deciding whether to live or to die because they are already on the threshold of death have a constitutionally protected interest that may outweigh the state's interest in preserving life at all costs. The liberty interest at stake in a case like this differs from, and is stronger than, both the common-law right to refuse medical treatment and the unbridled interest in deciding whether to live or die. It is an interest in deciding how, rather than whether, a critical threshold shall be crossed.

III

The state interests supporting a general rule banning the practice of physician-assisted suicide do not have the same force in all cases. First and foremost of these interests is the "'unqualified interest in the preservation of human life.'" That interest not only justifies—it commands—maximum protection of every individual's interest in remaining alive, which in turn commands the same protection for decisions about whether to commence or to terminate life-support systems or to administer pain medication that may hasten death. Properly viewed, however, this interest is not a collective interest that should always outweigh the interests of a person who because of pain, incapacity, or sedation finds her life intolerable, but rather, an aspect of individual freedom.

Many terminally ill people find their lives meaningful even if filled with pain or dependence on others. Some find value in living through suffering; some have an abiding desire to witness particular events in their families' lives; many believe it a sin to hasten death. Individuals of different religious faiths make different judgments and choices about whether to live on under such circumstances. There are those who will want to continue aggressive treatment; those who would prefer terminal sedation; and those who will seek withdrawal from life-support systems and death by gradual starvation and dehydration. Although as a general matter the state's interest in the contributions each person may make to society outweighs the person's interest in ending her life, this interest does not have the same force for a terminally ill patient faced not with the choice of whether to live, only of how to die. Allowing the individual, rather than the state, to make judgments "about the 'quality' of life that a particular individual may enjoy" does not mean that the lives of terminally ill, disabled people have less value than the lives of those who are healthy. Rather, it gives proper recognition to the individual's interest in choosing a final chapter that accords with her life story, rather than one that demeans her values and poisons memories of her.

Similarly, the state's legitimate interests in preventing suicide, protecting the vulnerable from coercion and abuse, and preventing euthanasia are less significant in this context. I agree that the state has a compelling interest in preventing persons from committing suicide because of depression, or coercion by third parties. But the state's legitimate interest in preventing abuse does not apply to an individual who is not victimized by abuse, who is not suffering from depression, and who makes a rational and voluntary decision to seek assistance in dying. Although, as the New York Task Force report discusses, diagnosing depression and other mental illness is not always easy, mental-health workers and other professionals expert in working with dying patients can help patients cope with depression and pain, and help patients assess their options.

Relatedly, the state and amici express the concern that patients whose physical pain is inadequately treated will be more likely to request assisted suicide. Encouraging the development and ensuring the availability of adequate pain treatment is of utmost importance; palliative care, however, cannot alleviate all pain and suffering. An individual adequately informed of the care alternatives thus might make a rational choice for assisted suicide. For such an individual, the state's interest in preventing potential abuse and mistake is only minimally implicated.

The final major interest asserted by the state is its interest in preserving the traditional integrity of the medical profession. The fear is that a rule permitting physicians to assist in suicide is inconsistent with the perception that they serve their patients solely as healers. But for some patients, it would be a physician's refusal to dispense medication to ease their suffering and make their death tolerable and dignified that would be inconsistent with the healing role. For doctors who have long-standing relationships with their patients, who have given their patients advice on alternative treatments, who are attentive to their patient's individualized needs, and who are knowledgeable about pain symptom management and palliative-care options, heeding a patient's desire to assist in her suicide would not serve to harm the physician-patient relationship. Furthermore, because physicians are already involved in making decisions that hasten the death of terminally ill patients—through termination of life support, withholding of medical treatment, and terminal sedation—there is in fact significant tension between the traditional view of the physician's role and the actual practice in a growing number of cases.

As the New York State Task Force on Life and the Law recognized, a state's prohibition of assisted suicide is justified by the fact that the "ideal" case in which "patients would be screened for depression and offered treatment, effective pain medication would be available, and all patients would have a supportive committed family and doctor" is not the usual case. Although, as the Court concludes today, these potential harms are sufficient to support the state's general public policy against assisted suicide, they will not always outweigh the individual liberty interest of a particular patient. Unlike the Court of Appeals, I would not say as a categorical matter that these state interests are invalid as to the entire class of terminally ill, mentally competent patients. I do not, however, foreclose the possibility that an individual plaintiff seeking to hasten her death, or a doctor whose assistance was sought, could prevail in a more particularized challenge. Future cases will determine whether such a challenge may succeed.

IV

In New York, a doctor must respect a competent person's decision to refuse or to discontinue medical treatment even though death will thereby ensue, but the same doctor would be guilty of a felony if she provided her patient assistance in committing suicide. Today we hold that the Equal Protection Clause is not violated by the resulting disparate treatment of two classes of terminally ill people who may have the same interest in hastening death. I agree that the distinction between permitting death to ensue from an underlying fatal disease and causing it to occur by the administration of medication or other means provides a constitutionally sufficient basis for the state's classification. Unlike the Court, however, I am not persuaded that in all cases there will in fact be a significant difference between the intent of the physicians, the patients, or the families in the two situations.

There may be little distinction between the intent of a terminally ill patient who decides to remove her life support and one who seeks the assistance of a doctor in ending her life; in both situations, the patient is seeking to hasten a certain, impending death. The doctor's intent might also be the same in prescribing lethal medication as it is in terminating life support. A doctor who fails to administer medical treatment to one who is dying from a disease could be doing so with an intent to harm or kill that patient. Conversely, a doctor who prescribes lethal medication does not necessarily intend the patient's death—rather, that doctor may seek simply to ease the patient's suffering and to comply with her wishes. The illusory character of any differences in intent or causation is confirmed by the fact that the American Medical Association unequivocally endorses the practice of terminal sedation—the administration of sufficient dosages of pain-killing medication to terminally ill patients to protect them from excruciating pain even when it is clear that the time of death will be advanced. The purpose of terminal sedation is to ease the suffering of the patient and comply with her wishes, and the actual cause of death is the administration of heavy doses of lethal sedatives. This same intent and causation may exist when a doctor complies with a patient's request for lethal medication to hasten her death.

Thus, although the differences the majority notes in causation and intent between terminating life support and assisting in suicide support the Court's rejection of the respondents' facial challenge, these distinctions may be inapplicable to particular terminally ill patients and their doctors. Our holding today in *Vacco v. Quill* that the Equal Protection Clause is not violated by New York's classification, just like our holding in *Washington v. Glucksberg* that the Washington statute is not invalid on its face, does not foreclose the possibility that some applications of the New York statute may impose an intolerable intrusion on the patient's freedom.

There remains room for vigorous debate about the outcome of particular cases that are not necessarily resolved by the opinions announced today. How such cases may be decided will depend on their specific facts. In my judgment, however, it is clear that the so-called "unqualified interest in the preservation of human life" (*Cruzan,* at 282) in not itself sufficient to outweigh the interest in liberty that may justify the only possible means of preserving a dying patient's dignity and alleviating her intolerable suffering.

Justice Souter, concurring in the judgment:
[Justice Souter concurred in the judgments in *Glucksberg* and *Quill* but differed from the Chief Justice in his assessment of whether and to what extent a Fourteenth Amendment "liberty interest" may in the future guarantee a right to assisted suicide. The greater part of Souter's lengthy opinion argues for a broader interpretation of substantive due process than Rehnquist would allow and, consequently, greater leeway for the judiciary to recognize new constitutional rights. In the concluding part of his opinion, which follows, he argues that legislatures are better equipped than courts "at this time" to address the question of assisted suicide.]

The state has put forward several interests to justify the Washington law as applied to physicians treating terminally ill patients, even those competent to make responsible choices: protecting life generally, discouraging suicide even if knowing and voluntary, and protecting terminally ill patients from involuntary suicide and euthanasia, both voluntary and non-voluntary.

It is not necessary to discuss the exact strengths of the first two claims of justification in the present circumstances, for the third is dispositive for me. That third justification is different from the first two, for it addresses specific features of respondents' claim, and it opposes that claim not with a moral judgment contrary to respondents', but with a recognized state interest in the protection of nonresponsible individuals and those who do not stand in relation either to death or to their physicians as do the patients whom respondents describe.

The state claims interests in protecting patients from mistakenly and involuntarily deciding to end their lives, and in guarding against both voluntary and involuntary euthanasia. Leaving aside any difficulties in coming to a clear concept of imminent death, mistaken decisions may result from inadequate palliative care or a terminal prognosis that turns out to be error; coercion and abuse may stem from the large medical bills that family members cannot bear or unreimbursed hospitals decline to shoulder. Voluntary and involuntary euthanasia may result once doctors are authorized to prescribe lethal medication in the first instance, for they might find it pointless to distinguish between patients who administer their own fatal drugs and those who wish not to, and their compassion for those who suffer may obscure the distinction between those who ask for death and those who may be unable to request it. The argument is that a progression would occur, obscuring the line between the ill and the dying, and between the responsible and the unduly influenced, until ultimately doctors and perhaps others would abuse a limited freedom to aid suicides by yielding to the impulse to end another's suffering under conditions going beyond the narrow limits the respondents propose. The state thus argues, essentially, that respondents' claim is not as narrow as it sounds, simply because no recognition of the interest they assert could be limited to vindicating those interests and affecting no others. The state says that the claim, in practical effect, would entail consequences that the state could, without doubt, legitimately act to prevent.

The mere assertion that the terminally sick might be pressured into suicide decisions by close friends and family members would not alone be very telling. Of course that is possible, not only because the costs of care might be more than family members could bear but simply because they might naturally wish to see an end of suffering for someone they love. But one of the points of restricting any right of assistance to physicians would be to condition the right on an exercise of judgment by someone qualified to assess the patient's responsible capacity and detect the influence of those outside the medical relationship.

The state, however, goes further, to argue that dependence on the vigilance of physicians will not be enough. First, the lines proposed here (particularly the requirement of a knowing and voluntary decision by the patient) would be more difficult to draw than the lines that have limited other recently recognized due-process rights. Limiting a state from prosecuting use of artificial contraceptives by married couples posed no practical threat to the state's capacity to regulate contraceptives in other ways that were assumed at the time of *Poe* to be legitimate; the trimester measurements of *Roe* and the viability determination of *Casey* were easy to make with a real degree of certainty. But the knowing and responsible mind is harder to assess.

Second, this difficulty could become the greater by combining with another fact within the realm of plausibility, that physicians simply would not be assiduous to preserve the line. They have compassion, and those who would be willing to assist in suicide at all might be the most susceptible to the wishes of a patient, whether the patient were technically quite responsible or not. Physicians, and their hospitals, have their own financial incentives, too, in this new age of managed care. Whether acting from compassion or under some other influence, a physician who would provide a drug for a patient to administer might well go the further step of administering the drug himself; so, the barrier between assisted suicide and euthanasia could become porous, and the line between voluntary and involuntary euthanasia as well. The case for the slippery slope is fairly made out here, not because recognizing one due-process right would leave a court with no principled basis to avoid recognizing another, but because there is a plausible case that the right claimed would not be readily containable by reference to facts about the mind that are matters of difficult judgment, or by gatekeepers who are subject to temptation, noble or not.

Respondents propose an answer to all this, the answer of state regulation with teeth. Legislation proposed in several states, for example, would authorize physician-assisted suicide but require two qualified physicians to confirm the patient's diagnosis, prognosis, and competence; and would mandate that the patient make repeated requests witnessed by at least two others over a specified time span; and would impose reporting requirements and criminal penalties for various acts of coercion.

But at least at this moment there are reasons for caution in predicting the effectiveness of the teeth proposed. Respondents' proposals, as it turns out, sound much like the guidelines now in place in the Netherlands, the only place where experience with physician-assisted suicide and euthanasia has yielded empirical evidence about how such regulations might affect actual practice. Dutch physicians must engage in consultation before proceeding, and must decide whether the patient's decision is voluntary, well considered, and stable, whether the request to die is enduring and made more than once, and whether the patient's future will involve unacceptable suffering. There is, however, a substantial dispute today about what the Dutch experience shows. Some commentators marshall evidence that the Dutch guidelines have in practice failed to protect patients from involuntary euthanasia and have been violated with impunity. This evidence is contested. The day may come when we can say with some assurance which side is right, but for now it is the substantiality of the factual disagreement, and the alternatives for resolving it, that matter. They are, for me, dispositive of the due-process claim at this time.

I take it that the basic concept of judicial review with its possible displacement of legislative judgment bars any finding that a legislature has acted arbitrarily when the following conditions are met: there is a serious factual controversy over the feasibility of recognizing the claimed right without at the same time making it impossible for the state to engage in an undoubtedly legitimate exercise of power; facts necessary to resolve the controversy are not readily ascertainable through the judicial process; but they are more readily subject to discovery through legislative fact-finding and experimentation. It is assumed in this case, and must be, that a state's interest in protecting those unable to make responsible decisions and those who make no decisions at all entitles the state to bar aid to any but a knowing and responsible person intending suicide, and to prohibit euthanasia. How, and how far, a state should act in that interest are judgments for the state, but the legitimacy of its action to deny a physician the option to aid any but the knowing and responsible is beyond question.

The capacity of the state to protect the others if respondents were to prevail is, however, subject to some genuine question, underscored by the responsible disagreement over the basic facts of the Dutch experience. This factual controversy is not open to a judicial resolution with any substantial degree of assurance at this time. It is not, of course, that any controversy about the factual predicate of a due-process claim disqualifies a court from resolving it. Courts can recognize captiousness, and most factual issues can be settled in a trial court. At this point, however, the factual issue at the heart of this case does not appear to be one of those. The principal enquiry at the moment is into the Dutch experience, and I question whether an independent front-line investigation into the facts of a foreign country's legal administration can be soundly undertaken through

American courtroom litigation. While an extensive literature on any subject can raise the hopes for judicial understanding, the literature on this subject is only nascent. Since there is little experience directly bearing on the issue, the most that can be said is that whichever way the Court might rule today, events could overtake its assumptions, as experimentation in some jurisdictions confirmed or discredited the concerns about progression from assisted suicide to euthanasia.

Legislatures, on the other hand, have superior opportunities to obtain the facts necessary for a judgment about the present controversy. Not only do they have more flexible mechanisms for fact-finding than the judiciary, but their mechanisms include the power to experiment, moving forward and pulling back as facts emerge within their own jurisdictions. There is, indeed, good reason to suppose that in the absence of a judgment for respondents here, just such experimentation will be attempted in some of the states.

I do not decide here what the significance might be of legislative foot-dragging in ascertaining the facts going to the state's argument that the right in question could not be confined as claimed. Sometimes a court may be bound to act regardless of the institutional preferability of the political branches as forums for addressing constitutional claims. Now, it is enough to say that our examination of legislative reasonableness should consider the fact that the legislature of the State of Washington is no more obviously at fault than this Court is in being uncertain about what would happen if respondents prevailed today. We therefore have a clear question about which institution, a legislature or a court, is relatively more competent to deal with an emerging issue as to which facts currently unknown could be dispositive. The answer has to be, for the reasons already stated, that the legislative process is to be preferred. There is a closely related further reason as well.

One must bear in mind that the nature of the right claimed, if recognized as one constitutionally required, would differ in no essential way from other constitutional rights guaranteed by enumeration or derived from some more definite textual source than "due process." An unenumerated right should not therefore be recognized, with the effect of displacing the legislative ordering of things, without the assurance that its recognition would prove as durable as the recognition of those other rights differently derived. To recognize a right of lesser promise would simply create a constitutional regime too uncertain to bring with it the expectation of finality that is one of this Court's central obligations in making constitutional decisions.

Legislatures, however, are not so constrained. The experimentation that should be out of the question in constitutional adjudication displacing legislative judgments is entirely proper, as well as highly desirable, when the legislative power addresses an emerging issue like assisted suicide. The Court should accordingly stay its hand to allow reasonable legislative consideration. While I do not decide for all time that respondents' claim should not be recognized, I acknowledge the legislative institutional competence as the better one to deal with that claim at this time.

Justice Ginsburg, concurring in the judgments:
I concur in the Court's judgments in these cases substantially for the reasons stated by Justice O'Connor in her concurring opinion.

Justice Breyer, concurring in the judgments:
I believe that Justice O'Connor's views, which I share, have greater legal significance than the Court's opinion suggests. I join her separate opinion, except insofar as it joins the majority. And I concur in the judgments. I shall briefly explain how I differ from the Court.

I agree with the Court in *Vacco v. Quill* that the articulated state interests justify the distinction drawn between physician-assisted suicide and withdrawal of life support. I also agree with the Court that the critical question in both of the cases before us is whether "the 'liberty' specially protected by the Due Process Clause includes a right" of the sort that the respondents assert. I do not agree, however, with the Court's formulation of that claimed "liberty" interest. The Court describes it as a "right to commit suicide with another's assistance." But I would not reject the respondents' claim without considering a different formulation, for which our legal tradition may provide greater support. That formulation would use words roughly like a "right to die with dignity." But irrespective of the exact words used, at its core would lie personal control over the manner of death, professional medical assistance, and the avoidance of unnecessary and severe physical suffering—combined.

As Justice Souter points out, Justice Harlan's dissenting opinion in
Poe v. Ullman offers some support for such a claim. In that opinion,
Justice Harlan referred to the "liberty" that the Fourteenth Amendment protects as including "a freedom from all substantial arbitrary
impositions and purposeless restraints" and also as recognizing that
"certain interests require particularly careful scrutiny of the state needs
asserted to justify their abridgment." The "certain interests" to which
Justice Harlan referred may well be similar (perhaps identical) to the
rights, liberties, or interests that the Court today, as in the past, regards
as "fundamental."

Justice Harlan concluded that marital privacy was such a "special
interest." He found in the Constitution a right of "privacy of the home"
—with the home, the bedroom, and "intimate details of the marital
relation" at its heart—by examining the protection that the law had
earlier provided for related, but not identical, interests described by such
words as "privacy," "home," and "family." The respondents here essentially ask us to do the same. They argue that one can find a "right to die
with dignity" by examining the protection the law has provided for
related, but not identical, interests relating to personal dignity, medical
treatment, and freedom from state-inflicted pain.

I do not believe, however, that this Court need or now should
decide whether or not such a right is "fundamental." That is because,
in my view, the avoidance of severe physical pain (connected with
death) would have to comprise an essential part of any successful claim
and because, as Justice O'Connor points out, the laws before us do
not force a dying person to undergo that kind of pain. Rather, the laws
of New York and of Washington do not prohibit doctors from providing patients with drugs sufficient to control pain despite the risk
that those drugs themselves will kill. And under these circumstances
the laws of New York and Washington would overcome any remaining significant interests and would be justified, regardless.

Medical technology, we are repeatedly told, makes the administration of pain-relieving drugs sufficient, except for a very few individuals
for whom the ineffectiveness of pain-control medicines can mean,
not pain, but the need for sedation which can end in a coma. We are
also told that there are many instances in which patients do not receive
the palliative care that, in principle, is available, but that is so for
institutional reasons or inadequacies or obstacles, which would seem

possible to overcome, and which do not include a prohibitive set of laws.

This legal circumstance means that the state laws before us do not infringe directly upon the (assumed) central interest (what I have called the core of the interest in dying with dignity) as, by way of contrast, the state anti-contraceptive laws at issue in *Poe* did interfere with the central interest there at stake—by bringing the state's police powers to bear upon the marital bedroom.

Were the legal circumstances different—for example, were state law to prevent the provision of palliative care, including the administration of drugs as needed to avoid pain at the end of life—then the law's impact upon serious and otherwise unavoidable physical pain (accompanying death) would be more directly at issue. And as Justice O'Connor suggests, the Court might have to revisit its conclusions in these cases.

Vacco v. Quill

United States Supreme Court
June 26, 1997

Chief Justice Rehnquist delivered the opinion of the Court:
In New York, as in most states, it is a crime to aid another to commit
or attempt suicide, but patients may refuse even lifesaving medical
treatment. The question presented by this case is whether New York's
prohibition on assisting suicide therefore violates the Equal Protection
Clause of the Fourteenth Amendment. We hold that it does not. . . .

The Equal Protection Clause commands that no state shall "deny
to any person within its jurisdiction the equal protection of the laws."
This provision creates no substantive rights. Instead, it embodies a
general rule that states must treat like cases alike but may treat unlike
cases accordingly. If a legislative classification or distinction "neither
burdens a fundamental right nor targets a suspect class, we will uphold
[it] so long as it bears a rational relation to some legitimate end."
(*Romer v. Evans*, 517 U.S. ___, ___ [slip op., at 10] [1996].)

New York's statutes outlawing assisting suicide affect and address
matters of profound significance to all New Yorkers alike. They
neither infringe fundamental rights nor involve suspect classifications.
These laws are therefore entitled to a "strong presumption of validity."

On their faces, neither New York's ban on assisting suicide nor its
statutes permitting patients to refuse medical treatment treat anyone
differently than anyone else or draw distinctions between persons.
Everyone, regardless of physical condition, is entitled, if competent,
to refuse unwanted lifesaving medical treatment; no one is permitted
to assist a suicide. Generally speaking, laws that apply evenhandedly
to all "unquestionably comply" with the Equal Protection Clause.

The Court of Appeals, however, concluded that some terminally
ill people—those who are on life-support systems—are treated differently than those who are not, in that the former may "hasten death"
by ending treatment, but the latter may not "hasten death" through
physician-assisted suicide. This conclusion depends on the submission that ending or refusing lifesaving medical treatment "is nothing

630

more nor less than assisted suicide." Unlike the Court of Appeals, we think the distinction between assisting suicide and withdrawing life-sustaining treatment, a distinction widely recognized and endorsed in the medical profession and in our legal traditions, is both important and logical; it is certainly rational.

The distinction comports with fundamental legal principles of causation and intent. First, when a patient refuses life-sustaining medical treatment, he dies from an underlying fatal disease or pathology; but if a patient ingests lethal medication prescribed by a physician, he is killed by that medication.

Furthermore, a physician who withdraws, or honors a patient's refusal to begin, life-sustaining medical treatment purposefully intends, or may so intend, only to respect his patient's wishes and "to cease doing useless and futile or degrading things to the patient when [the patient] no longer stands to benefit from them." (Assisted Suicide in the United States, Hearing before the Subcommittee on the Constitution of the House Committee on the Judiciary, 104th Cong., 2d Sess., 368 [1996] [testimony of Dr. Leon R. Kass].) The same is true when a doctor provides aggressive palliative care; in some cases, pain-killing drugs may hasten a patient's death, but the physician's purpose and intent is, or may be, only to ease his patient's pain. A doctor who assists a suicide, however, "must, necessarily and indubitably, intend primarily that the patient be made dead." (*Idem,* at 367.) Similarly, a patient who commits suicide with a doctor's aid necessarily has the specific intent to end his or her own life, while a patient who refuses or discontinues treatment might not.

The law has long used actors' intent or purpose to distinguish between two acts that may have the same result. Put differently, the law distinguishes actions taken "because of" a given end from actions taken "in spite of" their unintended but foreseen consequences.

Given these general principles, it is not surprising that many courts, including New York courts, have carefully distinguished refusing life-sustaining treatment from suicide. In fact, the first state court decision explicitly to authorize withdrawing life-saving treatment noted the "real distinction between the self infliction of deadly harm and a self determination against artificial life support." (*In re Quinlan,* 355 A. 2d, at 665 [1976].) And recently, the Michigan Supreme Court also rejected the argument that the distinction "between acts that artificially sustain life and acts that artificially curtail life" is merely a "distinction without constitutional significance—a meaningless exercise in semantic gymnastics," insisting that "the *Cruzan* majority disagreed and so do we." (*People v. Kevorkian*, 527 N.W. 2d, at 728 ([1994].)

Similarly, the overwhelming majority of state legislatures have drawn a clear line between assisting suicide and withdrawing or permitting the refusal of unwanted lifesaving medical treatment by prohibiting the former and permitting the latter. And "nearly all states expressly disapprove of suicide and assisted suicide either in statutes dealing with durable powers of attorney in health-care situations, or in 'living will' statutes." (*Kevorkian*, at 478-79. . . .) Thus, even as the states move to protect and promote patients' dignity at the end of life, they remain opposed to physician-assisted suicide.

New York is a case in point. The state enacted its current assisted-suicide statutes in 1965. Since then, New York has acted several times to protect patients' common-law right to refuse treatment. In so doing, however, the state has neither endorsed a general right to "hasten death" nor approved physician-assisted suicide. Quite the opposite: the state has reaffirmed the line between "killing" and "letting die." More recently, the New York State Task Force on Life and the Law studied assisted suicide and euthanasia and, in 1994, unanimously recommended against legalization. In the Task Force's view, "allowing decisions to forego life-sustaining treatment and allowing assisted suicide or euthanasia have radically different consequences and meanings for public policy."

This Court has also recognized, at least implicitly, the distinction between letting a patient die and making that patient die. In *Cruzan,* we concluded that "[t]he principle that a competent person has a constitutionally protected liberty interest in refusing unwanted medical treatment may be inferred from our prior decisions," and we assumed the existence of such a right for purposes of that case. But our assumption of a right to refuse treatment was grounded not, as the Court of Appeals supposed, on the proposition that patients have a general and abstract "right to hasten death," but on well-established, traditional rights to bodily integrity and freedom from unwanted touching. In fact, we observed that "the majority of states in this country have laws imposing criminal penalties on one who assists another to commit suicide." *Cruzan* therefore provides no support for the notion that refusing life-sustaining medical treatment is "nothing more nor less than suicide."

For all these reasons, we disagree with respondents' claim that the distinction between refusing lifesaving medical treatment and assisted suicide is "arbitrary" and "irrational." Granted, in some cases, the line between the two may not be clear, but certainty is not required, even were it possible. Logic and contemporary practice support New York's judgment that the two acts are different, and New York may therefore, consistent with the Constitution, treat them differently. By permitting everyone to refuse unwanted medical treatment while prohibiting anyone from assisting a suicide, New York law follows a longstanding and rational distinction.

New York's reasons for recognizing and acting on this distinction —including prohibiting intentional killing and preserving life; preventing suicide; maintaining physicians' role as their patients' healers; protecting vulnerable people from indifference, prejudice, and psychological and financial pressure to end their lives; and avoiding a possible slide towards euthanasia—are discussed in greater detail in our opinion in *Glucksberg*. These valid and important public interests easily satisfy the constitutional requirement that a legislative classification bear a rational relation to some legitimate end.

The judgment of the Court of Appeals is reversed.

It is so ordered.

Justice Souter, concurring in the judgment:

Even though I do not conclude that assisted suicide is a fundamental right entitled to recognition at this time, I accord the claims raised by the patients and physicians in this case and *Washington v. Glucksberg* a high degree of importance, requiring a commensurate justification. The reasons that lead me to conclude in *Glucksberg* that the prohibition on assisted suicide is not arbitrary under the due-process standard also support the distinction between assistance to suicide, which is banned, and practices such as termination of artificial life support and death-hastening pain medication, which are permitted. I accordingly concur in the judgment of the Court.

Notes

INTRODUCTION

MICHAEL M. UHLMANN

1. See, for example, Richard A. Epstein, *Mortal Peril: Our Inalienable Right to Health Care?* (Reading, Mass.: Addison-Wesley, 1997), 283-311.

2. The history and implications of the legal distinction between killing and allowing to die are comprehensively treated by Thomas J. Marzen et al., "Suicide: A Constitutional Right?," *Duquesne Law Review* 24 (1985): 1. The same authors revisit the subject in "'Suicide: A Constitutional Right?'—Reflections Eleven Years Later," *Duquesne Law Review* 35 (1996): 261.

3. David C. Thomasma discusses the impact of demography on thinking about death and dying in "Euthanasia as Power and Empowerment," in Robert H. Blank and Andrea L. Bonnicksen, eds., *Medicine Unbound: The Human Body and Limits of Medical Intervention* (New York: Columbia University Press, 1994), 210-27.

4. Wesley J. Smith, *Forced Exit: The Slippery Slope from Assisted Suicide to Legalized Murder* (New York: Times Books, 1997), 171. And see Robert Pear, "Expense Means Many Can't Get Drugs for AIDS," *New York Times,* February 16, 1997, 1.

5. Wesley J. Smith, "Euthanasia's Betrayal of Medicine," in Smith, *Forced Exit,* 142-80.

6. *Compassion in Dying v. State of Washington,* 79 F. 3d 790 (9th Cir. 1996).

7. See, for example, Russell Hittinger, "A Crisis of Legitimacy," *First Things,* November 1996, 25.

CHAPTER 1

"Classical, Christian, and Early Modern Thought: From Plato to Kant"

MICHAEL M. UHLMANN

1. Allan Bloom, Preface, *The Republic of Plato* (New York: Basic Books, 1968), xvii.

2. Genesis 1:3; Romans 14:7-12; I Corinthians 6:19.

3. Genesis 9:5-6; Exodus 20:13.

4. II Corinthians 4:16–5:10.

5. W. H. Lecky, *A History of European Morals,* as quoted in Nigel M. de S. Cameron, *The New Medicine: Life and Death after Hippocrates* (Wheaton, Ill.: Crossway Books, 1992), 116.

6. Auguste Comte, *A System of Positive Polity,* vol. 3, as quoted in Robert L. Barry, *Breaking the Thread of Life* (New Brunswick, N.J.: Transaction Publishers, 1994), 19.

7. On the rise and influence of the Hippocratic legacy, see Cameron, *The New Medicine,* 23-45; Ludwig Edelstein, "The Hippocratic Oath: Translation and Interpretation," *Supplement to the Bulletin of the History of Medicine,* no.1 (Baltimore: Johns Hopkins Press, 1943); Paul Carrick, *Medical Ethics in Antiquity: Philosophical Perspectives on Abortion and Euthanasia* (Dordrecht, Holland: D. Reidel Pub. Co., 1985), 59-98; and Leon R. Kass, "Is There a Medical Ethic? The Hippocratic Oath and the Sources of Ethical Medicine," in his *Toward a More Natural Science* (New York: The Free Press, 1985), 224-46.

8. Carrick, *Medical Ethics in Antiquity,* 134-35. On Pythagoreanism in general, see W. K. C. Guthrie, "Pythagoras and Pythagoreanism," *The Encyclopedia of Philosophy,* vol. 7 (New York: Macmillan, repr. ed., 1972), 37-39.

9. The relevant passage begins at 61b. Among the numerous general commentaries on Plato, perhaps none surpasses A. E. Taylor's *Plato: The Man and His Work* (New York: Macmillan, 1966), 57-83. Joseph Cropsey writes gracefully about the *Phaedo* in *Plato's World: Man's Place in the Cosmos* (Chicago: University of Chicago Press, 1995), 175-225.

10. Plato uses the word *phroura,* which could mean "guard-post" in the sense of a battle station, or "prison," i.e., a place of punishment. For a summary of the different meanings and their implications, see Leonardo Taran, "Plato, *Phaedo* 62A," *American Journal of Philology* 87 (July 1966): 326.

11. David Novak, *Suicide and Morality* (New York: Scholars Studies Press, 1975), 13.

12. Plato, *Phaedo,* 62c.

13. Ibid., 67c.

14. Plato, *Republic,* Bk. III, 405a-410a. See Allan Bloom, "Interpretive Essay," in his translation, *The Republic of Plato,* 307-436. On Platonic and Aristotelian thought touching suicide and euthanasia, see Carrick, *Medical Ethics in Antiquity,* and John M. Cooper, "Greek Philosophers on Euthanasia and Suicide," in Baruch Brody, ed., *Suicide and Euthanasia: Historical and Contemporary Themes* (Dordrecht, Holland: Kluwer Academic Publishers, 1989), 9-38. Although my own interpretation differs from Carrick's and Cooper's at critical points, I find them unusually thoughtful guides to the subject.

15. The relevant passages in the *Laws* will be found in Bk. IX, 854a3-854c5, 873c-d.

16. Ibid., 854c4-5.

17. Ibid., 873c-d.

18. Ibid.

19. The relevant passage in the *Nicomachean Ethics* will be found at 1138a5-14. Alasdair MacIntyre has written an accessible introduction to Aristotle's ethical theory in *A Short History of Ethics* (New York: Macmillan, 1966), 57-83. See also William E. May, "The Structure and Argument of the *Nicomachean Ethics,*" *New Scholasticism* 36 (1962): 1-28. On the relationship between Aristotle's ethical and political teachings,

see Harry V. Jaffa, "Aristotle," in Leo Strauss and Joseph Cropsey, eds., *A History of Political Philosophy* (Chicago: Rand McNally, 1963).

20. Aristotle, *Nicomachean Ethics,* 1136b3-12.

21. On the difference between the ancient and the modern understanding of law and justice, see Leo Strauss, *Natural Right and History* (Chicago: University of Chicago Press, 1953).

22. Aristotle, *Nicomachean Ethics,* 1138a.

23. Ibid., 1116a10-15.

24. An informative general study of Stoic thought is Eduard Zeller, *The Stoics, Epicureans, and Skeptics,* trans. O. J. Reichel (N.Y.: Russell and Russell, new ed., 1962). A good short introduction will be found in Philip P. Hallie, "Stoicism," *The Encyclopedia of Philosophy,* vol. 8 (New York: Macmillan, repr. ed., 1967), 19-22. John Cooper's "Greek Philosophers on Euthanasia and Suicide," 24-29, is also helpful, as is Carrick, *Medical Ethics in Antiquity,* 39-53, 127-47.

25. Carrick, *Medical Ethics in Antiquity,* 145.

26. John Finnis, *Natural Law and Natural Rights* (New York: Oxford University Press, repr. and corr. ed., 1986), 378.

27. Ibid., 377.

28. Cooper, "Greek Philosophers on Euthanasia and Suicide," 37, n. 20.

29. Carrick, *Medical Ethics in Antiquity,* 132-33.

30. On the transition from paganism to Christianity generally, see Henry Chadwick, *The Early Church* (London: Penguin Books, 1967). Christian thought about suicide, including Augustine's, and its influence on medical ethics are lucidly presented by Darrel W. Amundsen, *Medicine, Society, and Faith in the Ancient and Medieval Worlds* (Baltimore: Johns Hopkins University Press, 1996), 70-157. Excellent general introductions to St. Augustine will be found in Frederick C. Copleston, *A History of Medieval Philosophy* (Notre Dame: University of Notre Dame Press, 1972), 27-49, and Etienne Gilson, *The Christian Philosophy of St. Augustine* (New York: Random House, 1960).

31. Quoted from Copleston, *A History of Medieval Philosophy,* 42.

32. Augustine's argument with the Donatists is discussed by Chadwick, *The Early Church,* 219-25, and Geoffrey G. Willis, *Saint Augustine and the Donatist Controversy* (London: S.P.C.K., 1950).

33. Darrel W. Amundsen, "Suicide and Early Christian Values," in his *Medicine, Society, and Faith,* 70-126.

34. G. K. Chesterton's *Saint Thomas Aquinas* (New York: Sheed and Ward, 1954) is unsurpassed as a popular account of Aquinas's life and thought. Among the more notable commentaries are Joseph Pieper, *Guide to Thomas Aquinas* (New York: Pantheon Books, 1962), Etienne Gilson, *The Christian Philosophy of St. Thomas Aquinas* (New York: Octagon Books, 1983), and Copleston, *A History of Medieval Philosophy,* 179-98.

35. *Summa Theologiae,* II, II, Q. 81, art. 6.

36. Ibid., I, II, Q. 91, art. 1.

37. Ibid., I, II, Q. 91, art. 2.

38. Ibid., II, II, Q. 64, art. 6; see also II, II, Q. 124, art. 1. A thoughtful commentary on Aquinas's position will be found in David Novak, "Suicide and Human Nature in Aquinas," in his *Suicide and Morality,* 43-82. Two essays in Brody, ed., *Suicide and*

Euthanasia, are also useful: Joseph Boyle, "Sanctity of Life and Suicide: Tensions and Developments Within Common Morality," 221-50; and Tom L. Beauchamp, "Suicide in the Age of Reason," 190-93.

39. "Deliberate suicide seems to have ceased almost entirely with the establishment of Christianity, and to have continued in abeyance until the reign of philosophic skepticism." J. O'Dea, as quoted in Daniel M. Crone, "Historical Attitudes Toward Suicide," *Duquesne Law Review* 35 (1996): 20.

40. Gary B. Ferngren, "The Ethics of Suicide in the Renaissance and Reformation," in Brody, ed., *Suicide and Euthanasia,* 155-81.

41. Ibid., 166.

42. On Donne in general, see Evelyn Hardy, *Donne, A Spirit in Conflict* (London: Constable, 1942), R. C. Bald, *John Donne, A Life* (New York: Oxford University Press, 1970), and John Carey, *John Donne: Life, Mind, and Art* (New York: Oxford University Press, 1981).

43. Michael Rudick and M[argaret] Pabst Battin prepared a modern-spelling edition of *Biathanatos,* with an instructive introduction and commentary (New York and London: Garland Publishing, 1982).

44. Ibid., 1.

45. Ibid., 63-64.

46. E. C. Mossner's *The Life of David Hume* (Austin: University of Texas Press, 1954) is considered definitive. Mossner also wrote an entertaining shorter sketch, *The Forgotten Hume, Le Bon David* (New York: Columbia University Press, 1943). Among the more compelling studies of Hume's thought is Norman Kemp Smith's *The Philosophy of David Hume: A Critical Study of Its Origins and Central Doctrines* (London: Macmillan, 1941). On Hume, as on almost every philosophical subject, Frederick Copleston is instructive, engaging, and just in his assessment. See his *A History of Philosophy* (Garden City, N.Y.: Image Books, 1964), vol. 7, part 2.

47. Hume's essay on suicide was set in print but not published, for fear of scandal, during his lifetime. It made its first public appearance, and then only by an "anonymous" author, in 1777, the year after his death. It is included in a number of modern editions, e.g., David Hume, *Essays, Moral, Political and Literary,* ed. Eugene F. Miller (Indianapolis: Liberty Classics, 1987). Tom L. Beauchamp provides a succinct and intelligent reading in "Suicide in the Age of Reason," in Brody, ed., *Suicide and Euthanasia,* 199-206.

48. For a memorable discussion of Hume's skepticism about causation, see Hadley V. Arkes, *First Things* (Princeton: Princeton University Press, 1986), 59-67.

49. Ibid., 116, quoting Hume's *Treatise of Human Nature.* Arkes's commentary, at 116-31, on the distinction between "facts" and "values" is instructive.

50. Tom L. Beauchamp, "Suicide in the Age of Reason," 203, n. 12.

51. Ibid., 204.

52. Ibid., 202.

53. For a superb introduction to Kant, see Copleston, *A History of Philosophy,* vol. 6, part 5, 4. On Kant's ethical theory, H. J. Paton, *The Categorical Imperative: A Study in Kant's Moral Philosophy* (New York: Harper and Row, 1967), is always instructive. There are many English editions of Kant's moral writings, among them Immanuel Kant, *Critique of Practical Reason, and Other Writings in Moral Philosophy,* ed. and trans. Lewis W. Beck (New York: Garland Publishers, 1976).

54. *Groundwork of the Metaphysics of Morals,* as quoted by Copleston, *A History of Philosophy,* vol. 6, part 2, 116.

55. Kant's scattered references to suicide are collected and analyzed in Novak, *Suicide and Morality,* 83-113.

56. Tom L. Beauchamp, "Suicide in the Age of Reason," 208.

57. Ibid., 209.

58. Ibid., 208, quoting Kant, "The Doctrine of Virtue," from *The Metaphysics of Morals.*

59. Ibid., 210, quoting Kant's *Lectures on Ethics.*

60. Ibid., 211, quoting Kant's *Lectures on Ethics.*

CHAPTER 2

"The History of Suicide"

A. ALVAREZ

1. Quoted by E. H. Carr, *The Romantic Exiles* (Harmondsworth, 1949), 389.

2. Both quotations from Glanville Williams, *The Sanctity of Life and the Criminal Law* (New York, 1957, and London, 1958), 233.

3. See Emile Durkheim, *Suicide,* trans. J. A. Spaulding and G. Simpson (New York, 1951, and London, 1952), 327-30.

4. Giles Romilly Fedden, *Suicide* (London and Toronto, 1938), 223. In this section I have leaned heavily and gratefully on this learned but unusually readable book.

5. John Donne, *Biathanatos,* Part I, Distinction 3, Section 2 (Facsimile Text Society, New York, 1930), 58.

6. See Sigmund Freud, *Totem and Taboo,* vol. 13 of *Complete Psychological Works,* ed. James Strachey et al. (London, 1962), esp. 18-74.

7. See Durkheim, *Suicide,* 218.

8. Libanius, quoted by Durkheim, *Suicide,* 330.

9. Fedden, *Suicide,* 79-80.

10. Ibid.

11. Quoted by Helen Silving, "Suicide and Law," in Edwin S. Shneidman and Norman L. Farberow, eds., *Clues to Suicide* (New York, 1957, and Maidenhead, 1963), 80-81.

12. Donne, *Biathanatos,* 54.

13. Quoted by Fedden, *Suicide,* 54.

14. See Donne, *Biathanatos,* 64-65.

15. Ibid., 66.

16. Ibid., 60.

17. Ibid., 63, 65.

18. Gibbon, *Decline and Fall of the Roman Empire,* vol. 3, 401; quoted by Charles More, *A Full Enquiry into the Subject of Suicide* (London, 1790), vol. 1, 290.

19. Henry Morselli, *Suicide* (London, 1881), 3.

CHAPTER 3

"Do We Have a Right to Die?"

RONALD DWORKIN

1. In fact five justices—Justice O'Connor and the four dissenters—did declare that people have that right. But one of the dissenters, Justice Brennan, has retired, and it is not known whether Justice Souter, who took his place, agrees.

2. On July 1, 1990, the New York state legislature enacted a law, the "health care proxy bill," that provides for such delegation. Governor Mario Cuomo said that the *Cruzan* decision helped to break a logjam on the bill. See *New York Times,* July 2, 1990.

3. The well-publicized case of Janet Adkins, who killed herself using Dr. Jack Kevorkian's suicide machine in the back of his Volkwagen van, suggests the moral complexity of suicide provoked by illness, and the degree to which Americans are divided about the issues raised by such suicide. Adkins was fifty-three and in the relatively early stages of Alzheimer's disease. Her mental capacity had begun to diminish—she found tennis scoring and the foreign languages she used to speak too difficult, for example, though she had lost little physical capacity, and had recently beaten her 33-year-old son at tennis. She was still alert and intelligent, and had retained her sense of humor. But she wanted to die before the irreversible disease worsened; the life she would soon lead, she said, "is not the way I wanted it at all." She telephoned Kevorkian, whom she had seen on television discussing his device. They met in Michigan, chosen because assisting suicide is not a crime there, in a motel room where he taped a forty-minute conversation that recorded her competence and her wish to die. Two days later he inserted a needle into her vein as she lay in the back of his van, and told her which button to push for a lethal injection. Michigan prosecutors charged Kevorkian with murder, but the judge acquitted him after listening to the tape.

The case raises serious moral issues that the Cruzan case does not. Janet Adkins apparently had several years of meaningful life left, and Kevorkian's examination may not have been long or substantial enough to rule out the possibility that she was in a temporary depression from which she might recover while still competent. It is of interest that about half of the 250 doctors who wrote in response to a critical article in a medical journal approved of what Kevorkian did, while the rest disapproved.

4. I do not mean to deny that animal life might have intrinsic importance, too.

5. I do not mean that many people often reflect on their lives as a whole, or live according to some overall theory about what makes their lives good or bad. Most people define living well in much more concrete terms: living well means having a good job, a successful family, warm friendships, and time and money for recreation or travel, for example. But I believe that people take pride as well as pleasure in these concrete achievements and experiences, and have a sense of failure as well as displeasure when a job goes wrong or a friendship sours. Very few of them, perhaps, except those for whom religion is important, self-consciously think of their lives as an opportunity that they may either waste or make into something worthwhile. But most people's attitudes toward successes and failures do seem to presuppose that view of life's importance. Most of us think it is important that the lives of other people,

as well as our own, be worthwhile: we think it is a central role of government to encourage people to make something of their lives rather than just survive, and to provide some of the institutions, including the schools, necessary for them to do so. These assumptions are premises of liberal education, and also of the limited paternalism involved in stopping people from using drugs or wasting their lives in other ways, and in trying to prevent or discourage people who are depressed or despondent from killing themselves when they could in fact lead lives worth living.

That human life has intrinsic value in this sense—that it is important that a life go well once it has begun—obviously has important though complex implications for the abortion issue. In chapter 3 of this book [*Freedom's Law*] and in *Life's Dominion: An Essay on Abortion, Euthanasia, and Individual Freedom* (Knopf, 1993), I explored these implications. I argued that the idea that life has intrinsic value in the sense I described does explain many of our attitudes about abortion, including the opinion many people have that abortion even in an early stage poses moral problems. It does not follow that abortion is always wrong; indeed, it sometimes follows that abortion is morally recommended or required. I argued, moreover, that understanding our moral notions about abortion as flowing from respect for the inherent value of life reinforces the Supreme Court decision in *Roe v. Wade* that the state has no business coercing pregnant women to take a particular view about what the principle of respect for the inherent value of life requires.

CHAPTER 4

"The Right to Die—Again"

HADLEY V. ARKES

1. See Immanuel Kant, *Foundations of the Metaphysics of Morals* (Lewis White Beck trans., 1969), 58. This truism is also threaded through the works and writings of the Founders. The Founders' case for natural equality began with a recognition of the inequalities that existed in nature. No man was by nature the ruler of other men in the way that men were the rulers by nature of dogs and horses, and God was by nature the ruler of men. The polity was not made for animals. Human beings were suited by nature for politics because we were neither animals nor angels.

2. *Bouvia v. Superior Court ex rel. Glenchur*, 225 Cal. Rptr. 297, 304 (Ct. App. 1986).

3. Hadley V. Arkes, "'Autonomy' and the 'Quality of Life': The Dismantling of Moral Terms," *Issues in Law and Medicine* vol. 3, no. 2 (1987): 425-28.

4. *In re Jobes*, 529 A.2d 434, 439 (N.J. 1987).

5. *In re Guardianship of Grant*, 747 P.2d 445, 452 (Wash. 1987) *(en banc),* modified, 757 P.2d 534 (Wash. 1988).

6. *Bouvia v. Superior Court*, 304.

7. *Bouvia v. County of Los Angeles*, 241 Cal. Rptr. 239, 243 (Ct. App. 1987).

8. *Bouvia v. Superior Court*, 307.

9. Edmund Burke, "Letter to a Member of the National Assembly," 1791.

CHAPTER 5

"Ethical Issues in Physician-Assisted Suicide"

MARGARET PABST BATTIN

1. Numerous accounts of this case are available. See, among others, George Annas, "Physician-Assisted Suicide—Michigan's Temporary Solution," *New England Journal of Medicine* 328, no. 21 (May 27, 1993): 1572-76.

2. For a perceptive account of what it is like to have Alzheimer's disease, see Joseph M. Foley, "The Experience of Being Demented," in Robert H. Binstock, Stephen G. Post, and Peter J. Whitehouse, eds., *Dementia and Aging: Ethics, Values, and Policy Choices* (Baltimore: Johns Hopkins University Press, 1992), 30-43.

3. Timothy E. Quill, "Death and Dignity: A Case of Individualized Decision Making," *New England Journal of Medicine* 324, no. 10 (March 7, 1991): 691-94.

4. Up-to-date information on right-to-die legislation can be obtained from Choice in Dying, 200 Varig Street, New York, N.Y. 10014 [800-989-WILL].

5. *Compassion in Dying v. Washington,* no. C94-119R, 1994 U.S. Dist. LEXIS 5831, May 3, 1994, Judge Barbara J. Rothstein.

6. A. R. Omran, "The Epidemiologic Transition: A Theory of the Epidemiology of Population Change," *Milbank Memorial Fund Quarterly* 49, no. 4 (1971): 509-38.

7. S. Jay Olshansky and A. Brian Ault, "The Fourth Stage of the Epidemiology Transition: The Age of Delayed Degenerative Disease," in Timothy M. Smeeding et al., eds., *Should Medical Care Be Rationed By Age?* (Totowa, N.J.: Rowman & Littlefield, 1987), 11-43.

8. See Pius XII, "The Prolongation of Life."

9. Of course, there are exceptions. See, for example, Kenneth L. Vaux, *Death Ethics: Religious and Cultural Values in Prolonging and Ending Life* (Philadelphia: Trinity Press, 1992).

10. Data on the practice of euthanasia and physician-assisted suicide in the Netherlands are available in Paul J. van der Maas, Johannes J. M. van Delden, and Loes Pijnenborg, "Euthanasia and Other Medical Decisions Concerning the End of Life: An Investigation Performed upon Request of the Commission of Inquiry into the Medical Practice Concerning Euthanasia," published in full in English as a special issue of *Health Policy* 22, nos. 1 and 2 (1992), and, with Caspar W. N. Looman, in summary in *The Lancet* 338 (Sept. 14, 1991): 669-74.

11. Margaret P. Battin and Ezekiel J. Emanuel, "The Economics of Euthanasia: What Are the Potential Cost Savings from Euthanasia?," manuscript in progress.

12. C. G. Prado, *The Last Choice: Preemptive Suicide in Advanced Age* (Westport, Conn: Greenwood Press, 1990), 5.

13. Franklin G. Miller et al., "Regulating Physician-Assisted Death," *New England Journal of Medicine* 331, no. 2 (July 14, 1994): 119-23.

14. Prado, *The Last Choice,* 7.

15. In the Netherlands, euthanasia and physician assistance in suicide remain technical violations of the criminal law, but under a series of lower- and supreme-court cases, the physician who performs them will not be prosecuted provided certain guidelines are met.

16. On these issues see the special issue edited by myself and Thomas Bole, "Legal

Euthanasia: Ethical Issues in an Era of Legalized Aid in Dying," *Journal of Medicine and Philosophy* 18, no. 3 (June 1993).

17. See Thomas J. Marzen et al., "Suicide: A Constitutional Right?" *Duquesne Law Review* 24, no. 1 (Fall 1985):1-243, and many later papers drawing on this one.

18. These forms of abuse are discussed more fully in my "Voluntary Euthanasia and the Risks of Abuse," *Law Medicine, and Health Care* 20, no. 1-2 (Spring/Summer 1992):133-43; reprinted in my collection *The Least Worst Death*.

19. Chabot, a psychiatrist in the Netherlands, was tried in Spring 1994 for performing euthanasia for a woman suffering from untreatable depression, compounded by the disintegration of her marriage and the deaths of her two sons. Consultations were sought from a number of independent psychiatrists. Chabot was found guilty of a criminal offense because he had not followed the guidelines with due care (the consulting psychiatrists had not examined the patient in person), but no sentence was passed.

20. Jonathan S. Cohen et al., "Attitudes Toward Assisted Suicide and Euthanasia Among Physicians in Washington State," *New England Journal of Medicine* 331, no. 2 (July 14, 1994):89-94. Fifty-three per cent of respondents thought that assisted suicide should be legal in some situations, but only 40 per cent stated that they would be willing to assist a patient in committing suicide; 54 per cent thought euthanasia should be legal in some situations, but only 33 per cent stated that they would be willing to perform it.

21. *Rodriguez v. British Columbia* (attorney general), [1993] S.C.J. No. 94. The court held against Sue Rodriguez, a 42-year-old woman with ALS, who had claimed that section 241(b) of the Canadian Criminal Code, prohibiting the giving of assistance to commit suicide, violated her rights as a handicapped person who would soon become unable to end her own life.

22. Also see my "Voluntary Euthanasia and the Risks of Abuse."

23. Clyde H. Farnsworth, "Bungled AIDS Suicides Often Increase the Suffering," *New York Times,* June 14, 1994, B9, reporting Russel D. Ogden's study submitted for a master's degree in criminal law at Simon Fraser University.

24. Gerrit van der Wal, "Euthanasie en hulp bij selfdoding door huisartsen," Academisch proefschrift, WYT Uitgefgroep, Rotterdam, 1992; English summary p. 149.

25. George Annas, "Physician-Assisted Suicide," 1574.

26. Cathy Owen et al., "Cancer Patients' Attitudes to Final Events in Life: Wish for Death, Attitudes to Cessation of Treatment, Suicide and Euthanasia," *Psycho-Oncology* 3 (1994):1-9.

CHAPTER 7

"Jewish Views on Euthanasia"

BYRON L. SHERWIN

1. Talmud, *Pesahim* 75a.
2. Talmud, *Abodah Zarah* 18a.

3. *Sefer Hasidim,* ed. J. Wistinetzki and J. Freimann (Frankfurt: Wahrmann Verlag, 1924), no. 315, p. 100.

4. *Semahot* 1:1, 1:4. *The Tractate Mourning,* Eng. trans. Dov Zlotnick (New Haven: Yale University Press, 1966), p. 30.

5. Maimonides, *Mishneh Torah–Sefer Shofetim,* "Laws of Mourning," 4:5.

6. Jacob ben Asher, *Arba'ah Turim–Yoreh Deah,* para. 339.

7. Joseph Karo, *Shulhan Arukh–Yoreh Deah,* para. 339:1.

8. Solomon Ganzfried, *Kitzur Shulhan Arukh* (Lwow, 1860), *Yoreh Deah,* para. 194:1.

9. Talmud, *Abodah Zarah* 18a.

10. See Talmud, *Yoma* 84-85; Karo, *Shulhan Arukh–Orah Hayyim,* para. 329:4.

11. Talmud, *Baba Kamma* 91b; *Abodah Zarah* 18a; *Midrash Genesis Rabbah* 34:13; Maimonides, *Mishneh Torah–Sefer Nezikin,* "Laws of Murderers," 2:3.

12. Talmud, *Kiddushin* 42b; *Midrash Genesis Rabbah* 34:14.

13. See the gloss of Shabbatai ben Meir, *Siftei Kohein,* on Karo, *Shulhan Arukh–Yoreh Deah,* para. 336:1, in standard editions of the *Shulhan Arukh.*

14. *Sefer Hasidim,* ed. Wistinetzki, no. 316, p. 100.

15. See Isserles's gloss on Karo, *Sulhan Arukh–Yoreh Deah,* para. 339:1.

16. *Sefer Hasidim,* ed. Wistinetzki, no. 316, p. 100; Karo, *Shulhan Arukh–Yoreh Deah,* para. 339:1.

17. Isserles's commentary *Darkhei Moshe* to Jacob ben Asher, *Arba'ah Turim–Yoreh Deah,* para. 339:1.

18. *Sefer Hasidim,* ed. Wistinetzki, no. 316, p. 100. See Joshua Boaz on Isaac Alfasi's commentary to Talmud, *Mo'ed Katan* 16b, in standard editions of the Talmud with commentaries.

19. Jacob ben Samuel, *Beit Ya'akov* (Dyrenfurerth, 1696), no. 59.

20. *Sefer Hasidim,* ed. Reuven Margaliot (Jerusalem: Mosud ha-Rav Kook, 1960), no. 234, p. 208.

21. See, e.g., Leopold Greenwald, *Kol Bo al-Aveilut* (New York: Moriah Printing Co., 1947), 1:10, p. 21.

22. *Sefer Hasidim,* ed. Margaliot, no. 234, p. 208.

23. Immanuel Jakobovits, *Jewish Medical Ethics* (New York: Bloch Publishing Co., 1959), pp. 123-24.

24. Talmud, *Beitzah* 32b.

25. Israel Lipschutz, *Tiferet Israel* (Hanover, 1830) on Mishnah, *Yoma* 8:3; *Semahot* 1:1.

26. Mishnah, *Arakhin* 1:3; Talmud, *Arakhin* 6b.

27. Saul Berlin, *Responsa Besomim Rosh* (Berlin, 1793). In some subsequent editions, this responsum has been eliminated by the printer. No doubt the reason is that Berlin's view, which in effect redefines "suicide," is without precedent in halakhic literature.

28. *Yalkut Shimoni,* "Proverbs," no. 943.

29. Contemporary halakhists are divided on the question of whether "pulling the plug" is a form of withholding treatment (i.e., passive euthanasia), and therefore permitted, or an overt act of intervention designed to shorten life (i.e., active euthanasia), and therefore prohibited. See discussion and sources in J. D. Bleich, "The Quinlan Case: A Jewish Perspective," in Fred Rosner and J. David Bleich, eds., *Jewish Bioethics* (New York: Hebrew Publishing Co., 1969), p. 275, n. 2.

30. Talmud, *Ketubot* 104a.

31. Rabbenu Nissim on *Nedarim* 40a, in standard editions of the Talmud.

32. Hayyim Palaggi's responsum is found in vol. 1 of his collected responsa, *Hikkeke Lev* (Salonika, 1840), no. 50, pp. 90a-91a.

33. Talmud, *Niddah* 19b.

34. Talmud, *Sanhedrin* 45a, 52a; Talmud, *Baba Kamma* 51a; Talmud, *Pesahim* 75a.

35. Talmud, *Arakhin* 6b.

36. See, e.g., Rashi on Exod. 21:14.

37. *Sanhedrin* 78a; Maimonides, *Mishneh Torah–Sefer Nezikin,* "Laws of Murderers," 2:8.

38. See David M. Shohet, "Mercy Death in Jewish Law," *Conservative Judaism* 8, no. 3 (1952): 1-15.

CHAPTER 8

"Rethinking Life and Death: A New Ethical Approach"

PETER SINGER

1. The classic account of the shift from the Ptolemaic to Copernican models is Thomas Kuhn, *The Structure of Scientific Revolutions* (Chicago: University of Chicago Press, 1972).

2. Dr. L. Haas, from a letter in the *Lancet,* 2 November 1968, quoted from S. Gorovitz, ed., *Moral Problems in Medicine* (Englewood Cliffs, N.J.: Prentice-Hall, 1976), 351.

3. Clough's "The Latest Decalogue" can be found in Helen Gardner, ed., *The New Oxford Book of English Verse* (Oxford: Oxford University Press, 1978).

4. Thomas Aquinas, *Summa Theologica,* II, ii, q. 64, a. 5.

5. John Stuart Mill, *On Liberty* (London: J. M. Dent and Sons, 1960), 72-73.

6. This position is associated with Michael Tooley's influential article, "Abortion and Infanticide," *Philosophy and Public Affairs* 2 (1972): 37-65; for a slightly different argument to the same conclusion, see also Michael Tooley, *Abortion and Infanticide* (Oxford: Oxford University Press, 1983). Similar views have been defended by several philosophers and bioethicists, among them H. Tristram Engelhardt, Jr., *The Foundations of Bioethics* (New York: Oxford University Press, 1986); R. G. Frey, *Rights, Killing and Suffering* (Oxford: Blackwell, 1983); Jonathan Glover, *Causing Death and Saving Lives* (Harmondsworth, U.K.: Penguin, 1977); John Harris, *The Value of Life* (London: Routledge and Kegan Paul, 1985); Helga Kuhse, *The Sanctity of Life Doctrine in Medicine: A Critique* (Oxford: Oxford University Press, 1987); and James Rachels, *The End of Life* (Oxford: Oxford University Press, 1986) and *Created from Animals* (Oxford: Oxford University Press, 1991). See also my own *Practical Ethics* (Cambridge: Cambridge University Press, 1979, 2d ed. 1993).

7. For Augustine, see *Against Faustus,* bk. 15. ch. 7; for Luther, *Der Grosse Catechismus,* 1529, "On the Sixth Commandment"; and for Calvin, *Commentaries on the First Book of Moses Called Genesis,* on Genesis 38:8. I owe these references and other information in this paragraph to John T. Noonan, "Contraception," in Warren T.

Reich, ed., *Encyclopedia of Bioethics* (New York: The Free Press, 1978), vol. 1, 204-16. The Supreme Court case referred to is *Griswold v. Connecticut,* 1965.

8. Jodi L. Jacobson, "Holding Back the Sea," in Lester Brown et al., *State of the World, 1990: The Worldwatch Institute Report on Progress Towards a Sustainable Economy* (Washington, D.C.: Worldwatch Institute, 1990).

9. Peter Singer, "Sanctity of Life or Quality of Life," *Pediatrics* 72 (July 1983): 128-29; three protest letters were published with my reply in *Pediatrics* 73 (February 1984): 259-63, but the remainder of the letters are unpublished.

10. Vorstand der Bundesvereinigung Lebenshilfe für geistig Behinderte, *Ethische Grundaussagen,* Marburg, 1990 (my trans.). For an account of the events in Germany and their sequel up to 1991, see Peter Singer, "On being silenced in Germany," *New York Review of Books,* 15 August 1991; reprinted in Singer, *Practical Ethics,* 337-59.

11. Albert Schweitzer's ethic of reverence for life *may* be making this wider claim; the contemporary American philosopher Paul Taylor certainly does make it. I discuss and reject these views in my *Practical Ethics.*

12. Henry Longfellow, *The Song of Hiawatha,* Introduction, 91; quoted from *The Oxford English Dictionary,* 2d ed. (Oxford: Clarendon Press, 1989), vol. 7, 474.

13. For an argument that it could be as late as thirty-two weeks, see Susan Taiwa, "When is the capacity for sentience acquired during human fetal development?" *Journal of Maternal-Fetal Medicine* 1 (1992): 153-65.

14. For a full defense of this position, see Helga Kuhse and Peter Singer, *Should the Baby Live?* (Oxford: Oxford University Press, 1985).

15. For sources and further details, see Kuhse and Singer, *Should the Baby Live?,* ch. 5.

16. Here I have been influenced by Norbert Hoerster, "Kindestötung und das Lebensrecht von Personen," *Analyse & Kritik* 12 (1990): 226-44.

17. Thomas Hobbes, *Leviathan,* ch. 13.

CHAPTER 9

"Death With Dignity and the Sanctity of Life"

LEON R. KASS

1. Precisely such a (constitutionally protected) right to become dead, claimed by proxies on behalf of a permanently comatose other, is being asserted in the *Cruzan* case, now [1990] under review by the United States Supreme Court.

2. Some people, in contrast, are delighted with this polarized framing of the question. For they see it as the conflict between a vigorous humanism and an anachronistic otherworldliness foisted upon the West by the Judeo-Christian tradition. For those who deny the sacred, it is desirable to represent the arguments against suicide or mercy killing (or abortion) as purely religious in character—there being in truth, on their view, nothing higher than human dignity. The chief proponent of the recent "Humane and Dignified Death Act" in California is reported to have said that he was seeking to "overturn the sanctity-of-life principle" in American law.

3. Not all taking of human life is murder. Self-defense, war, and capital punishment

have been moral grounds used to justify homicide, and it is a rare moralist who would argue that it is never right to kill another human being. Without arguing about these exceptions, we confine our attention to murder, which is, by definition, unjust or wrongful killing. Everyone knows it to be wrong, immediately and without argument. Rarely do we ask ourselves why.

This is, of course, as it should be. The most important insights on which decent society rests—e.g., the taboos against incest, cannibalism, murder, and adultery—are too important to be imperiled by reason's poor power to give them convincing defense. Such taboos might themselves be the incarnation of reason, even as they resist attempts to give them logical demonstration; like the axioms of geometry, they might be at once incapable of proof and yet not in need of proof, i.e., self-evident to anyone not morally blind. What follows, then, is more a search for insight than an attempt at proof.

4. Non-religious readers may rightly express suspicion at my appeal to a biblical text for what I will claim is a universal or philosophical explanation of the taboo against murder. This suspicion will be further increased by the content of the text cited. Nevertheless, I believe the teaching of the passage, properly interpreted, stands free of its especially biblical roots, and offers a profound insight into the ground of our respect for human life.

5. This respect for human life, and the self-conscious establishment of society on this premise, separates human beings from the rest of the animals. This separation is made emphatic by the institution of meat-eating (Gen. 9:1-4), permitted to men here for the first time. (One can, I believe, show that the permission to eat meat is a concession to human blood lust and voracity, nor something cheerfully and happily endorsed.) Yet, curiously, even animal life must be treated with respect: the blood, which is identified as the life, cannot be eaten. Human life, as we shall see more clearly, is thus both continuous and discontinuous with animal life.

6. The second part of verse 6 seems to make two points: man is in the image of God (i.e., is god-*like*), and man was *made* thus by God. The decisive point is the first. Man's creatureliness cannot be the reason for avoiding bloodshed; the animals too were made by God, yet permission to kill them for food has just been given. The full weight rests on man's *being* "in the image of God."

7. In the first creation story, Genesis 1-2:3, man is created straightaway in God's likeness; in this second account, man is, to begin with, made of dust, and he *acquires* god-like qualities only at the end, and then only in transgressing.

8. Does this mean that those who murder forfeit their claim to be humanly respected, because they implicitly have denied the humanity of their victim (and, thus, in principle, of their own—and all other—human life)? In other words, do men need to act in accordance with the self-knowledge of human godliness in order to be treated accordingly? Or, conversely, do we rather respect the humanity of murderers when we punish them, even capitally, treating them not as crazed or bestial but as responsible moral agents who accept the fair consequences of their deed? Or is the capitalness of the punishment not a theoretical matter but a practical one, intended mainly to deter by fear those whose self-love or will-to-power will not listen to reason? These are vexed questions, too complicated to sort out quickly, and, in any case, beyond the point of the present discussion. Yet the relevant difficulty persists.

9. This is not necessarily to say that one should treat other people, including those

who eschew dignity, as if they lacked it. This is a separable question. It may be salutary to treat people on the basis of their capacity to live humanly, despite great falling-short or even willful self-degradation. Yet this would, in the moral sphere at least, require that we expect and demand of people that they behave worthily and that we hold them responsible for their own conduct.

10. The Homeric warriors, preoccupied with mortality and refusing to hide away in a corner waiting for death to catch them unawares, went boldly forward to meet it, armed only with their own prowess and large hearts; in facing death frontally, in the person of another similarly self-conscious hero, they wrested a human victory over blind necessity, even in defeat. On a much humbler scale, the same opportunity is open to anyone willing to look death in the face.

11. A perfect instance is the recent California Initiative. It proposed amending the name of the existing California statute from "Natural Death Act" to "Humane and Dignified Death Act," but its only substantive change was to declare and provide for "the right of the terminally ill to voluntary, humane, and *dignified* doctor-assisted *aid-in-dying*," "aid in dying" meaning "any medical procedure that will terminate the life of the qualified patient swiftly, painlessly, and humanely." A (merely) natural death is to be made "dignified" simply by having it deliberately produced by (dignified) doctors.

12. "Neither for Love nor Money: Why Doctors Must Not Kill," *The Public Interest,* Winter 1989, 25-46. [Also: "Why Doctors Must Not Kill," *Commonweal,* September 1992; reprinted in this volume.]

13. For a chilling picture of the fully rationalized and technically managed death, see the account of the Park Lane Hospital for the Dying in Aldous Huxley's *Brave New World*.

14. Once again we should be careful about our speech. It may be a great source of misery for *us* to see them in this state, but it is not at all clear that *they feel* or *have* misery. Precisely the ground for considering them beneath the human threshold is that nothing registers with them. This point is relevant to the "termination-of-feeding" cases, in which it is argued (in self-contradiction) that death by starvation is both humane and not in these instances cruel: someone who is too far gone to suffer from a death-by-starvation is, to begin with, not suffering at all.

CHAPTER 10

"The Gospel of Life"

POPE JOHN PAUL II

1. The expression "Gospel of life" is not found as such in Sacred Scripture. But it does correspond to an essential dimension of the biblical message.

2. Second Vatican Council, Pastoral Constitution on the Church in the Modern World *(Gaudium et Spes),* 22.

3. Cf. John Paul II, *Redemptor Hominis* (Encyclical Letter, 4 March 1979), 10.

4. Cf. ibid., 14.

5. Second Vatican Council, Pastoral Constitution on the Church, 27.

6. Congregation for the Doctrine of the Faith, Declaration on Euthanasia (*Iura et Bona;* 5 May 1980), II.

7. Ibid., IV.

8. Cf. ibid.

9. Pius XII, Address to an International Group of Physicians (24 February 1957), III; cf. Congregation for the Doctrine of the Faith, Declaration on Euthanasia, III.

10. Pius XII, Address to an International Group of Physicians, III.

11. Cf. Pius XII, Address to an International Group of Physicians; Congregation of the Holy Office, *Decretum de directa insontium occisione* (2 December 1940); Paul VI, Message to French Television: "Every life is sacred" (27 January 1971); Address to the International College of Surgeons (1 June 1972); Second Vatican Council, Pastoral Constitution on the Church, 27.

12. Cf. Second Vatican Council, Dogmatic Constitution on the Church *(Lumen Gentium),* 25.

13. Cf. Saint Augustine, *De Civitate Dei,* I, 20; Saint Thomas Aquinas, *Summa Theologiae,* II-II, q. 6, a. 5.

14. Congregation for the Doctrine of the Faith, Declaration on Euthanasia, I; Catechism of the Catholic Church, nos. 2281-2283.

15. *Ep.* 204, 5: *CSEL* 57, 320.

16. Second Vatican Council, Pastoral Constitution on the Church, 18.

17. Cf. John Paul II, *Salvifici Doloris* (Apostolic Letter, 11 February 1984), 14-24.

18. Cf. John Paul II, *Centesimus Annus* (Encyclical Letter, 1 May 1991), 46; Pius XII, Christmas Radio Message (24 December 1944).

19. Cf. John Paul II, *Veritatis Splendor* (Encyclical Letter, 6 August 1993), 97 and 99.

20. Cf. Catechism of the Catholic Church, nos. 1753-1755; John Paul II, *Veritatis Splendor,* 81-82.

21. Saint Augustine, *In Iohannis Evangelium Tractatus,* 41, 10; cf. John Paul II, *Veritatis Splendor,* 13.

CHAPTER 11

"Euthanasia and Christian Vision"

GILBERT MEILAENDER

1. Karl Barth, *Church Dogmatics,* III/4, ed. G. W. Bromiley and T. F. Torrance (Edinburgh: T. & T. Clark, 1961), 425.

2. I will be exploring some of the moral issues involved in euthanasia without taking up legal problems that also arise. I do not assume any answer to the question, "Should what is morally wrong be legally prohibited?"

3. James Rachels, "Euthanasia," in Tom Regan, ed., *Matters of Life and Death: New Introductory Essays in Moral Philosophy* (New York: Random House, 1980), 29.

4. Non-voluntary euthanasia occurs when the person euthanized is in a condition that makes it impossible for him to express a wish (e.g., senile, comatose). Involuntary

euthanasia occurs when the person euthanized expresses a desire *not* to be killed but *is* nevertheless.

5. Charles Fried, *Right and Wrong* (Harvard University Press, 1978), 27.

6. Cf. Joseph Butler, Dissertation "On the Nature of Virtue," appended to *The Analogy of Religion Natural and Revealed,* Morley's Universal Library edition (London: Routledge, 1884), 301: "The fact then appears to be, that we are constituted so as to condemn falsehood, unprovoked violence, injustice, and to approve of benevolence to some preferably to others abstracted from all consideration, which conduct is likely to produce an overbalance of happiness or misery; and therefore, were the Author of Nature to propose nothing to Himself as an end but the production of happiness, were His moral character merely that of benevolence, yet ours is not so." In other words, though the Creator may be a consequentialist, creatures are not! For a contrary view, see Peter Geach, *The Virtues* (Cambridge University Press, 1977), 95ff.

7. Whether this enlargement of the scope of our responsibility really works is another matter. Being responsible for everything may, for human beings, come quite close to being responsible for nothing. Charles Fried comments: "If, as consequentialism holds, we were indeed equally morally responsible for an infinite radiation of concentric circles originating from the center point of some action, then while it might look as if we were enlarging the scope of human responsibility and thus the significance of personality, the enlargement would be greater than we could support. . . . Total undifferentiated responsibility is the correlative of the morally overwhelming, undifferentiated plasma of happiness or pleasure" (*Right and Wrong,* 34).

8. It is a hard, perhaps unanswerable, question whether there might ever be exceptions to this general standard for Christian conduct that I have enunciated. There might be a circumstance in which the pain of the sufferer was so terrible and unconquerable that one would want to consider an exception. To grant this possibility is not really to undermine the principle, since, as Charles Fried has noted, the "catastrophic" is a distinct moral concept, identifying an extreme situation in which the usual rules of morality do not apply (*Right and Wrong,* 10). We would be quite mistaken to build the whole of our morality on the basis of the catastrophic; in fact, it would then become the norm rather than the exception.

One possible way to deal with such extreme circumstances without simply lapsing into consequentialism is to reason in a way analogous to Michael Walzer's reasoning about the rules of war in *Just and Unjust Wars* (New York: Basic Books, 1977). Walzer maintains that the rules of war are binding even when they put us at a disadvantage, even when they may cost us victory. But he grants that there might be "supreme emergencies" in which we could break the rules: namely, when doing so was (a) morally necessary (i.e., the opponent was so evil—a Hitler—that it was morally imperative to defeat him) and (b) strategically necessary (no way other than violating the rules of war was available for defeating this opponent). Reasoning in an analogous way, we might wonder whether the rule prohibiting euthanasia could be violated if (a) the suffering was so intense that the sufferer lost all capacity to bear that suffering with any sense of moral purpose or faithfulness to God, and (b) the pain was truly unconquerable. Whether such extreme circumstances ever occur is a question whose answer I cannot give. And even if such circumstances are possible, I remain uncertain about the force of this "thought experiment," which is offered tentatively.

9. This illustration is "inspired" by a different set of hypothetical cases offered by Paul Ramsey in "Some Rejoinders," *Journal of Religious Ethics* 4 (Fall 1976): 204.

10. In what follows I draw upon my own formulations in two previous articles: "The Distinction Between Killing and Allowing to Die," *Theological Studies* 37 (Sept. 1976): 467-70, and "Lutheran Theology and Bioethics: A Juxtaposition," *SPC Journal* 3 (1980): 25-30.

11. The passages cited in this paragraph may be found scattered throughout pages 336-42 and pages 401-2 of vol. III/4 of *Church Dogmatics*.

12. For what follows cf. C. S. Lewis, *Miracles* (New York: Macmillan, 1947), 129, and Paul Ramsey, *The Patient as Person* (New Haven and London: Yale University Press, 1970), 144.

13. Barth, *Church Dogmatics*, III/4, 368.

14. Ibid., 342.

15. George Orwell, "The Meaning of a Poem," in *My Country Right or Left, 1940-1943* (New York: Harcourt, Brace, Jovanovich, 1968), 133.

16. For a strong statement of such a case see James Rachels, "Active and Passive Euthanasia," *New England Journal of Medicine* 292 (1975): 78, 80.

17. William May, "The Metaphysical Plight of the Family," in Peter Steinfels and Robert M. Veatch, eds., *Death Inside Out* (New York: Harper & Row, 1974), 51.

CHAPTER 13

"A Fail-Safe Model for Justifiable Medically Assisted Suicide"

JACK KEVORKIAN

1. See G. Sumner, *Folkways: A Study of the Sociological Importance of Usages, Manners, Customs, Mores, and Morals* (New York: Dover, 1959).

2. See B. N. Cardozo, *The Growth of the Law* (New Haven: Yale University Press, 1924).

3. See C. Dickens, *Oliver Twist* (New York: Oxford University Press, 1987 ed.).

4. See L. Edelstein, *The Hippocratic Oath: Text, Translation, and Interpretation* (Baltimore: Johns Hopkins Press, 1943).

5. Jack Kevorkian, *Prescription: Medicide — The Goodness of Planned Death* (Buffalo, N.Y.: Prometheus Books, 1991).

6. Anonymous, "7 Deadly Days," *Time*, July 17, 1989, 30-60.

CHAPTER 18

"Active Voluntary Euthanasia:
Opening Pandora's Box"

D. ALAN SHEWMON

1. Leo Alexander, "Medical Science Under Dictatorship," *New England Journal of Medicine* 241 (1949): 39-47.

2. *Bouvia v. Superior Court,* 179 Cal. App. 3d 1127, 225 Cal. Rptr. 297 (Cal. App. 2 Dist. 1986).

3. Complaint par. 9, *Rodas v. ErkenBrack,* No. 87 CV 142 (Mesa Co., Col., Dist. Ct., filed Jan. 30, 1987), reprinted in *Issues in Law and Medicine* 2 (1987): 499-500.

4. President's Commission for the Study of Ethical Problems in Medicine and Biomedical and Behavioral Research, *Deciding to Forego Life-Sustaining Treatment* (1983), 275-97.

5. Derek Humphry, "Kubler-Ross Blames Patients' Families for Euthanasia," *Hemlock Quarterly* 14 (1984): 7.

6. Model Penal Code (1980) §210.5, comment 2.

7. Ibid., comment 5.

8. President's Commission, *Deciding to Forego Treatment,* 33, 73.

9. Ibid., 29, 30.

10. "The Hemlock Manifesto: Towards Accepting Voluntary Euthanasia," *Hemlock Quarterly* 8 (1982), insert; reprinted in Derek Humphry, *Let Me Die Before I Wake,* 3d ed. (1984), 100-114.

11. "The Hemlock Manifesto," §1.c.B.

12. See, e.g., sidebar for book advertisements, *Hemlock Quarterly* 10 (1983): 6.

13. M. Surber, V. Quinn, and D. Willner, eds., "Who Believes in Voluntary Euthanasia? A Survey of Hemlock Society Membership" (Hemlock Society, 1983), 22.

14. Derek Humphry and Ann Wickett, *The Right to Die: Understanding Euthanasia* (Harper and Row, 1986), 313; Humphry, "Mercy Denied to Roswell Gilbert," *Euthanasia Review* 1 (1986): 16, 17.

15. Derek Humphry, "Mrs. Bouvia's Sad Mistakes Are Lessons," *Hemlock Quarterly* 14 (1984): 1.

16. Derek Humphry, "The Suicide Shambles" (book review), *Hemlock Quarterly* 7 (1982): 1.

17. Derek Humphry, "Enigma of Double Suicide," *Hemlock Quarterly* 13 (1983): 1.

18. Ann Wickett, "Why Cynthia Koestler Joined Arthur," *Hemlock Quarterly* 18 (1985): 4-5.

19. Humphry, *Let Me Die Before I Wake,* 76.

20. P. Marx, *And Now . . . Euthanasia,* 2d ed. (1985), 23.

21. Joseph Fletcher, "Judge Every Case on Its Merits," *Hemlock Quarterly* 13 (1983): 4.

22. Van Till, "Dutch Doctors Get Guidelines," *Hemlock Quarterly* 14 (1984): 1, 2.

23. Note, "World Conference," *Hemlock Quarterly* 1 (1980): 1-2.

24. Senate Committee on the Judiciary, *Human Life Federalism Amendment,* 97th Cong., 2d Sess., 1982, S. Rept. 465, 50 n. 256.

25. Ibid., 3. In a highly publicized California incident, for example, many viable fetuses were among the nearly 17,000 found in a trash container. See Jones, "Stored Fetuses to be Studied Individually," *Los Angeles Times,* May 27, 1982, part 2, 1.

26. *Thornburgh v. American College of Obstetricians and Gynecologists,* 476 U.S.____, 106 S.Ct. 2169, 2190-91 (Burger, dissenting).

27. F. Wertham. *A Sign for Cain: An Exploration of Human Violence* (1973), 156. [Notes in the original article that are omitted here cite this book several times in this section on Nazi "euthanasia," along with R. Lipton, *The Nazi Doctors: Medical Killing and the Psychology of Genocide* (1986).]

28. Wertham, *A Sign for Cain,* 162.

29. Parachini, "The Netherlands Debates the Legal Limits of Euthanasia," *Los Angeles Times,* July 5, 1987, part 6, 1, 8, 9.

30. Ibid. Also: Fenigsen, "Involuntary Euthanasia in Holland," *Wall Street Journal,* Sept. 29, 1987, 29.

31. "The Hemlock Manifesto," §I.a, 3.

32. Joseph Fletcher, "Ethics and Euthanasia," *American Journal of Nursing* 73 (1973): 670-75.

33. Todres, Krane, Howell, and Shannon, "Pediatricians' Attitudes Affecting Decisionmaking in Defective Newborns," *Pediatrics* 60 (1977): 197-201.

34. American Academy of Pediatrics, Joint Policy Statement, "Principles of Treatment of Disabled Infants," *Pediatrics* 73 (1984): 559-60.

35. John Lorber, "Spina Bifida Cystica: Results of Treatment of 270 Consecutive Cases with Criteria for Selection for the Future," *Archives of Diseases of Childhood* 47 (1971): 871.

36. John Lorber, "Selective Treatment of Myelomeningocele: To Treat or Not to Treat," *Pediatrics* 53 (1974): 308.

37. Ibid.

38. McLone, Dias, Kaplan, and Sommers, "Concepts in the Management of Spina Bifida," *Concepts in Pediatric Neurosurgery* 5 (1985): 97-106.

39. Personal communication from Warwick J. Peacock, M.D., associate professor of pediatric neurosurgery at UCLA Medical Center.

40. Gross, Cox, Tatyrek, et al., "Early Management and Decision Making for the Treatment of Myelomeningocele," *Pediatrics* 72 (1983): 450-58.

41. Note, "Treating the Defective Newborn: A Survey of Physicians' Attitudes," *Hastings Center Report* 6 (April 1976): 2.

42. Kerenyi and Chitkara, "Selective Birth in Twin Pregnancy with Discordancy for Down's Syndrome," *New England Journal of Medicine* 304 (1981): 1525-27.

43. Warren, "On the Moral and Legal Status of Abortion," in R. Wasserstrom, ed., *Today's Moral Problems* (1975), 131.

44. Ibid., 136.

45. J. Glover, *Causing Death and Saving Lives* (1977), 164.

46. F. Clothier, "Euthanasia—The Physician's Dilemma," manuscript distrib. by the Euthanasia Educational Council (New York, 1972).

47. Joseph Fletcher, "Indicators of Humanhood: A Tentative Profile of Man," *Hastings Center Report* 2 (November 1972): 1-4.

48. Joseph Fletcher, "Moral Aspects," in T. Moore, ed., *Ethical Dilemmas in Current Obstetric and Newborn Care,* Report of the Sixty-Fifth Ross Conference on Pediatric Research (1973), 70-71

49. Joseph Fletcher, "Infanticide and the Ethics of Loving Concern," in M. Kohl, ed., *Infanticide and the Value of Life* (1978), 20 (emphasis in orig.).

50. Ibid., 15, 16.

51. Wanzer, Adelstein, Cranford, et al., "The Physician's Responsibility Toward Hopelessly Ill Patients," *New England Journal of Medicine* 310 (1984): 955 (reprinted in Society for the Right to Die, *The Physician and the Hopelessly Ill Patient* [1985]).

52. Ibid., 959.

53. Humphry and Wickett, *The Right to Die,* 129, 130.

54. Sim, "Alzheimer's Disease," *Hemlock Quarterly* 20 (1985): 7.

55. C. Everett Koop, "Ethical and Surgical Considerations in the Care of the Newborn with Congenital Abnormalities," in D. Horan and M. Delahoyde, eds., *Infanticide and the Handicapped Newborn* (1982), 89-106.

56. Humphry and Wickett, *The Right to Die,* 129, 130.

57. Ibid., 313.

58. *Death with Dignity: An Inquiry into Related Public Issues,* Hearings before the Special Committee on Aging, U.S. Senate, 92d Cong., 2d Sess. 30 (1972), statement of Hon. Walter W. Sackett, M.D., medical director of American Euthanasia Foundation and member of Florida House of Representatives.

59. R. Derzon (administrator, Health Care Financing Administration, U.S. Department of Health, Education, and Welfare), "Memorandum on Additional Cost-Saving Initiatives," June 4, 1977.

60. Gross, "Newborns with Myelodysplasia—The Rest of the Story," *New England Journal of Medicine* 312 (1985): 1632-34.

61. Letter to Editor, "Gov. Lamm Right—Now Supply Ways," *Hemlock Quarterly* 16 (1984): 6.

62. Deiden, "Pros and Cons of Suicide Literature," *Hemlock Quarterly* 16 (1984): 4, 5, 8.

63. R. Lifton, *The Nazi Doctors: Medical Killing and the Psychology of Genocide* (1986).

64. Alexander, "Medical Science Under Dictatorship," 46.

65. Wanzer, Adelstein, and Cranford, "The Physician's Responsibility Toward Hopelessly Ill Patients," 87, n. 118.

66. Derr, "The Real Brophy Issue," *Boston Globe,* November 18, 1985, 15.

67. President's Commission, *Deciding to Forego Treatment,* 73.

CHAPTER 19

"Assisted Suicide: The Dutch Experience"

HERBERT HENDIN

1. A. Camus, *The Myth of Sisyphus and Other Essays,* trans. Justin O'Brien (New York: Alfred Knopf, 1958).

2. H. Hendin, "New Directions in Suicide Research," *Hospital and Community Psychiatry* 37 (1986): 148-54.

3. E. Robins, C. Murphy, R. Wilkenson, et al., "Some Clinical Considerations in the Prevention of Suicide Based on a Study of 134 Successful Suicides," *American Journal of Public Health* 49 (1959): 888-99; T. L. Dorpat and H. S. Ripley, "A Study of Suicide in the Seattle Area," *Comprehensive Psychiatry* 1 (1960): 349-59; B. Barraclough, J. Bunch, B. Nelson, and P. Sainsbury, "A Hundred Cases of Suicide: Clinical Aspects," *British Journal of Psychiatry* 125 (1974): 355-73; D. C. Rich, D. Young, R. C. Fowler, "San Diego Suicide Study, I: Young vs. Old Subjects," *Archives of General Psychiatry* 43 (1986): 577-82.

4. Y. Conwell and E. D. Caine, "Rational Suicide and the Right to Die: Reality and Myth," *New England Journal of Medicine* 15 (1991): 1100-1103.

5. Robins, Murphy, Wilkenson, "Some Clinical Considerations"; Conwell and Caine, "Rational Suicide and the Right to Die"; Barraclough, Bunch, Nelson, Sainsbury, "A Hundred Cases of Suicide."

6. J. Brown, P. Henteleff, S. Barakat, and C. J. Rowe, "Is It Normal for Terminally Ill Patients to Desire Death?" *American Journal of Psychiatry* 143 (1986): 208-11.

7. Y. Conwell, E. D. Caine, and K. Olsen, "Suicide and Cancer in Later Life," *Hospital and Community Psychiatry* 41 (1990): 1334-39; T. L. Dorpat, W. F. Anderson, and H. S. Ripley, "The Relationship of Physical Illness to Suicide," in H. P. L. Resnick, ed., *Suicidal Behaviors: Diagnosis and Management* (Boston: Little, Brown, 1968).

8. S. Perry, "Suicidal Ideation and HIV Testing," *Journal of the American Medical Association* 263 (1990): 679-82.

9. Conwell and Caine, "Rational Suicide and the Right to Die."

10. P. J. van der Maas, J. J. M. van Delden, L. Pijnenborg, and C. W. H. Louwan, "Euthanasia and Other Medical Decisions Concerning the End of Life," *The Lancet* 338 (1991): 669-74.

11. K. Lebacqz and N. T. Englehardt, "Suicide and Covenant," in M. P. Battin and D. Mayo, eds., *Suicide: The Philosophical Issues* (New York: St. Martin's, 1980), 85-86.

12. M. P. Battin, "Manipulated Suicide," in Battin and Mayo, *Suicide: The Philosophical Issues*.

13. "Doctor in Suicides Assails U.S. Ethics," *New York Times,* November 3, 1991, A14.

14. J. Kevorkian, "A Fail-Safe Model for Justifiable Medically Assisted Suicide," *American Journal of Forensic Psychiatry* 13 (1992): 7-81. [Reprinted in this volume.]

15. The Hemlock Society, *Assisted Suicide: The Compassionate Crime* (Los Angeles, 1982).

16. D. Humphry, *Final Exit* (Eugene, Ore.: Hemlock Society, 1991).

17. P. Marzuk, K. Tardiff, C. Hirsch, et al., "Increase in Suicide by Asphyxiation in New York City after the Publication of *Final Exit,*" *New England Journal of Medicine* 329 (1993): 1508; B. Angelo, interview: "Assigning the Blame for a Young Man's Suicide," *Time,* November 18, 1991, 12.

18. A. Wickett, *Double Exit* (National Hemlock Society, 1989); T. Gabriel, "A Fight to the Death," *New York Times Magazine,* December 8, 1991, 46; G. Abrams, "A Bitter

Legacy—Angry Accusations Abound After the Suicide of Hemlock Society Co-Founder Ann Humphry," *Los Angeles Times,* "View" section, October 23, 1991.

19. R. Noyes, S. Frye, and C. Hartford, "Single Case Study: Conjugal Suicide Pact," *Journal of Nervous and Mental Diseases* 165 (1977): 72-75; D. Mehta, P. Mathew, and S. Mehta, "Suicide Pact in a Depressed Elderly Couple," *Journal of the American Cancer Society* 136 (1978): 136-58.

20. A. Hoche, "Vom Sterben," in *Aus der Werkstatt* (Munich: Jehmann, 1935), 210-32.

21. R. Brandt, "The Morality and Rationality of Suicide," in S. Perlin, ed., *A Handbook for the Study of Suicide* (New York: Oxford University Press, 1975), 61-76.

22. H. Hendin, "Seduced by Death: Doctors, Patients and the Dutch Cure," *Issues in Law and Medicine* 10 (1994): 123-68.

23. "Psychiater Vrijuit na Hulp," *Algemeen Dagblad,* Rotterdam, April 22, 1993, 1, 4; "Psychiater niet Gestraft voor Hulp bij Zelfdoding," *Volkskrant,* Amsterdam, April 22, 1993, 1, 3; Drozdiak, "Dutch Seek Freer Mercy Killing," *Washington Post,* October 29, 1993, A29, A32.

24. P. J. van der Maas, J. J. M. van Delden, and L. Pijnenborg, *Euthanasia and Other Medical Decisions Concerning the End of Life* (New York: Elsevier, 1992).

25. L. Pijnenborg, P. J. van der Maas, J. J. van Delden, and C. W. H. Louwan, "Life-terminating Acts Without Explicit Request of Patient," *Lancet* 341 (1993): 1196-99.

26. H. W. A. Hilhorst, *Euthanasie ni het Ziekenhuis* (Lochem-Poperinge: De Tijdstroom, 1983).

27. G. F. Koerselman, "Hoemondig Zijn Moderne Patienter?" *Med Tijdseter Geneesk* 14 (1986): 156-57; H. ten Have and G. Kimsna, *Geneeskunde Tissen Droon en Drama* (Kampen: R. O. K. Agora, 1987), 83-84.

28. "Psychiater Vrijuit na Hulp Bij Zelfdoding," *Algemeen Dagblad;* "Psychiater niet Gestraft voor Hulp bij Zelfdoding," *Volkskrant;* Drozdiak, "Dutch Seek Freer Mercy Killing."

29. "Doctor Unpunished for Dutch Suicide," *New York Times,* June 22, 1994, A10.

30. J. Keown, "On Regulating Death," *Hastings Center Report* 22 (1992): 39-43; A. M. Capron, "Euthanasia in the Netherlands: American Observations," *Hastings Center Report* 22 (1992): 30-33; J. Welie, "The Medical Exception: Physicians, Euthanasia, and the Dutch Criminal Law," *Journal of Medicine and Philosophy* 17 (1992): 419-37.

31. H. Brody, "Assisted Death—A Compassionate Response to a Medical Failure," *New England Journal of Medicine* 327 (1992): 1384-88.

32. D. Margolick, "Jury Acquits Dr. Kevorkian of Illegally Aiding a Suicide," *New York Times,* May 3, 1994, A1.

33. President's Commission for the Study of Ethical Problems in Medicine and Biomedical and Behavioral Research, *Deciding to Forego Life-Sustaining Treatment* (U.S. Government Printing Office, March 1983).

34. C. E. Koop, "The Challenge of Definition," *Hastings Center Report,* January/February 1993, Special Supplement, 2-3.

CHAPTER 20

"Aiding the Death of Young Children: Ethical Issues"

H. TRISTRAM ENGELHARDT, JR.

1. I am grateful to Laurence B. McCullough and James P. Morris for their critical discussion of this paper. They may be responsible for its virtues, but not for its shortcomings.

2. The concept of extraordinary treatment as it has been developed in Catholic moral theology is useful: treatment is extraordinary and therefore not obligatory if it involves great costs, pain, or inconvenience, and is a grave burden to oneself or others without a reasonable expectation that such treatment would be successful. See Gerald Kelly, S.J., *Medico-Moral Problems* (St. Louis: Catholic Hospital Association Press, 1958), 128-41. Difficulties are hidden in terms such as "great costs" and "reasonable expectation," as well as in terms such as "successful." Such ambiguity reflects the fact that precise operational definitions are not available. That is, the precise meaning of "great," "reasonable," and "successful" is inextricably bound to particular circumstances, especially particular societies.

3. I will use the term "euthanasia" in a broad sense to indicate a deliberately chosen course of action or inaction that is known at the time of decision to be such as will expedite death. This use of "euthanasia" will encompass not only positive or active euthanasia (acting in order to expedite death) and negative or passive euthanasia (refraining from action in order to expedite death), but acting and refraining in the absence of a direct intention that death occur more quickly (that is, those cases that fall under the concept of double effect). See note 4.

4. But both active and passive euthanasia can be appreciated in terms of the Catholic moral notion of double effect. When the doctrine of double effect is invoked, one is strictly not intending euthanasia, but rather one intends something else. That concept allows actions or omissions that lead to death (1) because it is licit not to prolong life *in extremis* (allowing death is not an intrinsic evil), (2) if death is not actually willed or actively sought (that is, the evil is not directly willed), (3) if that which is willed is a major good (for example, avoiding useless major expenditure of resources or serious pain), and (4) if the good is not achieved by means of the evil (for example, one does not will to save resources or diminish pain *by* the death). With regard to euthanasia, the doctrine of double effect means that one need not expend major resources in an endeavor that will not bring health but only prolong dying and that one may use drugs that decrease pain but hasten death. See Richard McCormick, *Ambiguity in Moral Choice* (Milwaukee: Marquette Univ. Press, 1973). I exclude the issue of double effect from my discussion because I am interested in those cases in which the good may follow directly from the evil—the death of the child. In part, though, the second section of this paper is concerned with the concept of proportionate good.

5. Raymond S. Duff and A. G. M. Campbell, "Moral and Ethical Dilemmas in the Special-Care Nursery," *New England Journal of Medicine* 289 (Oct. 25, 1973): 890-94.

6. Roger Pell, "The Agonizing Decision of Joanne and Roger Pell," *Good House-keeping,* January 1972, 76-77, 131-35.

7. This somewhat Kantian argument is obviously made in opposition to Kant's position that suicide involves a default of one's duty to oneself "to preserve his life simply because he is a person and must therefore recognize a duty to himself (and a strict one at that)," as well as a contradictory volition: "that man ought to have the authorization to withdraw himself from all obligation, that is, to be free to act as if no authorization at all were required for this withdrawal, involves a contradiction. To destroy the subject of morality in his own person is tantamount to obliterating it from the world" (Immanuel Kant, *The Metaphysical Principles of Virtue: Part II of the Metaphysics of Morals,* trans. James Ellington (Indianapolis: Bobbs-Merrill, 1964), 83; Akademie Edition, VI, 422-23.

8. Norman L. Cantor, "A Patient's Decision to Decline Life-Saving Medical Treatment: Bodily Integrity Versus the Preservation of Life," *Rutgers Law Review* 26 (Winter 1972): 239.

9. By "young child" I mean either an infant or a child so young as not yet to be able to participate, in any sense, in a decision. A precise operational definition of "young child" would clearly be difficult to develop. It is also not clear how one would bring older children into such decisions. See, for example, Milton Viederman, "Saying 'No' to Hemodialysis: Exploring Adaptation," and Daniel Burke, "Saying 'No' to Hemodialysis: An Acceptable Decision," both in the *Hastings Center Report* 4 (September 1974): 8-10; and John E. Schowalter, Julian B. Ferholt, and Nancy M. Mann, "The Adolescent Patient's Decision to Die," *Pediatrics* 51 (January 1973): 97-103.

10. An appeal to high costs alone is probably hidden in judgments based on statistics: even though there is a chance for a normal life for certain children with apparently severe cases of meningomyelocele, one is not obliged to treat since that chance is small, and the pursuit of that chance is very expensive. Cases of the costs being low but the expected suffering of the child being high will be discussed under the concept of the injury of continued existence. It should be noted that none of the arguments in this paper bear on cases where neither the cost nor the suffering of the child is considerable. Cases in this last category probably include, for example, children born with mongolism complicated only by duodenal atresia.

11. I have in mind here the issue of physicians, hospital administrators, or others being morally compelled to seek an injunction to force treatment of the child in the absence of parental consent. In these circumstances, the physician, who is usually best acquainted with the facts of the case, is the natural advocate of the child.

12. G. Tedeschi, "On Tort Liability for 'Wrongful Life,'" *Israel Law Review* 1 (1966): 513.

13. *Zepeda v. Zepeda,* 41 Ill. App. 2d 240, 190 N.E. 2d 849 (1963).

14. *Williams v. State of New York,* 46 Misc. 2d 824, 260 N.Y.S. 2d 953 (Ct. Cl., 1965).

15. Torts: "Illegitimate Child Denied Recovery Against Father for 'Wrongful Life,'" *Iowa Law Review* 49 (1969): 1009.

16. It is one thing to have a *conceptual* definition of the injury of continued existence (for example, causing a person to continue to live under circumstances of severe pain and deprivation when there are no alternatives but death) and another to have an *operational* definition of that concept (that is, deciding what counts as

such severe pain and deprivation). This article has focused on the first, not the second, issue.

17. H. Tristram Engelhardt, Jr., "Euthanasia and Children: The Injury of Continued Existence," *Journal of Pediatrics* 83 (July 1973): 170-71.

18. John Lorber, "Results of Treatment of Myelomeningocele," *Developmental Medicine and Child Neurology* 13 (1971): 286.

19. John M. Freeman, "The Shortsighted Treatment of Myelomeningocele: A Long-Term Case Report," *Pediatrics* 53 (March 1974): 311-13.

20. John M. Freeman, "To Treat or Not to Treat," in Freeman, ed., *Practical Management of Meningomyelocele* (Baltimore: University Park Press, 1974), 21.

21. John Lorber, "Selective Treatment of Myelomeningocele: To Treat or Not to Treat," *Pediatrics* 53 (March 1974): 307-8.

22. I am presupposing that no intrinsic moral distinctions exist in cases such as these between acting and refraining, between omitting care in the hope that death will ensue (that is, rather than the child living to be even more defective) and acting to ensure that death will ensue rather than having the child live under painful and seriously compromised circumstances. For a good discussion of the distinction between acting and refraining, see Jonathan Bennett, "Whatever the Consequences," *Analysis* 26 (January 1966): 83-102; P. J. Fitzgerald, "Acting and Refraining," *Analysis* 27 (March 1967): 133-39; Daniel Dinello, "On Killing and Letting Die," *Analysis* 31 (April 1971): 83-86.

23. Lorber, "Selective Treatment of Myelomeningocele," 308.

24. Positive duties involve a greater constraint than negative duties. Hence it is often easier to establish a duty not to do something (not to treat further) than a duty to do something (to actively hasten death). Even allowing a new practice to be permitted (for example, active euthanasia) requires a greater attention to consequences than does establishing the absence of a positive duty. For example, at common law there is no basis for action against a person who watches another drown without giving aid; this reflects the difficulty of establishing a positive duty.

CHAPTER 22

"Forgoing Life-Sustaining Treatment:
The Legal Consensus"

Alan Meisel

1. The states with appellate or federal trial-court right-to-die cases are Arizona, California, Connecticut, Delaware, Florida, Georgia, Illinois, Indiana, Louisiana, Maine, Massachusetts, Michigan, Minnesota, Missouri, Nevada, New Jersey, New York, Ohio, Rhode Island, Washington, and Wisconsin. There are appellate or federal trial-court cases in other states that are related but do not grapple with the core issues of forgoing life-sustaining treatment.

2. Thomas L. Hafemeister, Ingo Keilitz, and Steven M. Banks, "The Judicial Role in Life-Sustaining Medical Treatment Decisions," *Issues in Law and Medicine* 7 (1991):65.

3. *Superintendent of Belchertown State School v. Saikewicz,* 370 N.E.2d 417, 428 (Mass. 1977).

4. *Cruzan v. Director,* 110 S. Ct. 2841, 2852 (1990); quoting dissenting opinion of Justice Blackman in *Cruzan v. Harmon,* 760 S.W.2d 408, 428 (Mo. 1988).

5. President's Commission for the Study of Ethical Problems in Medicine and Biomedical and Behavioral Research, *Deciding to Forego Life-Sustaining Treatment* (Washington, D.C.: U.S. Govt. Printing Office, 1983).

6. *Cruzan v. Director* (1990).

7. *In re Grant,* 747 P.2d 445 (Wash. 1987).

8. *In re Browning,* 568 So. 2d 4 (Fla. 1990).

9. Throughout this paper, I use the term "incompetent patient" to refer both to patients who have been *adjudicated* incompetent by a court and to those patients who have not been adjudicated incompetent but in fact lack the capacity to make decisions about their medical treatment, making no distinction between the two because, for most purposes, the decision-making rights of and procedures for such patients are legally identical.

10. *In re Quinlan,* 355 A.2d 647 (N.J. 1976).

11. *United States v. George,* 239 F.Supp. 752, 754 (1965), quoting *In re President and Directors of Georgetown College* (1964) (patient's husband said that if court ordered transfusion the responsibility was not his).

12. *John F. Kennedy Memorial Hospital v. Heston,* 279 A.2d 670 (N.J. 1971).

13. No court appears to have *held* that the right to refuse treatment is absolute, although Judge Simons, of the New York court of appeals, remarked in his concurring opinion in *Fosmire* (1990) that "[t]he majority . . . for all practical purposes, leaves the right absolute." Perhaps the Florida supreme court's *Browning* decision (1990) comes the closest to finding the right to be absolute in its observation that "the right to make choices about medical treatment . . . encompasses all medical choices. A competent individual has the [state] constitutional right to refuse medical treatment regardless of his or her medical condition."

14. The standard enunciated by the Missouri supreme court in *Cruzan* is often referred to as the "clear and convincing evidence" standard. I prefer not to use this term because the standard at issue in *Cruzan* involved not merely a level of proof (i.e., clear and convincing evidence) but also what needed to be proved (the patient's actual intent, which is usually referred to in law as "subjective intent"). Two dissenting justices, Stevens and Brennan, recognized this. Justice Stevens's disagreement with the majority was, in his words, "unrelated to its endorsement of the clear and convincing standard of proof for cases of this kind." He agreed "that the controlling facts must be established with unmistakable clarity." The point of departure for him was "not how to prove the controlling facts but rather what proven facts should be controlling."

15. *In re A.C.,* A.2d 1235 (D.C. 1990).

16. *In re Estate of Greenspan,* 558 N.E.2d 1194 (Ill. 1990).

17. A health-care power of attorney is sometimes referred to as a health-care proxy or simply as a durable power of attorney. The term health-care power of attorney should be used to refer to the written instrument by which one appoints an agent to make heath-care decisions, and the term health-care proxy is more properly used to refer to that agent. The term durable power of attorney is overinclusive when used

in the health-care decision-making context. A durable power of attorney is a legal instrument that can be used to appoint an agent to make health-care decisions, but it can also be used to appoint an agent for a wide variety of other purposes.

18. American Medical Association, *Current Opinions of the Council on Ethical and Judicial Affairs* (Chicago, Ill.: AMA, 1986), 12-13.

19. *Cruzan v. Director,* 2852.

20. Ibid.

21. Ibid.

22. This statute is now revised—with the prohibition on the termination of tube-feeding eliminated—and is referred to as the Florida Health Care Directives Act.

23. "It's Over, Debbie," *Journal of the American Medical Association* 259 (1988): 272; Timothy E. Quill, "A Case of Individualized Decision-Making," *New England Journal of Medicine* 324: 691-94.

24. *In re Doe,* 418 S.E. 2d 3 (1992).

CHAPTER 23

"Are Laws Against Assisted Suicide Constitutional?"

YALE KAMISAR

1. For a careful, detailed analysis of the Michigan law, see George Annas, "Physician-assisted Suicide: Michigan's New Law," *New England Journal of Medicine* 328, no. 21 (1993): 1573-76.

2. See Thomas Marzen et al., "Suicide: A Constitutional Right?" *Duquesne Law Review* 24 (1985): 97-98; George Smith, "All's Well That Ends Well: Toward a Policy of Assisted Rational Suicide or Merely Enlightened Self-Determination?" *University of California Davis Law Review* 22 (1989): 290-91. See also Timothy E. Quill, *Death and Dignity: Making Choices and Taking Charge* (New York: Norton, 1993), 141.

3. Dan Brock, "Voluntary Active Euthanasia," *Hastings Center Report* 22, no. 2 (1992): 19 (emphasis added).

4. See Marzen et al., "Suicide," 68-100.

5. American Law Institute, *Model Penal Code and Commentaries,* Part I, § 2.10.5 at 94 (1985).

6. Marzen et al., "Suicide," 86, 100.

7. See Leon Kass, "Is There a Right to Die?" *Hastings Center Report* 23, no. 1 (1993): 34-35.

8. American Law Institute, *Model Penal Code,* 100.

9. Oliver Wendell Holmes, "The Path of the Law," in *Collected Legal Papers* (New York: Harcourt, Brace, 1920), 167, 187.

10. Sanford Kadish, "The Model Penal Code's Historical Antecedents," *Rutgers Law Journal* 19 (1988): 521.

11. See American Law Institute, "Model Penal Code" (tentative draft no. 9, 1959), 56-57.

12. See Marzen et al., "Suicide," 95.

13. *In re Quinlan,* 70 N.J. 10, 355 A.2d 647, 665, 670, and fn. 9 (1976).

14. *Cruzan v. Director, Missouri Department of Health,* 497 U.S. 261, 280 (1990). See also *Paris Adult Theatre v. Slaton,* 413 U.S. 49, 68, and fn. 15 (1973).

15. John Robertson, "*Cruzan* and the Constitutional Status of Nontreatment Decisions for Incompetent Patients," *Georgia Law Review* 25 (1991): 1174-75 and fn. 132.

16. See "The Supreme Court 1989 Term," *Harvard Law Review* 104 (1990): 257.

17. Louis Seidman, "Confusion at the Border: *Cruzan,* 'The Right to Die,' and the Public/Private Distinction," *Supreme Court Review,* 1992, 62.

18. See "The Supreme Court 1989 Term," 262.

19. Smith, "All's Well That Ends Well," 279-80. See also Mary Barrington, "Apologia for Suicide," in A. B. Downing, ed., *Euthanasia and the Right to Death: The Case for Voluntary Euthanasia* (Atlantic Highlands, N.J.: Humanities Press, 1969), 162 ("that voluntary euthanasia is in fact assisted suicide is no doubt clear to most people"); Raanon Gillon, "Suicide and Voluntary Euthanasia: Historical Perspectives," in Downing, *Euthanasia and the Right to Death,* 173-74 ("voluntary euthanasia is essentially a form of suicide, involving the assistance of others").

20. See Joseph Fletcher, *Morals and Medicine* (Boston: Beacon Press, 1954), 176; James Rachels, *The End of Life: Euthanasia and Morality* (New York: Oxford University Press, 1986), 86-87.

21. Quill, *Death and Dignity,* 142, 159.

22. Ibid., 160.

23. Ibid., 142.

24. Ibid., 143.

25. Brock, "Voluntary Active Euthanasia," 10. Brock is responding to Sidney Wanzer et al., "The Physician's Responsibility Toward Hopelessly Ill Persons: A Second Look," *New England Journal of Medicine* 320 (1989): 848. Although Wanzer and his co-authors stopped short of approving active voluntary euthanasia, they did not disapprove it.

26. Quill, *Death and Dignity,* 162.

27. Daniel Callahan, *The Troubled Dream of Life: Living with Mortality* (New York: Simon and Schuster, 1993), chap. 3. See also Leon Kass, "Neither for Love nor Money: Why Doctors Must Not Kill," *The Public Interest* 94 (1989): 32-33.

28. Alan Sullivan, "A Constitutional Right to Suicide," in Margaret P. Battin and David J. Mayo, eds., *Suicide: The Philosophical Issues* (New York: St. Martin's Press, 1980), 240.

29. See Alan Meisel, "Legal Myths About Terminating Life Support," *Archives of Internal Medicine* 109 (1991): 1498-99, discussing *Bouvia, McAfee,* and other cases.

30. Blackmun, J., joined by Brennan, Marshall, and Stevens, JJ., dissenting in *Bowers v. Hardwick,* 478 U.S. 186, 199-200 (1986), and Stevens, J., joined by Brennan and Marshall, JJ., at 216. In *Hardwick,* a 5-4 majority upheld the constitutionality of a Georgia law criminalizing homosexual sodomy.

31. The quotations are from Morris R. Cohen, *The Faith of a Liberal* (New York: Henry Holt, 1946), 70.

32. Sullivan, "Constitutional Right to Suicide," 243.

33. Philip Devine, *The Ethics of Homicide* (Ithaca: Cornell University Press, 1978), 188.

34. See George Colt, *The Enigma of Suicide* (New York: Summit Books, 1991), 37-38; Herbert Hendin, *Suicide in America* (New York: W. W. Norton, 1982), 185-86; David Clark, " 'Rational' Suicide and People with Terminal Conditions or Disabilities," *Issues in Law and Medicine* 8 (1992): 148.

35. Hendin, *Suicide in America*, 214. See also Herbert Hendin and Gerald Klerman, "Physician-Assisted Suicide: The Dangers of Legalization," *American Journal of Psychiatry* 150 (1993): 143-45.

36. Clark, " 'Rational' Suicide," 151-53.

37. Yeates Conwell and Eric Caine, "Rational Suicide and the Right to Die: Reality and Myth," *New England Journal of Medicine* 325 (1991): 1100-1102. See also James Brown et al., "Is It Normal for Terminally Ill Patients to Desire Death?" *American Journal of Psychiatry* 143 (1986): 208-11.

38. Conwell and Caine, "Rational Suicide and the Right to Die," 1101.

39. Quoted in Colt, *The Enigma of Suicide*, 342.

40. See Victor Rosenblum and Clark Forsythe, "The Right to Assisted Suicide: Protection of Autonomy or an Open Door to Social Killing?" *Issues in Law and Medicine* 6 (1990): 27. See also Yale Kamisar, "Some Non-Religious Views Against Proposed 'Mercy-Killing' Legislation," *Minnesota Law Review* 42 (1958): 990-93; David Velleman, "Against the Right to Die," *Journal of Medicine and Philosophy* 17 (1992): 664.

41. Margaret Pabst Battin, "Manipulated Suicide," in Battin and Mayo, *Suicide: The Philosophical Issues*, 169, 179.

42. Martin Marty and Ron Hamel, "Some Questions and Answers," in Ron Hamel, ed., *Active Euthanasia, Religion, and the Public Debate* (The Park Ridge Center, 1991), 27, 40.

43. The quotations are from Albert Alschuler, "Reflection," in Hamel, *Active Euthanasia*, 105, 107.

CHAPTER 24

"The Constitution and Hastening Inevitable Death"

ROBERT A. SEDLER

1. Robert Dixon, *"Bakke:* A Constitutional Analysis," *California Law Review* 67 (1979): 70.

2. Michigan Compiled Laws § 752.1027(3).

3. Ibid., 752.1027(1).

4. Yale Kamisar, "Are Laws Against Assisted Suicide Unconstitutional?" *Hastings Center Report* 23, no. 3 (1993): 38. [Reprinted in this volume.]

5. Ibid., 39.

6. Ibid., 40.

7. See the Supreme Court's classic discussion of this point in *Rescue Army v. Municipal Court*, 331 U.S. 549, 569 (1947). The concept of line of growth of constitutional doctrine is explained in Terrance Sandalow, "Constitutional Interpretation," *Michigan Law Review* 79 (1981): 1033-72.

8. See the discussion in Robert A. Sedler, "The Legitimacy Debate in Constitutional Adjudication: An Assessment and a Different Perspective," *Ohio State Law Journal* 44 (1983): 118-20.

9. *Skinner v. Oklahoma,* 316 U.S. 535 (1942).

10. *Griswold v. Connecticut,* 381 U.S. 479 (1965).

11. *Eisenstadt v. Baird,* 405 U.S. 483 (1972).

12. *Roe v. Wade,* 410 U.S. 113 (1973).

13. In *Planned Parenthood v. Casey* (112 Sup.Ct. 2791 [1992]), the Court affirmed that part of the *Roe v. Wade* decision, but held that the state could regulate the abortion procedure, even for the purpose of discouraging women from having an abortion, so long as the particular regulation did not impose an "undue burden" on the woman's decision whether to have an abortion.

14. Ibid., 2805-7.

15. As the Supreme Court has stated simply, "We assume that the United States Constitution would grant a competent person a constitutionally protected right to refuse lifesaving hydration and nutrition." *Cruzan v. Director, Missouri Department of Health,* 110 Sup.Ct. 2841, 2853 (1990).

16. There is no question, of course, that the state, in the exercise of its power to impose reasonable regulations on the practice of medicine, could constitutionally regulate physician participation in assisting the voluntary termination of life. Such regulations would be constitutional so long as they did not impose an undue burden on the decision of a competent terminally ill person to hasten the inevitable termination of life. For example, the state might limit physician participation in assisting the voluntary termination of life to practicing clinical physicians and/or to clinical physicians who have been directly involved in the care of the terminally ill patient. Such a regulation would be assumed to be constitutional, since it would not prevent the competent terminally ill patient from obtaining physician assistance in implementing his or her decision to hasten the inevitable end of life.

17. Kamisar, "Are Laws Against Assisted Suicide Unconstitutional?" 39.

18. Ibid., 36.

19. In *Roe v. Wade,* for example, the Court held that the state's interest in protecting potential human life was not of sufficient constitutional importance to outweigh the interest of the pregnant woman in bodily integrity and control of her own body until the pregnancy had reached the stage of viability.

CHAPTER 26

"Assisted Suicide in the United States: The 'Compassion' and 'Quill' Decisions"

VICTOR G. ROSENBLUM

1. ___ F.3d ___, 1996 WL 94848 (9th Cir., 1996).

2. ___ F.3d ___, 1996 U.S. App. LEXIS 6215 (2nd Cir., 1996).

3. Opinion at 23.

4. Idem at 39.

5. Idem at 31-32.

6. Idem at 48.

7. *Palko v. Connecticut,* 302 U.S. 319, 325 (1937).

8. *Moore v. City of East Cleveland,* 431 U.S. 494, 503 (1977)

9. Opinion at 25, *citing Bowers v. Hardwick,* 478 U.S. 186, 194 (1986).

10. Opinion at 17-18.

11. 410 U.S. 113 (1973).

12. 505 U.S. 833 (1992).

13. 413 U.S. 49 (1973).

14. 505 U.S. at 851.

15. 497 U.S. 261 (1990).

16. 448 U.S. 297 (1980).

17. 448 U.S. 340 (1980).

18. *Harris,* 448 U.S. at 325.

19. Idem.

20. New York State Task Force on Life and the Law, *When Death Is Sought: Assisted Suicide and Euthanasia in the Medical Context* (1994), ix.

21. Idem at 9.

22. Opinion at 29.

23. Idem at 28.

24. New York State Task Force, *When Death Is Sought,* 15.

25. House of Lords, *Report of the Select Committee on Medical Ethics* (U.K., 1994), 49.

26. Opinion at 43.

27. House of Lords, *Report,* 48.

CHAPTER 28

"The Legalization of Physician-Assisted Suicide: Creating a Potemkin Village"

DANIEL CALLAHAN and MARGOT WHITE

1. Franklin G. Miller et al., "Regulating Physician-Assisted Death," *New England Journal of Medicine* 331 (1994): 119-20.

2. The term "Potemkin Village" originally referred to sham villages created in eighteenth-century Russia to impress Empress Catherine II on her tours of the country.

3. New York State Task Force on Life and the Law, *When Death Is Sought: Assisted Suicide and Euthanasia in the Medical Context* (1994), 140, 131.

4. Timothy E. Quill et al., "Care of the Hopelessly Ill: Proposed Clinical Criteria for Physician-Assisted Suicide," *New England Journal of Medicine* 327 (1992): 1381.

5. Herbert Hendin, "Selling Death and Dignity," *Hastings Center Report* 25 (May-June 1995): 19.

6. Miller, "Regulating Physician-Assisted Death," 119.

7. Quill, "Care of the Hopelessly Ill," 1381-82.

8. Miller, "Regulating Physician-Assisted Death," 119.

9. Ibid, emphasis added.

10. Ibid., 121.

11. "Guidelines for Euthanasia," trans. Walker Lagerweg, *Issues in Law and Medicine* 3 (1988): 429, 431-33.

12. Miller, "Regulating Physician-Assisted Death."

13. John Keown, "Further Reflections on Euthanasia in the Netherlands in the Light of the Remmelink Report and the Van Der Maas Survey," in Luke Gormally, ed., *Euthanasia, Clinical Practice, and the Law* (London: Linacre Centre for Health Care Ethics, 1994).

14. Euthanasia is defined as "the *intentional* action to terminate a person's life, performed by someone other than the person concerned upon request of the latter."

15. John Keown, "Some Reflections on Euthanasia in the Netherlands," in Gormally, *Euthanasia, Clinical Practice, and the Law,* 227, 232.

16. "Medische beslissingen rond het levenseinde," Rapport van de Commissie onderzoek medische praktijk inzake euthanasie, Sdu Uitgeverij Plantijnstraat, 's-Gravenhage (1991) (quotation from Keown, "Further Reflections," 229). [Keown noted earlier that the Report had not been translated and that he was using a partial translation by Dr. Richard Fenigsen.] "Force majeure" is synonymous in Dutch usage with "necessity."

17. Ibid., 239.

18. Ibid., 235.

19. Charles H. Baron et al., "A Model State Act to Authorize and Regulate Physician-Assisted Suicide," *Harvard Journal of Legislation* 33 (1996), 4-5. [Reprinted in this volume.]

20. Ibid., 5.

21. Ibid., 10 (emphasis added).

22. Ibid., 11.

23. Ibid.

24. Ibid., 30-32.

25. Ibid., 19 (emphasis added).

26. *Compassion in Dying v. Washington,* No. 94-35534, 1996 WL 94848, at *7 (9th Cir. Mar. 6, 1996).

27. Ibid., *37.

28. Ibid., *36.

29. Ibid., *32. ("While defining the term 'terminally ill' is not free from difficulty, the experience of the states has proved that the class of the terminally ill is neither indefinable nor undefined. Indeed, all of the persons described in the various statutes would appear to fall within an appropriate definition of the term.")

30. Ibid., *26.

31. Ibid. (emphasis in the original).

32. Ibid.

33. Ibid., *62.

34. Ibid., *34.

Index of Names

Note: Court cases are listed in the Index of Cases that follows this Index of Names.

Index of Cases